Frontispiece (Colour Plate D). *Two monkies dressed in human clothing, one in the guise of a female vocalist, the other as a male musician with two drums upon his back (C109). 5⅞ ins. and 5⅛ ins. (14.9cm and 13cm). Chelsea c.1760, gold anchor mark. Chelsea red anchor prototypes were based upon originals made by J.J. Kändler at Meissen c.1747 known as the 'Affenkapelle'.*

Author's collection

18th Century English
PORCELAIN FIGURES
1745-1795

Peter Bradshaw, 1922-

Antique Collectors' Club

ISBN 0 902028 83 9

British Library CIP Data
Bradshaw, Peter
English 18th century porcelain figures.
1. Porcelain, English — Collectors and collecting
I. Title II. Antique Collectors' Club
738.2'0942 NK4485

Published for the Antique Collectors' Club
by the Antique Collectors' Club Ltd.

Printed in England by
Baron Publishing, Woodbridge, Suffolk

Antique Collectors' Club

The Antique Collectors' Club was formed in 1966 and now has a five figure membership spread throughout the world. It publishes the only independently run monthly antiques magazine *Antique Collecting* which caters for those collectors who are interested in widening their knowledge of antiques, both by increasing the members' knowledge of quality as well as in discussing the factors which influence the price that is likely to be asked. The Antique Collectors' Club pioneered the provision of information on prices for collectors and the magazine still leads in the provision of detailed articles on a variety of subjects.

It was in response to the enormous demand for information on "what to pay" that the price guide series was introduced in 1968 with the first edition of *The Price Guide to Antique Furniture* (completely revised, 1978), a book which broke new ground by illustrating the more common types of antique furniture, the sort that collectors could buy in shops and at auctions rather than the rare museum pieces which had previously been used (and still to a large extent are used) to make up the limited amount of illustrations in books published by commercial publishers. Many other price guides have followed, all copiously illustrated, and greatly appreciated by collectors for the valuable information they contain, quite apart from prices. The Antique Collectors' Club also publishes other books on antiques, including horology and art reference works, and a bull book list is available.

Club membership, which is open to all collectors, costs £8.95 per annum. Members receive free of charge *Antique Collecting,* the Club's magazine (published every month except August), which contains well-illustrated articles dealing with the practical aspects of collecting not normally dealt with by magazines. Prices, features of value, investment potential, fakes and forgeries are all given prominence in the magazine.

Among other facilities available to members are private buying and selling facilities, the longest list of "For Sales" of any antiques magazine, an annual ceramics conference and the opportunity to meet other collectors at their local antique collectors' clubs. Their are nearly eighty in Britain and so far a dozen overseas. Members may also buy the Club's publications at special pre-publication prices.

As its motto implies, the Club is an amateur organisation designed to help collectors to get the most out of their hobby: it is informal and friendly and gives enormous enjoyment to all concerned.

For Collectors — By Collectors — About Collecting

The Antique Collectors' Club, 5 Church Street, Woodbridge, Suffolk

This book is dedicated to my wife Mary who tolerated my idiosyncrasies for over a year whilst I was writing it.

If you were a Derby Shepherdess, and I were your Swain from Bow,
Beneath some emerald bocage we'd find a place to go —
Far from the Bulls of Planché, away from the dry-edge Boar,
Where we could be true lovers for a thousand years or more.

And if you went to Meissen, arrayed as Columbine,
Assuredly as Harlequin I'd wish to spend my time,
And not the whole of Kändler's band of Monkies and their tricks
Could ever stop me loving you until we cross the Styx.

Or, if you fled to Cathay, Immortal Kuan Yin,
I would forsake the Occident to be a fierce Kylin
To fight those silly Dogs of Fo and Dragons with five toes
That later I might stoop to kiss those lips of Famille Rose.

From Frankenthal to Nymphenburg, from Sèvres to Ching-tê Chên,
Which ever factory you chose, I'd find you just the same same —
In biscuit, in cold colours, or enamelled debonnaire,
The two of us shall always be a perfect matching pair!

Peter Bradshaw

Acknowledgements

I am indebted to Mr. George Savage who read my manuscript and made many extremely valuable suggestions which have been incorporated; he also most generously loaned numerous photographs of rare pieces some of which are in the Sigmund Katz Collection or were once in the Dudley Delevingne Collection.

It is a very great pleasure to thank Mr. Norman C. Ashton who invited me to see his magnificent private collection of dry-edge Derby figures and who also gave me illustrations of choice examples.

Dr. Bernard Watney assisted me in locating some obscure references and Miss Joanna Whiteley, of Sotheby Parke Bernet, also gave generously of her time and expertise in providing several photographs of figures and groups.

I am grateful to the following who provided me with photographs:

Mr. Bryan Bowden of Doncaster
Mrs. Kaye Chappell of Bakewell, Derbyshire
Dr. H.G.M. Edwards
Mr. Anton Gabszewicz of Christie's
Mr. Stafford Lorie of Grosvenor Antiques, London
Mr. David Love of Harrogate
Mr. and Mrs. John Mould
Mr. Simon Spero of China Choice, London
Mrs. Margaret Newton
Mr. Jeremy Pearson of Plymouth City Museum and Art Gallery
Miss Rosemary Bower of the Derby City Museum and Art Gallery
Mr. David Thorn of B. and T. Thorn, Budleigh Salterton, Devon
Mr. Robert Williams of Winifred Williams, London

I wish to acknowledge the generous help provided by Sotheby Parke Bernet, Christie's, and both Temple Newsam House, Leeds, and Saltram House, Plympton, Devon.

Contents

Continued

Colour Plates

Preface

Despite the undeniable elegance of eighteenth century English porcelain figures, there are some who regard them as little more than pale copies of Meissen originals. Although, it is true, many were based on prototypes created by J.J. Kändler and his associates in Dresden, there is a world of difference between the dramatically posed hard paste figures, clad in brilliant feldspathic glaze and strong dark enamels, and their soft paste English counterparts. Here, the harsh satire of Saxony was muted and transformed into something infinitely more charming, whilst any deficiencies in modelling are more than counterbalanced by the delicious soft pastes, the unctuous glazes, the delicate nuances of shade and colour and, sometimes, also by the glory of honey gilding. Comparison between the two is like that between an oil painting and a watercolour and there are many who prefer the less powerful rendering which they find better suited to the misty climate of these islands.

I wish, at the outset, to acknowledge my deep debt of gratitude to the late Mr. Thomas Thorn, of Budleigh Salterton, who first kindled the vital spark within me of the love of antique porcelain. He guided my purchases for many years, and from this kindly and scholarly man I learned so much of what I know today. I am also indebted to his son, David, who most generously granted me access to his library and treasures and gave me every possible assistance in my quest for knowledge. Without them both, there would have been no book.

When I embarked upon the formation of a modest collection, I soon discovered that a great deal of the information I sought was contained in books published many years ago that were out of print and difficult to obtain. One of the most enlightening, that shone out like a beacon in the darkness, was *English Porcelain Figures of the 18th Century,* by Arthur Lane (1961). According to the 'Introduction', this was planned as the second volume of a trilogy of which the first was to have considered the highly relevant matter of German Porcelain Figures and the third was to have dealt with Italian and French Porcelain Figures. Sadly, Mr. Lane died before completion of the supporting volumes and now, twenty years have elapsed. The time seemed right, therefore, to bring together under one cover information derived from widely dispersed sources that are germane to the subject and it is hoped that the present work will be of use and interest to the scholarly collector and dealer. The author has made only a few minor original contributions and is content simply to have assembled the pieces of an intriguing jigsaw that has been cut by others.

The first three chapters survey ceramic activities in China, at Meissen, and in the soft paste manufactories of North West Europe and indicate how they influenced porcelain modelling in this country. The impact of the works of French decorative artists and of the rococo taste is discussed in Chapter III, whilst other art forms, including sculpture, engravings and prints are reviewed in Chapter IV. The discovery and composition of soft paste and the methods by which the porcelain figure was constructed receive attention in Chapter V. The main corpus of the book is contained in Chapters VI to XI. Here, are provided historical summaries of the English eighteenth century factories concerned with figure production, followed by descriptions of paste and glaze, modelling characteristics, enamel colours, etc. The decline of the porcelain figure is discussed in Chapter XII and certain practical aspects concerning reproductions, fakes, restoration, etc. are considered in Chapter XIII together with some notes on collecting

In addition to discussions of many models made during the several phases of production, lists of models together with brief descriptions, sizes and where they are illustrated are provided in appendices — A to Q. These lists are fairly full and representative but no claim is made that they include all models known, and many informed readers will probably recall several that have been omitted. Many collectors have found the Derby list made out by John Haslem, which roughly covers the period 1772-1795, of considerable value when they wish to identify a specimen that bears a number upon the base. Accordingly, this list has been retained, though modified and brought up to date, in Appendix M. The disadvantages of leaving many blanks where either the identity or whereabouts of examples remains unknown are more than outweighed by the usefulness of Appendix M as it now stands.

Appendix R relates to marks found on figures, Appendix S to a survey of the Italian Comedy and Appendix T contains a few details of characters translated into porcelain which are based on Greek and Roman mythology.

The presentation of information in sections, while necessary for clarity, runs the risk of suggesting sudden alterations in the nature of materials or in styles of modelling and decoration. In fact, the whole process was effected by experimentation, trial and error. For example, there was no abrupt alteration of paste or glaze between the years 1745 and 1759 at Chelsea and yet the models are divided into four separate groups. It should be recalled that raised anchor figures may exhibit features of the earlier period and that during the period of the red anchor mark, continual modification of paste was taking place and probably well before the period of the gold anchor bone ash was incorporated in the paste. The dating of first issue of models, such as the Chelsea 'La Nourrice' (B50), or the Bow 'New Dancers' (H34), both of which were made for more than ten years, may be difficult especially if early examples are scarce. Some models are extremely rare, if not unique, and perforce must be viewed through glass or from a photograph when any error made by museum authorities is likely to continue uncorrected for a very long time. Although some museums and art galleries provide excellent catalogues and handbooks others, including the more august guardians of our artistic heritage, are found sadly wanting. The catalogues of the Lady Charlotte Schreiber Collection, for example, was last revised in 1928 and last printed in 1929! Even such antiquated copies are difficult to find and my own is dated 1915! Although some of the books listed in the bibliography may be equally hard to find, most are more readily available; and if the reader wishes to develop his interest further in a particular area, a few titles are suggested for each porcelain manufactory as a basis for further study.

PB

Chapter I

The Discovery and Development of Porcelain in the Orient and the Origins of the Ceramic Figure

The Birth of the Ceramic Figure

The ceramic figure was born as a substitute for blood sacrifice in the mists of ancient China. There, religious belief held that after the death of an important person his 'Superior Spirit' went on a trek to the mountains in the far north where lay the nine sources of the life supporting *Huang Ho* (yellow river) and where dwelt the Supreme Being, *Ti*. Upon this journey, which might last for one thousand years, the soul required for sustenance and comfort much the same as had been enjoyed by the body here on earth. Accordingly, during the Shang (1750-1111 B.C.) and earlier part of the Chou (1110-500 B.C.) dynasties, the demise of a man of consequence was closely followed by the slaughter of wives, concubines, soldiers and slaves as well as of horses, camels and even pet dogs. The bodies of the victims, together with jars of black millet wine, grain, meats, silks and precious stones, were entombed with the corpse of their lord. Excavations of the ancient Shang capitals of An-Yang, Lo-Yang, and Ch'ang-An, indicate that up to three hundred persons might perish at the interment of a king. Human and animal sacrifices were not limited to funerals for remains of soldiers and slaves have been found buried before important buildings and city gates. Specimens of Shang and Chou tomb furniture, including some splendid bronze vessels used in the macabre rites, were displayed at Burlington House, London, by the People's Republic of China in 1973/74.[1] Human sacrifice was certainly not limited to China and indeed the practice seems to have been world wide during the so called Prehistoric Era (2,000-1100 B.C.). In Europe, for example, the excavation of graves in Crete and on the Greek mainland dating back to the Minoan and early Mycenaean cultures have revealed secondary burials presumably of slaves or captives.

Ancient Shang dynasty bronze known as a Chüeh.

Some time between the fifth and the fourth centuries B.C., possibly as a consequence of the enlightened teachings of the sage K'ung-Ch'ui (Confucius), the episodic ritual slaughter became unacceptable and was discontinued. Henceforth only the emperor was deemed worthy to offer sacrifices of incense, meats, grain and wine, to the elemental gods to honour his ancestors and on behalf of his people. Excavations of late Chou (500-256 B.C.) and Han (206 B.C.-A.D. 220) tombs show that images replaced blood sacrifices. Those of the Han dynasty were mostly constructed of bronze and included equestrian warriors, chariots and their drivers and foot attendants laid out on the floor of the burial chamber in ranks like over large toy soldiers upon the nursery carpet.[2] Interspersed between these were lightly fired glazed pottery replicas of dwelling houses, farmsteads, and watch towers. It seems likely that other models carved of wood were originally included which have long since crumbled to dust. Interestingly enough, crudely fashioned clay models appear in tombs of the Mycenaean period preceeding the Dorian invasion of Greece in 1100 B.C.

The end of the Han empire was marked by a period of civil war known as the Six Dynasties (A.D. 221-580), during which the control of vital trade routes

1. *The Genius of China,* catalogue of the Exhibition of Archaeological Finds of the People's Republic of China, held at Burlington House, London, Sept. '73 to Jan. '74, pp. 61-90, ritual bronzes.
2. ibid., p. 18, bronze models.

into central Asia fell into the hands of foreigners. In the general recession of trade and decline that followed, the expensive bronze images were replaced by cheaper stoneware models. These display a focus of interest on stylised folds in drapery rather than upon the human form and examples exhibit expressionless faces with characteristically square chins and static poses. Women are portrayed as slender creatures with their hair piled high on their heads, dressed in long sleeved gowns.[3] The re-establishment of civil order during the Sui dynasty (A.D. 581-618) led to more natural representation of the human form and some delightful models of female musicians[4] were recovered from the tomb of the Princess Yung-Tai. These include two guitarists, flautist, harpist, players of reed-pipe and *hsiao* and a kind of mouth organ *(tsêng),* and two vocalists; surely the first pop group ever to be translated into ceramics!

T'ang dynasty tomb figure of a Bactrian camel covered in a straw coloured glaze c. AD 700.

During the T'ang dynasty (A.D. 619-906), tomb figures, or *Yung,* attained their highest level of development.[5] They were constructed of lightly fired soft buff earthenware and portray almost every aspect of contemporary life. There are slender girls dressed either in short jackets and long skirts, or large cloaks with a hood attached. Men wear tunics gathered with belts over trousers or have long boots. Horses resemble those broad backed muscular animals from Turkestan and are depicted standing, galloping, or ridden by hook-nosed foreigners. Pack horses laden with provisions for the sustenance of the soul are found together with splendid Bacterian camels. Models of fierce demons were intended to frighten off the would be tomb robber. Most display an economy of modelling detail and a vitality that anticipate the genius of Johann Joachim Kändler, the great *modellmeister* of Meissen, by nearly a thousand years. Though some figures were painted in unfired pigments over a coating of white slip, the best are resplendent in polychrome glazes of leaf-green, yellow, and brown — less often purple, orange-red and occasionally blue. These soft lead glazes were liberally applied and allowed to trickle down in rivulets which greatly enhance the artistic effect. Towards the middle of the dynasty, between A.D. 680-779, larger models were made and those of the ladies of the court show them wearing high waisted dresses and stoles or in loose robes with wide sleeves. The emperior Tai-tsung felt constrained to issue a series of edicts limiting the amount and size of tomb furniture and, had he not done so, there is little doubt that the living would have been impoverished to supply the needs of the dead. When the last T'ang occupant of the dragon throne "exhausted the mandate of Heaven", the land was once again swept by civil disorder and, in the less favourable economic circumstances that prevailed, the *Yung* virtually disappeared as burial rites and customs altered. The traditional reverence of the Chinaman for his ancestors who, like Catholic saints, may intercede for him with the Supreme Being, coupled with a fear of malevolent demons lurking in the burial areas, served to preserve the ancient tombs and their contents inviolate until the end of the nineteenth century so that the *Yung* remained hidden from western eyes and exerted no influence upon the eighteenth century potters. However, they are extremely important in the historical context of the development of the ceramic figure and from them were evolved the porcelain models of Ching-tê Chên and Tê Hua which reached Europe during the seventeenth and eighteenth centuries.

The development of terracotta figures in the Hellenistic world proceeded in parallel with the *Yung* of China. Primitive stylised models of mother goddesses[6] are found in late Minoan and Mycenaean graves and during the so called Archaic Period (650-500 B.C.) some stiffly posed expressionless replicas of Ceres, Aphrodite, Dionysus and Eros were made; the best of these originate from Boeotia north of Athens. Models were probably used in the home on private altars, though many were buried in trenches beside shrines and temples

3. *Chinese Ceramics* (London, 1974) by Michel and Cécile Beurdeley, pp. 68-69.
4. *The Genius of China,* op. cit., p. 138.
5. *Chinese Ceramics,* op. cit., pp. 80-93.
6. *Classical Terracotta Figures* (London, 1974) by J. Chesterman, pp. 24-32.

as votive offerings and were broken deliberately by the priests to prevent reuse. The advent of the classical period (500-300 B.C.) saw the development of a more natural style of modelling and a secularisation of subject matter. Some of the finest figures were made at Tanagra in Boeotia and include comely youths, maidens, gods and goddesses, grotesques, masks and even articulated children's toys.[7] The figures stand upon bases and were painted in matt colours upon a thin layer of white slip. During the last phase of Greek culture (330 B.C.-A.D. 100) some quite elaborate models were made for purely secular purposes in Alexandria, Attica, Boeotia, Myrina and in southern Italy. Roman terracottas (A.D. 100-500) are often emasculated copies of earlier Greek models although several new ones were added.

Terracottas from the ancient world, especially those that were excavated at Herculaneum and Pompeii, were overshadowed by the more important marbles and bronzes. Both had originally been brightly coloured but unfired pigments had either peeled away or faded. English potters working in the neo-classical style who turned to these relics for inspiration saw only white marble or buff terracotta. Models made at Derby after 1771 were increasingly left white and unglazed so that they might resemble faded marble and the models created after the beginning of the nineteenth century by Copeland, Mintons, and Coalport were fashioned from a stoneware that emulated Parian marble. For most of his models Josiah Wedgwood preferred to use black basaltes, which had a texture similar to that found in 'Etruscan' vases (which were in fact of late Greek origin) but he also created a few in creamware, together with busts in the Roman style. Only a few of the English porcelain models can be traced to an antique terracotta. There is a rare Chaffers' Liverpool model of 'Ariadne' reclining (030) made c.1760 after a Roman terracotta which was itself a copy of a Greek model.[8] The Derby Shepherd standing hat in hand (M396) followed a Roman terracotta of Antinous. However, most of the models after the antique were derived from contemporary plaster or terracotta replicas made by sculptors of the day. These will be described in Chapter IV.

The Discovery of Porcelain in China

Neolithic man learned to fashion hollow wares from moist clay which he hardened initially in the heat of the sun and subsequently in an oven or primitive kiln. During the period 4200 B.C. to 3500 B.C., a soft earthenware was fired at low temperature in the vicinity of Yang-Shao, in the province of Honan. The wares were assembled from coils of red or yellow earth, possibly with the assistance of a slow turntable, and were painted with whorls, geometrical shapes, and both human and animal masks, in unfired pigments of yellow, purple and black.[9] A parallel culture at Lung-Shan, in the province of Shantung, was associated with a much harder and crisper pottery which has a blackish hue and which was often burnished.[10] Both varieties are opaque, brittle, and by reason of their porous quality unsuitable for long storage of water. During the Shang dynasty (1700-1111 B.C.) the potters began to mix sand with the clay and improved design of kilns allowed far higher temperatures to be attained. The vitrification of silica in the sand at temperatures about 1,000°C enabled a much harder and less porous stoneware to be made which was often decorated with impressed rope patterns or incised designs.[11]

It was discovered during the Chou dynasty (1110-256 B.C.) that salt thrown into the hot kiln was deposited as a thin film over the surface of the wares and, after cooling, formed a tough water resistant skin or glaze. Chou pottery is rare but most examples have a yellowish glaze which, after two thousand

7. *Classical Terracotta Figures*, op. cit., pp. 57-75.

8. *Il Museo Archologico di Firenze* (Florence, 1912) by L.A. Milani, p. 313, nos. 40-41, pl. 152, Roman terracotta of Ariadne.

9. *Chinese Ceramics*, op. cit., pp. 11-22, pl. 1., figs. 1-7, neolithic pottery of the Yang-Shao culture.

10. ibid., figs. 8-9, neolithic pottery of the Lung-Shan culture.

11. ibid., pl. 2.

years' burial in damp soil, usually exhibits an attractive iridescence. The second important advance was the incorporation of a fine white china clay in the mix. This was called *Kao-lin* (kaolin), meaning high ridge, from which it was mined. This is a degradation product of feldspathic granite caused by chemical reactions in the ground, changes of temperature, and water seepage. The material at first complemented and eventually came to replace the earlier red earth that had been used. Towards the end of the dynasty, kiln temperatures of up to 1,250°C were achieved, and surviving specimens of stoneware are exceedingly hard and strong. Most of them remain opaque but there are a few which are faintly translucent when held up before a powerful light and these may be termed 'protoporcelains'. The period of the Warring States (433-221 B.C.) saw the introduction of tougher glazes formed from lead ore, silica, limestone and water and these assumed a green colour due to the presence of copper in the subsequent Han dynasty (206 B.C.-A.D. 220). Also at this time, small quantities of pulverised feldspathic granite, called *Pai-tung Tz'u* (petuntse) began to be incorporated in the paste. The name means white ceramic blocks and was acquired by the practice of pressing the powdered rock into small brickettes prior to use.

The first true porcelain was made in the T'ang dynasty in the ninth century. The proportion of petuntse had increased and the paste was compounded from this, kaolin, limestone, bracken-ash and water. Kiln temperatures of up to 1,350-1,400°C necessary for the formation of the new ceramic were now realised. Hard high temperature glazes, formed from kaolin, bracken-ash, lime and water were developed from the time of the Sung dynasty (A.D.906-1279). During the Ming (A.D.1369-1643) and earlier part of the Ch'ing (A.D.1643-1750) dynasties, further refinements evolved a white finely grained body and a brilliant tightly fitting and transparent glaze. Some figures and wares were covered with a single coloured glaze (monochrome), others with more than one colour (polychrome). Enamel colours derived from metallic ores mixed with gum were introduced as early as the T'ang dynasty but were not commonly used until after the reign of the Ming emperor Hsüan Tê (A.D.1426-1435). These were fixed to the fired glaze in a muffle kiln heated to about 600-700°C.

Te Hua blanc-de-Chine *figure of Ts'ai-shen, 13ins. (33cm), early 18th century.*

Hard Paste Porcelain

It has been shown how porcelain was evolved from earthenware, through stoneware and protoporcelain, over the space of more than a thousand years. Although the secrets of its manufacture were known to the Chinese as early as the ninth century A.D., it could not be made in Europe until 1709. The material was called hard paste, not only because it was a hard ceramic able to withstand marking with a metal file and the temperature of boiling water, but because it required a hot, or hard, fire for its manufacture. When struck with a metal object a musical note is emitted and when held against the cheek it feels exceedingly cold. If viewed before a powerful source of light its essential translucent quality and even density can be appreciated. Palpation of unglazed porcelain produces a smooth sensation to the exploring finger. When broken, the edges of the fragments resemble those of glass or marine shell (conchoidal fracture). The material is non-porous and strictly speaking does not need to be glazed and hence dirt and grease may readily be removed by scrubbing with soap and water. Most often it is covered with a tough scratch resistant feldspathic glaze and when enamel colours are applied they tend to sit upon the surface and stand out in slight relief.

Chinese Ceramic Figures

Following the break up of the T'ang empire the modellers refocused their

***Colour Plate A.** 'Scapino' (B37), a character from the Commedia dell 'Arte. 4½ins. (11.4cm). Chelsea c.1752, raised anchor mark. The model is a copy of a Meissen original.* Author's collection

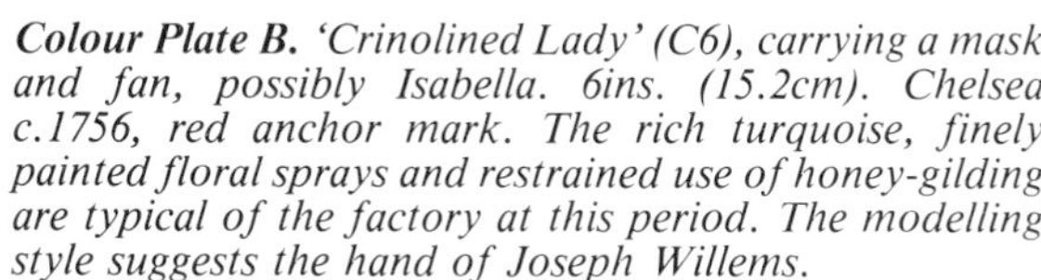

***Colour Plate B.** 'Crinolined Lady' (C6), carrying a mask and fan, possibly Isabella. 6ins. (15.2cm). Chelsea c.1756, red anchor mark. The rich turquoise, finely painted floral sprays and restrained use of honey-gilding are typical of the factory at this period. The modelling style suggests the hand of Joseph Willems.*
Author's collection

One of a pair of porcelain models of boys, decorated in famille verte *enamels, K'ang-hsi, 1662-1722.*

endeavours towards the creation of pottery and porcelain models for the living instead of the dead. Broadly speaking two centres were established and developed, the first at Ching-tê Chên, the second some seventy miles north of Amoy in the vicinity of Tê Hua.

Ching-tê Chên

Kilns probably existed at Ching-tê Chên, in the province of Kiangsi, since the time of the Han dynasty. In 1369, in the second year of the Ming emperor Hung Wu, an imperial kiln (Yu-yao Ch'ang) was erected on the southern slopes of the Pearl Hill. Around this there grew up a huge complex of privately owned ceramic factories. According to Père D'Entrecolles, by the first quarter of the eighteenth century the population amounted to nearly one million souls and there were three thousand kilns. The factories were chiefly concerned with production of useful wares many of which were made for export and sold at Canton. These were avidly sought by European kings and princes during the late seventeenth and early eighteenth centuries and prompted research into porcelain manufacture which was eventually successful at Meissen in 1709.

Ceramic models made during the Ming dynasty were not numerous and only a very few reached Europe. They consist of spirited replicas of fabulous animals and birds fashioned from red pottery and covered with yellow and green glazes that were produced as ridge-tiles. Others were made of buff stoneware and incorporated into items for the scholar's table, such as brush-pots, brush-rests, joss-stick holders and lamps which were often covered in polychrome glazes of yellow, green, and aubergine in the so called *san-ts'ai* (three colour) decoration. There are a very few free-standing models of Kuan Yin, goddess of mercy, of Taoist Immortals, seated emperors and grooms beside their horses.[12] These had no influence upon English porcelain factories.

Père D'Entrecolles was a Jesuit missionary who arrived in China in 1698 and died in Peking in 1741. He wrote two letters to Père Orry, the procurer of Chinese and Indian missions in Paris, which are dated 1st September, 1712, and 23rd August, 1722. In these, he gave detailed descriptions of porcelain manufacture at Ching-tê Chên. "Their huge workshops", he wrote, "have been to me a kind of Areopagus, when I have proclaimed Him, who fashioned the first man out of clay, and from whose hands we proceed to become vessels, either of glory or of shame." He noted how the two essential ingredients of porcelain, kaolin and petuntse, were mined, refined, and compounded with lime, bracken-ash and water to form a paste. Also, how this was kneaded beneath the feet of coolies to eliminate bubbles of air. "The Chinese who are employed at it find it difficult to attend church; they are only allowed to go if they offer substitutes, because as soon as the work is interrupted all the other workmen are stopped." He described the formation of glaze from kaolin, bracken-ash, and lime mixed with water and the methods of application to the raw porcelain wares either with a brush, or by dipping, or by spraying through a hollow bamboo screened with silk. The reverend father wrote of the preparation and use of underglaze blue and of enamel colours over the glaze. "The painting is distributed in the same workshop amongst a great number of workmen. One workman does nothing but draw the first colour line beneath the rims of pieces; another traces flowers, which a third one paints; this man is painting water and mountains and that one either birds or animals. Human figures are generally treated worst..." Drawings of earthenware boxes, or saggars, in which wares were placed and stacked in the kiln, and accounts of firing kilns with wooden billets were included.

Nearly all the Chinese figures imported into Europe during the late seventeenth and eighteenth century originated from Ching-tê Chên during the reigns of three emperors: K'ang-Hsi, Yung-Chêng, and Ch'ien-Lung. Many

12. *The Wares of the Ming Dynasty* (London, 1923, reprinted London and Tokyo, 1962) by R.L. Hobson.

One of a pair of cranes, 17ins. (43.2cm), decorated in famille rose *enamel colours,* Ch'ien-lung, *mid-18th century.*

relate to mythological birds and beasts such as the dragon *(lung),* kylin *(ch'i-lin),* lions of Fo *(shih tzu kou),* and phoenix *(fêng-huang),* or creatures connected with Taoist superstitions like the cockerel, deer, dog, hare, or tortoise. Representations of the Kuan Yin, Kuan Ti, or of the eight Taoist Immortals abound and there are models of the crane, heron, parrot and pheasant which appear to have been made for export to Europe. Père D'Entrecolles wrote: "The Chinese succeed best in grotesques, and in representation of animals. . . I have seen a cat painted after life, in the head of which a little lamp had been put to illuminate the eyes, and was assured that in the night the rats were terrified by it. They make here too many statuettes of Kuan Yin, a goddess celebrated throughout China, represented holding an infant in her arms, and worshipped by sterile women who wish to have children." The models made during the reign of the emperior K'ang-Hsi (1662-1722) were often decorated with monochrome or *san-ts'ai* (polychrome) glazes. Others were enamelled in a spectrum of greens, aubergine, yellow, red, and blue of the *famille verte* palette.[13] The same colours appear on useful wares of the period and were used to portray, amongst other things, stylised leaves and flowers. These avoided any three dimensional effects that might have been created either by perspective drawing or shading. During the reign of the emperior Yung-Chêng (1723-1735) a range of delicate rose-pinks, made from stanniferous gold chloride, were introduced into China from Europe which were called *fa-lang* (foreign colours), but are better known as *famille rose.* Afterwards, in the reign of Ch'ien-Lung (1736-1795) these colours came increasingly to dominate the decorative schemes of both useful wares and figures.[14]

Despite the vast number of models exported from China, they exerted practically no influence on the eighteenth century European modellers probably because their grotesque quality and subject matter made them objects of curiosity rather than patterns to be emulated. Nevertheless, in England, a magnificent pair of enamelled 'Pheasants' (P21) made at Plymouth, and a pair of 'Grotesque Birds' (G61) created at Bow, appear to have been based on originals manufactured at Ching-tê Chên. The stylised painting of flowers in the *famille verte* was copied and may be found as decoration on several Bow figures of the period 1755-65. Père D'Entrecolles's letters were published in *Descriptions de la Chine,*[15] by Jean Baptiste du Halde, which appeared in 1738 and came too late to influence the research by Johann Friedrich Böttger and Baron Ehrenfried Walther von Tschirnhaus at Meissen. However, the work was read by William Cookworthy, a chemist in Plymouth, who eventually established a porcelain manufactory at Plymouth and was the first person in England to make hard paste.

Tê Hua

Kilns had existed in the vicinity of Tê Hua, in the province of Fukien, since the T'ang dynasty but it was not until the end of the sixteenth or beginning of the seventeenth century that the inimitable white porcelain began to be manufactured by numerous potter families. This exquisitely beautiful material consists of a pure white tightly grained body which merges intimately with an immaculate milky glaze which has a pearl-like sheen. Called by the Chinese *Pai-Tz'u,* it was better known in Europe as *blanc-de-Chine.* Presumably the production of useful wares preceded that of models and these consist of rhinoceros horn cups bearing incised designs, libation cups, beakers, jars and vases adorned with moulded sprigs of plum or magnolia blossom. Wine cups, teapots and items for the scholar's table were also made in profusion. The perfection of paste and glaze made other adornment superfluous and enamel colours were employed only to hide defects on inferior specimens.

13. *Later Chinese Porcelain. The Ch'ing Dynasty 1644-1912* (London, 1965) by Soame Jenyns, p. 29, the famille vert palette; p. 35, K'ang-Hsi models.

14. *The Book of the Famille Rose* (London, 1927) by George C. Williamson.

15. *Descriptions de la Chine* (Paris, 1738) by Jean Baptiste du Halde, Vol. II, pp. 216-246.

Figures constitute the great glory of Tê Hua. The late W.B. Honey wrote of them: "... The best Fukien figures may indeed be held to be the finest porcelain figures ever made. They are an object-lesson in the principle that beauty in a porcelain figure depends absolutely upon the material of which it is made. In the Fukien figures the characteristic fragility and nervous delicacy of porcelain, as well as its senuous charm, play an indispensable part."[16] Early models are thickly potted and cast in one piece. The glaze is warm and has either a creamy or more rarely a slightly pink appearance. The inferior aspect is left open showing fire cracks and reddish-brown iron staining within. During the first half of the eighteenth century, models were more thinly potted and head and hands were often cast separately and inserted into the main section like corks in bottles. The glaze became colder and often presents a faintly blue or greenish tone. After about 1750, the paste becomes grey in colour and bases are often occluded by flat plates of rough paste perforated by a ventilation hole.

Fukien was a stronghold of Buddhism and this was reflected by the models. Images of the Buddha are, however, rare. Nine out of every ten models represent Kuan Yin (Plate 1). Although some have traced this deity back to a fertility goddess, most believe that the character started out as a male Bodhisattva, Avalokitesvara, and changed his sex to female during the

16. *Ceramic Arts in China* (London, 1945) by W.B. Honey, p. 134.

Plate 1. *Seated* blanc-de-Chine *figure of Kuan Yin, 10¼ins. (26cm). Tê Hua, c.1675-1700.* Author's collection

eleventh century. The two natures of the Buddha, infinite power and infinite compassion, were represented by Ta-shih Chih and Kuan Yin, but the goddess came to occupy a very special position in the Buddhist ethos and was also assimilated into the Taoist pantheon. She may be depicted with a child in her arms which she proffers to barren women, or standing upon a lotus bearing a willow wand symbolic of purity; again, she may be shown standing upon the waves as the protector of mariners and pirates, or scattering flowers, emblematic of blessings, upon the earth. The Jesuit missionaries were not slow to recognise her remarkable resemblance to the Virgin Mary, whose titles include Mother of God, Queen of Purity, Star of the Sea, and Genetrix of all Blessings. This probably accounts for her great popularity in Catholic Europe and why the royal collection of Augustus the Strong once contained twenty-six examples. Many of her models are illustrated.[17] English copies were made at Chelsea (B43) and at Longton Hall (O14).

Tê Hua blanc-de-Chine *model of Pu-tai Ho-shang, c.1720, copied at Meissen, St. Cloud and Chelsea (see plate 13, Chapter VI).*

Obviously less equivocal objects of Buddhist and Taoist veneration had scant appeal and many models, such as Kuan Ti, the god of war, found no echoes in Europe. However, the Immortal, Lu-tung Pin, was copied by Lund's Bristol factory in 1750 (Q13) and there are Longton Hall models of Shou-lao, the Founder of Taoism, and of Chun-li-Ch'uan. Bodhisattvas are those who have but one more earthly existence to complete before they can enjoy Buddhahood and one of these, famed for his love of children, was Pu-tai Ho-shang. [18] He is portrayed as a seated obese smiling monk with shaven head and was amongst the first of the models to be made at Meissen.[19] He was also adapted at Chelsea (A4) to serve as a pastil burner. Disciples of the Buddha, or Lo-Hans, were usually depicted standing, with shaven heads, bushy eyebrows, wearing cloaks but were overlooked by most European porcelain factories. Tê Hua also made models of secular figures and the Chelsea 'Boy carrying a gourd' (B42) is almost certainly copied from a Chinese original. Models of birds include pheasants and parrots made largely for export and some of these may have prompted the Chelsea 'Pheasant' (B31) and a pair of 'Parrots' (B29). A Longton Hall model of a 'Heron preening' (O23) most likely stems from a similar source. However, the Chelsea 'Crane' (B9), once believed to have been a copy of *blanc-de-Chine,* in fact was prompted by an engraving in the book *History of Uncommon Birds,* by George Edwards[20] published in 1743. The numerous mythological beasts incorporated into joss-stick holders, brush-pots, lamps and the like were ignored by potters in the west.

The use of moulded sprigs of plum blossom upon wares left in the white was copied at almost every eighteenth century European factory including Chelsea, Bow, and Derby. The same sprigged decoration is found also on a small group of soft paste English figures including 'Kitty Clive' (J10), a headless 'Actor' (Q7), a 'Putto emblematic of Spring' (Q1), and a seated 'Pug' scratching (Q6) which are ascribed to Derby c.1750.

The Japanese influence on English Porcelain Figures

The earliest Japanese pottery is reddish or grey in colour and unglazed. Tradition holds that between A.D. 1225 and 1227 Kato Shirozaemon visited China where he gleaned the secrets of producing and applying glaze from the Sung potters so that most wares created after this time were glazed. Further, in 1510, Gorodoyugo-Shonzui went from Japan to Ching-tê Chên and returned in 1515, bringing with him the ingredients necessary for porcelain manufacture. It is said that he continued in production until the raw materials became exhausted. Indigenous kaolin was discovered on the island of Kyushu, close to the town of Arita, and petuntse was quarried in the mountains of Izumiyama, towards the end of the sixteenth century. Porcelain factories were

17. *Blanc de Chine* (London, 1969) by P.J. Donnelly, pls. 81-86, examples of Kuan Yin.

18. ibid., p. 81, examples of Pu-tai Ho-shang.

19. *German Porcelain of the 18th Century* (London, 1972) by Erica Pauls-Eisenbeiss, Vol. I, p. 65.

20. *History of Uncommon Birds* (London, 1743) by George Edwards, pl. 45.

Japanese sake bottle decorated in the Kakiemon style, with stylised chrysanthemums and tendrils (Arita), c.1675-1700.

established at Kutani, in the province of Kaga, and at Arita, in Hizen. The quality of paste and glaze never approached the excellence of contemporary Chinese porcelain and the smudged purplish underglaze blue lacks the brilliance of the sapphire colour characteristic of Ching-tê Chên.

During the second quarter of the seventeenth century, Sakaida Kakiemon and members of his family, developed a brilliant enamel palette which included a vibrant green, light blue, pale yellow, aubergine, and a soft brownish red. These lovely colours were used to paint asymmetrical designs in a manner very different from the tightly formal and symmetrical decoration accomplished by the contemporary Chinese and European artists. Floral sprays including especially the chrysanthemum, camellia, lotus or peony, were placed in an arc across one side of a dish or plate leaving a large area in white. Sometimes instead, branches of plum, cherry, or prunus blossom were employed which were balanced by a stylised painting of an animal or bird. Shading and perspective drawing were omitted according to the fashion of the Orient. Some of the finest examples were painted for the Nabeshima family in which a single motif spilled over the edge of the ware to continue upon the reverse. The wares decorated at Kutani were decorated in a far less sophisticated way with often brownish-red enamel used in combination with purplish underglaze blue or alternatively in brilliant green.

The Portuguese and Spanish were amongst the first Europeans to trade with Japan but, in 1590, both were expelled, and there ensued two massacres of native Japanese Christians and a series of imperial edicts forbidding any contact with foreigners on pain of death. Despite the new laws the Portuguese managed to obtain permission to set up a trading post at Macao, whilst the Dutch enjoyed similar facilities on the island of Deshima close to the port of Nagasaki. During the last quarter of the seventeenth century, and first half of the eighteenth century, the East India companies of Portugal, the Netherlands, France and Great Britain brought back to their native lands huge quantities of Oriental porcelain including much that was of Japanese manufacture. Wares decorated by, or in the style of Sakaida Kakiemon were amongst those most highly prized and copies were made more especially at Meissen[21] and Chantilly[22] but also by almost every known porcelain factory in the west. Many decorative patterns, including those known as the banded hedge, the yellow tiger, the flaming tortoise, and the quail or partridge, were imitated at Worcester, Chelsea, Bow and Derby. Though the style of painting is more usually associated with useful wares, it was adapted for the adornment of the crinolines of Meissen figures and emulated by many English factories. The representation of flowers in flat washes of colour without shading or three dimensional drawing, common to China and Japan, became known in Europe as *Indianische Blumen*.

A second style of enamel painting effected in Japan was known as *Imari.* This was entirely foreign to the Japanese who evolved it in response to suggestions by European traders that they should reproduce designs more often employed for textiles. Patterns employ alternating dark grounds with areas left in the white with a preference for a blackish blue. Upon the coloured wash are placed stylised florettes, especially representing the chrysanthemum and daisy and diapers simulating brocade, whilst vases of flowers and other emblems appear upon the white. The palette includes an inky blue, a light blue, green, pale yellow, aubergine, blood red and a soft brown and the patterns may be accented by gilding. Known in England as the Japan Pattern, or Old Japan, it became immensely popular. A few porcelain figures display the style and amongst these the pair of Worcester 'Turks' (Q15) is perhaps the best example.

21. Christie's Sale Catalogue, 28.3.77, lots 40, 45, 46, 55, Meissen copies of Kakiemon wares.

22. *French Porcelains of the Eighteenth Century* (London, 1950) by W.B. Honey, col. pl. C, pls. 18-21, Chatilly copies of Kakiemon wares.

Chapter II

The Great Contribution made by Meissen

The dawn of the eighteenth century saw Augustus II king of Poland and Elector of Saxony. His nickname 'The Strong', had not been merited by his autocratic rule, nor yet by his ability to straighten a horse's shoe with his bare hands, but rather stemmed from his fathering of more than 350 children. Strange to relate, this lecherous prince found time for other persuits, including the collection of Oriental porcelain. He likened his chinamania to the craving for oranges once that fruit had been tasted, and few were better qualified to pass judgements on fruit and passion. In 1717, his craving for porcelain prompted him to trade a regiment of dragoons with Frederick William of Prussia for 127 items of Chinese porcelain including eighteen monumental vases. The exchange was concluded after hard bargaining and Frederick demanded and got 600 men of the requisite stature. Long before this affair, huge purchases of china from the east by Augustus had provoked a financial crisis which had been aggravated by an edict from the Chinese emperor, K'ang-Hsi, that henceforth all foreign devils must make payment in silver. China had, indeed, become the 'Bleeding Bowl of Saxony', as von Tschirnhaus had remarked. The only acceptable solution for a return to national solvency lay in the discovery of the secrets of porcelain manufacture and the establishment of a home based industry that would satisfy the requirements of an avaricious monarch.

The Graf Ehrenfried Walther von Tschirnhaus (1651-1708) was an influential citizen of Saxony who had been elected to the Paris Academy of Sciences in 1682. About 1694, he began research into the manufacture of ceramic materials, including porcelain, by use of burning mirrors and lenses. About this time, Johann Friedrich Böttger (1682-1719), who had been apprenticed to an alchemist named Zorn in Berlin, met von Tschirnhaus and doubtless the two exchanged ideas. Böttger was seeking the secret of the 'Philosopher's Stone', by which base metals might be transmuted to gold. Rumours that his quest had met with success reached the ears of Frederick William and he, ever eager to obtain gold with which to finance his military fantasies, began to show an unhealthy interest in the young man. In 1704, doubtless believing discretion to be the better part of valour, Böttger fled across the border into Saxony and enrolled as a medical student at Wittenberg. This proved to be a leap from the frying-pan into the fire. Frederick William's overtures for extradition alerted Augustus to the presence of Böttger in his domain. He was brought to Dresden under military escort, provided with a laboratory and assistants, and ordered to make gold. When he failed in this commission and attempted to escape, he was thrown into the rock of fortress of Königstein to sharpen his wits and, for a while, his life hung in the balance. However, he was an asset far too precious to extinguish and, accordingly, he was placed in the charge of Graf von Tschirnhaus and commanded to discover the secrets of porcelain manufacture. Together the nobleman and the prisoner worked for, though the place of captivity was often changed, Böttger remained incarcerated. Above the door of his cell he hung up the inscription: "Gott unser Schöpfer hat gemacht aus einem Goldmacher einen Töpfer."[1] In

1. Cited in *Porcelain through the ages* (2nd. edition 1963) by George Savage, p. 125: "God our creator has transformed a maker of gold into a potter."

1707, a red stoneware akin to the Chinese Yi-Hsing was made and, in January 1708, a small translucent white bowl was fired. Sadly, von Tschirnhaus died shortly before the final triumph of 28th March, 1709 when Böttger announced to his king: "I have made a good porcelain with a fine glaze." Augustus was overjoyed and Böttger was afforded every comfort except his liberty. The Royal Saxon Porcelain Manufactory was established in 1710 at Albrechtsburg Castle in the village of Meissen twelve miles from Dresden. Böttger was appointed works manager and commercial production started shortly before 1712.

Early Meissen vase (neck missing), c.1728, decorated in the Kakiemon *style with storks and* Indianische Blumen.

The first models to be made were copies of Chinese figures; Lo-Hans, the sage Pu-Tai Ho-Shang, and the goddess Kuan Yin. However, the king was anxious to promote a European style and ordered Johann Jakob Irminger, the court goldsmith, to supply drawings suitable for translation into porcelain. Between 1717 and 1727, a number of puppet-like models were made of freaks, peasants, characters from the Italian comedy and, perhaps inevitably, of Augustus II, by such artists as Georg Fritzsche and Göttfried Müller. It was high fashion during the seventeenth and eighteenth centuries to reserve a room in every *château* for the display of Oriental porcelain and Delftware. Augustus had dreamed of possessing a whole palace devoted to this end and, in 1717, purchased the Hollandische Palais from Graf von Flemming. The roof was altered to conform with the supposed Oriental style and the building renamed the Japanische Palais. The ground floor was used to house Augustus's Oriential collection whilst the upper floor was filled with the products of his Meissen factory. Eventually, some 40,000 items were amassed. In 1727, the sculptor Johann Gottlieb Kirchner (1706-1763) was appointed *modellmeister* and commissioned to produce porcelain models of animals and birds up to four feet in height. He was a competent artist though a slow worker and given to bouts of heavy drinking. He was dismissed in 1728 and an ivory carver, Johann Christoph Ludwig von Lucke engaged in his place. He too, proved unequal to the task and left Meissen. In 1730, Kirchner was reappointed. The massive scale proved inappropriate for the medium and enormous technical difficulties had to be overcome. Progress was painfully slow and, in 1731, Johann Joachim Kändler was appointed as Kirchner's assistant and, with his help, about fifty models, mostly in triplicate, were eventually completed though many were not delivered until after the death of Augustus II. The models have been described and many illustrated by Hugo Morley-Fletcher.[2]

Advances made in the modelling shop were paralleled in the field of enamel decoration. Early models were left in the white and some, including the large birds and animals, were painted with oil paint or covered with pigments suspended in lacquer, a method employed by Martin Schnell (1702-1740) for use in the furniture trade. Until 1719, a source of cobalt blue could not be found so that it was impossible to reproduce blue and white wares after the Oriental fashion which were so beloved by Augustus. Indeed, the standards of factory decoration were so deplorable that many pieces were sent to Augsburg where numerous artists lived who were familiar with the technique of enamelling upon glass. Some outside decorators, or *Hausmaler,* later became a thorn in the flesh of Meissen and several penalties were inforced upon any who were unfortunate enough to be brought before the Saxon courts. In 1718, the kiln master, Samuel Stölzel, defected to Vienna where he assisted Claude du Paquier in the establishment of a rival porcelain factory. The following year, Stölzel returned and made peace with his former employers by bringing with him the great colour chemist and artist, Johann Gregor Horöldt (1696-1775). Under Horöldt's direction, a fine range of enamel colours was developed, the paint shops were transformed and a formidable nucleus of artistic talent was

2. 'Meissen Beasts for Augustus the Strong' by Hugo Morley-Fletcher, *Connoisseur,* 1975, Vol. 189, No. 760, pp. 95-99.

assembled. Also in 1719, Böttger died at the early age of thirty-seven. During his long imprisonment he had sought refuge in the bottle and had become a hopeless alcoholic. In 1733, Kirchner left Meissen for the second time, Kändler became *modellmeister,* and Augustus II died. The large zoological models under construction were completed but little further interest was shown in the project which was soon to be forgotten.

Johann Joachim Kändler (1706-1775) was the son of a Protestant pastor, born in Fischbach near Dresden. He was apprenticed to the sculptor, Benjamin Thomae, and was profoundly influenced by the work of Balthazar Permoser. Kändler's genius was apparent from the moment he was appointed at Meissen. His large models display an amazing vitality and recapture the essence of the species that is altogether lacking in the stiffly posed, though anatomically correct, creations of Kirchner. It was said that he accomplished more in three months than his *modellmeister* had done in three years. Until 1735-36, Kändler was fully occupied with the plastic designs of the great baroque dinner services which culminated in the Swan service of 2,200 pieces made for Count Heinrich von Brühl, the prime minister and factory director. He then focused his remarkable talents upon the small scale porcelain model. There were no precedents other than those set by imported models from the east, the puppet-like creations of his predecessors, and the huge zoological images that he had himself helped to manufacture. He chose a scale, five to eight inches, that seems exactly right and stretched the medium to its limits and often seemingly beyond with knife sharp edges and projecting parts. Kändler appreciated that the new substance required a treatment all its own and that it was insufficient merely to reproduce in miniature larger plastic works of art. All unnecessary detail was, accordingly, eliminated and features hitherto moulded in the round were, instead, indicated by placement of enamel colour. He adopted the dramatic poses beloved by the Mannerist school of sculpture. Each model was intended to be viewed from any angle and to be a complete entity in its own right. Bases were kept as simple moulds or pads, sparsely decorated with leaves and flowers in a manner that did not compete for interest with the figure. Close collaboration with enamellers under the direction of Horöldt ensured optimum decoration which employed strong dark colours of the baroque palette applied between large passages left in the white and permitting reflections between interfaces covered with a mirror-like glaze. Sometimes the effect was enhanced by painted floral decoration. Initially, this was effected without shading or three dimensional drawing after the fashion of the Orient in a style called *Indianische Blumen.* The European style of more natural floral painting was introduced circa 1740 by Johann Göttleib Klinger and was known as *Deutsche Blumen.*

Meissen cup and saucer, c.1745, decorated in the European style with Deutsche Blumen.

Inspiration of subject matter came from book illustrations many of which were made available from the library of Count Brühl, from prints and engravings purchased at the annual trade fairs held at Dresden, Meissen and Leipzig, and also obtained from agents in Paris. Other sources were marbles and bronzes whilst some figures were modelled from life. Kändler's treatment was usually harsh, brilliant and satirical and, though he was capable of rare understanding, very little of his work displays empathy or tenderness. He was able, in a few inches of paste, to capture movement and emotion, but seldom grace and beauty. When more than one example of a model was issued, no two were ever decorated in quite the same manner so that each is a unique masterpiece. When, in 1764, Johann Joachim Winckelmann wrote in the *The History of Antiquity:* "Porcelain is generally modelled into ridiculous little puppets, and the childish taste it engenders has spread everywhere..." he revealed the depth of his own plebian prejudices more than any deficiency in the plastic art of Kändler and his associates.

In 1740-45, the rococo style reached Miessen from France and, within a few years profoundly influenced porcelain modelling. The hitherto dramatic poses were muted and figures were now intended to be viewed only from a particular aspect or in groups. The dark colours of the former palette became lighter to provide pastel shades of yellow, green and pink, whilst bases were decorated with C- and S-scrolls arranged in asymmetrical designs accented with gilt and enamel colour. Kändler was, essentially, a child of the Baroque and though never completely happy in the rococo, was forced to modify his former style. As the burden of his administrative duties steadily increased, he relied more and more on subordinate modellers and assistants.

Johann Frederich Eberlein (1697-1749) came to Meissen in 1735 and remained until his untimely death. Although he collaborated with Kändler and Reinicke, he also created many figures and groups of his own and is rightly famed for figures of Orientals, Levantines, and allegorical figures. His work displays a slender elegance that immediately distinguishes it from that of other artists and which is discernible even in copies fashioned in soft paste. He indulged a preference for almond-shaped eyes often on models relating to the European as well as the Oriental scene. Peter Reinicke (1715-1768), was appointed to Meissen in 1743, ostensibly as Kändler's assistant. Initially, he was employed roughing out models to the designs of his *modellmeister* who would then apply 'Corrections' before passing them to the mould makers. With the passage of time, Reinicke was allowed an increasingly free hand and eventually showed himself to be a competent artist. It is difficult to differentiate between the styles of master and pupil though it is probable that much of the credit properly owing to Reinicke was assumed by Kändler. Frederich Elias Meyer (1723-1785), was brought to Meissen to replace the ailing Eberlein in 1748; he left the manufactory at the request of Frederick the Great in 1761 to join his brother at the factory in Berlin. Meyer deliberately elongated the human form in a manner that recalls the paintings of El Greco and, to enhance the effect his models have small heads, strangely overhanging brows, and are placed upon tall bases. His work is, at its best, of oustanding merit, but much of it is over-detailed, fussy, and artistically unsuccessful. It is scarcely surprising that Meyer had frequent quarrels with Kändler who failed utterly to comprehend a style that was so very far removed from his own.

Meissen group emblematic of 'Hearing', from a set representing 'The Five Senses', 6ins. (15.2cm), c.1755, by F.E. Meyer.

Kändler had, as early as 1737, established a liaison with the Paris art dealer Jean Charles Huet, from whom he had purchased many engravings after Watteau, Boucher, Lancret, and by Huet's brother Christoph. Some fine groups including 'Ladies in Crinolines', made during the 1740s were based upon prints after *La Comédie Française.* When the momentum of Meissen's great creative force began to slow down, Kändler again visited the French capital and returned in 1749 with fresh material. The fruits of this are provided by a series of models and groups relating to *chinoiserie,* the idyllic pastoral and romanticised allegory which were issued between 1750-56. These were plagiarised by most European factories.

The lead established by Meissen over all potential rivals was prodigious and was retained until 1756. However, the defection of Samuel Stölzel in 1718, when he went with Christoph Hunger to Vienna, started a chain reaction. A Vienna workman, Joseph Ringler, gleaned the secrets of porcelain manufacture, so it is said, from a love affair with Claude du Paquier's daughter and he then embarked upon a circuitous journey stopping off for a while wherever he found persons prepared to purchase his knowledge. In this manner, porcelain factories were established at Künersburg (1750), Höchst and Strasburg (1751), Frankenthal (1753) and at Nymphenburg (1754). During his residency at

Künersburg, Ringler disclosed the arcanum to Johann Benkgraff who, in turn, assisted to found further porcelain works at Berlin (1752) under Wegely, and at Fürstenburg (1753). Each of these offshoots enjoyed a brief moment of glory but none possessed the necessary financial resources, the galaxy of talent or the organisation to pose any real or lasting threat to royal Meissen; not at least until 1756.

In 1740 Frederick the Great succeeded to the throne of Brandenburg and Prussia. The same year he invaded Silesia and obtained the necessary free passage for his troops through Saxony. In 1744, this procedure was repeated during the second Silesian campaign. On each occasion the Prussian troops behaved more like an army of occupation than as allies. In 1756, hostilities broke out for the third time and three columns, each of 20,000 Prussians, crossed the frontier of Saxony *en route* for Silesia. Frederick imposed harsh conditions upon which the non-belligerent status of Saxony depended. Augustus III was a man of peace but was unable to effect immediate demobilisation of his pathetic little army some units of which attempted to oppose the Prussian tide. Frederick used this as an excuse to occupy Dresden. Augustus and his ministers fled to Poland. The invading force then took possession of the Meissen works and endeavoured to dismantle the kilns with a view to their re-erection in Berlin. The plan proved impracticable and during the confusion many of the artists and potters, including Horöldt, fled. Frederick compelled the management that remained to provide him with dinner services, useful wares of all kinds and models, chiefly of allegorical subjects. When he had sated his appetite for porcelain, he compelled Augustus III to pay a huge indemnity and a high rent for licence to use his own property. Kändler stayed at his post but took great care to absent himself whenever Meissen was visited by Frederick who repeatedly tried to persuade him to work for him at the Berlin factory. Perhaps Kändler recalled the treatment meted out many years previously to Böttger.

The rape of the Meissen works effectively put a stop to the flow of new porcelain models in England. Nevertheless, Frederick had seized stocks of Meissen porcelain as spoils of war and these he gave to Carl Henrich Schimmelmann in lieu of payment for military supplies. Forbidden to dispose of these within the territories controlled by Frederick in order to protect the Berlin factory against unequal competition, Schimmelmann organised a series of auctions in Hamburg. These were most carefully stage-managed and much of what was sold fetched huge prices and eventually reached this country between about 1758-60. In this manner, useful ware and models manufactured at Meissen prior to the Seven Years War continued to flow, albeit in a steadily diminishing volume, into England where some of it served to inspire soft paste modellers.

The Prussian yoke was lifted in 1763 with the signing of a peace treaty and, although in reduced circumstances, the Meissen works was one of the few assets left in Saxony surviving the ravages of the hostilities. Kändler lived until 1774 but was by now out of touch with current European fashion in which the rococo had given place to neo-classical taste. A Frenchman, Michel Victor Acier (1736-1781), was engaged as *modellmeister* to be coequal with Kändler, whilst Count Camille Marcolini became director. A number of sentimental groups of mothers and children, cupids and mythological subjects were issued upon round or oval bases decorated with vertical gilded fluting. Many were left in the biscuit after the style of Sèvres, but the hard paste of Meissen produced a cold glittering and uncompromising appearance that compared most unfavourably with the beautiful *pâte tendre* of Sèvres. Sadly, by 1770, the French manufactories changed over to *pâte dure* when the great days of the

'Arlecchino' in mock greeting, 6ins. (15.2cm), c.1740, by J.J. Kändler.

porcelain figure came to an end.

In 1799, the Meissen factory was deeply in debt and Marcolini tendered his resignation; he was persuaded to remain at his post until 1813. The following year, the roar of cannon was once again heard by the citizens of Dresden, this time from the artillery of Napoleon I. The hegemony of Meissen had been broken in 1756 by military conquest and, after a brief and partial recovery, war and changing public taste further reduced the fortunes of the once great manufactory. Although there have subsequently been several minor revivals and some fine porcelain figures are still being produced, 1756 saw the disappearance of any significant influence exerted by Meissen upon the porcelain modellers in this country.

The Influence of Meissen Models upon English Factories

When, in 1756, the Prussian soldiery broke into Pfortin Castle, they found in the home of Count Brühl over 3,000 enamelled porcelain figures and groups. Clearly, from this evidence alone, the number of models produced before the Seven Years' War was prodigious and it is only possible, here, to mention those copied or adapted by porcelain factories in this country. This presupposes selection and much of outstanding merit, such as those models relating to court personages, the opera, the local political and social scenes, devotional pieces and crinoline groups, have been omitted.

The colourful characters of the *Commedia dell'Artre* formed the basis of some of the earliest models made by Kändler. Initially, these were inspired by engravings made by François Joullain after earlier etchings by Giacomo Calotto (1592-1635), in the *Histoire du Théâtre Italien depuis la décadence de la comedie latine,* by Luigi Riccoboni, published between 1726 and 1731. Most popular of the dramatis personae was *Arlecchino* (Harlequin), usually depicted in a round plumed or a conical hat, a mask either of tan or black, and motley. Models portray him dancing, scowling, in mock greeting,[3] alarmed, with pince-nez,[4] with a jug,[5] with a spyglass,[6] with slap-sticks,[7] with a bird[8] and, indeed, in almost every possible pursuit and engaged in all forms of mischief. Copies were made at Chelsea (C1), Bow (G6 and H1), Derby (K2 and M199), and Longton Hall (O44 and O45). Other models by Kändler include 'Arlecchino seated with Bagpipes', and companion 'Columbina seated with a hurdy-gurdy'.[9] These were copied at Chelsea (C2), Bow (H10) and Longton Hall (O46). The prototypes survive in many different forms some quite elaborate in which the bagpipes are shaped like a goat.[10] 'Pulcinella', the hunchback, was also a favourite of Kändler who delighted in showing him dancing in a conical cap.[11] An early pair of dry-edge Derby candlesticks incorporate 'Pulcinella' holding a lantern, and 'Arlecchino' dancing (K9), whilst a free-standing 'Pulcinella' (G9), created at Bow, leans against a tree-stump. There are several versions of the 'Avvocato',[12] mostly in tricorn hat, white mask, and gown decorated with rosettes. The Chelsea version (C3) wears a cap and ermine trimmed gown and another from Longton Hall (O4) stands reading from a book and both probably stem from lost Meissen prototypes.

In 1743-44, Peter Reinicke made a set of twenty comedy figures, after Joullain, to commemorate the marriage between the princess Wilhelmine and the Duke of Weissenfels. The bride's father, Frederick William, anxious to pre-empt the designs of his Empress for a matrimonial alliance between the houses of Hanover and Brandenburg, did not scruple to kick, punch, and pull the hair of the wretched girl till she agreed to wed a man twenty years her senior whom she did not love. The full set of porcelain models are illustrated by Dr. Erica Paul-Eisenbeiss,[13] whilst some of the engravings from which they were inspired are reproduced by Nathaniel Harris[14] and Hugh Tait.[15]

3. *Antique Porcelain Digest* (Bath, 1961) by C.M. and G.R. Scott, pl. 78, nos. 283, 284 and 285.
4. *German Porcelain of the 18th Century* (London, 1972) by Erica Pauls-Eisenbeiss, Vol. I, p. 279, Harlequin alarmed; p. 293, Harlequin with pince-nez.
5. ibid, p. 266, Harlequin with a jug of ale.
6. 'Miessen Beasts for Augustus the Strong', op. cit., p. 58.
7. *Festive Publication to Commemorate the 200th Jubilee of the Oldest European China Factory, Meissen* (Dresden, 1910 and reprinted 1972 by Dover Books) by Karl Berling, table 9, no. 237.
8. 'Meissen Beasts for Augustus the Strong', op. cit., p. 59.
9. ibid., pp. 84 and 85.
10. *German Porcelain of the 18th Century,* op. cit., p. 263.
11. ibid., p. 311.
12. ibid., p. 307.
13. ibid., pp. 302-321.
14. *Porcelain Figurines* (London, 1975) by Nathaniel Harris, p. 27, 'Baloardo', engravings by Joullain.
15. 'Commedia dell'Arte in Glass and Porcelain' by H.G. Tait, *Apollo,* 1963, Vol. 78, p. 263, fig. 4 'Scapino'; p. 266, fig. 11, 'Beltrame', engravings by Joullain.

'Scapino', standing cap in hand, 5¼ins. (12.7cm), c.1743/4, made by P. Reinicke as one of a set for the Duke of Weissenfels. This model was copied at Chelsea (see Colour Plate A).

'Pantalone' (Plate 26) in skull-cap, suit of red and long cloak, stands stooped with beard jutting forward, money-bag in hand; he was copied at Chelsea (B36 and C10) and Longton Hall (O5). 'Dottore Baloardo' (Plate 24) in broad-brimmed hat, leans backwards in histrionic pose with right arm akimbo and left arm elevated; there are Chelsea (C7) and Bow (H4) versions. Strangely, the model of 'Capitano Rogamondo' in tricorn hat, jacket, tight breeches and up-turned moustache, was ignored by English copyists and instead Reinicke's 'Narcissino' in wide-brimmed hat, long hair, linen tabs at neck and cummerbund with tabaro thrown over his shoulder was copied and issued as 'The Captain' (Plate 25, Chapter VI) at Chelsea (C9) and Bow (H7). Both Reinicke's models of 'Scaramuzzi' in soft cap, ruffle and tabaro were copied at Chelsea; one depicted walking with mincing steps (C14) was copied also at Bow (H9), the second with cloak slipping from off his shoulders is known only at Chelsa (C15). The varlet 'Scapino' in loose trousers and jacket, gathered with belt to which a purse is attached, stands in long cloak, cap in hand, bearded and laughing; there are Chelsea (Colour Plate A) (B37) and Bow (G10) examples and in the latter a mask may replace the cap. The tragi-comic 'Pedrolino' in brimmed hat, turn-back in front, ruffle and loose clothing, stands with both hands raised in horror and was echoed at Chelsea (C11) and Bow (H8). Other models of 'Arlecchino' disguised as a fisherman, and in a conical hat dancing, together with 'Columbina' with mask and slap-sticks were ignored by modellers in this country though 'Columbina dancing' found echoes at Chelsea (C4) and the same model was used married upon a single base to Arlecchino during the penultimate periods of production both at Chelsea (D17) and at Bow (I1).

Between 1740 and 1750, Kändler created several groups embracing characters from the Commedia dell'Arte after Boucher. The beautiful red anchor Chelsea group 'Columbina playing a lute whilst Pantalone conducts from a score' (C5) follows a Kändler original. Likewise, there is a Bow version (G11) of the 'Indiscretions of Harlequin',[16] in which Arlecchino seated upon the ground lifts the hem of Columbina's skirt as she sits upon the knee of Beltrame and regards her ankles with curiosity. The Meissen group of 'Harlequin making playful gestures to an infant' dressed in motley held by Columbina[17] appears in a strange Derby version (K2) where the characters look as if they were playing peek-a-boo under a leafing tree. Some of the Bow comedy groups were derived from engravings rather than via a Meissen prototype and sometimes the Saxon and the English models appear to have been based on different plates. Thus, the Bow group known as 'The Italian Musicians' (G13) depicts Columbina playing a mandoline seated on the left of Mezzetino who holds a musical score and sings, and was inspired by the engraving 'Belle, n'écoutez rien', by C.N. Cochin after Boucher.[18] The Meissen group[19] shows the roles and positions of the two characters reversed and was based upon the engraving 'Serenade Italien', by J. Daullé.[20] The satirical Meissen group, 'The Invalid Duped'[21] portrays a seated invalid kissing a girl who accepts refreshments proffered behind the back of her would-be lover by a clown, whilst a second clown behind the group makes derisive gestures. This theme was adapted at Derby to become 'Two Lovers and a Clown' (K21) by removal of the trappings of invalidism and omission of the second clown. Some charming models of children in Italian comedy costumes[22] found echoes at Derby (K24) and at Bow (H12).

Engravings after Watteau and Boucher inspired several figures and groups relating to Chinoiserie. 'Four Japanese'[23] by Kändler and 'Five Chinese'[24] by Eberlein were evidently ignored by English modellers. However, Chinoiserie groups made in 1750 by Reinicke and Meyer after Boucher's 'Les Délices de

16. *Festive Publication...*, op. cit., table 6, no. 344.
17. 'Meissen Beasts for Augustus the Strong', op. cit., p. 54.
18. *The Italian Comedy* (Paris, 1929, and reprinted New York, 1966) by Pierre Louis Duchatre, p. 37 'Belle n'écouter rien', by C.N. Cochin.
19. *Festive Publication...*, op. cit., table 9, no. 250.
20. *'Chelsea and Other English Porcelain Pottery and Enamel in the Irwin Untermyer Collection'* (Cambridge, Mass., 1957) by Yvonne Hackenbroch, Vol. II and *Connoisseur*, 1956, Vol. 138, p. 111, fig. 19.
21. *German Porcelain in the 18th Century*, op. cit., p. 277.
22. ibid., p. 317.
23. *Festive Publication...*, op. cit., fig. 121, nos. 2671 and 2672; fig. 122, nos. 2676 and 2677.
24. ibid., fig. 84, nos. 421, 435, 437, 439 and 444.

'Pedrolino' standing upon a tall rococo base, 9ins. (22.9cm), c.1745, by J.J. Kändler and J.F. Eberlein.

L'Enfance'[25] prompted two Chelsea groups. One of these portrayed a lady standing holding a steam kettle in one hand and pouring chocolate from a jug into a cup held by a Chinese boy. In the original Meissen group a third child crouches holding a bowl of fruit but in the Chelsea version the third figure was made separately and issued *en suite* (B40) suggesting that perhaps the engraving itself provided the source. The second group depicts a Chinese lady, a cat and a child playing with a diabolo (B39). Reinicke's 'Japanese Family'[26] seems to have provided the inspiration of a Bow group known as the 'Chinese Magician' (H13) which includes a Chinaman with a bear and a child standing upon a chair but, strangely, the beautiful 'Chinese Lovers' who read from a book in a trellised arbour,[27] based on an engraving from 'The Five Senses' by Gabriel Huquier after Boucher, were overlooked.

In 1714, a folio of one hundred engravings drawn by G. Scotin and other artists was published for M. de Ferriole, the French ambassador to the Sublime Port. This, which was entitled *Recueil de cent estampes représentant différentes Nations du Levant tirées sur les tableaux paints d'après Nature en 1707-1708, par ordres de M. Ferriole,* illustrated Turks, Negroes, Levantines, Bulgarians, Hungarians and others seen in the streets of Constantinople, and formed the basis of many Meissen models copied in this country. Eberlein's 'Turk in plumed turban', kneeling beside a sucrier[28] was imitated at Bow (G48) together with a fine 'Negress standing beside a basket',[29] though here (G47) the companion 'Negro' was ignored. Models of a 'Turk in a turban' and 'Levantine lady in a tall head-dress',[30] each seated beside a shell container are known in Chelsea (C70) and Bow (H15) versions, whilst a 'Standing Turk in cylindrical hat', and companion 'Levantine lady',[31] derived from Scotin's engraving 'Le Capi Aga ou Chef des Eunugues blancs', prompted Chelsea copies (C69). At Bow, the same 'Levantine lady' was paired with a 'Turk in turban and fur-edged cloak' (Plate 62, Chapter VII) (H14). In 1755, Kändler created 'Six Orientals in sumptuous dress'[32] which included a 'Persian' wearing a turban and holding a battle-axe, and companion Lady, in addition to a 'Turk in a stocking cap', standing with both thumbs tucked into his belt and a 'Levantine Lady'. The male figure of the last mentioned pair was copied at Longton Hall (O27 and O69) and at Chaffers' Liverpool factory (Q29). Kändler collaborated with Peter Reinicke to create a heavily armed 'Pandeur' and a 'Janissary'[33] who holds a short arrow in one hand and has a quiver slung across his back and was echoed by the Derby 'Abyssinian Archer' (K32). Kändler's 'Indian Prince' and 'Queen',[34] portrayed by a negro and negress in a feathered head-dress, were copied at Derby and Bow (H21) and, though the female figure also appears at Chelsea, her companion is a mirror image of the original (C66). A fine pair of prancing 'Horses with Grooms', represented as a blackamoor and a Turk with reins in their hands,[35] were adaptations of Guillaume Coustou's marble 'Horse Tamers' and were copied at Longton Hall (O68).

In 1736, Ravenet and Le Bas engraved drawings made by Boucher of peasants bearing farm produce to market, street criers, and itinerant musicians. The following year, the sculptor Édme Bouchardon produced sixty red chalk drawings of similar subjects. These were engraved by his friend Ann Claude Philippe de Tubières, Comte de Caylus, who published them in five sets, each of twelve engravings between 1737 and 1746. The folio was entitled: *Études prises dans le bas peuple, ou les cris de Paris,* and the sculptural character of the engravings prompted models of stocky peasants by Kändler and Reinicke issued between 1745 and 1747. The figures were rather freely adapted and it is difficult to identify the precise source for any specific character.[36] They were decorated in the strong dark colours of the baroque

25. *German Porcelain of the 18th Century,* op. cit., pp. 113, 115 and 119.
26. ibid., p. 113.
27. ibid., p. 117.
28. *Festive Publication....* op. cit., fig. 74, no. 771.
29. *Porcelain Figurines,* op. cit., p. 23.
30. *German Porcelain of the 18th Century,* op. cit., p. 103.
31. ibid., p. 105.
32. *Festive Publication....* op. cit., fig. 37, no. 1294, a 'Persian'; no. 1287, a 'Levantine lady'; no. 1286, a 'Turk' in stocking cap.
33. *Porcelain Figurines,* op. cit., p. 14.
34. *Antique Porcelain Digest,* op. cit., p. 149, col. pl. 4, fig. 12.
35. *Das Meissner Porzellan and seine and Geschichte* (Leipzig, 1900) by Karl Berling, fig. 97.
36. The engravings by the Count de Caylus, interleafed with the chalk drawings by Bouchardon, are in the British Museum.

palette and stand on mound bases. Many were copied by the English factories including a woman 'Vegetable Seller'[37] with her basket of wares over one arm wearing a head-scarf, which was echoed at Derby (J18), a pair of 'Fruit Sellers'[38] was copied at Bow (G30), and a standing 'Musician with a Hurdy-Gurdy'[39] at Chelsea (B54 and C31). the 'Absinth Seller', with tray of bottles,[40] found echoes at Bow (G26) and Derby (J19), whilst the 'Print Seller',[41] with samples in either hand and a pack on his back appeared in Chelsea (A11 and C33), Bow (G38) and Derby (Plates 90 and 111) (J20) where he acquired a female companion (K71). The 'Birdcatcher' and his 'Wife'[42] were copied at Chelsea (C21) where the female figure was adapted to provide a 'Flower Seller' (C29) with basket of blossoms over one arm.

Between 1752 and 1754, Kändler and Reinicke created a second series representing 'The Cries of Paris', based on watercolour sketches by Christoph Huet. There are about fifty models which stand on scrolled bases, are adorned in paler enamels and are more slender than the first set. Many, including 'Butter Seller', 'Orange Seller', 'Lemon Seller', and 'Cutler' by Kändler; the 'Water Carrier', by Eberlein, and 'Baker's Assistant', by Reinicke were not copied in this country. The fine pair of 'Cooks bearing Platters' were echoed at Chelsea (C23) and Bow (H27); the 'Jewish Pedlar' and 'Trinket Seller'[43] were plagiarised at Chelsea (C30) and Derby (K70); whilst the 'Savoyard Drummer'[44] with fife and tambour, was copied at Chelsea (C35). The 'Night Watchman' and 'Companion',[45] each with baskets of provisions and lantern, were not imitated at Chelsea until circa 1763 (D18). Other red anchor 'Cries' include 'Rat Catcher' (Plate 27, Chapter VI) (C34), 'Ballad Singer and her Child' (C16) whilst Bow versions include 'Tinker' (H42), 'Alchemist' (H23), 'Vintner' (G41), and 'Itinerant Musician' (H32). Some Meissen prototypes are illustrated in catalogues of the Emma Budge Collection,[46] C.H. Fischer Collection,[47] and Irwin Untermyer Collection.[48]

Somewhat similar models of fisherfolk include 'Fishwife with live Carp',[49] 'Fishwife holding a platter of Fish' (Plate 28, Chapter VI),[50] 'Fisherman in peaked cap' taking fish from his net,[51] and the 'Drunken Fisherman'[52] astride an eel-trap with his shirt stuffed with fish and one in either hand. All, except the first, were copied at Chelsea (C28, C24 and C25). Reinicke's beautiful 'Peepshowman'[53] and others based on Marcellus Laroon's 'Cryes of the City of London', were ignored by the modellers in England. Kändler also created a set of 'Small Artisans',[54] including 'Coppersmith', 'Butcher', 'Rope-maker', 'Potter', 'Tailor' and others, some of which are in Lord Fisher's Collection, in the Fitzwilliam Museum. The series also includes cooks[55] about various culinary tasks, either seated on brick plinths or standing before stoves. A rare Bow 'Cook in stocking Cap' tasting his forefinger over a saucepan (H28), and a Chelsea 'Cupid in Disguise' (D1) stem from the Meissen source. Many of the artisans display an over-dressed appearance with tie-wigs and red heeled, gold buckled shoes. Clearly they were intended to represent the nobility in fancy dress rather than humbler folk.

Other models of peasants are more in the genre of David Teniers, such as a 'Woodman with a Saw' and 'Companion with an Axe'[56] copied at Bow (Plate 64, Chapter VII) (H44). The Chelsea 'Ostler' (C44) and Carter (Plate 30, Chapter VI) (C38), 'Cooper seated upon a Barrel' (C39), as well as standing models of a 'Boy with up-turned basket of Fish' and 'Girl selling Fish' (H24) made at Bow, echo Meissen originals. Eberlein's 'Tyrolean Dancers'[57] portraying a swain dancing a gavotte with a peasant girl, reappeared at Chelsea (C48), Bow (H43), and Derby (K53).[58] Although the Chelsea group of a 'Dutchman dancing with his Wife' (C40) may have been copied from a lost Eberlein group, this appears highly unlikely on stylistic grounds and must

37. 'Meissen Beats for Augustus the Strong', op. cit., p. 54.

38. *Festive Publication*..., op. cit., fig. 130, no. 17.

39. *Porcelain Figurines*, op. cit., p. 44.

40. Sales catalogue of the Emma Budge Collection, 27-29 September, 1937, Hamburg, lot 826.

41. *Festive Publication*..., op. cit, table 11, nos. 554 and 557.

42. 'Lord Fisher's Collection of English Porcelain in the Fitzwilliam Museum', by Jack Palmer, *Transactions*, English Ceramic Circle, 1964, Vol. 5, pt. 5, pp. 252-257; fig. 228c, Meissen model; fig. 228d, Chelsea copy; fig. 228e, Chelsea adaptation of 'Flower Seller'.

43. *Festive Publication*..., op. cit., fig. 40, no. 2785.

44. ibid., fig. 94, no. 1768.

45. *Dresden China* (London, 1946) by W.B. Honey, pl. 52B.

46. See fn. 40.

47. *Katalog der Sammlung Alt-Meissner Porzellan des Herren Reutners und C.H. Fischer in Dresden* (Cologne, 1906) by C.H. Fischer.

48. *Meissen, Other Continental Porcelain, Faience and Enamel in the Irwin Untermyer Collection* (Cambridge, Mass., 1957) by Yvonne Hackenbroch, Vol. I.

49. *Apollo*, 1934, Vol. 20, No. 118, p. 182.

50. *Meissner Porzellan, 1710-1810* (Munich, 1966) by Siegfried Ducret, p. 230, fig. 948.

51. ibid., p. 224, fig. 917.

52. *Apollo*, 1934, Vol. 20, No. 118, p. 182.

53. 'Meissen Beasts for Augustus the Strong', op. cit., p. 88.

54. 'Early Dresden Figures: their origin and evolution' by Lord Fisher of Kilverstone, *Apollo*, 1934, Vol. 20, No. 118, pp. 178-186.

55. *German Porcelain of the 18th Century*, op. cit., p. 93.

56. 'Meissen Beasts for Augustus the Strong', op. cit., p. 86.

57. *German Porcelain of the 18th Century*, op. cit., pp. 81 and 83.

58. Fitzwilliam Museum, Cambridge, Lord Fisher Collection.

Meissen group known as the 'Tyrolean Dancers', 7½ins. (19.1cm), c.1735, by J.F. Eberlein, mounted in French ormolu.

surely be an original by Joseph Willems. The 'Peasant with a Hurdy-Gurdy' seated upon the ground[59] by Kändler was also reflected at Chelsea (B53).

Kändler created some magnificent devotional pieces which included statuettes and busts of saints and popes and culminated in the great altar garniture made for the empress Amalia of Austria[60] consisting of a crucifix, six candlesticks, twelve Apostles, ciborum, chalice, patten and a font. Such embellishments of the Roman Catholic faith found no sympathetic reception in a Protestant land. However, Kändler also made a series of models, in semi-humorous mood, of monks and nuns,[61] either standing with crucifix, rosary or breviary, or seated with missals. These, together with models of priests in birettas, were inspired by illustrations from contemporary and past books.[62] They proved very popular in England and copies were made at Chelsea (C104 and C105), Bow (H110-H117), Longton Hall (O70 and O71) and Chaffers' Liverpool (Q27).

Portrait models of members of the Saxon Court and their servants, the contemporary ballet and opera, and miners in their state uniforms were, not unexpectedly, ignored by English modellers. Strangely, two of the most humble people were immortalised in porcelain, namely Count von Brühl's 'Tailor' and his 'Wife'. The Count was a dandy who owned 650 dressing-gowns and three hundred suits in duplicate and probably spent more time with his tailor than with his cabinet colleagues. Anxious to have a new suit finished ready for a banquet, von Brühl rashly promised his tailor anything he liked to ask for if he could meet the deadline. The suit was duly delivered and the tailor asked to be able to attend the feast. It was impossible to acceed to this request so, instead, porcelain images of the tailor and his wife were created and placed upon the dining table. The worthy was lampooned in the order of knighthood holding a pair of scissors astride a bespectacled goat[63] and his wife upon a nanny-goat suckling a kid.[64] The Chelsea-Derby models of the 'Welsh Tailor' and his 'Wife' (M62) are said to have been adapted from this source.

A great many Meissen groups relate to allegorical subjects. Cesare Ripa's book, *Iconologia,* the first edition of which was published in 1593, illustrates personages from Greek and Roman mythology in their traditional dress, together with their appropriate accessories, and this probably provided a general guide to modellers. The name of Eberlein is especially associated with such models and groups. His 'Venus with a Dolphin and Cupid',[65] was adapted at Derby by omission of the Cupid to provide 'Aphrodite' (K77), whilst another Eberlein original was also copied at the same factory to give 'Cupid seated upon a Dolphin and Venus' (K95). His 'Charity',[66] represented by a standing woman with a babe upon her left arm, and handing an apple to a child at her side inspired copies at Bow (Plate 57, Chapter VII) (H73) by the Muses Modeller. Similar groups of a seated woman breast-feeding an infant with both a seated and a standing child, also known as 'Charity' issued at Chelsea (Colour Plate C) (D49) and Bow (H72) most probably follow a lost Meissen prototype. Eberlein portrayed 'Mercury'[67] in winged sandals and helmet bearing the caduceus; the Bow copy (G19 and H85) though less competently fashioned than that from Chelsea (C86) is by far the most appealing. A tall 'Diana' holding a long-bow beside her hound[68] in the act of selecting an arrow from a quiver upon her back, was based upon a seventeenth century bronze. Something of the slender elegance so characteristic of Eberlein's work is discernible even in the Derby soft paste copy (K11). Circa 1759, the same model was adapted at Longton Hall to provide the figure of a Red Indian Girl, emblematic of 'America' (O79) which was later issued from the same mould from the Plymouth factory in hard paste (P7). Eberlein was also responsible for 'The Antique Seasons',[69] which included four standing

59. 'Lord Fisher's Collection of English Porcelain in the Fitzwilliam Museum', op. cit., pl. 228a, Meissen model; pl. 228b, Chelsea copy.

60. *Antique Porcelain Digest,* op. cit., pl. 66, fig. 255.

61. *Katalog der Sammlung Alt-Meissner Porzellan...,* op. cit., pl. 4 *et seq.*

62. *Courte et solide Histoire de la Fondation des Ordres Religieux* (Amsterdam, 1688), engravings by Adrien Schoonbeck. Later edition Augsburg, 1692, engravings by Daniel Steudner. *Ordinum Religiosorum in Ecclesia Militanti Catalogus* (Rome, 1658), engraving by Filippo Bonanni. *Bref Historie de l'Institution des Ordres Religieux* (Paris) engravings by Odoardo Fialette.

63. *Festive publications...,* op. cit., fig. 47, no. 107, early version without base; fig. 48, no. 171, later version.

64. Ibid, table 15, no. 155.

65. ibid., fig. 70, no. 998.

66. ibid., fig. 96, no. 1688.

67. ibid., table 15, no. 198.

68. *English Porcelain of the 18th Century* (London, 1952) by J. Dixon, pl. 38.

69. *Derby Porcelain* (London, 1961) by F.Brayshaw Gilhespy, fig. 19, Derby 'Antique Seasons'; fig. 20, Meissen originals.

adult figures in classical robes beside putti, which found echoes at Derby (K75). His figure of 'Smell' from the 'Five Senses',[70] portrayed by a lady holding a posy to her nose, standing beside a flower-encrusted plinth upon which rests a perfume burner, was reproduced at Bow as 'Flora' (H78) and is also known in a Chelsea version (D47). These must not be confused with the Bow copy of the 'Flora Farnese' (H79). Although the source of many Chelsea allegorical figures is undetermined, the 'Rape of the Sabines' (C88) follows Eberlein's work[71] based upon a bronze by Giovanni da Bologna.

Kändler's set of 'Four Continents',[72] 'Small Continents',[73] 'Four Elements',[74] and 'Three Graces'[75] were, presumably, beyond the competence of the English copyists. It is possible, however, that the figure of Julius Caesar, emblematic of 'Rome', from Kändler's 'Four Ancient Kingdoms',[76] may be the source of the red anchor Chelsea 'Mars' (C85). Here, a Roman centurion in armour with cloak secured about his neck stands bare-headed. The later gold anchor 'Mars' (Plate 45, Chapter VI) (D45) together with several Derby versions (Plate 93, Chapter VIII) (J26) follows a different Meissen prototype in which the god wears a helmet and leans upon his shield.[77] 'Neptune with a Dolphin',[78] and 'Jupiter with an Eagle'[79] were copied both as individual models and as part of a set of the 'Four Elements' at Bow (H86 and H81) and Derby (K91 and K82); at Chelsea, the same two figures were used to represent 'Water' and 'Earth' but the model of 'Jupiter with an Eagle' representing 'Air' was replaced by 'Juno with her clothes blown out in the Wind' (D61). Kändler based his pair of reclining 'Water Deities'[80] on statuary of the Grenelle fountain in Paris and his work was plagiarised by Joseph Willems at Chelsea (C89). Kändler also created a set of 'Classical Season'[81] portrayed by four adult figures in antique robes, each attended by a putto, beside four rococo candlesticks, and these found echoes at Bow (H100).

Elias Meyer made two versions of the 'Four Quarters of the Globe'. The first[82] consists of two paired groups of seated children: 'Africa', a Blackamoor in an elephant head-dress sits facing 'Asia' a girl in stocking cap; the companion group shows 'Europe' as a white girl facing 'America' represented by a Red Indian. These were copied at Chelsea (C97) c.1756. The second[83] is composed of individual standing children in like dress with 'Asia', holding a perfume burner beside a crouching camel; 'Africa', with cornucopia and lion; 'Europe' crowned with orb and sceptre; and 'America', holding a long-bow beside a prairie dog. These were also copied at Chelse c.1759 (D60) and later at Derby (Colour Plate R) (K73) and Meyer's 'Antique Seasons' (M200)[84] consist of standing adult figures in classical robes, each beside a vase which found echoes at Bow (H91).

Models of putti and cupids were frequently employed to represent seasons, elements, the arts and sciences and these are too numerous to warrant individual mention. They may be depicted seated or standing, as individual figures, pairs or groups. For example, a pair of nude draped putti seated upon plinths, one with a terrestial orb the other with a star-spangled globe, issued at Chelsea and Bow to represent 'Geography' and 'Astronomy' (C95) follow Meissen prototypes. Reinicke's set of standing putti emblematic of the 'Four Seasons'[85] prompted a Longton Hall model of 'Summer' (O36) whilst similar standing putti upon a single base were issued from Chelsea (C101). The Derby factory evidently preferred to represent the 'Four Seasons' with four single seated putti (K74). Later Meissen models of the 1760s, include several groups, each of two cupids, representing such subjects as 'Commerce',[86] 'Astronomy'[87] and other arts and sciences created by Michel Acier and reproduced at Derby (M39-M45). Especially delightful, are 'Cupids in Disguise'. Kändler made these models often as humerous echoes of his earlier

70. *Dresden China,* op. cit., pl. XLVIB.
71. *Festive Publication...,* op. cit., table 10, fig. 110.
72. *German Porcelain of the 18th Century,* op. cit., pp. 135 and 137.
73. ibid., p. 143.
74. ibid., pp. 131 and 133.
75. ibid., p. 127.
76. ibid., p. 153.
77. *Koniglich, Sachsische Porzellan Manufaktur Meissen, 1710-1910* (Dresden, 1911) by Karl Berling, pl. 9, fig. 4.
78. *Festive Publication...,* fig. 96, no. 1688.
79. ibid., fig. 96.
80. *Katalog der Sammlung Alt-Meissner Porzellan...,* op. cit., pl. 4, no. 813.
81. Christie's Sale Catalogue, 28th March, 1977, lot 106.
82. Sotheby's Sale Catalogue, 9th June, 1963, lot 165.
83. *English Porcelain Figures of the 18th Century* (1961) by Arthur Lane, pls. 22B and 23B (Chelsea models). *Investing in Pottery and Porcelain* (1968) by Hugo Morley-Fletcher, p. 137 (Derby models).
84. *Bow Porcelain* (London, 1926) by Frank Hurlbutt, pl. 51B, set of Meissen models; pl. 51A, set of Bow copies.
85. *Festive publication...,* op. cit., table 11, nos. 2736A, 2736B and 2716.
86. ibid., fig. 164.
87. ibid., table 19, no. C46.

work. Thus, we find Cupid attired in the costumes of the Commedia dell'Arte as 'Pantalone', 'Columbina', 'Dottore Baloardo', and the 'Avvocato', or after the fashion of the 'Cries of Paris' in the guise of 'Hurdy-gurdy Player', or a 'Water Carrier'. The variations are almost limitless with Cupid as 'Shepherd' or 'Shepherdess', as a 'Huntsman', 'Wounded Soldier', 'Nursemaid', 'Playing Bagpipes', 'Carrying two flaming hearts', etc. Many may be seen in the Fitzwilliam Museum, Cambridge, in the collection of Lord Fisher,[88] in Saltram House, Plympton, and in Waddesdon Manor, Buckinghamshire; they are also illustrated in most of the catalogues relating to Meissen porcelain. The most accomplished of the English copies were made at Chelsea (C115 and D1) though others were later issued from Derby (M262-M278).

Long before Kändler's arrival at Meissen, models of freaks had proved popular, many based upon engravings made by Giacomo Calotto (1593-1635). His work had been reproduced by a number of different artists and published in 1716 at Antwerp as *Il Calotto Recusitato; oder Neu eingerichtes Zwerchen Cabinett,* accompanied by doggerel verses. A further set of twenty etchings by Calotto, 'Varie figure Gobbi',[89] prompted models of a 'Male' and 'Female Dwarf' which were copied at Chelsea (B56 and C106). The Derby 'Mansion House Dwarfs' (M227) stem from the same source. Huet's murals at Chantilly of monkeys dressed in human clothing, themselves probably prompted by Oriental designs, must have suggested to Kändler his models of a twenty-one piece monkey orchestra, called the *Affenkapelle.*[90] Indeed, two models may be traced to engravings after Huet.[91] Ten of these musicians were copied at Chelsea (C109) and issued as two sets each of five models. The rare 'Dog Orchestra' (D21) made at Chelsea may have sprung from a similar source.

When in 1749 Kändler returned from a trip to Paris, he brought back engravings after Watteau, Boucher, Lancret and others relating to La Comédie Française. A number of models of the 'Idyllic Pastoral' followed, including 'Liberty' and 'Matrimony'[92] issued in 1752 after Lancret. They portray a gallant standing beside a hound and a ram holding a bird aloft, whilst his lady holds open the door of an empty birdcage. Initial Bow copies (G37) show much of the original vigour which was to be dissipated in later versions (H63), and lost altogether in those made at Derby (K63), Longton Hall (O66), and Champion's Bristol factory (P31). Kändler's 'Shepherd with a Recorder', cross-legged before his dog, and companion 'Shepherdess with Posy' and blossoms gathered in her apron[93] found echoes at Chelsea (Plate 48, Chapter VI) (C57 and D80), Derby (Plate 109, Chapter VIII) (K64) and Bow (H66). There was, of course, no intention of representing rustic folk but, rather, lords and ladies in fancy dress. Hence the 'Shepherd feeding a Dog', and 'Shepherdess dressed in the height of Fashion' (Plate 165, Chapter XIII)[94] plagiarised at Chelsea (D75), together with the 'Imperial Shepherds' (Plate 49, Chapter VI) (D79). Here, the male figure wears a fine tricorn hat and long cloak and stands grasping a crook whilst proffering an apple; his companion holds a basket of flowers and gathers blossoms in her apron. Other English copies of Meissen pastoral subjects include 'The French Shepherds', copied at Chelsea (D78); the 'Dresden Shepherds', made at Derby (M55); 'Shepherd Bagpiper' in tricorn hat and companion 'Shepherdess', made both at Chelsea (C58 and D77) and Bow H65). The 'Boy Shepherd Bagpiper' in brimmed hat (Plate 70, Chapter VII), and companion 'Dancing Shepherdess' which are common to Bow (H60) and Derby (Plate 89, Chapter VIII) (J13) are likely to have been based on lost Meissen prototypes. Eberlein's 'Piedmontese Bagpiper',[95] readily identifiable by his broad plumed hat and voluminous cloak, was inspired by J. Dumont le Romain's engraving, and found echoes at Bow (H37). Models of 'Pierrot Dancing' and of a 'Dancing Girl mask in hand'

88. 'Love in Disguise' by Lord Fisher of Kilverstone, *Apollo,* 1955, Vol. 61, No. 364, pp. 183-188.

89. *Porcelain Figurines,* op. cit., pp. 56 and 57, Mansion House dwarfs together with engraving by Callot.

90. *Apollo,* 1964, Vol. 79, p. 365, fig. 2, the 'Affenkapelle'.

91. *Chelsea Porcelain at Williamsburg* (Virginia, U.S.A., 1977) by John. C. Austin, p. 134, engraving of 'Le Tambourin'; p. 135, corresponding model: p. 136, engraving of l'Organiste Ambulant; p. 137, model group.

92. *Das Meissner Porzellan and seine Geschichte,* op. cit., p. 131, fig. 195.

93. Fitzwilliam Museum Catalogue, no. 972.

94. *Festive Publication...,* op. cit., table 13, nos. 1331 and 1332.

95. ibid., table 17, nos. 1782 and 1784.

would seem to represent characters from the Commedia dell'Arte, but are unaccountably described by Karl Berling[96] as 'Dancing Shepherds'; they were copied at Derby (J14).

Blood sports in Saxony, as in most of Europe, during the eighteenth century were reserved for the aristocracy and savage penalties were meted out to those who dared to usurp their privileges. Hunting in Saxony was little more than a ritual slaughter of wild animals driven into a forest clearing, or even a town square, where they were shot to death at point blank range by ladies as well as their gallants. Kändler and Eberlein collaborated to create many models of 'Huntsman' with gun and dog, and companion 'Lady' with gun or falcon, less commonly with powder flask and game or with a pistol.[97] Their 'Huntsman in peaked cap' and 'Lady with Falcon'[98] prompted Chelsea copies (C55) whilst models in a similar genre made at Bow (Plate 71, Chapter VII) (H67, H68 and H69), Derby (L19) and Chelsea (D77 and D78) most probably stem from Meissen prototypes. Some groups by Kändler show 'Huntsman' and 'Lady' in romantic dalliance,[99] after the manner of Lancret and Boucher and such may well have inspired the beautiful Chelsa 'Huntsman kneeling before a Lady' who has a bird's nest in her lap, and the dry-edge Derby 'Huntsman flautist playing to a seated Lady' who has one hand upon his sleeve (Plate 168, Chapter XIII) (C54 and J17).

Many models of gallants and their ladies represent court personages but Kändler's 'Gentleman in a dressing-gown' blowing a kiss, and companion 'Crinolined Lady with a Fan'[100] were based on Filloeul's engraving 'Le Baiser Rendu' after J.B. Pater. The skirt of the lady was altered to conform with the current fashion in the Bow versions (H102). Eberlein's 'Lady in a crinoline' was paired with Kändler's 'Moustachioed Pole';[101] the female figure appeared at Chelsea (C68) without her partner and is sometimes called a 'Masquerader'. His group of 'An Actor offering his snuff-box to a Lady'[102] provided the basis for the dry-edge Derby model of a 'Snuff-Taker', emblematic of 'Smell' (J33) (Colour Plate L).

Almost every known musical instrumentalist was portrayed in the Meissen orchestra, but it is possible to name only a few here. Kändler's standing figure of a 'Lady with a mandoline'[103] was reproduced at Chelsea (C47). A 'Negro with a French Horn' and companion 'European musician' with the same[104] also found echoes at Chelsea (D85). A standing 'Man with fife and tambour' and his 'Lady with a triangle',[105] prompted models known as the 'Idyllic Musicians' common to Bow (H45) and Derby (K42). Other models, including the Derby 'Gentleman standing with a recorder' (J15), the Longton Hall 'Gentleman with a lute' and companion 'Lady flautist' (O47) along with many representatives of the large Bow orchestra (H48-H59), may be traced back to a Meissen source.

Augustus the Strong, like other rulers of the day, had an aviary containing all sorts of exotic birds at Moritzburg Castle not far from Dresden. Kändler was granted access to this as well as having specimens both dead and alive sent back to him from an African expedition. Kändler's birds are of outstanding merit and many, including small models of animals, were fashioned in what he termed *Feierabendarbeit* (leisure time). He was able to recapture in a few inches of paste the inimitable characteristics of each creature and this could only have been achieved after many hours of astute observation. Amongst the gems, are an 'Oakjay', a 'Magpie startled' and several 'Parrots'.[106] A charming pair of 'Bullfinches'[107] were echoed at Chelsea (C125 and C126) and Derby (K99 and K100); a farmyard 'Cockerel' and companion 'Hen',[108] as well as a 'Cob swan' and a 'Cygnet with a Pen'[109] were copied at Chelsea (B32). Buntings, finches[110] and canaries were almost certainly the inspiration behind

96. *Festive Publication ...*, op. cit., table 8, no. 297.

97. *German Porcelain of the 18th Century*, op. cit., p. 185.

98. 'Meissen Porcelain Copies of the 18th Century' by Yvonne Hackenbroch, *Connoisseur*, 1956, Vol. 137, pp. 149-153, fig. 16, 'The Falconers' by Eberlein and their Chelsea copies.

99. *German Porcelain of the 18th Century*, op. cit., p. 219.

100. 'Meissen Porcelain copies of the 18th Century', op. cit., p. 152, fig. 11, Kändler's Gallant and Lady; fig. 12, Bow copies.

101. *Festive Publication...*, op. cit., table 15, nos. 496 and 509.

102. *German Porcelain of the 18th Century*, op. cit., p. 177, 'An actor offering his snuff-box to a lady, the two seated upon the green sward'.

103. 'Lord Fisher's Collection of English Porcelain in the Fitzwilliam Museum', op. cit., pl. 228F, Meissen 'Lady with mandoline': pl. 228G, Chelsea Model.

104. *Festive Publication...*, op. cit., table 16, no. 1647.

105. *Meissner Porzellan, 1710-1810* (Ducret), op. cit., nos. 923 and 924.

106. *Festive Publication...*, op. cit., table 1., nos. 62 and 1127; fig. 36, no. 953.

107. *Meissner Porzellan 1710-1810* (Munich, 1966) by Rainer Rückert, nos. 1115 and 1116.

108. *Meissner Porzellan 1710-1810* (Ducret), op. cit., nos. 1137 and 1138.

109. *Meissen* (London, 1971) by Hugo Morley-Fletcher, p. 60.

110. *Meissner Porzellan, 1710-1810* (Ducret), op. cit., nos. 1113-1116.

many examples made at Chelsea (C125, 126, 130, 131 and 137), Bow (H129-135), and Derby (K106-111). Fine Derby woodpeckers (K122 and 123), and Bow parrots eating fruit (H139) also follow Meissen prototypes.

Kändler's animals also display great vitality and animation. His 'Nanny-Goat suckling a kid' was, possibly, based on a marble in the Vatican though his 'Billy-Goat' is likely to be original and both found echoes at Derby (J4). Peter Reinicke's 'Charging Bulls', inspired by engravings of Johann Elias Riedinger 'Auer Ochse im Zorn'[111] were also copied at Derby (J3). Kändler's 'Stag and Doe at lodge'[112] prompted late Derby versions (K146) and the earlier dry-edge pair are derived from an unknown source. There is a flock of Meissen 'Sheep', including standing 'Ewe' and 'Ram' with heads turned and rather broad backs, copied at Derby (J6), Bow (H155), Chelsea (B63) and Longton Hall (O17), as well as recumbent 'Ewe with Lamb'[113] also echoed at Derby (K144), Chelsea (B63), and Longton Hall (O15). A Chelsea 'Squirrel with a nut' (A18), later copied at Derby (K145), reflected a Kändler original. Standing and recumbent 'Bulls' and 'Cows with a calf'[114] may have been the basis for Derby (K128 and 129) and Bow (H152) cattle. The Meissen 'Monkey with fruit', and companion female 'Monkey with a baby' upon her back,[115] as well as several 'Cats seated', some with prey[116] provoked replicas at Bow (H150 and 151). Strangely, some delightful 'Bears', 'Lions' and 'Tigers', as well as 'Horses', 'Camels' and other beasts were over looked by the English copyists.[117]

Special mention must be made of the 'Pug'. In 1736, pope Clement XII excommunicated all Catholics who remained freemasons. This lead to the establishment of a superficially similar organisation permitted to the faithful called 'The Order of the Pug'. Thus, the animal became the symbol of a secret society popular amongst the nobility of central Europe. A number of porcelain groups were made at Meissen depicting men in the regalia of freemasonry and women, who were also admitted as members, with pug dogs. Single models of pugs were also produced in large numbers in almost every variety of pose and activity. Kändler's model of a 'Pug scratching' prompted an English soft paste copy which was once attributed to Bow but which is now thought to be a product of the Derby factory during the first tentative years of experimentation (Plate 159, Chapter XI) (Q6). Perhaps the most famous dog in Saxony was Count von Brühl's 'Pug', which was immortalised in porcelain seated upon a tasselled cushion with one paw raised.[118] English factories probably based their models on Meissen prototypes including Chelsea (B57, 59 and C123), Bow (G57, and G58), Derby (K137, 138 and 139), and Longton Hall (O21). Many other canine breeds were fashioned at Meissen of which the 'Pointer', 'Bologna terrier' and 'Bologna dog' serve as examples.[119]

111. 'Meissen Porcelain copies of the 18th Century', op. cit., fig. 10, engraving by Elias Riedinger.

112. *Meissner Porzellan, 1710-1810* (Ducret), op. cit., nos. 1150 and 1151.

113. ibid., nos. 1162, 1163 and 1166.

114. ibid., no. 1156. See also *Festive Publication...*, op. cit., table 4, no. 2687.

115. *Meissen*, op. cit., p. 47.

116. Saltram House Collection Catalogue, 1977, pl. VIB.

117. 'A Synonymous Concept — Porcelain Animals and Kändler' by Margot Newman, *Antique Dealer & Collector's Guide*, January 1971, pp. 74-80; pl. 2, elephants; pl. 3, bears; pl. 4, a camel; pls. 7 and 8, pugs; pl. 9, a heiffer; pls. 12 and 13, horses.

118. *Festive Publication...*, op. cit., table 10, no. 510.

119. ibid., table 4, no. 1124, a pointer; no. 2841, a Bologna dog; no. 333, a Bologna terrier.

Chapter III

The French Influence on English Porcelain Modelling

The French Connection

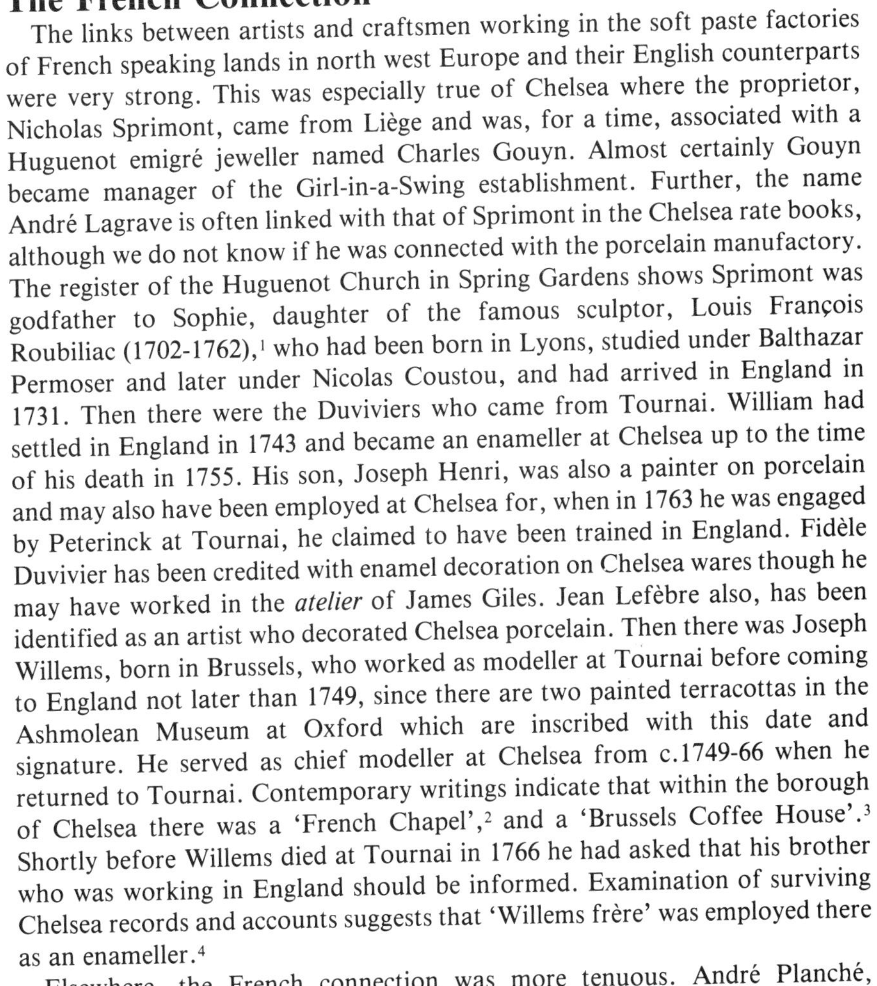

The links between artists and craftsmen working in the soft paste factories of French speaking lands in north west Europe and their English counterparts were very strong. This was especially true of Chelsea where the proprietor, Nicholas Sprimont, came from Liège and was, for a time, associated with a Huguenot emigré jeweller named Charles Gouyn. Almost certainly Gouyn became manager of the Girl-in-a-Swing establishment. Further, the name André Lagrave is often linked with that of Sprimont in the Chelsea rate books, although we do not know if he was connected with the porcelain manufactory. The register of the Huguenot Church in Spring Gardens shows Sprimont was godfather to Sophie, daughter of the famous sculptor, Louis François Roubiliac (1702-1762),[1] who had been born in Lyons, studied under Balthazar Permoser and later under Nicolas Coustou, and had arrived in England in 1731. Then there were the Duviviers who came from Tournai. William had settled in England in 1743 and became an enameller at Chelsea up to the time of his death in 1755. His son, Joseph Henri, was also a painter on porcelain and may also have been employed at Chelsea for, when in 1763 he was engaged by Peterinck at Tournai, he claimed to have been trained in England. Fidèle Duvivier has been credited with enamel decoration on Chelsea wares though he may have worked in the *atelier* of James Giles. Jean Lefèbre also, has been identified as an artist who decorated Chelsea porcelain. Then there was Joseph Willems, born in Brussels, who worked as modeller at Tournai before coming to England not later than 1749, since there are two painted terracottas in the Ashmolean Museum at Oxford which are inscribed with this date and signature. He served as chief modeller at Chelsea from c.1749-66 when he returned to Tournai. Contemporary writings indicate that within the borough of Chelsea there was a 'French Chapel',[2] and a 'Brussels Coffee House'.[3] Shortly before Willems died at Tournai in 1766 he had asked that his brother who was working in England should be informed. Examination of surviving Chelsea records and accounts suggests that 'Willems frère' was employed there as an enameller.[4]

'Belle n'Écoutez rien — Arlequin est un traître', engraving by C.N. Cochin after Watteau.

Elsewhere, the French connection was more tenuous. André Planché, manager and probably also modeller at Derby prior to 1756, was born in London of *emigré* Huguenot parents who fled from France shortly after the Revocation of the Edict of Nantes in 1685.[5] His brother, Jacques, according to Jewitt, was concerned with watch-making and later may have been associated with the London clock-smith, Benjamin Vulliamy, whose business placed orders with the Derby porcelain manufactory. Two modellers, Nicolas François Gauron, and Pierre Stephan, both from Tournai, came to work for William Duesbury c.1771, whilst the French speaking Swiss, Jean Jacques Spengler was also employed at Derby intermittently between 1790 and 1795. The father of the independent porcelain decorator, James Giles (or Gilles) is said to have come from Nîmes which had been a Huguenot stronghold and may have left during the Camisard revolt of c.1700. The style of painting large flowers upon the garments of porcelain figures from Derby and Bow, suggests

1. Register of the Hugenot Church, Spring Gardens, London: "Sophie Roubiliac, avec pour parain Nicolas Sprimont, 1744..."
2. *London Evening Post* of 19th December 1749: "Enquiries to be made of Mr. Brown against the French Chapel in Chelsea."
3. *Mortimer's Directory,* 1763: "Willems, Joseph, Modeller, at the Brussels Coffee House, Chelsea..."
4. Barton's weekly accounts of Chelsea factory from 1771: "Woolam, Painting Mottows to 46 seals..."
5. 'The Early Work of Planché and Duesbury' by Mrs. Donald Macalister, *Transactions,* English Porcelain Circle, 1928, No. 2, pp. 45-49.

the hand of a Frenchman who may have been employed by Giles. The repairer, Monsieur Thibauld (Mr. Tebo), who worked at Bow, Worcester, Plymouth, Bristol and Etruria was a Frenchman and so was Monsieur Soqui (or Saqui) the enameller of birds upon Plymouth wares, said to have come from Sèvres.

The French Decorative Artists

The influence of the French decorative artists upon the English ceramic scene was only marginally less than that exerted by the Meissen modellers. The most important by far were Watteau and Boucher. Antoine Watteau (1684-1721) studied under Gillot and Audran. Claude Gillot's name is linked with paintings of the Commedia dell'Arte, a subject that also fascinated his pupil, whilst Claude Audran was associated with designs for tapestries made by the Gobelins atelier. The work of Watteau became available to a wide public in over six hundred engravings made by different artists which were published by his friend, Jean de Julienne, as a folio entitled *Recueil de Julienne* in 1735. This has been described by Dacier and Vuaflart[6] who retain the original numbers allocated in the folio which here are given in parentheses. Charles Nicholas Cochin's engraving 'Belle, n'écoutez rien — Arlequin est un traître' (no. 82), inspired the beautiful Bow group known as the 'Italian Musicians'.[7] 'L'Amour au Théâtre italien' (no. 271) by the same artist, prompted a Chelsea model of 'Dottore Baloardo' (B34) which was taken from a figure in the foreground, and also the Bow group of 'Arlecchino in motley seated beside Coumbina' with his right arm about her waist and left hand elevated (G12). Several years following the death of Watteau, many of the engravings of his work were plagiarised in mirror image and allocated fresh titles. Thus, 'L'Amour au Théâtre italien', was reissued as 'La Comédie italienne', which was identified as the source of the last mentioned Bow group by Major Toppin.[8] Other engravings from the folio of Julienne, such as 'Pierrot Content' (no. 180) by Édme Jeurat and 'Pour Garder L'honneur d'une Belle' (no. 83) by Cochin, probably provided general guidance to Meissen modellers of comedy characters.

'Isabella', after a drawing by Antoine Watteau.

A second theme popularised by Watteau was the Westernised fantasy of the Orient known as the *chinoiserie*. The East India Trade had been established early in the sixteenth century by the Portuguese and by 1705 La Compagnie Royale du Chine had been founded in France. A shop in Paris owned by the dealer Gersaint was opened which sold Oriental *objets d'art*. Watteau, himself a collector of Chinese porcelain, painted the shop sign and, some years later, the trade card was engraved by Boucher. Watteau decorated the Château de la Muette with 'Les figures Chinoises et Tartares' which also appear in Julienne's folio of engravings (nos. 231-261). A raised anchor Chelsea model of a 'Chinese Boy' (B41) in leaf-shaped hat and a cloak, with both cheeks puffed out, was inspired by one of these. Michel Aubert's engraving, after Watteau, of 'Idole de la Déesse Ki Mao Sao dans le royaume de Mang au pays des Laos' (no. 260), prompted an ambitious Bow group of the goddess flanked by kneeling Chinamen (G45) of c.1754.[9] Another engraving by Laurent Cars of Watteau's 'Fête Vénitiennes' (no. 6), inspired a fine pair of Derby 'Minuet Dancers' (K51), whilst 'La Diseuse Daventure' (no. 30), also by Cars, was the source of a 'Fortune telling Group' depicting a gipsy woman with a babe upon her back and child at her side reading the palm of a young lady, made at Bow (I 13) and Chelsea (D114).

François Boucher (1701-1770) studied under Lemoyne, whom he assisted in the decoration of le Salon d'Hercule at Versailles. His style resembles that of Nicolas Lancret (1690-1743) who had been a fellow student. The Bow groups 'Liberty and Matrimony' (G37) and 'Two Lovers with a birdcage' (G42) follow Meissen originals based on Lancret. Boucher worked for Laurent Cars,

6. *Jean de Julienne et les graveurs de Watteau au XVIII siècle* (Paris, 1929) by E. Dacier and A. Vuaflart, 3 vols.

7. 'The Origin of Some Ceramic Designs' by A.J. Toppin, *Transactions,* English Ceramic Circle, 1948, Vol. 2, pl. CIIIa, engraving; pl. CIIIb Bow group.

8. ibid., pl. CIIc, engraving of 'La Comedie italienne'; pl. CIId, Bow porcelain group.

9. ibid., pl. CIIa, engraving of 'Ki Mao Sao' by Aubert; pl. CIIb, Bow porcelain group. Also *Porcelain* (London, 1962) by G. Hugh Tait, figs. 26 and 28 illustrating engraving and porcelain group.

in whose atelier he became an expert engraver, familiar with the work of Watteau. He was the friend of Juste-Aurèle Meissonier, sometimes called the father of the French Rococo, and was duly elected member of the Paris Academy in 1734. He was fortunate in being able to secure the patronage of Madame le Normant d'Étoilles, otherwise La Marquise de Pompadour, and rose to fame as court painter and artistic advisor both to Sèvres and the Gobelins atelier. His work, like that of Watteau, was widely dispersed through engravings. Mention has been made in Chapter II, of Meissen and Chelsea groups (B39 and B40) based on his 'Les Délices de L'Enfance', engraved by J.J. Balechou. Gabriel Huquier's *Livre de six feuilles représentant les cinq sens par différents amusements chinois sur les dessins de F. Boucher,* of 1740, were the likely basis for the dry-edge Derby 'Chinoiserie Senses'[10] (J34). Boucher's *Suite de Figures Chinoise,* that included 'Le Pêch Chinois', seems to have prompted the Chelsea 'Chinese Fisherman' (A9). His 'Décoration Chinoise',[11] engraved by P. Aveline,[12] inspired the Bow Chinoiserie group emblematic of Fire and Air (G44). The 'Chinaman standing beside a Table', once ascribed to Chelsea (A8) is probably a fragment of this Bow group of 'Fire'. A silver kettle decorated with the whole scene depicted by the engraving in relief bears the stamp of 'N. Sprimont'.[13] Aveline's 'La Bonne Aventure', after Boucher[14] was echoed by a delightful Bow 'Fortune telling Group' (G31). There are many other groups, including the Derby 'Huntsman with flute beside a seated Lady' (J17), and the Bow 'Gallant seated beside a Fishergirl' (G32) and 'Huntsman seated beside a Lady' (G33) that are very much in the genre of Boucher.

Boucher's painting of 1748, 'L'Agréable Leçon', was engraved by René Gaillard and translated into a biscuit porcelain group by Étienne Falconet in 1752. The Chelsea version (D72) (Plate 50, Chapter VI), enamelled and gilded, is in mirror image. Boucher was largely responsible for the creation of the idyllic pastoral myth, in which lords and ladies in rustic weeds made, incongruously, of silks and brocades, wiled away endless leisure hours in an Arcadian setting. Titles of his work which include 'Berger près d'une bergère endormie', and 'Berger et la Bergère représentant Louis XV et Mme. Pompadour', serve to emphasize that a charade was intended rather than realism. Some of the Meissen models on this theme have been described in Chapter II. Although most English models reflecting the myth were taken from Meissen originals based on the work of Boucher and Lancret, there are, however, some notable exceptions. Engravings by Simon François Ravenet[15] of 'Femme du Levant' and 'Dame de Constantinople', after Boucher, prompted a pair of raised anchor Chelsea models of Turkish ladies in sumptuous dress (B44). These, once in the Lady Ludlow Collection, are fussily detailed and artistically unsuccessful in porcelain. Ravenet's engraving of 'Fille de St. Jean de Patmos, Isle de l'Archipel',[16] also after Boucher, inspired a further raised anchor Chelsea model of a 'Gardener's Companion' (Plate 20, Chapter VI) (B52) in broad brimmed hat holding blossoms in a fold of her apron and standing beside a basket of flowers. This is altogether different from the 'Rose Seller' (B51), derived from a woodcut, in which the figure is dressed in lace cap and a dress with a ruffle at the neck and holds a basket in both hands. Boucher often made use of cupids in his romantic paintings and it is probable that many of the Girl-in-a-Swing and subsequent Chelsea 'toys' were inspired by these little fellows. Indeed, some of the etuis, scent bottles, and seals, actually bear such mottoes as 'Lien d'amitie', 'Gage de ma Tendress' and 'J'amerie l'innocence' to suggest a French derivation. Jean Daullé engraved several reclining muses, after Boucher, including Clio with lyre and quill in hand attended by Cupid bearing a parchment scroll, and Erato holding a tambourine, with flowers and a Cupid[17] which were translated into

10. Referred to in the *Mercure,* 1740.

11. Now in the Cooper Hewitt Collection, American Museum of Fine and Decorative Arts, Boston, U.S.A.

12. 'English Porcelain and Enamel from the Collection of Judge Irwin Untermyer' by Yvonne Hackenbroch, *Connoisseur,* 1956, Vol. 138, p. 109, fig. 12, Bow 'Fire'; fig. 13, Aveline's engraving.

13. 'Silver Shapes in Chelsea Porcelain' by Bellamy Gardner, *Transactions,* English Ceramic Circle, 1939, Vol. 2. No. 6, pp. 26-30, pl. XIa, Chelsea Figure, pl. XIb, engraving by Aveline; pl. XIc, silver kettle.

14. 'The Thomas Frye Period, 1755-1759' by G. Hugh Tait, *Apollo,* 1960, Vol. 71, p. 95, fig. IV, Bow group; fig. V, engraving by Aveline; p. 96, fig. VI, Boucher's 'La Bonne Aventure'.

15. 'Chelsea Porcelain Figures and the Modeller Joseph Williams' by Arthur Lane, *Connoisseur,* 1960, Vol. 145, pp. 245-251; p. 246, fig. 1, Chelsea 'Femme du Levant'; fig. 2, engraving by Ravenet; fig. 3, Chelsea 'Dame de Constantinople'; fig. 4, engraving by Ravenet.

16. ibid., p. 247, fig. 6, Ravenet's engraving; fig. 7, Chelsea 'Gardner's Companion'.

17. *Porcelain,* op. cit., fig. 28, engraving by Daullé; fig. 29, Derby model of 'Erato'; pl. 45, Derby model of 'Clio'.

'The Horse Tamers', bronze after marble by Guillaume Coustou. Wallace Collection.

porcelain first at Vincennes, later at Derby (K89 and 90), circa 1765. The attractive models created by Kändler of 'Cupids in Disguise', which were issued from the Meissen factory during the 1750s, and found echoes at Chelsea and Derby, may well have been suggested by the paintings of the French decorative artists of which the leading exponent was Boucher.

Other, perhaps lesser known, French speaking artists who influenced English porcelain modellers indirectly via Meissen, include Christoph Huet who has already been mentioned in Chapter II in connection with his watercolour sketches of the 'Cris de Paris'. His brother, Jean Charles, was Paris agent to Kändler. Christoph, created murals at Chantilly in the château of Henri de Bourbon, prince de Condé, though these were once erroneously ascribed to Watteau. They depict monkeys dressed as humans, some in the livery of the prince, hunting, engaged in tea parties or other activities. The concept of *Singerie* was most probably imported from the Orient and undoubtedly inspired Kändler's 'Affenkapelle'. There is no reason to suppose, as some have suggested, that the models were intended to lampoon the Dresden Court Orchestra. Only ten of the original twenty one monkey musicians were copied at Chelsea (C109). The late Derby Monkey Band[18] is unconnected with the Meissen figures.

A painting, now in the Louvre, by Laurent Cars, was adapted at the Girl-in-a-Swing factory to provide two groups. Both show a seated lady facing a gallant who reclines upon the ground; in one, the man fondles a lamb upon the lady's lap, in the other, which is in mirror image, the object of their attention is a dove (E10 and E11). Charles Lemoyne's painting of 'Hercules and Omphale' inspired a Vincennes porcelain group of the two characters attended by Cupid. In the Girl-in-a-Swing version (E13), the Cupid is omitted. Engravings by Carle van Loo were the basis of two Derby groups of c.1765, entitled the 'Dancing Lesson' (K48) and the 'Singing Lesson' (K49). In the first, a girl holds a dog upon its hind legs on a pedestal whilst a companion youth plays a hurdy-gurdy; in the second the companion holds a musical score. The more ambitious gold anchor Chelsea 'Dancing Lesson' (D63) may stem from the same source.

Nicolas Coustou (1658-1735), studied in Rome and became a member of the French Academy in 1693. he was engaged by Louis XIV to create sculpture for the adornment of Versailles, Le Trianon, and the Château de Marly. His terracotta study, after the antique *Gladiateur Borghese* dated 1683, is in the Louvre. This model, or a facsimile, was adapted and clothed to provide the Chelsea 'Fisherman with a Net' (C27). Coustou's major work was a marble depicting 'The Descent from the Cross'[19] now in Notre Dame Cathedral, Paris. This was completed c.1725 and inspired drawings by Joseph Willems[20] who later completed a porcelain 'Pietà' (C102) during both the red and gold anchor periods.

Guillaume Coustou (1677-1747), studied under Pierre Legros and was elected Academician in 1704. He, like his brother Nicolas, worked as a sculptor for Louis XIV. His prancing horses with attendant grooms, known as the 'Horse Tamers',[21] executed in 1743 for the Château de Marly replaced the equestrian statuary by Coysevox, but now face one another across the Champs Elysée. They were based on 'Bellerophon and Pegasus' by Bertoldo (1420-1491).[22] The Coustou marbles were adapted as porcelain models by Kändler who replaced the European grooms by a Turk and a Blackamoor[23] and these were reflected at Longton Hall (O68). Preliminary drawings for a fountain called La Pyramide,[24] at Versailles, made by François Girardon (1628-1715) inspired the Chelsea group of a Cupid riding a Sea-Horse (C78). Reference has already been made to Édme Bouchardon in connection with his

18. *Derby Porcelain* (London, 1971) by F.A. Barrett and A.L. Thorpe, pl. 123.

19. 'Origins of Design for English Ceramics of the Eighteenth Century' by Bernard Watney, *Burlington Magazine,* 1972, Vol. 114, No. 837, pp. 818-826; fig. 3, Chelsea group; fig. 4, marble by Coustou.

20. 'Chelsea Porcelain Figures and the Modeller Joseph Williams', op. cit., Appendix I, pp. 135-136 "...Qautre autres estampes, une tête peinte sur toile, un group représentant la Vierge et le Sauveur descendu de la croix, avec un adorateur..."

21. *Sculpture, Renaissance to Rococo* (London, 1969) by Herbert Keutner, no. 316.

22. *European Bronze Statues* (London, 1968) by Anthony Radcliffe, no. 59.

23. *Das Meissner Porzellan und seine Geschichte* (Leipzig, 1900) by Karl Berling, fig. 97.

24. 'Origins of Design for English Ceramics of the Eighteenth Century', op. cit.

'Pantalone', wood engraving by Giacomo Calotto.

drawings of 'Les Cris de Paris', which were engraved by his friend Ann Claude Philippe de Tubières, Comte de Caylus, and formed the basis of the first set of Meissen models by Kändler and Reinicke in 1747. Bouchardon also created the Grenelle fountain,[25] in Paris, from which source Kändler modelled his 'Reclining Water Deities'[26] which were copied by Willems at Chelsea (C89).

Finally, from a very different source, came the beautiful Chelsea raised anchor group of a Nurse and Child, known as 'La Nourrice' (Plate 21, Chapter VI) (B50), depicting a seated nurse breast feeding a baby in swaddling clothes. This was derived from a glazed earthenware group made in the sixteenth century by a successor of Bernard Palissy at Avon, near Fontainebleau.[27] It is possible that the original may have been intended to represent the Virgin Mary and Christ Child.

The Influence of the Soft Paste Factories of France

The appeal of French eighteenth century porcelain depends largely on the rare beauty of the *pâte tendre* and, where figures are concerned, upon their issue in the biscuit. When, in 1769, the discovery on French soil of the necessary raw materials allowed the potters to transfer to *pâte dure,* much of the artistic merit of the wares and figures was lost. It is a paradox that the triumph of Vincennes-Sèvres was due to an inability to make true hard paste porcelain whereas, at Meissen, which was first to discover the arcanum, the reverse obtained. The complex story of how soft paste porcelain was first made in France has been told by George Savage[28] and here mention is restricted only to a bare outline relevant to ceramic developments in this country.

Saint Cloud

It would appear that during the last quarter of the seventeenth century a number of *faience* factories were located at St. Cloud. One of these was owned by Pierre Chicanneau where, shortly before 1693, soft paste porcelain was successfully manufactured. In 1702, privileges were granted to Chicanneau's widow and two sons by Louis XIV. A second faience factory had been established by a Paris merchant, François Reverend who, in 1664, had also obtained the sole right to make porcelain in the 'Chinese manner, in and around Paris for a term of fifty years. This was probably under the management of one M. Morin and was suppressed by the decree of 1702. A third faience factory had existed at St. Cloud since before 1640. This was the province of the Trou family. Gabrile Trou, who was also bailiff to the Duc d'Orléans the future Regent of France, married Chicanneau's widow and effectively managed both factories until his death in 1746. He was succeeded by his son, Henri François, but the venture failed c.1766.

T.H. Clarke[29] has shown, that a number of early Chelsea pieces including models of seated Chinamen adapted to serve as teapots, tea-poys, or pastil burners (Plate 13, Chapter VI) were copied from St. Cloud prototypes despite their resemblance to Oriental *blanc-de-Chine* (A2, 3 and 4). Also, models of a seated 'Fisherman' and 'Fishwife'[30] designed as flower vases are known in red anchor Chelsea versions (C41), both enamelled and in the white. The St. Cloud factory was also famed for porcelain 'toys', including seals, scent-bottles, patch-boxes and etuis. Although no examples of English copies of these are known, their existence may well have prompted similar products both at the Girl-in-the-Swing and the Chelsea factories.

Mennecy

François Barbin founded a soft paste factory in the Rue de la Charonne,

25. *Baroque Sculpture* (London, 1965) by Harold Busch and Bernd. Lohse, pl. 169.
26. *Katalog der Sammlung Alt-Meissner Porzellan des Herren Reutners und C.H. Fsicher in Dresden* (Cologne, 1906) by C.H. Fischer, pl. 4, no. 813.
27. Sotheby's catalogue, 26-11-63, lot. 74, a glazed earthenware group of 'La Nourrice', 9ins. tall after B. Palissy. Also illustrated in *French Faience* (London, 1903) by M.L. Solon, p. 35, marked 'B.B.' and on this slender evidence was attributed to Berthélémy de Blénod.
28. *Seventeenth and Eighteenth Century French Porcelain* (London, 1960) by George Savage, chap. II, pp. 73-89.
29. 'The French Influence at Chelsea' by T.H. Clarke, *Transactions,* English Ceramic Circle, 1959, Vol. 4, pp. 45-52.
30. From the catalogue by Winifred Williams of the exhibition of eighteenth century White European porcelain held at 3 Bury St., St. James's, London, 10th-27th June, 1975, figs. 37 and 38, St. Cloud models.

Wood-engravings of 'Dwarfs' by Giacomo Calotto, from Varie figure Gobbi, *c.1623, which inspired the Chelsea-Derby 'Grotesque Dwarfs' (M227).*

Paris, in 1734. This was transferred in 1748 to Mennecy and, in 1773, to Bourg-la-Reinne. The body of early wares was white, and the glaze free from pinhole defects. The influence exerted by the factory on English porcelain modelling was negligible. A figure of a river deity leaning upon a dolphin holding a paddle[31] closely resembles one made by Gauron at Vincennes, but no English copy has been identified. There is, also, a pair of dwarfs[32] after etchings by Giacomo Calotto (Jacques Callot) which had also prompted Meissen models. Whether the raised and red anchor Chelsea dwarfs (B56 and C106) were based on the engravings, the Meissen or the Mennecy models remains undecided.

Chantilly

Ciquaire Cirou established a soft paste porcelain factory at Chantilly in 1735 which was under the patronage of Louis Henri de Bourbon, Prince de Condé. The prince was an admirer of the Kakiemon style and an avid collector of Japanese porcelains. It is not surprising, therefore, that the factory issued wares and a small number of models in the style beloved by the patron. Although the Kakiemon style of decoration was employed upon English porcelain models, this was usually copied from Meissen models and wares rather than from either Japan or Chantilly.

Tournai

François Peterinck, a potter from Lille, took over the management of a faience factory in 1751 that had existed at Tournai since the closing years of the seventeenth century. By the following year, soft paste was being manufactured with the help of Robert Dubois from Vincennes. Mention has already been made of the links between the Tournai and Chelsea factories. The fine Pietà[33] modelled by Nicolas Lecreux at Tournai, after a marble by Nicolas Coustou, closely resembles one created by Joseph Willems at Chelsea (C102) with omission of the draped cross. Another modeller, Nicolas François Gauron, who worked at Tournai between 1758 and 1764, later came to Chelsea, c.1770, to work for William Duesbury. His name appears in the Chelsea factory records of June 1773 when he was receiving the comparatively large sum for those times of 8s. 9d. per day. A number of models created at Tournai by Gauron were echoed by Chelsea-Derby versions. For example, the group of three putti on an irregular rock-like base about an obelisk representing Minerva crowning Constancy and Hercules killing the Hydra[34] found echoes at Derby (L11). The English version stems from different moulds, for it is slightly large and displays slight differences in detail whilst a leafing tree replaces the obelisk. The Tournai groups of two putti upon an irregular pad base beneath a tree, four of which represent the four elements[35] were repeated at Derby (M48).[36] Most French sources attribute the four pairs of "un garconnet et une fillette, porteurs d' attributs symbolique...", which comprise a set of 'The Four Seasons'[37] after Boucher, to Gauron. Four of these, including two boys emblematic of Spring and Winter, and two girls representing Summer and Autumn, were issued in debased forms at Derby[38] as 'The French Seasons' (Plate 125, Chapter VIII) (M123). Their modelling falls far short of the originals and they resemble stylistically and in genre the four 'Rustic Seasons' (Plate 151, Chapter X) (P36) made at the Bristol factory of Richard Champion. It seems that both were made by Pierre Stephan and were based upon the original work of Gauron. Stephan also worked at Tournai and amongst other Derby models and groups is credited with 'The Four Elements' represented by four individual standing figures (Plates 123, 124, Chapter VIII) (M3). These seem to have been adapted from a set of four chubbier models set

31. *French Porcelain of the 18th Century* (London, 1950) by W.B. Honey, pl. 48.

32. *Seventeenth and Eighteenth Century French Porcelain* op. cit., pl. 30B.

33. 'Porcelains de Tournay et de Chelsea-Derby' by H. Nichaise, *Revue Belge d'archeologie d'histoire de l'art,* 1935, Vol. 5, pp. 5-15, fig. 3, Tournai 'Pietà'; fig. 4, Chelsea 'Pietà'.

34. ibid., figs. 7 and 8, Tournai groups of 'Minerva crowning Constancy' and 'Hercules killing the Hydra'; figs. 9 and 10, Chelsea-Derby versions.

35. ibid., fig. 11, Tournai groups emblematic of Air and Earth; fig. 12, Chelsea-Derby versions.

36. 'Derby Biscuit' by T. Clifford, *Transactions,* English Ceramic Circle, 1969, Vol. 7, pt. 2, pp. 108-117; pl. 121B, Tournai group of 'Fire'; fig. 121C, Chelsea-Derby version.

37. 'Porcelaines de Tournay et de Chelsea-Derby', op. cit., fig. 4, eight Tournai figures emblematic of the 'Four Seasons' after Boucher.

38. ibid., fig. 2, Chelsea-Derby set of 'The Four French Seasons'.

Blind Beggar and Companion, engraving by Giacomo Calotto, c.1622, which inspired the Chelsea model of the 'Blind Beggar' (C17).

on high rock bases beside perfume vases issued at Tournai.[39] The design of one of them namely 'Air', a girl holding aloft a bird with a hunting horn, may be found in an ink drawing which is unsigned but which has been attributed to Lecreux. Most Tournai models survive both in biscuit and enamel versions; the former when made prior to 1760 exhibit a yellowish cast whilst after that date they have a bluish tinge.

Peterinck retired in 1796 after which the manufactory exerted little or no influence upon English modellers. It was managed by Jean Maximilien Joseph de Bettignies until 1817 and was later purchased by Peterinck's sons.

Vincennes-Sèvres

The defection of Robert and Gilles Dubois, Humbert Gerin (kiln-master), and François Gravant, from Chantilly led to the foundation of a soft paste porcelain factory in a building attached to the disused château of Vincennes by the nobleman Orry de Fulvy, in 1744. The brothers Dubois had been the key workmen, but they were dismissed for debauchery. Gravant, who had listened to them in their cups, had gleaned sufficient information to create soft paste for the proprietor. When Orry de Fulvy died the factory became virtually the private property of Louis XV, and in 1756 it was transferred to specially built premises at Sèvres for the greater convenience of Madame de Pompadour, who was deeply interested in the concern and lived close by, at Bellevue. The early paste presents an unattractive greyish hue and, according to Jean Jacques Bachelier, who became art-director in 1747, figures issued before his arrival were glazed and enamelled. Between 1749 and 1752 enamel colours were mostly discarded, and models were issued glazed but in the white. The sculptor Blondeau created eight models of children inspired by designs after Boucher depicting characters from the comic opera *La Vallée de Montmorency,* comprising 'La Petite Fille à la cage', 'Le Porteur d'oiseaux', 'Le Jeune Suppliant', 'Le Joueur de cornemuse', 'La Danseuse d'après Boucher', 'La Jardinier au table', 'Le Moissonneur et la Moissonneuse'.[40] Another sculptor, Louis Felix de la Rue, also modelled forty putti and children[41] which were based upon terracottas originally made in the workshop of François Duquesnoy (known as 'Il Fiammingo', 1594-1643). Similar terracottas by the same artist inspired Chelsea porcelain models (A5, 6 and 7) that will be discussed in a later section. De la Rue was probably responsible for a charming Vincennes group 'Enfants tenant un dauphin'[42] which may have been adapted from a bronze fountain at Versailles. The group was copied at Bow (G25) and also at Chelsea (C77) where the dolphin was replaced by an ugly fish. Other groups, emblematic of Music and Science[43] do not seem to have inspired copies elsewhere, but their style could possibly have prompted the early Bow Muses. There is one notable model of Mimi,[44] the favourite pet dog of Madame de Pompadour, seated upon a tasselled cushion, in white glazed porcelain. This recalls Kändler's model of a pug seated on a similar cushion[45] with one paw raised, representing the pet of Count von Brühl, and the Chelsea representation of 'Trump' (Plate 22, Chapter VI), William Hogarth's dog (B59).[46]

The artistic director at Vincennes was Jean Jacques Bachelier (1724-1805). Appointed in 1747, he collaborated closely with François Boucher who provided him with many designs suitable for translation into porcelain. One of the brightest stars in the galaxy of talent assembled under his direction, was Jean Hellot. He had been director of the Academy of Sciences and was a colour chemist of great skill. Under his aegis, the most exquisite ground colours were developed including *bleu du roi, bleu céleste, jaune jonquille, vert farcé, vert de mer,* and *rose pompadour.* Nothing produced in this country could equal the beauty of this palette though the Chelsea factory

39. Brussels Musée Cinquantenaire, cited in *Ceramics of Derbyshire 1750-1975* (1978) ed. H.G. Bradley, p. 22.

40. *Le Biscuit de Sèvres, recueil des modeles de la manufacture de Sèvres au XVIIIe siècle* (Paris, 1909) by E. Bourgeois and G. Lechevallier-Chevignard. See respectively pl. 1, no. 493; pl. 4, no. 511; pl. 1, no. 362; pl. 1, no. 367; pl. 4, no. 173; pl. 3, no. 357; pl. 4, nos. 436 and 437.

41. ibid., pl. 5, nos. 231-259. See also *Seventeenth and Eighteenth Century French Porcelain,* op. cit., pl. 68B.

42. 'The French Influence at Chelsea' by T.H. Clarke, *Transactions,* English Ceramic Circle, 1959, Vol. 4., pl. 24C.

43. *Seventeenth and Eighteenth Century French Porcelain,* op. cit., pls. 69A and 69B.

44. Catalogue of the Exhibition of White 18th Century European Porcelain, op. cit., fig. 20.

45. *Festive Publications to commemorate the 200th Jubilee of the Oldest European China Factory, Meissen* (Dresden, 1910) by Karl Berling, table 10, no. 510.

46. *Porcelain Figurines* (London, 1975) by Nathaniel Harris, p. 46.

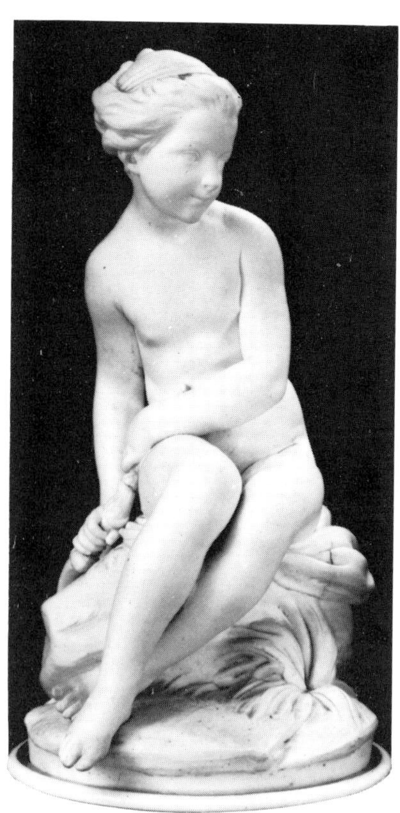

'Psyche' (paired with 'Cupid'), unglazed Sèvres figure after models by Falconet, c.1765.

attempted to imitate the enamel colours and issued 'marzarine blue', 'turquoise', 'pale yellow', 'pea-green', 'blue-green', and 'rose pink', which strangely was called 'claret'. The ground colours at Vincennes were broken up by reserves containing painted decoration such as flowers, birds, or scenes with human figures 'après Watteau'. The curvilinear outline of the cartouches were adorned with scrolls, thickly gilded by Étienne Henri le Guay and his assistants. Gilding was lavish, tooled, and sometimes engraved. In contrast, the brassy gilding used at Derby and Bow looks thin and garish and, even the beauty of the Chelsea honey-gilding, pales beside that of Vincennes and Sèvres. Decoration was the province of Jean Jacques Mathieu, but Bachelier retained overall control. Many pieces were mounted by Claude Duplessis, court goldsmith and gilt-bronze artist. It will be shown, later, how his work may have inspired the porcelain bocages used in this country.

François Gravant had continued to work at Vincennes and later at Sèvres where his research was directed to improvement of the soft paste (*pâte tendre*). In 1751, he announced a new formula which gave rise to an exceptionally lovely *pâte tendre* that had both a warm appearance had a velvety feel to the touch. Additional embellishment was superfluous and the absence of glaze permitted a sharpness of modelling detail that exactly suited Louis Felix de la Rue, Jean Baptiste Fernex, Pierre Blondeau, François Marie Suzanne and other sculptors who acted as modellers. In 1749, the Dauphine, Maria Josepha, presented her father, Augustus III of Saxony with 480 blossoms which had been made at Vincennes of tinted biscuit attached to metal stems arranged in ormolu mounted white glazed vases.[47] The Marquise de Pompadour is reputed to have delighted Louis XV by showing him her conservatory which, in the middle of winter, was filled with flowers — all made of porcelain! Indeed, biscuit flowers became something of a speciality of the factory and were also imitated at Chelsea where, during 1755, three thousand were sold. Madame de Pompadour had acquired white glazed models of 'Les Enfants après Boucher' made by Blondeau. In 1754, she ordered another set to be made in the biscuit. After this time few, if any, figures were glazed and enamelled. In England, a few figures had been issued in a rather unattractive grey biscuit at Bow but the medium was not popular owing to deficiencies of the body. At Chelsea, biscuit seems to have been utilized only for flowers. The Derby factory, as will later be shown, issued figures in biscuit after 1771 until well after the turn of the century. Though Derby biscuit never reached the excellence of Sèvres, it was extremely attractive.

The greatest of the Sèvres modellers was Étienne Maurice Falconet (1716-1791). He worked in close collaboration with Boucher who provided him with such designs as 'Figures in French Porcelain' which were engraved by Falconet (fils). Falconet made a series of groups relating to the contemporary drama, such as 'Le Baiser Donné', 'Le Baiser Rendu',[48] and 'Le Gouter Champêtre'[49] after the comedy *Anette et Loublin* which starred Madame Favert who served as the model. These were ignored by English modellers. Children depicted in a sentimental genre included 'Le Sabot Cassé',[50] 'La Mangeuse de gimblettes',[51] 'La Tournique, ou la Loterie', and 'La Lantern Magique'.[52] The last two of these prompted Chelsea-Derby groups of c.1775 which were known as 'The Game of Hazard' (M93) and 'A Raree Show' (M94) later to be described. Although the number of Sèvres biscuit children actually copied was small, a very considerable quantity of Chelsea-Derby figures are after the style of Boucher and Falconet, including 'Cupids riding Bucks' (M182), 'Cupid riding a Sea-Lion' (M197), a 'Boy seated beside a Dog' and companion 'Girl with a Cat' (M49). Perhaps the finest sculpture in porcelain

47. *Porcelain*, op. cit., fig. 15, illustration of biscuit bouquet in a vase now in the Zwinger, Dresden.

48. *Le Biscuit de Sèvres....* op. cit., pl. 8, nos. 94 and 95 (c.1765).

49. ibid., pl. 1, no. 398 (c.1752).

50. ibid., pl. 7, no. 543 (c.1760).

51. ibid., pl. 7, no. 400 (c.1757).

52. ibid., pl. 6, nos. 380 and 408 (c.1757). See also Schreiber Collection, no. 428 (no. 522).

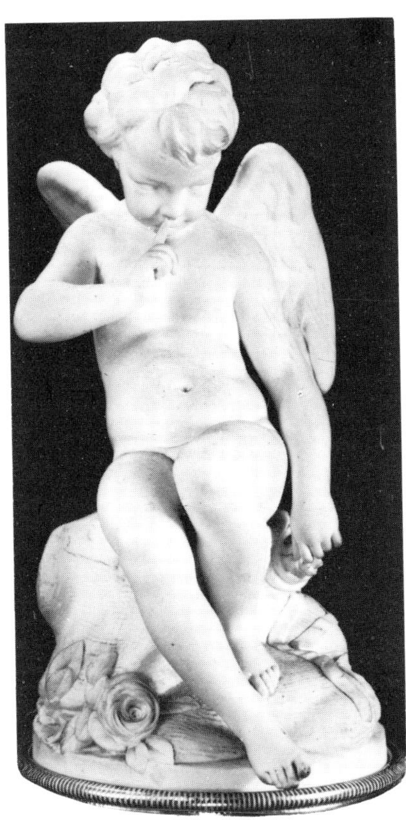

'Cupid' (paired with 'Psyche') unglazed Sèvres figure after models by Falconet, c.1765.

accomplished by Falconet relates to romanticised allegory, exemplified by 'Pygmalion amoureux de sa Statue',[53] 'Cupid and Psyche',[54] 'Pygmalion and Galathea',[55] and 'Leda with a Swan'.[56] The last mentioned was adapted in mirror image both at Meissen and at Chelsea (C84) with replacement of the attendant nymph by an inquisitive looking Cupid. Once again, only a few French prototypes were directly plagiarised though their sentimental manner of presentation is reflected by many Chelsea-Derby models and groups such as 'Procris and Cephalus' (M75), 'Prudence and Discretion' (M183), 'Bacchus with Nymphs on Mount Ida' (M376) and others. The fourth theme favoured by Falconet, which was the basis of many of his groups, was that of the 'idyllic pastoral myth'. Perhaps the best known example was his biscuit 'Le Leçon Agréable' (Plate 178) issued in 1752 that had been inspired by Boucher's painting of that title of 1748. Others include 'La Bergère des Alpes',[58] 'L'Oracle, ou le Noeud de Cravate,[59] 'Pensent-ils au Raisin?',[60] 'Le Mouton Favorite' and 'L'Education Sentimentale'. These were copied at Derby where they were called respectively: 'The Alpine Shepherdess' (M178 and M256), 'The Knot in the Cravat' (M177 and M255), 'The Grape Gatherers (M176), a pastoral group (L17), and 'A Lesson in Love' (L14). Amongst the last of the groups made by Falconet at Sèvres, were 'En Grande Toilette' which found echoes at Derby that are called by the banal names of: 'The Hair-dresser' (M84), 'The Shoe-black' (M81), 'The Stocking mender' (M79) and the 'Shoe maker' (M78). They were reissued during the first two decades of the nineteenth century.

In 1764, Madame de Pompadour died, and in 1766, Falconet without his patronne, had to face increasing criticism for his failure to conform to the neo-classical taste, and left France to work for Catherine the Great in Russia. Between 1768 and 1769, the exquisite *pâte tendre* was replaced by *pâte dure* and, in 1770, Boucher was found dead at his easel. Jean Jacques Caffieri was appointed head of the modelling department at Sèvres in place of Falconet but was, himself, superseded by Louis Simon Boizot in 1774. The golden age of Sèvres had passed and henceforth her influence upon English modellers was negligible until the nineteenth century.

Lunéville

A small, unimportant, ceramic factory had existed at Lunéville since 1731 which, forbidden to infringe the monopoly enjoyed by Vincennes and Sèvres, was forced to use a strange hybrid paste including pipe-clay intended to simulate biscuit. A talented modeller, Paul Louis Cyfflé, who had studied under Barthelemy Guibal, came to work at Lunéville first for a brief spell in 1752, and for several years after 1766 when he returned. His bust of 'Voltaire',[61] based upon a marble by J.P. Lemoyne made in 1748, was copied at Derby in 1773. He also modelled a group 'Belisarius and his daughter'[62] which was adapted by the Chelsea-Derby modeller Jean Jacques Spengler, c.1793, for a similar group in biscuit, whilst George Cocker also used the male figure in his own version with a lady, incongruously dressed in the fashion of the early nineteenth century.[63] Cocker, also copied other models by Cyfflé, namely the 'Cobbler whistling to a Starling in a cage',[64] and a 'Man playing a hurdy-gurdy with a Monkey holding a switch.[65] Interestingly enough, there are also Ralph Wood (senior) lead glazed versions of 'Chimney-Sweep,[66] 'Lady with a quail's nest in her apron',[67] and 'Falconer'.[68] The subject has been reviewed by Stuart G. Davis.

The Rococo Style

The use of a single branch of blossom, or a floral spray, on Kakiemon-

53. Seventeenth and Eighteenth Century French Porcelain, op. cit., pl. 70.
54. ibid., pl. 71B and 71C.
55. *French Porcelain of the Eighteenth Century,* op. cit., pl. 68.
56. ibid., pl. 70.
57. *Le Biscuit de Sèvres...,* op. cit., pl. 1, no. 313, model made in 1752.
58. ibid., pl. 9, no. 110, model made in 1766.
59. ibid., pl. 9, no. 481, model made in 1766.
60. ibid., pl. 1, no. 398, model made in 1752.
61. 'Some English Pottery and Porcelain Figures connected with Alsace Lorraine' by Stuart G. Davis, *Burlington Magazine,* 1927, Vol. 51, pp. 221-228; pl. I.C., Cyfflé's bust of Voltaire; pl. I.D., Derby version in Liverpool Museum.
62. ibid., Pl. II.A., Cyfflé's 'Belisarius and his daughter'; pl. II.B., Spengler's version in Liverpool Museum.
63. *Derby Porcelain* (London 1961) by F. Brayshaw Gilhespy, fig. 67, Samuel Cocker's group using Belisarius after Cyfflé.
64. 'Some English Pottery and Porcelain Figures connected with Alsace Lorraine', op. cit., pl. II.C, Cyfflé's 'Cobbler whistling to caged starling'; pl. II.D, Cocker's version.
65. *Crown Derby Porcelain* (London, 1951) by F. Brayshaw Gilhespy, fig. 172, Cocker's group of 'Hurdy-gurdy player and Monkey'.
66. 'Some English Pottery and Porcelain Figures connected with Alsace Lorraine', op. cit., pl. III.A, Cyfflé's 'Sweep'; pl. III.B, Ralph Wood pottery version possibly by Voyez.
67. ibid., pl.III.C., Cyfflé's 'Girl with Quail's nest'; pl. III.D, Ralph Wood pottery version.
68. ibid., pl. III.E, Cyfflé's 'Falconer'; pl. III.F, Ralph Wood version.

decorated porcelains imported from Japan may first have suggested to Europeans what Sir William Temple once called "the studied beauty of irregularity".[69] The Chinese concocted the curious *sharawadgi* to describe this quality. In 1751, Horace Walpole wrote: "I am almost as fond of Sharawaggi or Chinese want of symmetry in buildings as in grounds or gardens." Alternatively, asymmetry which is the essential component of the rococo style, may have been prompted by Paul Decker and other decorative artists who printed upon a single page both the right and the left halves of two different cartouches. The beginning of asymmetry in Europe have been traced to the designs of Jean Bérain I (1640-1711) during the closing years of the reign of Louis XIV. Juste-Aurèle Meissonier is generally regarded as a most important influence for, under his direction, the rococo style matured and flourished. Essentially the new taste was a reaction against the pomposity and monumental grandeur of the baroque. The hitherto massive proportions were scaled down, whilst majesty was replaced by elegance and pretentiousness by wit. It was likened to "the touch of a pretty woman smiling — always agreeable." Ponderous solidity was to give place to a sense of lightness, fluidity, and movement in which asymmetrical designs incorporated 'C' and 'S' shaped scrolls, water, rock-work and shells. The straight line yielded to the serpentine, the flat surface bulged and became *bombé,* the straight supports developed into cabriole legs, and perimeters of mirrors, panelling and of cartouches assumed extravagantly curvilinear forms. Both *singerie* and *chinoiserie* were accepted into the schemes so that carved and gilded mirrors frequently include cupolas, Chinamen, the phoenix and other Oriental emblems. The hitherto dark palette was muted to provide a pastel colour-scheme in which greens, pink, and yellow predominate.

The impact of the rococo upon Kändler and his fellow artists at Meissen has been described in Chapter II. Until c.1740, each porcelain figure had been a complete entity in its own right and, by reason of strong enamel colouring and dramatic pose, capable of competing successfully for interest with the architectural setting. Now, models were intended to be viewed in sets or groups, often owing to placement upon the dining table about a centrepiece only from a particular angle. Increasingly models were inspired by engravings and other two dimensional sources whilst some were made for display upon gilded wall brackets or upon the mantelshelf. It was inevitable that the finish of portions of models not meant to be seen was left in the rough. The importance of the model was reduced and, as additional ornament became more elaborate and profuse, it became subordinated to fulfill a purely decorative function. Such developments reached their zenith at Chelsea, Bow and Derby c.1765-70 when models and groups were not always easy to identify amidst a riot of gilt and enamel, sculptured bases and fan-shaped back-drops of leaves and flowers known as *bocage.*

The complex forms assumed by the bases of many English models during this period may, perhaps, be traced back to the work of the gilt-bronze specialist, Jean-Claude Duplessis, who was appointed to the Vincennes factory in 1747. There, he created ormolu mounts to embellish not only the factory products but also figures and wares imported both from Meissen and the Orient. His preference for scrolled and fenestrated mounts, including representation of water, shells, and marine life, was fully in accord with the spirit of the rococo and was echoed at Chelsea and at Bow, where some shell salts follow his designs. The strange bases of the early Bow 'Sphinxes' (G23) must also purely have been derived from French gilt-bronze mounts. Although arrangement of scrolls in asymmetrical patterns often assumed clumsy and ungainly forms upon the bases of early English models, by the early 1750s,

69. *The Garden of Epicurus* (1690) by Sir William Temple.

several figures including the Bow 'Liberty and Matrimony' (G37), and the dry-edge Derby 'St. Thomas' (Plate 91, Chapter VIII) (J23) and 'St. Philip' (J22) exhibit a more mature understanding of the rococo. Unaccountably, rococo scrolls are rarely if ever found upon the bases of Chelsea models until c.1756 when they are manifest upon the so called 'Family Groups' (C111 and 122).

Bocage was another feature adopted during the rococo period, which while it seems typically English, probably had its origins in France. There are many ormolu-mounted Meissen models with candle sconces attached together with leaves and stems of gilded bronze that terminate in large flowers fashioned in Chantilly enamel. Examples include a 'Chinaman' and a companion 'Lady with a parasol', in Saltram House.[70] Some quite early English porcelain models have holes that penetrate the back of the base or figure intended to accept brass fitments. Bow models emblematic of 'Taste' and 'Hearing' (H99) and dry-edge Derby figures representing 'Water' and 'Air' (J35) survive with their attachments intact which include, after the French fashion, brass candle-holders, leaves, and stems terminating in large porcelain flower heads. Probably, the high cost of bronze and a dirth of craftsmen skilled in fine metal work in England, prompted the idea of making these appendages entirely from slip. The first tentative attempts to apply leaves to the tree-trunk supports may be seen in the models of a 'Huntsman with his gun' and companion 'Lady with a falcon' (Plate 71, Chapter VII) (H67) made c.1755 at the Bow factory. Gradually, between 1756 and 1769, the number and density of these attached leaves increased to become first fan like projections containing flowers that did not extend above waist height but eventually enveloping the figure or group above and on both sides. Perhaps the best example of the late bocage is provided by the Chelsea gold anchor group known as 'The Music Lesson' (Plate 50, Chapter VI) (D72).

Models issued from Vincennes, and subsequently from Sèvres, eschewed colour from about 1751 and a few years later nearly all were left in the biscuit. English factories were unable to emulate this owing to the unattractive greyish hue of most of the soft pastes which fell far short of the whiteness of the French *pâte tendre*. Apart from a few biscuit models issued during the early 1750s by the Bow factory, the medium was not favoured in England until 1771. Denied the materials necessary to reproduce figures in the Sèvres manner, English artists instead adopted the style employed by that factory, of enamel decoration on useful wares, cabinet pieces and vases. Thus, we find ground colours upon the raiment of porcelain figures broken up with trefoil and quatrefoil reserves, often framed with gilt, containing stylised flowers, and diaper patterns intended to simulate brocades. When in 1771, William Duesbury of Derby, possibly helped by Nicolas François Gauron, introduced biscuit figures, the former style of enamel decoration together with bocages and other embellishments were abandoned.

Before completion of this brief review of the influence of the French Rococo upon eighteenth century English porcelain models, it seems appropriate to indicate how they were used to decorate the festive board. During the Middle Ages the table of a nobleman was usually decorated with images of castles, soldiers, courtiers, and animals as well as with armorial bearings fashioned from sugar and marzipan. During the reign of Louis XIV, the Sun King, more durable ornaments were created from silver though most of these were melted down for bullion during the financial crises of the latter years of the seventeenth century. In Italy, especially during the seventeenth century, silver, wax, and confentionary models were popular and these were arranged between the plates and dishes. It was a logical development, therefore, that when porcelain figures were first made at Meissen they should be employed to

70. The Saltram Collection (1977), no. 216T.

decorate the dining table. Some, indeed, were marked 'K.H.C.' or 'K.H.K.'[71] leaving no doubt as to their purpose. During the period 1733-36, Kändler introduced the novel concept of the plastic design of tureens, condiments and cruets which he included in his great baroque dinner services. Chinoiserie human and animal forms were used for sauceboats and other utensils of the *plât ménage*[72] whilst the famous Swan service[73] was later supplemented by free-standing models of pens, cobs and cygnets. By the year 1740, the small scale porcelain model had become an integral part of the fashionable dinner-table. There was generally a centre-piece, such as a *Temple of Minerva,* one example of which stands three feet nine inches in height,[74] or a model of a Dresden fountain complete with running water, or a representation of Mount Parnassus including a waterfall. Sir Charles Hanbury Williams went to a dinner attended by two hundred guests in Dresden given by Count Heinrich von Brühl and described the occasion in a letter dated 4th February, 1748, to his friend Henry Fox in London. "When dinner was brought on, I thought it the most wonderful thing I ever beheld. I fancyd myself either in a Garden or at the Opera. But I could not imagine I was at Dinner. In the middle of the table was the Fountain of the Piazza Navona at Rome, at least eight foot high, which ran all the while with Rose-Water, and 'tis said that piece alone cost six thousand Dollars. . ."[75] Around the central feature between one hundred and two hundred porcelain figures would be arranged. These would illustrate a theme or event relevant to the occasion, such as the opening of the Meissen Trade Fair, a visit of the opera or ballet to the Saxon court, a successful hunt or a performance given by the Comedia dell'Arte. Thus, table settings might include town houses surrounded by street vendors, theatrical characters, representations of the chase, or the ever popular allegorical fantasies. In 1753, Horace Walpole felt constrained to write: "Jellies biscuits, sugar-plumbs and creams have long given way to harlequins, gondoliers, Turks, Chinese, and Shepherdesses of Saxon china."[76]

In England nothing approaching the grandeur of the Saxon Court table decoration was ever attempted. Perhaps up to twenty or thirty models would be placed upon a patterned carpet composed of coloured marble chips down the centre of the board. Naturally, when the cloth was drawn, there was a high risk of damaging such fragile ornaments. George III is credited with having invented shallow trays made of silver to contain the marble chippings upon which the figures were placed so that they could be removed *en bloc* by footmen without hazard. Almost all the eighteenth century English factories advertised models, such as 'Love in Disguise for Desart', intended for table ornaments. Other models were designed to be displayed either upon the mantelpiece or on carved and gilded wall-brackets made by contemporary cabinet makers such as Thomas Chippendale. A small number of porcelain wall-brackets survive.

The rococo porcelain image makers had no comment to make about the social scene and strove only to create elegant playthings for the leisured classes. In this, they differed most profoundly from the earth potters of Staffordshire whose models and groups frequently illustrate a sermon on such perennial subjects as the evils of the demon drink or the virtues of hard work. This was at once the strength and the weakness of the rococo and, inevitably, there was a reaction against the excessive fripperies and hedonist philosophy that it expressed. The first signs of this came during the 1760s and early 1770s when a more ordered and disciplined *Louis Seize* style became manifest. This proved to be ephemeral and was, in turn, displaced by the neo-classical style, pioneered by Johann Joachim Wickelmann and others. The new style was essentially hostile to the small scale enamelled and gilded figure and its decline will be traced in Chapter XII.

71. "K.H.C.", *Königliche Hof Conditorei* (royal court confectionery). *"K.H.K."*, *Königliche Hof Könditorei* (royal court kitchen).

72. *Meissen* (London, 1971) by Hugo Morley-Fletcher, pp. 60, 63 and 64, items from the *plât ménage.*

73. ibid., p. 60, models of swans for the Swan Service.

74. *Burlington Magazine,* 1929, Vol. 55, pp. 188-190.

75. Victoria and Albert Museum, No. 246-1870. Part of the fountain mentioned by Sir Charles Hanbury Williams, more properly identified as a fountain of Dresden designed by Lorenzo Matteilli, not the Piazza Navona in Rome.

76. 'A Background to the earliest English Porcelain Figures' by R.J. Charleston, *Antique Review,* 1957, pp. 23-28.

Chapter IV

Other Art Forms that influenced the English Porcelain Modellers

The great Continental porcelain factories enjoyed rights and privileges undreamed of by potters in this country. Most were financed from the well nigh bottomless coffers of a powerful monarch who could always be relied upon to pump additional cash into the business whenever the need arose. The disbursement of rich sinecures lay in their gift, and it was possible to entice the very best sculptors, such as Johann Joachim Kändler, Franz Anton Bustelli, Simon Feilner and Étienne Maurice Falconet, into the modelling shops. The larger establishments were able to secure the services of chemists, gilders, painters, and decorative artists that were, in their several fields, the finest in Europe. In sharp contrast, the small privately owned English china works were usually founded with pathetically small working capital, enjoyed neither royal patronage, nor protection, nor privilege, and were entirely dependent for their survival upon commercial success. Modellers, together with other artists, were drawn from far less exalted social circles and proprietors were rarely able to commission the work of a sculptor, except for the rare occasion of a special order placed by royality. However, most sculptors both in England and on the Continent, created small workshop models in terracotta or plaster of their own work as well as studies after the antique which were available to the public at modest prices. François Duquesnoy (1597-1643), who created the great statue of St. Andrew now standing beneath the dome of St. Peter's, and who before his untimely death had been offered the Chair of Sculpture at the Paris Academy by Louis XIV, had himself made a large number of small terracottas. Many depict children engaged in various pastimes and forty of these were copied in porcelain by Felix de la Rue at Vincennes.[1] Others, including 'Boy asleep upon a Mattress' (A5), 'a Boy with a Reed-Pipe' (A6), and two models of 'A Boy seated upon Rocks' (A7), were copied at Chelsea between 1745 and 1749. After Duquesnoy's death, his designs passed into the hands of his brother who set up a school of sculpture at Antwerp. Amongst the pupils of this establishment were Peter Scheemakers and Michael Rysbrack both of whom settled in Britain in the second quarter of the eighteenth century. Peter Scheemakers (1681-1781), completed his training in Rome where he made a number of studies after the antique. In 1747, he offered a set of terracottas including Hercules, Flora, Venus, Faunus and the Zingara Woman for five guineas. This undersold the set made by Rysbrack in 1743 of Rubens, Van Dyck and Fiamingo Quenoy (Duquesnoy) issued at seven guineas. Scheemakers is perhaps best know for his statue of Shakespeare in Poet's Corner, Westminster Abbey. The bard is portrayed standing and leaning upon an architectural plinth on which rest books and a scroll. This mode of presentation became popular and was employed subsequently by artists in engravings, sculpture and porcelain to depict contemporary notables. The Derby 'Shakespeare' (K29) was created c.1758 after Scheemakers and paired with 'Milton' (Plate 122, Chapter VIII) (K28), which is also known in a

1. *Le biscuit de Sèvres au XVIII siècle* (Paris, 1909) by E. Bourgeois and G. Lechevallier-Chevignard, Vol. II, p. 6, 'Figurines par La Rue pour le Service du Roi. D'après François Fiamant.'

Chelsea version (A12). There are, however, minor differences in the facial expression and folds of drapery and they may have been derived from two sources. The Milton in Westminster Abbey is represented only by a bust made in 1737 by Rysbrack, so that the Chelsea and Derby models must have been inspired from elsewhere. In 1756, a terracotta of the poet was included in a sale of figures at Scheemakers's studio and it is possible that he made a set of such models of Poets from which the Derby Milton, and the Longton Hall Dryden (O80) may have been taken. Michael Rysbrack (1694-1770) sculpted a statue of the Flora Farnese for Sir Charles Hoare in 1760. Since the artist had never visited Italy, his work may have been based on Scheemakers's terracotta. However, the Bow model of 'Flora Farnese' (H79) is different from both the Rysbrack and Scheemakers versions.

A third talented sculptor, Louis François Roubiliac (1702-1762) arrived in England in 1731 from the Continent. He had studied under Balthazar Permoser who had exerted such a profound influence upon the young Johann Joachim Kändler. Roubiliac also had worked in the studio of Nicolas Coustou. After coming to London, Roubiliac became a close friend of Nicholas Sprimont who, in 1744, was godfather to the sculptor's daughter, Sophie.[2] The Chelsea porcelain head of a smiling child,[3] once believed to be in the likeness of Sophie Roubiliac, is now known in marble, terracotta and in bronze versions and is in the likeness of 'Endymion', by Agostino Cornacchini. Some have noticed a resemblance between the figure of Mary Myddleton, in a funerary monument by Roubiliac at Wrekham and the Britannia group (E16) made at the Girl-in-Swing factory to commemorate the death of Frederick Prince of Wales in 1751.[4] It is hardly likely that a small offshoot of the Chelsea manufactory would have had the means to commission work for a leading sculptor, and if the similiarity is other than fortuitous the model must surely have been based upon a drawing such as might have been produced by the sculptor for the guidance of potential customers. In 1762 Roubiliac died suddenly, and amongst his effects were four plaster models of a dog. The animal has been identified as 'Trump' (Plate 22, Chapter VI), the pet of William Hogarth, who included it in his self-portrait of 1745, and which is also immortalised in Chelsea porcelain.[5] Samuel Holland wrote of Hogarth: "It had been jocularly observed by him that there was a close resemblance betwixt his own countenance and that of his favourite dog, who had been his faithful companion for many years."[6]

Ornamentation of parks and gardens at Versailles with marble, lead, and bronze statuary for the delight of Louis XIV, had prompted a demand in England for decorative garden sculpture. As early as 1688 Caius Gabriel Cibber had supplied lead figures representing "Apollo, Pallas, and other mythological subjects", to the Duke of Devonshire for Chatsworth House. The sculptor, John Nost, who flourished between 1686 and 1729, also created lead figures of "Two Boys after Fiammingo, Perseus, Andromida, Mercury and Psyche", for Thomas Coke of Melbourne Hall. Some years before 1722 Andries Carpentière had established a business at Hyde Park Corner, adjacent to the atelier of John Nost, where he had issued statues of "Narcissus, Flora, Adonis, Apollo, Winter and Autumn". The Nost venture was taken over in 1739 by Sir Henry Cheere. Thus there existed numerous establishments engaged in copying antique statuary in lead, some of which may have served as a basis for porcelain models. In addition, a number of small plaster models, some painted to simulate bronze, were issued by artists such as John Cheere (1709-1787), brother of Sir Henry. Surviving examples of Shakespeare after Scheemakers, Milton, and the Zingara woman, are signed 'John Cheere'. The Zingara woman was copied in basaltes by Wedgwood and Bentley. An

2. Register of the Hugenot Church, Spring Gardens, London: "Sophie Roubiliac, avec pour parain Nicholas Sprimont...."

3. 'Sophie Roubiliac In Porcelain' by Bellamy Gardner, *Connoisseur,* 1938, Vol. 102, pp. 59-61.

4. *The Life and Works of Louis François Roubiliac* (London, 1918) by K.A. Esdaile, pl. 36.

5. Catalogue of the Irwin Untermyer Collection, Vol. 2, pl. 1, fig. 9.

6. 'Hogarth's Pug in Porcelain' by J.V.G. Mallet, *Bulletin of the Victoria and Albert Museum,* April 1967, Vol. III, No. 2, pp. 45-53.

Colour Plate C. *A group consisting of a woman breast-feeding a babe with two children at her side, emblematic of 'Charity' (D49). 7¼ins. (18.4cm). Chelsea c.1760, unmarked (gold anchor period).* John and Diana Mould collection

important innovation at this time was the invention, by Thomas Ripley and Richard Holt in 1730,[7] of artificial stone, which was in effect an extra hard terracotta. It provided a cheap alternative to lead for garden statuary and, in 1769, their factory was taken over by Eleanor Coade who appointed John Bacon as manager and sculptor. Among Bacon's first designs to be reproduced in artificial stone were a pair of fine lions created for Heaton Hall, Manchester which were used as the basis for the Plymouth porcelain models of 1770. John Haslem,[8] quoting from the *Life of John Bacon 1740-1799,* by Allan Cunningham, wrote... "Bacon, in 1754, when he was fourteen years of age, apprenticed himself to one Crispe, of Bow Churchyard, an eminent maker of porcelain, who taught him the art of modelling various groups and figures, such as the Deer and the Holly-tree, the Bird and the Bush, the Shepherd and Shepherdess, birds of all shapes, and beasts of every kind yet made for show or use in our manufactories." Nicholas Crispe, a jewellery by trade, and his partner Saunders, ran an artificial stone works in Bow Churchyard and it is probable that Cunningham confused this with Frye's china factory. Crispe was said also to have been associated with the mysterious porcelain manufactory either at Vauxhall or Lambeth. It is scarcely credible, as Haslem suggested, that Bacon should have been inspired by watching the baking of small models at a lesser known factory to take up a career as a sculptor. The possible link between Bacon and William Duesbury's Derby factory will be pursued in Chapter VIII. Haslem ascribes to Bacon Derby "Statuettes of Quin in Falstaff, and Garrick in Richard III", but supplies no supportive evidence and it is impossible to recognise his style in finished porcelain figures that have passed through their many formative processes. One might, however, reasonably suppose that Bacon's special skills would have been employed only for important models such as the groups representing the Royal Family[9] based on an engraving by Richard Earlom (1743-1822) after a portrait by Johann Zoffany. Such a commission might have come from Queen Charlotte herself. Mr. Timmothy Clifford[10] has noted that the ornaments and arrangement of garments around the neck of the porcelain model of the king do not conform with those in the Zoffany painting but almost exactly the same as those upon a bust of George III by Bacon now in Christ Church, Oxford. It seems, also, that a drawing made by the artist for a monument was supplied by Benjamin Vulliamy to Jean Jacques Spengler as the basis of a trial model of 'Astronomy' which served as decoration of a barometer.[11]

Other young sculptors working in London between 1784 and 1789 were recruited by the Swiss clocksmith, Benjamin Vulliamy, to make models which were dispatched by coach to Derby, which, if they met with approval, would be translated into porcelain. Such men included John Deare, Charles Peart, John Felix Rossi and others.[12] Joseph Lygo ascribed to Rossi models of 'Mars' (M114), 'Venus' (M115), and 'Diana' (M120), but the relatively low serial numbers allocated to them in John Haslem's factory list makes this very unlikely and for the same reason the model of 'Hygeia', usually paired with one of 'Aesculapius' (M99), mentioned in the Sales Catalogue of 1779, cannot have been created by Rossi who was first engaged to work for Derby in 1788. So far, it has not been possible to identify the work of these London sculptors. The model of 'Aesculapius', which stylistically resembles a terracotta now on the roof of the Derbyshire Royal Infirmary, is peculiar in that the figure holds not a caduceus but a club. Timothy Clifford[13] has suggested that this might have happened if the porcelain model had been adapted as a mirror image copy of the 'Farnese Hercules', by Giovanni da Bologna. In support of this contention it may be noted that 'No. 122' in Haslem's list is given as 'Hercules' and is, in fact, the same as 'Aesculapius' which is 'No. 99'. Before leaving the

7. 'Coade Stone' by K.A. Esdaile, *The Architect and Building News,* 1940, Vol. 161, pp. 94-96, 112-114.

8. *The Old Derby Porcelain Factory* (London, 1876, reprinted Wakefield, 1973) by J. Haslem, pp. 151-152.

9. *English Porcelain Figures of the 18th Century* (London, 1961) by A. Lane, pl. 73, the Royal Collection at Windsor Castle.

10. 'Derby Porcelain Figures', a lecture given by Timothy Clifford at Morley College, London, 13th November 1976.

11. *Derby Porcelain* (London, 1971) by F.A. Barrett and A.L. Thorpe, pl. 102.

12. Letters of Joseph Lygo to William Duesbury in the British Museum.

13. 'Derby Biscuit' by Timothy Clifford, *Transactions,* English Ceramic Circle, 1969, Vol. 7, pt. 2, pp. 108-117, pl. 126, 'Aesculapius'.

'The Rape of the Sabines', bronze group after the marble by Giovanni da Bologna. Wallace Collection.

subject of English sculptors, it may be added that the Chelsea-Derby model of 'Catherine Macaulay' an obscure historian who became regarded as a champion of liberty, may have been based on a marble created by J.F. Moore in 1777. She is usually paired with a model of 'John Wilkes' (M88).

The influence of the French decorative artists upon English porcelain figures, has been discussed in Chapter III, but there remain other sources of inspiration in the form of marbles and bronzes worthy of mention. Jean Bèrain (1640-1711) employed the Sphinx from ancient Egypt in European decorative sculpture and modified the creature by giving it the head and breasts of contemporary female personages. Examples of this design may be seen in the gardens of Chiswick House.[14] The porcelain sphinxes made at Champion's Bristol factory (P44) are much in this genre though other earlier models created at Chelsea and Bow were, most likely, inspired by engravings. The origins of many English porcelain figures based on foreign sculpture have been discovered, presented and discussed by Dr. Bernard Watney.[15] A bronze 'Leda and the Swan' by the sculptor Jean II Thierry (1669-1739)[16] prompted somewhat unexpectedly the Derby group representing 'Europa and the Bull' (K80), whilst the Derby porcelain group 'Leda and the Swan' (K86), may possibly have been derived from a lost pair to the Thierry bronze. A sixteenth century French bronze,[17] seems to have provided the basis for Friedrich Eberlein's fine model of 'Diana the Huntress', standing with long-bow in hand beside her faithful hound whilst selecting an arrow from a quiver slung upon her back. This was first reproduced at Derby c.1756 (K11), though there are a number of later versions.[18] Oddly, the same figure was adapted at Longton Hall, c.1759, to provide a model of a Red Indian in the set of large standing continents (O79) which were to reappear in hard paste Plymouth versions (P7). There is, also, at least one Chelsea-Derby set of the 'Four Quarters of the Globe (M200), in which the more usual Red Indian emblematic of America, is replaced by a juvenile in the same pose as that of the Longton model. An entirely different bronze of 'Diana and her Hound'[19] was adapted at Meissen to provide a model of both a 'Shepherd feeding a dog from a Scrip' and the companion 'Shepherdess'.[20] These, in turn, prompted gold anchor Chelsea models (Plate 165, Chapter XIII) (D75). It seems highly likely that a bronze by the sculptor Jacques Sarrazin (1588-1660),[21] may have inspired the Longton Hall porcelain group of 'Two Putti feeding a Goat' (Plate 136, Chapter IX) (O33), of which there are two versions both reproduced at the Plymouth factory (P1 and P4). Undoubtedly other French marbles and bronzes will later become identified as sources of both Meissen and English porcelain models and groups.

Flemish and Italian marbles and bronzes were also used as sources of inspiration by English porcelain modellers. The bronze group of 'The Rape of the Sabines' by Giovanni da Bologna (1529-1608)[22] found echoes both at Chelsea (C88) and Meissen and has already been mentioned. The same artist created a bronze of a 'Boy Bagpiper seated with legs crossed' which was the basis of the Bow model being issued both free-standing and as the finial of a pot-pourri vase.[23] Adaptation of his 'Farnese Hercules,[24] may, as has already been indicated, have prompted the Chelsea-Derby model of 'Aesculapius'. The marble 'Bacchus'[25] by Jacopo Sansovino (1486-1570) seems to have inspired modellers at several different porcelain factories. Firstly, at Chelsea c.1756 (C73), then at Derby (M193) where the model was issued with one of 'Ariadne' in 1775, and lastly a black basaltes version of the same was copied by Wedgwood and Bentley.[26] There are numerous bronzes depicting the goddess Minerva which portray her in crested helm wearing a cuirass and holding an oval shield and a spear. One of these, in the manner of Benvenuto Cellini[27]

14. *A Dictionary of Antiques* (London, 1968) by George Savage, p. 404.
15. 'Origin of Design for the English Ceramics of the 18th Century', by Bernard Watney, *Burlington Magazine,* 1972, Vol. 114, No. 837, pp. 818-826.
16. *French Bronze 1500-1800* (New York, 1968) by Jaques Fischer, pl. 55.
17. *Europaische Bronzestatuetten* (West Germany, 1967) by H.R. Weihrauch, fig. 472.
18. *English Porcelain of the 18th Century* (London, 1952) by J.L. Dixon.
19. *French Bronze 1500-1800,* op. cit., pl. 18.
20. *Festive publications of the Oldest China Manufactory in Europe, Meissen* (Dresden, 1910) by Karl Berling, table 13, nos. 1331 and 1332.
21. *Sculpture, Renaissance to Rococo* (London, 1969) by H. Keutner, no. 198.
22. *The Complete Encyclopaedia of Antiques* (London, 1962) by L.G.G. Ramsay, p. 1185, pl. 447a.
23. Schreiber Collection Catalogue, pl. 6, fig. 4.
24. 'Derby Biscuit', op. cit., pl. 126c.
25. *Italian Sculpture 1250-1700* (London, 1967) by F.M. Godfrey, fig. 158.
26. Wedgwood and Bentley Catalogue (1779), No. 9, 'Bacchus from Sansovino'.
27. *Burlington Magazine,* 1910, Vol. 16, p. 3, pl. 1.

'Hercules and the Kerynean Stag', bronze group, Renaissance. Wallace Collection.

may have been the basis of the many Meissen models that were copied at Derby (K87) and other English factories. The marble 'Lion', that stands with one paw upon a ball, at the foot of the steps leading up to the Loggia dei Lanzi in Florence, was reflected in porcelain models made both at Chelsea[28] and at Bow. A 'Boy Pedlar' or 'Pilgrim' (H38), with a pack upon his back and a staff in his hand, is known both in carved wood and in bronze versions[29] which for stylistic reasons have been identified as Flemish.

The Longton Hall group of 'Hercules and the Nemean Lion' (O28), may have followed one of several Italian bronzes attributed to Stefano Maderna (1576-1636) though it might equally have been based upon a seventeenth century Nurnberg ivory. The rather similar Longton group showing 'Hercules with the Kerynean Stag' (O29) was based on an engraving by Bernard Picart (1663-1733)[30] after Louis Cheron.[31] Francesco Fanelli, who worked in England between 1610 and 1640, created a bronze of the Infant Hercules on a galloping horse beside a baying hound[32] which prompted a pair of Longton Hall groups (O30) one in mirror image. The antique marble of a seated wild board, now in the Uffizi Gallery, Florence, was reproduced in bronze by the studio of Francesco Susini and other artists during the first quarter of the seventeenth century and there are also gilded bronze versions made in France during the eighteenth century. Either may have prompted the early Derby model (Plate 171, Chapter XIII) (J1) though in the porcelain version there is a more pronounced turn of the head and more powerful hind quarters. The companion 'Running Boar' may be original.

Porcelain modellers frequently adapted plaster models or terracottas after the antique to meet their needs and, when the positions of limbs had been altered and clothing had been added, the source was often difficult to identify. A terracotta of the 'Borghese Warror',[33] which was a favourite academic study, was the basis of the Chelsea 'Fisherman with a huge net' (C27). Another terracotta of 'Antinous', after the antique, was adapted at Derby to provide the Shepherd standing hat in hand (M396) by Spengler, though tradition attributes the model to William Coffee. Llewellyn Jewitt wrote that the original was in the possession of Mr. Joseph Wright of Derby. Spengler also modified the likeness of the ancient Capitoline Faun[34] to provide a 'Shepherd' and companion 'Shepherdess' each with a flute (M369).[35] A bronze after the antique by Massimiliano Soldani (1656-1740) of a 'Satyr with a Kid'[36] inspired the Longton Hall model of a 'Goatherd' (O50). Another ancient Greek statue representing Ariadne was copied in Rome [37] to become the basis of a Chaffers' Liverpool model (Q30) whilst by the addition of an asp about the arm of the lady, she was issued by the Staffordshire potters as Cleopatra.[38]

A number of book illustrations that were used for the basis of porcelain models have already been cited in Chapter II. These include several Flemish, French and Italian books illustrating habits worn by religious orders; Cesare Ripa's *Iconologia;* de Ferriole's *Recueil de cent estampes représentant les differentes Nations du Levant. . .;* and Luigi Riccoboni's *Histoire du Théâtre Italian. . . .* In 1743, *The History of Uncommon Birds,* by George Edwards, was published in four volumes in London. This contained coloured drawings of exotic birds and prompted rather more than twenty pairs of models of birds made at Chelsea between 1749 and 1753 (Plates 14, 15 and 16, Chapter VI) ,[39] which follow the originals fairly faithfully as to shape and colour. The 110 etchings made by Francis Barlowe (1626-1702) to illustrate the 1666 edition of *Aesop's Fables,* inspired a number of 'Fable Groups' at Chelsea during the period of the gold anchor, and some less well known ones from Bow.[40] Engraving No. 29, in the 1687 edition, also by Barlowe, is of Aesop and the pose and garments are similar to those of the red anchor Chelsea model[41]

28. *Transactions,* English Ceramic Circle, 1969, Vol. 7, pt. 2, pl. 130b.
29. Victoria and Albert Museum, No. A.52 — 1953, 'Bronze Pedlar'.
30. 'Engravings as the Origin of Design and Decoration for English 18th Century Ceramics' by Bernard Watney, *Burlington Magazine,* 1966, Vol. 108, No. 761, pp. 406-410, fig. 20. See also *Europaische Bronzestatuetten,* op. cit., fig. 405, bronze group.
31. 'Engravings as the Origin of Design etc.', op. cit., fig. 13, engraving signed 'Le Cheron inv: et ari incidere caepit B. Picart perfecit'; fig. 10, porcelain group of 'Hercules and the Kerynean Stag'.
32. *Europaische Bronzestatuetten,* op. cit., fig. 472, Fanelli bronze.
33. *French Bronze 1500-1800,* op. cit., pl. 18, 'Borghese Warrior'.
34. Répertoire de la sculpture Grecque et Romaine (Paris, 1903) by S. Reinach, Tome II, Vol. I, p. 135, fig. 5, the Capitoline Faun'.
35. *English Ceramics 1580-1830* (London, 1977) by R.J. Charleston and D. Towner, fig. 151, Derby 'Shepherd Flautist'.
36. *Apollo,* 1963, Vol. 77, p. 196, fig. 3, Soldani's 'Satyr'.
37. Il Museo Archologico di Firenze (Florence, 1910) by L.A. Milani, p. 313, no. 40-41, pl. 152, Roman model of 'Ariadne'.
38.'The King, the Nun and Other Figures' by Bernard Watney, *Transactions,* English Ceramic Circle, 1968, Vol. 7, pt. 1, pl. 52c, Chaffers' Liverpool model of 'Ariadne'.
39. 'The Chelsea Birds' by Bellamy Gardner, *Transactions,* English Porcelain Circle, 1931, No. III, pp. 55-63.
40. Chelsea Fables see Appendix D89-102 for models. For Bow examples of 'Fox and Goose at the Well' (pair of groups) see Appendix H146.
41. *Transactions,* English Porcelain Circle, No. 4, 1932, pl. VIa, Chelsea model of Aesop; pl. VIb, engraving by Francis Barlowe.

The 'Quan' or 'Guan' by George Edwards, History of Uncommon Birds, *Vol. I, plate 13.*

though in the porcelain version the character is portrayed as a hunch-back negro wearing the gold chain of a freeman. The idea of black Aesop seems to have sprung from an engraving made in 1665 by W. Hollar which was copied in 1673 by John Ogilby and included in his version of *Aesop's Fables.* Although the character of Aesop was included in David Garrick's farce *Lethe,* the role was played by Taswell as a white man. Etchings by Giacomo Calotto (1593-1635) in *Varie figure Gobbi,* published in the early 1620s prompted a pair of 'Grotesque Punches', otherwise known as the 'Mansion House Dwarfs' (M227) from Derby. *Les Metamorphoses d'Ovide,* by L'Abbé Banier, which appeared in several editions between 1767 and 1771, inspired the Chelsea-Derby group 'Procris and Cephalus' (M75) and a pair of figures making sacrifices (M14), the latter from the plate entitled 'Jason and Medea at the altar of Diana'. A.J. Toppin,[42] traced the origin of the early Bow muse, 'Clio' (G14) to an engraving by the Flemish book illustrator, D. Coster, in the works of L'Abbé de St. Real, which were published c.1700. The exceptionally fine raised anchor Chelsea figure of 'Isabella' (Plate 17, Chapter VI) (B35) was derived, somewhat unexpectedly, from a woodcut entitled 'Matrona di Orliens' (Plate 18, Chapter VI)[43] in a Venetian book on costume by Cesare Vecellio of 1590. A second woodcut, 'Donzelle Contadine di Parma', from the same work prompted another raised anchor model of a 'Rose Seller' (B51). The red anchor Chelsea 'Abbess of Cologne' (C104) was prompted by a woodcut, 'A Noble Canoness of Cologne' illustrating a book by Daniel Steudner published in 1693.[44]

Engravings were the most popular source of inspiration for the porcelain modellers. Thomas Frye, manager of the Bow works until 1759, was himself an accomplished artist who made several mezzotints, including one of the 'Queen of Sheba offering gifts to Solomon' painted by Paola Veronese. The peculiar head-dresses worn by women attendant on the queen are the same as those which appear on Bow porcelain 'Sphinxes'[45] which are said to be in the likeness of Peg Woffington taken from her portrait by Arthur Pond. These, which stand on rococo bases are totally dissimilar from others in the likeness of Kitty Clive mounted upon wedge shaped bases that have drapery over the back and breasts and which are known in both Chelsea triangle marked (A15) and Bow (G24) versions.[46] Possibly these were prompted by engravings made by J.F. Blondel in 1738. Standing models, as well as sphinxes, were made of 'Kitty Clive'[47] in the role of Mrs. Riot, or the Fine Lady, from David Garrick's farce *Lethe,* both at Bow (G1) and at Derby (Plate 87, Chapter VIII) (J10); these were taken from an engraving by Charles Mosley made in 1750 after the watercolour painting by Thomas Worlidge. The companion model of 'Henry Woodward' (G2), which was made only at Bow, was inspired by an engraving by James McArdell (1729-1765) after a portrait painted by Francis Hayman. McArdell made over two hundred mezzotints during his lifetime including studies of 'James Quinn as Falstaffe', 'Mary Duchess of Ancaster', 'David Garrick as Tancred', and of the Royal Family. The Derby models of 'Falstaff' (K27) after Francis Hayman's portrait, and the female 'Ranelagh Dancer' (K52) inspired by Thomas Hudson's painting of the Duchess of Ancaster, of 'Garrick as Tancred' (K30) which was the title role of *Tancred Sigizmunda* a play by Thompson that had its debut in London in 1744, and the three porcelain groups of the Royal Family (L7), which were prompted by the picture by Johann Zoffany, were all copied indirectly from McArdell's mezzotints. Here, it should be noted that the earlier Bow model of David Garrick as Falstaff (G3) came from a different source, namely an engraving by C. Grignion of David Garrick in that role.

Another Irish mezzotint engraver, Richard Houston (1721-1775),

42. 'The Origin of Some Ceramic Designs' by A.J. Toppin, *Transactions,* English Ceramic Circle, 1948, Vol. 2, No. 10, pp. 266-276, pl. CIa, engraving by D. Coster; pl. CIb, Bow model of 'Clio'.

43. *Degli Habiti Antichi e Moderni di tutto il Mondo: di nuovo Accresciuti molte figure* (Venice, 1590) by Cesare Vecellio. See also *Connoisseur, 1960,* Vol. 145, p. 247, fig. 7, Chelsea model of 'Isabella'; p. 247, fig. 8, 'Matron of Orleans', woodcut; p. 248, fig. 9, Chelsea model of 'Rose Seller'; p. 248, fig. 10, 'Peasant Girl of Parma', woodcut.

44. *Kurze und grundliche Historie von dem Anafang und Ursprung Gott-geweihten Orden aller Kloster Jungfrauen* (Augsburg, 1693) by Daniel Steudner. See also *Connoisseur,* 1960, Vol. 145, p. 250, fig. 19, Chelsea model of 'Abbess'; p. 250, fig. 20, 'Noble Canoness of Cologne', woodcut.

45. 'Thomas Frye 1710-1762' by T. Wynn, *Burlington Magazine,* 1972, Vol. 114, No. 827, pp. 79-84.

46. 'Some Consequences of the Bow Porcelain Special Exhibition' by Hugh Tait, *Apollo,* 1960, Vol. 71, pp. 181-185; p. 183, fig. IV, engraved 'Sphinxes' by Blondel; fig. III, Bow 'Sphinx after Peg Woffington'; figs. V and VI, 'Chelsea Sphinxes after Kitty Clive' (triangle); figs. X and XI, 'Bow Sphinxes after Kitty Clive'.

47. ibid., pp. 40-44; p. 42, fig. V, Mosley's engraving of Kitty Clive.

reproduced among other works two portraits by Sir Joshua Reynolds (1723-1792) which were echoed at Bow. One of these, 'The Marquis of Granby' (H107), shows John Manners in the uniform of Colonel-in-Chief of the Blues, wigless and without his hat, leading his men to victory. The incident traditionally took place on the field of Warburg in July 1760 when his lordship's bald pate became a rallying point during the hostilities. However, the model was most probably issued to commemorate the battle of Minden which took place in the preceding year. The second model is of General Wolfe (H109) who engineered the capture of Quebec from the French in 1759, but who died upon the battlefield at the moment of victory. The French engraver Charles Simon Ravenet, who spent much of his working life in this country, reproduced a plate of Charles Pratt, the Baron Camden, in the robes of Lord Chancellor, after Sir Joshua Reynolds, which was also translated into porcelain at Derby (L4). It would seem likely that Derby models of William Pitt, the Earl of Chatham (L6), John Wilkes (M126), General Conway (L5) and other notables such as Admiral Duncan (L2) and Lord Rodney (L1) were inspired by contemporary engravings of which there must have been a great many. The figure of 'Admiral Lord Howe' (M384), one example of which in the Victoria and Albert Museum is signed 'P. Stephan',[48] was prompted by Mason Brown's portrait of the admiral.

A pair of figures sculptured by Guido Reni had been drawn by Sir Robert Strange and formed the basis of a group of two nude but draped women standing stiffly on a flower encrusted base made at Chelsea and known as 'Liberality and Modesty' (D50). They were translated into porcelain without any concessions to scale or to the medium and are artistically unsuccessful. Some of the great artists of the world also provided material that led to models in porcelain. A mezzotint by William Panneels of work by Peter Paul Rubens (1577-1640) prompted the Chelsea gold anchor group of 'Roman Charity' (D48). This portrays the aged Cimon chained, a prisoner condemned to die by slow starvation, being breast fed by his daughter Pero who attempts thereby to save him. The dramatic impact of the original painting is largely lost in the group owing to the lavish decoration of the garments dictated by rococo taste. Two Chelsea pot-pourri vases, made in 1755, one decorated with models of 'Meleager in Roman dress with a Boar's head', and the other with 'Atalanta with long-bow and Hound',[48] were derived from paintings also by Rubens. Van Dyck's 'Time clipping the wings of Love', was engraved by Charles Phillips and echoed in the Chelsea-Derby group (M124). An example in biscuit is mounted with a clock by Benjamin Vulliamy and is in Buckingham Palace.[50] 'The Holy Family', by Raphael, now in the Louvre, was engraved by François Poilly and entitled 'La Petite Sainte Famille'[51] which was the basis of an exquisite, and possibly unique, group created at the Girl-in-a-Swing Factory (E24). Here, the boy Christ stands on the left of the seated Virgin and leans across her lap to greet St. John, also shown as a child, held by a kneeling St. Elizabeth. Huygh Voskuyl (1592-1665)[52] painted a picture 'Tobias and the Fish', now in the Staatsgemäldesammlungen, Munich, and this evidently prompted the Champion's Bristol model of a 'Boy frightened by a Dog' (P32). The allegorical painting made in 1649, by Carlo Maratti (1625-1713), now in the Hermitage, Leningrad,[53] depicting Galatea seated with her head turned towards the giant Polyphemus who appears in clouds above a distant cliff, was engraved by J. Audran and used as a guide for a Chelsea red anchor group of 'Galatea with a child Triton' (C81).

The subject of the 'Tithe Pig', engraved by Boitard in 1751, enjoyed immense popularity and prompted a set of three Derby models as well as a group (Plate 120, Chapter VIII) (M293). They depict a farmer holding tightly

48. Victoria and Albert Museum Catalogue No. C134-1937.

49. 'Rococo English Porcelain; a study in style' by J.V.G. Mallet, *Apollo,* 1969, Vol. 90, No. 90, pp. 100-113, pl. II.

50. 'A Masterpiece of Clockmaking' by L.G.G. Ramsey, *Connoisseur,* 1956, Vol. 38, p. 230, fig.1.

51. 'The Masterpiece of an unknown Craftsman' by P. Synge Hutchinson, *Connoisseur,* 1964, Vol. 168, No. 676, p. 97, fig. 1, porcelain group of the Holy Family; fig. 2, engraving after Raphael.

52. 'The Origins of some Ceramic Designs', (Watney) op. cit., pp. 267-275, pl. 181A, Bristol model; pl. 181B, painting by Voskuyl.

53. *Art Treasures of the Hermitage* (New York, 1977) by Pierre Descargues, p.121, plate of Maratti's painting.

'David Garrick as Richard III', mezzotint engraving by J. Dixon after Nathaniel Dance.

on to his pig whilst his wife proffers her tenth child to the astonished parson. A few models from the Girl-in-a-Swing factory were also based on engravings. A standing 'Boy in a tricorn hat' holding a fish (E5), emblematic of Water was based on Jacopo Amigoni's engraving, but the companion model representing Air seems to be original for the engraving of this element by Amigoni is clearly unsuitable for translation into porcelain being a gallant descending a ladder laid against a tree holding a bird's nest intended for a lady seated to the left of the picture.[54] The 'Fox and Stork at the well' (E26) was prompted by an engraving in the *Weekly Apollo* of 1752.

Angelica Kauffmann (1741-1803) arrived in England in 1766 and painted allegorical subjects both for private patrons and for Robert Adam in the neo-classical style. The name of this beautiful and talented Swiss artist was scandalously linked by the gossips of London with that of Sir Joshua Reynolds, who helped her to obtain commissions. The sculptor Nollekins caustically remarked that she was "a sad coquette. Once she professed to be enamoured of Nathaniel Dance; to the next visitor she would disclose the great secret that she was dying for Sir Joshua Reynolds."[55] Few have suffered her fate. A scoundrel, who impersonated his master, Count Horn of Sweden, set himself up with the trappings of nobility at Claridge's hotel, wooed, won, and bigamously married the poor lady. The miscreant was exposed and imprisoned but Angelica refused to marry her eventual husband, Antonio Zucchi, until the man who had wronged her had died. Much of her work is reproduced in stipple engravings, a technique introduced into England from France by William Wynne Ryland (1732-1783) who also enjoyed the doubtful distinction of having been judicially hanged for fraud. The copies of many of Angelica's paintings were made by Francesco Bartolozzi (1728-1815) who arrived in London in 1764 to engrave the royal collection and afterwards set up a school of engraving in the Metropolis. Probably several engravings attributed to him stem from the hands of his pupils. The Chelsea-Derby groups of 'Two Virgins awakening Cupid' (M195), 'Two Bacchantes adorning a bust of Pan with a garland' (M196), and 'Three Graces distressing Cupid' (M235), are after engravings by Bartolozzi from works by Angelica Kauffmann. A model of a 'Shepherd' with an end-flute and companion 'Shepherdess' (M389) were adapted from the engraving entitled 'The Shepherdess of the Alps'.[56] Two other groups modelled by J.J. Spengler at Derby, include 'Cupid disarmed by Euphrosyne' (M358) inspired by Thomas Burke's engraving,[57] and 'Palemon and Lavinia' (M366) which was probably copied from work by Louis Paul Cyfflé though this was based on C. Knight's engraving after Angelica Kauffmann.

54. 'The Origin of Some Ceramic Designs' (Toppin), op. cit., pl. XC, Amigoni's engravings.

55. *The Parkers of Saltram, 1769-89* (Rugby, 1970) by Ronald Fletcher, p. 76.

56. 'J.J. Spangler, a virtuoso Swiss modeller at Derby' by T. Clifford, *Connoisseur,* 1978, Vol. 198, No. 196, fig. 12a, engraving of 'Shepherdess of the Alps'; fig. 12b, Derby biscuit model of 'Shepherd with a flute' and companion figure of a 'Dancing Shepherdess'.

57. ibid., fig. 8a, Thomas Burke's engraving of 'Cupid disarmed by Euphrosyne'; fig. 8b, Derby biscuit group.

Chapter V

The Discovery and Development of Soft Paste and Methods by which English Models were Constructed

The Discovery and Development of Soft Paste

The quality of translucency which distinguishes porcelain from earthenware, suggested to the arcanists of the sixteenth, seventeenth and eighteenth centuries that china might be made with a white clay and glass. Accordingly, experiments were conducted along these seemingly promising lines. The first success in Europe was achieved by Francesco I de Medici, who became Grand Duke of Florence from 1574 to 1587, assisted by a maiolica potter, Flaminio Fontana. Some sixty specimens of this artificial soft paste porcelain survive, though the secret seems to have been lost after 1587. In 1673 exclusive rights were granted to Louis Poterat of Rouen to manufacture porcelain but, when the patent was renewed in 1694 it was stated that the secret was very little used, the petitioners devoting themselves to the manufacture of *faience*. Wares that survive are of a very glassy paste decorated with an inky underglaze blue and, when Poterat died in 1692, the secret perished with him. The subsequent establishment of soft paste manufactories at St. Cloud, Mennecy, Chantilly and Vincennes have been described in Chapter III.

In England John Dwight (1673-1703) was granted a patent on 23rd April 1671 for "A Transparent Earthenware commonly known by the name of Porcelain or China and Persian Ware". This would seem to have amounted to no more than a semi-translucent stoneware. Research continued after his death both in London and in the Provinces, and the first viable concern appears to have been established at Chelsea in about 1745. The similarity between the paste used at Chelsea and that of St. Cloud, both of which possess a high lead content, suggests that possibly a workman defecting from the French factory might have given the formula to Nicholas Sprimont. In a lengthy document written some time between 1752 and 1759 by Sprimont in the hope of prompting erection of tariff barriers against the importation of porcelain from abroad, he wrote: "The Undertaker, A Silversmith by profession, from a casual acquaintance with a Chymist who had some knowledge that way, was tempted to make a trial which, upon the progress he made, he was encouraged to pursue with great labour and expence..."

Who then was the Chymist? Severne Mackenna[1] and others have identified him as 'Thomas Briand' (or Bryand) who on 10th February 1743 was introduced to the Royal Society by a Dr. Cromwell Mortimer. The *Journal Book of the Royal Society* records that upon that day: "Mr. Bryant, a Stranger that was present, shew'd the Society several specimens of a sort of fine white ware made here by himself from native materials of our Own Country, which appear'd to be in all respects as good as any of the finest Porcelane or China ware: and he said it was much preferable for its fineness to

1. *Chelsea Porcelain, the Triangle and Raised Anchor Wares* (Leigh-on-Sea, 1948) by F. Severne Mackenna, pp. 9-11.

the ware of Dresden, and seem's to answer the Character of the true Japan. For when broken, it appears like broken sugar, and not like Glass as Dresden ware does; and that if it be heated red-hot, and immediately put into cold water, it will not fly or break..."[2] Dr. Mackenna suggested that Briand might be a Frenchman who had obtained knowledge of porcelain manufacture, possibly at St. Cloud, and had collaborated with Sprimont enabling him to establish the Chelsea factory. Further, he contended, the early Chelsea wares might be divided into two types: those which had been finely potted supposedly by the more experienced hand of Briand and which are marked with a triangle, and thicker unmarked wares that might represent the less accomplished efforts of Sprimont.

This attractive theory has been discounted by Arnold Mountford.[3] He pointed out that the name 'Briand' may appear in contemporary documents as 'Brian', 'Bryon', 'Bryan' as well as 'Bryand'. Further, he reminds us that in both the written and spoken parlance of the Staffordshire Potteries the letter 'D' may be either inserted into, or appended to, a word. This, 'Chimney' may become 'Chimnedy' and 'Hanley' may be 'Handley'. Certainly 'Brian' does not sound like the name of a Frenchman, though perhaps the same might be said of 'Tebo', itinerant repairer and modeller who is thought to have been Monsieur Thibauld! However, Mountford also discovered articles[4] drawn up between Thomas Briand, described as a painter, and Joseph Farmer a potter of Lane Delft, Burslem, dated 5th Feburary 1746. This agreement established a partnership between the two men intended to endure for the span of twenty-one years and to establish a small porcelain factory. Mrs. Briand was employed either making or painting ceramic flowers at one penny per dozen. In the event of her husband's death, she was to be made a partner. Briand died a pauper the following year and evidently there ensued some dispute between his widow and Farmer. A provision of the agreement had been contentious matters should be settled by reference "to two indifferent persons, each partner to choose one". Mrs. Briand called in Thomas Heath to protect her interests whilst Farmer invoked the assistance of John Wedgwood.

On 21st September 1748, Wedgwood wrote of the affair to his associates in London, John Weatherby and John Crowther. "You remember that I came in April with Mr. Heath to reconcile Mr. Farmer and Widow Briand; that Mr. Heath and I came to you and Mr. Fry, to hear what you had to say for or against Mr. Briand touching his behaviour in making china. And as I believe you gave but an ill character of him in it..."[5] The lengthy reply written by Weatherby, dated 24th September 1748 included the following denigration: "... If you remember we told you in a few words that we had nothing good to say of the deceased Briand (nor his wife), that we were greatly deceived by them, that they had from time to time made great promises to us of what they could do... but upon trial all promises ended in words, he never performed any one thing he pretended to know..."[6] Such evidence dubs Briand an impostor but sheds no light upon the possible identity of the 'Chymist' who provided the formula for the Chelsea paste.

Paul Bemrose[7] has shown that a potter named William Steers, from Hoxon in Middlesex, applied for a patent in 1742/43 for: "...the Art of making transparent Earthen Ware in Imitation of Porcelain or China Ware after a Method entirely new..." This does not appear to have been taken up by the petitioner. However, Steers had been employed at Limehouse and, unlike Briand, was no charlatan for in 1744/45 he went to the 'Pomona Potworks' at Newcastle in Staffordshire where he manufactured soft paste porcelain wares. Shards have been recovered from the factory site. This was a truly remarkable disclosure for it is certain soft paste was being made in the Midlands some four

2. 'The Earliest References to Chelsea Porcelain' by H. Bellamy Gardner, *Transactions,* English Porcelain Circle, 1928, Vol. I, No. 1, pp. 23-24.

3. 'Thomas Briand — a Stranger' by Arnold Mountford, *Transactions,* English Ceramic Circle, 1969, Vol. 7, pt. 2, pp. 87-95.

4. ibid., pp. 88 and 89.

5. ibid., from the John Wedgwood Papers in the City Museum, Stoke-on-Trent.

6. ibid., p. 93.

7. 'The Pomona Potworks, Newcastle, Staffs.' by Paul Bemrose, *Transactions,* English Ceramic Circle, 1975, Vol. 9, pt. 1, pp. 1-18. See p. 18, Appendix B, for Steers' petition.

years prior to the venture at Longton Hall that commenced in 1749/50 and before either the first Bow patent was taken out in 1744 or the earliest dated piece of Chelsea porcelain.

The Nature and Manufacture of Soft Paste

Soft paste is, essentially, an imitation of true porcelain made by suspending a white clay in glass. The several ingredients employed in its manufacture and the technical processes involved have been described by Donald MacAlister[8] and Arthur Hurst.[9] The results of chemical analyses of soft pastes associated with the different eighteenth century English porcelain factories are presented by George Savage.[10]

Clays are hydrated silicates which include mica and quartz as impurities and they are important constituents of soft paste upon which the plasticity of the material largely depends. A paste lacking plasticity is said to be 'short', one possessing this quality is described as 'fat'. Plasticity is related to the alumina content. The *pâte tendre* of Sèvres was so short and the alumina so low that it was necessary to mix it with soft soap before it could be either thrown or moulded. Shortness is one of the factors that may lead to surface tearing or full thickness firecracks due to unequal shrinkage of thinly and thickly potted areas during cooling. The Bow factory, as later will be shown, may initially have employed a fine white clay, known as 'unaker', obtained by the American potter André Duché from Savannah in Georgia. Hugh Tait[11] even suggested this source may have been used up to, and for some while after, the retirement of the proprietor, Thomas Frye, in 1759. However, Wedgwood sent an expedition to Virginia where the clay was mined and had to pay £500 for only five tons of unaker so that the high cost would probably have deterred most from importing it. The same unaker had been examined by Thomas Cookworthy of Plymouth and had been rejected because he had found an alternative source first at Tregonning Hill and later at St. Austell in Cornwall. Donald MacAlister cites *Groseley's Tour to London* of 1770 to show that Cornish clay was being used at Chelsea certainly as early as 1763.

When clay is heated with sand, which is a readily available source of silica, no reaction takes place unless an alkaline flux is added. However, if clay is heated either with pearl-ash (potassium carbonate) or soda-ash (sodium carbonate) obtained from incineration of ferns and marine plants, the salts crystalize out and the unstable mass crumbles. Also, if potash and sand are heated together a troublesome effervescence results. It is necessary, therefore, to convert the silica of the sand into an alkaline silicate by a process known as fritting. Lime (calcium oxide) was first prepared by heating limestone or granite in a lime-kiln. The lime and silica were then heated upon the floor of an oven and raked over at intervals. The alkaline silicate so formed was then mixed with potassium carbonate, small quantities of calcium oxide, and water to form a paste. In some instances fragments of lead glass, known as cullet, were added. The presence of cullet in a paste can be inferred by detection of a high content of lead oxide. Such glassy pastes which were used prior to 1750 at Chelsea and at the Girl-in-a-Swing establishment until c.1753, had a poor stability in the kiln, would not permit sharp edges to be created and caused sagging out of the perpendicular and distortion of unsupported projecting parts. Most soft pastes required a kiln temperature of about 1,100°C; if this rose much above 1,250°C, objects would collapse into a shapeless mass, whilst if it failed to reach 1,050°C, there was inadequate cohesion of particles. This narrow margin of safety inevitably caused huge kiln losses.

Devices designed to improve stability in the kiln included incorporation in the mix of either ground up pottery fragments, called grog, or Oriental

8. 'The Material of English Frit Porcelains' by D.A. Macalister, *Burlington Magazine*, 1927, Vol. 51, pp. 138-142, and ibid., 1928, Vol. 53, pp. 140-141.

9. 'Ceramic Construction' by Arthur Hurst, *Transactions*, English Ceramic Circle, 1937, No. 4, pp. 22-42.

10. *Eighteenth Century English Porcelain* (London, 1952) by George Savage.

11. 'The Bow Factory under Alderman Arnold and Thomas Frye' by H.G. Tait, *Transactions*, English Ceramic Circle, 1963, Vol. 5, pt. 4, pp. 195-216.

porcelain. The 1749 Bow formula included forty per cent. of calcined bone (i.e. cattle bones reduced to a calx by heat). The bone ash remained in suspension after firing giving the body a milky appearance and reduced translucency. Such a paste is phosphatic and may be identified chemically by the molybdic acid test. Phosphoric acid may be determined by this means in wares made at Chelsea after 1757 and in the Chelsea-Derby wares of the period 1770-84. Lowestoft figures and wares are also phosphatic. The paste invented at Lund's Bristol factory in 1749 was subsequently used at Worcester and her daughter factories. The formula containes soapstone, or steatite, which may be identified by a high content of magnesia, one part of which corresponds to three parts of the rock. This paste was stronger and harder than other soft pastes and permitted a crisper potting. Impurities in the paste include ferric salts which give rise to red-brown stains, and ferrous salts which cause a greenish discolouration.

Most soft pastes are covered with a glass, or glaze, made from lead acetate. This might be sprinkled over the figure as a powder or, more usually the powder was suspended in water into which the item was dipped. Prior to 1754 many factories opacified the glaze by inclusion of tin oxide so that underlying blemishes might thereby be concealed. Another practice, which will be mentioned in the appropriate sections, was the use of a pinch of cobalt, or smalt, to blue the glaze in an attempt to simulate the cold glittering appearance of feldspathic glaze on hard paste from Meissen.

Quality control of raw materials was primitive in the eighteenth century, and it is scarcely surprising that analysis of drillings from different figures made at the same time and at the same factory, should give widely different results. Further, competence in the performance of tests is not enough to ensure accurate estimations unless there is continuity of experience and the laboratory is geared to carry out several analyses per week. Many of the published results arise from sporadic activity by researchers often hampered by the necessity to take only very small samples. It seems to the author patently absurd to express results of analyses of porcelain to two places of decimals or more!

Soft pastes are less hard than true porcelain. They will often crack when placed in contact with boiling water, will mark with a metal file and, when broken, the edges of the fracture resemble the surface of a sugar cube. Unglazed surfaces absorb dirt and become stained and such marks cannot readily be removed by scrubbing with soap and water. Palpation of exposed biscuit gives a sensation of stroking pummice and the material feels less cold than true porcelain. Usually, the covering soft lead glaze displays abrasions and scratch marks best seen with a hand lens. Enamel decoration appears to be within, or even beneath, the surface of the glaze. Transillumination, not usually possible where a figure is concerned, will often show areas of increased translucency which are called according to size either tears or moons, and often also a faint colour that may be peculiar to the factory of origin.

Modelling for Translation into Porcelain

The master model was usually fashioned from wax or clay with tools that have altered little over the years. Occasionally, some other medium would be employed, and one modeller at Nymphenburg, Franz Anton Bustelli, preferred to carve in lime wood. In England, the first phase of modelling, which may be called the formative years, began c.1745 and ended between 1751 and 1752. During this time, few porcelain models from Meissen were imported and the techniques evolved by Kändler and his associates remained unknown to English modellers. Here, it was considered sufficient simply to reduce the scale of larger plastic work without making any special concessions to the medium. Figures were stiffly posed, like garden statues, and some, including a group known as the 'Rustic Lovers' (E12) made at the Girl-in-a-Swing factory, have indentations into the cornea of both eyes, a device employed by sculptors who wish to obviate the appearance of blindness otherwise evident in uncoloured statues. Until 1751, enamel colours were rarely used on figures so that all features had to be represented in the round. Likewise decoration of garments was effected with applied slip. The 'Muses Modeller' at Bow dressed his models in large earrings, necklaces, and ruffles imparting to them a fussy appearance. He created heavy lidded prominent eyes, ungainly noses, half open mouths and receding foreheads and chins. The modelling of Chelsea figures prior to 1750, lacks sufficiently deep relief to be entirely convincing. Nicholas Sprimont may himself have served as modeller before 1749 and though capable of producing fine models in silver was at this time unfamiliar with the demands of the new medium of porcelain. The crude Longton Hall models that were issued between 1750 and 1753, suggest there was no skilled modeller upon the factory staff. Although those made at the Girl-in-a-Swing establishment are naïve and display great simplification of drapery, they possess a certain charm with their deeply set eyes, Greek noses, tapering hands and feet and tasteful placement of accessories.

In 1751, Meissen models from the collection of Sir Charles Hanbury Williams were loaned to the proprietor of Chelsea. Within months, the chief modeller, Joseph Willems, began to eliminate from his work all unnecessary detail and to suggest features hitherto represented in the round with enamel colour. This tidying up process was soon emulated at other English manufactories though each evolved an individual style of modelling. After 1752-53, almost every model made in this country followed a Meissen prototype. Joseph Willems's figures have a stately appearance lacking animation owing to his failure to represent secondary postural adjustments that normally accompany action; they have finely chiselled features with broad foreheads, widely spaced eyes and *retroussé* noses whilst drapery seems to have been copied from blanket thick material. The 'Muses Modeller' at Bow must have played an important role in effecting the improvements for some of his earlier traits are recognisable even though muted. His later work imparted to models an impish inclination of the head, an unnatural twist to the torso just above the hips and slight flexion of both knees which overall created a magnificent sense of movement. Some Derby models made, possibly by André Planché between 1752 and 1755, mostly follow Meissen originals but display rather sharp facial features, large mouths and finely sculptured drapery. These contrast favourably with the later Derby figures of 1756 to 1769 which are stiffly posed like dolls with their long noses, narrow faces and eyes that stare vacantly into space. At Longton Hall, between 1754 and 1758, it is probable that more than one modeller was employed but one created some exceptionally fine figures with a robust realism that has much in common with the products of the Staffordshire potteries. The subject of modelling styles will receive fuller treatment in appropriate sections of chapters that follow.

The brilliance and satire of Meissen rarely survived intact when translated into soft past. In general, the less attractive excesses such as the 'Freaks', the 'Crinoline Groups', and models relating to the local scene in Saxony, were ignored in England. Here, severe limitations were imposed by the deficiences of the medium so that unsupported projection of limbs and sharp edges could not be reproduced. The differences were enhanced too by the pastel colouring and thick soft glazes of the English copies.

The third phase of English modelling followed the Prussian rape of Meissen though, as has been shown in Chapter II, models made at that factory before

1756 continued to flow into England, albeit in a diminishing stream. Now it was the turn of Sèvres to assume the mantle of greatness and to become the arbiter of porcelain taste. The brilliant satire of Saxony gave place to the elegance and beauty of France, exemplified by the exquisite biscuit models and groups made by Étienne Falconet and his colleagues mentioned in Chapter III. The previous preoccupation with the Commedia dell'Arte, the Cries of Paris and chinoiserie waned and interest refocussed upon themes such as romanticised allegory, the idyllic pastoral and the French theatre. Increasingly the English copyists adapted to the new fashion though ignoring the contemporary Parisian drama; they also favoured models of obese and weary looking Cupids based on 'Les enfants d'après Boucher'. Unfortunately, the French taste also included a cloying sentimentality which found expression in replicas of sickening children simpering at their mothers' skirts or performing tasks which were more properly the province of the artisan. If these were sugary in their original biscuit forms, when clad in enamel and gilt they became totally unprepossessing. Denied a paste sufficiently refined to emulate the French biscuit, the models were mounted upon highly sculptural bases within a frame of bocage and garishly decorated in enamels and gilt. In such settings, the figure was reduced in importance to fulfil a purely decorative function and, accordingly, modelling standards fell. Joseph Willems of Chelsea, became under employed and was listed in *Mortimer's Directory* of 1763 as available for giving drawing lessons. Another Chelsea modeller, probably a pupil of Willems, created some rather crude models with small heads, steeply arched eyebrows, swan necks, long torsos and short thick legs. Modellers at Bow shared in the reduced standards; models from Chelsea were plagiarised, old models reissued in debased forms and very little of merit was produced. The high rococo found similar expression at Derby and here the overall standards, although still falling below those of Chelsea, were maintained.

The fourth phase commenced after the absorption of Chelsea by Derby in 1770 and the discovery of a paste suitable for the issue of figures in the biscuit. Immediately, there followed a reassertion of the importance of the model and many of the added fripperies of the rococo were abandoned in favour of a more disciplined *Louis seize* style. This, the Chelsea-Derby era, lasted until 1783 and saw the arrival at Derby of Nicholas François Gauron and Pierre Stephan from Tournai. Some of their work conducted at the French factory is described in Chapter III, whilst many of the contributions they made at Derby are detailed in Chapter VIII. One further artist, possibly the greatest ever to work at Derby, was Jean Jacques Spengler. He arrived in London in 1790 and was to model for the Derby factory intermittently until 1795. He continued to work in the romantic manner and to create a slender elegance and grace that is readily identifiable. His models are described and listed in Chapter VIII.

The final period of decline commenced with the departure of Spengler and lasted until the failure of Derby in 1848. Many of the old copies of French models, first made in the 1770s, were reissued and some new rather artless models appear. These receive a brief mention in Chapter VIII but are, strictly, beyond the scope of the present work. The decline of the porcelain figure is also dealt with in Chapter XII. It is impossible to better the comments of Timothy Clifford:[12] "...The reasons for this decline were mostly social for increasingly under Michael Kean and Robert Bloor figures were made for cottages not castles; a little girl kneeling upon a cushion inscribed 'Good-night Mother' had a more ready sale in Scunthorpe or Wapping than, for instance, the 'Rape of Persephone'."

12. 'Derby Biscuit' by Timothy Clifford, *Transactions,* English Ceramic Circle, 1969, Vol. 7, pt. 2, pp. 108-117.

Construction of the Moulds

When the clay or wax master model had been completed, it was dissected into pieces each one of which would be suitable for casting. Usually 'V' shaped incisions were employed to facilitate reassembly. Interlocking moulds were constructed of plaster of Paris by the mould maker. These were composed of between three and five segments so enabling casts to be removed without damage.[13] Solid squeezes of clay were taken initially and assembled to serve as a guide to repairers responsible for piecing together the castings. When a large demand for a particular model was anticipated, a lead master model might be cast.[14]

Casting

Two methods, press moulding and slip casting were used. Most soft paste Continental factories, Bow, Lowestoft, and Lund's Bristol, favoured press moulding. In this process, semi-solid paste was pressed by hand into each mould. Arms, legs and relatively slender portions might be cast solid though, almost invariably, the main central segment relating to torso and perhaps one leg, would contain a central cavity. Some rare Bow models,[15] and a Longton Hall 'Heron' are solid cast. Press moulded models have thick walls and are, hence, heavy, whilst inspection of the interior, which in a few models may be possible by the absence of a base-plate, reveals a rough surface often bearing the impressions of fingers or marks of tools. The model of 'Lu-tung Pin' (Q13), made at Lund's Bristol factory, is exceptional for although it is press moulded the interior was wiped smooth.

The process of slip casting was adopted at all other English manufactories including Chelsea, Derby, Longton Hall, Girl-in-a-Swing and the Plymouth and Bristol factories of Cookworthy and Champion. Peripheral portions, such as arms and legs, were often cast in the manner described above but the main section, including often one leg together with the torso and tree-stump support, would be inverted and filled with liquid slip. A layer of dessicated paste would form adjacent to the plaster, the thickness of which would depend upon the time allowed before the excess of slip was poured off. Models cast in this way are thin walled and hence light in the hand and, when inspection of the interior is feasable, a smooth surface will be seen. A single mould would suffice for about twenty press mouldings or fifteen slip castings before definition of detail became unacceptably blurred. The first few castings were the most sharp and these were reserved for models intended for issue in the biscuit at Derby after 1771.

Assembly of the Castings

The assembly of a figure from its separately cast portions was the duty of a skilled craftsman known as a 'repairer' who had it within his power to make or mar the final achievement. Slight shrinkage of castings due to dehydration facilitated their removal from the moulds without damage. Often, the repairer would refer to a master model, assembled from clay squeezes, for guidance relating to the correct posture for limbs, and would attach castings to one another with liquid slip which served as cement; a procedure known as 'luting'. When this had been done, a wet brush might be drawn over the junctions to render them inconspicuous, whilst at Bow the repairers often sharpened up features with an edged tool or knife. Some accessories, such as musical instruments, guns and trophies, were either modelled by hand, made in a pitcher mould, or stamped out of a sheet of paste with a die, much as a chef creates decoration for pastry. The plaster mould for the triangle held by the female member of the 'Idyllic Musicians' was recovered from the

13. *Chelsea, Bow and Derby Porcelain Figures* (Newport, Wales, 1955) by Frank Stoner, pl. 63, a dissected model and a clay squeeze.

14. *The Cheyne Book of Chelsea China and Pottery* (London, 1924) by Reginald Blunt, pl. 45, a lead master model of 'Pantalone'.

15. 'Evidence that some early Bow figures were cast solid' by Peter Bradshaw, *Journal of the Northern Ceramic Society,* 1972-73, Vol. 1, pp. 41-44.

Stratford-le-Bow site in 1921 by Aubrey Toppin.[16] Often a clever repairer would adapt one basic model to serve many different purposes. For example, the figure of Britannia required only the replacement of the cross of St. George upon her shield by a moulded replica of the head of Medusa to become Minerva. Again, the addition of a cornucopia and a lion and removal of the shield would transform the lady into Cybele who might be issued simply as a goddess or emblematic of Earth in a set of the Four Elements.

The design of the base was usually considered to lie in the province of the repairer. Many shapes characteristic of the different phases of production at the several manufactories have already received mention and others will be described in later chapters. In short, the early bases were usually simple mounds or rectangles, more rarely shaped as plinths with swags formed with applied slip. However, some quite elaborate forms are found on models made at the Girl-in-a-Swing factory which were favoured especially for representations of birds. The use of asymmetrical arrangements of scrolls appeared first on Bow models of c.1752, including 'Liberty and Matrimony' (G37), 'Charity' (Plate 57, Chapter VII) (G15) and a pair of candlestick figures of boys with flowerpots upon their heads (G49). By about 1758-60, the Bow bases became increasingly elaborate with table like forms elevated upon short cabriole legs (Plate 80, Chapter VII) and, later, sculptural features included comma and slot fenestrations (Plate 66, Chapter VII). The first dry-edge Derby models stand upon steep mounds but, by c.1754-55, rococo scrolls appear and are evident on models of 'St. Philip' and 'St. Thomas' (Plate 91, Chapter VIII) (J22 and 23). During the first few years of the proprietorship of William Duesbury, between 1756 and 1758, the steep mounds give place to wide flat bases edged with symmetrically arranged scrolls (Plate 115, Chapter VIII). Once again, during the 1760s the Derby bases became more elaborate though rarely to the same extent as those of Bow. Later, between 1770 and 1783, Derby bases recapture something of their earlier simplicity with irregular pads (Plate 123, Chapter VIII), rectangles, circular and octagonal shapes some adorned with vertical fluting or a Greek key-fret pattern. Strangely, the Chelsea bases remained simple almost discoid mounds (Colour Plate B) until c.1756 and even during the period of 1759 to 1762 these continued to be issued though the increasing use of complex forms with short curved legs and dependant 'U' scrolls (Plate 50, Chapter VI) becomes evident. High bases decorated with symmetrically arranged scrolls after the manner of the *Louis*

16. 'Bow Porcelain — Recent Excavations' by A.J. Toppin, *Burlington Magazine,* 1922, Vol. 40, pp. 88.

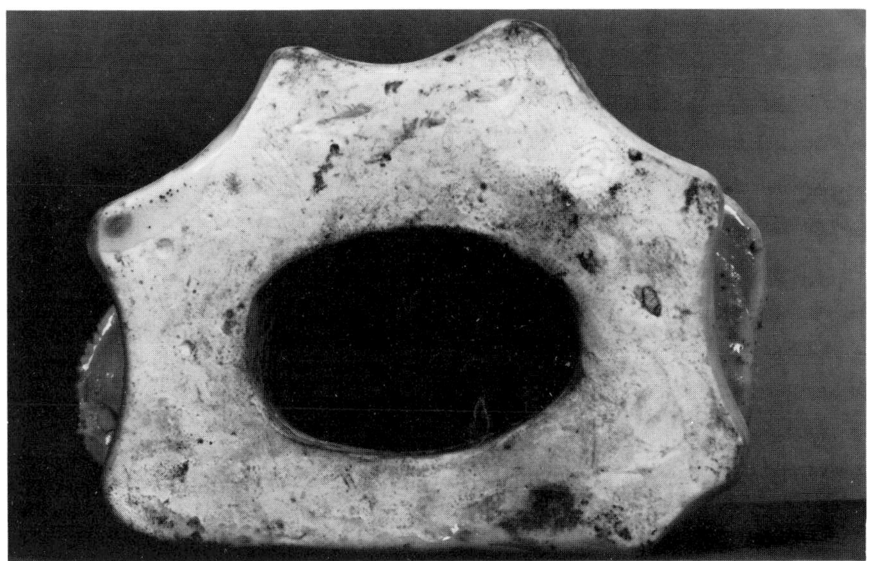

Plate 2. *Inferior aspect of a dry-edge Derby model of 'Kitty Clive' (J10), c.1750, showing a flat unglazed surface to a star-shaped base devoid of any base plate.* George Savage, Sigmund Katz Collection

seize style were issued at Plymouth (Plate 144, Chapter X) between 1768 and 1770 but, following the move to Bristol, many assumed a rectangular or relatively simple shape.

It was standard practice at nearly all the factories to occlude the under surface of the base with a plate of paste. A few exceptions in which the base was left open include Bow models of a seated 'Boy with bagpipes', 'Henry Woodward' and 'Kitty Clive' as well as the Derby version (Plate 2) of the last mentioned figure. Cookworthy's Plymouth figures are invariably devoid of base plates so that their smooth glazed interior may be seen (Plate 3). This immediately distinguishes them from Longton Hall models cast from the same mould. The under surfaces of most models made prior to 1756 are flat (Plate 4) though after this time those made both at Chelsea and at Bow are concave (Plate 5). Base plates are perforated by ventilation holes to allow escape of gases expanded in the heat of the kiln within the central cavity. These apertures may be funnel shaped on Derby figures created prior to 1756. Their resemblance to the holes made by a carpenter to accept the head of a screw has led to them being called 'screw-holes' (Plate 6). Less often other forms may be found such as two cylindrical holes arising from a punched out oval depression. Models from elsewhere display ventilation holes of variable size the largest of which are found on those made at Derby from 1770-84 (Chelsea-Derby period) which may admit the tip of a finger. Derby and Bow figures may also exhibit a second aperture that penetrates the back about an inch to an inch and a half from the lower edge and passes horizontally to enter the central cavity. This was intended to accept a metal fitment attached to a candle sconce or additional decoration. Most often those pertaining to the Bow factory are triangular or square (Plate 7) in section whilst those of Derby are circular (Plate 8), though there are many exceptions to this general rule.

The modelling of leaves and flowers was another task allocated to the repairer. Derby leaves may have a pin-hole on their inferior surface where they have been lifted out of a mould by a sharp pointed instrument. They are thin, sharp edged with serrated borders and relatively small in scale to the model. Those made at Chelsea prior to 1753 resemble oak leaves though subsequently they lose this characteristic and acquire serrated edges though they are generally larger and thicker than those of Derby. Bow leaves made before 1755

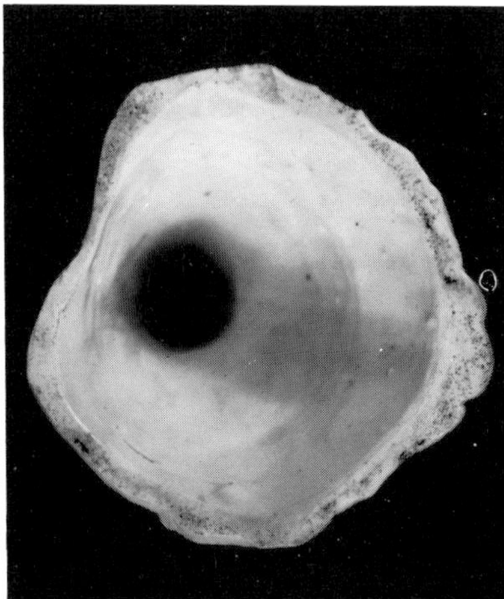

Plate 3. *The under surface of a Plymouth model of a musician (P10) showing absence of a base plate and the smooth, glazed interior.* Author's collection

Plate 4. *The inferior aspect of a Bow toper (H26), c.1756, showing the flat ground surface and small ventilation hole.* Author's collection

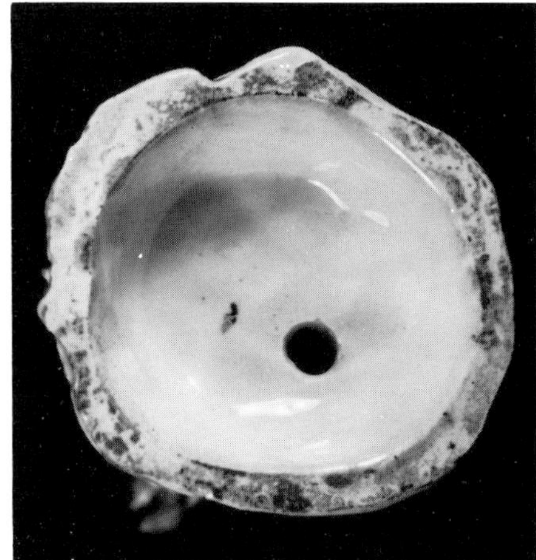

Plate 5. *Inferior surface of a Bow musician (H45), c.1760, showing the glazed, concave central portion perforated by a small ventilation hole and a flat circumferential rim ground free of glaze.* Author's collection

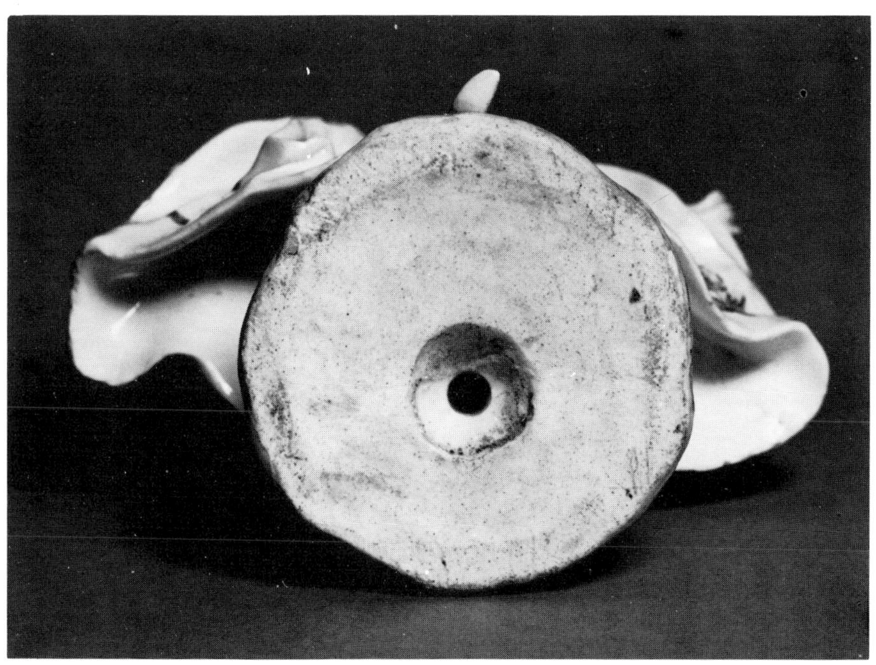

***Plate 6.** The under surface of a dry-edge Derby model of a 'Dancing Girl' (J14), showing the unglazed surface and a funnel-shaped ventilation hole (screw-hole).* David Thorn collection

are canoe shaped but between 1756 and 1765 they become spiky like holly leaves and are large in scale; late Bow leaves have smooth contours and may exhibit moulded dorsal veins.

The aggregations of leaves and flowers known as bocages have already received mention. After 1760 they became complex and assumed absurd proportions. The assembly of these must have required the patience of Job and the application of a compulsive obsessional neurotic for, in such examples as the gold anchor Chelsea groups of 'The Music Lesson (Plate 50, Chapter VI) (D72) and 'The Dancing Lesson' (D63), upwards of a hundred leaves and flowers had to be individually luted to their supports. One repairer at Bow, seems to have deliberately twisted the leaves before assembling them in order to produce a more natural appearance. A few Plymouth models display bocages, such as the 'Gardener holding a basket of Fruit' and companion 'Lady holding a basket of Flowers' (P11). These seem to have been constructed by affixing the leaves to a plate of paste in much the same manner as that used by John Walton and other modellers in pottery.

The nature of flowers both in bocages and upon the superior surface of bases may indicate the factory of their origin. Most Chelsea blooms are rather flat and open and may consist of four or five shaped petals radiating from a central mound or a concave disc with a serrated circumference; a few appear to have been individually modelled. Flowers made at Bow are often large in scale, saucer shaped and either rounded or, more often, with long pointed petals few of which survive intact. At Longton Hall prior to 1753, flowers were represented by little more than rosettes but, after 1754, they become very large and either have the form of a rose with strangely rectangular petals or resemble cabbages. Very few Derby models made prior to 1756 are decorated with moulded flowers and the few examples consist of tightly rolled blossoms like rose buds or look like daisies. The early Duesbury models of 1756 to 1758 nearly always display moulded and modelled flowers that are inappropriately large for the model. These are like huge open roses with ragged edged petals. By about 1758-60, the flowers become much smaller and take a number of different forms. Many are stellate, or trumpet-shaped, others are discoid, or

Plate 7. *Square hole intended to accept a brass fitment in the back of a Bow musician (H45), c.1760.* Author's collection

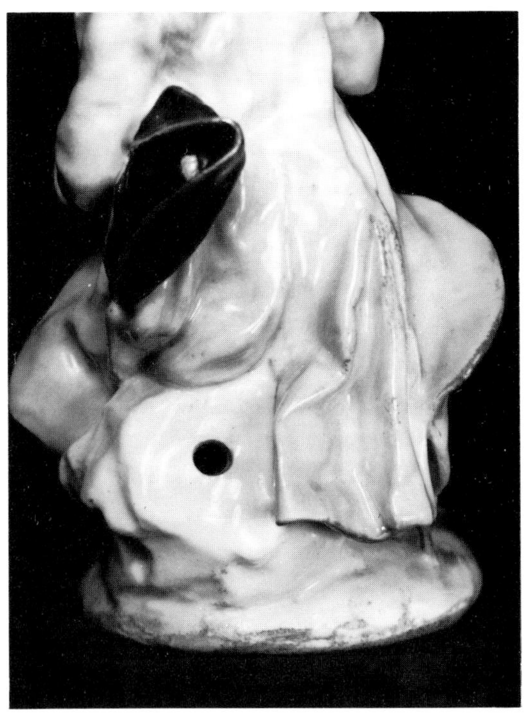

Plate 8. *Circular hole intended to accept a brass fitment in the back of a dry-edge Derby model of a snuff-taker (J33).* Author's collection

bun like in appearance, whilst there are a few which seem to have been fashioned individually by hand. Plymouth blossoms are also pleomorphic and may be saucer shaped, with five or six petals, like serrated discs, or resemble crocuses with the tips of the petals turned back. They are often crowded together in bocages almost touching one another as may be seen in the 'Two Putti feeding a Goat' (Plate 143, Chapter X) (P1) in the City Museum and Art Gallery, Bristol.

The last duty of the repairer was to incise or impress any marks that might be required and these, for the purpose of convenience, may be considered under four categories. The first, relate to factory of origin. For example, a figure in the City Museum and Art Gallery at Derby, mentioned by Chaffers,[17] is incised 'New D', (New Dresden) and seems to be unique. A script 'D' or 'Derby' is known upon a few early Derby creamers, but is unknown on figures. Further, Brayshaw Gilhespy[18] mentions the mark 'W.D. & Co.', incised upon a Derby bagpiper now in the British Museum which, presumably, stands for 'William Duesbury and Company'. Many Chelsea figures issued prior to 1750, are marked with an incised triangle, the alchemist's sign for fire, whilst models created between 1750 and 1753 may bear a small oval medallion bearing upon it an embossed anchor within an oval (raised anchor mark) (Plate 9). Some examples of the rare Lund's Bristol figure of the sage 'Lu-tung Pin' are impressed 'BRISTOLL'. Bow models rarely, if ever, bear a factory mark. Chelsea-Derby models may bear the device of a crown and crossed batons over a script letter 'D' which is incised. More commonly they were left unmarked or were enamelled overglaze.

The second category of marks relating to the repairer are those indicating the date of manufacture. A model of Henry Woodward in the Irwin Untermyer collection bears the date 1750, whilst some versions of the Bristol

17. *Marks and Monograms on European and Oriental Pottery and Porcelain* (London, 1965) by William Chaffers, 15th revised edition, Vol. 2, p. 200.

18. *Derby Porcelain* (London, 1961) by F. Brayshaw Gilhespy, p. 41.

'Lu-tung Pin' have the same date impressed. A rare Chelsea model of a 'Boy asleep on a Mattress', is incised 'June ye 26th 1746', and this is the earliest known date marked upon any English porcelain model.

The third type of mark relates to workmen, especially repairers. The device 'To.' is thought to stand for Tebo or Thibault, a Bow repairer who later worked at Worcester, Cookworthy's Plymouth and Bristol factories, and Etruria where the same mark may be found. An incised star, made with four intersecting lines, was the mark of Isaac Farnsworth, whilst an impressed triangle refers to Joseph Hill — both repairers who may have been employed occasionally as modellers. The letter 'B', may have been intended to denote selection for issue in the biscuit whilst 'G' presumably indicated the model was to be glazed. Other capital letters, 'R' and 'J' may be found, the significance of which is unknown. There is no justification for the belief that the letters 'B' and 'R' stood for Bacon and Roubiliac or Rysbrac.

The fourth type of mark concerns numbers allocated in the Derby Factory List, probably commencing in 1772. These are incised upon the bases of Chelsea-Derby and later Derby models as well as other numbers concerned with size (Plate 10). These are described in the appropriate section.

The First Firing

When the repairer had completed his work, models were placed in earthenware boxes, called saggars, designed to protect them from fumes and smoke. The floor was first sprinkled liberally with sand to prevent adherence of the model base, whilst vents in the roof and walls ensured an even distribution of heat. Ceramic props were certainly used at Bow to support projecting portions

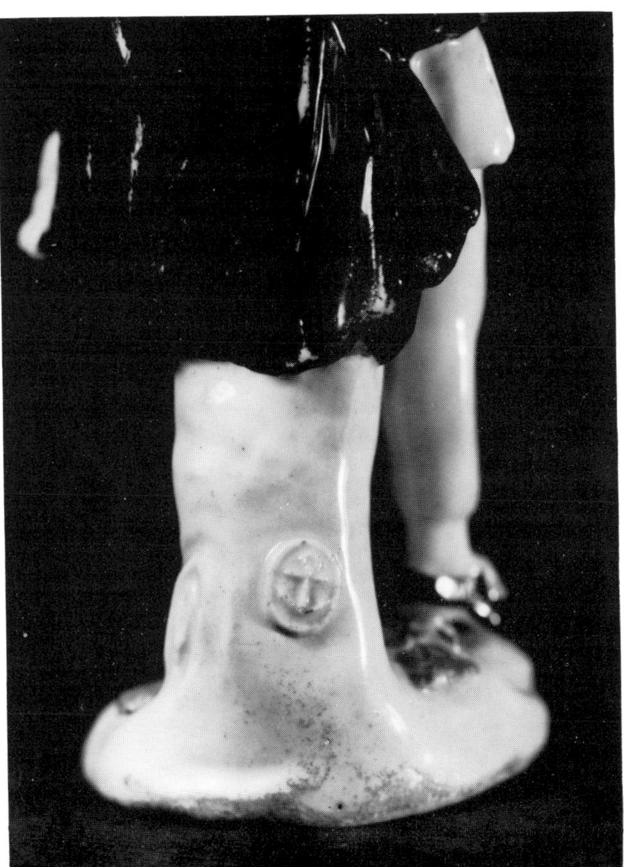

***Plate 9** (left). Reverse of Chelsea model of 'Scapino' (B37), c.1752, showing applied oval medallion bearing a raised anchor within an oval.* Author's collection

***Plate 10** (below). Inferior aspect of a Chelsea-Derby model of a fisher-girl, emblematic of Water (M3), c.1773, showing flat glazed surface, patchmarks, large ventilation hole and incised 'No. 3', and the word 'Second'. These correspond to No. 3 in Haslem's list and intermediate size.* Author's collection

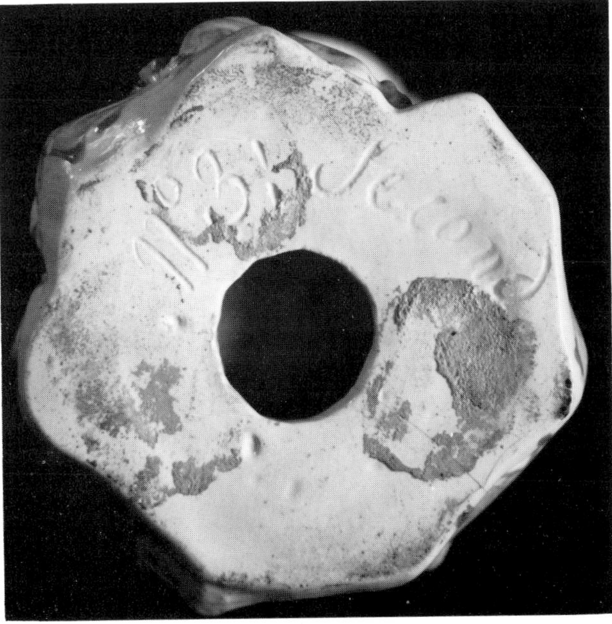

Colour Plate E. *Neptune standing beside a dolphin emblematic of Water, and Ceres holding a cornucopia beside a lion representing Earth, from the set of the 'Four Elements' (H100). 7½ins. (19.1cm). Bow c.1760. The floral sprays are painted in monochrome upon the robe of Ceres and in polychrome on the mantle of Neptune.* Author's collection

Colour Plate F. *A 'Turk' standing with his left hand on his hip and his right outstretched (H14). 7½ins. (19.1cm). Bow c.1754. The facial features, which have been sharpened up with a knife, display traits associated with the Muses Modeller, and colouring includes sealing-wax red and blue, pale yellow, and gold-purple. This model is rare since it has been cast solid.* Author's collection

of figures, such as an outstretched arm, which might otherwise sag out of alignment in the heat of the biscuit kiln[19] and it is probable that this practice was common to all other manufactories. The props were made of clay or from some similar material that would shorten by the same proportion as the model for otherwise they would not have fulfilled their purpose. The absence of such props amongst excavated kiln furniture of eighteenth century English manufactories may indicate no more than their failure to have survived intact though some have argued that they were not commonly used. Saggars were stacked upon shelves in the kiln where those on top received the greatest heat. Great care was taken to seal all kiln ports to ensure a slow rise of temperature, and an equally slow cooling when the fire had been struck. If this was not done wares might suddenly fragment or become reduced to a shapeless mass. Most kilns were fired with wooden billets and fed by hand with the aim of achieving a temperature of 1,100° to 1,200°C. which was maintained for about twenty hours before being allowed to cool over a number of days. Firemen were immediately recognisable by the absence of hair and eyebrows from working in the fierce heat.

Figures and wares removed from the kiln after the first burning are said to be in the biscuit. Many were unsuitable for sale owing to instability in the kiln and were deemed wasters. Less severe imperfections included sideways drooping, found in the same dry-edge Derby and Girl-in-a-Swing models, sagging of limbs out of their intended position, tearing of the surface of the paste, and full thickness fire-cracks. The last mentioned are most frequently seen around the circumference of ventilation holes while surface tearing is more usual over thickly potted areas. Grey, or even yellow, staining is a common feature of Plymouth and Bristol figures, where kiln temperatures of around 1,350°C. were required for the burning of hard paste. The coal fired kilns at Longton Hall also produced yellow discolouration of useful wares prior to 1753 but figures which were protected in conical saggars seem to have escaped such blemishes. Some imperfections are almost invariably present on eighteenth century English porcelain figures.

Application of Glaze and the Second Firing

The porous nature of soft paste made it necessary to seal the surface with a lead glass or glaze. The material employed consisted of lead acetate, an

19. Contained in a personal communication from David Redstone in 1979.

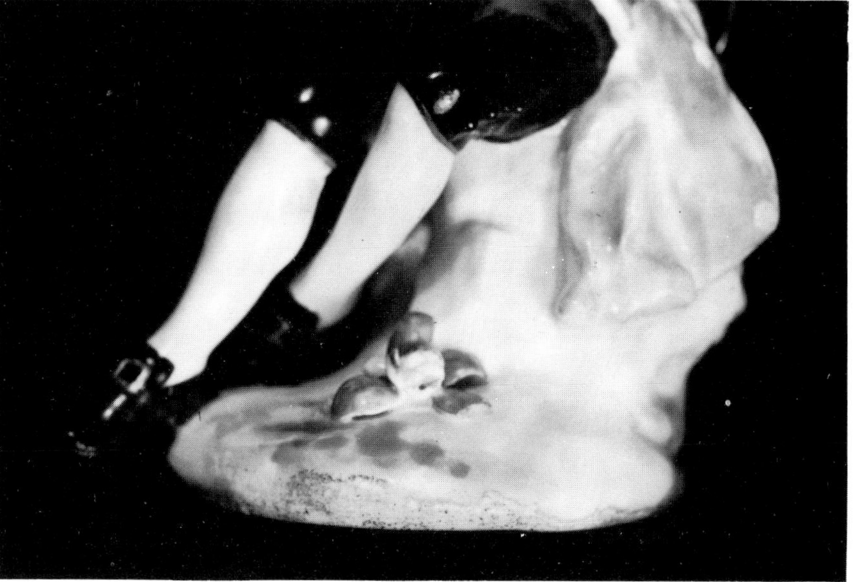

Plate 11. *The large mound base of the Derby snuff-taker (J33), showing the dry-edge and rim of exposed biscuit.* Author's collection

Plate 12. *Inferior aspect of a Derby model of Africa (K73), c.1760 showing the flat glazed surface three patch marks, and large ventilation hole.* Author's collection

alkaline flux, and water. The first Bow patent taken out by Heylyn and Frye in 1744 included the formula of a lead glaze which was applied by dipping and other establishments appear to have used similar materials and methods. It was once believed that powdered lead acetate was sprinkled over the model prior to 1756 at Derby though evidence will later be presented to discount this theory. Various stratagems were devised to prevent aggregation of glaze beneath the base thereby impairing its level stance. Prior to 1756 at Derby coverage with glaze stopped short of the inferior circumference of the base leaving a rim of exposed biscuit known as a dry-edge (Plate 11). At Longton Hall before 1753 any surplus glaze upon the lower surface was wiped off before the replacement in the kiln for the second, or glost, firing. Elsewhere, at Chelsea and at Bow, evenness of the inferior surface was restored by grinding. Another problem was the prevention of adherence of a glazed base to the floor of the saggar. After c.1756 the Derby factory used three or four small pads of clay known as stilts upon which the figure stood. Subsequent removal of these left oval or round unglazed patches which over the space of more than two hundred years have become discoloured by absorption of foreign particles. These are called 'patch' marks and are a feature of nearly all Derby models issued between 1756 and 1795. (Plate 12). Very rarely, faint patch marks may be found on Chelsea figures though if any marks remain after the grinding, mentioned above, they are usually small points of exposed biscuit caused by spur-like stilts. At Longton Hall similar pointed spurs or knife like blades of pottery arranged radially within a circle were used for the support of figures and when any traces remain after firing these take the form of points or faint radial lines.

A few hours in the glost-kiln at 900 to 1,000°C were sufficient to fix the glaze to the body. Failure to eliminate air bubbles led to pin-hole defects when they expanded and ruptured the surface. Sometimes the glaze would fail to adhere to the paste leaving dry patches. If the glaze contracted more than the paste during the cooling fine fissures or crazing developed. When the reverse obtained the glaze might flake off altogether. Iron impurities were sometimes manifest by brown spots with slightly raised black centres, known as sanding or bird's eyes. Surface staining by smoke and fumes have already been described.

Enamel Decoration

Enamel colours were rarely used for the decoration of English eighteenth century figures before 1751. A number of early examples bear traces of oil-paint and gold leaf, deep in crevices, indicating that they had once been adorned with cold colours. The proportion of models left white steadily declined until by 1755 the majority were enamelled. Enamels were extracted from metallic ores, ground to a fine powder and blended with an oily medium so that they might be applied with a brush. Blue was obtained from cobalt, a colour that exhibits a greyish hue when contaminated with iron and has a purplish cast in the presence of manganese. Cobalt, almost alone of the metallic substances, is able to withstand the heat of a glost-kiln without degradation of colour and may, accordingly, be painted underglaze. This was done at Longton Hall to produce Littler's blue, at Chelsea to create Mazarine blue, and was also introduced at Bow as a substitute for overglaze enamel during the closing period of production. Iron is the basis of both a black and a red, manganese provides a purplish-pink and a puce, copper can be manipulated to create either a bluish-green or turquoise, whilst lead, tin, and copper give a range of yellows. A fine pink may also be obtained from trichloride of gold and a yellow-green from chrome though the latter was not introduced until c.1795. Pigments were mixed with an alkaline flux with a low melting point enabling them to be fixed to the surface of the glaze at a temperature of about 700°C maintained for a few hours in a muffle-kiln.

Colours of enamels in their raw state look very different from their final appearance since they develop in the heat of the kiln. The modern practice of including vegetable dyes which burned off to assist decorative artists was unknown in the eighteenth century. Kiln temperature was critical and the methods by which it was controlled were crude. Often, throughout a firing, plugs would be removed from ports in the kiln allowing inspection of the colour of the flames. Some enamels require a temperature for their maturation that will cause others to become debased. Modern methods employ several different firings commencing with high-temperature colours and reducing kiln heat at subsequent burnings. In the eighteenth century, most often, a single firing had to suffice. Results were therefore uncertain. For example, when stanniferous trichloride of gold is heated the following colours result at different temperatures: brownish-red at 650°C, rose-pink 850°C, rose-purple at 870°C, purple to violet at 900°C and at 1,000°C all traces of colour disappear. The need to fire all enamels at one time probably accounts for the muddy turquoise and dirty greens associated with the Derby factory during the period 1756 to 1769. Other factors leading to the modification of enamel colours included the acidity or alkalinity of the material and the amount of oxygen in the kiln. Normal firing is said to take place in an oxidising kiln whereas if the carbon monoxide content is increased by, for instance, throwing in damp wood, it becomes a reducing kiln. The oxygen content was particularly important where copper colours were concerned.

Metallic impurities impart irridescence to eighteenth century enamels, which is a quality lacking in modern chemically pure colours. They were applied most thickly at Chelsea and most thinly at Derby during the period between 1756 and 1760. This partly accounts for the deep rich colour of Chelsea models and the almost pastel shades of streaky enamel seen on the products of Derby that has led to the generic term 'pale family'. The thickness of enamel used at Bow was intermediate. The range of palette at all factories was initially very restricted and colours were applied in plain washes between large passages left white. These were sometimes decorated with painted flowers either in the Oriental or the European style. Flesh tints were frequently omitted entirely or were limited to faint daubs of orange-red upon lips and cheeks. Gradually, with the passage of time, the quality of the colours improved and their range increased. The palette and decorative style peculiar to each factory will be described in the appropriate sections.

Until about 1760, a proportion of figures from all English factories were painted by artists working independently. William Duesbury, who was to become proprietor of the Derby manufactory, worked in a London studio as an independent decorator between 1751 and 1753.[20] Although much of his work was effected in oil paint he also used 'Hinamel' on models from 'Bogh', 'Chelsay', and 'Staffartshire'. Other independent artists include Thomas Hughes of Clerkenwell[21] about whom little is known, and John Bolton who had his atelier in Kentish Town prior to 1755, after which he moved to Lambeth and later to Champion's Bristol factory.[22] James Giles took over the Kentish Town establishment, but transferred his studio first to Cockspur Street and later to Berwick Street in Soho, London.[23] Llewellyn Jewitt states that Giles was latterly financed by William Duesbury before being declared bankrupt in 1776 and that he died in 1780. Almost certainly the Giles workshop gave employment to a number of artists some of whom have been associated with the painting of dishevelled birds, cut-fruit, armorials, landscapes and flowers and their contribution towards the decoration of porcelain figures will later be considered.

Gilding

Gilding is rare on figures made before 1754. A few early Bow Muses have gilt laid upon a dark blue ground on the base and an example of 'Henry Woodward' in Lord Bearsted's collection has gilding upon a brown enamel ground. Rubbed gilding is seen on the raised anchor Chelsea 'Scapino' (Colour Plate A) and the dry-edge Derby 'Lady eating grapes' emblematic of Taste in the Broderip collection. The author's 'Snuff-taker' (Colour Plate L) representing Smell also shows unusually fine gilding. After about 1754-75 standards of gilding improved and gold is seen upon the edges of garments, buttons, shoe-buckles, and on accessories such as musical instruments. Between c.1758-60 and 1770 gilding became lavish and was used upon the base and on candleholders to accent scrolls as well as being incorporated into designs simulating brocade upon garments. After 1770 a more ascetic neo-classical style eschewed gilding which was either sparingly applied or omitted altogether.

Two methods of gilding were used known as honey-gilding and mercury-gilding. The first employed a paste of gold powder mixed with honey which was brushed on to the porcelain and fired at about 600°C in a muffle-kiln. The brown colour that resulted was burnished with an agate pencil to reveal a sumptuous gold. Mercury-gilding used an amalgam of mercury and gold, called 'goldwater', which was mixed with fat dissolved in alcohol. The mercury vapourised in the kiln and a thin, brilliant gold was deposited on the surface of the glaze. The technique was adapted from that used to gild bronze furniture mounts which were extremely popular in contemporary France but many of the workmen engaged in the work became ill and died of mercury poisoning.

Honey-gilding was used, *par excellence,* at Sèvres and at Chelsea and may also be found on a few early Bow models. Elsewhere mercury-gilding was standard practice. The quality of gilding deteriorated during the terminal years of production at Bow and presents a thin and coppery appearance.

Transfer-printing

Transfer-printing was brought to Battersea from Birmingham for use in the enamelling trade. The technique was known to John Sadler of Liverpool and Richrd Holdship of Worcester amongst others. The same process was employed in the calico printing industry and one such business, owned by

20. *William Duesbury's London Account Book 1751-1753* (London, 1931) by Mrs. Donald Macalister, English Ceramic Circle Monograph.

21. 'Thomas Hughes, First Enameller of English China of Clerkenwell' by W.H. Tapp, *Transactions,* English Ceramic Circle, 1939, Vol. 2, No. 6, p. 20.

22. 'The King, the Nun and Other Figures' by Bernard Watney, *Transactions,* English Ceramic Circle, 1968, Vol. 7, pt. 1, pp. 48-58.

23. *Worcester Porcelain and Lund's Bristol* (London, 1966) by F.A. Barrett, pp. 13, 30, 36, 47-52. See also 'A Decorator of Porcelain and Glass — James Giles in a new light' by R.J. Charleston, *Transactions,* English Ceramic Circle, 1967, Vol. 6, pt. 3, pp. 292-316.

Joseph Wimpey and Richard Emery, was situated adjacent to the Bow works in Stratford. The required design was engraved upon copper-plates and deepened with cutting tools since a greater depth was necessary for printing on porcelain than upon cloth. There are two basic techniques. In the 'hot process', heated pigment is wiped over the engraved copper plate and a sheet of tissue-paper pressed down upon the surface by a roller. The paper is then trimmed, peeled off the plate, and applied wet side downwards upon the glazed surface of porcelain. During the firing the paper burned away leaving the design fixed to the glaze. In the 'cold process', cold oil is applied to the surface of the copper plate, and a bat of glue replaces the tissue-paper. The design is transferred to the surface of unglazed porcelain upon the bat which after being pressed down is removed. Powdered pigment is then blown over the surface and the piece is fired. Both methods allow complex designs to be reproduced rapidly by relatively unskilled labour.

Although transfer-printing was used extensively on useful wares, there are only a very few examples of figures decorated in this manner. Perhaps the best known is the Longton Hall model of 'Britannia' (O78). This has a detachable stand which bears transfer-printed scenes illustrating the Seven Years War, executed by John Sadler and Guy Green of Liverpool. Whether Sadler and Green purchased Longton Hall porcelain for decoration and sale, or served as independent decorators under contract to the factory is not determined.

Plastic Surgery

Most of the eighteenth century porcelain factories suffered huge kiln losses where up to thirty per cent of figures may be reduced to a shapeless mass. Naturally every effort was made to salvage wares and models which displayed only relatively minor defects. When, for example, secure stance of a figure was lacking this might be rectified by the application of a small pad of paste beneath the inferior surface of the base. More rarely, the perpendicular alignment might be restored by a wooden wedge, as may be seen in a model of a canary made c.1750 at Chelsea.[24] Distortion of models was especially liable to occur at Plymouth and Bristol where higher kiln temperatures were necessary for the firing of hard-paste. There is a model of an old man, emblematic of Winter from the Bristol set of 'Classical Seasons' (P37) in the Bristol City Museum and Art Gallery,[25] in which a pad of paste has been inserted between the undersurface of one foot and the superior surface of the base in order to make the shortened and deformed leg less noticeable. Further, it is not unusual to find that fire-cracks have been filled with soft paste and fired prior to enamelling. Dark brown specks in the glaze were often adapted to simulate the body of an insect to which legs and wings were added in enamel colour, though this was largely confined to useful wares. More severe defects created by smoke-staining and sanding might be overlaid with opaque colour or gilding. When in 1815 Robert Bloor purchased the Derby manuafctory, he gave orders that models displaying defects which had been retained in store as unsaleable should be decorated with dark opaque enamel colours and gilding to conceal their blemishes and sold. This explains why some soft-paste English figures created in the late 1780s and '90s are decorated in the brash style and brassy gilding associated with the period of the late Regency.

24. Saltram House Catalogue, No. 269T.

25. No. 42 in the catalogue of the Bristol Bicentenary Exhibition, 1770-1970, held at the City Museum and Art Gallery.

Chapter VI

The Chelsea and Girl-in-a-Swing Manufactories

Part One — Historical survey and figures made prior to 1753

Nicholas Sprimont (1716-1771) was born the son of Pierre Sprimont and his wife, Gertrude, née Goffin, in Liège and was apprenticed silversmith to his uncle, Nicholas Joseph Sprimont of Rue du Pont in that city. The exact date when Sprimont came to England is not known. Since, however, he married Ann Protin, spinster of the parish of St. Ann's, Westminster Batchal, in Knightsbridge Chapel on 13th November, 1742, he presumably needed time to meet, woo and wed her, and his arrival cannot have been much later than January, 1742. Evidence has been presented by A. Grimwade[1] to suggest Sprimont may have worked with another Huguenot silversmith named Paul Crespin. Both men lived in Compton Street, both created silver and silver-gilt wares in a similar style, and both supplied Frederick, Prince of Wales. Sprimont registered his mark as 'plateworker' in the Goldsmiths' Hall on 25th January, 1743. A pair of highly sculptural sauceboats, one incorporating Venus the other Adonis, each seated with a dolphin, some crab salts, a kettle and stand, together with other items representative of his work, have been reviewed by Dr. Bellamy Gardner,[2] and are also mentioned by John Mallet.[3] A fine drawing of a design for a tureen in Sprimont's hand survives, and there is too a centre-piece depicting two goats standing side by side head to tail dated 1747.[4] This recalls the early 'Goat and Bee' creamers made at Chelsea. Sprimont certainly continued to practise his trade until 1747. Examination of relevant rate-books, shows he resided in a house upon the north side of Compton Street until 1747 and, in 1745, leased additional premises in the form of an adjacent 'Back Shop'.

Sprimont was a friend of the sculptor, Louis François Roubiliac, and acted as godfather to his daughter in 1744. Roubiliac was one of a coterie of artists that included William Hogarth, George Michael Moser, the German enameller and engraver, and Hubert Gravelot, the French book illustrator. This was centred upon the St. Martin's Lane Academy, and Old Slaughter's Coffee House, immortalised in Thackeray's *Vanity Fair*. John Mallet has drawn our attention to this avant-garde group who became exponents of the new rococo taste. However, though Compton Street was within easy walking distance of St. Martin's Lane, their artistic innovations had little or no impact upon the Chelsea porcelain manufactory.[5] Unfortunately, the rate-books for the critical period, 1743-47, are missing, but those pertaining to the Chelsea area survive from March 1748 onwards.[6] These indicate that Monmouth House, Lawrence Street, was rated to 'Mr. N. Sprimont' from not later than the last quarter of 1747. This building had been erected by a Mr. James Chase, son of John Chase apothecary to King William III[7] and the uncle of Sir Everard Fawkener

1. 'Crespin or Sprimont? An unsvolved problem of Rococo Silver' by A. Grimwade, *Apollo,* 1969, Vol. 90, No. 90, pp. 126-127,
2. 'Silvershapes in Chelsea Porcelain' by Bellamy Gardner, *Transactions,* English Ceramic Circle, 1939, Vol. 2, No. 6, pp. 26-30.
3. 'Rococo English Porcelain: a study in style' by J.V.G. Mallet, *Apollo,* 1969, Vol. 90, No. 90, pp. 100-111.
4. Victoria and Albert Museum.
5. 'Rococo English Porcelain: a study in style', op. cit., p. 103.
6. 'The Earliest References to Chelsea Porcelain' by Bellamy Gardner, *Transactions,* English Porcelain Circle, 1928, No. 1, pp. 16-24; p. 18, Chelsea rate-books.
7. 'Payments by Sir Everard Fawkener to Nicholas Sprimont' by Eric Benton, *Transactions,* English Ceramic Circle, 1976, Vol. 10, pt. 1., pp. 54-58.

from whom Sprimont most probably acquired the lease. It had also been the residence of the widow of the ill-fated Duke of Monmouth and, subsequently of his daughter the Lady Isabella Scott, until 1738. It was demolished in 1834. Sprimont leased additional premises in St. Lawrence Street and Church Lane East in 1750, and again in 1751, whilst in 1755 he rented buildings on the Waterside. A more precise location of the properties which formed the Chelsea China Works is given by John Mallet.[8] Unlike the Bow factory, which was custom-built, Chelsea was a conglomeration of adapted dwellings and never amounted to much more than a cottage industry, albeit one which specialised in supplying the luxury end of the trade. As shown by Mrs. Elizabeth Adams,[9] who surveyed surviving insurance policies, Chelsea never employed more than one hundred men whilst the number at Bow was three hundred in 1755 which was only slightly less than the number engaged at royal Sèvres.

Some have held that porcelain was made at Chelsea prior to the arrival of Sprimont. Since the earliest wares bear the incised date '1745', this would only leave two years before Sprimont was known to have leased Monmouth House. It is true that Dr. Severne Mackenna[10] has illustrated a 'Goat and Bee' jug with an incised date which he reads as '1743'. If this is a correct reading, the piece stands alone and might then represent the results of experimental rather than commercial production. There is no justification for the belief that Thomas Briand either managed a porcelain factory or assisted Sprimont to set one up at Chelsea in view of the observations made by Arnold Mountford.[11] Another possible contender for the proprietorship of a pre-Sprimont Chelsea Porcelain Factory is Charles Gouyn, also a Huguenot *emigré,* mentioned in *Mortimer's Universal Directory* of 1763, as a jeweller who lived in Bennet Street, in the parish of St. George's Hanover Square. The register shows that most of his thirteen children were baptised in the church between 1737 and 1748. Although there is every reason to believe Gouyn may have entered into a partnership with Sprimont between 1745 and 1749, which terminated owing to some disagreement, there is not one shred of evidence to support the contention that Gouyn managed a porcelain factory in the borough of Chelsea, or elsewhere, prior to 1745. Further reference will be made later of the role possibly played by Gouyn in the mysterious Girl-in-a-Swing factory.

The establishment of a successful porcelain works would necessitate capital assets almost certainly beyond the possession of a silversmith not long registered at the Goldsmiths' Hall. William Chaffers[12] cited the writings of a workman named Mason: "I think the Chelsea Manufactory began about the 1748 or 1749. I went to work [there] in about the year 1751. It was first carried on by the Duke of Cumberland and Sir Everard Fawkener, and the sole management was intrusted to a foreigner of the name of Sprimont..." The British Minister in Dresden, Sir Charles Hanbury Williams, wrote in a letter dated June 1751: "I received a letter about ten days ago from Sir Everard Fawkener who is, I believe, connected with the manufacture of China at Chelsea..." Such evidence, albeit indirect, suggested that Sir Everard Fawkener was at least a financial sponser of the Chelsea venture.

Eric Benton,[13] has now provided the final proof in the discovery of Bank of England records of payments made by Sir Everard. The first, dated 16th August 1746 was to a 'Premonte'; all subsequent entries show the recipient was 'Sprimont' and altogether a sum of £1,495 was made over to him between August 1746 and April 1748. It is not clear, however, whether monies were paid on behalf of the Duke of Cumberland or by Sir Everard in his own right. Sir Everard Fawkener (1693-1758), had been a classical scholar, interested in antiquities, and worked for his father's company in Aleppo, before becoming British Ambassador at Constantinople from 1738-43. His brother was a

8. 'The Site of the Chelsea Porcelain Factory' by J.V.G. Mallet, *Transactions,* English Ceramic Circle, 1973, Vol. 9, pt. 1, pp. 115-131.

9. 'The Bow Insurances and related Matters' by Elizabeth Adams, *Transactions,* English Ceramic Circle, Vol. 9, pt. 1, pp. 67-108.

10. *Chelsea Porcelain, the Triangle and Raised Anchor Wares* (Leigh-on-Sea, 1948) by F. Severne Mackenna, pl. 1, fig. 1.

11. 'Thomas Briand — a Stranger' by Arnold Mountford, *Transactions,* English Ceramic Circle, 1969, Vol. 7, pt. 2, pp. 87-95.

12. *Marks and Monograms on European and Oriental Potter and Porcelain* (London, 1965) by William Chaffers, 15th revised edition, Vol. II, p.292.

13. 'Payments by Sir Everard Fawkener to Nicholas Sprimont', op. cit., pp. 54-58.

director of the Bank of England in 1743. After returning to this country, Sir Everard became secretary to the king's younger brother, the Duke of Cumberland. He accompanied his master upon the Scottish campaign of 1745 and probably did not return to the metropolis until the following year. It is most unlikely that the Duke himself had any financial stake in the Chelsea works, but he certainly provided a valuable liaison with the Court circle.

The skills possessed by Sprimont in drawing and plastic designs for silver were probably employed to good use in the modelling shop of the new porcelain factory, at least until 1749. His widow wrote in a legal deposition dated 1776, five years after his death, "...by his superior skill in the arts of drawing, modelling and painting [he] instructed and perfected several apprentices, workmen and servants therein, so that they were capable of executing the porcelain in the highest perfection."[14] Earlier Sprimont himself had written that he had established at Chelsea "...a nursery of thirty lads from the parishes and charity schools, & bred to designing & painting...".[15] However, in 1749 Joseph Willems arrived in this country from Tournai and, most probably in the same year, was engaged as modeller at the works. Pierre Joseph Willems (1715-1766), was born in Brussels, married and worked as modeller at Tournai, and came to England not later than 1749 since there are painted terracotta figures of a 'Dancing Boy' and 'Dancing Girl'[16] bearing that date and his signature which are now in the Ashmolean Museum, Oxford. He was clearly a trusted employee for the Chelsea Rate Books of 1755 up to 1758 often couple his name with that of Sprimont, viz, "Mr. Willems or Mr. Sprimont — Church Lane East, Rent £4 — taxes 11/-". Exhibition Catalogues of the Society of Artists of Great Britain between 1760 and 1763[17] list exhibits displayed by 'S. Williams' many of which can be related to contemporary Chelsea porcelain models. These include 'Charity', 'Leda', and 'Cleo' [*sic*] known in gold anchor marked Chelsea, as well as 'Generosity', 'Heroic Virtue', and 'Sincerity', which are more difficult to identify. Mortimer's *Universal Directory* of 1763, bears the entry "Willems, Joseph, Modeller, At the Brussels Coffee House, Chelsea; this artist teaches Drawing, Modelling, and has modelled for the Chelsea China Manufactory." At this time Willems probably took on such work part time owing to reduced demands upon his time by Sprimont. A review by Major Tapp[18] of documents drawn from the Archives of the Tournai Porcelain Works, which were destroyed during the late war, shows that Willems returned to Tournai in March 1766, to work for François Peterinck and died there in November of the same year.

At first Sprimont conducted sales of his wares upon the factory premises. An advertisement in the *Daily Advertiser*, which appeared between 21st and 24th February, 1749, reads, "The Undertaker of the Manufactory of China Ware hereby acquaints the Publick, that he has prepared a large Parcel of that Ware, consisting of Tea and Coffee Pots, Cups and Saucers of various forms, besides several other Things as well for Use as Ornament, which he hopes to offer to Sale on Thursday next the 28th. instant, at the Manufactory at Chelsea, from which Time the Warehouse will be open constantly, and attendance given."[19] Evidently, the sale was a success for on 8th March, 1749, a further notice in the same journal reads: "Mr. Sprimont takes the Liberty to acquaint the Publick that the favourable Reception and General Approbation his China Ware has met with, makes it necessary for him to suspend all further Sale thereof at his Ware-house after tomorrow that he may have Time to make a sufficient Quantity of such Things..."[20] The notice then invites private orders and continues "... He, also gives notice, that he has no sort of Connection with, nor for a considerable Time past has put any of his Ware into that Shop in St. James's Street, which was the Chelsea China

14. 'Further History of the Chelsea Porcelain Manufactory' by Bellamy Gardner, *Transactions*, English Ceramic Circle, 1942, Vol. 2, No. 8, p. 140.

15. *The Ceramic Art of Great Britain* (London, 1877) by Llewellyn Jewitt, Vol. 1, pp. 171-172.

16. 'Chelsea Figures and the Modeller Joseph Willems' by Arthur Lane, *Connoisseur*, 1960, Vol. 145, p. 249, figs. 12-14.

17. *The Society of Artists of Great Britain 1760-1791, The Free Society of Artists 1761-1783, a Complete Dictionary* (London, 1907) by A. Graves.

18. 'Joseph Willems, china modeller, died 1766' by W.H. Tapp, *Connoisseur*, 1938, Vol. 101, pp. 176-182.

19. *Chelsea Porcelain, the Triangle and Raised Anchor Wares*, op. cit., pp. 18-19.

20. ibid., p. 19.

Warehouse." This was the first hint that Sprimont was troubled by a rival concern purporting to sell 'Chelsea Porcelain'. On January 9th, 1750, the *Daily Advertiser* gave advance notice of a sale proposed for the 'Month of March next', but this was postponed and a further announcement on 15th May, 1750 read: "Chelsea Porcelain. The Publick is hereby informed that the Sale-Warehouse at the Manufactory there will from henceforth be constantly open, and new Products are daily produced, and brought into the Sale-room, and the Publick may be assured that no Pains will be spared to extend this Manufacture to as great a Variety as possible, either for Use or Ornament."[21] Once again a disclaimer was added, "Note, the Quality and Gentry may be assured, that I am not concern'd in any Shape whatsoever with the Goods expos'd to Sale in St. James's Street, called the Chelsea China Warehouse. N. Sprimont." On 29th January there was a response to this unequivocal statement, in the *General Advertiser* of 1751. "Chelsea China Warehouse. Seeing it frequently advertised, that the Proprietor of Chelsea Porcelain is not concern'd in any Shape whatsoever in the Goods expos'd to Sale in St. James's Street, called the Chelsea China Warehouse, in common justice to N. Sprimont (who signed the advertisement) as well as to myself, I think it incumbent, publickly to declare to the Nobility, Gentry &c. that my China Warehouse is not supply'd by any other Person than Mr. Charles Gouyn, late Proprietor and Chief Manager of the Chelsea House, who continues to supply me with the most curious Goods of that Manufacture, as well Useful as Ornamental, and which I dispose of at very reasonable Rates. S. Stables." Such evidence[22] suggests that Gouyn was once proprietor and manager of the Chelsea factory and associated with Sprimont for some time prior to March 1749 when the first advertisement appeared. Further, it seems the two men separated and that after this Gouyn was able to provide Stables with Chelsea wares which may possibly have been given to him by Sprimont in lieu of cash as repayment for capital invested or perhaps a loan that he could not then repay.

Sales at the Chelsea warehouse were not the only method of conducting business. Advertisements appearing in the *London Daily Advertiser* between 1751 and 1753 indicate that Sprimont made items to order for other concerns. For example, one of these reads "China knives and Forks of the Chelsea Manufactory, in the greatest variety of most beautiful Dresden Patterns, mounted and sold by Nathaniel Jeffreys — Cutler to His Majesty...".[23] In the spring of 1751 Sprimont wrote to his patron, Sir Everard Fawkener, asking him to obtain through the good offices of the British Minister in Dresden models of Meissen manufacture which he might have copied at Chelsea. The diplomat in question was Sir Charles Hanbury Williams who already owned a collection of Meissen porcelain, including one hundred and sixty-six figures, which was stored during his absence abroad in Holland House, the home of his friend, Henry Fox. Sir Charles wrote to Fox from Dresden, in a letter dated 9th June, 1751, "...I received a letter about ten days ago from Sir Everard Fawkener who is, I believe, concerned in the manufacture of China at Chelsea. He desired me to send over models for different Pieces from hence in order furnish [*sic*] the undertakers with good designs; and would have had me send over fifty or three-score pounds worth. But I thought it better and Cheaper for the manufacturers to give them leave to take any of my China from Holland House and copy what they like..."[24] This action, as has already been shown in a previous section, had a profound effect upon the modelling of the porcelain figure, not only at Chelsea, but throughout this country.

The practice of holding regular sales on the factory premises seems to have been discontinued between 1753 and 1754 and to have been replaced by public

21. *Chelsea Porcelain, the Triangle and Raised Anchor Wares,* op. cit., p.20.

22. *Contributions towards the History of Early English Porcelain* (Salisbury, 1881) by J.E. Nightingale, p. v.

23, *Chelsea Porcelain, the Triangle and Raised Anchor Wares,* op. cit., p. 20.

24. 'A notable service of Meissen porcelain' by the Earl of Ilchester, *Burlington Magazine,* 1929, Vol. 55, p. 188.

auctions. One of the earliest notices to have survived appeared in the *Public Advertiser,* between 29th March and 26th April, 1754. "To be Sold by Auction by Mr. Ford. At his Great Room in the Haymarket, on Wednesday next and fourteen following Days, Sundays excepted: The large, valuable and entire Stock of the Chelsea Porcelaine brought from the Manufactory there and the Warehouse in Pall-Mall; consisting of Epargnes and Services for Desserts, beautiful Groupes of Figures &c. complete Table Sets of round and oval Dishes, Tureens and Plates, with the greatest Variety of other useful and ornamental Pieces, all warranted True Enamel."[25] The specific mention of 'True Enamel' was in no way superfluous as many pieces, including figures, had hitherto been issued either in the white or covered in unfired cold pigments. By the time of the advertisement, the vast majority of wares were enamelled. The notice continued, "The Undertaker of this Manufactory...humbly hopes this Manner of offering his Works to the Publick will meet with favourable Encouragement...he will positively not open his Warehouse, nor exhibit any Articals to Sale, after this time next year." This suggests that the idea of annual public auctions was then novel. Having met with success possibly greater than expected, Sprimont postponed the last seven days of the sale and, on 11th April the following paragraph was added to the previous advertisement. "At the particular Desire of the Nobility, &c., that have honor'd the Auction with their Company, the remaining seven Days of the Sale are adjourn'd to Friday next, and to oblige the Curious, the lots of those Days will be exhibited to View on Wednesday and Thursday next." It is probable that the reason for the postponement was that Sprimont had meanwhile acquired the stock of the Girl-in-a-Swing factory which seems to have failed at about this time. A speciality of this works was a variety of scent bottles, etuis, seals, and patch boxes known collectively as 'toys'. Notices in the *Public Advertiser* between 23rd November and 21st December, 1754, were concerned exclusively with such small items. "All the entire Stock of Porcelain Toys, brought from their Warehouse in Pall Mall; consisting of Snuff-Boxes, Smelling-Bottles, Etwees and Trinkets for Watches (Mounted in Gold and unmounted) in various Beautiful Shapes, of an Elegant Design, and curiously painted in Enamel...Nothing of the above kind was in their former Sale, nor will any Thing of the same Sort as this be sold from the Manufactory till after next year...Most of the above Things are in lots suitable for Jewellers, Goldsmiths, Toy-Shops, China-Shops, Cutlers and Workmen in those branches of Business..."[26] Mention of gold mounted porcelain toys naturally suggests the work of a jeweller such as Charles Gouyn. Miss Kate Foster[27] believes that these were created by Charles Gouyn at the Girl-in-a-Swing factory prior to 1754 and that it is possible to identify a later group made at Chelsea after this date.

The products of the Chelsea manufactory reached a pinnacle of good taste and excellence within a decade of its foundation. The expansion of factory premises and the opening of a warehouse have already been mentioned. Unfortunately, the earliest insurance policy for the manufactory discovered by Mrs. Elizabeth Adams[28] dates to 27th June, 1760, so it is not possible to show increased valuations for building, stock, and equipment over this period or to compare developments with those at Bow. However, by 1754-55, Joseph Willems had digested the techniques of modelling after the style of Meissen, and a fine range of enamel colours was available to the decorative artists as well as honey-gilding. Further, it is probable that porcelain toys, after the manner of those created at the Girl-in-a-Swing manufactory, were being made at Chelsea after 1754. Perusal of the Catalogue of Sale pertaining to the auction held by Mr. Ford in the Great Room in the Hay Market, between 10th

25. *Contributions towards the History of Early English Porcelain,* op. cit., p. ix.

26. ibid., p. x.

27. 'Chelsea Scent Bottles — Girl in a Swing and Another Group' by Kate Foster, *Transactions,* English Ceramic Circle, 1967, Vol. 9, pt. 1, p. 73.

28. 'The Bow Insurances and Related Matters', op. cit., p. 73.

and 25th March, 1755, provides a glimpse of the glory that belonged to Chelsea in that year.[29] A further great sale took place in 1756.[30] However, in 1757, in lieu of the usual notice, there appeared in the *Public Advertiser* an announcement on 15th February, "The Publick is hereby acquainted that the Chelsea Porcelain Manufactory has been very much retarded by the sickness of Mr. Sprimont; nevertheless several curious Things have been finished, which will be exposed to Sale at the Warehouse in Piccadilly, some time the beginning of March, of which more particular Notice will be given."[31] William Chaffers,[32] again citing the writings of Mason: "Mr. Sprimont...having amassed a fortune, he travelled about England, and the manufactory was shut up for about two years; for he neither would let it, or carry it on himself. I went to work at Bow for a short time, which was carried on by a firm, but I don't recollect their names. I went to work again at Chelsea for Mr. Sprimont after being absent two or three years."

Much has been written about the possible nature of Mr. Sprimont's illness; some have suggested it might have been related to lead poisoning, a common hazard in the ceramic industry of the day, or to gout whilst others, with less charity, have attributed his indisposition to over indulgence in food and drink. Whatever the diagnosis, it is certain that there were other factors which contributed to the temporary closure of the factory. Sir Everard Fawkener became financially embarrassed a few years before his death in 1758, and it is understood that in 1757 he sold his interests in the Chelsea works to Sprimont. Faced with the necessity for raising a large sum of money at short notice Sprimont was probably forced to give up the lease of much of the property, and to exercise many other drastic economies facilitated by temporary closure. The warehouse in Pall Mall was given up and replaced by another in Piccadilly but he retained his house upon the Terrace at Richmond where he resided until the lease expired in 1762. The sale of Sir Everard's estate took place in 1759, and in the same year the Chelsea factory reopened. Workmen who had obtained temporary employment at Bow, such as Mason, and at other factories further afield now returned to their alma mater. It has been suggested that workmen who had been engaged at Bow had learned the secret of the paste, which included bone-ash, and disclosed this information to Sprimont after their services were re-engaged at Chelsea. However, by 1759 this knowledge was not confined to Bow. It is of great interest that George Savage has identified phosphates in some red anchor wares of c.1755.[33]

The annual auction sales were resumed, but they were now conducted by Mr. Burnsall at his Great Auction-Room in Charles Street, Berkeley Square. They were arranged for the spring months of either March or May for the three years of 1759, 1760, and 1761. Part of the Sale Catalogue covering the period 30th April to 4th May, 1761, is reproduced by Dr. F. Severne Mackenna.[34] Preceding notices announced: "The Proprietor, N. Sprimont, after many years Intense Application, has brought this Manufactory to it's present Perfection; but as his indisposition will not permit him to carry it on much longer, he takes the Liberty to assure the Nobility, Gentry and others, that next year will be the last Sale he will offer to the Publick."[35] When the auction had been completed Sprimont took up residence in his house at Knightsbridge leaving the day to day management of the factory to his clerk, Francis Thomas, who was supervised only by infrequent visits from Ann Sprimont. No public auction took place in 1762, but on 7th January, 1763, the following notice appeared in the *Public Advertiser,* "N. Sprimont, Proprietor of the Chelsea Porcelain Manufactory, takes the Liberty to give Notice that he proposes to have a Sale some time in March next, at Mr. Burnsall's, in Charles-street, Berkley Square, of all the last two Years Produce...In a short

29. *Chelsea Porcelain* (London, 1922) by William King.

30. *Contributions towards the History of Early English Porcelain,* op. cit., pp. xi-xiv.

31. ibid., p. xv.

32. *Marks and Monograms on European and Oriental Pottery and Porcelain,* op. cit., Vol. 2, p. 292.

33. Personal communication from George Savage in 1978.

34. *Chelsea Porcelain, the Gold Anchor Wares* (Leigh-on-Sea, 1952) by F. Severne Mackenna, pp. 81-95.

35. *Contributions towards the History of Early English Porcelain,* op. cit., pp. xxi.

time after he will likewise dispose, at his Manufactory at Chelsea, of everything in general belonging to it, viz all the unfinished Porcelain and Materials; his valuable and great variety of Models; all the Moulds, Mills, Kilns, Presses, &c. together with all the Outbuildings; and as he will retire farther into the Country, all his Household Furniture will be sold at the same time..."[36] One may wonder why William Duesbury did not then make a bid for the Chelsea Works; possibly the expense of expansion and development of his own factory at Derby left him short of liquid assets.

In 1764 Chelsea was once again put up for sale and, for the second time, no acceptable offers seem to have been made. In that same year Sprimont vacated Monmouth House and seems to have conducted his remaining business from buildings upon the west side of Lawrence Street which he had leased for the first time in 1750. In 1766 the properties were rated at £30, in 1767 at £19, so it is likely that a further decline of activity ensued.[37] Joseph Willems left Chelsea in 1766 for Tournai. A third attempt to sell the Chelsea works was successful in May, 1769. The price paid was £600 and the purchaser was James Cox, a London exporter of mechanical clocks, automata and musical-boxes. The new owner had no prior knowledge of the ceramic industry, and obviously intended to entrust the management of his factory to the clerk, Francis Thomas. However, Thomas died a few months later and, accordingly, Cox resold Chelsea to William Duesbury for £820. Before relinquishing control Sprimont had removed a quantity of stock to his home, and this was sold on 14th February, 1770, by Mr. Christie at his Great Room, Pall Mall. "A Catalogue of all the remaining curios and truly matchless Pieces of Chelsea Porcelaine, consisting of Beautiful Vases, Antique Urns, Perfume Pots... Variety of Figures, very large and curious Groups (particularly, two of ROMAN CHARITY) beautiful Toilet Boxes of various Shapes and Sizes, and Other Articles; many of them in Mazarine Blue, Crimson, Pea-Green, and gold..."[38]

Dr. Bellamy Gardner,[39] has shown that after Sprimont's death in 1771, his widow married Mr. John Chetwood, councillor-at-law, of Chancery Lane. Also, in Hilary Term, 1776, a legal action was filed against the widow of Francis Thomas, but was eventually abandoned owing to her becoming "Disordered in her senses". In summary, it was alleged that Nicholas Sprimont had "in or about the year 1750" built the Chelsea works, and "by his labours brought it to a degree of perfection hitherto unknown in this Kingdom". That "sometime in the year 1752, Mr. Sprimont employed one Francis Thomas, a person totally a stranger to that business and who was then in indigent circumstances as clerk or book-keeper...at a salery or wage of £100 a year...". When Thomas died in 1770, his estate was valued at more than £7,000, a sum impossible to have been secured by honest means. The stock which Sprimont had sold for £525 to a Mr. Thomas Morgan in 1770, it was alleged, was worth more than £2,000, whilst Thomas Morgan was none other than Francis Thomas. There would seem to have been a *prima facie* case against Thomas for abusing the trust placed in him by his employer, and for running the Chelsea works more for his own profit than for the benefit of Nicholas Sprimont.

The lease on the factory buildings acquired by Duesbury had been secured by Sprimont in 1759 for fourteen years, and this he extended for two consecutive periods of ten and four years. The site was vacated in 1784. The period 1770-84, known as Chelsea-Derby, will be described in Chapter VIII.

36. *Contributions towards the History of Early Porcelain,* op. cit., pp. xxvii and xxix.

37. 'The Site of the Chelsea Porcelain Factory', op. cit., pp.124.

38. *Contributions towards the History of Early English Porcelain,* op. cit., p. xxxi.

39. 'Further History of the Chelsea Porcelain Manufactory', op. cit., pp. 136-142. *Chelsea Porcelain, the Gold Anchor Wares,* op. cit., pp. 37-39.

Chelsea Figures made before 1750

The Paste and Glaze

Analysis of the early Chelsea figure of Milton (A12) shows[40] the paste to contain silica 62 per cent, lime 16 per cent, lead oxide 11.5 per cent, alumina and iron 5 per cent whilst the soda and potash together amount to 4.5 per cent. The high content of lead indicates inclusion of cullet in the mix, and accounts for its poor stability in the kiln and the lack of sharpness in modelling detail. The relatively low alumina explains the shortness of the paste which, together with rather meagre potting, accounts for surface tears and firecracks so frequently found on wares and models. Transillumination of flat wares reveals an uneven density due to inadequate mixing of ingredients, although, where figures are concerned, this form of scrutiny is rarely possible. The failure to eliminate air-bubbles from the paste, which in the heat of the kiln expanded and burst through to the surface, imparted pitting to the body best seen with a hand-lens. The exposed biscuit has a greyish hue and is often stained; the discolouration very frequntly extends for some distance beneath the glaze itself. Thinness of potting explains why figures feel unexpectedly light in the hand. Opacification of the glaze with tin oxide imparts to it a warm milky appearance, though the surface is generally married with numerous pin-hole defects. The glaze is also thin and badly rubbed, which may be the reason for its lack of lustre, and also for a dry feeling when it is stroked.

The Bases

Bases are mostly simple mounds, rectangles, or pads, akin to those of contemporary sculpture, and the majority are devoid of ornament. Occasionally oak leaves made of slip with fine central veins are applied. Undersurfaces are flat and usually ground free of glaze though some times spur or stilt marks may be seen. Traces of glaze may remain within slight hollows and the transition between exposed biscuit and glaze is tapered and smooth, unlike the heaped up edge, like treacle, found in dry-edge Derby figures issued before 1756 in which the inferior aspect is left unglazed. The ventilation holes are circular, cylindrical, and intermediate in size.

Enamel Colouring

Enamel colours do not seem to have been used for decoration of figures until after 1750. A few white models exhibit unfired pigment deep in the folds of drapery.

Marks

Probably more than half the models that survive are unmarked; the remainder bear a small incised triangle, the alchemist's symbol for fire, upon the inferior surface of the base. The slightly ploughed up appearance of the edges serves to distinguish the incised from the impressed mark. An example of the group known as 'Rustic Lovers' (A10) in the British Museum is marked with a crown and trident in underglaze blue which also may be found on Chelsea useful wares. Goat and Bee creamers usually have 'Chelsea' incised in script together with a date which is usually 1745.

The Models

The highly plastic forms of several items which are not, strictly speaking, figures, justifies their inclusion here. The 'Goat and Bee Creamer' (A1) is said to have been taken from a silver original made in 1737 by Edward Wood[41] though the authenticity of the alleged prototype has been questioned. There are also tea-pots, each fashioned as a Chinaman seated cross-legged in loose robes, with a detachable conical hat as the lid, and carrying either a cockerel, or a parrot, or a snake as a spout (A2). Others without such appendages were

40. 'Girl in a Swing Porcelain and Chelsea' by A. Lane and R.J. Charleston, *Transactions*, English Ceramic Circle, 1962, Vol. 5, pt. 3, p. 137.

41. *Connoisseur,* 1926, Vol. 76, p. 237, article by Bellamy Gardner.

Plate 13. *'Grotesque Chinaman' as a pastil burner (A4), after the Meissen model of Pu-tai Ho-shang. 5¼ins. (13.1cm). Chelsea c.1746.*
Sotheby Parke Bernet

issued as tea-poys (A3). Although one might suppose that these were based on Chinese *blanc-de-Chine* models, T.H. Clarke[42] has shown that they follow originals made at St. Cloud. A 'Grotesque Chinaman' with open mouth (Plate 13) (A4) made as a pastil burner, follows Meissen models which were based on a *blanc-de-Chine* of Pu-tai Ho-shang. Three early Chelsea figures imitate terracottas representing children created by the Flemish sculptor, François Duquesnoy (1594-1644). They include a 'Boy seated with a reed-pipe' (A6), two models of 'A Boy seated upon rocks' (A7), and a 'Boy asleep upon a mattress' (A5). The last mentioned may be seen in the British Museum in the Wallace Elliot Collection which is incised 'June ye 26 1746', whilst there is a terracotta in the Casa Buonotti in Florence and both bronzes and ivory carvings of the same subject are known.[43] A rare model of a 'Chinaman' (A8), leaning upon a small table upon which rests a tea-pot, illustrated by Dr. Bellamy Garnder,[44] looks from the photograph to be a fragment of the Bow group emblematic of 'Fire' (G44). Both are taken from an engraving after Boucher's 'Décoration Chinoise'. More precise identification is not possible without handling a specimen. The model of a 'Chinese Fisherman' (A9) stands upon an irregular pad base strewn with marine life beside a basket and a net; he wears loose robes and a conical hat turned back in front and is derived from the engraving 'Le Pêche Chinois', after Boucher.

Possibly the first model to have been made by Joseph Willems at Chelsea was that of 'Ceres' (A13) who stands stiffly in wreath of corn husks holding a reaping-hook. Here, the drapery is deeply moulded though the overall result is more appropriate for garden statuary than for a porcelain figure. Indeed, it is possible that Willems copied it from a lead or terracotta which may have been created by an artist such as John Cheere. Altogether more pleasing is the group known as 'Rustic Lovers' (A10) of which one example in the British Museum is marked with an underglaze blue crown and trident. The rustic swain sits with a peasant girl facing him upon his right knee; his right arm is about her waist, his left hand which the lady restrains, lies on her knee. There is a slightly different version in the Sigmund Katz Collection, showing coverage of the youth's left hand with the hem of the dress or, as Lane and Charleston so aptly say, "in a

42. 'The French Influence at Chelsea' by T.H. Clarke, *Transactions,* English Ceramic Circle, 1959, Vol. 4, pp. 45-57.

43. 'Three Sleeping Children, a Further Observation' by William Little, *Connoisseur,* 1952, Vol. 129, p. 35, no. I, Chelsea porcelain model; no. II, ivory carving; no. III, a Vincennes porcelain model listed as 'Enfant endormi sur un matelas' by Felix de la Rue.

44. 'Sir Hans Sloane's Chelsea Porcelain Heirlooms in the possession of Major R.C.H. Sloane-Stanley' by Bellamy Gardner, *Transactions,* English Ceramic Circle, 1939, Vol. 2, No. 6, pp. 26-30: pl. XIa, porcelain model; pl. XIb, engraving after Boucher taken from the *Louvre Inventaire General,* Vol. II, No. 1415, fig. 9.

more purposive position".[45] A less sophisticated version of the group, ascribed to the Girl-in-a-Swing factory, is in the National Museum of Ireland, Dublin, and this serves to link the two porcelain establishments. The Chelsea model of 'Milton' (A12), shows minor points of difference over the facial features and folds in drapery from the Derby model of the poet (K28). Possibly they were based on a terracotta issued by either Scheemakers or some other sculptor as indicated in Chapter IV.

Only one Chelsea figure of the first phase of production is known that echoes a Meissen prototype and this is the 'Print Seller' (A11) which is a copy from the 1747 series of the 'Cries of Paris', by Kändler and Reinicke.[46] There is a rare pair of 'Sphinxes' (A15) mounted upon wedge shaped bases adorned with rococo scrolls[47] in the likeness of the actress Kitty Clive. These, which are marked with the incised triangle, may have been based on a watercolour by Charles Worlidge via Chalres Mosley's engraving showing her in the role of Mrs. Riot.[48] They antedate both the Bow 'Sphinxes'[49] and standing model,[50] as well as the Derby figure.[51] Although, the concept of the sphinx arose in ancient Egypt, it had been reintroduced into decorative sculpture by Jean Bérain (1640-1711) usually adapted to include the head and breasts of a well known personality. An example of his work may be seen in the grounds of Chiswick House.[52] A similar carved sphinx is incorporated into a giltwood chair designed by William Kent, now in the Ionic Temple at Rievaulx Terrace.[53] A bust of the Duke of Cumberland (A14) is, perhaps, more familiar in a raised anchor version and may also be found in Staffordshire pottery. The Staffordshire figures usually have ceramic plinths attached whereas those made at Chelsea seem to have been supplied with shaped wooden stands during both periods.

A fine pair of tawny owns (A19) anticipate the raised anchor aviary that was to follow. A pair of finches (A17) are copies of Vincennes originals; they perch upon tall bases adorned with applied leaves made of slip. These take the form of oak leaves with fine embossed central veins which Frank Tilley noticed on other Chelsea wares of the period.[54] Several small models of animals include a recumbent 'Pug upon a tasselled Cushion' (B57), a delightful 'Squirrel eating a Nut' (A18), and a superbly fashioned greyhound dog and companion bitch (A16).

Before concluding this section, it is necessary to explain certain omissions. A number of models, chiefly of animals and birds, are illustrated in the *Cheyne Book of Chelsea China and Pottery*[55] and have been omitted owing to either erroneous attribution or to the difficulty in making an assured identification from rather small photographs. A head and shoulders of 'George III as Prince of Wales', mounted upon a shaped plinth which appropriately bears the device of three embossed feathers,[56] has been reallocated from Chelsea to the Longton Hall factory (083). A bust of 'George II' (Plate 163, Chapter XI) which was the subject of a paper by the late Dudley Delevingne,[57] has been attributed by Dr. Bernard Watney[58] to Chaffers' Liverpool (Q25) because of the paste, glaze and method of press casting employed in its manufacture.

Figures made at Chelsea between 1750 and 1753

The Paste and Glaze

Between 1749 and 1751 the paste evolved to become more tightly grained, more plastic, and less glassy. The amount of lead oxide fell to around 0.55 per cent, whilst the alumina rose to about 6 per cent; other ingredients showed little change with silica 65 per cent, lime 25 per cent and soda and potash together 4.3 per cent.[59] Figures were more thickly potted and hence are heavier; firecracks, tears, sagging out of alignment, and pitting are all less evident.

45. 'Girl in a Swing Porcelain and Chelsea', op. cit., pl. 135c, Girl-in-a-Swing version of 'Rustic Lovers'.

46. *Porcelain Figurines* (London, 1975) by Nathaniel Harris, p. 47.

47. 'Some consequences of the Bow Special Exhibition, Alderman Arnold and Thomas Frye 1748-1759' by G.H. Tait, *Apollo*, 1960, Vol. 71, No. 705, p. 184, fig. V.

48. ibid., p. 183, fig. IV.

49. *Eighteenth Century English Porcelain* (Bungay, 1952) by George Savage, pl. 39.

50. *English Porcelain Figures of the 18th Century* (London, 1961) by Arthur Lane, pl. 37.

51. 'Some consequences of the Bow Special Exhibition etc.', op. cit., p. 40, fig. I.

52. *A Dictionary of Antiques* (London, 1970) by George Savage, p. 404.

53. *Treasures of the National Trust* (Frone & London, 1976), ed. R. Fedden, pl. 73 (col.).

54. 'The Clue of the Oak Leaf: Its Place in Identifying Unrecorded Triangle Period Chelsea' by F. Tilley, *Antique Collector,* 1950, Vol. XXI, pp. 13-15.

55. *The Cheyne Book of Chelsea China and Pottery* (London, 1924), ed. Reginald Blunt.

56. *Chelsea and Other English Porcelain Pottery and Enamel in the Irwin Untermyer Collection* (Cambridge, Mass., 1957) by Yvonne Hackenbroch, pl. 2, fig. 10.

57. 'The Bust of George II' by Dudley Delevingne, *Transactions,* English Ceramic Circle, 1960, Vol. 5, pt. 4, pp. 236-248.

58. 'The King, the Nun and Other Figures' by Bernard Watney, *Transactions,* English Ceramic Circle, 1968, Vol. 7, pp. 48-58.

59. 'Girl in a Swing Porcelain and Chelsea', op. cit., p. 138.

Exposed biscuit is white and transillumination of flat wares reveals an uneven density due to imperfect mixing of constituents. The glaze remained opacified with tin but became thicker, more glossy, and feels slightly greasy or wet in the hand. Pinhole defects are less numerous. The former warm and creamy appearance gives place to a cold glitter resulting from the inclusion of smalt. The distinctly blue tinge is most noticeable in crevices where the glaze lies most thickly. This is exemplified by the model of a 'Chinese Boy' (B42) with his mouth open carrying a gourd over his shoulder in the Fitzwilliam Museum, Cambridge, which gives the impression that the little fellow has been eating bilberries!

The Bases

Bases mostly retain simple mound, pad, or rectangular forms until towards the end of 1751 when many, after the Meissen fashion, were decorated with moulded and enamelled leaves and flowers. The bird models usually stand on tall bases shaped like truncated cones with their lower circumferences flared outwards to which are applied leaves, insects and flowers. Until c.1752, leaves resemble those of an oak tree but later have less indented and finely serrated edges. Inferior surfaces of bases are flat, ground free of glaze, and are perforated by ventilation holes of intermediate size.

Enamel Colours and Decorative Style

Enamel colours, first introduced for figures c.1751, were increasingly popular and the number of models left white steadily declined until, by 1755, the majority were coloured. The palette included canary yellow, a dull opaque leaf-green, a glossy brick-red, a warm purplish-brown, and black. A pale turquoise, an opaque medium blue which has a violaceous hue, were available not later than 1754 and probably earlier. Enamels were thickly applied over small areas leaving large passages white. Portions representing flesh were covered with the palest buff with a faint orange-red upon the cheeks. Eyelids and eyelashes were depicted with lines drawn in brown, irises are usually brown or grey, whilst the pupils are painted in purplish-black. A distinctive use of short and thin brush strokes in two or more shades of the same colour were used to portray hair. Areas left in the white were often embellished with floral sprays, with a preference for use of a single bloom or of sprigs, outlined in brownish-red filled with flat washes after the manner of *Indianische Blumen*. In some examples stylised flowers are interspersed with patterns composed of lines, dots, and circles intended to draw the whole together in one comprehensive design. Very frequently, flowers have red pointed petals and these may be mixed with smaller flora of violet blue and yellow. During this early period gilding was rarely used and when present, is watery, pale and rubbed, as can be seen upon the facings of Scapino's jacket (Colour Plate A). We do not know the proportion of models decorated outside the factory, though the number is likely to be less than obtained at Derby or Bow. The London Account Book of William Duesbury covers the period from November 1751 to August 1753.[60] The earlier entries more frequently pertain to figures from Chelsea than from other factories though this may indicate no more than a lack of precision in keeping records. Notes are in the calligraphy of several different persons. Undoubtedly, much of the work of Duesbury was effected in cold colours which have long since peeled away leaving only traces deep in crevices. However, there is specific mention of 'Hinamil' for which he charged nearly double the rate for oil paint. Chelsea models that passed through the atelier include "Drooping Bird ... Bird ... Goldfinchis ... Flapwing Birds ... Houls [Owls] ... Doggs ... Hare ... Gouts [Goats] ... Ships [Sheep] ... Doctor ... Nurs [Nurse] ... Jupetors ... Junose ...

60. *William Duesbury's London Account Book, 1751-1753* (London, 1931) by Mrs. Donald Macalister, English Ceramic Circle monograph.

Dominoes [Harlequins] ... Chafashinds [Capuchins, i.e. Monks] and Sphinks." No work can with certainty be ascribed to Duesbury but some tentative attributions are mentioned in Chapter VIII. In 1754, Duesbury left London for Longton Hall and ceased to work as an independant enameller.

Marks

Most models have small oval medallions bearing the device of a small embossed anchor within a circle, applied either to the back of the figure, its support, or to the upper aspect of the base. A few raised anchors dating to the period 1752-53 are enamelled red and there is one model of 'Isabella' (Plate 17), now in the Victoria and Albert Museum, on which the anchor is coloured violet. There is no justification for the belief that red enamelled raised anchors indicate decoration by William Duesbury himself.

The Modelling

The modelling characteristics peculiar to Joseph Willems have been described by Arhur Lane.[61] These include rather long heavy bodies, squat necks and short thick legs. Models lack the representation of those postural adjustments that normally accompany action, such as tilting of the pelvis or shoulder girdles and altered curvature of the spine. This failing imparts to them a stately dignified appearance lacking animation. Drapery seems to have been modelled from blanket-thick material and is arranged in deep triangular folds favoured by the baroque style. Faces have broad foreheads, widely spaced eyes, full curving cheeks terminating in pointed chins, and lips are parted in a half-smile. Ear lobes may stand out from the neck as they do in a person sufferent from mumps, whilst in profile the nose is retroussé and there is a hint of a double chin. The head and eyes are slightly turned to one side and the gaze is either above or below the horizontal. Willem's models of peasants

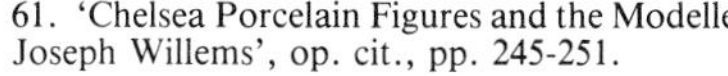
61. 'Chelsea Porcelain Figures and the Modeller Joseph Willems', op. cit., pp. 245-251.

Plate 14 (above). 'Parakeet' (B19). 5ins. (12.7cm). Chelsea c.1752, mark of the raised anchor.
George Savage

Plate 15 (right). 'Crested Red Butcher Bird' (B6). 6¾ins. (17.1cm). Chelsea c.1751, after George Edwards.
Sotheby Parke Bernet

recall those painted by David Teniers, and his women, whether simple rustics or fine ladies, display the bored upper-class look. Limitations imposed by an unstable paste necessitated a relatively small scale, five to eight inches, and the avoidance of poses with unsupported projecting limbs. Most of the earlier tendency to reproduce excessive detail disappeared after 1752 when the lessons learned from inspection of Meissen models had been fully digested.

The Models

Perhaps the best known of all Chelsea models are the birds many of which are based on coloured engravings included by George Edwards, one time librarian to the Royal College of Physicians, in his book *The History of Uncommon Birds.*[62] This was published between 1743 and 1747 in four volumes and copies may be seen in the British Museum. It was common practice for sea captains in the eighteenth century to bring back from foreign parts exotic birds which they either sold or presented to members of the aristocracy or landed gentry. Edwards made his drawings by visiting aviaries that contained such birds in many different country estates. Rather more than twenty pairs of models were made at Chelsea (B1-B22) during the period of the raised anchor mark which follow the shape of the originals fairly well, but often have a brighter and different coloured plumage, suggesting that some may have been taken from black and white engravings. Examples are illustrated in Plates 14, 15 and 16. They are four to eight and a quarter inches tall and stand on mound or chimney-pot bases adorned with moulded leaves and flowers as well as painted insects. They are rather stiff and lack the animation of others copied from originals by Kändler. Both enamelled and white versions are known. The most ambitious, and certainly the most successful, are the 'Black and white Chinese Pheasants' (B2), and 'Little Hawk

62. 'The Chelsea Birds' by Bellamy Gardner, *Transactions,* English Porcelain Circle, 1931, No. III, pp. 55-62.

Plate 16. *'Whip-Poor-Will or Lesser Goat Sucker' (B22). 6½ins. (16.5cm). Chelsea c.1752, raised anchor mark.*
Sotheby Parke Bernet

Owls' (B17). The bases of coloured specimens are left white, with moss represented by a transparent pale turquoise laid over a purplish-black vermiculation, and dull green leaves. Edwards, himself, had no very high opinion of the models and wrote: "Several of our manufacturers that imitate china, have filled the shops in London with images modelled after figures in my History of Birds, most of which are sadly represented as to shape and colouring..." History records a different verdict for upon the rare occasions when raised anchor Chelsea birds come up at auction, huge sums are bid to secure them. Although the London Account Book of William Duesbury contains such entries as "Boolfinchis, Peeping Birds, Topnot Birds, Chelsay Phesons, King Fishiars, and Hostrigis", it seems unlikely that many of the birds after Edwards passed through Duesbury's studio. Probably, those listed followed Meissen originals which display such a contrasting sense of animation that they may instantly be identified. Some of these are listed in the Appendices (B23-B32). There are, also, a few small models of finches and canaries[63] copied from Vincennes prototypes whilst others, including an ungainly and somewhat angular peacock[64] seem to have been made in the likeness of imported models from China.

63. 'The French Influence at Chelsea', op. cit., pp. 45-57.

64. *Chelsea Porcelain, the Triangle and Raised Anchor Wares,* op. cit., pl. 35, fig. 73.

Plate 17. *'Isabella' (B35), enamelled violet, inspired from woodcut shown in plate 18. 9½ins. (24.1cm). Chelsea c.1750, mark of a raised anchor. Now in the Victoria and Albert Museum.* Winifred Williams

Plate 18. *A woodcut of 'Nobile Matrona Francese di Orliens', from Cesare Vecellio's* Degli Habiti Antichi e Moderni di tutto il Mondo *(Venice, 1590), pp. 269-270.* Winifred Williams

Amongst the more attractive human models are those relating to the Commedia dell'Arte. A semi-grotesque representation of 'Dottore Baloardo' (B33) in the Untermyer Collection, wears a brimmed hat over a head-scarf, white ruff, and long purple cloak; he was copied from Peter Reinicke's original based upon an etching by Calotto[65] and is seven inches tall. Another model, eleven and a quarter inches in height, of 'The Doctor'[66] in the Sigmund Katz Collection, was inspired by a figure in the foreground of an engraving by C.N. Cochin, entitled 'L'Amour au Théâtre italien', after Watteau. Here, the figure wears the traditional black mask with covers only his forehead and nose; he is dressed all in black with a long cloak whilst a letter inscribed 'Memoire Disabella 1750', is tucked into his belt (B34). This presumably relates to the death of the doctor's daughter Isabella in a particular scenario whilst the date may refer to that when the model was first issued. A similar model, once in the Lady Ludlow Collection at Luton Hoo, is a modern copy and is discussed in Chapter XIII. 'Isabella' (Plate 17) (B35) was inspired by a woodcut entitled 'Nobile Matrona Francese di Orliens' (Plate 18) in a book illustrating costumed by Cesare Vecellio, published in Venice in 1590.[67] There are three other Comedy models, each about four and a half inches tall after Peter Reinicke's originals which are five and a half inches in height. The difference is accounted for by shrinkage of the soft paste copies by about one fifth in the kiln. They include 'Pantalone' (B36), bearded with skull-cap and voluminous cloak holding a money-bag; 'Scapino' (Colour Plate A) (B37), leaning against a tree-trunk, cap in hand, with a purse and dagger attached to his belt; and 'Scaramuzzi' (B38) who walks with mincing gait as if balancing upon a tight-rope. The last two varlets wear a short cape, or *tabaro,* to denote their humble status.

Plate 19. *Bust of the Duke of Cumberland (B49). 5½ins. (14cm). Chelsea c.1750, mark of the raised anchor.* George Savage

Allegorical subjects, which during the subsequent phase of production were to become so popular, were restricted to a group representing 'Europa and the Bull' (B45), a further version of the 'Sphinx' (B47), a pair of which in Chatsworth House, has the head and breasts of a woman and stands on a rectangular base, and the 'Head of a smiling Girl' (B48), once erroneously thought to be in the likeness of Sophie Roubilliac but probably copied from a French marble or bronze of *Endymion.*

A funerary group embodying Britannia (B46) shows her as a rather stern-looking lady in plumed helmet and cloak who sits with a trident in her left hand, regarding a blank shield held in her right, whilst at her feet there is a lion. This commemorates the tragic death from pneumonia of Frederick Prince of Wales in 1751. Although the prince was a model husband and a great patron of the arts, as well as being a keen cricketer, he did not enjoy a good press and has been quite unjustifiably remembered in the doggerel:

"Here lies poor Fred who was alive and is dead.
We had rather it had been his father.
But as it's just poor Fred who was alive and is dead
There's no more to be said."

Arthur Lane suggested that the shield upon the model may once have born a portrait of Frederick painted in cold colours. Both this Chelsea group and another created at the Girl-in-a-Swing factory (E16) must have been issued shortly after 31st March, 1751, when the event took place. Another commemorative model is a small bust of the Duke of Cumberland (Plate 19) (B49), first issued c.1746. Dr. Bellamy Gardner[68] suggested it might have been based on a medal struck to celebrate the victory over the Scots at Culloden but since it is intended to be viewed full-face, this seems improbable.

Two models of ladies in Levantine dress (B44), which stand upon square bases, were inspired by engravings made by Ravenet after Boucher entitled

65. *Dresden China* (London, 1946) by W.B. Honey, pl. 42B.

66. *Eighteenth Century English Porcelain,* op. cit., pl. 10.

67. *Degli Habiti Antichi e Moderni di tutto il Mondo: di nuovo accresciuti di molte figure* (Venice, 1590) by C. Vecellio; see an article in *Connoisseur,* Vol. 145, by Arthur Lane, figs. 7 and 8.

68. 'Origins of Design in old Chelsea Porcelain' by Bellamy Gardner, *Connoisseur,* 1940, Vol. 106, pp. 3-6, no. I, model; no. II, medal struck in 1746.

'Femme du Levant' and 'Dame de Constantinople'. Their dresses are sumptuous and both desport huge turbans but they fail as models owing to an excess of detail represented in the round. A rare 'Gardener's Companion' (Plate 20) (B52) is derived from another engraving by the same artist 'Fille de St. Jean de Patmos, Isle de L'Archipel'. The lady wears a brimmed hat and stands beside a tree-trunk upon which is a basket of flowers whilst she gathers further blossoms in her apron. There is, also, a model of a 'Rose Seller' (B51) which seems to have been prompted by a wood-cut of c.1590 depicting a peasant girl from Parma. She may be distinguished from the 'Gardener's Companion' by her lace cap, apron and dress which has a ruffle at the neck and also by a basket of flowers which she grasps in both hands. The engraver, J.J. Balechou, reproduced Boucher's 'Les Délices de L'Enfance', which prompted two Chelsea and several Meissen chinoiserie groups. The first Chelsea group depicts a standing Chinese lady holding a kettle in her left hand and pouring with her right chocolate from a jug into a cup held by a boy; a third figure issued separately *en suite* is of a crouching boy with a bowl of fruit (B40). As has been noted in Chapter II, all three figures were cast together at Meissen. The second Chelsea group includes a Chinese lady with a child and a cat playing with a string toy like a diabolo (B39). This has no Meissen counterpart and was based upon the engraving entitled 'Le Mérite de Tout Pais'. There is a delightful Chinese boy (B41) with cheeks puffed out wearing a

***Plate 20** (left). 'Gardener's Companion' (B52). ¾ins. (22.9cm). Chelsea c.1750, mark of the raised anchor.*
Sotheby Parke Bernet

***Plate 21** (above). 'La Nourrice' (B50). 7¼ins. (18.4cm). Chelsea c.1752, red anchor mark.*
Winifred Williams

leaf-shaped hat, after Watteau. A second 'Chinese Boy' (B42) who is bare-headed, and holds a gourd over his left shoulder, follows an Oriental blanc-de-Chine original and a seated 'Kuan Yin' (B43) stems from a similar source.

Models copied from Meissen originals included a peasant, seated upon the ground playing a hurdy-gurdy (B54), and a male 'Dwarf in a tall hat' (B56), and also a peasant musician, first created by Kändler in 1736, with his long grey hair hanging down his back and mouth open as if about to sing;[69] his partner, a peasant woman, wearing a head-scarf playing a similar instrument, was not copied.[70] The Chelsea male 'Dwarf' (B56) did not acquire a mate until after 1753 (C106). Both were based on etchings by Giacomo Calotto, though were most probably copied from Meissen prototypes or similar models issued at Mennecy.[71] An exceptionally beautiful group of a seated nurse breast-feeding an infant, known as 'La Nourrice' (Plate 21) (B50), was copied from a glazed earthenware original created by an unknown potter at Avon, near Fontainebleau, during the seventeenth century.[72] There, a pottery works had been established by Bernard Palissy (1510-1590) and a number of fine models resplendent in polychrome glazes had been issued shortly after his death. The Chelsea version enjoyed great popularity for no less than ten examples passed through the studio of William Duesbury and the same group continued to be made during the period of the red anchor mark. Possibly it was intended to represent the Virgin Mary and the Christ Child for, amongst the effects of Joseph Willems listed after his death was a terracotta of 'The blessed Virgin with the infant Jesus asleep'.

Amongst models of animals the most interesting by far is one of a pug (Plate 22) (B59) which has been identified as 'Trump', the favourite pet dog of William Hogarth.[73] A terracotta of the animal was made by Louis François Roubiliac and came up for sale after the death of his widow in 1789. According to Arthur Lane,[74] the engraving upon which the terracotta was based appears in Samuel Ireland's *Graphic Illustration of Hogarth,* published in 1799. A mirror image Chelsea porcelain model has come to light in the

69 . *German Porcelain of the 18th Century* (London, 1972) by Erica Pauls-Eisenbeiss, Vol. I, p. 119.

70. ibid., p. 85.

71. *Seventeenth and Eighteenth Century French Porcelain* (London, 1952) by George Savage, pl. 30B.

72. Sotheby's Sale Catalogue, 26th November, 1963, lot. 74.

73. 'Hogarth's Pug in Porcelain' by J.V.G. Mallet, *Victoria and Albert Museum Bulletin,* 1967, Vol. III, No. 2, pp. 45-53.

74. *English Porcelain Figures of the 18th Century* (Lane), op. cit., p. 31, footnote 1.

Plate 22. *'Trump' (B59), the pet dog of William Hogarth. Chelsea c.1750.* George Savage

collection of Lionel Geneen.[75] The two were probably taken from plaster replicas made by Roubiliac of which four were recovered from his studio following his death in 1762. Another 'Pug on a cushion' (B57) is comparatively crude in contrast but there is a magnificent pair of seated hounds (B58). Paired groups, one of 'Recumbent Kids' (B61), the other a pair of goats (B60) are particularly attractive and there are also lions including a lion couchant (B62). There remain several models of sheep which are portrayed both standing and recumbent, singly or in groups of two. Standing ewes and companion rams and separate models of lambs are mounted on oval bases the upper surfaces of which are sometimes covered with a dull green, whilst russet-brown and black may be used to accent features. Most follow Meissen prototypes and exist in Derby and Bow versions. They were presumably used to form pastoral scenes along with shepherds and shepherdesses on the dining-table. There seems to be a dirth of illustrations of these animals owing to competition for limited space in books for more important figures and for similar reasons examples have nearly always been banished from display cabinets of museums to languish and gather dust in reserve collections.

75. 'Rococo English Porcelain: a study in style', op. cit., p. 111, footnote 12.

Plate 23. *A 'Toper' (B64). 8½ins. (21.6cm). Chelsea c.1752-53, unmarked but period of raised anchor. A previously unrecorded model.*
Simon Spero

Part Two — Chelsea figures made between 1752 and 1769

Figures made between 1752 and 1757 (Red Anchor)

The Paste and Glaze

Between 1752 and 1757, there were gradual improvements made to both paste and glaze by the process of trial and error. The glassy body, with its high content of lead oxide, which had been unstable in the kiln and presented a greyish hue, gave place to one that was closer grained, contained only a trace of lead oxide, was more plastic and stable in the kiln and had a whiter colour. The earlier surface pitting of the biscuit was also eliminated. The new material, by about 1756, contained silica 64.75 per cent, lime 25 per cent, alumina 6 per cent, alkalis 4.5 per cent and 0.5 per cent of lead. This permitted sharper modelling detail, representation of projecting parts in more ambitious poses and, also, a larger scale. The old glaze had been thick, blued, opacified and displayed numerous pin-hole defects. This became thin, transparent, faintly straw-coloured and surface defects were almost entirely eliminated. Sanding, crazing, and smoke staining are rarely seen. Transillumination of flat wares of this period show areas of increased translucency which, if large, are known as 'moons', or if small, as 'tears'. These, however, are difficult to demonstrate in figures owing to their irregular contour and thickness.

The Bases

Although useful wares made at Chelsea were amongst the first to reflect the rococo style, the use of asymmetrically arranged 'C' and 'S' scrolls is rare upon figures until 1756. A few models retain rectangular bases often with the superior edges smoothed, but the vast majority stand upon shallow mounds which are, at times, almost discoid. The upper surface is usually adorned with moulded leaves and flowers and, where single figures are concerned, often create an overcrowded appearance. Groups upon larger pad bases do not give this impression. After 1756 scrolls moulded in low relief and often gilded appear, which are tastefully and elegantly arranged in a manner that bespeaks complete familiarity with the rococo style. The inferior surface of the base is flat, perforated by a ventilation hole of intermediate size, and ground to ensure level stance. The smooth, rather greasy feeling on palpation of this area is distinct from the slightly uneven and rough sensation when unground biscuit is palpated. After 1756 a few bases are concave underneath and glazed though there is a flat circumferential rim that has been ground free of glaze. Similar alteration in the style of bases occurred at Bow, though examination of these usually shows particles of sand and frit adherent to the glaze seldom evident on Chelsea models. The earlier oak leaves applied to bases now give place to others with finely serrated edges which are thicker than those associated with Derby and less spiky than those of Bow. It is also uncommon to find moulded dorsal veins. Flower heads are open and rather flat and mostly have four or five petals though some are little more than saucers with saw-tooth circumferences and a few others are fashioned individually by hand.

The Marks

Many figures are unmarked; others display a small and carefully drawn anchor in red enamel placed on the back of the model, or the tree-stump support, or the base.

Enamel Colours

The range of the palette increased and the quality of the enamels improved between 1752 and 1761. Although, turquoise had been introduced c.1753, since it appears in the 'Maypole Group', the colour was initially pale and tended to flake away from the glaze. Later it evolved into a deep rich hue that some have identified as the 'pea green' (perhaps 'peacock green') of the advertisements in the Sale Catalogue of 30th April, 1761. The green which, hitherto, had been dull, opaque and lifeless gave place to both a transparent yellow-green and a delightful blue-green. A strong vermilion complimented the older, glossy brownish red and other innovations included pale yellow, a light blue with a mauvish cast, a warm brown and a spectrum of delectable violets and mauves. The deep purplish blue which is often rather uneven and was called 'Marazine blue', was first mentioned in the Sales Catalogue of 27th March, 1755. However, the beautiful rose pink was not issued until 1761.

The Decorative Style

Colours were always applied thickly and hence it is very uncommon to see individual brush strokes that are associated with Derby or the streaky effect peculiar to some Bow models. Until 1756-58, enamels were used in plain washes between large passages left in the white. Flesh tints amount to scarcely more than a suspicion of palest buff heightened over cheeks and lips with orange-red. The deep salmon-pink cheeks of Derby figures are not encountered. Pupils are purplish-black, irises are grey, brown or a greyish-pink whilst lashes and eyelids are suggested by lines drawn in a warm brown. Eyebrows are often shown with a series of short diagonal strokes in black or brown, whilst hair is depicted by plain washes upon which a very fine irregular pencilling may be laid. This never presents the heavy regular lines characteristic of contemporary Bow models. Overall, there is a commendable restraint in decoration which enhances the artistic effect and this is nowhere more apparent than on the Beggars (C17-C20), some examples of which may be seen in the Victoria and Albert Museum. These are largely left white with small placements of warm brown, yellow, and black enamel which most perfectly accent the great beauty of the paste. Other models display painted floral decoration on their garments which is frequently in the Kakiemon style, though here the manner is more likely to have been derived indirectly through Meissen than direct from Japanese wares. Sometimes this is effected in a monochrome of blue or vermillion and may then include large flower heads, either with lobed contours with segmental divisions, or with flame shaped petals, arranged about small open circles and associated with scroll-like leaves and stems. Examples include a 'Levantine Lady',[76] a 'Lady 'Sporter' ',[77] and a group of 'Vintners',[78] all in the Untermyer Collection. Alternatively, floral sprays outlined in a warm brown may be filled in with washes of iron red, yellow-green, and a delicious light blue which has a violaceous hue. An example of this type of polychrome floral painting is provided by the group 'Columbine and Pantalone'[79] in the Untermyer Collection and recalls some of the best *famille verte* decoration of the K'ang-Hsi period. More often, however, the achievement is less remarkable and includes widely spaced sprigs consisting of a single blossom, frequently a red flower with pointed petals, and between five and nine leaves of a yellow-green colour. This may be seen upon the dress of the 'Lady in the Crinoline' (Colour Plate B). In some red anchor figures similar floral sprigging is interspersed with patterns formed from lines, circles and dots which serve to unite the whole into a coherent design. This feature may be observed upon the dress of a 'Polish lady' in a crinoline[80] in the Cecil Higgins Museum, Bedford. More rarely, floral sprays may be omitted altogether and the decoration limited to patterns created with stars, circles,

76. Untermyer, pl. 21, fig. 36.
77. ibid., pl. 24, fig. 32.
78. ibid., pl. 32, fig. 53.
79. ibid., pl. 38, fig. 31.
80. *Chelsea Porcelain, the Red Anchor Wares* (Leigh-on-Sea, 1951) by F. Severne Mackenna, pl. 68, fig. 135.

dots, and lines such as may be seen upon the dress of the female partner in the group of 'Tyrolean Dancers'.[81] Although decoration of figures in the style of *Deutsche Blumen* was favoured at Derby and at Bow, it is uncommonly found upon red anchor Chelsea figures.

The upper surface of bases was usually left white though some were covered by a pale wash of transparent green laid upon a yellow ground which produces a pleasingly variegated effect rarely found on models from other factories. The tips of moulded flower-petals were usually touched with red, yellow, blue, or pink, whilst their centres are either yellow or dark brown and surrounded by a circumferential ring of brown dots, a feature rarely seen on Bow or Derby flowers. Honey-gilding was employed with restraint and application limited to suitable accessories, such as musical instruments, shoe buckles, and the edges of garments.

Modelling

The modelling traits associated with Joseph Willems have been described above. These, though muted, continue to be evident. Willems showed his preference for the baroque style long after it had been displaced by the rococo. His copies of Kändler's 'Water Deities' reclining (C89), for example, recapture something of the Mannerist representation of the figure of Adam by Michelangelo in the Sistine Chapel of the Vatican. The supercilious expressions on the faces of Willems' models of women are epitomised by his peasant woman wearing a linen cap and bearing a sheaf of corn, emblematic of Summer (Plate 38) (C98). However, his more serious representations of the Five Senses (C94) perfectly exemplify the deep triangular folds of drapery and poses of the Grand Manner. Willems was a good draughtsman and much more

81. Untermyer, pl. 35, fig. 38.

Plate 24. *'Dottore Baloardo' (C7), striking an histrionic pose. 5½ins. (14cm). Chelsea c.1755.*
Sotheby Parke Bernet

Plate 25. *A model traditionally known as 'The Captain' (C9). 5½ins. (14cm). Chelsea c.1755, red anchor mark. This is a copy of Peter Reinicke's model of 'Narcissino' created c.1743-44 at Meissen.*
Sotheby Parke Bernet

than a mere copyist, for his fine 'Beggars' (Plate 29) (C17-C20), and 'Carpenter' (C22), are in no way inferior to other 'Cries of Paris' created by Kändler and Reinicke and his adaptation of the marble by Nicolas Coustou to create the Chelsea Pietà was completely successful and brilliantly executed from the artistic viewpoint. These larger models became possible after 1755 when a stronger paste was introduced.

The Models

Many copies were made of Peter Reinicke's models of the Commedia dell'Arte including 'Columbina' (C4) dancing in a jaunty hat; 'Dottore Baloardo' (Plate 24) (C7) in a brimmed hat and cloak striking an histrionic pose; 'Pedrolino' (C11) wearing ruff, loose garments and hat with hands raised up in horror; and 'Arlecchino' (C1) in motley. The Chelsea model of 'The Captain' (Plate 25) (C9), as noted previously, is a copy of Reinicke's 'Narcissino', who stands wearing a wide brimmed hat and baggy trousers with a cloak thrown over his left shoulder. There are two versions of 'Scaramuzzi': the earlier raised anchor version (B38) was reissued though in at least one illustration he is wrongly named 'Mezzetino';[82] in the new model he stands with his cloak slipping off his shoulders (C15). A rare 'Avvocato' (C3) wearing a doctor's hat and ermine trimmed gown probably follows a Kändler original. The red anchor representation of 'Pantalone' (Plate 26) (C10) which portrays him wearing a large soft cap and holding a money-bag in his left hand, is altogether different from Reinicke's original model. This has been called, quite wrongly, 'Pantalon Ançien' after the engraving of that title made by François Joullain after Giacomo Calotto.[83] There is, in fact, a Kändler model

82. *Chelsea Porcelain, the Red Anchor Wares,* op. cit., pl. 65, fig. 130.

83. *Histoire du Théâtre italien...*(Paris, 1928-31) by Luigi Riccoboni, pl. 3, engraving of 'Pantalon Ancien'.

***Plate 26.** 'Pantalone' (C10). 5¾ins. (14.6cm). Chelsea c.1755, red anchor mark. Note the money-bag is held in the left hand whereas in the raised anchor version it is in the right.* Sotheby Parke Bernet

***Plate 27.** 'The Rat Catcher' (C34), from the Cries of Paris. 5¾ins. (14.6cm). Chelsea c.1756.* Sotheby Parke Bernet

of Pantalone who has both hands behind his back which echoes the engraving.[84] Some models of Pedrolino show him seated with a drum attached to his belt playing an end-flute (C13), others depict him standing with tambourine and end-flute (C12). The first of these recalls the 'Savoyard Drummer' which was created by Kändler and Reinicke for their set of Paris Cries, whilst the second is reminiscent of the male member of the 'Idyllic Musicians' issued at Bow (H45) and Derby (K42). A rather beautiful 'Lady in a crinoline' (Colour Plate B) (C6) is tentatively identified as Isabella carrying a mask and a fan. Minor variations are known in which she holds a musical score,[85] or a book[86] or may be paired with a gallant wearing a tricorn hat and huge waistcoat who stands with his left hand in his pocket.[87] Unaccountably, this same pair have been ascribed to the Ansbach factory.[88] The male figure bears more than a passing likeness to Simon Feilner's model of 'Cynthio del Sole'[89] made at Höchst c.1752. Most of the groups relating to the Commedia dell'Arte were made at Bow, but there is one very lovely Chelsea example depicting Columbina playing a lute, whilst Pantalone holds a score and conducts (C5) copied from a Kändler original. Models of 'Arlecchino seated with bagpipes', paired with 'Columbina playing a hurdy-gurdy' (C2) are known in Bow, Derby, and Longton Hall.

There are only two Chelsea versions of characters modelled by J.J. Kändler and Peter Reinicke for their 1745-47 series of the Cries of Paris. The first, 'Print Seller', was copied first in white prior to 1750 (A11) but was reissued in a more sophisticated form resplendent in enamel colours (C33). He is shown with a pack upon his back and a map in either hand and, in some exaples, one of the charts portrays America. The second model is a peasant standing wearing a tricorn hat and playing a hurdy-gurdy (B54). Other representations of Paris Cries followed those of the second set by Kändler and Reinicke based on a watercolour sketched by Christoph Huet and issued c.1752 at Meissen. Chelsea examples include a seated lady 'Ballad Singer' with song-sheets in her hand and a child at her side (C16), a 'Savoyard Drummer' (C35) with his drum suspended from his waist-band and an end-flute held to his lips, and a pair of male and female 'Bird Catchers' (C21) carrying huge cages. Oddly enough, the model of the woman was adapted at Chelsea to provide a 'Flower Seller' (C29) by replacement of the cage by a basket of flowers. There is a 'Rat Catcher' (Plate 27) (C34) seated with a ferret and trap, a 'Jewish Pedlar' wearing a fur-lined hat with a tray of samples suspended about his neck by a strap and his companion 'Trinket Seller', who has a box of gewgaws attached to her belt (C30). A pair of 'Cooks' (C23) portray a man wearing a turban and woman in a linen cap both of whom wear aprons and carry platters of food before them; they are known in Bow versions (H27). There is also a group, known as the 'Itinerant Musician' (C32) composed of a man with bagpipes walking beside a child and a dog.

Strangely, Pierce Tempest's *Cryes of the City of London* evoked no response from the Chelsea modellers. The fine illustrations by Marcellus Laroon (1653-1702), the Dutch painter and engraver, had prompted Meissen replicas of a quack doctor and other contemporary characters which must have been available in London. Joseph Willems was not content simply to imitate the work of other modellers and made a fine 'Carpenter' (C22) that seems to be original. He stands in tricorn hat with a bag of tools over his left shoulder and is in no way inferior to the artisans made by Kändler which included a carpenter amongst them. Closely allied to the Paris Cries are the fishermen of the red anchor. 'The Drunken Fisherman' (C25), which may be seen at Saltram House (No. 267.T.), typifies the satirical Kändler style even in the copy.[90] The figure stands with shoulders hunched, holding a fish in either

84. *German Porcelain of the 18th Century,* op. cit., p. 289.
85. *The Cheyne Book of Chelsea China and Pottery,* op. cit., pl. 10, no. 146.
86. *English Porcelain Figures of the 18th Century* (London, 1924) by William King, fig. 14 (right hand model).
87. *An Illustrative Encyclopaedia of British Pottery and Porcelain* (London, 1966) by G.A. Godden, p. 78, pl. 78.
88. *A Dictionary of Antiques* (London, 1970) by George Savage, p. 9.
89. *Antique Porcelain Digest* (Newport, 1961) by C.M and G.R. Scott, pl. 97, fig. 332d.
90. *Meissner Porzellan 1710-1810* (West Germany, 1966) by S. Ducret, p. 224, fig. 917.

hand, astride an eel-trap his shirt stuffed with fish and an inane grin upon his face; he wears a stocking cap, waistcoat over an open shirt and trousers rolled up. Also at Saltram, is another fisherman (C24) in a peaked cap, shirt and breeches rolled up, who stoops to take fish from a net gripped between his knees to transfer them into a basket.[91] A third fisherman (C26) in the Untermyer Collection is dressed in a similar fashion apart for a brimmed hat; he holds a large fish in his left hand and has his right ready to catch it should it wriggle free. This model may have been based on a watercolour by Christoph Huet entitled 'Live Carp', though the likeness may be no more than fortuitous. The fourth fisherman (C27), leans backwards his weight upon his right leg and holds the pole of a huge net in his left hand so that it comes to lie almost horizontally across the back of his neck, whilst grasping a fish in his right hand. Dr. Bernard Watney[92] has shown how the model was adapted from the 'Borghese Warrior' which was a favourite academician's study after the antique. The warrior is illustrated by Jacques Fischer[93] and there is an example fashioned by Nicolas Coustou in the Louvre dated 1683. Rather strangely, there seems to be only one Chelsea 'Fishwife' (Plate 28) (C28). She stands in linen cap, dress and apron, bearing in both hands a platter of assorted fish. Arthur Lane[94] suggested that she might have been created by Joseph Willems but, in fact, she represents a copy of a Meissen figure, most probably fashioned by Kändler and Reinicke.[95] The ratio of four men to one woman belies common experience of sea-faring folk and it is likely that further examples of fishwives, possibly copied from many available Meissen models, will come to light.

Brief mention has already been made of the Chelsea 'Beggars' (Plate 29). The 'Italian Beggars' (C18) are standing figures, the one in wide-brimmed hat, shirt sleeves and ragged breeches which terminate at the knees, with arms

91. *Apollo,* 1934, Vol. 22, No. 118, p. 182.

92. 'Origins of Design for English Ceramics of the 18th Century' by Bernard Watney, *Burlington Magazine,* 1972, Vol. 114, No. 837, pp. 818-826, pl. 36.

93. *French Bronze 1500-1800* (New York, 1968) by Jacques Fischer, pl. 18.

94. *English Porcelain Figures of the 18th Century* (Lane), op. cit., p. 68.

95. *Meissner Porzellan 1710-1810,* op. cit., p. 230, fig. 948.

Plate 28. *The 'Fishwife' (C28), from the Cries of Paris. 7⅞ins. (20cm). Chelsea c.1755.*
George Savage, and Sigmund Katz Collection

Plate 29. *The 'Blind Beggar' (C17), and 'Italian Beggar' (C19). 7½ins. (19.1cm). Chelsea c.1754.*
Victoria and Albert Museum

folded; the other (C19) wears a tricorn hat and gathers a blanket about his person whilst extending a pouch in his right hand which in some examples contains a silver coin. The 'Blind Beggar' (C17) wears a headscarf and cloak and extends his tricorn hat for alms; he is often paired with a 'Beggar Woman' (C20) though she looks more like a peasant woman on her way to market with vegetables in a basket. These all appear to be original creations by Willems.

A group known as the 'Tyrolean Dancers' (C48), consist of a swain holding the left hand of a peasant girl in his right, with his left arm about her waist as he whirls her round in a gavotte. The magnificent sense of rhythm and movement, rare in English porcelain models, reflects the creative skill of Eberlein who fashioned the original Meissen version.[96] The first Meissen group portrays the swain bare-faced and was issued c.1735; the Chelsea copy follows a later edition in which the male dancer wears a face mask.[97] There is a group of 'Dutch Dancers' (C40). This depicts a stiffly posed Dutch farmer dancing arms linked with his wife, the two facing in opposite directions. They are mentioned in the Chelsea Sale Catalogue of 29th March, 1756: "Lot 12, Two fine figures of a Dutchman and his wife dancing". They epitomise the stately appearance and lack of any sense of movement that characterises the work of Joseph Willems and must surely be from his hand. Nevertheless, Zimmermann writes[98] that Eberlein made two groups "showing Dutch and Tyrolean dancers". It is thus possible that the first mentioned has been lost and some have suggested the Chelsea pair may have been based upon the missing group. Prior to his arrival in this country in 1749, Willems must have been familiar with the paintings of rustics made by David Teniers and other Flemish artists and, indeed, his signed pair of painted terracottas of 'Dancing Peasants' recall such work. Porcelain models in this genre include an 'Ostler' (Plate 30) (C44) in jacket and breeches holding a whip with his pipe stuck into the band of his broad brimmed hat; also a 'Carter' (Plate 30) (C38), who is in similar dress but with his trousers gathered below the knees with ribbons, holding a mug of ale.

96. *German Porcelain of the 18th Century*, op. cit., pp. 80-83, an early example of 'The Tyrolean Dancers' by Eberlein.

97. *Meissen and Other Continental Porcelain, Faience and Enamel in the Irwin Untermyer Collection* (Cambridge, Mass., 1957) by Yvonne Hackenbroch, fig. 84.

98. *Meissner Porzellan* (Leipzig, 1926) by E. Zimmermann, p. 152.

Plate 30. *A 'Carter' (C38) (left) and companion 'Ostler' (C44). 4½ins. (11.4cm). Chelsea c.1755, red anchor mark.* Christie's

A 'Cooper' (C39), seated upon a cask with barrel hoops over his shoulder, echoes a Kändler original. There is a magnificent 'Drunken Peasant' (C45) as well as a 'Dancing Peasant' (C46) who, in the *Cheyne Book of Chelsea China and Pottery,* unaccountably assumes Irish nationality! Undoubtedly, the most ambitious of all English porcelain groups is that known as 'The Maypole Dancers' (C43), an example of which is in the Fitzwilliam Museum, Cambridge. It appears to have been built up piecemeal from separately moulded figures rather than to have been conceived as a single entity. A horseshoe of six dancers who hold hands and face outwards include a lord of the manor with his lady, a bailiff and his wife and a peasant man and woman; a drunk and a fiddler stand in the centre upon a mound beside a tree-stump. The quality are finely attired: the lord in a fine turquoise coat and full-bottomed wig and his spouse in a dress adorned with floral sprigs whilst the remainder are left largely in the white with accents of yellow, brown and black. It is stated in the Cheyne Book, that three of the rustic figures were based on those in a painting by David Teniers (fils) entitled 'Rural Fête', dated 1645, then in the possession of Sir Otto Beit. Dr. Bernard Watney pointed out that in the social climate of eighteenth century central Europe, no lord would dance with his lady amongst his social inferiors so that the camaraderie of the Chelsea group was a sop to more liberal English opinion. Other rustic folk include a 'Boy Fisherman' and companion 'Girl with fish in her Apron' (C36), a 'Boy holding a Bird' (C37), a 'Woman with a Mandoline' (C47) and others, which follow originals by Kändler. Two exceptionally fine 'Fruit Sellers' (Plates 31 and 32) (C42), each seated beside a basket, some intended for sweetmeats others containing porcelain fruit, were derived from designs by Sebastien Le Clerc.[99] A pair of seated 'Fisherman' and 'Fishwife' (C41) are, like their St. Cloud originals, adapted to serve as flower holders.[100]

99. Folio of engravings entitled 'Oeuvres choisies' (Paris, c.1765) by Sebastien le Clerc (1716-1784).

100. From the catalogue by Winifred Williams, of the Exhibition of White 18th Century European Porcelain held 10th — 27th June, 1975, at 3 Bury Street, St. James's, London, figs. 37 and 38, St. Cloud models.

***Plate 31.** A male fruit seller seated beside a pierced basket (C42). 9½ins. (24.1cm). Chelsea c.1755, red anchor mark.*
Grosvenor Antiques

***Plate 32.** A female fruit seller (C42). 9ins. (22.9cm). Chelsea c.1755, red anchor mark.*
Grosvenor Antiques

***Plate 33.** A 'Levantine Lady' adjusting her head-dress (C69). 6½ins. (16.5cm). Chelsea c.1756.*
George Savage

The theme of the idyllic pastoral that, during the period following 1759, came to dominate the modelling scene, was foreshadowed by a few red anchor examples. The 'Shepherd playing a Recorder', standing cross-legged beside his dog and his companion 'Shepherdess with flowers in her apron', and a posy in her right hand (C57) were copies of originals made c.1746 by Kändler;[101] they are known both in contemporary and later versions and were made at Derby and Bow as well as at Chelsea of c.1763 (Plate 47). The Chelsea 'Troubador playing a guitar', and companion 'Lady playing a Piccola' (C59), a seated 'Pierrot playing a Drum' paired with a 'Girl flautist in linen cap' (C50), all echo Meissen prototypes. One similar model of a 'Man playing upon a saltbox' (C52), may be original for the story is told in Croker's edition of Boswell's *Johnson,* on page 143, of strange happenings in Ranelagh Gardens, Vauxhall... "About this time, a song was given by Beard, accompanied on the salt-box by Brent, the fencing master, whilst Skeggs played on the broomstick as bassoon..." The performers then sang recitative, airs and choruses in masquerade.[102] The Chelsea Sales Catalogue of 1755, mentions, "Lot 34, a figure of a man playing on a salt-box". Other items mentioned in the same catalogue are, "Two very beautiful groups, one a man and woman with a bird's nest...", which must refer to that of a 'Huntsman in a jockey cap kneeling to examine a bird's nest in the lap of a seated Lady' (C54), and "...the other ditto, with a bird cage". The last mentioned recalls the Meissen group 'Two lovers with a Bird Cage' but in fact this rare group is different and may be seen in Upton House.[103] It portrays a seated gallant and lady reclining with a bird's cage between them, possibly an adaptation of 'Liberty and Matrimony'. A 'Dancing Girl' holding out her skirts in a fan (C53) echoes Kändler's model of 1745,[104] whilst a 'Huntsman with a tricorn hat' in riding boots with a falcon, and 'Lady with a riding whip' (C55) also reflect Meissen originals.[105]

The tales of travellers returning from the Middle and Far East, must have stimulated interest in foreigners and in turn prompted porcelain models relating to this subject. Many made at Meissen are described in Chapter II. Some were based on the set of a hundred engravings made by various artists including G. Scotin published by Le Hay of Paris in 1714 and entitled *Receuil des cents estampes représentent les différentes Nations du Levant.* They were drawn by order of the French ambassador to the 'Sublime Port', Monsieur le Comte Charles de Ferriol who, when he was first appointed, refused to divest himself of his sword, as was customary in Islam before entering the presence of the Sultan, on the grounds that to do so would tarnish the honour of his sovereign. He had been lucky to escape mutilation and death for the offence. The engravings, some of which are reproduced by J.I. Smith,[106] portray characters then seen about the streets of Constantinople including Hungarians, Armenians, Bulgarians, Persians, Turks and Levantines. Chelsea models of 'Seated Turk' in a plumed turban, and companion 'Levantine Lady' in tall head-dress (C70) beside shell containers, follow originals created c.1748 by Kändler and Reinicke[107] from this source. Models of 'Turk in tall hat', and 'Levantine lady' adjusting her head-dress (Plate 33) (C69) also echo Meissen prototypes inspired by plate 5 of de Ferriol's folio called *Le Capi Aga ou Chef des Eunugues blancs.*[108] The Chelsea 'Negro in turban' wearing loose robes gathered by a sash, with a quiver upon his back and longbow in hand (C66) is a mirror image of the Meissen original and thus dissimilar to other English copies, though the companion 'Negress in crown and Cloak', with right hand elevated to her face, follows the Saxon prototype without alteration. The two are described in the 1755 Chelsea Sales Catalogue as: "Two very fine black figures of an Indian Prince and a Queen". It was the eighteenth century

101. Lord Fisher Collection in the Fitzwilliam Museum, Cambridge, cat. nos. 488 and 489.

102. *The Cheyne Book of Chelsea China and Pottery,* op. cit., p. 59, no. 216.

103. Lord Bearsted Collection, Upton House, Warwickshire, cat. no. 21, pl. I.

104. Sammlung Muehsam, Vienna, sale catalogue of Glueckselig, April 1925, lot 94.

105. 'Meissen Porcelain and Copies of the 18th Century from the Collection of Judge Untermyer' by Yvonne Hackenbroch, *Connoisseur,* 1956, Vol. 137, p. 153, fig. 15.

106. 'An 18th Century Turkish Delight' by J.I. Smith, *Connoisseur,* 1964, Vol. 156, No. 705, pp. 215-219.

107. *German Porcelain of the 18th Century,* op. cit., Vol. I, p. 103.

108. *Katalog der Sammlung Alt-Meissner Porzellan des Herrn Rentners C.H. Fischer in Dresden* (Cologne, 1906) by C.H. Fischer, p. 146, no. 958.

Colour Plate G. *A selection of Bow models, c.1760-65: left, 'Winter', portrayed by a seated man in a cowled coat extending his hands over a brazier, from the 'Rustic Seasons' (H92). 6ins. (15.2cm). Centre, a sportsman holding a gun (H69). 5½ins. (14cm). Right, 'Taste', represented by a youth eating grapes, from the set of the 'Five Senses' (H99). 6ins. (15.2cm).*
John and Diana Mould collection

Colour Plate H. *Two groups, one with a nanny-goat suckling a kid, the other with a billy-goat, each being adorned with flowers by putti (H118). 7ins. (17.8cm). Bow c.1760.*
John and Diana Mould collection

Plate 34 (left). 'Chinaman' with a large moustache (C62). 7ins. (17.8cm). Chelsea c.1754, red anchor mark. Private collection

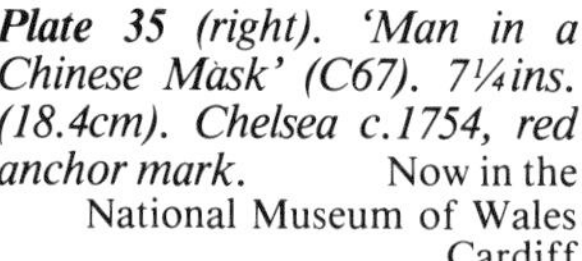

Plate 35 (right). 'Man in a Chinese Mask' (C67). 7¼ins. (18.4cm). Chelsea c.1754, red anchor mark. Now in the National Museum of Wales Cardiff

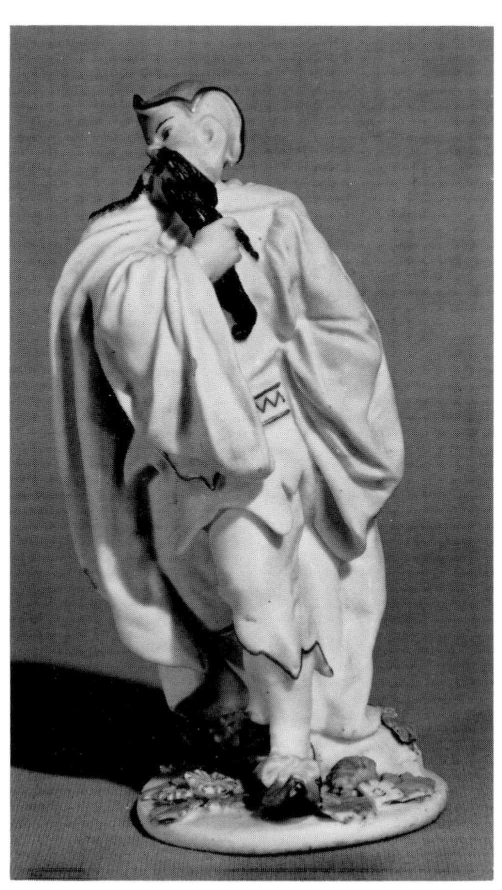

custom to refer to all natives of Eastern and African countries as 'Indians'.

Most chinoiserie models may be traced to engravings after Watteau or Boucher though, often, the English figure was taken indirectly from Meissen. Examples include a standing Chinaman with a huge moustache and arms folded (Plate 34) (C62), and the 'Man in a Chinese Mask' (Plate 35) (C67), now in the National Museum of South Wales, Cardiff. Also, smaller models of a 'Chinaman in conical hat' who stands with hands concealed within voluminous sleevs (C60), a most charming and attractive pair of 'Chinese Boy with fife and Girl with drum' (C63), and a magnificent group of four 'Chinese Musicians' (C65). The last mentioned are arranged in a ring facing outwards and include a youth holding a bell in his left hand who clasps with his right that of a small boy who also holds aloft a bell in his right hand; a girl with tambourine and bell and an older female child who plays a fife. Unlike another large Chelsea group of the 'Maypole Dancers', which was assembled piecemeal from separate models, the 'Musicians' were clearly designed as a whole and cast accordingly. The Chelsea Sales Catalogue of April 8th, 1756, lists "Lot 82. A most magnificent Lustre in the Chinese taste, beautifully ornamented with flowers, and a large group of Chinese figures playing music". An example is in the Judge Irwin Untermyer Collection and is finely illustrated in the catalogue.[109]

Other models of foreigners include the so called 'Spanish Sportsman' and companion 'Lady' (C71). The reason for the prefix 'Spanish' is not known, though from their elaborate dress, they may well have been prompted by characters in a contemporary drama. The male is dressed in tricorn hat bearing a plume, a scarf, coat, breeches and gaiters, whilst his elegantly attired lady wears a wide brimmed hat turned up on one side and a riding habit; both are seated before game and hold a gun. A delightful model of a lady in a crinoline wearing head-scarf, jacket and full skirt which she lifts with her right hand to

109. Untermyer Collection, pls. 29, 30 and 31 (colour) fig. 39.

display her petticoat (C68) has often been termed a 'masquerade figure'. Her left hand, which is against her breast, in some versions holds a mask which has lead to her erroneous identification by some authors as an Italian Comedy character, possibly Isabella. A fine example is in the Cecil Higgins Museum, Bedford. I am indebted to John Mallet for pointing out that she is, in fact, a copy of a Meissen model made by Kändler in 1743 to partner a swashbuckling and moustachioed model of a Pole created by Friedrich Eberlein.[110] She is, thus, 'Polish Lady', though it is improbable that Joseph Willems who made the Chelsea version knew of her intended nationality for the male figure was overlooked.

Nicholas Sprimont was concerned largely with the upperclass market composed of ladies and gentlemen who were familiar with Latin and Greek, and steeped in the legends and myths of ancient allegory. This may account for the relatively large numbers of models issued by the Chelsea factory relating to allegorical subjects. Most of those which date from between 1753 and 1757 are mounted upon plain square or rectangular bases devoid of ornamentation and stand rather stiffly posed some ten to twelve inches tall.

Though most other English porcelain factories based their allegorical figures on prototypes from Meissen, Chelsea also tapped some different sources that have not been identified. The model of 'Ceres' (Plate 36) with corn-husks and a reaping hook (C76) appears to be a refined version of an earlier figure issued

110. *Festive Publication to commemorate the 200th Jubilee of the Oldest European China Factory, Meissen* (Dresden, 1910) by Karl Berling, table 15, nos. 496 and 509.

***Plate 36.** 'Ceres' (C76), the goddess of crops and vines. 12¾ins. (32.4cm). Chelsea c.1755, red anchor mark.* Winifred Williams

in 1749 (A13). A rare 'Jupiter' with an eagle (C82) an example of which is in the Eckstein Bequest, is described in the Sale Catalogue of 1755 as "exceeding fine". 'Bacchus' (C73), crowned with vine leaves holding a bunch of grapes and a goblet in either hand, is reminiscent of a bronze by Jacopo Sansovino (1486-1570).[111] Probably most of these models were based on plaster or terracotta replicas obtained from the studios of many different sculptors. However, the group depicting 'Venus' holding a flaming heart (C93), and models of 'Mercury' in winged helmet and sandals bearing the caduceus (C86) and of 'Diana' holding a long-bow standing beside her hound (C79), in common with Bow and Derby versions, stem from Meissen originals. Possibly some will eventually be traced back to bronzes of which a great number survive. This is especially likely in the case of the Chelsea model of 'Apollo' (C72) wearing a laurel chaplet and holding a lyre which resembles several bronze replicas made in the fifteenth, sixteenth and seventeenth centuries, though the precise source remains undetermined. One Chelsea group depicting 'Flora with two Cupids' (C80), stands sixteen inches tall and in the Sale Catalogue of 15th April, 1756, is described as "Lot 76. A most grand Lustre, richly chas'd and gilt, decorated with flowers, and a large group of Flora and Cupids in the middle". This was undoubtedly intended as a centrepiece for the dining-table. Perhaps the largest of all red anchor groups is that of 'Una and the Lion' (C91) standing twenty-six inches tall. Possibly, this figure may have been adapted by the repairer to serve as Britannia mentioned in the Sale Catalogue of 1756 which seems to have been lost. 'Mars' (C85) is attired in the armour of a Roman centurion and stands bare-headed with a cloak draped about his neck. It has been suggested in Chapter II that he may have been adapted from Kändler's model of Julius Caesar. He is quite unlike the gold anchor 'Mars' (D45) which is almost identical with one issued over a number of years at Derby (J26), both derived from a Meissen original.[112] The Sale Catalogues of 1755 and 1756 list 'Juno' and 'Minerva' but no examples of either have yet come to light. A pair of reclining river deities (C89) probably follow Kändler's models based on Édme Bouchardon's marbles representing the Seine and the Marne on the Grenelle fountain.

The group depicting the 'Rape of the Sabines' (C88), like Kändler's 'Rape of Persephone',[113] stem from a bronze by Giovanni da Bologna,[114] an example of which is displayed in the Wallace Collection in London. The would be ravisher is shown staggering beneath the weight of a buxom wench who appears to be more amused than frightened by the action. Boucher's painting of 'Leda with an attendant Nymph and a Swan', now in the National Museum of Sweden in Stockholm, prompted a biscuit group by Falconet at the Sèvres factory.[115] Both the Meissen and the Chelsea (C84) versions are mirror images of the original and replace the nymph by a winged Cupid and substitute an absurdly amorous bird for the aggressive cob. Most repulsive is a group showing 'Cronus eating his Son' (C90), possibly intended to be an allegory of 'Time devouring the Hours', and said to have been based on a painting by Peter Paul Rubens. 'Perseus and Adromeda' (C87) depicts the damsel chained to a rock and menaced by a monster with her rescuer holding the head of Medusa with crested helm, sword and shield. 'Galatea' (C81) shows the goddess embracing a child triton seated upon rocks beneath which water flows. It is a somewhat free adaptation of a painting by Carlo Maratti now in the Hermitage in Leningrad,[116] probably taken from an engraving by J. Audran. The group of 'Two Children with a Fish' (C77) seems to have been adapted from the Vincennes 'Enfants tenant un Dauphin' by Felix de la Rue[117] by replacement of the dolphin with an extremely ugly fish. Often referred to as a 'rose-holder', it is in fact a taperstick though in most specimens the drip-pan has been lost.

111. *Italian Bronze Sculpture 1250-1700* (London, 1968) by F.M. Godfrey, fig. 158.

112. *Königlich, Sächsische Porzellan Manufaktur Meissen, 1710-1910* (Dresden, 1911) by Karl Berling, pl. 9.

113. *Festive Publication*..., op. cit., fig. 53, no. 1836.

114. *The Complete Encyclopaedia of Antiques* (London, 1962) by L.G.G. Ramsey, p. 1185, pl. 447A.

115. *French Porcelain of the 18th Century* (London, 1950) by W.B. Honey, pl. 70.

116. *Chelsea and Other English Porcelain, Pottery and Enamels in the Irwin Untermyer Collection*, op. cit., Vol. II, pp. 68 and 69, pl. 28, fig. 52.

117. 'The French Influence at Chelsea', op. cit., pp. 45-57, pl. 24C.

There is a set of three small groups, all free standing without bases, which were probably intended for use as table decorations. They include a 'Boy riding a Hippocampus' (C78) which Bernard Watney has shown was derived from a preliminary sketch made by François Giradon (1628-1715) for La Pyramide fountain at Versailles. Possibly a similar source inspired 'Leda kneeling beside a Dolphin' (C83) and a 'Boy astride a Seal' (C75). Models of 'Meleager with the Calydonian Boar's head', and 'Atalanta with her long-bow and hound' (C92) are mounted upon the bases of two rococo perfume vases which are in the British Museum. A set of small bustos of Pagan gods (C74) follow Meissen originals but are less artistically pleasing than similar Bow busts emblematic of the Four Seasons (H98).

Closely allied to the gods and goddesses of mythology are the sets of models representing the Five Senses, Four Seasons, Four Elements, Arts and Sciences and Four Quarters of the Globe. The Chelsea Senses (C94) are represented by dramatically-posed, seated adults in classical robes arranged in deep triangular folds in the grand manner of the baroque style. They are about twelve inches tall and over large to appeal to most private collectors. Smell is a man with a hound beside a perfume vase; Taste is a lady with a flat basket of fruit upon her knee; Feeling is a lady with a tortoise at her feet and a falcon in her lap; Hearing is a lady with a mandoline beside a deer; Sight is a man with an eagle. The Arts and Sciences (C95 and 96) are portrayed in lighter mood as nude draped putti, each seated upon a shaped plinth in mirror positions with globes upon one knee; a terrestial globe for 'Geography', a star-spangled globe for 'Astronomy' (Plate 37). These, together with models of standing putti emblematic of 'Astrology' with a canvas upon which are painted planetary symbols, and 'Painting' holding an appropriate picture follow Meissen prototypes. 'The Four Quarters of the Globe', or 'Four Continents' (C97) (for Australia had not then been discovered), are represented by two groups, each of two seated children facing one another, after originals by Friedrich Elias Meyer.[118] Africa, a blackamoor wearing an elephant head-dress, sits upon a lion facing Asia who is a Levantine girl in a stocking cap; America, a Red Indian, may in one version sit upon a seal[119] and in another on an alligator[120] facing Europe, who is a white girl with a sceptre and orb. 'The Four Seasons' at Chelsea, as at other porcelain factories, were presented in a number of different ways. Perhaps the best known are the 'Rustic Seasons' (Plate 38) (C98) composed of standing adults in peasant attire. Spring is a lady with a basket of flowers wearing a wide-brimmed hat secured by a scarf tied about her neck; Summer is another peasant woman dressed in a linen cap, dress and apron holding a corn-sheaf in both hands; Autumn is a young rustic with a vine of grapes; Winter is an old man in a fur-trimmed hat, large overcoat holding a basket of charcoal in his right hand and warming his left upon it. An early Longton Hall set of Seasons are exact copies (O6) whilst the Chelsea version of Spring was used at the Bow factory to represent 'Columbina' (H59). There is a different set of standing adult figures mounted upon the bases of rococo style candlesticks in the form of tree branches to which leaves are attached (C99). The Child Seasons (C100) consist of four pairs of children, each couple placed on either side of a candlestick upon a scrolled base. Both of the last two mentioned follow Meissen originals. A group of four putti (C101) standing beneath a tree upon a mound base was reissued later in a more elaborate form. Strangely, no Chelsea examples of the Four Elements appear to have been made until after 1759.

***Plate 37.** Putto seated with a celestial globe, emblematic of 'Astronomy' (C95). 4¾ins. (12.1cm). Chelsea c.1756. Similar models were made at Bow.* George Savage

118. Sotheby's sale catalogue, 9th July 1963, lot 165.

119. *Chelsea Porcelain, the Red Anchor Wares*, op. cit., pl. 69, figs. 136 and 137.

120. *Chelsea, Bow and Derby Porcelain Figures* (Newport, Wales, 1955), by Frank Stoner, pl. 21.

Religious subjects do not readily lend themselves to the medium of porcelain except, perhaps, when they receive the attention of a genius like Kändler. Clearly the representation of saints as images had less appeal in a Protestant

Plate 38. *'The Four Rustic Seasons' (C98). 5-5½ins. (12.7-14cm). Chelsea c.1756, red anchor mark.* Christie's

Plate 39. *'Nun standing with breviary and rosary' (C104). 7½ins. (19.1cm). Chelsea c.1755.* George Savage

country than in the Catholic lands of central Europe. Nevertheless, Willems came to England from Brussels and Tournai and had become familiar with the more tangible expressions of piety. His 'Pietà' (C102) depicts the Virgin Mary seated holding the dead body of Christ in sorrow whilst his hand is venerated by an angel. This was an adaptation of the marble by Nicolas Coustou now in the choir of Notre Dame in Paris.[121] The porcelain masterpiece was reissued after 1759. A second exceptionally fine religious group depicts the Virgin seated beside a terrestial globe upon which stands the Holy Child (C103). There are a number of minor variations of this devotional piece one of which is in the Cecil Higgins Museum, Bedford, another was once in the Lady Ludlow Collection. In the last mentioned the Christ Child holds a cross and the globe displays a circumferential band upon which appear the Roman numerals XII, I, II, III, IIII, V, and VI. There are, in addition, painted maps labelled Persia, India, and China, and the word 'March'. These features suggest that the whole group may have been derived from an ornamental clock. There is a fine model of an 'Abbess' (C104) recognisable by a ruff at the neck of her habit and inspired by a late seventeenth century woodcut entitled 'A noble Canoness of Cologne, St. Maria im Capitol'.[122] In one example of this model the underskirt exposed at one point where the habit is raised is painted with floral sprigs upon a brilliant canary ground.[123] This style of decoration is present in the woodcut and it should be recalled that ladies of fashion in many Catholic countries of those times ended their days in convents. There is no reason, therefore, to suppose that the porcelain model represents a lady in masquerade as a nun, such as Columbina from the Commedia dell'Arte. There remain a few standing monks and nuns (Plate 39) (C104) holding rosaries, missals or crucifixes and some delightful seated versions (C105) that are echoes of Meissen originals.

Models of freaks and dwarfs never enjoyed popularity in England. A Chelsea model was made of a 'Female Dwarf' (C106) after Calotto to serve as the partner of the 'Male Dwarf' in a tall hat (B56) that first appeared during the period of the raised anchor mark. Similar models made at Meissen and Mennecy have been mentioned earlier. The Sale Catalogue of 1756 mentions several times "a set of 5 musical figures representing monkies in different attitudes", and "a beautiful set of 5 monkies in different attitudes playing on music".[124] These may be identified as ten different monkey musicians (Colour Plate D, Frontispiece) (C109) copied from Kändler's 'Affenkapelle'.[125] They include the conductor in periwig and jacket holding a baton and a musical score in his upraised hands; a female musician with a hurdy-gurdy, four male musicians wearing tricorn hats and jackets one with pipe and tambour, one with a French horn, one bearing a drum upon his back and his partner holding two drum-sticks. Another male musician, who wears a wig but is hatless, plays a shawm and there is a group composed of an organist astride an unclad monkey on all fours with an organ mounted upon its back. The last mentioned is known with several minor variations and seems to have been based upon an engraving after Huet[126] which depicts a third figure inflating the fundament of the unclad animal with a pair of bellows whilst it also blows into an organ pipe. The same source also inspired the musician with pipe and tambour. In all known versions of the Monkey Band, the conductor is larger than the other figures. Other grotesques include a large model of 'Aesop' (C107), depicted as a hunch-back negro wearing the gold chain of a 'freeman'. This seems to have been based upon the frontispiece, drawn by Francis Barlow, of the 1687 edition of Aesop's Fables. A droll 'Fox dressed as a Poacher' (C108), in the Untermyer Collection, stems from the same work.

Towards the end of 1756, a number of family groups were issued and these

121. 'The Origins for English Ceramics of the 18th Century', op. cit., fig. 3, Chelsea pietà; fig. 4, marble by N. Coustou.

122. *Kurze und grundliche Historie van dem Aufang und Ursprung Gott-geweihten Orden aller Kloster Jungfrauen* (Augsburg, 1693) by Daniel Steudner, pl. XIV. See *Connoisseur*, Vol. 145, p. 250, fig. 20.

123. *Transactions,* English Ceramic Circle, 1933, Vol. 1, No. 1, pl. 1.

124. Chelsea Sale catalogues; third day on 12th April, 1756, lot 18; seventh day on 16th April, 1756, lot 51.

125. *Animals in Pottery and Porcelain* (London, 1966) by John P. Cushion, p. 21.

126. *Chelsea Porcelain at Williamsburg* (Williamsburg, Virginia, 1977) ed. John C. Austin, p. 136, 'L'organiste Ambulant'; p. 134, 'Le Tambourine'.

bridge the periods of red and gold anchor for the same group may appear bearing either mark. Bases show the new style with scrolls and arabesques picked out in gilt whilst many have short curved legs; inferior surfaces are now concave and glazed though they retain a flat circumferential rim which has been ground. These under surfaces also appear on contemporary Bow models though these, unlike Chelsea ones, may display particles of frit caught up in the glaze. The groups also show the bocages which were later to dominate gold anchor models. Some of the family groups relate to musical entertainments (C110 and C111), others to alfresco meals (C112) in which a husband, wife holding a baby, and a child are grouped about a table under a tree. Other variations include 'Fruit Gatherers' (C114) and a fish vendor's group (C113).

A second series of models also spans the red and gold anchor period, namely the 'Cupids in Disguise' (C115). These had been created at Meissen by Kändler and had probably been inspired by 'Les Enfants d'après Boucher'. The great majority reflect in humerous vein more serious representations employing adult figures. For example, models from the Italian Comedy were echoed by Cupid as Arlecchino, Dottore Baloardo, Pantalone and Columbina; the Cries of Paris are represented by 'Cupid as a Water-Carrier with a Hurdy-Gurdy', or as a 'Fishwife'. There are Cupids portraying 'Huntsman' and 'Lady Companion', as 'Shepherd' and 'Shepherdess'. A few are entirely new including 'Cupid as a Wounded Soldier'. The full range of Meissen prototypes is large but only a few were issued prior to 1757 from Chelsea. The 1755 Sales Catalogues mention seventeen lots relating to winged Cupids: "Six beautiful small figures of different sorts, representing Love in Disguise for Desart". Those of 1756 list a total of fifty-six including "Six beautiful Cupids, representing Love in Disguise playing on different sorts of music, for desart". Those issued before 1757, are usually four and a quarter to four and three quarter inches tall and are mounted upon mound bases decorated with asymmetrically arranged gilt scrolls but have no flowers applied to their superior surfaces whilst the inferior aspects are flat and devoid of glaze. Further, areas which represent flesh are left in the white and are touched with faint daubs of orange red over cheeks and lips. Most often if any tricorn hat is depicted it is coloured black. In general, the colour scheme is restrained and rather drab. Models are described in the Appendices (C115) and later versions (D1). Such is the appeal of these delightful porcelain images that few can suppress a smile of satisfaction when they first encounter them. It is scarcely remarkable, therefore, that when after a temporary closure, the Chelsea factory reopened in 1759, they continued to be reproduced and many new models added. Perhaps the most outstanding of them all is the 'Wounded Soldier' who is shown with wooden leg, one arm in a sling and a patch over one eye standing in a bullet torn tricorn hat. Dr. Karl Berking once wrote: "Kändler was quite in his element when creating those robust little Cupids in all imaginable impersonations, poses and costumes."[127]

Small models of animals, mentioned in the Sales Catalogues of 1755 and 1756 were most probably intended for the decoration of the dining table along with shepherds and shepherdesses, for on 30th March, 1956, lot 23, are advertised: "two ewes and two lambs of different sorts, two goats, a fox and two dogs for desart". Again we read included in lot 89 "two cows and two sheep". Many sets were available on several days of the sale. On 9th April, 1756, lot 6, "a cow and three calves, one suckling, the other two lying down..."; on 14th April, lot 91, "a fine Bantom Cock and Hen", etc., etc. Some of these may be readily recognisable though others do not appear to have survived. Illustrations of farmyard animals are rarely provided owing to pressure upon space for more important subjects whilst for similar reasons

127. 'Love in Disguise' by Lord Fisher of Kilverstone, *Apollo*, 1955, Vol. 61, No. 364, pp. 183-188.

many end up in reserve collections of museums and are unseen by the public. None are, perhaps, especially remarkable saving a fine lion (Plate 40) (C119) with one paw upon a sphere. Bow versions are also known and both are based on marbles at the foot of the steps leading up to the Loggia dei Lanzi, in Florence.[128] A squirrel eating a nut is shown in Plate 41 (C122). A selection of other animal models is listed (C116-C123) in Appendix C.

The popularity of models of birds seems sharply to have declined after 1753 when the last examples of the aviary based on illustrations by George Edwards in his *History of Uncommon Birds* appear to have been created. Most of the red anchor Chelsea birds are based upon Meissen prototypes and display a far greater animation than the raised anchor ones derived from George Edward's illustrations. Perhaps the most outstanding example is the 'Barn Owl' (C124),

128. *Transactions*, English Ceramic Circle, 1969, Vol. 7, pt. 2, pl. 130B.

Plate 40. *Standing Lion (C119), after a Florentine marble. 10ins. (25.4cm) long. Chelsea c.1753.* George Savage, late Dudley Delevingne Collection

Plate 41. *A Squirrel eating a nut (C122). 4½ins. (11.4cm). Chelsea c.1755.* George Savage

Plate 42. *A pair of pheasants (C135). 5½ins. and 4¾ins. (14 and 12.1cm). Chelsea c.1754.* Sotheby Parke Bernet

though the 'Peacock and Peahen' (C134), and a brace of 'Pheasants' (Plate 42) (C135) are also very fine. A few representative examples are given in Appendix C. Owing to the lack of any up to date catalogue and the inadequacy of black and white photographs as a basis for accurate attribution, it is not always possible to be sure that all of the models listed are of Chelsea origin.

Figures made between 1759 and 1769 (Gold Anchor)

The Paste and Glaze

Probably the Bow secret of improving the stability of the paste in the kiln by inclusion of bone-ash was known to Sprimont long before the Chelsea works reopened in 1759. Analysis reveals 45 per cent silica, 12 per cent alumina, 14.25 per cent phosphoric acid, no lead and only traces of potash and soda.[129] The product had a very white body, and owing to increased plasticity, sharper definition of modelling detail became possible. Tearing of the paste and fire-cracks were reduced and more ambitious poses with projecting limbs became feasable together with the adoption of a larger scale. Transillumination of flat wares of this period shows that the moons and tears had been entirely eliminated by more thorough mixing of the ingredients. The glaze became thin and transparent, though displaying a faint straw colour; crazing became commonplace, however, owing to the unequal coefficients of expansion between paste and glaze.

The Bases

Some models issued between 1759 and 1761 retain the former style of a mound base adorned with applied leaves and flowers. A few others, which are oval or rectangular, were painted to simulate marble. Increasingly, however, bases assume more complex forms with short curved legs between which are dependant 'U' scrolls and embossed 'C' and 'S' arabesques picked out in lavish gilding. However, though some are quite elaborate the Chelsea bases never became as flamboyant as those on which contemporary Bow models were mounted. The under surfaces were glazed, concave, but with a wide circumferential rim ground free of glaze which feels greasy to the touch. Ventilation holes are generally small and cylindrical in section.

Enamel Colours and Decorative Style

The study of ground colours on wares of Vincennes and Sèvres led to the development of "New Colours which have been found this year by Mr. Sprimont, the Proprietor, at very large Expence, incredible Labour, and close Application, all highly finished, and heightened with Gold peculiar to that fine and distinguish'd Manufactory".[130] Colours included 'Mazarine blue', an under glaze purplish-blue emulating the *gros bleu* of Vincennes and first mentioned in the Sale Catalogue of 1756, and 'Claret' (or crimson) which was a rose-pink in imitation of the beautiful enamel known as *rose Pompadour.* This was unrivalled in England though the Longton Hall pink is very fine. Another new colour was 'Pea-Green' about which there is some dispute. Some hold it to be turquoise (possibly Peacock green) simulating the Sèvres *bleu céleste,* others believe it was copied from the more banal *vert farcé.* The first suggestion would seem unlikely since turquoise was used on the coat of a figure in the Maypole group issued c.1753 whilst pea green was advertised as an innovation.

Enamels were applied thickly in association with honey-gold and, until c.1760, models retain something of their earlier simplicity and charm, as may be exemplified by the Ranelagh dancers (D22). Later, more flamboyant decoration became usual. Areas representing flesh were painted in a uniform

129. 'Ceramic Construction' by A Hurst, *Transactions,* English Ceramic Circle, 1937, No. 4, pp. 22-42.

130. *Contributions towards the History of Early English Porcelain,* op. cit., p. xix.

buff, heightened with pink on lips and cheeks. Eyes and hair continued to be represented in the earlier style, but almost every available area of garments was smothered with enamel and gilt. Ground colours were broken up by trefoil- and quatrefoil-shaped reserves filled with florettes, lines, and dots arranged in patterns intended to simulate brocade. The restraint previously exercised in the matter of gilding was now abandoned altogether, and gold was scattered over the clothing of figures and their bases in a way that greatly reduced the artistic impact of the model.

The Marks

A number of figures are unmarked. Many others bear a small gilt anchor which is placed, most often, on the back of the model or its base, though occasionally it may be partially concealed in folds of drapery. It is never found upon the under surface of the base. The gold anchor is placed centrally within the area enclosed by the foot rim on useful wares. Occasionally, the anchor may be drawn in brown or red enamel. When this is done, the device is less carefully painted than true red anchor marks and may be devoid of either ring or cross piece, or both, whilst the shank may penetrate the crown at the base which has a pointed instead of a rounded form.[131] Some miniature figures, toys, and Cupids in disguise, may have two anchors, either red or brown or gold, sometimes combining one painted in enamel with another of gold. Some useful wares, especially those with *chinoiserie* decoration, may bear an anchor in underglaze blue. Incised or enamelled letters, 'A', 'T', 'G' and 'R' may also be found which are probably the marks of repairers.

The Modelling

Until now the size of models had been limited by inadequacies of the paste and, though some quite large figures were made, the average size was five to seven inches. Inclusion of bone-ash in the mix made it possible to adopt a larger scale and 'Una and the Lion' (D39), probably issued in 1756, was twenty-seven inches tall. Many feel the smaller size most appropriate for the medium. Joseph Willems continued as chief modeller until 1766 when he left for Tournai where he died the same year. Examination of his more ambitious work, such as 'Apollo and the nine Muses' (D35 and 36), justifies the supposition that he was a frustrated baroque sculptor who loved the 'Grand Manner'. Characteristics of his modelling style have been described. Models created by another unnamed artist appear at Chelsea from about 1759. These display long torsos and short limbs suggesting their modeller was a pupil of Willems but they differ from the master's style on account of small heads, arched eyebrows, rose-bud mouths, long swan-necks and doe-like eyes. The figure of Mars (Plate 46) (D45) serves as an example.

During the period 1759-61, several models, such as the 'Ranelagh Masqueraders' (D22-D32), 'Charity' (D49) and some shepherds and shepherdesses (D80) were issued on mound bases with fairly simple enamel decoration and were without bocages. Later, the bocage grew first to waist height and finally came to envelop the model above and on both sides. Such is evident both in the group known as 'The Dancing Lesson' and 'The Music Lesson' (D63 and D72). These, however, retain the fine modelling of the figures from the hand of Joseph Willems. Others, like the paired groups of 'Huntsman and Lady' (D69 and D70) in the Untermyer Collection, display puppet-like figures amidst huge bocages flanked by candle sconces where the identity of subject matter has been subordinated to become unrecognisable in the riot of enamel, gold, bocage and elaborate forms of their bases. The Chelsea bocages are composed of flat, relatively thick leaves with serrated edges of more than one size and include flowers of different forms.

131. *Chelsea Porcelain, the Gold Anchor Wares,* op. cit., pp. 63-64.

During the last phase between 1765 and 1770, many old models were reissued in debased forms and often two would be married upon a single base where they sit or stand with vacant stare, frozen in the act of a meaningless gesture. Although human subjects were portrayed with scant respect for detail, there were several fine models of animals relating mostly to Fable subjects made as chamber candlesticks (D89-D102) which are most attractive. In these the bocage serves as a foil to display the stories from Aesop or La Fontaine in an amusing and altogether delightful manner.

The Models

Mention has already been made in the preceding section of 'Cupids in Disguise' made during the closing years of the red anchor period. Many of the old models were reissued together with several new ones, all of which were based on Kändler's prototypes. The gold anchor examples are slightly larger than the earlier Chelsea ones and stand about four and three quarter to five and a quarter inches tall upon bases adorned both with asymmetrically arranged scrolls as well as moulded and applied leaves and flowers. Their colouring is generally brighter and includes the new rose pink; tricorn hats, which hitherto had invariably been covered with black enamel, were now coloured pink, green, yellow or blue. In addition, areas representing flesh which formerly had been left in the white and touched only with a faint

Plate 43. *'The Night Watchman', from the Cries of Paris (D18). 5¾ins. (14.6cm). Chelsea c.1760.*
Victoria and Albert Museum

orange-red over lips and cheeks, were now covered with a pinkish buff enamel. Further, the inferior surface of bases display a domed and glazed central area with a flat ground circumferential rim which was normal practice after 1757. A selection of different models is provided in the appendices (D1). Here, it is only possible to single out a few for special mention, such as 'Cupid in a brimmed hat with a money-bag' (money changer) and 'Cupid as a Drummer'[132] both of which were copied from Cupids mounted upon the sides of a Meissen vase,[133] and 'Cupid as a wounded Soldier' which is sometimes wrongly called a 'Beggar' of which a white Meissen example was exhibited by Robert Williams.[134] Strangely enough, the Chelsea Sales Catalogues of 1761, make no direct reference to 'Cupids', but there are frequent descriptions of items such as "six small figures of different characters for Desart". Part of the charm of these delightful little fellows is due to the sense of *déjà vue* that they engender by recreating in a humerous manner such topics as the Commedia dell'Arte, the Idyllic Pastoral, the Small Artisans, or the Cries of Paris which had been previously portrayed in more serious models.

Cupids were also modelled individually and in groups for ornamentation of porcelain clocks (D5). Cupids without wings, or more properly 'putti', were also made (D2), with a bunch of grapes simulating Bacchus; carrying two flaming hearts; with a wreath of flowers; or standing with hands clasped.

'Family Groups',, also mentioned in the previous section, were reissued and new versions added. Most consist of three of four figures mounted on a legged base picked out with gilded scrolls either beneath a leafing tree or before a bocage. A representative selection is provided in the Appendices (D7-D16).

'The Night Watchman', an addition to the Cries of Paris series, was issued c.1760 (Plate 43) (D18).

The 'Monkey Band' was reissued in the more garish colouring and gilding of the gold anchor period (Colour Plate D, Frontispiece) and there also appears a 'Dog Orchestra' (D21) which includes a conductor, female vocalist, and three instrumentalists respectively with French horn, pipes of Pan and a violin. Other grotesques are 'David Gaborisco' (D19) a dwarf in Cossack uniform brandishing a sword with a severed head at his feet, and his companion 'John Coan' (D20) in Beefeater's costume with a large hound. Letters upon cards comprising the name John Coan are scattered over the base with one held in the mouth of the dog. The story of this pathetic freak is told by E.J. Wood.[135]

The masked ball in Ranelagh Gardens, Vauxhall, given on 24th May, 1759, to celebrate the birthday of George Frederick, Prince of Wales, prompted a series of some fourteen different models known as the 'Ranelagh Masqueraders' (D22-D32). They wear fancy dress costumes similar to those worn by figures in a print depicting the event by Bowles after Maurier[136] though clearly some other source was tapped. They stand seven and three quarters to eight and a half inches tall upon mound bases adorned with gilt scrolls and applied leaves and flowers and retain much of the charm and simplicity of decoration more usually associated with the period of the red anchor. Eleven models are in the Colonial Williamsburg Foundation collection[137] whilst others are illustrated by Dr. Severne Mackenna[138] and Arthur Lane.[139] These, which include three pairs namely 'Jack O'Green and Lady', 'Soldier and Vivandière', 'Fiddler and Lady with hurdy-gurdy' are described in Appendix D. Larger models, eleven and a half to twelve inches, on more elaborate bases are sometimes called the 'Vauxhall Revellers' (D33) which include a man in Turkish costume and a lady in Levantine dress holding a flower. The 'Vauxhall Singers' (D34) consist of the figure of an actor in plumed hat and cloak holding a mask in his left hand and companion Turkish lady in a stocking cap and fur edged cloak wearing a mask.

132. *Apollo,* 1955, Vol. 61, No. 364, p. 183, figs. 1 and 4.

133. ibid., p. 186, colour plate.

134. From the catalogue by Winifred Williams of the exhibition of White 18th Century European Porcelain held 10th — 27th June, 1975, at 3 Bury Street, St. James's, London.

135. *Giants and Dwarfs* (London, 1868) by E.J. Wood. "John Coan was born at Twitshill, Norfolk, in 1728. When aged one year he was of average size but, in 1744, when he was sixteen he measured only 36 inches, and at 22 he was 38 inches and weighted 34 pounds. He was many times presented to royalty and was exhibited at Bartholomew Fair with Edward Bamford the giant of Shire Lane, with whom he is portrayed in an engraving by Roberts in 1771. He played the role of 'Fine Gentleman' in Lethe at Tunbridge Wells and amused visitors by recitation of prologues and speeches from other plays. In 1762, aged 34, he began to display evidence of infirmity more usual in advanced life. For the last two years of his life he was employed at the Dwarf Tavern, in Five Fields, Chelsea, to entertain customers by Pinchbeck. He died on 28th March, 1764, aged 36."

137. *Chelsea Porcelain at Williamsburg,* op. cit., col. pl. and pls. 130-139.

138. *Chelsea Porcelain, the Gold Anchor Wares,* op. cit., pl. 54, figs. 104 and 105; pl. 55, figs. 106 and 107.

139. *English Porcelain Figures of the 18th Century* (Lane), op. cit., p. 25.

Allegorical subjects are well represented both by reissue of earlier models and by new ones. Two stiffly posed nude women who stand upon a flower encrusted base are, somewhat oddly, known as 'Modesty and Liberality' (D50). These were inspired by engravings made by Sir Robert Strange of sculpture by Guido Reni. They are artistically unsuccessful for their modeller failed to make any concessions necessitated by the smaller scale of the medium. Models of 'Venus holding a flaming heart' (C93) and 'Leda and the Swan' (C84), were reissued in the newer style on scrolled bases before bocages topped by candle holders (D37 and D38) (Plate 44). 'Mars' (Plate 45) (D45) which follows a Meissen prototype and stands in a helmet before a shield with right arm akimbo[140] closely resembling a dry-edge Derby version (J26) taken from the same source. He may be mounted beside a candlestick when his companion is either 'Minerva' or 'Venus with a Cupid' (D45) (Plate 45). Two rare models in Lord Bearsted's collection at Upton House, relate to two of the twelve labours of Hercules. One of these, 'Hercules and Omphale' (D40) shows Hercules seated with the distaff whilst Omphale stands holding his club attended by a Cupid; the other 'Slaying the Hydra' (D41) portrays Hercules weilding a bronze axe at the multiheaded hydra whilst Iolaus stands holding a flaming brand with which to seal the severed necks. Both are on scrolled bases before tree-like bocages, the last mentioned containing the golden apples of the 'Hesperides. 'Perseus and Andromeda' (D53), in the British Museum,

140. *Königlich, Sächsicshe Porzellan Manufaktur Meissen, 1710-1910,* op. cit., pl. 9, fig. 4.

Plate 44. *'Leda and the Swan' with an attendant cupid (D38). 10¼ins. (26cm). Chelsea c.1762, gold anchor mark.*
Sotheby Parke Bernet

Plate 45. *'Venus' with Cupid, and companion 'Mars' (D45). 7½ins. (19.1cm). Chelsea c.1765, gold anchor mark.*
Grosvenor Antiques

follows the design of the earlier red anchor version (C87) but is more detailed. The monster in the piece, according to Bellamy Gardner[141] was taken from an illustration in Topsell's *Historie of Four Footed Beasts and Serpents,* published in 1608. 'Juno and the Peacock' (D43), is perhaps more familiar in the Derby version. 'Neptune holding a paddle' (D52) and 'Jupiter seated in his Chariot' (D42) were once in the Bellamy Gardner Collection. There are also two groups, both portraying 'Mercury in winged helmet addressing Venus' (D44). However, 'Pryamus and Thisbe' and the 'Death of Adonis', mentioned in the Chelsea Sale Catalogue of 1761, have not as yet been identified.

The set of Apollo and the Nine Muses (D35 and D36) are amongst the most impressive of all Chelsea models. They are portrayed in the grand baroque manner so much favoured by their creator, Joseph Willems. They stand overall fifteen and three quarter inches tall on detachable stands shaped like little bombé commodes. The complete set may be seen in Upton House, Warwickshire. A fine 'Roman Charity' (D48), described in 1770 as "a Group available either on a pea-green or mazarine blue detachable plinth, sumptuously gilded", was taken from an engraving made in 1624-30 by William Panneel of the painting by Rubens now in the Prado, Madrid. The group illustrates the legend of how Pero saved Cimon, her aged father, condemned to die in prison from slow starvation by giving him her own breast milk. The dramatic impact of the painting is severely impaired by the florid decoration upon the porcelain group which was made to comply with the prevailing rococo taste. Another smaller group, known as 'Charity' (Colour Plate C) (D49), depicts a seated woman who breast feeds an infant with two children, one seated and one standing on either side of her; this is also known in a Bow version.

The Four Seasons are represented by several different sets and groups. In one version, Spring is a lady with a basket of flowers paired with Winter who is

141. 'Animals in Porcelain' by Bellamy Gardner, *Transactions,* English Ceramic Circle, 1934, No. 2, pp. 17-21, pl. VIIIa, 'Hercules slaying the Hydra'.

Plate 46. *The Four Elements (D61). 8½ins. (21.6cm). Chelsea c.1760, gold anchor mark. See Colour Plate E for Bow versions of 'Earth' and 'Water'.*
Grosvenor Antiques

a man in hat, coat, and muff; the companion group shows Summer as a lady with a corn sheaf who stands beside Autumn who is a youth with a basket of grapes (D54). The 'Allegorical Seasons' (D57) also has two groups with Winter as a man in stocking cap and fur-lined boots skating beside a girl with blossoms in her apron emblematic of Spring; Summer is a girl with corn whose right hand rests upon the shoulder of a gardener with fruit in his apron who represents Autumn. A 'Group of Four Putti' with appropriate accessories, stand on a single mound base beneath a tree (D58), as well as four pairs of putti on scrolled bases beside rococo candlesticks (D59) which were also issued as Seasons. The 'Four Quarters of the Globe' (D60) echo models of standing children by Meyer. Africa, a blackamoor in an elephant head-dress, steps over a lion and holds a cornucopia; Asia, a Levantine girl with a perfume vase, stands beside a crouching camel; Europe, a girl wearing a crown, holds an orb and sceptre (and looks rather like Queen Victoria); America is a Red Indian in skirt and feathered head-dress holding a long-bow. The 'Five Senses' (D62) are debased versions of earlier red anchor models (C94) set before bocages. The 'Four Elements' (Plate 46) (D61) were copied from models by Friedrich Eberlein and include Fire as an effeminate youth, possibly Vulcan, standing beside a flaming urn on a plinth; Water as Neptune pouring water from a bucket with a dolphin; Earth as Persephone with cornucopia and a lion; Air as a lady, possibly Juno, her veil and raiment blown by the wind, standing beside an eagle. A similar set was made at Bow.

The rising influence of Sèvres that followed the sack of the Meissen factory in 1756, was reflected in England by a series of models and groups relating to the idyllic pastoral theme based on engravings after Boucher and Lancret but

Plate 47. *'Shepherd playing a recorder' and companion 'Shepherdess with flowers' (D80). 8¼ins. and 8ins. (21cm and 20.3cm). Chelsea c.1765, gold anchor mark.*

Plate 48. *Shepherd playing a recorder standing cross-legged beside his dog (C57). 7¾ins. (19.7cm). Chelsea c.1760, marked with a carelessly drawn red anchor.*

Author's collection

mostly copied from Meissen prototypes. There are models of a 'Shepherd playing a recorder standing beside his dog' and companion 'Shepherdess with flowers in her apron holding a posy standing beside a lamb' (Plate 47) (D80) that were first issued without bocages in the red anchor period (C57) (Plate 48) and which echo Kändler originals. Likewise, the 'Shepherd bagpiper', and 'Shepherdess with a lamb' (D77) were restyled earlier copies of Meissen prototypes. The 'Shepherd in cockaded hat', taking bread from a scrip to feed a hound is dressed in the height of fashion, with beribboned cloak, and knickerbockers gathered with garters below the knees, whilst his 'Shepherdess' more closely resembles an elegant lady of the court than a rustic (Plate 165, Chapter XIII) (D75). They too follow Kändler originals of c.1750.[142] The 'French Shepherds' (D78) show the man with a lamb beneath one arm and a basket of flowers at his side and his companion holds a similar basket and a posy in either hand. Grandest of all are the 'Imperial Shepherds' (Plate 49) (D79). The bucolic scene includes also models of reapers and their wives (D73 and D74), sportsmen and ladies (D69-D71), gardeners and their companions (D67 and D68) as well as the more sophisticated gallants and their inamorata (D64-D66). Some examples are paired upon single bases which are elevated upon short curved legs decorated with scrolls picked out in gold, and have huge bocages either topped by or flanked with candleholders (D70 and D71). Within such settings one may be excused for failing to recognise the subject or to be able to distinguish between gallants, shepherds and musicians or tell the

142. *Festive Publication...*, op. cit., table 13, nos. 5 and 7.

Plate 49. *'The Imperial Shepherds' (D79). 10¼ins. (26cm). Chelsea c.1765, gold anchor mark.*
Grosvenor Antiques

difference between a peasant woman and a fine lady. 'The Music Lesson' (Plate 50a) (D72), adapted from the biscuit group by Falconet (Plate 50b) after Boucher, bears little resemblance to the French original and the eye is distracted by the riot of enamel colour, gold, sculptured base and massive bocage. A similar group called 'The Dancing Lesson' (D63) was inspired by Carle van Loo's engraving after Boucher and is almost a pair to the 'Music Lesson'. The Arcadian setting is the same but the figures are different and the rustic swain plays a hurdy-gurdy whilst his companion holds a dog dressed in a jacket upon its hind legs on a plinth. The same subject was translated into porcelain at Derby in a smaller and greatly simplified version (K48). Other less ambitious Chelsea models portray a 'Gallant holding a birdcage' and companion 'Lady with a dog' (D66).

Porcelain models of foreigners seem to have passed out of fashion. There are, however, figures of a Chinaman and a Chinese lady each of which is seated beside a vase (D81), a 'Coolie with a basket' (D82) and a pair of 'Chinese Musicians' posed in gazebos topped with cupolas and flanked with candleholders (D83). A pair of kneeling 'Blackamoors' with hands elevated to support candle sconces (D84), recall red anchor models of the Indian Prince and his Queen (C66).

Musicians are amongst the most attractive of all Chelsea figures and most follow Meissen originals. Examples of copies are provided by a pair of French horn players (D85) consisting of a seated negro and companion white man playing instruments. There is a seated gentleman 'cellist (D86), and a pair of seated figures, one a 'Rustic with a flute', the other a 'Lady with a lute' (D87) which are mounted within trellissed arbours. A standing man with a drum attached to his left sleeve which he beats with a drum-stick, whilst at the same time playing a three holed pipe (D88) is common to Bow where he is paired with a lady playing a triangle (H45) though at Chelsea it would seem only the male was modelled.

Plate 50a *(below left). 'The Music Lesson' (D72), after Etienne Maurice Falconet's 'La Leçon agréable' (see plate 50b). 15ins. (38.1cm). Chelsea c.1763, gold anchor mark.*
Sotheby Parke Bernet

Plate 50b *(below right). 'La Leçon agréable', a Sèvres biscuit group by Etienne Maurice Falconet c.1752, based on Boucher's painting of 1748.*
Sotheby Parke Bernet

A magnificent group portraying 'George III, Queen Charlotte and a Page' (D113) is in the Irwin Untermyer Collection. The king stands in coat, long waistcoat, knee-breeches, and buckled shoes, his hat under his left arm, beside his consort who is elegantly dressed in a corsage trimmed with roses, jewellery, and a crinoline; a page supports the monarch's cloak. The group has affinities with the engraving by James MacArdell after portraits by Johann Zoffany, possibly painted to commemorate the royal wedding of 1761. The Derby set of three groups (L7) of the Royal Family seem to have been made about a decade later. A rather ugly 'Fortune telling group' (D114), listed in the Sale Catalogue of 1761 where it was described as "a Fine groupe of a gypsy telling a lady's fortune under a tree, upon a rich gilt ornament foot", included a babe upon the back of the crone and her standing child. It was based upon 'La Diseuse Daventure', by Antoine Watteau. The painting was engraved by Laurent Cars but it is more likely that the Chelsea factory copied one by Robert Hancock. A late Bow version was probably copied from the Chelsea group (I13).

Some extremely attractive groups relating to *Aesop's Fables,* mounted on scrolled bases before bocages, were issued as chamber candlesticks. These seem to have been loosely based upon the engravings of Francis Barlow which illustrated the 1666 edition, published in London, though some may have been inspired by plates after Barlowe in the 1687 version, which contained rhymes by Mrs. A. Behn, some of which are cited below. 'The Goat in the well looking up at the Fox' (D89) illustrates Fable LX, whilst the 'Fox in the well looking up at the Wolf' (D90) illustrates Fable VIII. The first victim was admonished for the stupidity of falling in, whilst the second was asked how he came to be there, and neither obtained the help he sought. The 'Dog in the manger barking at a brown and white Ox' (D91) portrays Fable XXIX which reads:

"An Envious Dog in a full manger lay,
Nor eats himselfe, nor to the Ox gives way,
Who griev'd reply'd — ah grudge not me that meat,
Which (cruell) thou thy selfe disdainst to eate.
Morall
Thus aged Lovers with young Beautys live,
Keepe off those joys they want the power to give."

The pair 'Ass laden with game birds and other provender eating thistles and regarded by a starving dog' (D92), illustrates Fable VI which has the following verse:

"A sordid Ass, while on his back he bore,
Of chosen delicates, a plenteous store;
His courser Appetite with Thistles treats,
And starves beneath his load of nobler meats.
Morall
Profuseness is a farr less dangerous vice
Than the Ill natur'd damning Avarice."

The model of 'Two Foxes beneath a fruiting vine' (D98) depicting Fable XCIII concerning the sour grapes, requires no further explanation. Less familiar is Fable XX echoed by a group of a 'Fox attacked by a hound and a Cat up a tree' (D97).

"The Fox pretends a thousand shifts t'ave found,
To save him from the hard persuing Hound,
The Catt but one, who climes the Tree amaine,
Anon the dogs persue, and Renards slaine
Morall
One Action where discretion is its guide,
Transcends all the results of noys and pride."

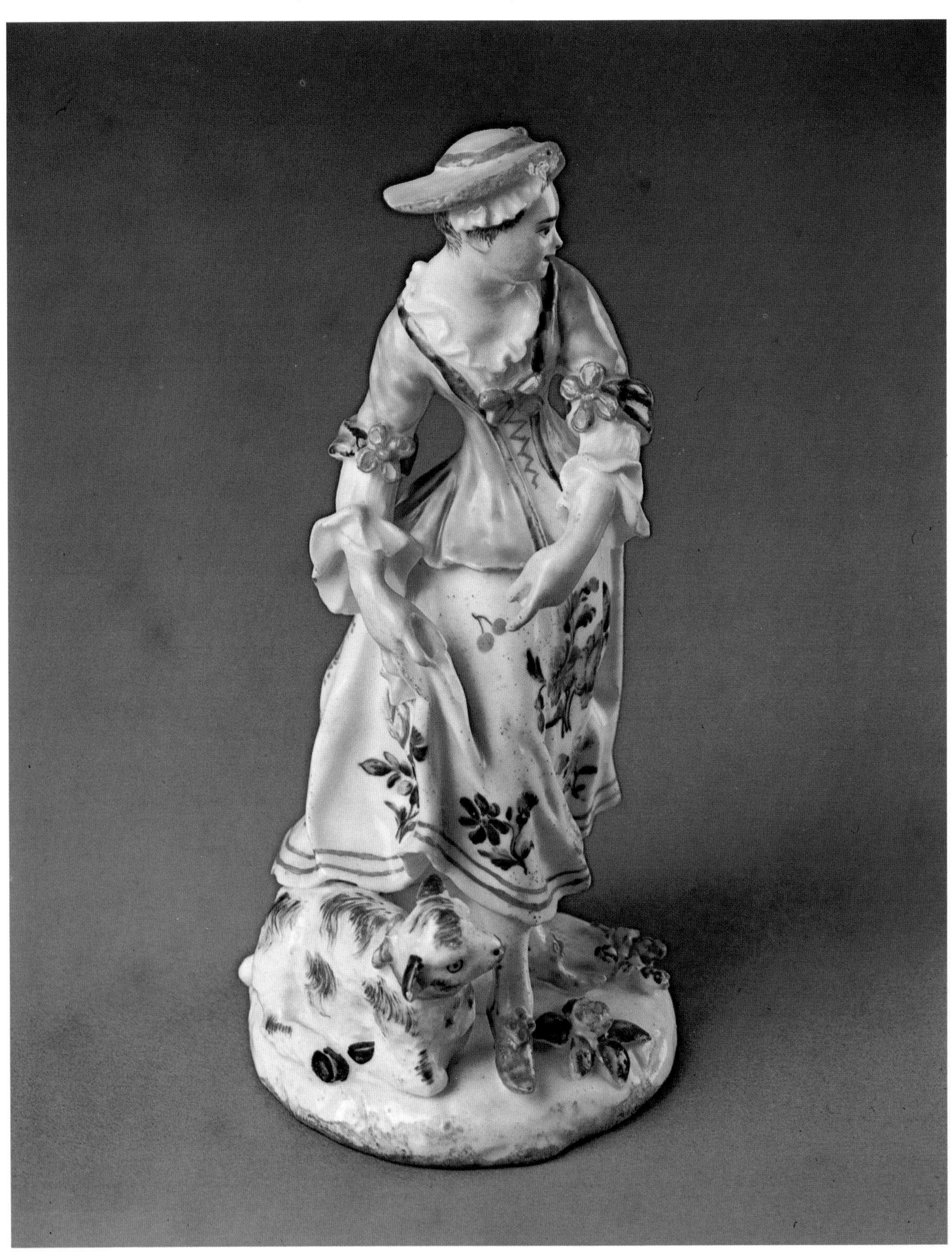

Colour Plate I. *'The dancing Shepherdess' (J13). 6½ins. (16.5cm). Dry-edge Derby. The brilliantly enamelled floral sprays, which include the device of a double cherry, are in a style attributed to the studio of James Giles.*
Norman C. Ashton collection

Other Fable groups are listed in Appendix D. There are also some fine animal groups in the genre of fable but possibly stemming from some other source, including the fine pair of candlesticks incorporating a 'Leopard assailed by dogs' (D103), 'A Stag attacked by hounds' (D108), 'Fox with Game' and companion 'Dog with Game' (D104). John Mallet who has identified the source of many of the engravings and rhymes of Fable Groups in Lord Bearsted's Collection,[143] considers that two animal groups 'Tiger and Fox' (D102), in which the tiger attempts to remove an arrow head from its flank, and the 'Leopard and the Fox' (D101) may relate to Fables XXXI and LVIII respectively which are as follows:

"The Tyger boasts to guard the Beasts from harme,
Since his tough hide so well his vitals arme,
Which the young hunter heareing sent a dart,
That pierc'd the fancy'd victor to the heart.
Morall
So the young Hero on his strength relying,
Rendered him more remark's and worthyer dying."

And

"The Leopard, for the Splender of his hide,
Boasts himself Lord of Beasts, the Fox replyd
Tho thou the fairest art of all beast kind,
Other excell in beauties of the mind.
Morall
Not the gay spark that in guilt Coach does roule
Can forme the Hero, but the nobler soule."

Mr. Mallet also considers that two other groups, 'The Cock with a Jewel' (D94) and the 'Vain Jackdaw' (D93) may more properly be ascribed to the Chelsea-Derby period on the grounds of their paste and the brilliant overglaze blue used in the plumage. These are also in the Lord Bearsted's Collection and in the Untermyer Collection. It is notable that the 'Jay' of the fable has become a 'Jackdaw' in the porcelain group. Yvonne Hackenbroch,[144] cites the explanatory rhymes included in the 1666 edition viz:

"A graine of Barley and a gem did dwell
Ith' caskett of a dunghill as their cell,
Till the rude clawes of keene hungry Cock
Did that dull cabinett of Dirt unlock,
And having rak't them forth w'ith cheape disdaine
Waves y'e bright gem, to taste y'e coarser graine."

The rhymes in the 1687 edition pertaining to Fable I and Fable XLVII are quoted by Mr. Mallet in the catalogue of the Bearsted's Collection. The second rhyme concerning the Jackdaw (1666 version), reads:

"With gaudy feathers the Ambitious Jay
Purloin'd from Peacocks did herself array,
And y'e other Jays with coy neglect disdaines,
Her selfe ('mongst Peacocks mix't) a Peacock fayns.
But they her borrow'd pride does soon detect
And her disrob'd of her faire plumes reject.
When being confin'd againe to live with Jays
Her triviall pride each with just scoffs repay."

The fable of *Le Corbeau et le Renard,* made famous by La Fontaine, prompted the porcelain group of a 'Crow with cheese in its mouth and a Fox' (D100). The tale is told of how the Fox first flattered the Crow upon the beauty of its plumage and then intimated that it probably also sang divinely. When the unsuspecting bird opened its mouth to warble, the fox seized the

143. Catalogue of porcelain in Lord Bearsted's Collection, p. 13.
144. Untermyer, pls. 46 and 47, fig. 76.

cheese that fell from its beak and ran away.

Other animal and bird candlestick groups were also manufactured at this period and a pair of rabbit candlesticks are illustrated in Plate 51.

The Chelsea Miniature Figures

Miniature figures of between seven eighths of an inch up to three inches tall, averaging two and a half inches, were made at Chelsea from approximately 1754 onwards though the first to be advertised may have originated at the Girl-in-a-Swing factory. They were slip cast. Those marked with a red anchor include a 'Gardener pushing a Wheel-barrow', 'Lady in picture hat riding a galloping Horse', 'Girl with a Dove seated beside a Dalmation'; a double red anchor may be found on models of a 'Gallant with hat under his arm', a 'Gardener pushing a Roller', 'Huntsman with gun at the Ready', a 'Highlander', and a 'Poet with a book'. Unmarked models include 'Pierrot' and a 'Monkey seated upon a green mound'.

Etuis (needle-cases)

These are between three and a half and four and a half inches long and may be mounted in gilded base metals or gold. Some examples include a 'Partridge in a Wheat-sheaf', the upper half of a 'Lady holding a basket of Chestnuts', 'Three Nude Children around a Column', 'Three Graces', 'A Nosegay', 'John Barleycorn', a 'Female Bust', the 'Infant Bacchus', and the head of a 'Masked Columbine'. There are also 'Cranes amidst Sea-Grass', 'Cupids', 'Doves', and others. Many bear French mottoes.

Plate 51. *Pair of rabbit candlesticks with large bocages (D106). 9¼ins. (24.8cm). Chelsea c.1765.* Sotheby Parke Bernet

Bonbonnières and Patch-boxes

These may also date to c.1755 though most are post-1759. They are usually oval with hinges and other fitments of gold. They are between two and a half and three and a half inches in diameter and their lids are often decorated with miniature figures such as a 'Lady with a Dog', 'Basket of Fruit', 'Shepherd and Shepherdess', 'Boy playing with two lambs', 'Boy with a Pig', 'Three Children at a Peep-Show', 'Venus and Cupid' and various animals such as 'Lion and Cock', a 'Camel', 'Birds with Fledglings' and 'Billing Doves'. There are also a number in the form of heads such as a 'Pirate', 'Pierrot', 'Ladies' some masked and others in bonnets. Some may be designed as cane handles.

Illustrations of these and other examples may be found in *Chelsea Toys* (1925), by G.E. Briant; *Chelsea and Other English Porcelain, Pottery & Enamel in the Irwin Untermyer Collection* (1957), by Yvonne Hackenbroch; and 'Chelsea Scent Bottles — Girl in a Swing and Another Group' by Kate Foster, *Transactions,* English Ceramic Circle, 1967, Vol. 6, pt. 3, pp. 284-291.

Scent Bottles

The vast majority of the Chelsea toys are scent bottles. They take a great number of different forms and examples are illustrated by Arthur Lane and R.J. Charleston,[145] Miss Yvonne Hackenbroch,[146] Miss Kate Foster,[147] G.E. Briant[148] and by Reginald Blunt.[149]

We are indebted to Miss Kate Foster for her observations which enable scent bottles made in England at this period to be divided into two groups. In the first group, the paste has a greenish cast and is covered by a glassy glaze both of which may be found in larger models made at the Girl-in-a-Swing factory. Enamel painting of these is minutely detailed and usually includes floral sprays centred on a yellow and pink cabbage rose which are found upon garments and both the upper and lower surfaces of the bases. Often, the flowers are accompanied by paired cherries. Human hair often has greyish streaks, tree-trunks are brown, and moulded leaves which have serrated edges are coloured a bluish-green. The majority of items are gold mounted and the evidence suggests that they were made by the jeweller, Charles Gouyn, at the Girl-in-a-Swing manufactory between 1749 and 1753. The Chelsea Sale of 1754 included a number of toys which probably represented the residual stock of the splinter Chelsea factory which had been acquired by Nicholas Sprimont. Miss Foster lists forty-three different models.

There are fifty items in the second group which are fashioned from a much white paste clad in a thinner glaze. Enamelled decoration is less skilfully composed and, instead of delicately painted floral sprigs, there are washes of plain colour especially of turquoise, puce, and yellow. In a few examples that have floral painting they take the form of single widely spaced roses most frequently of a pink colour. These appear upon the inferior surface of bases together with a wreath of leaves. Human hair is nearly always chestnut, leaves are a greenish-blue and, rather oddly, are attached to garments instead of to branches or tree-trunks. Mounts are of gilded base metal. This group has been ascribed to Chelsea. Examples are listed in Appendix F.

145. 'Girl in a Swing Porcelain and Chelsea', op. cit., pp. 111-144.

146. *Chelsea and other English Porcelain, Pottery and Enamel in the Irwin Untermyer Collection,* op. cit., pls. 61-73.

147. 'Chelsea Scent Bottles — Girl in a Swing and Another Group', op. cit., pp. 284-291.

148. *Chelsea Toys* (London, 1925) by G.E. Briant.

149. *The Cheyne Book of Chelsea China and Pottery,* op. cit.

Part Three — Girl-in-a-Swing figures, 1749-1753

In 1920, a pair of white glazed porcelain models of a 'Dancing Girl' (E3) and a 'Youth wearing a plumed hat' playing a hurdy-gurdy (Plate 53) (E2) were presented by Lt. Col. Kenneth Dingwall to the Victoria and Albert Museum.[150] Two years earlier the same donor had made a gift of another figure of a 'Girl seated on a swing' suspended between two tree-stump supports (Plate 52) (E1).[151] These three models, together with some others, were described and discussed by William King in 1922[152] who ascribed them to the first period of production of the Chelsea manufactory and were thought to have been made under the supposed proprietorship of Charles Gouyn. With the passage of time further examples have come to light which today amount to rather more than thirty models and groups. These were reviewed by Arthur Lane and R.J. Charleston[153] who presented evidence to justify their separation from other early Chelsea models. Since the name of this factory is unknown, it has come to be called the 'Girl-in-a-Swing' manufactory. The possiblity that it once existed on a site close to the present 'World's End Tavern', is suggested by an advertisement.[154]

Simeon Shaw,[155] not usually regarded as the most reliable of historians, wrote in 1829 "...Carlos Simpson, 63 years of age, [in] 1817, was born at Chelsea; to which place his father, Aaron Simpson, went in 1747, along with Thomas Lawton, slip maker, Samuel Parr, turner, Richard Meir, fireman, and John Astbury, painter, all of Hot Lane; Carlos Wedgwood, of the Stocks, a

150. Victoria and Albert Museum, nos. C.328-1919 and C689-1920.

151. ibid., no. C.587-1922.

152. *Chelsea Porcelain* (London, 1922) by William A. King.

153. 'Girl in a Swing Porcelain and Chelsea', op. cit., pp. 111-140.

154. Personal communication from George Savage in 1978.

155. *History of the Staffordshire Potteries* (Hanley, 1829), by Simeon Shaw.

***Plate 52.** The 'Girl in a Swing' (E1). 6ins. (15.2cm). Girl-in-a-Swing factory c.1750.*
Victoria and Albert Museum

good thrower; Thomas Ward, and several others, of Burslem, to work at the Chelsea China Manufactory. They soon ascertained that they were the principal workmen, on whose exertions the excellence of the Porcelain must depend, they then resolved to commence business on their own account at Chelsea, and were in some degree successful; but at length owing to disagreement amongst themselves, they abandoned it and returned to Burslem, intending to commence there the manufactory of China; but soon after their return Aaron Simpson died, the design was relinquished and each took the employment quickly offered in the manufacture of white stone ware..." Without corroboration this testimony would not bear scrutiny but, the register of St. Luke's Church, Chelsea. records the birth on 4th December, 1754, of "Careless [*sic*], son of Aaron Simpson and Elizabeth his wife".[156] Thus, there are reasons to suppose that in 1747 a gang of workmen who possessed all the skills necessary for the establishment of a porcelain factory arrived at Chelsea from the Staffordshire Potteries. Although there is no direct link between these men and Nicholas Sprimont, the time of their arrival coincides approximately with the first payment made by Sir Everard Fawkener to 'Premonte', dated 16th August, 1746.[157]

Mention has been made in the history of the Chelsea factory earlier in this chapter, of a series of advertisements and notices appearing between 3rd March, 1749, and 15th May, 1750, which indicate that Nicholas Sprimont was anxious to disassociate himself and his factory from some rival concern in the neighbourhood. It will be recalled that the final notice dated 15th of May, 1750, read: "...I am not concerned in any Shape whatsoever with the goods expos'd to Sale in St. James's Street, called the Chelsea China Warehouse. N. Sprimont." The wording gives the impression that the warehouse in question stocked porcelain that had been made at a factory other than the main Chelsea works. Moreover, on 29th January, 1751, there was a rejoinder "...My China Warehouse is not supplied by any other person than Mr. Charles Gouyn, late Proprietor and Chief Manager of the Chelsea House who continues to supply me with the most curious goods of that manufacture...S. Stables." These exchanges appeared in the *General Advertiser*.

Charles Gouyn was a jeweller who might very properly be associated with gold-mounted porcelain toys, which have been shown to exist in a paste similar to that of the larger Girl-in-a-Swing models. The corpus of evidence supports the view that Charles Gouyn was a financial sponsor and partner of Sprimont when he first established the Chelsea porcelain factory c.1745. Further, at some time after this, and preceding the date of the first advertisement in March, 1749, the two men parted. It seems likely that at this early phase of production, Sprimont would have lacked the funds required to reimburse Gouyn's investment and may have repaid the debt with porcelain stock which was later sold to the china-dealer, Stables. It would also seem likely that Gouyn set up a small porcelain works in the borough with the help of workmen who had defected from Sprimont and that the products of this establishment included etuis, scent-bottles, patch-boxes and seals as well as the larger Girl-in-a-Swing figures. This factory seems to have failed some time between 1752 and 1754, since Sprimont appears to have obtained the stock which he advertised for sale in November, 1754.

Girl-in-a-Swing Models c.1749-1753

The Paste and Glaze

Arthur Lane and R.J. Charleston[158] have given the results of both spectroscopic and chemical analysis of the paste. This includes silica 64 per cent, lead oxide 16 per cent, alumina 3 per cent, lime 11 per cent, and about 1

156. 'Chelsea, the Triangle Period' by Mrs. Donald Macalister, *Transactions*, English Ceramic Circle, 1935, Vol. 1, No. 3, p. 27.

157. 'Payments by Sir Everard Fawkener to Nicholas Sprimont', op. cit., pp. 54-58.

158. 'Girl in a Swing Porcelain and Chelsea', op. cit., pp. 136-137.

per cent of both soda and potash. The high lead content bespeaks the inclusion of cullet, and the poor stability of the paste in the kiln is evidenced by fire-cracks, sagging and sideways drooping of figures. Most of the models are relatively small in size. The body looks solid and dense, though it usually presents a greyish, or even a greenish, hue. A glassy glaze usually exhibits pin-hole defects and sanding; it is thin, closely fitting, and both more opaque and whiter than the raised anchor Chelsea glaze.

The Bases

Broadly, three distinct forms have been identified. The greater number consist of irregular shaped pads with flat upper surfaces which have bevelled, or chamfered, edges. Less often, single figures stand on plain rectangles. The third variety is complex and probably derived from a silver shape. These are hexagonal in plan, with long front and back sides of convex contour and two short concave surfaces upon either side. All facets are longer along their lower border than upon the surface of the base. Ventilation holes are often large, and the flat under surface has been wiped free from glaze to ensure level stance. Often, small semilunar incisions, like finger nail parings, are seen upon the upper surface.

Marks

No factory or workmen's marks are recorded.

Enamel Colours

About fifty of the seventy-five known specimens are in the white, and it seems unlikely therefore that any enameller was employed at the factory. At least two decorative styles have been identified amongst enamelled examples most probably the work of independent decorators. The most common decoration consists of floral sprigs with small leaves scatted over dresses and also seen on the bases. These nearly always include one large crimson rose with a thick curved stem whilst other flowers include tulip-like blooms with yellow highlights upon iron red petals. These, together with leaves and stems, are outlined in purple. A pale orange-red appears on faint daubs upon lips and cheeks but other fleshtints are omitted. Human hair is indicated by painted streaks of chocolate brown, deep yellow-brown, or black. Dresses are frequently edged with narrow borders of a rather bright light blue, or crimson. A similar style has been recognised on an English decorated Meissen 'Figure of Winter',[159] a raised anchor Chelsea bird,[160] and upon a 'Chinese Teapot'.[161] Arthur Lane and R.J. Charleston recognised a second rather similar form of decoration in which large flowers are outlined in black and smaller ones in purple. Here, the arrangement of blossoms is more sophisticated and they include both a crimson and a yellow rose. They consider that this style may be a more mature form of the first as the artist gained experience. An altogether different type of floral painting was attributed to James Giles. Bubbling and loss of lustre of the glaze of coloured examples suggests that they were enamelled at least six months after manufacture. The palette is generally brighter and includes an orange and a yellow-green, purple, crimson and yellow. A double purple line, or a pink border, is usually found at the hem of dresses and the design may include representation of a double cherry. Pale gilding may also be found. This style is described in greater detail in Chapter VIII, and may also be found on Derby, Chaffers' Liverpool, and Girl-in-a-Swing figures as well as upon English decorated Chinese and Worcester wares.

The Modelling

Most of the models are four and a half to six inches in height and droop sideways away from the perpendicular. The modeller took great care to avoid

159. Untermyer, pl. 132B. Museum of Fine Arts, Boston, no. 55.410.
160. ibid., pl. 132C.
161. A private collection.

postures requiring the projection of unsupported limbs. For example, the group 'Hercules and Omphale' (E13) was copied from a Vincennes original in which Hercules holds the distaff in his right hand.[162] In the English version, the distaff is omitted and the hand represented hanging meaninglessly upon his thigh, for there would have been little chance of reproducing the posture of the original. The heads of human subject are curiously flat topped and their faces are often triangular, terminating in pointed chins; eyes are deeply set, mouths firmly incised yet having a sensitive appearance, the upper lips are short and noses thin, straight and in line with the forehead in profile. Bernard Watney[163] has seen in them a resemblance to stucco figures in the Rotunda Chapel, Dublin, fashioned in 1755 by Bartholomew Cramillion. This date would be appropriately about a year after the supposed failure of the Girl-in-a-Swing factory, though tradition dictates that the artist came to Ireland direct from Italy, not England. Hands and feet of the porcelain figures are elegant, small and tapering whilst drapery is greatly simplified yet charmingly accented by carefully fashioned ribbons, bows or rosettes. Moulded leaves are large in scale with fine branching dorsal veins and serrated edges; they are flat and may be accompanied by rosette-like flowers which are totally unconvincing.

Models

The group known as the 'Rustic Lovers' (E12) has clearly been copied from a Chelsea original (A10) but is slightly smaller and far less accomplished. The 'Girl in a Swing' (Plate 52) (E1) herself, sits upon a seat suspended between two tree trunks to which leaves are attached. Apertures in the tree stumps indicate that either additional leaves or flowers are missing. The modelling is at once naïve and charming. A male 'Musician in plumed Hat' (E2) stands

162. *Seventeenth and Eighteenth Century French Porcelain,* op. cit., pl. 67A, Vincennes group. Also *English Porcelain Figures of the 18th Century* (Lane), op. cit., pl. 34, Girl-in-a-Swing group.

163. 'Decorations for English 18th Century Ceramics' by Bernard Watney, *Burlington Magazine,* Vol. 114, pp. 818-826.

***Plate 53.** 'Dancing Girl' (E3) and companion male 'Musician in a plumed Hat' (E2). 5¾ins. (14.6cm). Girl-in-a-Swing factory c.1751.*
Private Collection

upon a rectangular base holding a hurdy-gurdy and he is paired with a 'Dancing Girl' (Plate 53) (E3) who holds her skirt out in a fan with both hands. Artistically unsuccessful are two groups each depicting a lady seated upon a tree stump with a reclining gallant at her feet, which are in mirror image of one another; in one (E10) the pair fondle a lamb, in the other a dove (E11). The inspiration of these models and groups remains undetermined.

Fine models of vinters, of which there is an enamelled pair in the Irwin Untermyer Collection, probably follow Meissen prototypes. The male figure leans upon a tall pannier of fruit whilst his companion, a girl, rests against a tree trunk with a bunch of grapes in one hand (E17 and 18). It is possible that 'Winter' (E22), represented by a youth blowing upon his fingers, and 'Autumn' (E21), a boy with grapes, may be based upon lost Meissen models.

An engraving by Jaopo Amiconi,[164] who worked in this country between 1729 and 1739, was adapted to provide a model of a man in a tricorn hat holding a fish in both hands, emblematic of Water (E5). The engraving, however, shows a bare-headed youth holding a fishing net beside a seated girl with a basket of fish. In another porcelain group, now in the Kulturhistoriska Museum, Lund, in Sweden,[165] emblematic of Water (E7), a hatless man stands beside a seated girl. Amiconi's engraving portraying Air, consists of a gallant descending a ladder from a tree with a bird's nest intended for a seated lady. Clearly, this was unsuitable for translation into porcelain and accordingly the modeller was forced to rely upon his own imagination and created a strange group of 'A Girl standing with a basket in both hands and reclining Gallant' who supports a large bird upon his right thigh whilst clutching another smaller bird on his left side (E6). An engraving of 'The Dying Nymph', that appeared in *Bickham's Musical Entertainer* of 1739, prompted a pair of delightful candlestick figures of a 'Sleeping Girl' (E19) and a 'Boy with one finger to his lips' (E20) as if calling for silence. A group of a lady receiving a bird's nest from a kneeling gallant (E8) recalls engravings after Boucher of the idyllic pastoral.

The death of Frederick, Prince of Wales, on 31st March 1751, prompted a funerary porcelain group of 'Britannia lamenting', holding a handkerchief to her tear-stained face, with a shield and a lion at her side and a cameo bearing the likeness of the Prince in a head and shoulders relief (E16). The example in the Victoria and Albert Museum[166] shows a miserable dog-like animal, scarcely resembling the king of beasts, whilst upon the group in the Irwin Untermyer Collection,[167] the lion is finely modelled, possibly after a bronze prototype. Mention in Chapter IV is made of the suggestion that Roubiliac may have created the group owing to the resemblance between the figure of Margaret Myddelton on funerary sculpture by that artist and the figure of Britannia. There is no evidence to support this contention other than a fortuitous facial likeness. The Girl-in-a-Swing group compares favourably with another made at Chelsea (B46), both of which must have been issued shortly after the tragic event.

A group depicting Hercules and Omphale (E13) was adapted from one made at Vincennes based upon the painting executed in 1724 by François Lemoyne. A third figure in the original model was omitted and minor alterations effected, made necessary by the instability of the paste in the kiln. Other allegorical groups, 'Ganymede and the Eagle' (E14), and 'Europa and the Bull'(E15) are sometimes incorporated into candlesticks and were probably derived from lost prints. An exquisite, and possibly unique, representation of 'The Holy Family' (E24) was taken from François Poilly's engraving after Raphael,[168] the original of which is in the Louvre. The Virgin Mary is shown seated with Christ standing at her left side looking over her lap to greet St.

164. 'The Origin of some Ceramic Design' by A.J. Toppin, *Transactions,* English Ceramic Circle, 1948, Vol. 2, No. 10, pp. 266-276. Pl.XCc, engraving of 'Water'; pl. XCa, engraving of 'Air', both after Amiconi.

165. 'Girl in a Swing Porcelain and Chelsea', op. cit., pls. 130a and 130b, groups of 'Water' and 'Air' from the Kulturhistoriska Museum, Lund, Sweden.

166. ibid., pl. 126B.

167. Untermyer, pl. 1, fig. 9.

168. 'The Masterpiece of an Unknown Craftsman' by P. Synge Hutchinson, *Connoisseur,* 1968, Vol. 168, No. 678, pp. 96-98, pl. 1, the porcelain group; pl. 2, engraving by Poilly after Raphael.

John represented as a boy held by his kneeling mother, St. Elizabeth. Another religious model is of the 'Mater Dolorosa' (E9) depicted as wearing a veil with arms crossed over her breast. It is likely this was based upon one of many ivory carvings of the subject.

There is a very rare model, once in the Dudley Delevingne Collection, of a lady standing beside a plinth upon which a lamp burns (Plate 54) (E25). This is reminiscent of the early Vincennes model of 'Amitiée', adapted from sculpture by Etienne Falconet, though the precise source has not yet been identified. Another model, attributed to the Girl-in-a-Swing factory by Mr. Robert Williams, portrays a 'Gallant in a huge tricorn hat seated upon a rock' (E23).

Several models of finches (E28-E30) are known, mostly mounted upon hexagonal shaped bases with heads half turned to the left or right and some of these are adapted as candlesticks. One of the most attractive is the 'Finch with wing displayed', of which one example was in the Lady Ludlow Collection and another in the Sigmund Katz Collection. There is a 'Hound Bitch' (E31), with rather prominent eyes, in the Victoria and Albert Museum,[169] whilst the companion 'Hound Dog', is in the Boston Museum of Fine Art.[170] Bow versions of these are also known (H158). Finally, there is a fable group of 'Fox and Stork at the Well' (E26), which was prompted by an engraving in the *Weekly Apollo* of 1752.[171] These models and groups, together with the porcelain toys mentioned earlier, and some rare examples of useful ware, comprise the output of the so-called Girl-in-a-Swing manufactory.

169. Victoria and Albert Museum, Cat. no. C.236-1921.

170. Boston Museum of Fine Arts, Cat. no. 30.365, from the Alfred Hutton Collection.

171. 'Primitive Chelsea Porcelain' by Bellamy Gardner, *Connoisseur,* 1942, Vol. 109, p. 35, nos. II and III, respectively the porcelain group and the engraving.

Plate 54. *A Lady standing beside a plinth upon which a lamp burns (E25). 7ins. (17.8cm). Girl-in-a-Swing c.1752. Possibly based on a Vincennes model representing Amitié.* George Savage

Chapter VII

The Bow, or Stratford-Langthorne, Factory

Although a great deal has been written about the Bow manufactory since the Bow exhibition of 'Special Porcelain 1744-1776', held at the British Museum in 1959-60, no comprehensive book has been published on the subject since that written by Frank Hurlbutt in 1926.[1] Accordingly, the historical review given here is rather more detailed than that provided for the other English porcelain factories.

Events in the American Colonies prior to the establishment of the Bow manufactory are germain to the subject. In 1736, Roger Lacy, who was agent to the Chirokee Indians for the state of Georgia, persuaded a potter named André Duché to settle in Savannah.[2] André Duché (1709-1778) had carried out research into the manufacture of porcelain after the Oriental manner and, by about the year 1738, claimed to have succeeded in his task. He steadfastly refused to dispatch specimens of the white clay that he had employed to the 'Trustees of Georgia' in England. His application for a grant to visit England had been rejected but, after many complications and inconveniences that included his arrest, he came to London at his own expense and arrived on 26th May, 1745.[3] Presumably he wished either to register a patent or to find a market for the sale of his china clay, samples of which he brought with him. Indirect evidence suggests that he met William Cookworthy for, on 30th May, 1745, Cookworthy wrote from Plymouth to a surgeon in Penryn named Richard Hingstone: "I had lately with me the person who had discovered the china-earth. He had several samples of china-ware of their making with him, which were, I think, equal to the Asiatic. It was found in the back of Virginia where he was in quest of mines. . . He has gone for a cargo of it, having bought the whole country of the Indians where it rises. They can import it for £13 per ton."[4] It seems probable that the person mentioned in the letter was Duché. Cookworthy appears to have shown scant interest in the white earth possibly because even at this early date he had found supplies of a suitable clay on Tregonning Hill in Cornwall.[5] On 6th December, 1744, a patent was granted to "Edward Heylin, in the parish of Bow, in the county of Middlesex, merchant and Thomas Frye, of the parish of West Ham, in the county of Essex. A New Method of manufacturing a certain kind of mineral, whereby a ware might be made of the same nature or kind, and equal to, if not exceeding in goodness and beauty, china or porcelain imported from abroad. The material is an earth, the product of the Chirokee nation in America, called by the natives UNAKER. . ."[6] Other ingredients included "pot-ash, sand and flints pulverised to a powder. . ." It is highly improbable that any wares fashioned from this non-phosphatic body could have been successfully fired and none have survived. It seems likely that Heylyn and Frye met Duché and that the application for the patent was intended to secure their rights to use unaker or, possibly, to stake a claim to the manufacture of a frit porcelain when it became known that Nicholas Sprimont of Chelsea was also in the race. Hugh Tait[7] has suggested the unaker was used by Bow at least until the retirement of Frye in 1759. He thought that the cost of transporting the earth across the Atlantic

1. *Bow Porcelain* (London, 1926) by Frank Hurblutt.

2. From the catalogue by H.G. Tait to the Exhibition of Bow Porcelain 1744-1776 of documentary material to commemorate the bicentenary of the retirement of Thomas Frye, held at the British Museum Oct. '59 – April '60.

3. *The Colonial Records of Georgia* (Atlanta, 1908) by A.D. Candler, supplement to Vol. IV, p. 242.

4. *The Ceramic Art of Great Britain* (London, 1877) by Llewellyn Jewitt, Vol. I, pp. 320-321.

5. ibid., pp. 323-326.

6. *Marks & Monograms on European & Oriental Pottery and Porcelain* (London, 1965) by William Chaffers, 15th revised edition, Vol. II, p. 271.

7. 'The Bow Factory under Alderman Arnold and Thomas Frye' by H.G. Tait, *Transactions*, English Ceramic Circle, 1963, Vol. 5, pt. 4, p. 200.

ocean might have been reduced by negotiation with ship owners who would have vessels returning in ballast from the New World. However, the Port of London records have only one entry to support this contention, dated to the 1743-44, "Earth unrated, 20 tons — value £5: imported into London from Carolina". Duché may have remained in England for several years but was living in Norfolk, Virginia, between 1754 and 1766.[8]

Edward Heylyn (1695-1765) was born in Westminster, the son of John Heylyn who became Master of the Worshipful Company of Saddlers. Edward was created a Freeman of the City of London in October 1718.[9] His name also appears in the Bristol Burger's Roll of Potters, dated 15th July, 1731. He had interests in Bristol, where he ran a business for the importation of copper ore and may possibly have been connected with Lowdin's Glass House and the factory of Benjamin Lund. In London, he owned a Glass House and might have been involved in the Limehouse manufactory. He must have met Thomas Frye at the Saddlers' Company. Heylyn, together with Robert Rogers, was gazetted bankrupt at Bristol in August 1737 some years before his association with Bow, and for a second time in August 1757, when it appears he ceased to be an active proprietor of the manufactory. He spent his declining years upon the Isle of Man where he died in 1765.

Thomas Frye (1710-1762) was born near Dublin and came to England c.1734. His eldest child was baptised in St. Olave's Church, Old Jewry, on 10th October, 1735. Like many of his fellow Irish artists, such as Houston, Purcel, McArdell and Spencer, he was a mezzotint engraver. His work included engravings of George II, Queen Charlotte, David Garrick, Captain Cook and the Duchess of Northumberland.[10] He was commissioned to paint Frederick, Prince of Wales, in 1736 and the portrait was presented by Thomas Sherman in July 1741 to the Saddlers' Company.[11] Later, he painted Princess Augusta, and also Dr. Jeremy Bentham in his academic robes, which is now in the National Portrait Gallery. Frye was a competent miniaturist and was even compared in this field to the great Cooper. Dr. Bernard Watney[12] suggested that Frye might have come to West Ham to engrave copper plates for the calico printing industry which had originally been established in the locality by William Sherwin in 1676. Mrs. Elizabeth Adams[13] pointed out that the Calico Works of Joseph Wimpey (fils) and Richard Emery was located in a field close to the Bow manufactory. Further, that in 1756 one of Frye's pupils, William Pether, was awarded a prize by the Society of Arts for 'Designs of flowers, fruit, foliage and birds proper for weavers, embroiderers or calico printers, by boys under seventeen'.[14] The venue of Heylyn's Glass House in Stratford must have been ideal for experimentation into the manufacture of porcelain. Why an artist of repute like Frye should have become involved in such a venture remains a mystery. Nevertheless he did and provided the artistic genius that guided the Bow works until his retirement in 1759.

A third important character to be connected with the factory during the early years was George Arnold who became the Master of the Worshipful Company of Drapers, Alderman of Cheap Ward, and Governor of St. Thomas's Hospital. *The West Ham Poor Account Books* during the second quarter of the year 1749-50 refer to the Bow factory as 'Alderman Arnold and Company', though by the 1750-51 the entry had been amended to read 'Frye and Company'. John Ainslie[15] discovered evidence in the Court Book for 1744 that George Arnold purchased property in Bow, Middlesex, during the autumn of that year and shortly before 1750 acquired additional land adjacent to this site. Although no wares survive that have been attributed to Bow prior to 1750, it is interesting to read in the 1748 edition of Daniel Defoe's *Tour of Great Britain,* edited by Samuel Richardson, of a porcelain factory recently set

8. *English Blue and White Porcelain* (London, 1973) by Bernard Watney, 2nd edition, pp. 10-11, footnote 8.

9. 'The Bow Factory under Alderman Arnold and Thomas Frye', op. cit., p. 9.

10. 'Thomas Frye 1710-1762' by Thomas Wynn, *Burlington Magazine,* Vol. 114, No. 827, pp. 79-84.

11. From the Records of the Saddlers' Company, cited in *English Blue and White Porcelain,* op. cit., p. 7.

12. ibid., p. 12.

13. 'The Bow Insurances and Related Matters' by Elizabeth Adams, *Transactions,* English Ceramic Circle, 1973, Vol. 9, pt. 1, p. 68.

14. ibid., p. 68.

15. *Court Book 1744,* Record Office, County Hall, London.

up in the village of Bow, before the traveller crosses Bow Bridge into Essex.[16] On 25th June, 1752, the *London Daily Advertiser* carried the obituary notice: "William Arnold Esq:, Alderman of Cheap Ward, President of St. Thomas's Hospital, one of the principal proprietors of the Porcelain Manufactory at Bow..." Here the name of 'William' had been written in error for 'George'. William, his brother, survived him as President of the Hoare's Bank. For many years it was believed that George Arnold was, as stated in the obituary, one of the proprietors of Bow but Mrs. Elizabeth Adams has shown by a scrutiny of the Bow insurance policies (see below) that this was not so and that his role was limited to that of a financial sponsor.

The site of the Bow factory has been established by three necessarily limited excavations. The first, made in 1867, was made during the digging of the foundations of Bell and Black's match factory when shards were recovered some of which are now in the Victoria and Albert Museum. The second was effected in 1921 and reported in 1922 by Aubrey Toppin.[17] A third limited dig in 1969 was supervised by Drs. John Ainslie and David Redfern when fragments of blue and white ware were recovered. The Bow works were situated on what is now the north side of Stratford High Street, upon the Essex side of the river Lea, and was separated from Bow bridge by a distance of about two hundred and fifty years where there were once tenement buildings and an inn known as the 'New Canton'. An account of the Bow works was written in the lid of a cardboard box containing a Bow porcelain bowl made for the enameller Thomas Craft who had himself decorated it and written the inscription.[18] "The above manufactory was carried on for many years by Mssrs. Crowther and Weatherby, whose names are known almost over the world; they employed 300 persons; about 90 painters (of which I was one), and about 200 turners, throwers etc: were employed under one roof. The model of the building was taken from that at Canton in China; the whole was heated by two stoves on the outside of the building and conveyed through flues or pipes and warmed the whole, sometimes to an intense heat, unbearable in winter. It now wears a miserable aspect, being a manufactory for turpentine, and small tenaments...T, Craft, 1790." Clearly the Bow works was, unlike the Chelsea factory, custom-built and something more than an array of converted tenement buildings. This description receives support from an insurance policy dated 7th July, 1749, with the *Sun Insurance Company,* discovered by Mrs. Elizabeth Adams[19] which records "Workhouses in one building 173 feet long Brick", "A House Elaboratory", possibly an experimental laboratory, "Timber constructed Workhouse and Millhouse", as well as utensils and stock together insured for a sum of £4,000. The amount is, as Mrs. Adams pointed out, four times that of the largest of Liverpool's factories owned by John Dunbibin and Ralph Coventry, whilst the number of employees was only slightly less than were working at royal Sèvres during its heyday.

The occupation of 'potter' does not occur in the baptismal register of Bow Parish Church[20] until the first quarter of 1748 and it is therefore unlikely that commercial production of porcelain was commenced in that locality much before the last quarter of 1747. On 17th November 1749, a second patent was taken out in the name of Thomas Frye alone.[21] "...For a new method of making a certain ware, which is not inferior in beauty and fineness, and is rather superior in strength than earthenware that is brought from the East Indies, and is commonly known by the name of China, Japan, or porcelain ware. Animals, vegetables, and fossils, by calcining, grinding, and washing, are said to produce an insoluble matter named *virgin earth,* but some in greater quantities than others, as all animal substances, all fossils of the calcareous kind, as chalk, limestone, &c.; take therefore any of these classes, calcine it,

16. 'The Bow Factory under Aldeman Arnold and Thomas Frye', op. cit., pp. 195-216.

17. 'Bow Porcelain — Recent Excavations' by A.J. Toppin, *Burlington Magazine,* 1922, Vol. 40, pp. 88-91.

18. *Marks & Monograms on European & Oriental Pottery and Porcelain,* op. cit., Vol. 2, pp. 277-278.

19. 'The Bow Insurances and Related Matters', op. cit., pp. 69-70, *et seq.*

20. ibid., p. 68.

21. *Marks & Monograms on European & Oriental Pottery and Porcelain,* op. cit., p. 271.

grand and wash it in many waters; these ashes are mixed in certain proportions with flint, 'white pebble or clear sand,' and with water, made into balls, highly burned and ground fine, and mixed with a proportion of pipeclay it is then thrown on the wheel, and when finished, dried, burnt, and painted with *smalt or saffer,* when it is ready to be glazed with a glaze, made first by making a glass with saltpetre, red lead, and *sand flint, or other white stones,* grinding it up well, and mixing it with a certain proportion of white lead, adding a little smalt to clear the colour. After dripping and drying, the articles are put in cases and 'burned with wood till the surface is clear and shining'." This, then, was a formula for a phosphatic paste due to the incorporation of bone ash in the mix.

The Bow insurance policy of 1749, mentioned above, refers to the proprietors as "Edward Heylin, Thomas Frye, John Weatherby and John Crowther on their China Manufactory in Stratford Road in the County of Essex..." John Weatherby came from Staffordshire and, he and John Crowther are listed in the *London Directories* of 1744 as "Potters at St. Catherine's near the Tower". They had been in correspondence with John Wedgwood in connection with the dispute between Briand's widow and Farmer in 1748 to which reference has been made in Chapter V. Mrs. Elizabeth Adams[22] has found insurance policies which indicate that Weatherby and Crowther owned "Glass and Materials in their seven warehouses at the Glass-House near Green Yard, in East Smithfield", and "a Warehouse and contents at Woolward's Warf, St. Catherines". They are described in these policies as "Dealers in Glass, China and Earthenware".

No wares or figures survive that were made of the non-phosphatic paste and none can be dated to before 1750. Small cylindrical ink-wells, marked 'Made at New Canton 1750' are amongst the first which were clearly intended partly as advertisements. Most are decorated in underglaze blue; a few are enamelled in brownish red, yellow, green and blue. Cups and coffee cans which are rather heavily potted, globular tea-pots, plates, many of which are octagaonal, and tankards represent the early stock in trade. Models show a degree of competence that bespeaks previous experience though lacking familiarity with Meissen prototypes until about 1752. Some have thought the early models have an affinity with Staffordshire salt glaze figures. Since the name of this artist is unknown he has come to be known as the 'Muses Modeller' after a set of models.

In 1753 a warehouse was acquired in Cornhill which was announced in the Derby Mercury of 9th March: "BOW CHINA WARE. Was opened on Wednesday the 17th February near the Royal Exchange in Cornhill with a Back Door facing the Bank, in Threadneedle-street, for the Convenience of all Customers both in Town and Country; where all sorts of China will continue to be sold in the same manner as formerly at Bow, with Allowance made to wholesale Dealers."[23] A notice appeared on 24th March in *Aris's Birmingham Gazette* seeking additional painters and modellers. "This is to give Notice to all Painters in the Blue and White Potting Way, and Enamellers on China-Ware, that by applying to the Counting House at the China Works near Bow, they may meet with Employment, and proper Encouragement, according to their Merit; Likewise Painters brought up in the Snuff-Box Way, Jappanning, Fan-Painting, &c. may have Opportunities of Trial; wherein, if they succeed, they shall have due Encouragement. N.B. — At the same House, a person is wanted who can model small Figures in Clay neatly."[24] Although there ensued an improvement in the style of modelling during the year 1754 when Meissen prototypes were studied, the Muses Modeller appears to have played a leading role since his earlier traits remain identifiable even though they were muted.

22. 'The Bow Insurances and Related Matters', op. cit., p. 75.

23. *Contributions towards the History of Early English Porcelain* (Salisbury, 1881) by J.E. Nightingale, p. xlv.

24. ibid., p. xlv.

The strong Bow paste was eminently suitable for useful wares and a vast amount of inexpensive blue and white seems to have been made from the commencement of production. This must have provided the profit necessary to permit manufacture of more elaborate decorative wares and figures. Hugh Tait[25] cites an advertisement that appeared in a Boston newspaper in November 1754. "Just imported by Philip Breaching, and to be Sold at his house in Fifth Street, a Variety of Bow China, Cup and Saucers, Bowls &c. . . ." Since no explanatory note was appended it would seem that the good citizens of Boston were no strangers to Bow wares. Exports made to the New World, the West Indies and Ireland contributed to the Bow success story. The extent of the expansion of trade may be gauged from the Bow insurance policies.[26] The original sum assured in November 1749 had been £4,000, and this rose to £6,500 in 1750, and £8,650 in 1755. Additions made to factory premises included a Mill for grinding pigments, a Fuel Store, a second Kiln House, a Slip House, and a Drying House and valuation of transport facilities rose from £25 to £100. The values of stock show a similar increase. The Bow Account Books[27] show that the annual cash flow was £6,573 in the year 1750/51, and had reached £11,228 in 1756/57 and if the last figure is corrected for bills outstanding, it reaches the then huge sum of £18,115 8s. 9d. In the same period takings at the Cornhill Warehouse averaged £120 a week.

In 1753, John Bowcocke was appointed general clerk to the manufactory. He had been a purser in the royal navy. The so called *Bowcocke Papers,*[28] consist of documents once in the possession of Lady Charlotte Schreiber which have been lost, and further letters, a note book and sundry items now in the British Museum which were displayed in the exhibition of 1959-60. Part of the contents of the former portion was published in the *Art Journal* of 1839. Mention has already been made of the *Bow Account Book.* Miscellaneous letters addressed to and written by John Bowcocke, notes relating to his family tree and designs and drawings made by Walter Jones and Bridget Bowcocke are included. Those of a "Fluter and Companion, 3/- and 4/6 each", together with the corresponding porcelain models, were displayed in the exhibition of 1959-60. Perhaps the most interesting documents are note books containing memoranda of the day-to-day running of the manufactory in the year 1756. One entry reads: "March 27, Quy. What's to be done with bud sprigs; what quy. of Cupids and B (Boys) is wanted white; what floras &c." Moulds for slip decoration, which were used in the form of prunus and bud sprigs were recovered from the factory site.[29] An order for fire-bricks entered on 28th April is followed by the memorandum: ". . . but mind, 200 of them are for the Glass House and 1,500 for the China Factory — see that a correct account is sent to each". Later, on 7th May, we read: "Quy. Whether any Windsor bricks were received at the Glass House which is charged to the porcelain compy:?" It will be recalled that Heylyn had interests in both concerns. "May 4. What is meant by 36 white men with salt-boxes?", and on 7th May: "Whether any bucks is wanted? There was five pairs sent down, and only one pair came back. Send what does there is in town, and send down the Bow books." Today 'Bucks' and 'Does' are relatively scarce whilst 'White men with Salt-Boxes', may be similar to those issued at Chelsea as 'Rat Catchers' from the Paris Cries. The all too familiar subject of damaged stock is also mentioned: "June 18. Allowed Mr. Fogg, In a Pero's broken hat, 1s.; in 2 Turks, 3s".

Lists of clients make interesting reading. Notables include the Duchesses of Leeds and Portland, the Duke of Argyll, the Lady Cavendish and the Lady Stairs and Colonel Griffin of Brook Street. Lesser mortals were Mr. Legg, of Birchen Lane, Mr. Fahy, Mr. White, Mrs. Ann Howard of Broad Mead,

25. From the catalogue of the Exhibition of Bow Porcelain 1744-1776, op. cit., p. 12.
26. 'The Bow Insurances and Related Matters', op. cit., pp. 69, 70, 77-79.
27. *Marks & Monograms on European & Oriental Pottery and Porcelain,* op. cit., pp. 272-273.
28. ibid., pp. 274-276.
29. 'Bow Porcelain — Recent Excavations', op. cit., pp. 224-233.

Bristol, and a dealer named Fogg, of Swallow Street, London, who made a number of purchases. A memorandum of 6th May 1756 reads: "Mrs. Whitfield to have 1 p. white biscuit candlesticks". Biscuit wares and figures are more often associated with the Derby factory after 1771, but several early figures and these candlesticks were made at Bow many years earlier. An account made out to: "Richard Dyer at Mr. Bolton's, enameller, near the Church Lambeth", shows that Bow porcelain was being decorated outside the factory as late as 1756. Some of the figures available in 1756 were: 'Harlequins', '1 small Flutter white', '1 small Fidler and Companion', 'Swans, wings open', 'Enamelled Pero 6s.', 'Turks', 'Cooks', etc. The 'Shepherd Imperial 7s.', are more familiar in Derby and Chelsea versions than in Bow porcelain, whilst 'Boars' recall the fine models made at Derby by Planché. 'Sporters' have been related without cause to models copied from Meissen prototypes emblematic of 'Liberty and Matrimony', but might equally be one of many pairs of Huntsman and Lady. 'Sesens' are known in numerous forms though the qualifications 'some with detachable plints [plinths], are unfamiliar today.

Until 1757, most of the products were sold either upon the factory premises, or in the Cornhill Warehouse. On 24th March, 1757, an announcement in the *Public Advertiser* read: "To be Sold by Auction by Mr. Cock & Co: at their New Auction Rooms in Spring Gardens, leading into St. James's Park, on Tuesday next. The very extensive and Valuable Production of the Bow Porcelain Manufactory consisting of many compleat and useful Services, and Abundance of curious and Ornamental Pieces. To be seen from Friday next till the Sale..."[30] On 6th and 7th April, the following addendum was appended: "All Orders are received and executed as usual at the *Bow China Warehouse* in Cornhill..." This was clearly intended to indicate that the former sales venue had not been abandoned for this purpose. Some items that remained over from the sale were readvertised in a further notice on 25th April: "Sale by Auction *COCK & CO*...."[31] On 9th December, and on many subsequent days the *Public Advertiser* carried the notice: "At Bow China Warehouse in the Cornhill are a great variety of useful and ornamental Wares of the Manufactory greatly improved: and for the convenience of the Nobility and Gentry, their Warehouse on the Terrace in St. James's Street, is constantly supplied with every Thing new, where it is sold as at Cornhill, with the real Price marked on each Piece without Abatement."[32]

Also in 1757, the *London Weekly Advertiser* carried the notice: "Bankrupts...Edward Heylyn, of Cornhill, Merchant, Dealer and Chapman...", but this event seems to have had no adverse effect upon the Bow manufactory. Two further sales took place in 1758, both of which were advertised in the *Public Advertiser*.[33] "To be Sold by Auction by Mr. Lambe, At his House in Pall Mall on Feby. 27, and five following days. A Large and Valuable Collection of Fine Porcelain or China, from the Manufactory at Bow; consisting of Perfume Pots, beautiful Groups of Figures, Jars, Beakers, Birds, Beasts &c:...put in such lots as are fit for private Families and Dealers." The second sale, announced on 10th April, included "All the intire Stock of their Warehouse, on the Terrass in St. James's Street, of Birds, fine Essence Pots, beautiful Groups, and other Figures of Birds, Beasts...". The same year, John Bowcocke travelled to Ireland where he remained for eight months in order to promote sales and set up agencies. Upon his return, he was presented with the famous bowl, known as the 'Bowcocke Bowl'.[34] Decorated in underglaze blue and white, it is inscribed 'John & Ann, BOWCOCK, 1759', and is described in the *Bowcocke Papers* relating to the pedigree of the Bowcocke family as: "On a punch-bowl is John and Ann Bowcock 1759, on

30. *Contributions towards the History of Early English Porcelain*, op. cit., p. xlv.
31. ibid., p. xlvi.
32. ibid., p. xlvii.
33. ibid., pp. xlviii-xlix.
34. Catalogue of the Exhibition of Bow Porcelain 1744-1776, op. cit., fig. 33, no. 125, the 'Bowcocke Bowl'.

the inside is himself landing and sailors with staffs in their hands." It has been suggested that the occasion for the presentation may have been either in recognition of a successful business trip, or upon Bowcocke's tenth wedding anniversary, or to celebrate his promotion to the post of factory manager. However, there is evidence to suggest that Ann Bowcocke died during his absence in Ireland. Dr. Bernard Watney[35] cites a letter, now in the *Entwistle Papers,*[36] written on 21st August, 1922, by Miss K. MacIntire, whose mother had once owned the Bowcocke Bowl. The relevant passage reads: "Mrs. Bowcock died and was buried whilst he was away (of plague). The poor man was never the same again after, as the family believed she had been buried alive."

In 1759, Frye retired for reasons of ill health and his artistic genius and managerial skills were lost to the factory. He travelled to Wales for convalescence and returned to his home in London where he died in 1762, most probably from pulmonary tuberculosis. We know very little of the craftsmen and artists who worked at Bow, except that Frye's two daughters, Sarah and Elizabeth, and also Thomas Craft who has earlier been mentioned, were employed as painters. Craft, writing of the famous bowl had written in 1790, "Th's Bowl, was made at the Bow China Manufactory, at Stratford-le-Bow in the County of Essex, about the year 1760, and painted there by Thomas Craft, my Cypher is in the Bottom; it is painted in what we used to call the Old Japan taste, a taste at the time much esteemed by the then Duke of Argyle...I took it in a box to Kentish Town, and had it burned there in Mr. Giles's kiln, cost me 3s., it was cracked the first time of using it..."[37] Mrs. Elizabeth Adams[38] has shown that after leaving Bow, Thomas Craft set up in business as a 'Callico Printer', which he insured in a policy taken out on 20th February, 1771, with the Sun Company.

On 15th October, 1762, the *London Chronicle* carried the obituary: "Mr. John Weatherby, one of the Proprietors of the Bow China Warehouse in Cornhill, died at his home on Tower Hill."[39] The following year, John Crowther was gazetted bankrupt, and notices appeared on 12 March, and both the 19th and 30th May, 1764, in the *Public Advertiser,* "To be Sold by Auction, On Wednesday next and the following day, at the Large Exhibition Room in Spring Gardens. The Remaining Part of the Large Stock in Trade of JOHN CROWTHER, a Bankrupt, near Stratford, and the Bow Warehouse in Cornhill: consisting of a large Quantity of the finest Porcelain, chose out of the said Collection, in curious Figures, Girandoles and Branches for Chimney Pieces, Compotiers, Leaves. &c:, fine Deserts of fine old Partridge and Wheatsheaf Pattern..."[40] Nobody has yet explained how this bankruptcy of the only surviving proprietor could have failed to lead to the immediate closure of the Bow manufactory which continued to operate until c.1776. Some, including Llewellyn Jewitt, suggested that William Duesbury, then proprietor of Derby, might have financed Bow until his final purchase in 1776. One of the most important factors contributing to Crowther's financial troubles must surely have been the flooding of the porcelain factory by water from the river Lea which was graphically described in the *Gentleman's Magazine* of October, 1762: "The Works at Bow were overflowed in such a manner that the current rushed through the great arch [the entrance] in like manner as the tide runs through the arches of London Bridge."[41]

The decline of the Bow factory, like its earlier rise to greatness, is mirrored in the insurance policies which have been published by Mrs. Elizabeth Adams.[42] In July, 1763, the factory equipment, buildings, and stock were assured for the sum of £4,900. This was only £900 more than the valuation in the very first insurance policy of November, 1749. Part of this decline can be

35. *English Blue and White Porcelain,* op. cit., p.21.

36. Liverpool Public Library, D.Q. 6573/26.

37. Catalogue of the Exhibition of Bow Porcelain 1744-1776, op. cit., p. 43, no. 111, the 'Craft Bowl', illus. fig. 37; no. 112, the inscription in the cardboard box.

38. 'Ceramic Insurances in the Sun Company archives, 1766-74' by Elizabeth Adams, *Transactions,* English Ceramic Circle, 1978, Vol. 10, pt. 1, p. 4.

39. *Marks & Monograms on European & Oriental Pottery and Porcelain,* op. cit., p. 277.

40. *Contributions towards the History of Early English Porcelain,* op. cit., p. 1.

41. *The Gentleman's Magazine,* Oct. 1862, Vol. XXXII.

42. 'The Bow Insurances and Related Matters', op. cit., pp. 67-110.

accounted for by the revaluation of the long workshop from £1,000 to only £300, but other items were included that were not formerly detailed such as 'nine kilns', three for enamelling, two for glazing, four unspecified, and a 'dipping house' together with other sundry constructions. In 1766, the sum assured, which for the first time included cover for household property and items of personal apparel, had fallen to £3,400. By the following year this figure rose to £4,200. Subsequent policies might have shed light on the proprietorship and trading position but, unfortunately, they were found to be in a condition that precluded evaluation.[43] However, in 1766, a new warehouse in St. Mildred's Court was opened which contained stock valued at £1,000 which by 1777 had risen to £1,300. Further, in 1770, two new porcelain modellers were engaged so that, presumably, a profitable business was being conducted at least until this time.

Llewellyn Jewitt[44] wrote: "Crowther sold his entire concern — works, moulds, tools, &c., to Mr. William Duesbury who not only held the Derby China Works but, as previously stated, had purchased those of Chelsea, Giles, and one at Vauxhall, thus became the proprietor of the Bow works as well, and was therefore the largest holder either in those or later days. Mr. Duesbury, as he did with those of Chelsea, removed moulds, models, implements, &c., to Derby, and Bow was brought to a close. The next year, 1777, John Crowther became an inmate of Morden College, Blackheath, being elected to the foundation on 17th March, and he was still there in 1790." No documents were produced to support this contention but, if it is true, the failing Bow factory could almost certainly have been had for a song. It is very strange, however, that there are only two Chelsea-Derby models that might possibly have been cast from old Bow moulds. These are said to include a 'Huntsman holding a gun', and a companion 'Lady with flowers' (M50) which have been illustrated.[45] It is fitting to end this brief historical review of the Bow manufactory with the closing words written within the lid of the cardboard box that once contained the Craft Bowl. "...Mr. Weatherby has been dead many years; Mr. Crowther is in Morden College, Blackheath, and I am the only person of all those employed who annually visit him. — T. Craft, 1790."

Bow Figures made between 1750 and 1754 (Muses Modeller)

Paste and Glaze

No figures or wares fashioned from the non-phosphatic paste of the 1744 formula survive and there are no figures that can be dated earlier than 1750. Analysis of the paste of the first period of production reveals: 40 per cent silica, 16 per cent alumina, 24 per cent lime, and 17 per cent phosphoric acid. The last mentioned indicates incorporation of 40 per cent bone ash in the mix. This imparts the quality of milky opaqueness to the body due to small phosphate particles held in suspension and transillumination displays, in consequence, only a faint translucency of the more thinly potted portions of useful ware. There is considerable variation in the appearance of the body to the naked eye which ranges between a greyish colour, evident in the model of 'A Negress with a Basket' (G47), to a warm creamy white displayed by models such as 'Kitty Clive' (G1) in the Untermyer Collection. The paste is tight grained but tending to be short and may, accordingly, exhibit surface tearing and sometimes deep firecracks in the base of figures whilst edges tend to chip and flake off. It is densely radio-opaque and models are very heavy though this quality is in part due to press casting. The glaze is soft and thick, and varies between having a mushroom hue to being of a creamy colour. Crazing is

43. 'Ceramic Insurances in the Sun Company archives, 1766-74', op. cit., pp. 2-4.

44. *Marks & Monograms on European & Oriental Pottery and Porcelain,* op. cit., p. 277.

45. *Transactions,* English Ceramic Circle, 1969, Vol. 7, pt. 2, pls. 124C and 124D, Chelsea-Derby models of 'Sportsman' and companion *English Porcelain Figures of the 18th Century* (London, 1961) by Arthur Lane, col. pl. B, model of a Bow 'Sportsman and his Lady' (group).

rarely seen but there may be conspicuous pitting of the surface, and sanding, due to the presence of iron impurities, is fairly usual.

The Bases

Until about 1753, most bases were plain rectangles left unadorned, or shallow mounds or pads decorated with applied flowers and leaves. Occasionally, painted decoration may be seen upon the superior surface. About 1752-53, a sight of Meissen models prompted the use of clumsy 'C' and 'S' scrolls which were usually picked out in a purplish black displaying a very imperfect understanding of rococo taste. A few models were provided with detachable stands which were embellished with swags in high relief together with trophies. These include 'Henry Woodward' and 'Kitty Clive' in the Untermyer Collection. Rarely, the inferior surface may be left open revealing the rough irregular surface of the interior peculiar to press moulding. Usually, however, there is a base plate with a flat surface which is perforated by a ventilation hole of intermediate size and most often ground to facilitate level stance.

Enamel Colours

Enamel colours first appeared on Bow figures c.1751-52, though many now seen in the white were once adorned with unfired pigments. The early palette included pale yellow, a powdery brownish red and a lifeless opaque medium blue (known respectively as 'sealing-wax red' and 'blue'), a blue-green, both a grey and a black with a purplish cast, and a thin streaky manganese pink, known as 'gold-purple'. Colours were applied less generously than at Chelsea but more thickly than at Derby, in washes between large passages of white. The juxtaposition of pink and red often resulted in a discordant yet attractive appearance. Gilding was seldom used during this first period and when present may be laid upon a base of brown enamel as may be seen upon the model of 'Henry Woodward' in Lord Bearsted's collection[46] though in the case of some of the Muses it may take the form of tracery upon a dark blue ground on the bases.

The Decorative Style

Flesh tints are frequently omitted altogether or confined to the palest buff, heightened with orange-red upon the cheeks and lips untidily painted in brownish-red. Eyebrows are black and steeply arched, eyelashes and lids suggested by lines drawn in a greyish brown and irises most usually are grey or brown. Hair is portrayed by a wash of buff or brown overlaid with fine pencilling. Garments left in the white may display floral sprays outlined in black, rather large in scale, covered with flat washes of yellow, red and blue. Some take a 'V' shape as may be seen upon one model of 'Charity'[47] and 'Two Lovers with a Birdcage',[48] whilst others take the form of stylised leaves and florettes in a monochrome of either red or blue as may be seen upon the dress of the Chinese lady in the group emblematic of 'Air' in the Untermyer collection.[49] The proportion of Bow models decorated outside the factory is unknown. Certainly 'Bogh Figars' are amongst the entries in the account book of William Duesbury prior to 1754 whilst the Bowcocke Papers record that as late as 1756 wares were being sent to "Richard Dyer, at Mr. Bolton's, enameller near the Church, Lambeth". It will also be recalled that Thomas Craft took his famous bowl "...to Kentish Town and...burned there in Mr. Giles kiln".

The Modelling Characteristics

Only one modeller, called the 'Muses Modeller', seems to have worked at Bow before 1754. He gave his figures small heads, prominent heavy-lidded

46. Upton House, Warks., Porcelain Catalogue, no. 1.
47. *English Porcelain Figures of the 18th Century* (Lane), op. cit., pl. 42.
48. ibid., pl. 38.
49. Untermyer Collection, pl. 74, fig. 239.

eyes, receding forehead and chin, open mouth and clumsy nose. Drapery is deeply cut, often adorned with applied slip and many of the women have outsize ear-rings as well as beaded necklaces and lace ruffles at the neck and cuffs. The initial absence, and later paucity, of enamel colour made it necessary to reproduce all features in the round and this created an over detailed and fussy effect. Angular projection of unsupported limbs was avoided and figures were supported by thick vertical props thinly disguised as tree-stumps. Close scrutiny of models may show that details were sharpened up by the repairer with a knife or edged tool and this feature seems unique to Bow.

Some authorities have remarked on the presence of two groups of Bow models made before c.1754; the larger one displaying the characteristics associated with the Muses Modeller, the other showing a greater competence and sophistication of execution which might represent the work of a second more accomplished artist. Here it may be noted, however, that in general those figures which are based on a Meissen prototype, such as the standing 'Negress' (G47) and the characters from the Italian comedy (G6-G13) and the Cries of Paris (G26-G29, and G38), reflect the more mature techniques and styles of their original modellers whereas those Bow figures and groups based on prints, which almost certainly include the Muses (G14) and 'Lady attended by a Page' (G36) number amongst the most crude and unattractive. Nevertheless this cannot be the sole explanation for the very fine replicas of Kitty Clive (G1) and Henry Woodward (G2) which are traditionally thought to follow respectively a watercolour painting and an engraving, and certainly owe nothing to Meissen. Whether these figures were based on some intermediate three dimensional source, such as a small bronze or terracotta, or whether we must invoke the hand of another porcelain modeller remains an open question.

The Marks

Although the title 'New Canton' appears on ink-wells often with the date 1750 or 1751 in underglaze blue, marks on figures are usually restricted to planetary symbols that are most often incised which are shown in Appendix R. An example of 'Kitty Clive' in the Untermyer Collection is incised 1750, whilst there are several early models, including some of the Muses, incised 'T', or 'To'. The vast majority of models are unmarked.

The Models

Amongst the best known Bow models are those of Henry Woodward (G2) as the 'Fine Gentleman', and Kitty Clive (G1) as 'Mrs. Riot', from David Garrick's farce *Lethe* which had its debut in 1740 at Drury Lane. The plot related to fashionable characters from the contemporary London scene who, during their passage across the Styx in Charon's boat, poured out their troubles to old Aesop in order to gain access to the healing waters of Lethe. Garrick wrote of the Fine Gentleman, "Faith, my existence is merely supported by amusements. I dress, visit, study, taste, write sonnets; by birth, travel, education, and natural abilities I am entitled to lead the fashion. I am the principal connoisseur at all auctions, chief arbiter at assemblies, professional critic at the theatres and a Fine Gentleman everywhere." The model shows him standing, hands in pockets, wearing a tricorn hat and huge foppish waistcoat. In some versions he has a sword. The inspiration came from James McArdell's mezzotint after the portrait by Francis Hayman.[50] Garrick wrote of Mrs. Riot, "She lies in bed all morning, rattles about all day; sits up all night; she goes everywhere and sees everything; knows everybody and loves nobody; ridicules her friends, coquets with her lovers, sets 'em together by their ears, tells fibs, makes mischief, buys china, cheats at cards,

50. 'Some Consequences of the Bow Special Exhibition' by H.G. Tait, *Apollo,* 1960, Vol. 71, No. 705, pt. 1, pp. 40-44, pl. V.

keeps a pet dog and hates parsons." Her model portrays her in a lace cap, lace trimmed jacket wearing a crinoline and carrying a dog beneath her right arm. Based upon Charles Mosely's engraving of an earlier watercolour by Thomas Worlidge which was mentioned in an inventory of the contents of Strawberry Hill made in 1764 for Horace Walpole: "Mrs. Catherine Clive, the excellent comedienne, in the character of the Fine Lady in Lethe; in water-colours by Worlidge". Most examples are in white though an entry in the London Account Book of William Duesbury reads: "For enamelling Mrs. Clive three shillings". There are enamelled models of Kitty Clive and Henry Woodward in Lord Bearsted's Collection; the general colouring and gilding on the former suggests the hand of James Giles but upon the latter are rather tightly painted floral sprigs upon the dress that have been tentatively attributed to Duesbury.[51] Other models relating to the theatre are of an unknown 'Actor' and 'Actress', both in Turkish dress (Plate 55) (G5), and 'David Garrick as Falstaff' (G3) showing the knight in a plumed hat holding a sword and an oval shield after Truchy's engraving of a painting by Francis Hayman.[52]

51. *Eighteenth Century English Porcelain* (London, 1952) by George Savage, pls. 52 and 53.

52. 'The Origin of Some Ceramic Designs' by A.J. Toppin, *Transactions,* English Ceramic Circle, 1948, Vol. 2, No. 10, pp. 266-276, pl. CIc, engraving after Francis Hayman's portrait; pl. CId, Bow model.

***Plate 55.** Model of an 'Actress' wearing Turkish costume (G5). 7½ins. (19.1cm). Bow c.1752.*
George Savage

***Plate 56.** The Muse 'Polyhymnia' (G14). 6½ins. (16.5cm). Bow c.1751-52.*
Victoria and Albert Museum

Italian Comedy figures are mostly rather small and mounted on rectangular bases and follow some of Reinicke's originals. These include 'Columbina dancing' (G8), 'Scapino' (G10), and 'Arlecchino wearing a mask and motley' (G6). Others copy originals by Kändler, such as 'Pulcinella the hunchback' leaning against a tree-stump (G9), and 'Columbina' dressed in a brimmed hat holding a basket of grapes (G7). There are also three fine groups. 'The 'Indiscretions of Arlecchino' (G11) is a faithful copy of Kändler's original and has been described in Chapter II. Another rare group shows 'Arlecchino seated beside Columbina', his left arm encircling her waist, his right elevated (G12), whilst the third group portrays Isabella playing a mandoline seated on the left of Mezzetino who holds a musical score and sings, and is known as the 'Italian Musicians' (G13). The last mentioned follows engravings after Watteau entitled, respectively, 'L'Amour au Théâtre italien',[53] and 'Belle, n'écoutez rien'.[54]

Amongst the best known Bow models relating to mythological subjects are Apollo and the Nine Muses (G14). Thalia is in the Boston Museum of Fine Arts and stands holding a mask. Calliope remains unidentified. The remainder are illustrated by A.J. Toppin.[55] Clio stands beside a tome inscribed 'The History of Wales' with a quill in her hand; Erato has flowers in her lap and is attended by Eros whose quiver hangs from a tree-stump; Euterpe sits holding a recorder with musical trophies at her feet; Melpomene stands with a goblet in one hand and a dagger in the other; Polyhymnia (Plate 56), who alone amongst the Muses has wings, holds a laurel chaplet over an obelisk to which she points with her right hand; Terpsichore stands with one arm raised in the position of the dance; Urania stoops over a celestial globe holding a pair of dividers. They are ugly wenches between six and a quarter and six and threequarter inches in height and exemplify the modelling traits peculiar to Bow models made between 1750 and 1754. The name of the modeller remains unknown but, possibly, his name might have been Wales or he may have been a Welshman in view of the title of the book held by Clio. A.J. Toppin[56] has shown that Clio was probably inspired by the frontispiece of the *Works of the Abbé de Saint Real,* engraved by D. Coster and published c.1700. The sources that prompted the other Muses are unknown but the misspelling of their names, which may be scratched upon the base or tree-stump support, has led some to suppose they were copied from engravings that bore French captions which were imperfectly understood by the repairer. For example, Clio is written 'Clion', Erato appears as 'Eraton', Melpomene becomes 'Polimne' whilst Terpsichore is incised 'Terpssicore'. Most examples are white and in the rare coloured specimens the daubs of red upon their cheeks, the absence of flesh tints, the steeply arched black eyebrows and the deep red smudged lips recall the make up of a circus clown. Dresses may be adorned with rather large and widely spaced flowers in blue and brownish red whilst a blackish blue upon the bases may be relieved by a gilded design that is usually badly rubbed.

Several of the models of mythological subjects are copies of more sophisticated Meissen originals. These include Mercury (G19) in winged helmet bearing a caduceus, Minerva (G21) as a warrior goddess, Justice (G18) in classical robes leaning upon a pile of books and holding a short sword and the scales in either hand, and Charity (Plate 57) (G15) depicted as a woman standing in antique robes with a babe upon her left arm and handing an apple to a child standing at her right side. Although there is a Meissen version of Charity, both may possibly have been based on a lost print or a baroque bronze representing Fecondité. Neptune who stands astride his dolphin (G22) may stem from a similar source. Later versions (H86) show the god standing meekly beside the creature. A pair of allegorical figures said to portray Hope

53. 'The Origin of Some Ceramic Designs', op. cit., pl. CIIc, engraving 'L'amour au Théâtre italien'; pl. CIIb, Bow porcelain group.

54. ibid., pl. CIIIa, engraving 'Belle, n'écoutez rien'; pl. CIIIb, Bow group of Italian musicians.

55. 'Some Early Bow Muses' by A.J. Toppin, *Burlington Magazine,* 1929, Vol. 54, p. 190, pls. Ia-c; p. 191, pls. IIa-d.

56. 'The Origin of Some Ceramic Designs', op. cit., pl. CIa, engraving D. Coster; pl. CIb, Bow model of 'Clio'.

(Plate 58) (G16) and Justice (G18) were displayed at the exhibition to mark the half centenary of the English Ceramic Circle in 1977.[57] The first named is a woman standing in classical attire leaning upon the shaft of an anchor. It will later be mentioned that in 1773, Josiah Wedgwood gave drawings of 'Hope and the Conquered Province' to the Derby modeller, Pierre Stephan, as the basis for a trial model. The identity of the second model is doubtful since objects held by the lady are invariably damaged or missing and she has been called 'Minerva' or even 'Metis'. There are two different pairs of sphinxes. One pair with head and breasts of an unidentified woman is in the baroque style with drapery about the neck and follows an engraving by J.F. Blondel (G24).[58] The other are said to be in the likeness of the actress Peg Woffington (G23) and are placed upon elaborate rococo bases. Many hold they are based on a portrait by Arthur Pond. Michael Wynn[59] has pointed out that the head-dress worn by the actress is the same as those upon the heads of women attendant on the Queen of Sheba in the painting by Paolo Veronese and it is interesting that Thomas Frye himself made a mezzotint engraving of the work. The tale is told of when Peg Woffington had appeared in male costume upon the boards she was incautious enough to remark to an actor, "I do declare sir half of London took me for a man." This provoked the inevitable retort,

57. *English Ceramics 1580-1830* (London 1977) by R.J. Charleston and D. Towner, no. 137.
58. 'Some Consequences of the Bow Special Exhibition', op. cit., p. 183, fig. IV.
59. 'Thomas Frye 1710-1762', op. cit.

***Plate 57.** 'Charity' (G15). 9¾ins. (24.8cm). Bow c.1751, by the Muses Modeller.* Temple Newsam House, Leeds

***Plate 58.** 'Hope', a lady in classical robes leaning upon an anchor (G16). 8¾ins. (22.2cm). Bow c.1752-54, by the Muses Modeller.* George Savage

"Madam, the other half know you to be a woman!" The charming group of 'Two Putti struggling with a Dolphin' (G25) echoes a Vincennes model.[60]

Some early Bow models may be original though they were probably based on engravings. They include a 'Thames Waterman' with the badge of a 'fowled anchor' upon his uniform (G40), a seated lady who is sewing (G34), a spirited dancing sailor and his lass (G39) and three groups which possess great charm by reason of the naïvety of their modelling. The 'Lady accepting refreshment from a Page' (G36) was once in the Culdwell Collection.[61] A 'Huntsman seated beside a Lady wearing riding habit' (G33) is in the National Museum of Ireland, Dublin, and resembles the 'Gallant seated beside a Fishergirl' (G32). The 'Lady wearing a Crinoline playing a lyre' (G35) stands upon an elaborately scrolled base which anticipates by nearly a decade the later forms.[62] A seated 'Sportsman with a gun' and companion 'Lady with a dog' (G43) provide examples of Bow biscuit figures from the collection of Dr. Bernard Watney. The 'Fortune Teller' depicting a gipsy man reading the palm of a young lady (G31) was inspired by an engraving 'La Bonne Daventure' after Boucher.[63]

Bow copies of the 1752-53 Kändler and Reinicke Cries of Paris include the 'Absinth Seller' with tray of wares and a bottle in one hand (G26), a pair of 'Fruit Vendors' (G30), a 'Print Seller' (G38), a 'Hurdy-gurdy Player' (G27), and a 'Vintner' represented by a youth holding a bunch of grapes who stands cross-legged beside a pannier of fruit (G41). There are several beggars and two beggar women (Plate 59) (G27-29). One of the women holds a baby in a crib (G29). Engravings after Lancret were the basis of the group 'Lovers with a

60. 'The French Influence at Chelsea' by T.H. Clarke, *Transactions,* English Ceramic Circle, 1959, Vol. 4, pp. 45-47, pl. 24c, Vincennes group.

61. "English White Porcelain in the Collection of Mr. C.H.B. Culdwell' by W.B. Honey, *Apollo,* 1928, Vol. 8, pp. 329-334, fig. III.

62. ibid., fig. IV.

63. 'Some Consequences of the Bow Special Exhibition', op. cit., fig. V.

Plate 59. *'Beggar' and companion 'Beggar Woman' (G28). 6¾ins. (17.1cm). Bow c.1754.*

George Savage

birdcage' (G42) and also of the paired models of a sportsman holding aloft a bird, standing beside a hound and a ram, and a lady who holds open the door of an empty birdcage, known as 'Liberty and Matrimony' (G37). Both were copied from Meissen prototypes. The last mentioned were reissued in debased form both at Bow (H63) and at other English factories where the underlying Freudian connotations were completely lost. A waster of the base of the early Bow sportsman was recovered from the Stratford Langthorn site by A.J. Toppin in 1921.[64]

Chinoiserie groups, emblematic of Air and Fire (G44), were inspired by P. Aveline's engravings after Boucher in 'Décoration Chinoise'.[65] The Elements are represented by a lady leaning upon a birdcage whilst holding aloft a bird and gesticulating to a seated Chinaman who has beside him another bird and a flying fish, and a Chinaman standing beside a stove pouring tea into a cup held by a seated compatriot. They are too complicated to be successful as groups. Rare coloured examples are in the Untermyer Collection. Another most ambitious porcelain group depicts a 'Chinese Goddess flanked by two kneeling Chinamen' (G45). This was taken from Michel Aubert's engraving after Watteau of 'Idole de la Déesse Ki Mao Sao dans le Rayaume de Mang au pays des Laos'.[66] The 'Negress standing beside a basket' (G47), a 'Turk wearing a plumed turban' kneeling beside a sucrier (G48), and a pair of busts mounted on shaped plinths representing a Mongolian prince and his princess (G46) are all based on Meissen prototypes. However, there is a pair of models of boys with flower pots upon their heads (G66) intended to serve as candlesticks which stand nearly fifteen inches tall and may have been adapted from bronze fire-dogs made in the seventeenth century.[67]

The Bow models of animals and birds have a certain charm even though they fall far short of those created by Kändler and his associates at Meissen. Paired groups of 'Ewe reclining with a Lamb' and 'Nanny-Goat with a kid' (G49 and 50) are only about three inches tall and yet are most attractive. Lions, usually modelled as pairs, are depicted lying down with their heads turned (G53), seated with one paw resting upon a tree-stump (Plate 60) (G52), or upon a globe (G54) but the finest of all is a prowling beast which, like the Chelsea version, is based on a Florentine marble. The popularity of the 'Pug' at Meissen was mirrored at Bow where the animal is shown recumbent on a tasselled cushion (G56), standing (G57), or seated upon a square base (G58). An oustanding model of a retriever stands with mouth open with one paw upon a dead bird (G59). There is also an exceptionally rare model of a 'Fox with game' (G51).

During this early phase of production, the Bow aviary is small and includes a crane (G60), a heron (G62) and an ostrich (G63) which may be based on oriental originals. A pair of 'Grotesque Birds' (G61) may possibly have been intended to represent cormorants though they could have been adapted from *blanc-de-Chine* representations of the Chinese 'Phoenix'. A pheasant standing upon a rocky mound (G65) bears a resemblance to a Longton Hall pair of pheasants (O25). There is also a fine pair of owls (G64) which recall the style of the raised anchor Chelsea models of hen harriers (B28).

Bow Figures made between 1755 and 1765

Paste and Glaze

Bone-ash continued to be used in the Bow paste throughout the lifetime of the factory and, from the seventeen to eighteen per cent of phosphoric acid detected by analysis, some forty to forty-five per cent was included in the mix.

64. 'Bow Porcelain — Recent Excavations', op. cit.

65. *Louvre Inventaire General,* Vol. II, no. 1415, fig. 9, 'Décoration Chinoise', after Antoine Watteau.

66. *Porcelain* (London, 1962) by H.G. Tait, fig. 28, engraving by Aubert; fig. 26, Bow porcelain group.

67. *English Porcelain Figures of the 18th Century,* (Lane) op. cit., p. 89.

Plate 60. A pair of lions, each with one paw upon a tree-stump (G52). 4⅛ins. (10.5cm). Bow c.1752-54.
George Savage

Other constituents remained virtually unaltered. However, the milky whiteness of the paste which today is so greatly appreciated was not at that time considered admirable for it was the aim to simulate the cold flitter of Meissen hard paste. In order to achieve this end, after 1760, both paste and glaze were blued with a pinch of cobalt. Accordingly, inspection of figures issued after this date shows that the brownish tint seen deep in the folds of garments has been replaced by a bluish hue. The glaze became thinner and hence obscuration of modelling detail was reduced. The brown specks with black centres, known as sanding or bird's eyes, continued to be evident and are most readily detected upon areas left in the white. Other blemishes, such as crazing, dry patches and staining are relatively infrequent.

The Bases

Reference has already been made to the use of clumsy 'S' and 'C' scrolls for adornment of the base of some models in the late 1753/54 period. These were usually picked out in a purplish black or purplish grey enamel in a style that displayed imperfect understanding of the rococo. By about 1754/55, scrolls become lighter in form and are more elegantly arranged. However, until 1756, a large proportion of models continued to be issued upon plain mounds or irregular pads which are devoid of scrolls but have flowers and leaves moulded and enamelled upon their superior surface in the old baroque fashion developed during the 1730s at Meissen. There are some which combine the two and have moulded and enamelled scrolls around the circumference of the mound and flowers upon the top. The inferior surface is invariably covered with a flat plate of paste perforated by a small ventilation hole and has been ground to facilitate level stance. Circa 1758, the design of the bases assume greater importance and many quite elaborate forms may be recognised. Nearly all of these have a glazed concave under surface surrounded by a flat circumferential ring which has been ground. This is very similar to bases favoured during the period of the gold anchor at Chelsea. In both, the ventilation hole is small and cylindrical in section though often fine particles of frit or sand may be adherent to the glazed concave area which is rarely seen on Chelsea examples. Some bases are elevated upon four short 'S', or cabriole, legs with a dependent 'U' scroll between the front pair. These were initially enamelled in a deep vermillion or purplish black. Between 1760 and 1765, modelling of legs and scrolls became more elaborate and their colouring more varied and complex, as may be evident on a large model of Minerva (H84). In some instances, including many models of musicians, there are two 'S' shaped legs to the base in front whilst a single straight support is provided at the back. By 1765, some highly scuptural bases were developed incorporating scrolls with comma or vertical slot shaped fenestrations. Examples of the first mentioned are illustrated by the 'New Dancers' (H34). Horizontal apertures, which may penetrate the figure from the back to enter the central cavity, are usually square or triangular in section though there are exceptions.

Enamel Colouring

Until about 1758, the simplicity of the earlier style of decoration was preserved though the range of enamel palette increased. Parallel with this development, an ever diminishing proportion of models were issued in the white. Notable additions included a turquoise, introduced c.1755, which is finer than that of Derby but lacks the deep richness of the Chelsea colour; it also tended to flake off the glaze until c.1760. An opaque light blue was also developed together with an inimitable emerald green which was vibrant and transparent. The earlier yellow-green was retained and combined upon leaves in bocages with the emerald green to create a pleasingly variegated effect. The dry sealing-wax red was now complemented by a crimson-purple and the pale yellow by a deep lemon yellow. Towards 1760, a beautiful violet blue was introduced. The previous warm browns, purplish-grey, gold-purple and black continued to be employed.

The Decorative Styles

Until about 1756-58, enamels were applied as plain washes, often of strangely pleasing discordant colours between large passages of white. Areas representing flesh were left either uncoloured or were tinted the palest buff heightened with a suspicion of orange-red upon the cheeks. Eyelids, eyebrows, and eyelashes were all suggested by lines drawn in a purplish brown whilst irises were usually grey, brown or very rarely a violet hue.[68] Pupils were a purplish black. Hair was indicated by a wash of colour over which pencilling in a purplish grey or black was overlaid. This has a rather even and mechanically contrived appearance and is dissimilar from that seen on models painted at other contemporary English factories. Pockets, buttons, and flaps of garments may be drawn in black, dark brown or red and are best seen upon pale ground colours of clothing. Gilding is rare and, when present, pale and watery. Those accessories such as shoe-buckles, which might properly be gilded, are usually left uncoloured. Floral painting upon garments is usually small in scale and in the style of *Indianische Blumen*. Simple stylised blooms outlined in black are filled with flat washes of red, blue, yellow or purple and leaves with a yellow-green. Naturally represented blossoms, after the fashion of *Deutsche Blumen,* are larger in size but less common. Most, include a large dull blue flower, a deep yellow bell and a crimson rose with highlights left white. Both varieties of painting were carried out in the factory but there is a small group of figures adorned by an independent decorator. These display flowers outlined in black with a thread-like spray winding behind the main flower.[69]

After 1756-58, the overall decoration became more elaborate. Plain washes were broken up with reserves, often trefoil or quatrefoil in shape, sometimes framed with scrolls of gilt, in which are painted florettes, patterns made of dots, stars, circles and lines, intended to simulate brocade. Similar compositions cover garments left in the white though in a few models issued between 1758 and 1765 this is replaced with floral designs in the European taste executed in a very bright palette. Areas representing flesh are now completely covered with a medium buff colour heightened with iron red patches over the cheeks. Eyes are, most often, painted after the manner favoured at Meissen with irises of orange-pink though some retain the former

68. 'Evidence that some 18th Century English Porcelain Figures have blue eyes' by Peter Bradshaw, *Journal of the Northern Ceramic Society,* 1977, Vol. 2.

69. 'The King, the Nun and Other Figures' by Bernard Watney, *Transactions,* English Ceramic Circle, 1968, Vol. 7, pt. 1, p. 54.

more usual colours of brown and grey. Pencilling of hair is less prominent and sometimes omitted. Gilding of a somewhat brassy appearance was employed not only upon the edges of garments, buttons, and musical instruments but also within enamel decoration upon dresses, waistcoats and coats. Indeed, very little of the paste remains visible beneath the plethora of gilt and enamel adornment. The change in style is also seen on bases where the deep crimson purple employed to delineate scrolls is joined by turquoise, dark blue and other colours as well as by gilding. The moulded leaves upon the superior surface of bases as well as those used in bocages were initially yellow-green, later emerald and after about 1760 both shades give a variegated effect. Some display branching dorsal veins drawn in purple or deep brown. Moulded and applied flowers have their tips touched with red, yellow, blue, or purple and have either yellow or dark brown centres. The ring of dots around the centre so commonly seen on Chelsea flowers of the same period either do not occur or are exceptionally rare. By 1765, the delightful simplicity of decoration was completely destroyed and the dramatic impact of the figure itself lost.

The Marks

Many Bow figures are unmarked and no single device was used by the factory. The early inkwells marked 'New Canton' supply the explanation for the later use of pseudo-Chinese characters which are drawn in underglaze blue. Most are meaningless though, either accidentally or deliberately, the ideogram for jade appears on many models. These are illustrated by William Chaffers.[70] Other marks include the capital letters: 'B', 'F', 'G', 'I', 'K', 'P', and 'X', as well as a strange letter 'A' which has a V-shaped cross-piece. There is no justification whatsoever for associating the letter 'R' with Rysbrack or Roubiliac, or the letter 'B' with Bacon. The letters are, almost certainly, the marks of repairers, painters or gilders. The incised marks 'T' and 'To' are now thought to be the devices used by the repairer Tebo, or Thibauld, who worked at Bow until about 1768 when he served as modeller for the Worcester and Champion's Bristol factory. In 1774 he went to work for Wedgwood at Etruria. Occasionally an underglaze crescent, akin to that which was used at Worcester, may be found on Bow figures. The overglaze marks of an anchor and dagger, usually in red enamel but occasionally in gilt, usually accompanied by an underglaze blue 'B', may be evident on figures issued between 1760 and 1768 and probably signify decoration in the studio of the independent porcelain enameller, James Giles. It has been suggested that after the bankruptcy of Crowther in 1762, William Duesbury may have run the Bow factory and sent much of the ware and figures to Giles whom he also financed before purchasing his business.

The Modelling

After 1753-54, the pop-eyed, heavily nosed, men and ungainly wenches disappear as the Muses Modeller acquired the simplified modelling style learned by inspection of Meissen prototypes. Nevertheless, the earlier distinctive traits remain identifiable although they were muted. Thus, forehead and chin are perceptably receding and eyes are more prominent than those of Chelsea and Derby models though the noses were modified to become tip-tilted and the mouth was indicated now only by enamel colour. There is an impish inclination of head, and an unnatural twist of the body just above the hips that is characteristic of Bow models in this period whilst slight flexion of both knees gives them a sense of rhythm and movement and a toy-like quality which contrasts favourably with contemporary Derby figures that are stiffly posed and stare vacantly into space. Tree-stump supports of figures issued between 1754 and 1755 are often adorned sparsely with moulded leaves and by

70. *Marks & Monograms on European & Oriental Pottery and Porcelain,* op. cit., pp. 283-286.

Plate 61. 'Pantalone' (H3) from the Commedia dell' Arte, after Reinicke's prototype. 4ins. (10.2cm). Bow c.1756. Author's collection

about 1755-58 this foliage became more dense and included flowers. These stood out like fans on either side but rarely extended above waist height. Subsequently bocages developed to emulate the gold anchor Chelsea style. Leaves prior to 1755, confined to the superior surface of bases, are canoe-shaped but, by about 1756, they assume the appearance of holly with spiky edges and are rather large in scale to the figure. After about 1765, their perimeters become more regular and are either serrated or smooth like the foliage of a laurel bush. These may have rather clumsy moulded dorsal veins. Flowers are also rather large and are saucer shaped with either rounded petals or, more often, long pointed petals few of which have survived intact.

The Models

The number of different models made at Bow between 1755 and 1765 was prodigious and here it is possible only to give a representative selection. Bow models of characters from the Commedia dell'Arte, like those of Chelsea, are mostly copied from the set made by Peter Reinicke for the Duke of Weissenfels. They include 'Columbina' (H2) dancing, 'Dottore Baloardo' (H4) striking a pose, 'Mezzetino' (H6) in his traditional costume and soft hat, 'Pedrolino' (H8) whose hands are elevated in horror or surprise, and 'Pantalone' (Plate 61) (H3) in his long gown who in one version has unaccountably lost his money-bag. The Bow figure known as 'the Captain' (H7), like his Chelsea brother, is a copy of Reinicke's Narcissino. A few models follow originals by Kändler including 'Arlecchino seated with bagpipes' and 'Columbina playing a hurdy-gurdy' (H10), a pair of 'Boy dressed as an Arlecchino' and 'Girl attired as Columbina' (H12), and 'Arlecchino wearing mask and motley' (H1). The last named may have been based upon a figure in the background of the engraving by C.N. Cochin 'Belle, n'écoutez rien', after Watteau. There is, also, a tall and stiffly posed figure in a long skirt representing 'Isabella' (H5) who may possibly have been adapted

Plate 62. 'Turk' and companion 'Levantine Lady' (H14). 8ins. (20.3cm). Bow c.1760. An earlier version of the Turk is shown in Colour Plate F.
Grosvenor Antiques

from a shepherdess. Also, a lady in a brimmed hat with a basket over her right arm who holds a posy in her right hand, has been called Columbina[71] but she seems to have been copied from the red anchor Chelsea figure emblematic of Spring (C98) from the set of the 'Rustic Seasons' and here has been listed as a 'Lady in brimmed hat' (H59). Only one model relates to the contemporary English theatre and that is of 'David Garrick as Falstaff' (H11) inspired by C. Grignion's engraving of a painting by Francis Hayman. This is different from the Derby and Chelsea-Derby versions which depict James Quinn in the role.

Foreign personalities by reason of their colourful dress were eminently suitable for translation into porcelain and their popularity is underlined by the number common to Bow and Chelsea based on Meissen prototypes. A seated 'Turk in a plumed turban' and companion 'Levantine Lady in a tall head-dress', each beside a shell container (H15) and a standing 'Levantine Lady adjusting her head-dress' (Plate 62) (H14) are examples. However, the Bow partner of the last named was a 'Turk' in a plumed turban wearing a fur-edged cloak (Colour Plate F) (H14) in place of the Chelsea 'Turk in a tall hat' (C69). They were based on engravings in the de Ferriol folio previously mentioned. There are some charming models of a Turkish Boy wearing a turban and a cloak and a 'Lady' in tall head-dress (H16), a 'Youth in Turkish costume' (H17) who owing to his pose with one hand upon his breast may represent an actor, and a 'Turkish Dancing Girl' (H18) who typifies the Bow style with her tiny head impudently inclined and body twisted at the hips to produce a sense of rhythm and movement. Common to Chelsea and Bow are the models of 'Indian Prince', depicted as a negro wearing a crown, and his 'Indian Queen' portrayed by a negress in a feathered head-dress (H21). A group showing a 'Turkish lady being proferred refreshments by a Negro Page' (H20) follows a Kändler original. Chinoiserie seems to have passed out of fashion and was represented only by the group known as the 'Chinese Magician', composed of a Chinaman, a bear and a child standing upon a chair (H13). This was reissued after 1765 in a more elaborate style (I 3) and was based on an engraving after Boucher.

71. The Saltram House Collection (1977); no. 260.T.

Plate 63. *A pair of cooks (H27). 7ins. (17.8cm). Bow c.1755.* George Savage

Bow examples of the Cries of Paris mostly follow those made between 1752 and 1753 by Kändler and Reinicke after watercolour sketches by C. Huet. Most of the Bow copies are based on different characters to those of Chelsea. They include an 'Alchemist' with a tray of bottles (H23), a 'Rat Catcher' who stands with a box and a ferret with a monkey upon his shoulder (H39), a 'Tinker' with an assortment of pots and pans (H42), and a 'Pedlar with a begging bowl' (H35) sometimes paired with a 'Woman with a tray of trinkets'. There is an 'Itinerant Musician' who has a magic lantern upon his back and who is shown turning the handle of a barrel-organ (H32), and a 'Knife Grinder' (H30). A pair of cooks bearing platters of food (Plate 63) (H27) are often incised with the letter 'B' and are known in Chelsea versions (C23). Another model of a cook standing beside a stove with a saucepan, tasting the contents with his finger (H28), was copied from a figure in Kändler's 'Small Artisan' series and is not, strictly speaking one of the Paris Cries. Although this model was not copied at Chelsea, interestingly enough, there is a Chelsea version of Kändler's 'Cupid as a Cook' (D1) which was based upon the adult model.

Several Bow models portray peasants after the manner of Teniers but were derived from Meissen prototypes. These include a woodman with a axe (Plate 64) and woodman with a saw (H44), a male toper drinking from a bottle and a companion lady with a glass of wine (H33), and two versions of a 'Boy Toper', one showing him seated upon a tree-stump (Plate 65) (H26) the other astride a cask (H25). A girl fish vendor, standing beside a pail of fish and companion boy with an up-turned creel (H24) follow originals by Kändler. Models of a peasant and companion girl dancing with arms akimbo (H36) are known also in candlestick adaptations. The Bow 'Tyrolean Dancers' (H43) after Eberlein, show the rustic swain bareface and thus differs from the Chelsea and Derby versions in which the youth wears a grotesque mask (C46 and K53). Another pair of models are known as the 'New Dancers' (Plate 66) (H34), presumably to distinguish them from the 'Tyrolean Dancers' which may have been the 'old dancers'. There are Derby and Longton prototypes of these figures.[72] The pair consist of a boy in brimmed hat turned up at one side waring a jacket and trousers whilst his companion has a picture hat with a plume, a laced bodice and an apron over her long skirt; both have their arms raised before them as if dancing. They are about the most common of all Bow models and may be found mounted upon mound, legged, or fenestrated bases, single or as a group, with and without bocage and both free standing and incorporated into candlesticks. A Chaffers' Liverpool version of the male figure is also known.[73] The 'Piedmontese Bagpiper' (H37) is immediately identifiable by his broad-brimmed plumed hat, long cloak and massive musical instrument. He follows a Meissen model based upon an engraving by J. Dumont le Romain. A pilgrim with a pack upon his back and a staff in his hand (H38), mounted upon a square base, is known in carved wood and bronze versions.

A triste damsel, sometimes called the 'Lady with a Handkerchief' (Plate 67) (H41) gives the appearance of having stepped out of a contemporary drama, but she is really a 'Sailor's Lass'. Bernard Watney recalled that the model had been coupled with one of a 'Sailor' in the sale of the collection of William Bemrose, at Nottingham, in 1909. Confirmation of the identity of the lady was obtained by finding a paired group composed of the models before a bocage.[74] It has never been ascertained whether the object held by the wench is a handkerchief to dry the tears of impending separation or a purse containing the 'wages of sin'.

There are Many different musicians in the Bow orchestra, mostly seated and issued as pairs based somewhat freely on Meissen originals. Many are mounted

72. From the Catalogue by Winifred Williams of the Exhibition of Early Derby Porcelain 1750-1770 held at 3 Bury St., London, January 1973, fig. 20, Derby 'New Dancers', c.1756. *Longton Hall Porcelain* (London, 1957) by Bernard Watney, pl. 50A, Longton Hall 'New Dancers'.

73. 'The King, the Nun and Other Figures', op. cit., pl. 55B, Chaffers Liverpool 'New Dancer'.

74. *Porcelain Figurines* (London, 1975) by Nathaniel Harris, p. 52.

***Plate 64** (left). A woodman with an axe (missing) H44). 5¾ins. (14.6cm). Bow c.1755.*
George Savage

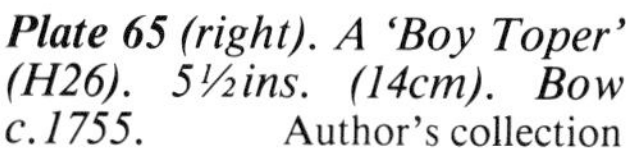

***Plate 65** (right). A 'Boy Toper' (H26). 5½ins. (14cm). Bow c.1755.* Author's collection

***Plate 66.** 'New Dancers' (H34). 7¾ins. and 7½ins. (19.7cm and 19.1cm). Bow c.1765. Mounted on highly sculptural bases with comma shaped fenestrations.* Author's collection

***Plate 67.** A 'Sailor's Lass', sometimes called the 'Lady with a handkerchief' (H41). 7½ins. (19.1cm). Bow c.1756-58.*
Author's collection

upon table-like bases which have two short and curved legs in front and a straight support behind. They are extremely attractive, especially those issued prior to 1760 which are clad in pale colours and have large passages left in the white. They include a 'Gentleman with a Flute' and 'Lady with a Mandoline (Plate 68) (H51), a 'Lady with a Zither' and a 'Boy with drum and fife' (H50), all four of which are seated and a standing 'Trumpeter' and 'Lady with a Triangle' (H52) to mention a few examples. The 'Boy with reed-pipe' and companion 'Lady with Tambourine' (H57), examples of which are in the Untermyer Collection, are later models and show a greater complexity of detail and more brash style of decoration. The standing man with fife and tambour attached to his sleeve (Plate 69) and companion lady with a triangle, often named the 'Idyllic Musicians' (H45) and are known also in Derby versions (K42). Owing to the long plumes attached to the hat and head-dress of the models they may be called the 'flambé musicians'. There are two models, both standing upon shaped plinths, of a drummer boy and a companion boy flautist (H48). A vase decorated with four cartouches that has models of three children emblematic of 'Music', 'Drama' and the 'Dance' (H168) was issued to commemorate the death of the composer Handel in 1759.

During the decade 1760 to 1770, the theme of the erotic pastoral became increasingly popular. Later versions of 'Liberty and Matrimony' (H63), however, became emasculated and lost the vigour of the first copies of the Meissen originals of 1752. Now, instead of the sportsman holding aloft a bird, he clutches a nest of fledglings in both hands at waist level whilst his insipid companion grasps a lantern-like bird-cage. Models of a small 'Shepherd Bagpiper' (Plate 70) wearing a wide brimmed hat standing beside his dog and

Plate 68. *'Gentleman with a flute' and 'Lady with a mandoline' (missing) (H51). 7ins. (17.8cm). Bow c.1756. Incised mark of a script G.* George Savage

Plate 69. *A musician with three-holed pipe and tambourine, one of the 'Idyllic Musicians' (H45). 7¾ins. (19.7cm). Bow c.1760.*
Author's Collection

Colour Plate J. *Four models from a set of four pairs of figures emblematic of the 'Four Seasons' (J32). 5¾ins. to 7½ins. (14.6cm to 19.1cm). Dry-edge Derby c.1754/5. 'Spring', a lady holding a posy, with flowers gathered in her apron; 'Summer', a woman holding a bird's nest, and a harvester holding a corn-sheaf; 'Winter', an old man holding out one hand over a brazier with the other in a muff.* Norman C. Ashton collection

Colour Plate K. *'Venus and Cupid' (J30). 7½ins. (19.1cm). Dry-edge Derby c.1753/4. The rather heavy appearance of painted floral sprays in a limited palette are in a style sometimes attributed to William Duesbury.* Norman C. Ashton collection

companion 'Dancing Shepherdess' who is shown lifting her skirt with both hands as if about to dance (H60) are known in dry-edge Derby versions (Plate 88, Chapter VIII) (J13). A larger 'Bow Shepherd Bagpiper wearing a tricorn hat' standing with a pig-like dog and a sheep, is partnered by a 'Shepherdess with blossoms gathered in her apron' (H65). One example of the male figure has the letters 'I.B. 1757' (possibly for John Bowcocke) within a circle upon the bagpipes.[75] The same models were later reissued upon gilded and scrolled bases and some of them are marked with a red anchor and dagger which is a device thought to have been used by James Giles, the independent decorator.[76] Other examples of the pastoral theme are provided by models of a shepherd standing cross-legged playing a recorder beside a recumbent dog, and a shepherdess who has flowers and a lamb (H66). There are several versions of this pair some of which incorporate candle sconces and bocages. The Meissen prototypes are in the Fitzwilliam Museum, Cambridge.[77] The 'Sportsman in a peaked cap' leaning upon a gun, with game in his right hand, has as his companion a lady wearing a riding habit, who has a hooded falcon upon her wrist (Plate 71) (H67). Another couple consist of a 'Sportsman in a tricorn hat' holding a gun horizontally by its middle, and a 'Lady holding a pistol' (H69). These and other similar models stem from Meissen originals mostly by Kändler and Reinicke. Models of gardeners and their wives (Plate 72) (H61) are mostly included in sets at Bow representing the Four Seasons rather than issued as pairs. There are some fearsome 'Pugilists' (H64) stripped to the waist and often with heads shaven examples of which are in the Victoria and Albert Museum.

75 From the catalogue of the Exhibition of Bow Porcelain 1744-1776, op. cit., no. 101, fig. 31.

76. ibid., no. 150.

77. Collection of Lord Fisher, Fitzwilliam Museum, Cat. no. 972.

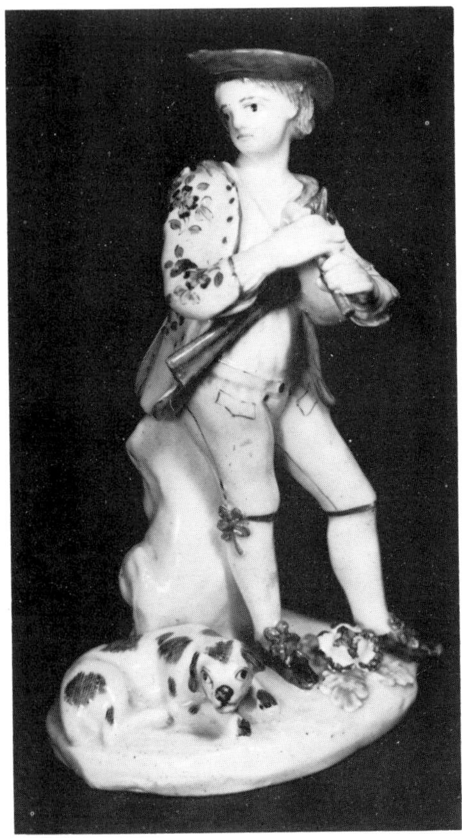

Plate 70. *The 'Boy Shepherd Piper' (H60). 6¼ins. (15.9cm). Bow c.1755. For Derby version see Plate 89.* Author's collection

Plate 71. *Lady holding a hooded falcon and companion 'Sportsman in a peaked hat' with a gun holding game beside a dog (H67). 7½ins. (19.1cm). Bow c.1756.* Author's collection

Some models of mythological subjects echo Meissen originals and these include Apollo (H70) wearing a laurel wreath and carrying a lyre, Jupiter (H81) with an eagle, Mercury clad in winged helmet and sandals bearing the caduceus (H85), and Minerva with an owl (H84). The last mentioned may have been based on the model at the summit of a centrepiece known as the 'Temple of Minerva' created by Kändler c.1745.[78] The Bow version of Mars (H83) has lion mask epaulettes and Diana (H76) with her hunting dog follows Eberlein's original. A model of 'Flora' (H79) stands eighteen inches tall and may be based either on Rysbrack's statue or a terracotta by Scheemakers of the 'Flora Farnese'. There is another Bow 'Flora' (H78) portrayed as a lady standing and holding a posy to her nose beside a flower encrusted plinth upon which rests a perfume burner. It is a copy of Eberlein's figure emblematic of Smell from his set of the Five Senses; no other models from the set appear to have been copied at Bow. Some examples are incised 'Faustina'. John Bowcocke's Memorandum Book contains the entry dated 21st May, 1760: "3 fostina 3s. 6d. each — 10s. 6d."[79] According to Jean Plaidy, during the reign of George II there were two famous sopranos, one named Faustina, the other Cuzzoni.[80] 'Fame' (Plate 73) (H77) is represented as a winged angel with a trumpet. Neptune (H86) stands tamely beside his dolphin and is often paired with Jupiter (H82) astride an eagle which may be a reissue of an earlier model since the Neptune of the preceding phase of production rode his dolphin (G22). Venus is depicted standing with one breast bared carrying a torch

78. *Porcelain,* op. cit., p. 54, 'The temple of Minerva' from the collection of the Marquis of Bath, Longleat.

79. *Bow Porcelain,* op. cit., p. 70.

80. *Newsletter of the Northern Ceramic Society,* No. 31, Sep. 1978, item 17. 'Notes and Queries' by Mrs. Margaret M. Newton.

Plate 72. *Bocage group of gardener and companion woman with flowers (H61). 10ins. (25.4cm). Bow c.1765. The ring of dots around the centre of each flower and the thin bocage are features more usually associated with Chelsea.*
Sotheby Parke Bernet

Plate 73. *'Fame' portrayed as an angel with a trumpet (missing) (H77). 7½ins. (19.1cm) approx. Bow c.1760.* Private collection

Plate 74. *'The Four Seasons', represented by individual standing putti (H97). 6ins. (15.2cm). Bow c.1765.* Grosvenor Antiques
Late Lady Ludlow collection

(H89), and also reclining looking into a square mirror (H90) and this version is also used with minor modification to serve as Sight in the set of the Five Senses (H99).

The 'Antique Seasons' (H91) consist of men and women wearing classical robes standing beside vases and follow originals by Eberlein.[81] The 'Rustic Seasons' (H92) are represented by seated men and women in contemporary dress: Spring is a girl wearing a picture hat and holding a posy seated beside a basket of flowers; Summer is a girl wearing a hat with the brim turned back in front beside a corn sheaf with corn stalks in her lap; Autumn is a youth holding a goblet and a bunch of grapes in either hand; Winter is a man wearing a heavy overcoat with a cowl pulled over his head who leans forward to warm both hands over a brazier. A variant of Winter shows the same figure who leans upon a short stick with one hand and holds his other over a charcoal container that has two handles. There is also a set of 'Standing Rustic Seasons' (H94) in which Spring is a peasant woman with flowers in her apron standing beside an up-turned basket of flowers; Summer is a similar woman beside a corn sheaf; Autumn is a youth who stand astride a cask holding grapes beside a vine; Winter is a rustic who warms both hands over a charcoal container suspended from his belt. Another set depicts young bloods and their girls in which they stand with appropriate accessories with the exception of Winter who wears his tricorn hat to which are attached ear-flaps, and who has both hands in a fur muff (H93). The 'Classical Seasons' (H95) utilize standing adult figures in classical dress each attended by a putto and placed beside a candlestick and are copied from Kändler's originals. Four putti (Plate 74) (H97) which are stiffly modelled wearing respectively flowers, corn stalks, grapes, and holly which form chaplets and diagonal cross bands, also were intended to portray the seasons and a set was once in the Lady Ludlow

81. *Bow Porcelain,* op. cit., pl. 51a, the Bow 'Antique Seasons', pl. 51b, the Meissen Seasons by Eberlein.

Plate 75. Three small bustos of Flora, Ceres and Bacchus, emblematic of Spring, Summer and Autumn (H98). 5⅝ins. (14.3cm). Bow c.1758. George Savage

Plate 76. A rare model of a Lady stroking a dog, emblematic of 'Feeling' from the set of the Five Senses (H99). 6½ins. (16.5cm). Bow c.1755. Private Collection

Plate 77. 'Lady in a Crinoline holding a Fan' (H104). 7½ins. (19.1cm). Bow c.1760. Grosvenor Antiques

Collection. Lastly, there are four bustos (H98), each upon a shaped plinth, which depict Flora, Ceres, Bacchus, and Saturn, three of which are shown in Plate 75.

Complete sets of Bow Senses (H99) must be exceedingly rare. Feeling is a seated lady who strokes a spaniel that has one paw upon her lap (Plate 76); Sight is a lady seated before a square hand mirror adjusting her hair; Hearing is a gentleman with a lute; Taste is a youth eating grapes beside a pannier; Smell is a girl who holds a posy to her nose. The 'Four Elements' (Colour Plate E) (H100) include Neptune standing beside a dolphin; Cybele with a cornucopia and a lion; and Vulcan portrayed as a youth beside a flaming urn. The same three figures were issued at Chelsea where the fourth, emblematic of Air was Juno beside an eagle, her veil and clothing blown out by the wind. More often this is replaced in the Bow version by the model of Jupiter astride an eagle. The 'Four Quarters of the Globe'[82] exist only in the form of paired figures beside chamber candlesticks but were later reissued as individual figures (I 17).

Portrait models include General Wolfe (H109), the captor of Quebec, who died upon the Heights of Abraham in the hour of his triumph; the Marquis of Granby (H107) in the uniform of Colonel-in-Chief of the Blues to commemorate the victory at Minden; and Frederick the Great (H101) the 'Prussian Hero'. Gallants and their ladies were often based on models of members of the Dresden court. Kändler's 'Gentleman in a Dressing-gown', leaning forward to blow a kiss to a 'Lady in a Crinoline' who holds a fan had been inspired by J.B. Pater's engraving 'Le Baiser Rendu'.[83] The first Meissen models were devoid of bases which enhanced the sense of intimacy between the pair. Bow copies (H102) are most often mounted upon tall rococo bases which impart an altogether different feeling of detachment. Further, the dress of the Bow paramour has been altered to include flounces in keeping with the prevailing fashion. There is a Bow 'Gallant' in a huge waistcoat (H103), paired with a 'Lady' in elbow length sleeves and a quilted underskirt. These recall

82. Upton House, Collection of Lord Bearsted, Cat. no. 4.

83. *Porcelain Figures of the 18th Century* (Vermont, U.S.A., 1949) by David Rosenfield, p. 42, Meissen models.

Plate 78. *'A seated Nun' reading the Divine Office (H116). 5¾ins. (14.6cm). Bow c.1753/4, after a Meissen prototype of c.1744 by J.J. Kändler.* Author's collection

Höchst models of 'Cynthio del Sole' and 'Isabella' by Simon Feilner. A 'Lady in a Crinoline and holding a Fan' (Plate 77) (H104) is also after a Kändler prototype and there is also a Hussar in fur lined shako and dolman' (H108).

Few models were made for devotional purposes though there are a number of semi-humorous representations of Monks and Nuns. A few are depicted standing (H111, H112 and H113) (Plates 79a and 79b) but the vast majority are seated reading from books (H114-H117) (Plate 78). These may hold their missal in both hands, or have one hand lying free upon their lap; most attractive of all are those with one hand poised in the air about to turn over a page when male and female are in mirror image positions. A rare model of a bishop in a mitre (H110) has his right arm raised in benediction.

Before completing a review of human figures, it is necessary to mention a large number of stiffly modelled putti, or according to the catalogues, 'Girls' and 'Boys'. Literally thousands of these were issued both from the Bow and Derby factories and were exported to the Continent where they enjoyed great popularity. Most are nude with garlands of blossoms slung diagonally from the left shoulder and chaplets upon their brows. Most common, are those who carry flower-pots or baskets of flowers held in both hands; a few grasp posies in either hand and there are others holding puppies (H121). Girls have a queue of hair at the back, narrower brows, and their modesty drape hangs from the left hip, an arrangement reversed for boys. Putti were also incorporated into candlesticks (Plate 80) (H122) and there are two charming groups of putti adorning goats with flowers (Colour Plate H) (H118). Examples of a Derby 'Boy with Posies' (Plate 102, Chapter VIII) and a Bow 'Putto with a Puppy' (Plate 81) are illustrated.

The Bow aviary is large and many examples of models are illustrated in the catalogues of the Lady Ludlow[84] and the Judge Irwin Untermyer[85] collections.

84. *The Catalogue of the Lady Ludlow Collection* (London, 1932) by Arthur Hatden.

85. *Chelsea and Other English Porcelain, Pottery and Enamels in the Irwin Untermyer Collection* (Cambridge, Mass., 1957) by Yvonne Hackenbroch.

Plate 79a. *A standing nun (H113). 7ins. (17.8cm). Bow c.1760.* George Savage

Plate 79b. *A standing monk (H113). 7ins. (17.8cm). Bow c.1760.* George Savage

Plate 80. *Pair of candlesticks decorated with seated putti and flowers, mounted on bases with 'S' shaped legs and dependent 'U' scrolls (H122). 7½ins. (19.1cm). Bow c.1765.* Sotheby Parke Bernet

Plate 81. *A 'Putto with a puppy' (H121). 4¾ins. (12.1cm). Bow c.1760.* Author's collection

Bow birds display an admirable sense of movement which has been achieved by unnatural twisting of the normal anatomy in a manner also used to represent human subjects. They are mostly decorated in rather bright and unreal plumage and in consequence have a toy-like quality. The effect is quite different from that created by the pale Derby birds which perch like stool pigeons. They are also generally larger in scale. Amongst the most appealing are pairs of pheasants (H143 and H144), 'Parrots eating fruit' (H139), a fine kestrel (H136), and a pair of superb owls (H138). There are a great number of finches (H129-H135), and two versions of 'Cockerel' and 'Hen' (H128), one hen being portrayed with three chicks (H147). Two beautiful pairs of birds in bocages topped by candle holders include 'Buntings in a cherry tree' (H127) and a pair of 'Song Birds' (H148).

The menagerie embraces the usual models of cows and bulls (H152), ewe and ram (H155), and some amusing cats with prey (H150 and H151). There are also a few rather unsatisfactory farmyard groups (H153 and H154). There are two rare fable groups (H156 and H157) portraying the 'Fox dining with the Stork', and the 'Stork dining with the Fox', repasts at which the visitor went hungry. 'Squirrels eating nuts' (H164) also exist in early Chelsea (A18) and Derby (K145) versions. A fine pair of seated hounds (H158) were probably copied from Chelsea prototypes (B58). There are other models including several pairs of monkies (H161 and H162), and a seated pug (H163) that follow Meissen originals.

Figures made at Bow between 1765 and 1776

Paste and Glaze

Although chemical analysis of the paste of late Bow wares and figures shows little modification from that initially employed, imperfect firing greatly altered the appearance of the body which is most evident on useful wares. The paste displays a dull grey colour and is almost completely opaque after the fashion of stoneware. The glaze is generally thinner but has an unpleasant bluish tinge which is most clearly seen deep in crevices of garments on models. Imperfections, such as firecracks, sanding, and pinhole defects in the glaze, are notable features and a number of models also show crazing.

Bases

Almost every model is mounted upon an elaborately shaped base of which there are several forms. Some are after the fashion of ormolu mounts with scrolls in high relief and either comma or vertical slot fenestrations. Others take the form of a double inverted 'U', whilst some have 'S' shaped legs between which are dependant 'U' scrolls. Inferior surfaces of more complex forms are glazed apart from the feet of legs, whilst simpler ones have glazed domed central areas surrounded by a ground flat rim which is greasy to the touch and may have particles of frit adherent to it.

Enamel Colours

The inimitable emerald green was replaced by a thick opaque yellow green and the sparkling enamel dark blue by an inky underglaze colour. Watery turquoise and pink appear liberally, chiefly upon bases where they are associated with a pale watery gilding. Areas representing flesh are covered with a deep buff, heightened with orange-red upon lips and cheeks. The process, which commenced c.1758-60 of breaking up ground colours with reserves filled with diaper and brocade patterns, was developed until eventually scarcely a square inch remained that was not covered with some decoration. The debased standards of flower painting on dresses is best seen with a hand lens.

Modelling Characteristics

Many models were reissued from old moulds or were copied from gold anchor Chelsea prototypes and very few new figures were issued. The decline in the importance of the figure model to become little more than part of a decorative design was nowhere more apparent than at Bow. They become stiff and doll-like and are off set by huge bocages, candle sconces, and highly sculptural bases. A certain carelessness in assembly was usual, often leading to odd features that could not be corrected after burning, such as a hand erroneously placed like a flower in a bocage which necessitated coverage of the stump of the wrist with leaves and flowers.[86]

Models

The number of new models issued after 1765 was small. There is a strange 'Arlecchino' with an oddly pointed head, paired with 'Columbina', each dancing. They may appear on two high scrolled and fenestrated bases or married on a single wide and flat base edged with scrolls (I1). A 'Fortune Telling group' (I13) based on the engraving by Laurent Cars of Watteau's 'La Diseuse Daventure', is almost identical to a gold anchor Chelsea version (D114). By comparison with the early Bow group (G31) after Boucher's 'La Bonne Aventure', the later group seems ugly, with a crone standing with babe upon her back and a child at her side examining the palm of a young lady.

A great number of older Bow models were reissued, often with minor alterations, in a debased form. The model of 'Columbina seated with a Hurdy-Gurdy' (H10), formerly paired with one of 'Arlecchino with Bagpipes', reappears married to a 'Gentleman with a Violin' which had hitherto (H54) been totally unconnected with Columbina. The two play an unexpected duet before a bocage. Separate models of 'Arlecchino' in motley and 'Columbina' (H1 and H2) first intended as a pair, were reissued on a legged base before a huge bocage topped by a candle sconce. The group known as the Chinese

86. Example once owned by David Thorn.

Musician (H13) depicting a chinaman standing beside a child who is upon a chair and a bear, loses the beast and the figures are remounted in a gazebo topped by a cupola in the new flambouant style (I3). The beautiful simplicity of the two groups of 'Putti garlanding a Nanny-Goat' and 'Billy-Goat' (Colour Plate H) (H118) issued in the early 1760s, is dissipated in the later adaptations which include the addition of candle holders (I4). Indeed, nowhere is the reduced importance of the model more evident than at Bow during the closing years. Individual standing youths and girls, that had so charmingly represented the Four Seasons (H93), are rearranged in pairs embracing Summer and Autumn and Spring and Winter with the inevitable bocages and elaborately sculptured bases (I8). The pair of early seated figures of 'Sportsman with gun' and 'Lady with dog' (G43) of c.1755, biscuit examples of which are in the collection of Dr. Watney, were brought together devoid of identifying accessories and placed before a water fountain on gilded base topped with leaves and flowers (I12). The fine pair of 'Huntsman in peaked cap with Gun' and 'Lady in riding habit with hooded Falcon' (H67) unaccountably acquire huge hounds as well as a plethora of ornament (I10). Debased versions of the 'Idyllic Musicians' (H47) and 'Shepherd playing a Recorder' with 'Shepherdess holding a posy' (H47) serve to underline the general decline of artistic and modelling standards (I15 and I11). The 'New Dancers' (H34) in their updated adaptations cease to dance and, instead, stand like waiters holding open the lids of sweet-meat containers (I16). Probably the 'Rustic Seasons' (Plate 82) (I7) composed of single standing figures of peasants with the appropriate accessories are the most pleasing of the late Bow models.

Plate 82. *The Four Seasons, represented by standing figures with grapes, corn, flowers and holly, Autumn, Summer, Spring and Winter respectively (I 7). 7ins. (17.8cm). Bow c.1770, red anchor and dagger mark.* Grosvenor Antiques

Plate 83. A Gardener standing hat in hand with fruit and vegetables in his apron, emblematic of Autumn (I 9) 13ins. (33cm). Bow c.1766-70. Adapted from a Chelsea prototype included in the 'Allegorical Seasons'. Victoria and Albert Museum

A number of models were taken, or so it would appear, from gold anchor Chelsea moulds. The large standing figure of a gardener (Plate 83) with fruit gathered in his apron and his lady companion who holds a posy and has secured flowers in her apron (I9) were taken from figures in the gold anchor Chelsea groups known as the 'Allegorical Seasons' (D57) and were issued on detachable stands. The large Bow version of the muse Clio, who holds a scroll in her hand (I5), originated as one of Willems set of the Nine Muses (D36). However, a very unattractive pair of Mars who wears a helmet with four divergent plumes and Minerva (I6) may have been original or older models altered beyond recognition.

During the final years, Bow reissued many of the old models several times so that they became increasingly small and modelling details became more and more blurred. The earlier candlestick figures representing the 'Four Quarters of the World' now reappeared on pierced pedestal bases before small bocages extending up to waist level. They may be seen in Saltram House[87] and include Africa as a negress with a lion; America as a Red Indian girl with one foot upon an alligator; Asia as a Levantine girl who carries a casket and has a guitar at her feet; Europe as a small version of Britannia leaning upon a shield (Plate 84) (I17). Many other models that were greatly reduced in size by recasting from moulds made by application to a fired model, were employed to form groups. These marry figures that were often not previously connected and place them before debased small leafed bocages in scenes devoid of all meaning.

87. The Saltram Collection (1977), No. 244.T, the 'Four Quarters of the Globe'. Lord Bearsted Collection, Upton House, Cat. no. 4, candlestick version.

Plate 84. *The 'Four Quarters of the Globe', standing on pierced pedestal bases (I 17). 5¼ins. (13.3cm). Bow c.1766.* Sotheby Parke Bernet

Chapter VIII

The Derby Factories

Part One — Historical survey and figures made prior to 1756

When in 1775, George Holmes (modeller) and Constantine Smith (enameller) wrote seeking employment from Josiah Wedgwood at Etruria, they intimated that they had both worked at Derby[1] for the previous twenty-eight years. Taken at face value, this presupposes the presence of a porcelain factory in that city as early as 1747. In 1809, William Locker, who was then clerk of the Derby porcelain manufactory, wrote: "About 1745 a man, said to be a foreigner in very poor circumstances, living at Lodge Lane [Derby], made small articles in china, such as birds, cats, dogs, sheep, and other small ornamental toys, which he fired in a kiln in the neighbourhood belonging to a pipe-maker named Woodward. Mr. Duesbury frequently visited this image-maker and took great interest in his small factory, and becoming desirous of improving the art, he engaged his services to his own account..."[2] It is scarcely credible that the porcelain we now associate with the first production at Derby could have been burned successfully in a pipe-clay oven. Further, the earliest dated Derby items to have survived are creamers incised '1750'. William Duesbury, moreover, was working as an independent porcelain decorator in London at least as early as November 1751 up to August 1753, if not later, and was subsequently at Longton Hall. It is impossible, therefore, to accept Locker's account of the beginnings of the Derby factory. However, there are a number of relatively primitive porcelain porcelain models which have recently been ascribed to Derby, which here are presented in a separate section under the title of 'Experimental Derby' in Chapter XI.

Certainly there was a foreigner connected with Derby at an early phase of production. Llewellyn Jewitt[3] has identified him as André Planché (1727-1809) and we are indebted both to him and to Mrs. Donald MacAlister[4] for most of what is known about this craftsman. He was born in London of Huguenot parents and, in 1740, was apprenticed goldsmith to Mounteney in the Metropolis. Thus, if Planché ever completed his training, he would have done so in 1747, the year mentioned by Holmes and Smith. His youngest brother Jacques, according to Jewitt, "made his way to Geneva, where he learned the business of watch-making". It is possible that Jacques later became associated with the Swiss clocksmith, Benjamin Vulliamy, in London. Jewitt wrote of André, "I believe he went into Saxony, and there learned the art of making porcelain at Dresden...I have proof he was in Derby eight years — how much longer I know not..." No evidence in support of this contention is presented.

The register of St. Alkmund's Church in Derby, which was situated close to St. Mary's bridge before it was demolished, contains entries pertaining to André Planché. Recorded are the baptisms of Paul, his first born son on 21st September, 1751; James, his second son on 12th October, 1754; James, his bastard son by Margaret Burrows on 4th March, 1754; and William, his third legitimate son on 3rd July, 1756. The burial of his son James on 11th

1. 'Thomas Hughes, first enameller of English China, of Clerkenwell' by W.H. Tapp, *Transactions,* English Ceramic Circle, 1939, Vol. 2, No. 6, p. 60.

2. *Marks & Monograms on European & Oriental Pottery & Porcelain* (London, 1965) by W. Chaffers, 15th edition, Vol. II, p. 189.

3. *The Ceramic Art of Great Britain* (London, 1878) by Llewellyn Jewitt, Vol. II, pp. 57-66.

4. 'The Early Work of Planché and Duesbury' by Mrs. Donald Macalister, *Transactions,* English Porcelain Circle, 1929, No. 2, pp. 45-59.

December, 1754, is also recorded. This documentary evidence indicates the residence of André Planché in the parish of St. Alkmund's at least as early as September 1751 until about the autumn of 1756.

Until fairly recently, it was supposed that early Derby porcelain figures were made at a factory on Cockpit Hill upon the west bank of the river Derwent a few miles south of the centre of the city. A ceramic factory had been established there since 1751 which was managed by John Heath (banker), William Butts, Thomas Rivett and Ralph Stean. However, the first products seem to have been limited to white and brown saltglazed stoneware, though Donald Towner has shown some blue and white porcelain may also have been manufactured.[5] A notice in the *Derby Mercury* of 26th January, 1753, reads "We hear that yesterday morning, the body of a man who appeared to have been a considerable time in the water, was taken from the river [Derwent] near Borrowash. 'Tis said he was one of the Workmen belonging to the China Works near Mary Bridge, and he had been missing since Christmas Eve..." St. Mary('s) Bridge is nearly three miles up stream from Cockpit Hill which cannot be described as 'near' this factory. It would seem fairly certain that a second porcelain manufactory was referred to in the notice and that this was probably adjacent to the bridge upon the east bank of the river Derwent in the parish of St. Alkmund's.

Amongst the earliest specimens of Derby porcelain to have survived are three creamers. One in the Victoria and Albert Museum is incised 'Derby 1750', another in the British Museum bears the mark 'D. 1750', whilst the third is marked 'D'. All are made from a non-phosphatic paste which has a lead oxide content of about two per cent. They are decorated with sprigs of leaves and flowers with strangely up turned edges in applied slip.[6] A model of the actress Kitty Clive (J10) has almost identical sprigging upon the superior surface of its star-shaped base and is made of a similar paste.[7] A further sixty-odd models are known in the same style and paste but without the applied decoration which have been listed by F.A. Barrett and A.L. Thorpe.[8] Some of these, including St. Philip (J22), St. Thomas (J23), Pluto and Cerberus (J29) and a 'Gentleman playing a recorder' (J15), were reissued after 1755 when the Derby factory was under the management of William Duesbury. Further, the figure of a seated putto holding grapes, representing Autumn from the set of the Four Seasons (J31) was later modified after 1755 to serve as a candlestick (K10). It would see, therefore, that the early group of models listed by Barrett and Thorpe resulted from a stream of production which, though modified, was continued at Derby during the proprietorship of Duesbury. The London Account Book of William Duesbury lists many Derby figures that passed through his studio. They include 'Darbyshire Dansers', Darby Figars', 'Wild Boors', 'Darby Sesens', and others. Some are clearly identifiable amongst surviving models. The links between Derby and these early figures are further strengthened by the discovery amongst stock and factory equipment sold in 1848 when the Derby factory failed, of moulds pertaining to these early models. There is, for example, a mould from which a clay squeeze produced the head of a Chinese lady wearing a strange head-dress resembling an inverted egg-cup and this matches that upon the model in a chinoiserie group from the Five Senses, emblematic of Sight.[9]

In summary, it is probable André Planché arrived in Derby some time between 1747 and 1751 and lived in the Parish of St. Alkmund's where he worked in a porcelain factory close to St. Mary's Bridge. This factory specialised in high quality porcelain figures and, possibly, Planché was their modeller. He may have been financed by John Heath who certainly had a stake in the Cockpit Hill works. Towards the end of 1755, an agreement was

5. 'The Cockpit Hill Pottery, Derby' by Donald Towner, *Transactions*, English Ceramic Circle, 1967, Vol. 6, pt. 3, pp. 254-267.

6. *Apollo*, 1960, Vol. 71, p. 40, fig. IV.

7. ibid., p. 41, fig. III, Kitty Clive non-phosphatic model with sprigged decoration on the base.

8. *Derby Porcelain* (London, 1971) by F.A. Barrett and A.L. Thorpe, Appendix IX, pp. 193-198.

9. *Chelsea, Bow and Derby Porcelain Figures* (Newport, 1955) by Frank Stoner, clay squeeze of chinoiserie group lady's head. *Derby Porcelain*, op. cit., pl. 16, the porcelain group.

drawn up between Heath, Duesbury and Planché which was probably never signed. The reasons for this are unclear though possibly the extra marital adventures of Planché with Margaret Burrows may have offended the conscience of such Midlands' worthies as Duesbury and Heath. After 1756 Planché disappears from the Derby ceramic scene. The deterioration in the quality of the paste, glaze and standard of modelling that ensued after his departure surely invalidates the suggestion that Planché continued to work for Duesbury.

The second phase of production commenced with the arrival in Derby of Duesbury as part owner and manager during the first quarter of 1756. William Duesbury (1725-1786), was born at Longton, the son of a currier from Cannock, Staffordshire. He married Sarah James of Shrewsbury and, at the age of twenty-six, if not earlier, became the proprietor of a London atelier for the decoration of porcelain from 'Bogh', 'Chelsay', and 'Staffartshire'. His London Account Book for the period November 1751 to August 1753 has already been mentioned.[10] According to Llewellyn Jewitt[11] Duesbury went to Longton Hall in 1754, where he most probably worked as an enameller for William Littler. Some have suggested that Duesbury met Jacques Planché whilst he was at Longton Hall and the latter introduced him to his brother André. However, Jacques was almost certainly working elsewhere as a clocksmith either in Zurich or in London. A strange legal document was drawn up between William Duesbury, father and son, which was signed and is dated 27th September, 1755. This transfers ownership of all the elder man's money, goods, and chattles to his son in exchange for an undertaking "to provide for the said William Duesbury [senior] during the term of his natural life, good and sufficient meat, drink, washing and Lodging, wearing apparel, and all other necessaries whatsoever..."[12] This arrangement may have been the only means open to William Duesbury *(fils)* to raise sufficient money with which to purchase a share in the Derby porcelain factory with Heath who had invested £1,000 of his own in the venture. This was the prelude to the second agreement, which is unsigned, and therefore may either never have been enacted or may simply be a copy of a signed original that has been lost. "Articles of Agreement between John Heath of Derby in the County of Derby Gentleman, Andrew Planche of ye same Place China Maker & Wm. Duesbury of Longton in ye County of Stafford Enameller. Made and enter'd into the 1st of Jany., 1756..." This document is reproduced in full both by Llewellyn Jewitt[13] and by Barrett and Thorpe.[14]

The *Derby Mercury* of 30th July, 1756, included the advertisement "To be sold, a free hold estate consisting of 7 houses and a barn, situated all together near St. Mary's Bridge, Derby, which are now occupied by Mr. Heath and Company in the China Manufactory and let at £10 per annum exclusive of all taxes." This refers to a site acquired by John Heath from a Mr. Shepherdson of Kings Newton on lease, and must have been the works run by Planché. The property was readvertised for sale on 25th October, 1756. There is a conveyance, dated 1st August, 1880, now included amongst the *Bemrose Papers,*[15] which mentions the transfer of the Shepherdson properties to John Heath & Company on 19th November, 1756, in earlier deeds. Shortly before the transfer in April 1756, a number of other plots, which were adjacent to the Shepherdson site, had been acquired by Heath. Dwelling-houses upon this land had been "converted into and then continued to be Workshops and employed by Sd. W. Duesbury and Company as such in the making of China".[16] In 1764, additional land abutting upon Calver Close was purchased, although this was not used for factory buildings until the closing years of the eighteenth century during the proprietorship of Michael Kean.

10. *William Duesbury's London Account Book 1751-1753* (London, 1931) by Mrs. Donald Macalister, English Ceramic Circle Monograph.

11. *The Ceramic Art of Great Britain,* op. cit., pp. 66-67.

12. ibid.; also *Chelsea Porcelain, the Gold Anchor Wares* (Leigh-on-Sea, 1952) by F. Severne Mackenna, p. 36.

13. *The Ceramic Art of Great Britain,* op. cit., p. 64.

14. *Derby Porcelain* (Barrett & Thorpe), op. cit., pp. 178-179.

15. Duesbury MSS included in the 'Bemrose Papers', now in the British Museum.

16. ibid.

On 14th December, 1756, and for several days following, an advertisement carried in the *Public Advertiser* read: "To be sold by Auction by Mr. Bellamy, By Order of the Proprietors of the DERBY PORCELAIN Manufactory, at a commodious House in Prince's Street Cavendish Square. This and three following days. A curious Collection of Fine Figures, Jars, Sauceboats, Services for Deserts, and great Variety of other useful and ornamental Porcelain, after the finest Dresden models, all exquisitely painted in Enamel... This and the following Days will be sold some of the finest of the Derby Porcelain and foreign China."[17] This, it will be recalled, was the year in which the Prussian armies overran Meissen and, doubtless William Duesbury hoped to capture the market and fill the vacuum created by the event. He seems to have concentrated his efforts on imitation of porcelain models which had been one of the glories of the Saxon manufactory. Instructions were issued that clay models should first be roughed out in the nude to ensure correct anatomical proportions before garments were added. The early warm glaze was deliberately blued with cobalt in an attempt to simulate the cold glitter of Meissen hard paste clad in a sparkling feldspathic glaze. In May, 1757, a notice appeared in the *Public Advertiser* announcing the sale of property owned by Mr. Thomas Williams, a china dealer, which included the following statement: "At the large Auction Room facing Craig's Court near the Admiralty, Whitehall, there were numbers of Quality and Gentry, who expressed great satisfaction at seeing the extensive Number of foreign, and a great Variety of the English Manufactories; and admired at the great Perfection the Derby Figures in particular, are arrived to, that many good Judges could not distinguish them from real Dresden. This is the first day of the said Sale. May 17th 1757."[18] No informed person was likely to have mistaken the doll-like Derby figures of this period, clad in blued lead glaze and pale colours, for the dynamic models created at Meissen by Kändler and his associates. It was as well for Duesbury that the Trade Descriptions Act was not then on the statute book!

On 28th January and again on 11th February, 1758, the *Public Advertiser* carried the notice: "The Proprietors of the Derby China Company beg leave to acquaint the Nobility and Gentry that they have fix'd their Porcelain to be sold by their Factor, Mr. Williams, at his large Foreign China Warehouse up one Pair of Stairs, formerly known by the name of Oliver Cromwell's Drawing-Room, facing Craigg's Court, near the Admiralty, consisting of a great Variety of Figures, the nearest the Dresden... the great Demand there is for them, has encouraged the Proprietors to enlarge their Manufactory, and [they] have engaged double the Number of Hands they used to employ, which will enable them to send to the said Warehouse every week [a] great Variety of Goods..."[19] However, in April, 1758, the Warehouse in Craigg's Court had to be demolished for road-widening and by 1763, if not before, Mr. Williams the 'China Dealer' had moved to an address in Pall Mall.

In 1763 forty-two boxes of porcelain were dispatched from Derby for sale in London.[20] Amongst their contents were many figures described as 'Large Brittanias', 'Large Quarters' (the Four Quarters of the Globe), 'Jupiter', 'Juno', 'Ledas', 'Europa', 'Mars and Minerva', 'Neptune', 'Milton and Shakespeare', 'Diana', 'Sets of Elements' and others. Some were listed as 'Tumblers', which may have been Harlequins, whilst 'Bird Catchers' might refer to Liberty and Matrimony (K65). One is left wondering why shepherds have the prefix 'Spanish', and what ever became of 'Huzzars 2nd size'? 'Large Pidgeons' and 'Chickens' are not often encountered nowadays, whilst 'Bucks on Pedestals' and 'Small Rabbits' are unfamiliar to most collectors. We know very little about the names of the modellers, painters and other artists who

17. *Contributions towards the History of Early English Porcelain* (Salisbury, 1881) by J.E. Nightingale, pp. lxvii-lxviii.

18. ibid., p. lxix.

19. ibid., pp. lxx-lxxi.

20. *The Ceramic Art of Great Britain,* op. cit., pp. 68-69.

worked at Derby before 1770. It is likely that this anonymity was the outcome of a deliberate policy by employers anxious to retain their small force of skilled labour and to protect those who had defected from other rival establishments and thereby been in breach of contract. Barrett and Thorpe[21] have drawn attention to the model of a youth in the Leverhulme Collection which bears the incised 'George Holmes did this figer 1765' upon the base. This was presumably the same Holmes mentioned at the beginning of this chapter.

The huge commercial success of the Derby porcelain factory under the management of Duesbury and Heath is undeniable. If technical and artistic standards fell sometimes below those of Chelsea, it should be remembered that by 1763, Nicholas Sprimont was vainly attempting to sell a failing enterprise. Duesbury's failure to make a bid for Chelsea when it was first put up for sale is hard to explain. However, he purchased the factory equipment and stock from James Cox in February, 1770, for the sum of £820. This was just £220 more than Cox had paid Sprimont less than six months before. The lease of the Chelsea site was due to expire in 1773. Duesbury renewed the lease in 1770 for a period of ten years and later extended it by a further three years. The period when Duesbury was engaged both at Chelsea and at Derby, which lasted from 1770 to 1784, is known as Chelsea-Derby.

The third phase of production commenced with the acquisition of the Chelsea works in 1770, and might properly end with the vacation of the London site in 1784. However, when the focus of interest concerns figures, it is more convenient to cover the models included in a factory list supplied by John Haslem that were issued up to approximately 1795. The paucity of documentation hitherto evident now gives way to a spate of letters, accounts, and other material relating to almost every aspect of activity in the factory. These may be found in the Derby Public Library, and in the *Bemrose Papers* in the Department of Mediaeval and Later Antiquities of the British Museum. However, many of the Bemrose Papers relate to account books of the period 1795-1819, and to events that followed the death of William Duesbury II in 1796.[22] Information is also available in letters written by Joseph Lygo, the London agent for the Duesburys, who wrote each week to his employer in Derby from London. Unfortunately, most of Duesbury's replies are lost. Some of the Lygo correspondence is reproduced by Llewellyn Jewitt[23] and relevant material has also been summarised by Barrett and Thorpe[24] and by Arthur Lane.[25] Only a small fraction of this pool of information has, so far, been sifted, edited and published and here only very brief extracts will be provided.

The Chelsea premises seem to have been used for the manufacture of ornamental vases which, during the period of the gold anchor mark, had proved popular. A few figures, some marked with an anchor intersecting a script letter 'D' in gilt, may have been made in London, but there are some bearing this device that were cast from Derby moulds. The work force seldom amounted to more than twelve men and was often smaller. Weekly accounts mention the names of Richard Boyer and Richard Barton, who were responsible for potting and glazing. Others include Roberts, whose task was "Grinding of Case Clay and working the Bruisers", and Inglefield, who was paid for "Cleaning the Bisket Work to be Glas'd". The duties of a man named Piggot were not disclosed but a modeller called Gauron was on the payroll for June 1773 and received 8s. 9d. per day. This was a very high wage for one of the most accomplished painters employed at Derby, Zachariah Boreman, earned no more than 5s. 3d. Other work carried out at Chelsea may have included the making of seals, scent-bottles, *étuis,* and patch-boxes. These had provided a profitable business for Sprimont and no doubt Duesbury was eager

21. *Derby Porcelain* (Barrett & Thorpe), op. cit., p. 26.
22. 'The Derby China Factory Sites on Nottingham Road' by F.A. Barrett, *Transactions,* English Ceramic Circle, 1959, Vol. 4, pt. 5, pp. 26-44.
23. *The Ceramic Art of Great Britain,* op. cit.
24. *Derby Porcelain* (Barrett & Thorpe), op. cit., Appendix V.
25. *English Porcelain Figures of the 18th Century* (London, 1961) by Arthur Lane, Appendix II. Abstracts from the Duesbury and the Derby Porcelain Factory 1755-1795, Victoria and Albert Museum.

to continue production.

J.E. Nightingale[26] has published the *Catalogue of the Last Year's Produce (being the first public sale) of the CHELSEA and DERBY Porcelain Manufactories,* which took place on Wednesday 17th April, 1771, and the three following days. The sale was conducted by Mr. Christie at his Great Room in Pall Mall. The catalogue contains the first mention of figures issued in biscuit: on April 17th, "Lot 19. A fine group of the Virtues, with Minerva crowning Constancy with a garland of flowers, and Hercules killing the Hydra, in biscuit, £3 3s.". Fine quality biscuit had been made at Vincennes since 1751 and had later been introduced at Tournai. The link between Tournai and Derby may well have been Nicolas Francois Gauron whose earlier work has been described in Chapter III. Born in 1736 in Paris, he may possibly have visited London and been apprenticed silversmith to Jacob Gauron in 1750. In 1754, he was at Vincennes as modeller and a figure of a river deity is incised with his name. The records of Mennecy also include the name Gauron, though no models from his hand have been identified from this factory. In 1758, he became chief modeller at Tournai. A number of biscuit groups made by Gauron at this factory later appeared at Derby and these have been described in Chapter III. After leaving Tournai in 1764, his whereabouts are uncertain, but he most probably arrived at Chelsea shortly before the retirement of Sprimont in 1769. One explanation for his high remuneration may be that he assisted in the development of a paste suitable for issue in biscuit. Models attributed to Gauron when he was working for Duesbury are listed in Appendix L.

The Sale Catalogue of 17th April, 1771, also records "Lot 37. A pair of sitting figures, elegantly decorated with fruit and flowers, and most curiously work'd with lace. £2 12s. 6d.". These have been identified by Timothy Clifford as the 'Pair of Sitting Fruit and Flowers', bearing the number '8', in Haslem's factory list.[27] The models are copies of originals made by Michel Acier, who is credited with the discovery of reproducing lace in porcelain at Meissen by dipping lace into liquid slip and attaching it to the figure; in the heat of the kiln the material burns away leaving an exact replica in porcelain. Another pair of models mentioned in the same catalogue is "Lot 60. A pair of sitting figures, a gentleman reading, and a lady knotting [*sic*], most curiously ornamented with lace. £5 5s.". The catalogue also serves to date the first issue of models.

In 1773, Duesbury opened a London showroom in what had been the Old Castle Tavern in Bedford Street, Covent Garden. William Wood was placed in charge, and that same year the premises were visited by George III. It is probable that, in order to facilitate the retail business, William Wood allocated numbers to models which were incised upon their inferior surface as well as being listed. This may have been initiated shortly before the showroom was stocked, c.1772-73. John Haslem[28] reproduced a list of three hundred and ninety items which he called 'A Price List of Groups and Single Figures'. This contains several gaps and a few errors and though he includes prices for items mentioned, he gives neither the date when the list was compiled nor the source of his information. However, it has proved useful to collectors who wish to ascertain the identity of a numbered model. Another very similar list was provided by William Bemrose.[29] This, he said, was "A List made out, and a valuation put thereon, in 1819 by four old employees named Soar, Longdon, Farnsworth, and Hardenberg, for the purpose of a Chancery suit, Duesbury versus Kean." Three hundred and ninety-seven models are included. It should be noted that several models known to have been made between 1770-73, such as 'Minerva crowning Constancy and Hercules killing the Hydra', 'Field

26. *Contributions towards the History of Early English Porcelain,* op. cit., pp. xxix-xxx.

27. 'Derby Biscuit' by Timothy Clifford, *Transactions,* English Ceramic Circle, 1969, Vol. 7, pt. 2, pp. 108-117, pls. 124A and 124B.

28. *The Old Derby China Factory* (London, 1876) by John Haslem, pp. 170-178, the Derby factory list.

29. *Bow, Chelsea and Derby Porcelain* (London, 1898) by William Bemrose.

Marshall Conway', 'Baron Camden', and others, do not appear on either the Haslem or the Bemrose list. Further, models known to have been available in the 1750s and '60s, such as 'Shakespeare', 'Milton', 'Falstaff', and the 'Tithe Pig', group, have been allocated high numbers which might erroneously suggest they had been made after those bearing lower ones. Haslem suggested that by about 1780, the number 300 had been reached. This would permit the conclusion that, in the seventeen years between 1773 and 1780, over three hundred sets, models or groups were issued. Further, we know a modeller named Spengler (or Spangler) modelled a shepherdess, which is numbered 395, and that he left Derby in 1795, so that in the fifteen years between 1780 and 1795 only ninety-five items were issued. This would make the earlier figure of 300 in seventeen years seem improbable, and there is good reason to question the validity of Haslem's assertion. It appears, that new models introduced after 1772/73 were given numbers in chronological sequence but when old models were reissued in either original or modified versions, they were given the next available number. It follows, that precise dating of issue cannot be accomplished from Haslem's or Bemrose's lists.

A second modeller named Pierre Stephan (Mr. Stevens) came to Derby from Tournai. The absence of his name from the records of that factory,[30] which were destroyed during the Second World War, must have been an over sight for there is a bill, dated 14th October, 1769, in the Archives de la Ville de Bruxelles, which reads "...4 figures les elemens de Stephan..."[31] According to Frank Hurlbutt,[32] he was first engaged to work at Chelsea by Nicholas Sprimont but, in September 1770, signed a three year contract with William Duesbury to work for a weekly wage of £2 12s. 6d. Models made by Stephan are listed in Appendix L. After honouring his contract, he left Derby to work at Wirksworth, and both letters and bills survive to confirm this.[33] He married Catherine Yates when she was six months pregnant on 3rd August, 1773, in St. Alkmund's Church, Derby and the same register carries an entry pertaining to the baptism of his daughter Frances, on 24th October of that same year. Whilst he was at Wirksworth he wrote to Josiah Wedgwood a letter that has been reproduced by Major Tapp.[34]

"Sir,

I was informed some time agoe by sevral persons...that you gave great encouragement to Artists in the Modelling branch, at which time I was engaged with Mr. Duesbury of Derby, and since then with the China factory at Wirksworth both [of] which I am now disengaged from..."

He then asks to be employed, preferably for at least part of the time in London, and concludes

"...hope you will be so kind as to favor me with a line as soon as possible as I shall leave this place in a fortnight or three weeks at the farthest which will much oblige.

Your most Obed't Hble serv't
P. Stephan.

Wirksworth, 9th May 1774. P.S. please to direct for me at the Post Office in Wirksworth. N.B. I work in Figures, Vasses, or any sort of Useful as Business may require."

Wedgwood gave Stephan drawings of 'Hope' and 'The Conquered Province', which he had obtained in London, as the basis for two trial wax models. When these had been completed in August, 1774, Wedgwood paid him £2 10s. 0d. and shortly afterwards wrote to his partner, Thomas Bentley.[35] "...I have received and examined Mr. Steven's moulds of Hope and the Conquered Province, and am glad to find the drawing and the proportions so well preserved, but in everything else they are infinitely short of

30. *English Porcelain Figures of the 18th Century* (Lane), op. cit., p. 105, footnote 6.

31. 'Tournai Porcelain and English Ceramics' by M. Jottrand, *Transactions*, English Ceramic Circle, 1977, Vol. 10, pt. 2, pp. 130-135, Appendix III.

32. *Old Derby Porcelain and its Artist Workmen* (London, 1925) by Frank Hurlbutt.

33. 'The Wirksworth China Factory' by Terence Lockett, *Northern Ceramic Society Journal*, Vol. 1, pp. 45-57.

34. 'Wirksworth China' by W.H. Tapp, *Antique Collector*, November 1932, pp. 389-394.

35. *The Life of Josiah Wedgwood* (London, 1866) by Eliza Meteyard, Vol. II, pp. 326-327.

the exquisite originals. The drapery is hard and unfinish'd & the characters of the Faces are those of common mortals of the Lower Class. The armour in the Conquer'd Province comes out too much a great deal. The face of the figure is crooked, greatly so and there is a total want of finishing in both pieces. They are in my opinion far from being equal to our figures of the same class... Mr. Stevens can do it better than us, if he would bestow a little more attention and labour upon them." Despite these strictures, Wedgwood gave Stephan employment. Stephan probably continued to model freelance for both Duesbury I and II, as well as providing models for Richard Champion at Bristol.

In 1776, George III, accompanied by the Duchess of Ancaster, visited the Bedford Street showrooms. After this event, Duesbury was entitled to use the prefix 'royal' before his Derby factory and to incorporate the device of a crown into the factory mark. Although found on useful wares, the mark is rare on figures issued much before 1782.

The possible role played by the sculptor John Bacon has been mentioned in Chapter IV. Certainly he received two payments from Duesbury, one in 1769 and the other in 1772, but this may have been for plaster or terracotta models intended for instruction of craftsmen in the modelling shop. It is difficult to accept Haslem's statement that Bacon was responsible for 'Statuettes of Quin in Falstaff and Garrick in Richard III'.[36] Timothy Clifford[37] made the interesting observation that the model of George III (L7), which together with two groups portraying the Royal Family were based on Johann Zoffany's portrait, does not faithfully follow the source. The details of cravat and the arrangement of clothing about the neck and shoulders, however, are almost identical to those upon a bust of the monarch by Bacon in Christ Church, Oxford. Certainly such important models and groups would be the most likely to have been commissioned from a sculptor but after passing through many formative stages necessary for their construction it is almost impossible to identify the style of even a famous sculptor in a porcelain model.

J.E. Nightingale[38] has published extracts from sale catalogues issued between February 1773 and December 1783. These help to establish the dates when certain specific models became available. Information provided by the letters of Joseph Lygo, who in 1776 replaced William Wood as London representative and manager of the Bedford Street showroom,[39] relates to the abandonment of the Chelsea site. In a sale on 11th December, 1783, were offered "all the remaining Finished and Unfinished Stock of the Chelsea Porcelain Manufactory in Lawrence Street, near the Church, Chelsea... with all Buildings and Fixtures thereto belonging". On 18th February, 1784, Richard Bower, who had been entrusted with supervision of clearing the site, wrote "We are pretty forward in pulling down buildings at Chelsea." By March, 1784, all moulds and equipment which had not been sold or destroyed were transferred to Derby.

The correspondence of Joseph Lygo covers the period 1777 to 1797, but most of it concerns matters after 1786. Much of it has been condensed and summarised by F. Brayshaw Gilhespy.[40] From the letters we learn of the Swiss clockmaker, Benjamin Vulliamy, who became an important customer of the Derby factory in about the year 1780. He placed orders with Duesbury for biscuit figures which he used on his clocks and ornamental barometers. Examples of his work may be seen in the Bank of England, Syon House and in the Victoria and Albert Museum. He was an exacting client, who often engaged the services of a young sculptor in London and, if he approved the wax model, would send it by coach to Derby for translation into biscuit porcelain. He also purchased models from Josiah Wedgwood. Vulliamy

36. *The Old Derby China Factory,* op. cit., p. 152.

37. from a lecture given on 'Derby Figures and Vases' by Timothy Clifford, at Morley College, London, on 12th October, 1976.

38. *Contributions towards the History of Early English Porcelain,* op. cit., pp. 44-80.

39. *Derby Porcelain* (Barrett & Thorpe), op. cit., Appendix V.

40. *Derby Porcelain* (London, 1961) by F. Brayshaw Gilhespy, pp. 65-71.

obtained models from John Deare (1759-1798) in 1784 but, in 1785, the young sculptor took up residence in Rome where he remained for the remainder of his life. Other sculptors who modelled for Derby include B.F. Hardenburg, Charles Horwell, Charles Peart, Henry Webber, and John Charles Felix Rossi. According to Jewitt,[41] Hardenberg came to Derby in 1788 and was dismissed in 1789 for "repeated idleness and ignorance". Peart is said to have worked for Duesbury between 1787 and 1788 and Rossi made models for Derby between 1787 and 1788. Unfortunately it has proved impossible to identify the work of any of these artists and the information abstracted from the letters of Joseph Lygo is often at variance with the known or generally accepted facts. For example, Lygo attributes to Rossi the models of 'Aesculapius' (M99), 'Venus' (M115), 'Mars' (M114), and 'The New Diana' (M120). The porcelain model of Aesculapius stylistically resembles the terracotta statue upon the roof of the Derbyshire Royal Infirmary which somewhat improbably has been attributed to William Coffee. It is paired with a model of 'Hygieia' and is listed in the Sale Catalogue of May, 1779, a date some nine years before Rossi was engaged by Duesbury. Further, the numbers allocated to all the models mentioned above, which range between ninety-nine and one hundred and twenty, seem far too low to relate to the period 1787-1788. Lygo stated also that Rossi created a "female Sacrifice figure from drawings Mr. Vulliamy gave him from one of his books. . .in 1788". This model is incised 'No. 14.'

Constantine Smith, mentioned at the beginning of this chapter, was employed as an enameller by William Duesbury from 1756 and may have worked previously for André Planché. He is credited with the discovery of a saxe blue that bears his name. His son, William, was not apprenticed to him until 1773 and cannot, therefore, have played any important role in the invention though some have given him this distinction. Certainly the clear brilliant enamel was used on useful wares, though only a few models, after 1770. Another man, mentioned in the Lygo letters, Mr. Charles, was a mould maker. In the spring of 1786, Joseph Lygo wrote to his employer to inform him that the demand for porcelain figures in the Metropolis had sharply declined. The great days of the small scale porcelain figure were almost over. Later, in November 1786, William Duesbury died.

William Duesbury was succeeded by his son of the same name and although he suffered from poor physical health, he proved to be a hard working and efficient proprietor until his death in 1796. During the decade of his management Derby enjoyed a golden age, though this related more to useful ware and cabinet pieces than to figures. Exquisite landscapes were painted by the brothers Robert and John Brewer, figures by James Banford and Richard Askew, flowers by Quaker Pegg and William Billingsley, and naval and harbour scenes by George Robertson, to give but a few names from a galaxy of talent. Most models were now issued in biscuit and became rather large in scale under the influence of the neo-classical style. Despite the unfavourable climate of opinion, as far as porcelain figures were concerned, one great modeller arrived at Derby in 1790 whose name was Spengler.

Jean Jacques Spengler (or Spängler), was a French speaking Swiss of German extraction. Born in 1755, he was the son of Johann Adam Spengler, director of the Zurich Porcelain Manufactory and one time modeller at Höchst. Spengler (fils) may have been apprenticed to the sculptor and modeller J.V. Sonnenschein whose style is similar to his own, and was probably employed at the Zurich factory as modeller between 1772 and 1777. None of his work of this period has been identified. His subsequent life and work have been reviewed by Timothy Clifford.[42] Spengler left Zurich after the death of his mother and his father's remarriage to a woman who was only

41. *The Ceramic Art of Great Britain*, op. cit., pp. 109-110.

42. 'J.J. Spängler, a virtuoso Swiss modeller at Derby' by Timothy Clifford, *Connoisseur*, 1978, Vol. 198, No. 196, pp. 146-153.

Colour Plate L. *'Smell', represented by a gentleman taking snuff, from the set of the 'Five Senses' (J33). 6¼ins. (15.9cm). Dry-edge Derby c.1755. The model displays violet-blue eyes matching the coat-cuffs, and fine gilding.* Author's collection

Colour Plate M. *'Sight', represented by a gentleman in a cap and dressing-gown looking at his reflection in a hand mirror (missing), from the set of the 'Five Senses' (J33). 6¼ins. (15.9cm). Dry-edge Derby c.1755. The floral painting in monochrome is in a style associated with John Bolton.* David Thorn collection

Colour Plate N. *'Taste', represented by a lady eating fruit, from the set of the 'Five Senses' (J33). 6½ins. (16.5cm). Dry-edge Derby c.1755. The brilliant floral sprays and pale gilding are in the manner of James Giles.* Norman C. Ashton collection

twenty-six years of age. His movements between 1770 and 1790 are uncertain but, he appeared in London in the spring of 1790 where he met Joseph Lygo who wrote of him to Duesbury as "a foreigner who wants employment as a modeller". He successfully completed a trial model of Astronomy from drawings supplied to him by Vulliamy and, after several misunderstandings due to Spengler's temperament and the language barrier, an agreement was signed between the modeller and William Duesbury II in July, 1790. Under the terms of this contract, Spengler was to work at Derby at a weekly wage of two guineas for a period of three years. He proved to be a poor attender at the works, refractory to discipline, and frequently in debt. After borrowing money from his employer, Spengler absconded but was arrested shortly afterwards attempting to embark for the Continent at Ramsgate. He was imprisoned, but released upon a promise to mend his ways and repay his debts out of his wages. Towards the end of 1791, he returned to Derby. In 1793, Joseph Lygo wrote "I could not get the beautiful figure of Rosina without buying it at that price of 6 shillings. Spengler is going to model it — have not found a male figure to match it and S wants to do one of his own idea. He is on his own making two female girls with a little poultry before them for two guineas. . .two pair female figures with dead bird." When Spengler's contract expired, he left Derby, walked to London and, when he found the friend upon whom he called was away, stole his money and was caught red-handed. Lygo wrote to Duesbury "Spengler is the greatest rascal I ever had anything to do with — it would a been well if you had not imployed him here." Spengler was next seen passing through Derby dressed in rags, having taken to the road. He returned to the porcelain works in the first quarter of 1795 when he was shown monuments of Westminster Abbey and is said to have modelled 'Two Sitting Boys'. Written upon a letter, in a calligraphy supposedly that of William Duesbury II, is the memorandum "July 11, 1795. I have given Spengler notice". Spengler left Derby in that year and his subsequent fate is unknown. His Derby models are listed in Appendix N.

William Coffee, came to Derby in 1791. Llewellyn Jewitt writes of him "I believe he was employed as a fireman at Coades [Eleanor Coade's Artificial Stone Works, Lambeth], and here, no doubt, being a clever fellow, picked up his knowledge of modelling and of mixing bodies."[43] He may well have assisted in the firing of the terracotta figure of Aesculapius but could scarcely have created such a sophisticated model. After his arrival at Derby, Coffee was found to have a natural ability to make small models and, in 1794, a contract was signed between him and Duesbury II. Coffee was to receive either 3s. 6d. for a ten hour day, or "at a rate of 7s for any single human figure up to 6 inches high whether standing or in any other action which if standing would be 6 inches hight; and that all figures shall be roughed out naked in correct proportions before draped."[44] Haslem's Derby Factory List includes "Numbers 335-359. Twenty-five — Spangler's and Coffee's Figures and Groups". Only one of these, No. 359, has been identified which is a gardener.[45] An unidentified group, No. 379, was also attributed to Coffee, by Lygo who wrote "Number 359. The figure is one of the most stupid things I ever saw. . .", and he added "The figure of Apollo is very vulgar about the bosom, for sure never such bubbys was seen and so much expos'd — the design is pretty enough."[46] On 8th December, 1794, the manager of the Derby works, Charles King, wrote to Duesbury who was in London "Mason has had some conversation with me about Coffee's work, he thinks it so very imperfect as not to answer your purpose however low it may come. . ." When, in 1795, Spengler finally left Derby, Coffee's wages were increased doubtless in the hope that he would be able to assume the role of an expert modeller. Evidently

43. *The Ceramic Art of Great Britain* by Llewellyn Jewitt, 2nd edition (1883), p. 94.
44. *Derby Porcelain* (Barrett & Thorpe), op. cit., p. 86.
45. *The Ceramic Art of Great Britain* (1878), op. cit., Vol. II, p. 96.
46. ibid., p. 96.

Coffee was unequal to the task for within a few months he left and accepted employment in a small factory near Burton-on-Trent, owned by Sir Nigel Gresley. In 1796, Coffee returned to Derby to set up his own business which specialised in terracotta garden statuary. He may possibly have supplied the porcelain factory with models as a freelance after the year 1800.

Although not strictly within the province of this book, the following summarises the events which followed Duesbury's death in 1796. Michael Kean, who under Duesbury II had been factory manager, married his widow in 1798 and the company traded under the title of Duesbury and Kean. Kean was an Irish miniature painter of some repute. In 1779, he had been awarded the Society of Fine Arts' Medal, and had also exhibited at Burlington House between 1786 and 1790. Although the decline in popularity of the porcelain figure continued, there was an increased demand for finely decorated cabinet pieces and useful wares. Under his direction, the factory prospered and new buildings were erected on Calver Close. Unfortunately, the marriage of convenience proved to be unhappy and, in 1811, Kean sold his shares in the business to the father-in-law of William Duesbury III, William Sheffield. Sheffield, in turn, resold to his factory manager, Robert Bloor in 1815. Bloor was compelled to raise cash to pay off the loan of £5,000 necessary to accomplish the purchase and to pay the agreed annuities to surviving members of the Duesbury family. Accordingly, he ordered porcelain models which had been removed from sales owing to defects and placed in store, to be decorated in a manner that would render them saleable. So it is that models, fashioned in an eighteenth century soft paste, are today found clad in dark opaque enamels and brash gilding appropriate to the taste of the late Regency. Though some have criticised Bloor for taking this action, without it the factory would almost certainly have failed. As things turned out, Bloor became 'potter to his majesty king George IV' and the business flourished. In 1826, Bloor began to exhibit signs of mental incapacity and was admitted to an 'asylum' where he remained until his death in 1846. The Derby factory was managed during this period by Thomas Clarke until the closure of the works in 1848.

The gilder, Sampson Hancock, who had been employed by Bloor, purchased many of the old figure moulds at the sale following the closure of the Nottingham Road works in 1848. Some of the products of the factory set up in King Street, Derby, by Stevenson and Hancock will be mentioned in Chapter XIII. In 1877, this factory was absorbed by the Royal Crown Derby Porcelain Company. Another small porcelain works was established in 1826, at Friar Gate, Derby, by George Cocker who had previously been a modeller employed by Duesbury II. The works speciality was biscuit figures. In 1841, Cocker moved to London where he contined to make figures until about 1853. Some of these models, which may be mistaken for the products of the Nottingham Road, Derby, manufactory, are listed in Appendix N.

Figures made at Derby prior to 1756

Paste and Glaze

The early Derby paste is glassy, due to inclusion of cullet in the mix and contains silica 70 per cent, lime 20.5 per cent, alumina 5.5 per cent, lead oxide 2 per cent, and magnesia rather more than 1 per cent. Thus, it is non-phosphatic and non-steatitic. The body lacks the milky opacity associated with bone ash and has a faintly bluish tinge; despite the high lead oxide, stability in the kiln seems to have been fairly satisfactory and only a few models show slight sideways drooping from the perpendicular whilst tearing of the surface and firecracks are not common. Some figures, such as St. Philip and St. Thomas, are very heavy though the majority exhibit no more than average weight. The quality of the glaze is variable between specimens. At its best, it is thin, transparent, glossy and faintly blue but a few models, such as the 'Map Seller' in the Ashton collection, have a warm, almost creamy, glaze while there are others where it resembles candle grease. Crazing and dry patches are rarely seen. The glaze usually stops short of the inferior circumference of the base leaving a rim of exposed and sullied biscuit known as a dry-edge. The inferior edge of the glaze has a slightly heaped up rim like treacle and in this way is dissimilar from the smooth tapered junction between glaze and biscuit that is evident after the inferior surface has been ground. Enamelled models often display a glaze which over the upper parts of the figure is bubbled, cloudy, and lacks lustre. This may be due to refiring in a muffle kiln by an independent decorator a year or more after the model was issued in the white. Some have suggested that glazing of dry-edge Derby figures was carried out by insufflation of powdered lead acetate over the surface rather than by dipping into a vat of liquid. If this was done, it could not have been standard practice. Mr. Ashton pointed out to me how, on his figure of a 'Girl holding a Bird's Nest', emblematic of Summer, the glaze had failed to reach the interior of the hollow nest. The most likely explanation is that when the inverted figure was dipped, entrapment of an air bubble prevented the glaze from entering the nest. Further, many dry-edge models have a horizontal hole which penetrates the back to enter the central cavity. One would expect during dipping some glaze might enter through this aperture and later, when the figure was placed the right way up, might trickle down upon the inside to appear in the ventilation hole. In fact the author has seen irregular blobs of glaze in the ventilation holes of four dry-edge models all of which had horizontal holes. The inferior surface of the base is unglazed, and feels both slightly rough and uneven, thereby distinguishing it from one that has been ground. The purpose of the dry-edge seems to have been to prevent droplets of glaze collecting upon the inferior surface and interfering with level stance.

The Bases

The majority of models stand upon large steep mounds or irregular pad bases which lack embellishment, though a few have sharply moulded leaves and tightly rolled flowers applied to their upper surface. A rare example of Kitty Clive (Plate 87) has plum blossom moulded in slip after the fashion of useful wares made of *blanc-de-Chine* imported from Tê Hua. Most models are supported by a sturdy prop thinly disguised as a tree-stump, and this, as has previously been indicated, may be perforated by a circular horizontal hole intended for the acceptance of a brass fitment attached to a candle holder. Some bases, including those of St. Philip (Plate 91) and St. Thomas, display moulded 'S' and 'C' scrolls and flowers with narrow pointed petals radiating from heaped up centres like Michaelmas daisies, and these have large lanceolate leaves. Probably the more elaborately decorated bases date to c.1754-55. The model of the goddess Cybele is known in two versions: one mounted upon a low mound base, the other standing upon a high truncated cone adorned with applied vine leaves, fruit and flowers. It is probable that the latter is the later of the two and some examples may have been issued in 1755-56 during the transitional period between the management of Andrew Planché and William Duesbury. The under surfaces of nearly all these early Derby bases are flat though there are a few models of ewes and rams where they are slightly concave. This may have happened during the first firing from unequal shrinkage of the paste by accident. Ventilation holes may take several different forms. Many are small, round, and cylindrical. In a few of these there are two apertures, both of which may originate from a small punched out oval depression. Lastly, the hole may be funnel shaped like that made by a carpenter to accept the head of a screw (Plate 6, Chapter V). Occasionally a thin pad of applied paste is attached to the inferior surface to restore level stance when distortion or sideways leaning would otherwise make this impossible.

Marks

Figures of this period are usually unmarked.

Enamel Colours and Decoration

It seems very unlikely that a small factory which specialised in figures would have issued some two thirds of their models in the white had there been an enameller upon the staff. Some figures bear traces of gold leaf, which evidently had been attached with size, and of having been painted with cold pigments, but amongst enamelled specimens several styles of decoration have been recognised which may also be seen upon wares and figures of other contemporary factories thereby indicating the hand of independent decorators. At present it is only possible to make tentative attributions.

The London Account Book of William Duesbury, covering the period from November, 1751, to August, 1753, survives and contains entries pertaining to decoration of specifically Derby models as well as others some of which may well have originated from the same factory.[47] One entry reads: "How to colour group, gentleman Busing a lade — gentlm a gold trim'd cote, a pink wastcot and trim'd with gold and black Breeches and socs, the lade a flowrd sack with yellow robings, a black stomegar, her hare black his wig powdr'd." Much of Duesbury's work was probably in unfired pigments though he also used 'Inhamils' for which he charged a great deal more. Bills submitted for the decoration of Derby porcelain were always higher than for London wares presumably because the cost of transport was included. Mention is made of: "1 Darbyshire Sesen 1/-...1 Darbyshire sitting Sesen 1/-...2 prs dansing Darby figs 6/-...1 pr large Darby figures 4/6...1 pr Darby figars large 8/-...". Other items likely to have been from Derby include: "Chines men...Wild Boors...and Staggs". The style of decoration peculiar to Duesbury is unknown. It has been suggested that his palette showed a predominance of yellow, yellow-green, and puce, and that he painted large open flowers and heavy dark leaves with no great skill or artistic distinction. He has also been associated with the 'Star-Cross' type of decoration. This consists of four trifid symbols resembling birds' feet, arranged in a cross centred either upon a small circle or a dot. It may be seen upon a chinoiserie group, emblematic of Taste, in the Victoria and Albert Museum. Although Duesbury may possibly have opened his decorating atelier prior to November 1751, we know from Llewellyn Jewitt[48] and William Bemrose[49] that Duesbury was at Longton in 1754, so any decorative style appearing upon wares and figures from more than one factory after this date cannot be attributed to him.

Several different styles of floral painting have been described and discussed by Dr. Bernard Watney.[50] One of these, which is also found on Chaffers' Liverpool figures and English decorated Chinese wares, is tentatively ascribed to John Bolton. Here spiky sprays, usually centred upon a tightly rolled cabbage rose or an anemone in semi-profile, are outlined in purplish black and painted in a rather dry palette (Colour Plate K). Occasionally the central blossom faces downwards against the stem and there is usually a sketchy trail of Michaelmas daisies curving above the bouquet. Single flowers may include a yellow harebell, a flower head with almost rectangular petals and, most common of all, a whiskered heartsease. Leaves include both broad and lanceolate forms, the former often with their tips turned back. Painted insects

47. *William Duesbury's London Account Book,* op. cit.

48. *The Ceramic Art of Great Britain* (1878), op. cit., p. 66.

49. *Longton Hall Porcelain* (London, 1906) by William Bemrose, records registration of William Duesbury's daughter, Ann, born at Longton on 3rd October, 1754.

50. 'The King, the Nun and other Figures' by Bernard Watney, *Transactions,* English Ceramic Circle, 1968, Vol. 7, pt. 1, pp. 48-58.

are often associated with this form of decoration when it appears upon useful ware but not on figures. Rare variants may be executed as a blue or puce monochrome (Colour Plate M). Examples in polychrome include the 'Lady with a Parrot', emblematic of Feeling, in the Statham Collection,[51] 'Cybele' mounted upon a low mound base in the collection of Robert Williams,[52] a goat, in the Schreiber Collection,[53] and the 'Dancing Shepherdess' in the Victoria and Albert Museum.[54] A monochrome example emblematic of Sight is in the collection of Mr. David Thorn. Dr. Watney recognises a somewhat similar form of painting by a less accomplished hand, possibly effected at an earlier date by the same artist, where there is a characteristic thick curved stem but this has not been identified upon figures.

In the same paper Dr. Watney identifies an entirely different form of floral painting which he considers to be by James Giles. This artist probably took over John Bolton's Kentish Town studio c.1755. According to Llewellyn Jewitt the business was eventually purchased by William Duesbury in the late 1770s. The style of decoration is found upon Worcester wares, Chaffers' Liverpool figures, Girl-in-a-Swing models and scent bottles, and on dry-edge Derby figures. The palette is very much brighter than that of John Bolton, and incorporates a yellow-green, orange-red and an attractive violet (Colour Plate I). A frequently recurring feature is the use of a purplish-grey to represent shadow over flowers and leaves. This appears to be a brown colour under yellow and a black beneath green. Almost invariably, either distributed between floral sprays, or adjacent to the hem of a dress, there are paired cherries which amount almost to a signature. Hems and borders of female garments are often decorated with a double line or a broad band of pink or purple. Flesh tints are pale buff, mouths large and untidily painted, eyes are generally ringed with a dark brown continuous line. Hair is lightly pencilled. This style may be seen on the 'Dancing Shepherdess', in the Statham Collection,[55] a 'Boy Shepherd Piper',[56] a 'Lady with a Parrot' emblematic of Feeling[57] and a 'Lady with a basket of Fruit' emblematic of Taste[58] all three of which are in the Lord Fisher Collection in the Fitzwilliam Museum, Cambridge. Some have suggested that the double cherry was a rebus 'Deuce Berry' for 'Duesbury'. This theory is attractive, but unfortunately untenable. The double cherry appears upon an English decorated Chinese bowl inscribed 'John and Sarah Jeffreys 1756', as well as on a Worcester coffee can which from its style cannot be earlier than 1756. It will be recalled that by the autumn of 1754 Duesbury had given up his London decorating atelier and was working

51. 'The King, the Nun and other Figures', op. cit., pls. 57A and 57B, 'Feeling'.
52. ibid., pl. 57C, 'Cybele'.
53. ibid., pl. 57D, 'a Goat'.
54. ibid., pls. 58A and 58B, 'Dancing Shepherdess'.
55. ibid., pl. 65A.
56. ibid., pl. 64A.
57. ibid., pl. 64D.
58. ibid., pls. 68A and 68B.

***Plate 85.** Standing 'Ewe' and companion 'Ram' (J6). 4½ and 4ins. (10.8 and 10.2 cm). Dry-edge Derby, c.1750-52.* N.C. Ashton collection

at Longton Hall.[59] Following this he was fully occupied with managership and part proprietorship of the Derby factory and can scarcely have simultaneously continued as an independent decorator. Further, the same style of decoration, with or without the double cherry, may be associated with a red anchor mark which, in association with a red dagger, is usually accepted as the mark used by the Giles studio.

Pale gilding of rather poor quality appears upon the hem of the skirt worn by the lady emblematic of Taste in the Broderip Collection;[60] also upon the crown and edges of the robes of 'Cybele' both in the Victoria and Albert Museum and in the author's collection (Colour Plate O). Gilding of fine quality is evident upon edges of garments, buttons, garters and the snuff-box of the 'Snuff-Taker' (Colour Plate L) emblematic of Smell also in the author's collection. This possibly unique model is peculiar for having violet-blue eyes which match the cuffs of the coat he wears.

The Modelling

Dry-edge Derby figures are amongst the finest made in this country. Arthur Lane[61] wrote: "Generally speaking the figures assumed to have been made by Planché between 1750 and 1755 show little Meissen influence. They could very readily be mistaken for French porcelain by reason of the creamy quality of the paste and the broad manner of handling it..." However, many of the models hitherto believed to be original are, as will be shown, taken from Meissen prototypes. The figures tend to lean away from the perpendicular and some have rather large mouths accentuated by enamel in coloured specimens. Drapery is attractively and convincingly portrayed and there is a sense of movement entirely lacking in later Derby models.

The Models

The two most desirable of all early Derby models are the 'Wild Boars' (Plate 171, Chapter XIII) (J1), one seated, the other running. Tradition dictates that the first was copied from a marble by Pietro Tacca now in the Uffizi Gallery, Florence, but it might just as well have been taken from frontispiece of the 1666 edition of Aesop's Fables, engraved by Francis Barlow, from innumerable inn signs that still survive, or from the stone sculpture of a seated boar, paired with a fox in Chatsworth House. A pair of 'Charging Bulls' (J3) were copied from originals by Peter Reinicke which had been inspired by the engravings 'Auer Ochse im Zorm',[62] by Johann Elias Riedinger. A marble in the Vatican was the basis of a 'Nanny-Goat suckling a Kid' (Plate 175,

59. *The Ceramic Art of Great Britain* (1878), op. cit., p. 66.

60. 'The King, the Nun and other Figures', op. cit., pl. 57D.

61. *English Porcelain Figures of the 18th Century* (Lane), op. cit., p. 100.

62. 'English Porcelain and Enamel from the Collection of Judge Irwin Untermyer' by Yvonne Hackenbroch, *Connoisseur,* 1956, Vol. 138, p. 108, fig. 10, engraving by J.E. Riedinger of 'Bulls in a rage', fig. 11, dry-edge Derby models.

***Plate 86.** A pair of seated 'Lions' (J9). 3½ins. (8.9cm). Dry-edge Derby c.1750-52.*
N.C. Ashton collection

Chapter XIII) (J4), though the Derby model and companion 'Billy-Goat' (Plate 176, Chapter XIII) were, most probably, from the intermediate source of Kändler's prototypes. The Derby 'Dog' and 'Cat' (J8), and group of a 'Nanny-Goat being milked by a naked Boy' (J5), also follow Meissen prototypes. The 'Stag' and companion 'Doe' at lodge (J2), seem to be original and may have been prompted by one of the very numerous illustrations contained in almost every contemporary book about the chase. It may also be recalled that the stag is the crest of the city of Derby. There is a fine group of recumbent 'Ewe and Lamb' and several standing rams and ewes (Plate 85) (J6 and J7), issued in different sizes, which are also known in Chelsea and Bow porcelain versions.[63] These may, possibly, have been moulded from small bronzes. There is also a pair of dog-like lions (Plate 86) (J9).

Models of human subjects are more numerous and that of Kitty Clive as Mrs. Riot (Plate 87) (J10) shows only minor differences from the Bow version (G1) in the folds of the drapery and a double instead of a single ruffle at the neck. The Derby model is slightly smaller and instead of being mounted on a rectangular base with a detachable stand, has a pad base adorned with prunus blossom in slip. The Italian Comedy had little impact on the Derby modellers until 1756, but one pair includes 'Arlecchino' leaning against a tree-stump with one arm raised and the other behind his back, and 'Columbina' dancing (J11). A male dancer dressed as Pierrot, and companion 'Dancing Girl' who holds a

63. 'Some Early Derby Porcelain' by A.L. Thorpe, *Connoisseur,* 1960, Vol. 146, p. 261, fig. 4, dry-edge Derby group of 'Ewe and Lamb'.

***Plate 87.** 'Kitty Clive as Mrs. Riot', from David Garrick's farce* Lethe, *mounted on a star-shaped base (J10). 9¾ins. (24.8cm). Dry-edge Derby c.1750.* George Savage

***Plate 88.** Figure of 'an Actor', possibly from the Commedia dell 'Arte (J12). 6¾ins. (17.1cm). Dry-edge Derby c.1752.* N.C. Ashton collection

mask (J14) might well be taken from the Commedia dell'Arte (though Karl Berling lists them as 'Dancing Shepherds'),[64] as also may be the 'Figure of an Actor' (J12) (Plate 88). 'A Boy Shepherd Piper' (Plate 89) in brimmed hat standing beside his hound and his partner the 'Dancing Shepherdess' with a lamb (J13) are known too in contemporary Bow versions (H60). They were later to be reissued at Derby in Scottish dress as 'Boy Shepherd' and 'Dancing Shepherdess' (K53A) and must all have been taken from Meissen prototypes. They must not be confused with another pair, common to Bow and Derby, of 'Shepherd in tricorn hat with Bagpipes' and 'Shepherdess with blossoms' (H65). The Cries of Paris found echoes at Derby with models copied from originals by Kändler and Reinicke of 'Absinth Seller' (J19) with his tray of samples and a bottle in one hand, a 'Lady Vegetable Seller' (J18), and the 'Print Seller' (Plate 90) (J20) with charts in either hand and a pack upon his back. Models of a pair of seated 'Bagpipers' (J16) were once represented in the Wallace Elliot Collection.

A very beautiful group depicts a 'Huntsman flautist with recumbent Lady' who has one hand upon his sleeve (Plate 168, Chapter XIII) (J17) and this recalls the 'Idyllic Pastoral' created by Watteau, Lancret and Boucher and translated into porcelain at Meissen. Two rather late dry-edge models stand upon bases bearing moulded 'C' and 'S' scrolls and daisly-like flowers; these are St. Thomas (J23) (Plate 91) in Roman armour with a cloak wrapped about his right arm and both a broken orb and sword at his feet, and St. Philip (J22)

64. *Festive Publication to Commemorate the 200th Jubilee of the Oldest European China Factory, Meissen* (Dresden, 1910) by Karl Berling, table 7, nos. 1784 and 1782.

Plate 89. *A 'Dancing Shepherdess' beside a lamb, and 'Boy Shepherd Piper' with a dog (J13). 6¾ins. and 7¼ins. (17.1 and 18.4cm). Dry-edge Derby c.1752-54. (See Plate 70 for Bow Shepherd.)* N.C. Ashton collection

Plate 90. *A 'Print Seller', from the Cries of Paris (J20). 6¼ins. (15.9cm). Dry-edge Derby c.1753-55.* N.C. Ashton collection

Plate 91 (left). 'St. Thomas' (J23), represented as a man standing barefoot in Roman dress, with a tattered cloak. 9½ins. (24.1cm). Dry-edge Derby c.1754-55.
N.C. Ashton collection

Plate 92 (right). A 'Chinaman and boy' (J21), intended to serve as a watchstand. 9½ins. (24.1cm). Derby c.1755-56.
Winifred Williams

represented by a bearded man in soft cap and ragged mantle standing barefoot regarding a crucifix. Although St. Thomas has sometimes been called 'King Lear', his identity is assured by the finding of similar pottery versions which form a set of saints complete with identifying labels.[65] A rococo watchstand, incorporating a 'Chinaman and Boy' (J21) (Plate 92) follows a Meissen original.

Although almost all the models so far mentioned stem from Meissen prototypes, others especially those relating to allegorical subjects come from a variety of sources. The author possesses two eighteenth century bronzes after the antique of Pluto stepping over Cerberus, which bears a close resemblance to the porcelain group (J29), and 'Aphrodite holding aloft a mirror towards which a child Centaur reaches'. The last mentioned was adpated by the replacement of the centaur by a cupid to provide the porcelain Venus and Cupid (Colour Plate K) (J30). Neptune (J28) in crown and cloak stands beside his dolphin and looks for all the world as if he had just stepped down from a baroque fountain. Mars (Plate 93) (J26), clad in the helmet and armour of a Roman centurion, leans upon his shield; both he and a later gold anchor Chelsea version (D46), imitate a Kändler model[66] which, according to Mr. T. Clifford, may have been based upon a lost statue of Louis XIV by Martin Dejardins (1640-1694). The companion model of Minerva, in crested helm and cuirass holding a spear and shield upon which is emblazoned the head of Medusa, was adapted from a garden statue by John Cheere.[67] Both models continued to be reissued over a period of many years suitably adapted to conform with the current style. The goddess Cybele (Colour Plate O) (J25) appears in flowing robes and turret crown beside a lion; her distinction from

65. *The Earle Collection of Early Staffordshire Pottery* (London, 1915) by C. Earle, nos. 133 and 136, 'Thomas' and 'Philip', Victoria and Albert Museum, No. C36-1944.

66. *Königlich, Sächsische Porzellan Manufaktur Meissen 1710-1910* (Dresden, 1911) by Karl Berling, pl. 9, fig. 4.

67. *Sculpture in Britain 1530-1830* (London, 1964) by W.H. Whinney, pl. 107B.

Plate 93 (left). 'Mars' (J26), represented as a centurion in Roman armour. 6¾ins. Dry-edge Derby c.1752-54.
N.C. Ashton Collection

Plate 94 (right). A robed figure emblematic of 'The Arts' (J24). 6½ins. (15.9cm). Dry-edge Derby c.1755.
Sotheby Parke Bernet

either Persephone or Demeter seems to have been unclear in the mind of her creator for she proffers fruit and holds a cornucopia. The figure emblematic of the Arts (Plate 94) (J24), in the museum of the Royal Crown Derby Porcelain Company, sports a laurel wreath and wears robes possibly borrowed from Apollo though he stands amidst art and musical trophies.

'The Four Seasons' (Plate 95) (J31), are represented by four models of seated putti; 'Spring' with a basket of flowers; 'Summer' with a corn sheaf and corn stalks upon his lap and in one hand; 'Autumn' sits upon an up-turned basket with a bunch of grapes; 'Winter' sits huddled in a cloak stretching out his diminutive hands over a basket of charcoal placed upon the ground. About 1760, the figure emblematic of Autumn from this early dry-edge set was incorporated into a candlestick (K10) an example of which is in the Derby Museum and Art Gallery. One of the finest of all sets of porcelain figures emblematic of the Four Seasons (J32) consists of four pairs of single figures in rustic garb. Although the source of these has not been identified, they are reminiscent of models of peasants made by Friedrich Eberlein some years earlier. 'Spring' is a man wearing a tricorn hat with a basket of flowers over one arm and a posy in one hand, and a woman (Colour Plate J) dressed in a hat, laced bodice, and skirt gathering blossoms in her apron; Summer is a reaper wearing a brimmed hat (Colour Plate J and Plate 96) with a sheaf of corn, and a woman (Colour Plate J and Plate 97) holding in her left hand a bird's nest filled with eggs to which she points with her right; Autumn is a vintner (Plate 98) wearing a wide hat and holding over his shoulder a square pannier of fruit attached to a pole, and a woman wearing a head-scarf gathering grapes in her apron; Winter is a man wearing a fur hat and heavy overcoat holding a muff in one hand and extending the other over a brazier

Plate 95. *'The Four Seasons' (J31), represented by four draped seated putti, 4ins. to 5¼ins. (10.2cm to 13.3cm). Dry-edge Derby c.1750-52.*
N.C. Ashton collection

(Colour Plate J), and a woman wearing a head-scarf who warms both hands over a brazier (Plate 99). The last mentioned pair are sometimes wrongly called 'Old Age'.

There are two different sets emblematic of the Five Senses. One of these is composed of seated men and women in contemporary dress (J33). 'Taste' (Colour Plate N) is a lady holding a bunch of grapes to her mouth in her right hand with a circular basket of fruit upon her knee. This model was adapted c.1756-57 to become a 'Lady with a mandoline' (K14). 'Feeling' is a lady stroking a parrot on her lap which pecks her fingers; 'Smell' (Colour Plate L) is a gentleman taking a pinch of snuff and holding a snuff-box in his left hand; 'Sight' (Colour Plate M) is a gallant in a night-cap and dressing gown looking at his reflection in an oval hand mirror. Barrett and Thorpe[68] describe Sight as a man with a bird and they cite an illustration[69] to support this contention. However, the photograph to which they refer shows the same gallant devoid of either mirror or an ornithological companion so, for all three of them, the bird has flown! The same authors indicate that Hearing is a girl with a cage full of birds, and though this may be true, examples are unkown to the author. However, there is a model in the Museum of the Royal Crown Derby Porcelain Company of a seated lady who holds a musical score in her left hand whilst the position of her right suggests that she may once have grasped a musical instrument. She is slightly smaller than other members of the series and may be an adaptation from an earlier model that has been lost. A most peculiar version of the snuff-taker appeared recently in which he holds a lantern-like birdcage upon his knee with his right hand and has a flagon in his left.[70] This is simply an example of faulty restoration. Until now, these models of the Senses have been regarded as original. However, the Snuff-taker and Lady emblematic of Taste echo figures in Kändler's group of 1744 listed as 'An Actor offering his snuff box to a lady, the two seated upon the green sward'.[71] Both the 'Snuff-taker' and 'Gallant with a mirror' have breeches of black enamel as does the man in the Meissen group. It seems very likely that Meissen prototypes will be discovered for other models in this series.

The second representation of the Five Senses is composed of five Chinoiserie groups (J34) which were most probably based on a series of engravings illustrating supposed Chinese pastimes in Gabriel Huquier's folio after Boucher called Senses.[72] 'Sight' is a Chinese lady who holds aloft a bird in her

68. *Derby Porcelain* (Barrett & Thorpe), op. cit., p. 195.

69. *Apollo,* Dec. 1928, p. 322, No. IX.

70. Sotheby's Sale Catalogue, 27th April 1976, lot 76.

71. *German Porcelain of the 18th Century* (London, 1972) by Erica Pauls-Eisenbeiss, Vol. 1, p. 177.

72. *Livre de six feuilles representant les cinq Sens par differentes amusements chinois sur les dessin de F. Boucher* by Gabriel Huquier. This work was advertised in the *Mercure,* 1740. See *The Ceramics of Derbyshire 1750-1975* (Tiverton, 1977) by H.G. Bradley, p. 10.

***Plate 96** (left). A harvester with corn, emblematic of 'Summer' (pair to Plate 97), from the set of the 'Four Seasons' (J32). 6¼ins. (15.9cm). Dry-edge Derby c.1752-54.* N.C. Ashton collection

***Plate 97** (right). A girl holding a bird's nest containing a clutch of eggs, emblematic of 'Summer' (pair to Plate 96), from the set of the 'Four Seasons' (J32). 6½ins. (16.5cm). Dry-edge Derby c.1752-54.* N.C. Ashton collection

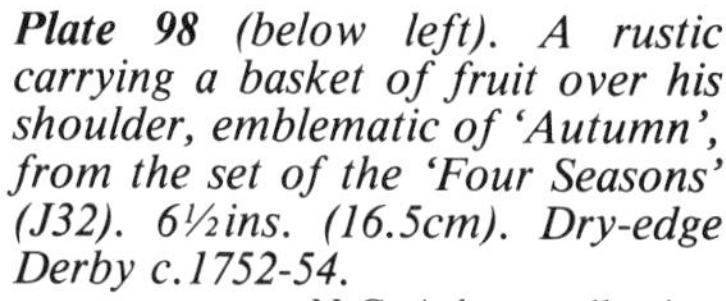

***Plate 98** (below left). A rustic carrying a basket of fruit over his shoulder, emblematic of 'Autumn', from the set of the 'Four Seasons' (J32). 6½ins. (16.5cm). Dry-edge Derby c.1752-54.* N.C. Ashton collection

***Plate 99** (below right). A lady warming her hand over a brazier, emblematic of 'Winter', from the set of the Four Seasons (J32). 6½ins. (16.5cm). Dry-edge Derby c.1752-54.* Sotheby Parke Bernet

***Plate 100** (left). Chinoiserie group emblematic of 'Feeling' (J34), showing a Chinaman about to strike a boy. 8½ins. (21.6cm). Dry-edge Derby c.1752-54.* Winifred Williams

***Plate 101** (right). Chinoiserie group emblematic of 'Smell' (J34), showing a child reaching up to grasp a flower held by a youth. 8¾ins. (22.2cm). Dry-edge Derby c.1752-54.* N.C. Ashton collection

left hand and gesticulates to a seated Chinaman; 'Feeling' (Plate 100) is a Chinaman in a conical hat about to strike a boy upon the cheek; 'Smell' (Plate 101) is a Chinese youth standing with a flower held up to his nose which a child stretches up to grasp; 'Hearing' is a Chinese lady with a lyre standing beside a child; 'Taste', which is also known as 'the Quack Doctor', is a Chinaman examining a phial standing beside a boy who leans upon a basket containing bottles. Most examples of these fine groups, including those in the N.C. Ashton Collection, are white. Some enamelled versions, including one of Taste,[73] exhibit the 'star-cross' pattern of decoration in which trifid symbols, like the imprint of birds' feet, are used to form crosses or stars. This relatively unsophisticated form of painting has, perhaps without just cause, been associated with William Duesbury. Other groups are decorated by a different hand with great restraint employing touches of pale yellow, iron red, a discordant puce and black to produce a most pleasing effect. Mention has been made earlier of the recovery of a mould, from which the head of the Chinese woman in the group emblematic of Sight was cast, which could be traced back to the Derby sale of 1848.

There are two other chinoiserie models. The first, which is emblematic of 'Air' is a seated boy with shaven head, wearing a loose jacket and trousers with a ruffle at his neck; he looks up towards his right hand which is raised and upon which he may once have held a bird. The second wears a broad brimmed hat and is seated holding what may have been a fishing rod and is emblematic of 'Water' (J35). The boy representing Air seems to have been adapted from the figure in the chinoiserie group mentioned above representing Taste. One pair, in the white, retains their original brass fitments terminating in large porcelain flowers.[74] An enamelled pair are in the Leslie Godden Collection.[75]

73. *English Porcelain Figures of the 18th Century* (Lane), op. cit., col. pl. D.

74. *Derby Porcelain* (Barrett & Thorpe), op. cit., pl. 13.

75. *Ceramics of Derbyshire 1750-1975*, op. cit., fig. 4.

Part Two
Derby figures, 1756-1795, with brief mention of later models, 1796-1848

Porcelain Figures made at Derby, 1756 to 1769

Paste and Glaze

Following the departure of André Planché from the Derby Porcelain factory and the commencement of William Duesbury's management, models were issued in a chalky paste that is very light in the hand. The paste employed up to c.1758 was glassy, and unstable in the kiln causing the sagging of projecting limbs and leaning away from the perpendicular. Larger models, such as Cybele (J25) which may be regarded as a transitional piece spanning the Planché/Duesbury periods, and 'Diana' (K11), show large and wide fire-cracks. Analysis of the figure of a 'Lady with a Mandoline' (K14) showed the body to contain silica 70 per cent, lime 20 per cent, alumina 5 per cent, and lead oxide 2 per cent. This almost certainly included cullet. However, after about 1758 a closer grained and more compact paste was evolved which was more stable in the kiln. Analysis of the model of Diana (K79) in the Victoria and Albert Museum, which is a later version of the one cited above and was probably issued c.1764, revealed silica 74 per cent, lime 22 per cent, alumina 5 per cent, and only a trace of lead oxide.[76] These models are heavier in the hand, display fewer firecracks and other imperfections such as sagging and leaning away from the vertical.

The early Duesbury glaze of 1756-58 is opacified with tin oxide so that underlying faults in the body might be hidden. It is also blued with cobalt in an attempt to simulate the cold glitter of Meissen hard paste clad in feldspathic glaze. At some time between 1758 and 1760, this practice of blueing was discontinued though opacification of the glaze may be seen on models issued as late as 1765. However, some models made as early as 1760 are covered with a transparent and faintly straw coloured glaze which creates a warm appearance. Difficulties in fusing glaze to body led to dry patches where the glaze failed to adhere. Sanding is far less common than on contemporary Bow models and crazing is relatively rare. Indeed, by about 1765, most of the imperfections in the glaze had been eliminated. Glazing appears to have been effected by dipping for it covers the under surface leaving three or four oval patches of exposed biscuit known as patch marks, to which reference has already been made. This is almost the trade mark of Derby figures until 1795, though there are a few which do not show this feature or may exhibit a dry-edge that were made c.1756-57.

The Bases

During the period 1756-58 the bases, which had previously been steep mounds, became wide, flat and edged with symmetrically arranged 'C' and 'S' scrolls. The under surfaces of these bases are often slightly concave and glazed whilst ventilation holes are generally small and cylindrical though a screw-hole may occasionally be found. Other bases of this period are mounds that have U-shaped excavations at the front and sides which create an appearance of free-standing legs, though, in fact the central portion always remains flat in contact with the table top. By about 1758-59, the inferior surfaces are flat, glazed and display the patch marks that have been described. At about the same time, the wide flat bases give place to small shallow mounds. Some of

76. Victoria and Albert Museum, No. 769-1925.

these are adorned with leaves and flowers made from slip, others show moulded scrolls arranged in asymmetrical patterns in the rococo taste. After 1760-62, the forms of the bases show great variation. Those that retain a fairly simple form are small mounds with their sides cut to become vertical. Others become increasingly complex with scrolled legs, leaves and flowers combined in distracting and restless designs. After about 1765, free-standing legs appear on bases though these never reach the height or complexity of those seen on contemporary Bow models. Ventilation holes vary a great deal in diameter, some are quite small, others will admit the tip of the finger. Holes piercing the figure, support, or base, from behind are usually round though triangular and square holes may occasionally be found.

The Marks

Very few Derby models made during this period are marked; the incised 'New D', standing for 'New Dresden', is found on a pair of 'Gardener' and 'Gardener's Companion'.[77] A group of a 'Sportsman and a Lady'[78] is incised with a triangle and the letters 'TxT', whilst another has the mark 'T.T.L.' These, as well as faintly incised letters and crosses, are probably workmen's symbols.

Enamel Colours and Decorative Styles

The term 'Pale Family' has been coined to describe Derby models issued between 1756 and about 1760 on account of their pale, almost pastel, colouring. The enamel palette included a smoky pink, both a deep lemon and a pale straw yellow, turquoise which is blotchy and often muddy, an orange-red, and a spectrum of uncertain greens. Green was the Achilles' heel of the manufactory for, although initially an opaque yellow-green was used, later it became darker and varied from a bluish-green to a brownish-grey. Enamels were applied as thin meagre washes, like oil-paint mixed with a surfeit of turpentine, in which the marks of brushes remain visible. Gilding prior to 1758 was mostly pale, watery and rubbed and is likely to have been effected outside the factory, probably in the atelier of James Giles. Later, the factory introduced mercury-gilding which has a brassy appearance.

Until approximately 1760 areas representing flesh were either left in the white with faint orange touches upon the cheeks and lips, or were covered with a wash of the palest buff heightened with red. Between 1760 and 1769 figures exhibit salmon pink patches upon their cheeks. The size of the mouth, which in the dry-edge period had been large, is now reduced and indicated with deep brownish-red in a stylised manner. Eyelids and lashes are painted with lines drawn in a warm brown, irises are either grey or brown, or occasionally greyish pink, after the fashion favoured at Meissen, whilst pupils may be dark brown or black. Washes of colour overlaid by thin irregular pencilling are employed to represent hair.

The names of factory enamellers are mostly unknown to us. More than one style has been recognised. Floral painting upon garments in the European taste is usually in a scale inappropriately large for the figure. One artist, known as the 'Cotton Stem Painter', used a rather dry palette of iron red, deep yellow, green and brown and his work stands out in slight relief upon the glaze. Floral sprays invariably contain one large flower outlined in red and left partially uncoloured, as well as half open blossoms like anemones. Leaves are lanceolate, with one edge smooth, the other ragged and stems are like threads. An example is illustrated by Barrett and Thopre.[79] Another altogether dissimilar style of painting is executed in a wider range of colours including an attractive rose-pink, pale blue, clear pale yellow, indigo and violet. In sharp contrast with the previous work, these enamels have sunk deeply into the glaze

77. *Derby Porcelain* (Barrett & Thorpe), op. cit., pl. 52. This model is in the Derby City Museum and Art Gallery. See Appendix K 13.

78. Model group in the British Museum, No. C/D 63.

79. *Derby Porcelain* (Barrett & Thorpe), op. cit., col. pl. C, 'a Derby mug, c.1756, in the style of the Cotton Stem painter'.

and do not stand out in slight relief; they have a soft yet rich appearance. Carefully drawn floral sprays most often centre on a pink rose upon which highlights have been left white, whilst a mauve iris with everted petal tips is generally included. Both of these two artists seem to have worked at Derby between 1756 and 1769 and, during this period, the number of models decorated outside the factory steadily diminished.

Painting in the Oriental manner was especially favoured and was accomplished in a palette that was dominated by iron red. This colour was used to depict stylised florettes which either had flame shaped petals or lobed contours within which radial lines create the impression of petals. These were arranged about a small open circle, often touched with gilt and included other daisy-like flowers that were coloured pale yellow and blue. The decoration in some models is restricted to patterns formed by combinations of lines, dots, circles, stars and crosses and a small number exhibit the stylised peacock's eye, after the manner employed on useful wares at Sèvres.

After 1758-60, as obtained elsewhere, the plain washes of colour were broken up by irregular shaped reserves filled with florettes and diaper patterns created in enamel and gilt. Until this time any gold used had been restricted to buttons, shoe-buckles, edges of garments and accessories such as musical instruments. Now, it was liberally applied to pick out scrolls upon bases as well as being placed over the surface of clothing.

The Modelling.

Models issued before 1759 were generally rather small, ranging between four and a half and six and a half inches tall though a few exceptions, such as the model of Diana were twelve and a half inches in height. Although correct anatomical proportions were preserved, Derby figures of this period lack any sense of movement and are posed stiffly like dolls staring vacantly into space. They have, nevertheless, a certain charm due in part to the naïvety of their modelling and in part to the lack of any sense of scale between model and other ornament. For example, a Candlestick Group (K7) in the Derby Museum and Art Gallery portrays two people and a dog looking up at a bird perched in a tree encrusted with flowers. The bird is larger than the dog and almost as big as the figures of the boy and girl, whilst the huge flowers dwarf the human forms. Large flowers which have ragged petals are a feature of this early group of the Pale Family and may be seen in the illustration of Cybele (Colour Plate O) (J25) where they are larger than the head of the attendant lion. Another example is shown in Plate 102 (K148). Many dry-edge models were reissued in slightly altered forms and several new models were added. After c.1758, the gay disregard for scale was corrected and improvements in the paste allowed much bigger models to be produced. Towards the end of this phase, some extremely large figures especially of gods and goddesses were issued. The faces of Derby models of the Duesbury I era are long and narrow and noses are proportionately lengthy whilst lips are represented in a formal and contrived manner and are much smaller than those of the dry-edge models. The models issued after 1756 lack the animation and the toy-like quality of Bow and the finely chiselled features of Chelsea.

***Plate 102.** A 'Putto' garlanded with flowers (K148). 4¼ins. (10.8cm). Derby c.1756, Pale Family.*
Author's collection

The development of the Derby bocage may be traced back to about 1760 and closely follows the pattern set at Chelsea during the gold anchor period. The Derby leaves are flat, small, and have sharp serrated edges; they lack the moulded dorsal veins and the spiky appearance of the Bow foliage and are smaller and thinner than those made at Chelsea. Flowers may be little more than small discs with saw-tooth circumferences, but others are either stellate, trumpet-shaped, or resemble small hot-cross buns; a few appear to have been modelled separately by hand. The Derby flora are also smaller in scale than those of Bow or Chelsea and an undue proportion of those included in bocages are coloured blue or white. Others are painted with two or three concentric circles of yellow, red, blue, puce, or white. These contrast with the large blossoms made prior to 1759.

The Models

A number of models first issued before 1756 reappear with some modifications. The seated lady, emblematic of 'Taste' (Colour Plate N) from the set of the Five Senses (J33) was modified and reissued as the 'Lady with a Mandoline' (Plate 103) (K14) with a scrolled instead of a mound base. A 'Gentleman playing a Recorder' (J15) who had stood hatless upon a mound, acquired both a tricorn hat and a base excavated to create the impression it was elevated on legs, to become a gentleman flautist (Plate 104) (K12). The 'Boy Shepherd Piper (Plate 89) (J13) made a fresh debut in Scottish dress, whilst his companion, the 'Dancing Shepherdess', had the position of her hands altered and was given a new dress with flounces in keeping with the fashion of the day (K53A). The 'Pierrot' (J14) reappeared in debased form with a dreary looking woman wearing an apron (K15) instead of his earlier partner who had been a dancing girl. Fresh versions of St. Philip (K93) and St. Thomas (K94) were also issued.

New models made during the period of the Pale Family include a gentleman and a lady (K16), each seated holding a shell container, and an adaptation of Kändler's group, the 'Invalid Duped'. The first Derby version of the latter is only five and a half inches tall and shows the Arlecchino proffering a plate of refreshments, behind the back of the invalid, to the lady, which she accepts

Plate 103 (left). A 'Lady with a Mandoline' (K14). 5ins. (12.7cm). Derby c.1756-58, adapted from the dry-edge Derby figure emblematic of 'Taste' (J33) (Colour Plate N). David Love

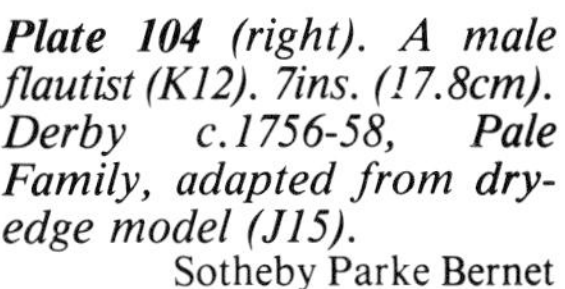

Plate 104 (right). A male flautist (K12). 7ins. (17.8cm). Derby c.1756-58, Pale Family, adapted from dry-edge model (J15). Sotheby Parke Bernet

(K21). Later versions measure up to thirteen inches and are mounted before bocage, and may portray the clown holding a platter before the invalid, which he ignores (K31). Another group depicts 'Arlecchino in motley standing beside Columbina' (K1), the two placed upon a wide flat base edged with scrolls. Kändler's group of 'Arlecchino making playful gestures to a baby held by Columbina' appears in an odd Derby version, where the figures seem to be playing peek-a-boo beneath a leafing tree (K2). 'Diana' (K11) with long-bow and hound recaptures something of the slender elegance of Eberlein's original, in which the goddess is shown selecting an arrow from a quiver suspended upon her back. Later editions of the 1760s are larger and more garishly decorated (K79). A small model of a 'Naked Child seated beside a vase' (K20), which is only three inches tall, also follows a Meissen original.

Other models are of uncertain origin. There are stiffly posed models of a boy with corn husks in his hand (Plate 105) and a girl with flowers, each seated and representing, respectively, 'Summer' and 'Spring' (K18), and known in Longton Hall versions (O39). A model of a 'Boy kicking his legs' paired with one of a 'Girl seated with her hat on her lap' (Plate 106) (K3) show an unusual degree of animation and must surely follow lost Meissen originals. A pair of standing dancers (K4), both with their arms extended in front of them, would seem to be the prototypes of the Bow 'New Dancers' (H34) and are also known in Longton Hall versions (O48).

A candlestick incorporatng a 'Putto eating grapes' (Plate 107) (K10) is an adaptation of the figure issued as Autumn from the dry-edge set of the Four Seasons (Plate 95) (J31). Probably a pair of candlesticks which include 'Arlecchino dancing' and 'Pulcinella carrying a lantern' (K9) were based on Kändler's original models. Branched candlesticks in the Derby Museum and Art Gallery include those that have been mentioned and the boy and girl with a dog looking at a bird in a tree (K7), and two dogs looking up at a squirrel (K8).

Models issued after 1759 up to the purchase of the Chelsea factory in 1770, form the main stream of production. These include Shakespeare (K29) standing and leaning against a pile of books on a plinth, and Milton (K28) in

***Plate 105** (left and right). 'Spring', portrayed by a girl seated with flowers, and 'Summer', a boy with corn in his hand (missing) (K18). 4½ins. (11.4cm). Derby c.1756-58, Pale Family.*

George Savage

***Plate 106.** Seated boy and girl (K3). 6ins. (15.2cm). Derby c.1756-58, Pale Family.*
Winifred Williams

***Plate 107.** A 'Putto eating grapes' incorporated into a candlestick (K10). 9ins. (22.9cm). Derby c.1756-58, Pale Family, adapted from a dry-edge Derby model emblematic of 'Autumn' (J31) (Plate 95).*
George Savage

like fashion with a scroll of parchment, both probably derived from terracottas after Scheemakers. They must have been popular since they were reissued many times and were still being made c.1790 when their early scroll bases were replaced with others in the neo-classical style. David Garrick, actor, dramatist and Poet Laureate, was modelled in the title role of 'Tancred' (K30) wearing a shako and fur-lined dolman with gilt facings, from the play *Tancred and Sigismunda,* by James Thompson, which had its London debut in 1745. The model is often paired with one representing a street vendor (K25), which has sometimes been identified erroneously as the actress Colly Cibber in the role of a vivandière. The lady would have been seventy-four years of age when the play opened so that one must seek some alternative identity since it seems improbable that a model of Garrick would be coupled with one of a street trader. Another actor, James Quinn, was shown in the popular role of Falstaff (K27) wearing a plumed hat, cuirass, and baggy breeches holding in one hand a sword and in the other an oval shield. The model was based on James McArdell's engraving after Francis Hayman's portrait.

Models of foreign personages include a fine 'Abyssinian Archer' (K32), and a 'Negress' who adjusts her head-dress with her left hand whilst proffering an apple in her right (K33), both after Kändler. A pair of 'Blackamoors' (K34) each with a shell container, and 'Four Blackamoors' (addorsed) (K35), possibly intended as a salt, also follow Meissen prototypes. A dancing 'Levantine Lady', and companion 'Turk' (K37) may represent an actress and actor in stage costumes from the contemporary drama. Chinoiserie is sparsely portrayed in a pair of rococo candlesticks, each incorporating two Chinese boys (K39).

The Derby orchestra is a great deal smaller than the one from Bow. The 'Gentleman flautist' (Plate 104) has already been mentioned. Amongst the best known are models of a 'Boy standing with fife and tambourine' (K5), a similar 'Youth with pipe and tambourine' (K46), and the pair known as the 'Idyllic Musicians' (K42) known also in Bow versions (H45). A bagpiper and lady with a mandoline (K43) both sit in gazebos topped by cupolas mounted on very elaborate legged bases and may be seen in the Derby Museum and Art Gallery. The 'Singing Lesson' (K49) is portrayed by a girl who holds open the mouth of a dog perched upon its hind legs on a plinth, whilst a youth holds a song-sheet. The 'Dancing Lesson' (K48) depicts a similar pair with a dog dressed in motley dancing and the youth playing a hurdy-gurdy. They are both after engravings by Carle van Loo. A fine pair of 'Minuet Dancers' (K51) who wear long cloaks and lean strangely backwards, were taken from Laurent Cars engraving after Watteau entitled 'Fêtes Venitiennes'. The Tyrolean Dancers (K53) follow one of several versions after Eberlein issued at Meissen. In contrast with the splendid set of Chelsea Ranelagh revellers, only two 'Ranelagh Dancers' (K52) were made at Derby, though these were issued in several different sizes. The male figure stands magnificiently attired with a letter in his right outstretched hand inscribed 'Domini Lucretiae'; his elegant lady wears plumes in her hair and has a cameo suspended from her shoulder which was the ticket of admission to the masked ball held in Ranelagh Gardens, Vauxhall. Major Toppin[80] has shown how the female model was inspired by a mezzotint by James McArdell of the portrait of Mary, Duchess of Ancaster, painted in 1757 by Thomas Hudson.

Pastoral subjects after engravings by Boucher were usually taken by way of Meissen models. They include the 'Italian Farmer' holding a cockerel and the farmer's wife holding a hen (Colour Plate Q) (K56). They continued to be issued over more than a decade, and later examples[81] are mounted in front of bocages, whilst there are also Doccia versions.[82] The 'Dresden Shepherds' (Plate 108) (K60) consist of a standing shepherd with a lamb beneath his right arm and a posy in his left hand, and a shepherdess with a bunch of flowers and

80. 'Francis Place, Holdship and the Ranelagh Figures' by A.J. Toppin, *Transactions*, English Ceramic Circle, 1951, Vol. 3, pt. 1, p. 70.

81. Victoria and Albert Museum. Examples on mound bases, c.1758, No. C.673-1925; examples on scroll bases, c.1763, No. C.1002-1917.

82. *Italian Porcelain* (London, 1954) by Arthur Lane, col. pl. C.

Plate 108. *'The Dresden Shepherds' (K60). 6ins. (15.2cm). Derby c.1765.* David Love

blossoms gathered in her apron. They exist both as free-standing models and as candlesticks. The 'Shepherd playing a recorder' who stands cross-legged before his dog, and companion 'Shepherdess holding flowers' gathered in her apron (Plate 109) (K64), together with a 'Shepherd proffering an apple' and holding a basket of fruit to his breast, and 'Shepherdess with a crook' in a jaunty hat (K63), all have Meissen prototypes. A pair of 'Singing Shepherds' (K58), each in mirror pose with one hand on hip and the other elevated, may be seen in the Museum of the Royal Crown Derby Porcelain Company. A pair of chamber candlesticks 'Children with flowers' (K149) is illustrated in Plate 110.

Plate 109 (above). A shepherd playing a recorder standing beside his dog (left), Shepherdess with flowers in her apron beside a sheet (right) (K64). 8ins. and 8½ins. (20.3cm and 21.6cm). Derby c.1765. (Chelsea versions plate 47). Shepherdess holding a posy and flowers (centre) (K62). 8ins. (20.3cm). Derby c.1760. Sotheby Parke Bernet

Plate 110 (left and right). A pair of chamber candlesticks of 'Children with flowers', each with a loop handle (K149). 6¾ins. (17.1cm). Derby c.1765. George Savage

The theme of the 'Tithe Pig' (a later version of which is shown in Plate 120), inspired by an engraving made in 1751 by J.S. Muller after Boitard, proved popular with its gentle dig at the established church and has been reviewed by H.B. Lancaster.[83] At Derby, it was translated into porcelain as both a group (K54) and as a set of three separate models. Elsewhere, wares from various factories were transfer printed to illustrate the subject by Sadler and Green of Liverpool and some of these also carry one or more verses of which the following is an example:

"The Parson comes, the Pig he claims,
And the good Wife with Taunts inflames,
But she quite Arch bow'd low and smil'd —
Kept back the Pig and held the Child.
The Priest look'd gruff, the Wife look'd big,
Zounds, Sir quoth she, no Child, no Pig!"

The porcelain models portray the farmer's wife proffering her tenth born child to the parson whose hands are raised in astonishment, whilst the farmer retains a tight hold on the tithe pig.

Only a few models of the Cries of Paris were copied at Derby which include a 'Jewish Pedlar' in a fur-lined hat with a tray of wares suspended by a strap about his neck, and companion 'Woman with a box of trinkets' suspended from her belt (K70). These are unusually large and stand some ten and a half inches tall. An earlier model of the 'Print Seller' (J20) was reissued in a more sophisticated rendering (Plate 111) (K71) and acquires a lady map seller (Plate 112) as his companion. There are several models, both of rustics and of ladies

83. 'The Origins of the Tithe Pig Pottery Group' by H. Boswell Lancaster, *Connoisseur,* 1940, Vol. 105, pp. 253-255, no. I, Derby porcelain group; no. II, Sadler print; no. III, Toby jug inscribed 'I will have no child tho' the X pig'.

Plate 111 *(left). 'The Print Seller' from the Cries of Paris (K71). 6½ins. (16.5cm). Derby c.1760.*
George Savage

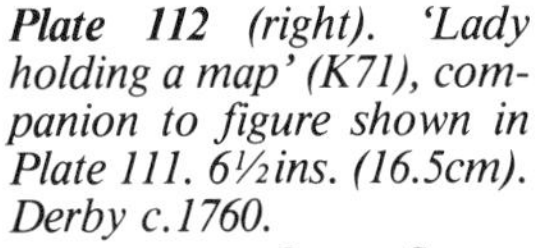

Plate 112 *(right). 'Lady holding a map' (K71), companion to figure shown in Plate 111. 6½ins. (16.5cm). Derby c.1760.*
George Savage

and their gallants, placed beside containers which were intended, according to size, to hold sweetmeats or comfits. The last mentioned were breath sweeteners, aromatic for men, scented for women, which in the days of poor dental hygiene were necessary to render close conversation over the dinner-table acceptable. Examples include a 'Gallant', and companion 'Lady' holding open the lids of square hampers (K68) and a 'Gallant', and a 'Lady' standing beside a dog and a sheep and oval containers (K69).

The 'Five Senses' (K72) are illustrated in the *Cheyne Book of Chelsea China and Pottery* where they are erroneously identified as Chelsea. Each Sense is represented by either a seated boy or girl. 'Taste' is a youth holding a bunch of grapes up to his mouth beside a leopard; 'Sight' is a boy with a spy-glass beside an eagle; 'Feeling' is a girl attended by Cupid whose quiver is suspended from a tree-stump; 'Smell' is a young man who holds a posy up to his nose beside a hound; 'Hearing' is a lady with a lute beside a white swan. They are over nine inches in height but fall far short of the grandeur of the Chelsea Senses by Willems. The Four Quarters of the Globe (Plate 113) (K73) were moulded from the Chelsea models (D60) which, in turn, had been copied from the work of Friedrich Elias Meyer described in Chapter VI. The earliest Derby versions appear on simple mound bases, and are rather stiff in appearance; later models were more elaborate both in their moulded detail and enamel decoration and stand upon scroll bases adorned with gilt. A few late examples have labels, some written in German, which identify each figure. They are amongst the most common of all sets of models and continued to be issued until well into the nineteenth century.

Plate 113. *'Asia', a Levantine girl with a camel, and 'Africa', a Blackamoor with a lion, from the set of the 'Four Quarters of the Globe' (K73). 7¼ins. (18.4cm). Derby c.1860, copied from Chelsea models and reissued in later versions (see Colour Plate R).*
Author's collection

Plate 114. *'The Classical Seasons' (K75), after Meissen originals by J.F. Eberlein. 9ins. Derby c.1758.*
George Savage

The Four Seasons were portrayed at Derby, as at other contemporary factories, in a number of different ways. The 'Classical Seasons' (Plate 114) (K75) are composed of standing models of men and women in classical robes, each attended by a child, and follow Meissen originals by Eberlein. 'Spring' is a lady in a floral dress who holds a posy to her nose and stands beside a putto bearing a basket of flowers; 'Summer' is a lady holding corn stalks who is attended by a putto who carries a corn sheaf; 'Autumn' is a youth decked in vine leaves holding a goblet and a bunch of grapes accompanied, in most versions, by a putto bearing grapes; 'Winter' is an old man in a hooded cloak who stands arms folded whilst a putto carries logs to a fire burning in a brazier. Some may prefer to identify the models as Flora, Ceres, Bacchus and Vulcan. Another set representing the Four Seasons depicts rather similar standing figures in antique robes beside vases from which sprout flowers, corn, grapes, and flames (K76). These follow prototypes by F.E. Meyer. There are also models of 'Four seated Putti' (K74) with appropriate accessories. A pair of 'Grape Vendors' (Plate 115) seated with baskets of grapes on their laps (K55) and a group composed of a peasant woman with grapes in her apron standing beside a farmer who has one arm about her waist, sometimes called 'Lovers with grapes' (Plate 116) (K57), may both have represented Autumn though the remaining three Seasons have not yet been identified.

Models of allegorical subjects most often follow Meissen prototypes. 'Pluto and Cerberus' (Plate 117) (K92), and 'Aphrodite' with a dolphin (K77) are copies of originals by Eberlein created c.1740 at Meissen. 'Europa and the Bull' (K80) depicts a long nosed woman with her left breast bared placing a garland about the neck of a pug-like bull, whilst 'Leda and the Swan' is portrayed by a rather similar lady beside a swan with an S shaped neck (K86); both may have been adapted from bronzes by Jean Thieny. The familiar figure of 'Mars' (K87) in the guise of a Roman centurion is a more elaborate version of an earlier model (J26). He may have as his companion 'Minerva' in crested helmet and cuirass, who holds an oval shield, upon the centre of which is the

Plate 115. *A pair of seated 'Grape Vendors' (K55). 5¼ins. (13.3cm). Derby c.1758, Pale Family.* Author's collection

Plate 116. *A pair of 'Lovers with Grapes' (K57), possibly emblematic of Autumn. 6¼ins. (15.9cm). Derby c.1760. For Bow group in which the same figures are adapted to hold flowers (Plate 72).* George Savage

Plate 117. *Pluto and the three-headed dog Cerberus (K92). 7ins. (17.8cm). Derby c.1760.* George Savage

head of Medusa, and a spear (K87). Mars and Venus were also issued as candlesticks (Plate 118) (K88). Models of Britannia (Plate 118) (K78) were issued in several sizes and some seem to have been adapted from Minerva. Justice (K85) stands holding in her left hand the scales and in her right a short sword, whilst 'War' (K97) is represented as a youth standing amidst the trophies of battle. Both of these models were issued c.1760 and probably in that same year 'Jupiter riding in a chariot with an eagle' (K83) and 'Juno in a chariot' with a peacock (K84) were issued. Two groups, one of the reclining muse, Clio, with a lyre, holding a quill in her hand, being lectured by a Cupid holding a scroll (K89), the other of the muse, Erato, recumbent holding a tambourine and attended by Cupid bearing flowers (K90) both follow originals made at Sèvres by Etienne Falconet.

The spirited animal models made most probably by André Planché prior to 1756 gave promise of even better things to come which, sadly, were not to be realised. Most of the Derby animal models issued between 1756 and 1769 are banal, and of these there are a great number some of which are listed in Appendix K. Farmyard livestock includes a standing 'Cow suckling a Calf' and 'Bull' (K128), a pair of recumbent cows (K129), standing or reclining ewes and rams, some with lambs (K140-K144). There are, also, many dogs including pugs (K137-K139), and pointers (K136) and some rather prosaic horses (K133). A pair of 'Stag' and companion 'Doe' at lodge (K147) follow Meissen prototypes.

Plate 118. *'Mars' dressed as a Roman centurion (left) and companion 'Venus with a Cupid' (right) (K88). 8ins. (20.3cm). Derby c.1765. Britannia (centre) standing beside a lion and with trophies at her feet (K78). 10ins. (25.4cm). Derby c.1765.* David Love

The Derby aviary is fashioned generally on a smaller scale than that of either Chelsea or Bow. The colouring of plumage is rather pale and more natural than the bright colouring of the Bow models. Derby birds lack animation and usually perch on bases shaped like chimney-pots with flared lower edges, or truncated cones, which are encrusted with flowers and leaves. The majority are tits (K98-K99), finches (K100, K106 and K108-111), buntings (K101-K102) and canaries (K103-K105). There are a few which show an admirable animation and these, which include two pairs of woodpeckers (K122 and K123), and two parrots eating fruit (K114), are copies of Meissen originals. After about 1760 some elaborate candlestick groups were made that include two birds with a nest often containing fledglings in a bocage. Examples include 'Two Finches with a nest of Fledglings' in a cherry bush topped by a candle sconce (K124), and a pair of 'Fabulous Birds in a Bocage' (K125). Only a fraction of the total number of animal and bird models are reviewed here, though some further examples are listed in Appendix K.

Derby Figures made between 1770 and 1795

Paste and Glaze

When William Duesbury purchased the Chelsea factory in 1770, he acquired with it expertise relating to paste, glaze, and enamel colours. Analysis of the Chelsea-Derby paste reveals silica 42 per cent, lime 24 per cent, alumina 16 per cent, phosphoric acid 24 per cent, soda 1 per cent, and only traces of magnesia, potash, and lead oxide.[84] The phosphoric acid level indicates the inclusion of some 44 per cent of bone-ash, and this ingredient accounts for the milky opaqueness of the body. It also made it possible to create larger models in more ambitious poses with unsupported projection of limbs. Surviving factory accounts include a bill "March to July, 1770 — Mr. William Johnson, for Ten Bags of Bone Ash from London...". The improved plasticity of the paste due to the clay, is reflected by the high level of alumina and this led to elimination of surface tearing, firecracks, sagging out of alignment, and other blemishes. Unfortunately, the use of the Chelsea glaze upon the new body led to crazing due to unequal coefficients of expansion between the two. However, the earlier dry patches, sanding, and smoke-staining became rare. Further, by about 1780, a thin, transparent, and glossy glaze was evolved which was well-nigh perfect.

The Bases

Between 1770 and about 1780, most figures were mounted on irregular rock-like pads which were enamelled a pale green and decorated with appropriate accessories, such as flowers, shells, or garden implements picked out in natural colours. Those that display more elaborate bases show the newer symmetry of arrangement in the *Louis Seize* style which include 'C' and 'S' scrolls and shell motifs. A very few continue to be issued on bases elevated upon legs adorned with gilded and enamelled scrolls. Many of the smaller models of allegorical subjects appear on plain square or rectangular stands. There are several groups depicting Cupids which represent such subjects as Commerce or Astrology which are mounted on high rectangular bases which are pierced and show scrolls that are left white.

After 1780, most bases are cylindrical, octagonal or rectangular after the style of the neo-classical taste and many have vertical fluting, circumferential gilt bands, or towards 1795 the Greek key-fret pattern. Most ventilation holes between 1770 and 1780 are fairly large and will often admit the tip of a finger. Later, they become very much smaller. Inferior surfaces of bases remain flat and continue to display patch marks.

84. *Derby Porcelain* (Barrett & Thorpe), op. cit., p. 120.

The Marks

Reference has already been made to incised numbers which appear upon the inferior surface of Derby models made after 1772 up to about 1795. These correspond fairly accurately with a factory list drawn up by John Haslem, though there are many unfilled gaps and a few errors. Appendix M provides a similar list based on Haslem, in which models are briefly described and such additional information as is known to the author has been inserted. For example, Haslem erroneously transposed the numbers relating to the 'Virgin Mary' and the 'Prudent Mother' and this amendment together with other corrections has been made. The marks themselves include a script 'No.', followed by Arabic numeral(s). There may also be incised in script letters 'Size', followed either by the word 'First', 'Second', or 'Third', or by the appropriate Arabic numerals. Size 1, was the largest, size 2 intermediate, size 3 small but a few models were issued in as many as six sizes. Two figures marked in this way are shown in Plate 119. Models issued after 1795 may retain their old numbers.

A few models and groups fashioned from Chelsea moulds between 1770 and about 1774, are marked with an enamelled or gilt script letter 'D', intersected by an anchor which may take several forms illustrated in Appendix R. Although the patronage of the Derby factory by George III entitled the use of the prefix 'Royal' or inclusion of the device of a crown, they do not appear on porcelain figures until about 1782. At this time, a crown surmounting crossed batons, flanked by three dots arranged in a triangle, above the script letter 'D' were introduced. The device was carefully drawn in red or blue enamel, though occasionally it was impressed.

The impressed letter 'B', is said by Haslem to have been applied to unfired assembled models selected for issue in biscuit and, owing to blemishes acquired by some of these in their firing, a few enamelled models and groups may bear the mark. Likewise, the impressed letter 'G' may have been used to

Plate 119. *A pair of Gardeners (M292). 4¾ins. (12.1cm). Chelsea-Derby c.1782. Incised 'No. 292, Second Size'.* Author's collection

indicate that a model was intended to be glazed and enamelled. Other impressed letters such as 'R' and 'K' most probably refer to workmen. An impressed triangle, was the mark of Joseph Hill, and an incised star made with four intersecting lines, was the sign used by Isaac Farnsworth — both repairers. Occasionally numerals appear without the prefix 'No.', and the significance of these is unknown.

Enamel Colours and Decorative Style

Acquisition of the Chelsea colour chemistry led to an immediate improvement in the quality, and an extension in the range, of the Derby enamels. Until this time greens had been unpredictable and had sometimes emerged from the muffle-kiln as a muddy sage or greyish blue both of which had a matt surface. Now, a clear transparent light green was introduced and used liberally on bases as well as upon the figure and accessories. Unfortunately its lack of any variation between models reduces the interest when several are viewed as a group. The blotchy turquoise was replaced by a thick glossy light blue and the streaky pink was superseded by a pale but even colour. Neither the blue nor the pink approached the richness of the Chelsea peacock green and rose Pompadour. A spectrum of mauves, purples and browns were developed and an unpleasant light orange made its first appearance. A saxe blue was invented by Constantine Smith but this was rarely used on figures though it is evident on groups depicting the 'Cock on the Dunghill' (D94) and the 'Vain Jackdaw' (D93) which necessitates their reallocation from Chelsea to Derby. The enamel was used chiefly as a substitute for the earlier underglaze blue that had proved to be unsatisfactory. Colours were applied more generously than previously and all brush marks were completely eliminated.

Gilding had been lavishly applied between 1760 and 1765 but was now either used sparingly to accent some special feature or omitted altogether. The irregular reserves of the rococo fasion were also abandoned and clothing was covered in plain washes of more natural colours. Frequently dresses were painted with small scale flowers in monochrome in the style of *Deutsche Blumen*. These might be a deep purple upon a paler shade of the same colour or in a contrasting colour such as purple upon pale green or yellow. Alternatively, larger flowers drawn in brownish red and accented with gilt might be placed beside smaller blossoms in violet-blue and pale yellow with green leaves in the style of *Indianische Blumen*.

The striking salmon-pink cheeks of the earlier period had begun to fade in the period 1765-1769 and uniform flesh tints were used instead. These were a medium buff heightened with a suspicion of orange-red upon cheeks. Lips had been depicted in a rather stylised manner but after 1770 these are more naturally represented. Eyelids and eyelashes continued to be pencilled in a warm brown and irises were either grey, brown, or orange-pink, whilst pupils were painted dark brown or purplish-black. Hair was portrayed by a plain wash of buff, brown or grey upon the surface of which very fine irregular lines were placed in some areas. Dark hair is relatively uncommon.

Biscuit Figures

Derby biscuit figures are first mentioned in the Sale Catalogue of 17th April, 1771, and continued to be made until the first quarter of the nineteenth century. During the first phase between 1771 and 1793, the biscuit models are close grained and faintly translucent in their more thinly potted areas. They have an ivory colour which is quite distinct from the pure white of Sèvres or the bluish tinge peculiar to Tournai, whilst French models lack the Derby patch marks and factory devices upon the under surface of their bases and, owing to their construction by press moulding, are heavier in the hand. The surface is flawless, smooth to the touch and presents a satin-like surface sheen. This last mentioned quality may initially have been created by accident when droplets of glaze remaining over in the kiln vapourised and were deposited upon the surface of models as a fine mist. After 1794, the effect was contrived either by painting glaze on the inner walls of the saggars or including a small cup of glaze with the models. This gave a more predictable surface sheen and the process was known as smear glazing. At some time between 1795 and 1810, the soft paste body was altered to one of bone china. During this time, biscuit figures exhibit a chalky white appearance, are dry and slightly rough to the touch, and lack the surface sheen. These characteristics also are found on the models made by George Cocker at his small Friar Gate factory in Derby.

Modelling Styles

The chief problem relating to any description of modelling styles peculiar to the different artists is that it is necessary first to make the correct attributions and this cannot be done with any degree of certainty. Models made at Tournai by Nicholas François Gauron have been mentioned in Chapter III and several of these reappear at Derby in the same style but clearly were cast from different moulds. He seems to have shown a preference for creating groups of figures, which are often cupids, arranged upon an irregular rock-like base about a central feature such as a leafing tree or an obelisk. His work does not display any peculiar traits by which it can be identified and those groups and figures tentatively ascribed to him are listed in Appendix L. He appears to have been a competent modeller of no small merit.

Pierre Stephan was a second Derby modeller to have come from Tournai though his work whilst at the French factory has not been identified. A Derby model of Admiral Lord Howe (M384) is signed 'P. Stephan', and another model in a similar style of Admiral Lord Rodney (L1) is known in a black basaltes version from Josiah Wedgwood's factory at Etruria where it is known that Stephan modelled. A set of four standing children with large heads, smirking faces with rounded cheeks, and rather short arms, are poor copies of models included in a set of eight made by Gauron at Tournai, and are known as 'the French Seasons' (Plate 125) (M123). These stylistically resemble the Bristol 'Rustic Seasons' (P36) and many other models which are attributed to Stephan. However, figures in a very different style including a beautiful 'Pastoral Group' (M12), the 'Four Elements' (Plates 123 and 124) (M3) and groups after Angelica Kauffmann (M195, M196 and M235) have also been ascribed to the same artist and it is difficult to believe that the two styles stem from the hand of one man. Here, it should be remembered, Josiah Wedgwood had no high opinion of Stephan's trial models of 'Hope' and 'The Conquered Province' (page 173-174) which leads one to suppose that the modeller was far less skilled than Gauron.

The style of Jean Jacques Spengler can readily be identified since much of his work has been named in the Lygo letters. He was amongst the first of the porcelain modellers working in England to be influenced by the neo-classical style though his presentation remains idealised and a trifle sentimental. Faces of his figures have Greek profiles with forehead and nose in one straight line, short upper lip and rounded chin. He spared no pains faithfully to reproduce the smallest folds of drapery and, if to the modern eye his work seems too detailed, he was nevertheless an artist of considerable distinction.

The role of William Coffee as modeller was probably limited to the provision of small figures of animals, some of which were used to compliment human subjects fashioned by other artists, others issued in their own right.

Judging from the 'Recumbent Setter' (L31)[85] incised 'W. Coffee', and a 'Spanish Pointer' (L30) which is fashioned in the same style, he possessed very limited skill. Here, one recalls the adverse comments about his work made by Joseph Lygo, and also by Charles King (page 177).

The Models

The following descriptions of models and groups are arranged under subject matter rather than in chronological order. A number, relating to the scandal of John Wilkes (1727-1797), first appeared in 1764, but are more familiar in the later versions of 1770-74 when his election to Parliament rekindled public interest in the affair. Wilkes had been arrested after publication in 1763, of a libellous attack on George III for his illiberal policies, in issue number 45 of the *North Briton*. Charles Pratt, then Chief Justice of Common Pleas, declared his detention to be illegal and he was promptly released. He became something of a folk hero and those associated with his cause enjoyed a measure of reflected glory. The model of Wilkes (M126), depicts him with his characteristic squint after the manner of Scheemakers' Shakespeare; he stands with his cloak thrown over his shoulder, one hand on hip, the other resting upon a plinth from which hang two scrolls inscribed 'Bill of Rights', and 'Magna Charta', whilst at his feet a putto holds the Cap of Liberty and a tome entitled 'Lock on Govt'. The model of Pratt (L4) was based on Ravenet's engraving after the 1766 painting by Sir Joshua Reynolds, made to commemorate his appointment to the office of Lord Chancellor under the administration of Lord Chatham. He stands in full-bottomed wig in robes of scarlet and ermine. General Sir Henry Conway (1721-1795), a cousin of Horace Walpole, had incurred the wrath of the government by his adverse criticism of the way in which the matter had been handled in the House of Commons. His temerity was rewarded by dismissal from the post of Officer to

85. *The Ceramics of Derbyshire 1750-1975*, op. cit., no. 42.

***Plate 120.** 'The Tithe Pig group' (M293). 6ins. (15.2cm). Derby c.1772. This group was first issued c.1765 (K54) and continued to be popular until the end of the 18th century.* George Savage

***Plate 121.** 'A Boy with a Puppy' and companion 'Girl with a Lamb', known as the 'French Shepherds' (M57). 6ins. (15.2cm). Chelsea-Derby c.1775.* David Love Antiques

the Royal Bedchamber, and he was deprived of his command. Later, he was reinstated, and his model (L5) shows him after he had been promoted to the rank of field-marshal, baton in hand, leaning against a cannon, with a putto at his feet holding a shield bearing upon it the device of a Moor's Head, which was his crest. The model of Wilkes is often paired with one of Catherine Macaulay (M88). In 1777, a statue of this lady by J.F. Moore was erected in the chancel of St. Stephen's Church, Walbrook, portraying her in classical robes, quill in hand, leaning against a pile of volumes of her *History of England.* The porcelain version is said to have been adapted from the sculpture, which was hurriedly removed in the following year after she had married a man named William Graham, who was her junior by thirty-five years. Although she was regarded by many as a champion of liberty, Wilkes evidently did not greatly admire her, for he once described the lady as "painted up to the eyes" and "looking as rotten as an old Catharine pear"![86]

***Plate 122.** Milton (M297), standing beside a plinth holding a scroll inscribed 'Into the Heav'n of Heav'ns I have presum'd, an earthly guest & drawn Empyreal air'. 10¼ins. (26cm). Derby c.1790. A reissue of a model of c.1758 in the neo-classical style.* George Savage

There are several models of admirals and other notables including Admiral Lord Rodney (L1), and the companion figure of Admiral Hood. Another sea-lord, who is possibly Sir Adam Duncan (L2), is in Lord Bearsted's Collection in Upton House, Warwickshire. A model of Admiral Lord Howe (M384) was based upon the portrait by Mason Brown depicting him on the deck of the *Queen Charlotte* after his victory over the French fleet on the Glorious First of June, 1794.[87] An example in the Victoria and Albert Museum is incised 'P. Stephan'. There is a group portraying William Pitt (L6), who in 1766 became Lord Chatham. He stands beside a plinth to which is attached a plaque inscribed "Viscount Pitt of Burton Pynsent, Earl of Chatm Lord Keeper of His Majesty's Privy Seal", and at his feet kneels a Red Indian girl who has beside her an alligator. The kneeling girl is doubtless intended to signify the honour due to the noble lord for his liberal policies concerning the American Colonies. This group is wrongly identified by William King[88] as having been made at Chelsea. A bust of Jean Jacques Rousseau (L8), adapted from a painting of 1716 by J.H. Tarval, is paired with one of Alexander Pope (L9) based on an engraving by J. Smith of a portrait by Sir Godfrey Kneller. The most magnificent of all Derby groups are those representing the Royal Family (L7) which were inspired by a mezzotint of Earlom after the painting by Johann Zoffany.[89] In 1773, the manager of the Bedford Street London warehouse, William Wood, wrote of these "Their present majesties, the king and queen, and the royal family, in three grouped pieces in biscuit. The centre piece represents the king in Vandyke dress, on a blue and gold basement, supported by four lions leaning on an altar richly ornamented in blue and gold, with hanging trophies of the polite arts and sciences. The crown, munde, and sceptre reposing on a cushion of crimson, embroidered, fringed, and tasselled in gold. 14 inches." The other two companion groups portray Queen Charlotte with two of the royal children, and a group of four children. The whole set is now in the Royal Collection in Windsor Castle.

The earlier models of Milton (K28) and Shakespeare (K29) were reissued on octagonal bases decorated with vertical fluting in the neo-classical taste (Plate 122) (M297 and M305). Also, 'James Quinn as Falstaff' (M291) in plumed hat, doublet and baggy hose, holding a sword and shield, taken from James McArdell's engraving of the portrait by Francis Hayman. Some of the models include a bill of fare attached to the belt of Falstaff which reads:

Sack	£2 - 2 - 0
Capon	0 - 2 - 0
	0 - 1 - 0
Bread	- - ½
	£2 - 5 - 0½.

86. *Catalogue of Lord Bearsted's Collection* (Plaistow, 1964) by J.V.G. Mallet, pp. 18-19, no. 55.

87. Victoria and Albert Museum, No. C.134-1937.

88. *English Porcelain Figures of the Eighteenth Century* (London, 1925) by William King, fig. 36.

89. 'English China Collections of the Past' by Bellamy Gardner, *Transactions,* English Ceramic Circle, 1937, No. 4, pp. 23-27, plate IXd; portrait pls. IXa, IXb and IXc, porcelain groups.

Colour Plate O. *'Cybele' (J25), the Phrygian earth goddess, wearing a turret crown standing beside a lion and a cornucopia. 9¼ins. (23.5cm). Derby c.1756. The large flowers (almost as large as the lion's head) are usually associated with the period 1756-58 and the enamelled floral sprays are in the manner of James Giles.* Author's collection

Colour Plate P. *A huntsman standing beside a seated lady, playing a flute (J17). 6¼ins. (15.9cm). Dry-edge Derby c.1754/5.* Norman C. Ashton collection

Colour Plate Q. *A pair of models often called the 'Italian Farmers' (K56). 7½ins. (19.1cm). Derby c.1760. Originals were created by J.J. Kändler at Meissen and Doccia versions are also known.* David Thorn collection

The subject must have been exceedingly popular for models of up to fifteen inches tall continued to be issued well into the nineteenth century. A model of 'David Garrick as Richard III' (M21) was inspired by John Dixon's mezzotint of a painting by Nathaniel Dance of c.1771. Miss Barnette Craven[90] has shown that the same model was reissued in the 1790s with a new head in the likeness of John Philip Kemble, who succeeded Garrick in the role. Further, in about 1815, the second version was painted to resemble Edmund Kean who was currently playing the stage part and this final version was issued in the dark opaque enamels and brash gilding of the Bloor period. The attribution to John Bacon of the models of Quinn and Garrick cannot be substantiated. The popularity of models of characters from the Commedia dell'Arte seems to have waned despite such stage productions as *Harlequinade* that ran in London. There is only a single pair of models representing 'Arlecchino in plumed hat and motley' bearing slapsticks, and 'Columbine dancing' (M199).

A large number of porcelain groups made in imitation of originals by Maurice Etienne Falconet have been mentioned in Chapter III. They include 'The Hair Dresser' (M84) shown as a man-servant dressing the hair of a seated lady, 'The Shoe Black' (M81) which portrays a maid polishing the shoes of a standing gallant, 'The Stocking Mender' (M79) consisting of a man stooped to repair the stocking of a standing lady, and 'The Shoe Maker' (M78) in which a cobbler fits a shoe to the foot of a seated lady. Many copies of pastoral themes made by Falconet after Boucher have also been noted in Chapter III. 'The knot in the Cravat' (M177), shows a seated lady adjusting the cravat of a squatting gallant; 'The Alpine Shepherdess' (M178) portrays a beau seated upon the green sward holding the hand of a shepherdess who sits upon a mound; 'The Grape Gatherers' (M176) are represented by a rustic swain seated offering his girl grapes whilst a sheep eats the posy he was prepared for his beloved. There is a pastoral group (L17), probably inspired by 'Le Mouton Favorite' by Boucher, composed of a seated lady who strokes a lamb upon her knee whilst warding off a caress from an admirer. Other groups, after Falconet, include 'A Raree Show' (M94) in which a dog and two children watch a peep-show whilst a third acts as showman, and 'A Game of Hazard' (M93) in which three children operate a fortune telling device. The 'Boy dancing with Girl' (L21) is based on Falconet's 'La Danse Allemande' after Boucher,[91] and shows the pair side by side facing in opposite directions with hands clasped as if about to dance a reel. Many of these Derby versions of the 1770s and 1780s were reissued after the beginning of the nineteenth century in debased forms, clad in dark enamel colours and brash gilding of the Bloor period and several of these carry the device of two crossed 'Ls' simulating the factory mark of Sèvres.

'The Four Elements' (M48) closely resemble Tournai biscuit groups made by Gauron. Earth is represented by one putto with a spade and another with flowers; Fire depicts two putti at a grindstone; Water consists of a putto with a fish and another with a basket; Air is portrayed by two putti robbing a bird's nest. Each pair stands upon a tall rock-like base which has a leafing tree in the centre. A different version of the Four Elements (M3) includes four standing adult figures with Earth (Plate 123) as a gardener leaning upon a spade and lifting a pot plant from a plinth; Fire is a youth who ignites a faggot in his left hand with a burning-glass held aloft in his right; Water (Plate 124) is a fishergirl standing with a rustic net and fish caught up in her apron; Air is a girl who holds a bird in her up-stretched hand. The Four Quarters of the Globe (Colour Plate R) (M200) are similar to those previously made at Chelsea (C97) and Derby (K73) though the Red Indian girl emblematic of America may, in some sets, be replaced by another based upon the Longton Hall model, whilst

90. 'Derby Figures of Richard III' by Barbette Craven, *Transactions,* English Ceramic Circle, 1977, Vol. 10, pt. 2, pp. 95-98, pl. 40a, models of Garrick, Kemble and Kean; pl. 40b, mezzotint by Dance; pl. 41a, a wax relief of Kemble; pl. 41c, a print of Kean by Cruikshank.

91. *Le Biscuit de Sèvres, Recueil des Modeles de la Manufacture de Sèvres au XVIIIme Siècle* (Paris, 1909) by Emile Bourgeoise and Georges Lechevallier-Chevignard, pl. 11, no. 170.

***Plate 123** (left). A gardener, emblematic of 'Earth', from the set of the 'Four Elements' (M3), probably by P. Stephan. 10ins. (25.4cm). Chelsea-Derby c.1773, incised 'No. 3, Size 1'.*
Author's collection

***Plate 124** (right). A fishergirl, emblematic of 'Water', from the set of the 'Four Elements' (M3), probably by P. Stephan. 8½ins. (21.6cm). Chelsea-Derby c.1773, incised 'No. 3, Second Size'.*
Author's collection

***Plate 125.** 'The French Seasons' (M123). 8½ins. (21.6cm). Derby. First created c.1775, attributed to P. Stephan and incised 'No. 123', the examples illustrated are c.1790 and are mounted on cylindrical bases.* Grosvenor Antiques

Europe may acquire a recumbent horse, also after the manner of the Longton version (Colour Plate T) (O79). The earlier Derby models were combined to form a group about an obelisk in a variation of the Continents (M295).

There are a great many different models and groups which represent the Four Seasons. The 'Antique Seasons' (M5) consist of adult figures in classical robes standing upon plinths which include Flora wearing a diadem of flowers with blossoms in her hand and gathered in her robe; Ceres with a chaplet of corn stalks with a corn sheaf; Bacchus crowned with vine leaves and holding in one hand a goblet and in the other a bunch of grapes; Saturn wearing a soft hat and with a brazier. The same figures are included about a leafing tree as a group (M248). The 'French Seasons' (Plate 125) (M123) have already been mentioned in connection with models made at Tournai by Gauron and copies probably made by Stephan at Derby. Spring is a youth in a tricorn hat and contemporary dress who holds a posy in both hands; Summer is a bare-headed girl in a floral dress who holds a sheaf of corn; Autumn is another girl wearing a head-scarf, laced bodice and apron who dances holding a basket of fruit and a bunch of grapes; Winter is a bare-headed youth who carries a bundle of faggots upon his right shoulder. Traditionally, they are attributed to Stephan. The 'Grotesque Seasons' (M47) are truncated standing models of peasants with appropriate accessories, whilst there are also 'Seated Seasons' (M61) portrayed by seated rustic boys and girls which have an unnatural twist to their bodies immediately above the hips. Stiffly modelled standing 'Rustic Seasons' (M35) were issued both as individual figures and as two paired groups (M68). Halsem lists the 'Chelsea Seasons' (M125) which include models of a lady with a basket, and a gentleman with a gun, both of which were available as a single pair (M50). The same figures were included as a group of four arranged about an obelisk (M294). The complex group illustrated by William King[92] which consists of a shepherd and shepherdess reclining beneath a tree upon a mound base surrounded by four pairs of putti, one pair representing each season, looks like French biscuit, but without inspection cannot be ascribed to any particular factory.

'The Five Senses' (M59) are adaptations of earlier models (K72) already described. Groups, each of two Cupids, represent the 'Arts and Sciences' (M39-M45) which stand on pierced bases. 'Commerce' consists of a cupid examining a parcel whilst his companion writes in a ledger; 'Music' shows a cupid standing with one hand upon the shoulder of his fellow who plays a fiddle; 'Painting and Sculpture' are represented by a cupid sculpting a bust and another seated with a brush and canvas; Astrology and Astronomy are two cupids, one holding a telescope, the other with a pair of dividers pouring over a globe; 'Architecture' shows two cupids beside a ruined fluted column. The sixth group in the series may be 'Poetry' or 'Geography' and is unknown to the author. All were copies of originals by Victor Michel Acier of Meissen. There are two very different groups representing 'Music' (M216) and 'Poetry' (M217). The first, consists of a lady dressed in classical robes standing before a ruined column playing a flute; upon the top of the column and about her feet are musical trophies and two attendant children, one holding a violin, the other a musical score, are at her side. The second shows a similar arrangement with the central figure holding a lyre, one putto holding a quill and another a scroll.

The pantheon of gods and goddesses is large, and many are represented in an idealised and romantic manner. Models are often between four and eight inches tall and mounted on square or rectangular bases. Mars (M114), shown as a Roman centurion, echoes an earlier model and may be paired either with Minerva (M121), or with a group including Venus holding up a mirror and

92. *English Porcelain Figures of the 18th Century* (King), op. cit., fig. 55.

Cupid who reaches up to grasp it (M115). These, together with Apollo (M116) wearing a laurel chaplet and holding a lyre, Jupiter (M117) with a thunderbolt and his eagle, Neptune (M118) and Juno (M119) and her peacock, all follow earlier Derby versions. Britannia (M258) which was available in three sizes seems to have been based upon garden statuary such as that made by John Cheere. The 'Antique figure of Justice' (M162) is different from the earlier Justice (K85), and consists of a tall blind-fold lady in classical dress and sandals holding a sword in her right hand the point of which is lowered. She is usually paired with 'Antique Wisdom' (M161) represented by a similar lady who wears a helmet and extends an orb in her right hand. Examples may be seen in the Plymouth City Museum and Art Gallery. Other allegorical figures received more serious treatment. Bacchus (M193) crowned with vine leaves carries a goblet and may have been based on a marble by Jacopo Sansovino now in the Bargello, Florence.[93] The companion model is Ariadne (M194). 'Winged Time' (M222) stands one foot on a globe holding an hour-glass, and may have been an adaptation of Giovanni da Bologna's marble Venus in the Bobli Grotto.[94] 'Time clipping the wings of Love' (M124) is portrayed by a bearded man docking the wings of Cupid with shears and was inspired by Charles Phillip's engraving after Van Dyck. There are three groups based on mezzotints by Francesco Bartolozzi after Angelica Kauffmann including 'Three Graces distressing Cupid' (M235), 'Two Virgins awakening Cupid' (Plate 126) (M195) and 'Two Bacchantes adorning a bust of Pan' with a wreath (M196).

Another group, 'Procris and Cephalus' (M75), shows the huntsman, Procris, bending over his beloved aghast to find her breast pierced by the javelin he had cast at a venture. This was based on Noel Mire's engraving made in 1768 after Charles Monnet's illustration in the second volume of Le Mire and Basan's edition of *Ovid's Metamorphoses.*[95] The companion group, Renaldo and Armida (M76), was inspired by an engraving by Pierre de Bailliu, after a painting by Van Dyck, to illustrate the fourteenth canto of Tasso's *Gerusalemme Liberata,* published during the seventeenth century.[96] Here, the sourceress Armida who had been bent on the destruction of Renaldo as he slept was so overcome by his beauty that, instead, she covers him with leaves and flowers. A model of Aesculapius, usually paired with Hygieia (M99), may be a mirror copy of the Farnese Hercules for he carries a club in place of the caduceus.[97] Further, No. 122 in Haslem's list, which is the same model, is identified as 'Hercules'. 'The Three Arts', a group of three ladies, representing Poetry, Painting, and Science (L13) was based on an etching by Marcantonio Raimondi after a design by Raphael.[98] A pair of sacrifice figures (M14), portraying a youth in classical dress standing at an altar upon which rests a lamb, and companion girl sacrificing a goat, were based on engravings by the Flemish artist, Charles Monnet, entitled 'Jason and Medea at the altar of Diana' from *Les Metamorphoses d'Ovide,* by L'Abbé Banier, which appeared in Paris between 1767 and 1771. Two charming models depicting a girl looking into a hand mirror with a snake twined around her right hand, and Cupid standing with one finger to his lips, both standing beside urns resting on flower encrusted plinths, are known as 'Prudence' and 'Discretion' (M15). They recall the work of Falconet but their precise source is not known.

'Cupids' are disinguished from 'putti' by their diminutive wings, though both were probably inspired by *les enfants d'après Boucher.* Many were modelled after gold anchor Chelsea prototypes which had been based on originals by Kändler. The Derby versions of these 'Cupids in Disguise' (M262-M278) stand on irregular pad bases coloured pale green and generally lack the dynamic quality and the sharpness of modelling detail of their Chelsea

93. 'Derby Biscuit' by Timothy Clifford, *Transactions* English Ceramic Circle, 1969, Vol. 7, pt. 2, pl. 127a, Derby model; pl. 127b, marble by J. Sansovino.

94. ibid., pl. 127c, model of 'Winged Time'.

95. 'Two Chelsea-Derby groups and their Prototypes' by William King, *Connoisseur,* 1924, Vol. 69, pp. 211-213, no. I, porcelain group of 'Procris and Cephalus'; no. IV, engraving by Noël le Mire.

96. ibid., p. 212, no. II, porcelain group of 'Renaldo and Armida'; no. III, engraving by P. de Bailliu.

97. 'Derby Biscuit', op. cit., pl. 124c.

98. ibid., pl. 128a, group representing 'Poetry, Painting and Science'; pl. 128b, engraving by M. Raimondi.

forebears. Other Cupids, taken from a different source, are shown in a variety of pastimes such as riding bucks (M182), riding a dolphin or a swan (M185), astride a sealion (M197), or perhaps with less elan seated with a cat or dog (M213) or with a falcon (M214). Some of the groups of Cupids depict them as 'Four Cupids hunting' (Plate 127) (M251), 'Four Cupids bird's-nesting' (M234), and representing 'Music' (M333). These are amongst the most attractive of the smaller biscuit models and, after the fashion of Gauron, place the figures around a leafing tree upon an irregular rock-like base.

Many models of children receive misleading identities in Haslem's factory list. 'Grotesque Boy and Girl' (M101) refers to a rustic boy eating an apple and his companion girl consuming curds-and-whey with bowl and spoon. 'Fruit and Flowers' (M8) are represented by seated figures of a boy and girl. The boy has an inverted hat filled with vegetables upon his lap, the girl wears a brimmed hat and holds flowers; both were available in 1771. 'Cat and Dog,

Plate 126. *A group depicting 'Two Virgins awakening Cupid' (M195). 11½ins. (29.2cm). Derby biscuit c.1778.*
Derby City Museum and Art Gallery

Plate 127. *A group of 'Four Cupids Hunting' (M251). 7⅜ins. (18.7cm). Derby biscuit c.1784.*
Derby City Museum and Art Gallery

William and Mary' (M362) consists of seated figures of a boy who holds a cocked hat over the head of a dog, and a girl who holds a cat by the fore-paws and feeds it from a spoon. Haslem's entry 'Flute and Cymbal' (M10) refers to models of a seated pair of musicians, the boy with a flute, the girl with a hurdy-gurdy. However, his 'Pair of dancing Figures' (M365) includes three small models of a girl with a tambourine, a girl with cymbals, and a boy playing a French horn. Two of these appear as decoration painted by James Banford on two coffee cans in the Derby Museum and Art Gallery and the source seems to have been an engraving by C. White.

Models illustrating pastoral themes have already been mentioned among the copies made of the work of Falconet. Others include a fine 'Pastoral Group' (M12), ascribed to Stephan, composed of a shepherd piper serenading a sleeping shepherdess who reclines at the base of a fountain which serves as a candlestick. 'The Dresden Shepherds' (M55) (an earlier version is illustrated in Plate 108) are represented by a shepherd who stands holding a basket of fruit against his breast with his left hand whilst proffering an apple in his right, and a shepherdess with blossoms secured in her apron by her right hand, offering a posy in her left. 'The French Shepherds' (M57) (Plate 121) consists of a boy standing bare-headed and bare-foot, supporting a puppy with his right hand which has leapt up and has both front paws on his chest to reach a ball held in his left hand, and a girl, likewise, holding a lamb in both arms. There are also 'Singing Shepherds' (M60) who stand in mirror positions, one hand on hip the other raised, bare-headed and with mouths open. The 'Shepherds with Garlands' (M56) mentioned by Haslem are unknown to the author though they might possibly be reissues of earlier models (K61).

Religious subjects are generally considered too serious to be translated into porcelain but Derby made one fine devotional piece, a group of 'The Three Marys' (L25). This has a socket which was presumably intended for the attachment of a crucifix. A somewhat banal representation of 'Madonna and Child' (M138) portrays her seated in a chair holding a rather large baby with flowers in her lap. There is a very similar model, known as 'The Prudent Mother' (M140) composed of a seated lady reading a book with a standing child at her left side. Both are mounted on octagonal fluted bases and their factory numbers in Haslem's list are reversed in error. There are several individual models of monks and nuns (M102-M133), which in general follow the forms first issued at Chelsea and Bow but which are inferior in their execution. There are two attractive groups depicting a nun kneeling before a seated Abbess, and a nun confessing to an abbot, the latter reminiscent of Abelard and Heloise.

'Grotesque Punches' (M227) relates to a pair of dwarfs wearing tall hats which were adapted from etchings by Giocomo Calotto.[99] Traditionally, however, they are equated with two midgets who once stood bearing advertisements outside the Mansion House in London. Some examples of the models are painted to include notices attached to their head gear. One announces a forthcoming sporting event, another reads "Sale, on the premises of John Humble, who is going to Spike Hall". Spike Hall was contemporary slang for the workhouse which was generally surrounded by spiked railings.

The work of Jean Jacques Spengler spans the period of 1790-95 and falls appropriately at the end of this section. Timothy Clifford[100] has described many models attributed to the artist which have been mentioned either in the Lygo correspondence or in the Bemrose Papers. Spengler's trial model of 'Astronomy'[101] was based on drawings supplied by Joseph Lygo. Other examples of work probably carried out whilst he was in London include

99. *Porcelain Figures* (London, 1975) by N. Harris, pp. 56-57, col. pl. of the two Derby dwarfs and a reproduction of an engraving by Calloto.

100. 'J.J. Spängler, a virtuoso Swiss modeller at Derby', op. cit., pp. 146-155.

101. *Derby Porcelain* (Barrett & Thorpe), op. cit., pl. 102.

'Morning' and 'Noon', each represented, according to Llewellyn Jewitt, by a lady standing in classical dress beside an urn, 'Meditation', and a group of the 'Three Graces'. The last mentioned are probably not the same as 'The Three Arts' (L13), which has already been described, and none of these models and groups have been identified. Spengler's style has recieved brief mention and his models display a slender elegance and an attention to fine detail. His group 'Palemon and Lavinia' (M366) was based on an engraving by C. Knight, after Angelica Kauffmann, that illustrated the 1788 edition of *The Seasons,* by James Thomson. The beautiful Lavinia is portrayed standing wearing a soft cap, dress and apron, with her eyes averted from her lover, Palemon, who tenderly holds her left hand in his. The maiden had been forced by poverty to work in the corn fields which once belonged to her father and became the object of attention by Palemon who is the son of the new owner. The group 'Cupid disarmed by Euphrosyne' (M358), shows Cupid standing with right hand extended to grasp his long-bow and quiver that are held by the kneeling Euphrosyne. It was inspired by an engraving by Thomas Burke[102] after Angelica Kauffmann. The shepherd standing with an end-flute, and companion dancing shepherdess who holds a crook (M389) were adapted from the engraving by F. Bartolozzi[103] after Angelica Kauffmann. The 'Russian Shepherds' (L20) were based upon an engraving by J.B. Tillard made in 1782 after work by J.B. le Prince entitled 'Les Bergers Russes'. The group consists of a Russian peasant with a beard, dressed in tunic and boots, seated with a guitar at the feet of a lady whilst behind the couple there is a third figure of a boy playing a pipe who faces away from them. Perhaps the most poignant groups is that of 'Belisarius and his Daughter' (M370), based on C. le Vasseur's engraving after earlier work by Humbert Gravelot of 1767. However, Spengler most probably copied the group from one made at Lunéville by Louis Paul Cyfflé.[104] The disgraced Byzantine general, old, impoverished and blind, is portrayed staff in hand with his left hand upon the shoulder of his youthful daughter. The Lunéville version stands on a rectangular base adorned with swags in high relief; that made by Spengler is more slender and is mounted on a shallow cylindrical base. The example in the Liverpool Museum may be unique.[105]

Not all of Spengler's work is so impressive. His shepherd and companion shepherdess, each with a flute (Plate 128) (M369) were adaptations of the ancient Capitoline piping faun, in Rome.[106] A gardener standing with flowers in a pot on a plinth (M359), apart from the absence of a tricorn hat, closely resembles another made by Stephan portraying Earth (M3) (Plate 119).

The sentimental mood of the late eighteenth century found expression in two figures with a dead bird (M363). This pair of models consist of a lady wearing a bonnet leaning upon an empty birdcage regarding a dead bird held in her hand, and a youth digging a diminutive grave. The shepherdess feeding a sheep with hay who stands with one hand resting on a gate (M395) may have been inspired by J. Hogg's engraving of 'Adelaide', published in 1787, after Francis Wheatley.[107] Some had, until corrected by Timothy Clifford, supposed this model to have been 'Rosina' mentioned by Joseph Lygo. The companion shepherd, standing cap in hand beside a dog and a sheep (M396),was adapted from a terracotta after an antique representation of Antinous, once the favourite of the emperor Hadrian. Tradition holds that Spengler left Derby after completing the shepherdess and that the companion shepherd was made by William Coffee. However, the style is that of Spengler and it seems incredible that such a fine model should have been created by an artist who included amongst his works some crudely fashioned animals. Models comprising 'The Proposal' (M372) portrays a gallant who stands with one

102. 'J.J. Spängler, etc.', op. cit., p. 151, fig. 8a, engraving by T. Burke; fig. 8b, porcelain group.

103. ibid., p. 154, fig. 12b, porcelain models; fig. 12a, engraving by F. Bartolozzi.

104. 'Some Early Pottery and Porcelain Figures connected with Alsace Lorraine' by G.S. Davis, *Burlington Magazine,* 1927, Vol. 51, pp. 221-228, pl. IIa, Cyfflé's group of Belisarius and his daughter; pl. IIb, Spengler's group.

105. Liverpool Museum catalogue No. M.1340.

106. *Repetoire de la sculpture Grecque et Romaine* (Paris, 1903) by S. Reinach, Tome II, Vol. I, p. 135, fig. 5, 'the Capitoline Faun'.

107. 'J.J. Spängler etc.', op. cit.

Plate 128 (left). 'Shepherd with a flute' (M369). 10ins. (25.4cm). Derby biscuit c.1790-93. Probably modelled by J.J. Spengler and adapted from the 'Capitoline Faun'.
Grosvenor Antiques

Plate 129 (right). 'Flora' (M390), represented by a girl wearing classical robes, standing before a ruined column holding a U-shaped garland (possibly modelled by J.J. Spengler). 10ins. (25.4cm). Derby biscuit c.1795. Marked with an impressed triangle, also a script 'D' and crossed batons incised.
Dr. H.G.M. Edwards collection

hand upon his heart, and a lady who has one hand raised as if to dismiss his protestations of love. A 'Dancing Girl' (M382) with her hair secured with a band about her forehead, stands holding out her skirt with her left hand and has her right upon her hip.

Other models have been ascribed to Spengler for stylistic reasons. These include a group of four putti, emblematic of the Four Seasons (M388), and 'Bacchus standing beside three Nymphs' (M376), of which there is a clay model in the Castle Museum, Nottingham. Recently a model of 'Flora' (Plate 129) (M390) has come to light and I am grateful to Dr. H.G.M. Edwards for the photograph of this beautiful figure from his collection. The lady stands wearing classical robes before a ruined pillar holding in each hand the ends of a U-shaped garland. She seems to have been inspired by an engraving by Grignion after Brabdoin, published in Paris in 1771, entitled 'An Opera Girl of Paris in the Character of Flora'.[108] Here it should be pointed out that according to John Haslem 'No. 390', is the group 'Gaultherus and Griselda' which was probably based on an engraving by James Thomson in *The Seasons*.[109]

Only a few models can be ascribed to William Coffee with any degree of certainty. Although Haslem lists 'Nos. 335 to 359' as "25 Spangler's and Coffee's Figures and Groups", only one of these, No. 359, has been identified as a gardener (M359) who stands bare-headed leaning upon a spade with his clenched right fist pressed against his cheek. He cannot have been responsible, as some have suggested, for the 'Grotesque Seasons' (M47), or for models of Hygieia and Aesculapius (M99), because the latter were mentioned in the Sale Catalogue of 1779, some twelve years before Coffee arrived at Derby. One is left with the possibility that he modelled a 'Scotsman' and his 'Lass' (M378), and the banality of these is there for all to see. His signed model of a 'Recumbent Setter' has already been mentioned[110] and also a 'Spanish

108. 'Liverpool Printed Tiles' by Anthony Ray, *Transactions,* English Ceramic Circle, 1973, Vol. 9, pt. 2, p. 61, Appendices D5-26, a design on a tile.

109. *The Seasons* (1730-34) by James Thomson. A first edition is in the British Museum.

110. *Ceramics of Derbyshire 1750-1975,* op. cit., no. 42.

Plate 130. *'Sailor' and his 'Lass' (M316). 7½ins. (19.1cm). Derby c.1820. The pair were first issued c.1790 and incised 'No. 316'. Reissued models are marked 'No. 372'.* Grosvenor Antiques

Pointer'(L30) fashioned in a similar style and based on a wood engraving by Thomas Bewick (1753-1828) which illustrated his book *The General History of Quadrapeds,* published between 1790 and 1792.

The majority of models made at Derby lack attribution to any known artist. Sometimes a source can be identified but often this is obscure. Models described as a sailor and his lass (Plate 130) (M316), for example, were intended to represent Woodward and Nancy Dawson as sailor and lass from Gray's ballad 'The Farewell of Sweet William to Black-eyed Susan' according to R.L. Hobson. These and many others are listed in Appendix M.

Derby Figures made between 1796-1848

Paste and Glaze

After the death of William Duesbury II in 1796, the factory gradually phased out soft paste in favour of bone china. Franklin Barrett and Arthur Thorpe have published entries taken from a note book once owned by Robert Bloor.[111] These list the ingredients of several formulae employed to produce a hard paste body. They include bone-ash, china-clay, china-stone, flint, and traces of smalts which were found necessary to disperse the yellow hue that otherwise would have resulted after burning. The glaze was feldspathic and very hard. Its toughness resisted scratch marks and abrasions whilst enamel colours tended to sit upon the surface and, often, to flake away from the glaze.

The Bases

Older models that were reissued during this period, often retain their irregular pad bases. Others stand on bases shaped like plinths and some incorporate pierced scroll work picked out, very often, in gilt. New models were usually issued on shallow and rather wide cylinders which might be decorated with a circumferential band of gold. Octagonal bases bearing the Greek key fret pattern are also encountered though many of these were associated with subsequent models issued by Stevenson and Hancock from their factory in King Street, Derby. Patch marks are rarely seen and generally

111. *Derby Porcelain* (Barrett & Thorpe), op. cit., Appendix IV.

are replaced by faint indentations caused by pointed spurs. Under surfaces of bases have rather small flat ventilation holes.

The Marks

Some models which had earlier been copied from Sèvres originals and which were reissued, bear the two crossed 'Ls'.[112] Those copied from a German source more usually have the crossed swords[113] imitating the device employed at Meissen. However, these two marks may be applied to late Derby models incorrectly. Incised factory list and size numbers may also be present. The use of other Arabic numerals or of capital letters most likely indicate workmen's marks. The mark of crossed batons surmounted by a crown over a script letter 'D' may also be found either in puce or blue until approximately 1820. After this date, the mark is often very carelessly drawn in red.

Enamel Colours and Decorative Style

Shortly before the commencement of the nineteenth century, the almost pastel Derby palette gave place to one that included dark opaque enamels including dark blue, deep maroon, a greyish dark blue-green, an opaque yellow green (chrome green), orange, a pale yellow and a chocolate brown. Garments such as breeches, waistcoats and skirts were frequently painted with vertical stripes in two or more contrasting colours. The ponderous effect of the dark ground colours was sometimes relieved by delicately pencilled small flowers and leaves in gilt. This effect recalls that produced at Sèvres where the underglaze *gros bleu* formed a base for most beautiful gilt decoration. Unfortunately, however, at Derby a brassy gilt arose from the purchase of cheap gold from Read and Lucas of Sheffield, and by the process of mercury gilding. Flesh tints, that up to this time had been a maukish buff, now became almost a tan or a pinkish-buff. Many figures are now depicted with dark hair whilst a high proportion exhibit china blue eyes. The rather drab effect overall was enhanced by the tendency of enamels to flake away from the glaze.

The Models

The reissue of figures and groups mentioned in Haslem's list formed the bulk of the models. There should be little difficulty in recognising them for what they are by reason of the hard paste used for their construction, debased modelling standards, careless assembly, the dark opaque enamel colouring and brassy gilding. New models are largely undistinguished. They are not, strictly speaking, within the province of this work and those wishing for a fuller survey should refer to the work of John Twitchet and Betty Bailey.[114]

Samuel Keys (senior) had been apprenticed gilder to William Duesbury I in 1785, and his two sons Edward and Samuel Keys, later became modellers at Derby. Edward worked at the factory between 1815-1826 and is best known for his small models mounted on wide shallow cylinders relating to Dr. Syntax. These were based on Thomas Rowlandson's illustrations in the book *The Tour of Doctor Syntax,* by William Coombe, which was published in 1810. Most are four to six inches tall and naturally coloured with captions upon their bases. These are listed in Appendix N. Edward Keys is also credited with six models of Paris Cries, an extremely ugly set of seated monkey musicians, and a series of 'Characters of London', inspired by Pierce Egan's *Life in London,* published c.1715. John Haslem also attributes to this artist many models of animals including 'Elephant with driver', 'Elephant without driver', 'Lean Cows', 'New sitting Pugs', 'Small sitting Foxes', 'Small standing Sheep', 'Rabbits on plinths', 'Large Horses', 'Bucks', 'Does', 'Pony', 'Cats on cushions', 'Cats with prey', 'New Poodle Dogs', 'Lion and Lioness', and a 'Peacock'.

Samuel Keys (junior) worked at Derby until 1836 and created a number of

112. 'The Shoe Maker' (M78) and 'Shoe Black' (M81), both in the Derby City Museum and Art Gallery, are marked with crossed 'Ls' in blue.

113. Seated boy and companion seated girl (M8), and the 'Girl tatting' (M314), all in the Derby City Museum and Art Gallery, are marked with crossed swords in blue.

114. *Royal Crown Derby* (London, 1976) by J. Twitchet and Betty Bailey.

small models of stage characters. Perhaps the best known of which are the actor, Liston, in the roles of Paul Pry, Mawworm, and Domini Sampson, and of the actress Madame Vestris, in her title role singing 'Buy a Broom', and of Miss Foote as Little Jockey. It is said that Liston bought the model of himself as Paul Pry. Samuel Keys also created a large pair of models of Hebe and Innocence. These are twenty-eight inches tall and are said to have been enamelled by Leonard Lead with floral sprays upon the plinths beside which the figures were placed, whilst they were gilded by Samuel Keys (senior).

Another modeller working at Derby during this period was George Holmes, who was credited by Haslem with a group of four seated persons, emblematic of the Four Seasons, as well as with small replicas of animals and birds. When, in 1836, Samuel Keys left Derby, supervision of modelling was taken over by John Whitaker. Models attributed to him include stags, dogs, 'Leaping Stag', and a 'Peacock amongst Flowers'. His models of human subjects include an 'Eastern Lady', a 'Guitar Player', a 'Child seated in an arm-chair', a 'Boy' and companion 'Girl', each with a dog, and the group depicting 'Mazeppa on a wild horse chased by Wolves' after the theatrical performance by Ada Isaacs Meucken, who played the male part. It is improbable that any models were made after 1840 and the factory failed in 1848.

The Derby Factory at Friar Gate managed by George Cocker

George Cocker had been apprenticed modeller to Derby under the management of William Duesbury II and in 1808 left to take up work at Coalport. None of the work done by this artist prior to this period has been identified. After a brief adventure at Jackfield, where he attempted to found a porcelain factory, he was employed at Worcester until 1826, when he returned to Derby. There he set up a small factory at Friar Gate, where he seems to have specialised in the manufacture of biscuit figures. This business was transferred to 8, Chenies Street, Bedford Square, London, in 1840-41. In 1853, the London factory was closed and Cocker went to work at Minton's. Although models from Cocker's factories are, strictly speaking, beyond the compass of eighteenth century English porcelain figures, they receive this brief mention owing to the fact they may be mistaken for the products of the main Derby factory in the Nottingham Road. They are chalky white, light in weight, and feel dry and like fine glass-paper to the touch. Models fall far short of the high standards which obtained at Derby during the eighteenth century and often the subject matter is different. Some examples are listed in Appendix N. They include William Wilberforce seated and reading from a book, Hannah More, also seated, wearing a crimped cap, and the forbidding Douglas Fox famed in the local contemporary Derby scene for his diatribes against the 'demon drink'. The wider politcal arena is represented by Sir Robert Peel, Admiral Lord Nelson, and Queen Victoria. The group of a 'Cobbler whistling to a caged Starling'[115] is copied from an original made at Lunéville by Louis Paul Cyfflé, whilst there is a very strange group in which the standing figure of Belisarius is used beside a young lady wearing a bonnet, who looks as if she had just left an early nineteenth century vicarage garden-party.[116] Cocker's group of a 'Hurdy-gurdy Player standing beside a Monkey which holds a switch'[117] was copied from a Meissen prototype. Further models may have been made in the London factory and amongst these are the 'Rape of the Sabines', a 'Roman Matron', a 'Boy with a Hurdy-gurdy', and the 'Dying Drunk'. Marks, which are usually impressed, include 'Cocker Derby', 'G. Cocker', or, when the modeller was George Cocker's son David, 'D. Cocker'.

115. 'Some English Pottery and Porcelain Figures connected with Alsace Lorraine', op. cit., pl. IIc, 'Cobbler with caged Starling' by L.P. Cyfflé; pl. IId, version by George Cocker.

116. ibid., pl. IIa, 'Belisarius and his Daughter' by L.P. Cyfflé; *Derby Porcelain* (Gilhespy), op. cit., fig. 76, group including Belisarius by George Cocker.

117. ibid., fig. 172.

Chapter IX

The Longton Hall Factory

The Five Towns of the north-west Staffordshire Potteries which today form the conurbation of Stoke-on-Trent include Burslem, Hanley, Longton, Stoke, and Tunstall. The manor house of Longton, or Longton Hall, is said to have been built in the period and style of Queen Anne in wooded countryside close to neighbouring coal-mines. Here, in 1749 or 1750, William Jenkinson leased the property from one, Obediah Lane, and set up a soft paste porcelain manufactory. Very little is known about the earlier life of Jenkinson though he was certainly a gentleman of some wealth and property with mining interests which may have prompted him to fire his kilns with coal. He was probably the first potter to do so in England. He is also credited with the invention of a steam-pump designed to evacuate water from underground workings. There is a legal agreement of 1753 that later will be described in which an earlier document is cited stating that Jenkinson "had obtained the Art, Secret or Mystery of making porcelain in imitation of China Ware, at Limehouse...". Also mentioned in this document are the assets of the proprietor which include stocks of porcelain wares available in 1751. These would presuppose the manufacture of porcelain some time before 1751 when the list was issued. A pair of models of 'Seated Pugs' (O21) exist which are attributed to Longton Hall and incised '1750'

Until William Bemrose's book,[1] little was known about the Longton factory. Further information was presented by Mrs. Donald MacAlister who established the nature and the form of some of the early wares.[2] She also drew attention to a small group of models, made from a non-phosphatic and glassy paste which were covered with a very thick glaze. The obscuration of modelling detail by the glaze and its shimmering appearance when viewed in sunlight, due to the presence within it of myriads of tiny air bubbles, prompted the generic name of 'Snowmen'. These were initially ascribed to Derby but the attribution was changed to Longton Hall when matching shards were discovered upon the factory site. The nature of these discoveries has been described by Bernard Watney,[3] who has also listed many of the Snowmen models.[4] Dr. Watney has pieced together the clues that he unearthed by a remarkable series of investigations and detective work to provide the history of the Longton Hall porcelain factory.[5]

The second important person, after Jenkinson, to walk on the Longton stage was William Littler (1725-1784). He was the son of an earth-potter of the same name who worked in the parish of Burslem and died in 1729. Following his father's death, William, together with three other children, was brought up by his mother, née Sara Shaw. William Littler's brother-in-law was Aaron Wedgwood and the two men collaborated to invent a liquid glaze containing flint, clay and 'zaffer', which eliminated the surface pitting that hitherto had been a feature of saltglaze stoneware. They are also reputed to have discovered an underglaze blue for the decoration of stoneware that was later employed on Longton Hall porcelain. Although this colour was called 'Littler's blue', the secret was known in Staffordshire long before the time of Littler. The third character in the Longton saga was William Nicklin who was an advocate by profession and came from Newcastle-under-Lyme. A deed of partnership was

1. *Longton Hall Porcelain* (London, 1906) by William Bemrose.

2. 'The Early Work of Planché and Duesbury' by Mrs. Donald Macalister, *Transactions*, English Porcelain Circle, 1929, Vol. 1, No. 2, pp. 45-59 and 'Early Staffordshire China' *Transactions*, English Ceramic Circle, 1933, Vol. 1, No. 1, p. 44.

3. 'Longton Hall Factory Site' by Bernard Watney, *Connoisseur*, 1955, Vol. 136, pp. 94-97.

4. 'Porcelain Figures of the Snowman Technique' by Bernard Watney, *Connoisseur*, 1957, Vol. 139, pp. 149-153.

5. *Longton Hall Porcelain*, (London, 1957) by Bernard Watney.

drawn up on 7th October, 1751, between "William Littler, late of Hanley Green in the Parish of Stoke-on-Trent, Earth Potter", William Jenkinson and William Nicklin that was intended to endure for fourteen years. In this venture, Littler received two shares and the other two proprietors had three each. Littler was then a bachelor and twenty-six years of age.

Some have sought to identify Littler as the 'Potter from Limehouse', mentioned by Right Reverend Dr. Pococke in his account of a visit to Newcastle-under-Lyme in 1750. It seems hardly credible that his lordship would have confused Newcastle in Staffordshire with Stoke-on-Trent and we now know from Paul Bemrose[6] that there was a potter named William Steers at the Pomona Potworks in Newcastle, so that further comment is superfluous. Jenkinson was very probably the dominant partner, Littler the works manager, and Nicklin seems to have fulfilled the role of no more than a financial sponsor. One of the first notices relating to the porcelain works appeared on 27th July, and for several subsequent days, in 1752, in *Aris's Birmingham Gazette.* "This is to acquaint the public that there is now made by William Little and Co, at Longton Hall near Newcastle, Staffordshire, A Large Quantity, and Great Variety, of very good and fine ornamental PORCELAIN or CHINA WARE, in most fashionable and genteel Taste. Where all Persons may be fitted with the same at reasonable Rates, either Wholesale or Retale."[7]

A second agreement, dated 25th August, 1753, provides an important milestone in the evolution of the business for, at this time, William Jenkinson, who had been the driving force behind the factory, withdrew. The first phase of production may conveniently be considered to cease with this event. Jenkinson promised: "Not in any time during the remainder of the said Term of Fourteen Years...to make or cause to be made of the said Porcelain or Ware in Imitation thereof which is now made at Longton Hall..."[8] Three of his five shares were sold to Nathaniel Firmin, the new partner, for £950; of the remaining two shares he gave one each to William Nicklin and William Littler for "divers other good causes and valuable considerations". Jenkins retired to Oswestry and later moved to Lambeth where he died in 1771. Nathaniel Firmin is described in the Longton agreements as a 'water gilder', but elsewhere is 'merchant tailor and button maker' whose business was conducted at 'The Red Lion over against Norfolk Street in the Strand'. By water gilding is understood use of an amalgam of mercury and gold, known as 'liquid gold', or 'gold water'. This special expertise may have proved useful in the decoration of porcelain. However, only six months later, Nathaniel Firmin died, and, in accordance with a provision of agreement his shares were inherited by his son Samuel.

Between 1753 and 1755 only one dealer's notice appeared in the press that was relevant to the porcelain factory. This was in the *Manchester Mercury* on 10th and 17th of December, 1754:[9] "the first produce of the factory at Longton near Newcastle in Staffordshire of Porcelain and China Ware..." Excavations on the Longton site have revealed kiln furniture and shards. Figures seem to have been fired on a number of different supports. The most common of these were pottery rings with radial spokes which are triangular in section; others are sharp spurs of clay, whilst fragments of porcelain seem occasionally to have been used. Figures were contained in conical saggars not encountered at other factories. Only a very few models were enamelled prior to 1753 which will later be described. Although William Duesbury decorated figures from 'Staffartshire', presumably Longton Hall, at his London studio between 1751 and 1753, and was resident in Longton in 1754, no examples of his work on Longton wares or figures has yet been identified. Littler's wife,

6. 'The Pomona Potworks, Newcastle, Staffs.' by P. Bemrose, *Transactions,* English Ceramic Circle, 1973, Vol. 9, pt. 1, pp. 1-18.

7. *Contributions towards the History of Early English Porcelain* (Salisbury, 1881) by J.E. Nightingale, p. lii.

8. 'Porcelain Figures of the Snowman Technique', op. cit., p. 65.

9. ibid., p. 65.

Jane, is mentioned in an agreement of 1755, when she received one guinea per week for work in the factory. The name of John Hayfield was also mentioned. He was a skilled enameller and was probably the artist who by reason of his landscapes on porcelain became known as the 'Castle Painter'. The hand of an independent decorator, who painted roses with wavy petals and leaves, known as the 'Trembly Rose Painter', may also be found on Longton Hall figures and ware.

The difficulties encountered by Littler in running a porcelain factory on a limited budget in Staffordshire, must have been enormous and, in 1755, outstanding debts could not be met. The factory depended for its survival on investment of fresh capital and this was provided by a Bakewell clergyman named Robert Charlesworth (1717-1771). The new sponsor had interests in local lead mines and was a man of property. He consented to the advance of £1,200 only if his conditions were accepted. These included the disclosure of the means by which the porcelain was made, the acquisition of one third of the company shares, and submission to himself of the monthly accounts for scrutiny. The agreement was signed on 1st September, 1755. A supplementary agreement, in which he made further capital advances, was signed on 1st October, 1757. Details of both are provided by Bernard Watney.[10] The terms were harsh for Charlesworth reserved the right in the second agreement to dissolve the partnership and withdraw his investment unless one or more of the partners put up £2,000, or were able to show that by October 1759 the factory stock was worth not less than £1,000. Littler did everything within his power to establish a favourable trade balance by promoting sales. Between 4th and 10th April, 1757, the *London Public Advertiser* announced the forthcoming auction by Mr. Ford "at his Great Room at the Upper End of St. James' Haymarket... A Quantity of new and curious Porcelain or China, both useful and ornamental, of Longton Hall Manufactory..." On 10th, 11th and 12th June, 1757, *Aris's Birmingham Gazette* carried the addition "...A Variety of curious useful Ornaments for Deserts, with Figures and Flowers of all Sorts, made exactly to Nature, allow'd by the best Judges to be the finest in England..."[11]

The third, and final phase of production followed the signing of the document of October 1757. By now, Littler knew the survival of the factory hung in the balance and he attempted to capture part of the market for cheap blue and white useful wares. On 12th July, 1758, *Aris's Birmingham Gazette* bore the following advertisement: "This is to acquaint the public that there is now to be Sold by William Littler & Co., at Longton Hall, near Newcastle in Staffordshire, Great Variety of all Sorts of Useful and Ornamental Porcelain or China Ware Blue and White, and also Enamelled in the best and most lively colours; to wit, Services of Dishes and Plates, Tea and Coffee Equipages..."[12] A London Warehouse was opened to promote sales in the Metropolis which was announced in the *London General Evening Post* of 3rd October, 1758: "Longton China-Warehouse At the Corner of St. Paul's Churchyard next Watling Street, London, is now open. Where may be had a great variety of fine china ware useful and ornamental, both blue and white and finely enamell'd..." Sadly within the year this warehouse had closed. Presumably the more fragile useful wares from Longton were unable to compete successfully with the cheap, durable blue and white made at Bow.

During the last two years some of the finest models ever made in England were produced at Longton Hall, probably with the assistance of craftsmen who during the temporary closure of the Chelsea factory had migrated north. Some useful ware, and at least one model were transfer printed by Sadler and Green of Liverpool. Whether the Longton wares were purchased by this firm

10. 'Porcelain Figures of the Snowman Technique', op.cit., pp. 55-64, Appendix A.
11. *Contributions towards the History of Early English Porcelain,* op. cit., p. lx.
12. ibid.

for printing and resale, or were sent there for decoration, is uncertain. On 9th June, 1760, Robert Charlesworth announced in *Aris's Birmingham Gazette* the dissolution of the Longton Hall partnership which he considered to have taken place from 23rd May of that year. He named Samuel Boyer as his agent with powers to recover debts outstanding to the company. On 30th June, 1760, also in *Aris's Birmingham Gazette,* Littler made reply. "It's not in Robert Charlesworth's Power to dissolve the Partnership therein mentioned without Consent of the rest of the Partners. . . that the said William Littler and Co. are far from Expectation of any Credit on the said Charlesworth's Account and are very desirous to execute any proper Instrument for the Dissolution of the said Partnership, on having fair Accounts settled, and Damages paid by the said Charlesworth for his many Breaches of Covenant. . . And as the said Littler and Co. are a Majority of the said Partners, and have, by Articles of Partnership Effects, but in all Matters of Moment their Decision is final. . . And that all Gentlemen, Ladies and others, may be fitted at Longton aforesaid, with much better Wares than ever, at reasonable Rates, by William Littler and Co." Littler's bold bluff was called when Samuel Firmin gave his support to Charlesworth's declaration. The stock and equipment were seized by Charlesworth's agents and sold by auction at Salisbury. The sale commenced on 8th September, 1760, and included "Upwards of ninety thousand Pieces of the greatest variety of Dresden Patterns, in rich enamel'd, pencil'd, Blues and Gold; as Figures and Flowers. . . superbly furnish'd, equal to a National factory, so eminently distinguish'd, with a profusion of useful and ornamental Articles. . . ". The choice of venue may have been determined by the good communications by inland waterways, and the desirability of holding the sale far away from ceramic manufactories. However, Bernard Watney has discovered that a member of the Firmin family resided in Salisbury.

The subsequent fate of Littler had for long remained uncertain. Arthur Lane[13] found records, papers and letters, some in the possession of the Duke of Atholl, to show that Littler was engaged in a decorating business at West Pans, near Musselburg, in Scotland, at least as early as 1764. On 3rd October of that year records confirm that "William Littler — China Maker at West Pans, was created an honorary Burgess of Musselborough". This was a necessary preliminary to enable him to establish a porcelain factory in the neighbourhood. Letter headings upon bills indicate that Littler made both stoneware and porcelain in addition to enamelling wares which he may have salvaged from Longton Hall. One heading reads "All kinds of Useful and Ornamental China, particularly Very Fine Mazareen and Gold Enamel'd China. Also all kinds of Stone Ware, such as fine gilded and Japand Black and Tortoise Shell Ware &c. . . . ". Bernard Watney[14] later visited the area and carried out excavations which by the circumstances then obtaining, were necessarily restricted. It is now certain that after the collapse of Longton Hall, Littler set up a small factory at West Pans. There is no evidence that he made any porcelain figures. The factory was operating until at least 1770. Littler died a pauper in Burslem in 1784, at the age of fifty-five.

Longton Hall Figures made between 1749 and 1753

Paste and Glaze

Although only a few Longton Hall figures have been submitted to chemical analysis, both Arthur Lane[15] and Bernard Watney[16] agree the constituents include lead oxide 8-10 per cent, silica 73 per cent, lime 9 per cent, and alumina 4 per cent. The material is glassy, akin to the triangle mark Chelsea and the Girl-in-a-Swing pastes, though it is more coarsely textured. Cullet was

13. 'William Littler of Longton Hall and West Pans, Scotland' by Arthur Lane, *Transactions,* English Ceramic Circle, 1961, Vol. 5, pt. 2, pp. 82-94.

14. 'The West Pans Story — The Scotland Manufactory' by Bernard Watney, *Transactions,* English Ceramic Circle, Vol. 6, pt. 2, pp. 167-176.

15. *English Porcelain Figures of the 18th Century* (London, 1961) by Arthur Lane, p. 114.

16. *Longton Hall Porcelain* (Watney), op. cit., p. 29.

certainly included in the mix. The Longton Hall paste is short and this quality prevents modelling of fine detail whilst lack of stability in the kiln gave rise to leaning away from the perpendicular and to sagging of unsupported projecting parts. Firecracks and surface tearing of the paste are common. The fired body is sugary white which contrasts sharply with the yellowish hue of contemporary useful wares from the factory. The protection of models in conical saggars, to which reference has been made, may account for the difference. The glaze is almost a pure glass and is very thick so that it fills in crevices and folds and obscures modelling detail. Dry patches are evident, where it has failed to adhere to the body, and the inclusion within its substance of myriads of tiny air bubbles creates a shimmering effect in sunlight. Droplets of glaze are usually found in dependent areas, especially about the base, where a brownish discolouration may form a scum line. Some sanding as well as crazing are generally present.

The Bases

Bases are usually simple in form like small mounds, pads, or rectangles. Often those on figures intended as a pair are of a different size. A Jacobite group known as 'Fame' (O10) in the Sigmund Katz Collection, now in the Museum of Fine Arts, Boston, is mounted on an irregular pad to which are applied shells and marine plants fashioned of slip. A few models, like the pair of candlestick figures of a 'Gallant' and a 'Lady' (O9) display rather clumsy incised rococo scrolls. The under surfaces are generally flat and either brushed or wiped free of glaze, though owing to slight depressions, some patches of glaze remain behind. Very occasionally, sufficient glaze is present to exhibit small pinhead spur marks or faint radial lines. Ventilation holes vary a great deal some being large enough to admit the tip of a finger. Many bases are unadorned; a few have applied leaves and flowers made of slip. Flowers are either small rosettes, or seeded roses, or strawberry with appropriately shaped flat leaves. A model of a 'Turkeycock' (O24) has vine leaves and grapes instead of flowers.

Enamel Colours

Almost all models made between 1749 and 1753 are white though there are a few exceptions that include standing ewes and rams (O17), and groups of both 'Ewe and Lamb' (O15) and 'Goat, recumbent suckling a kid' (O16) which have manganese applied underlaze to snouts, eyes, feet and horns. There are similar models, which probably date to 1753-54, painted in enamel which have brownish-red or purplish black patches upon the animals and features picked out in black; also moulded leaves and flowers upon supporting props and on the bases are yellow-green and puce. Enamelled examples of 'Ceres',[17] 'Arlecchino'[18] and of a woman emblematic of Summer[19] may date to the period 1753-54 or have been decorated outside the factory.

Marks

The device of crossed swords in underglaze blue may be found on the back of bases or supports of animals that follow Meissen originals. A seated pug (O21) is incised '1750'.

The Modelling

The sophistication of the subject matter contrasts sharply with the artless modelling of the Longton Snowmen figures which have heads like the tops of clothes pegs, oval faces with rather flat features, eyes and mouth indicated with simple incisions, and hinge-like fingers which resemble bunches of bananas. Drapery is naïvely depicted and is wholly unconvincing. About sixteen models of humans follow Meissen originals whilst there are some

17. 'Porcelain Figures of the Snowman Technique', op. cit., fig. 9b, 'Ceres' (enamelled).
18. Sotheby's, 6-12-77, lot 28, 'Arlecchino' (enamelled).
19. 'Porcelain Figures of the Snowman Technique', op. cit., fig. 11.

twelve others that are known in saltglaze stoneware. A pair of 'Pheasants'[20] show an unusual modelling competence that was evident when biscuit wasters were found. Here, the overall effect was impaired only by the thickness of the glaze.

The Models

The unskilled modelling is amply portrayed in the group representing 'Fame on the crest of the wave' (Plate 131) (O10), below which stands a gingerbread-like Bonny Prince Charlie shaking the paw of the British lion flanked by two pug dogs. The Scottish army of the wretched Young Pretender reached Leek in Staffordshire, only a few miles from Longton, on their march south in the rebellion of 1745. This odd group probably stemmed from the hand of a craftsman with Jacobite sympathies and may be seen in the Jessica and Sigmund Katz Collection. There are two variations of 'Cupid at Vulcan's forge' (O11) and evidently a version was also issued at Worcester (Q18), for fragments were recovered from the factory site. These may have been based on a bronze. The source of models of a Gallant and companion Lady (O9), both bare-headed, seated cross-legged, is unknown; these were later reissued as candlesticks.

Surprisingly a fairly large number of first period figures follow Chinese prototypes, most probably *blanc-de-Chine* imported from Tê Hua. There are two different models of a seated 'Kuan Yin' (O14). One is similar to a Chelsea model and was probably cast from a Chelsea mould, for in one Longton

20. 'The Rare and the Curious' by Frank Tilley, *Antique Collector,* July 1964, pp. 107-112, figs. 5 and 6, pheasants (glazed); fig. 7, pheasant (biscuit).

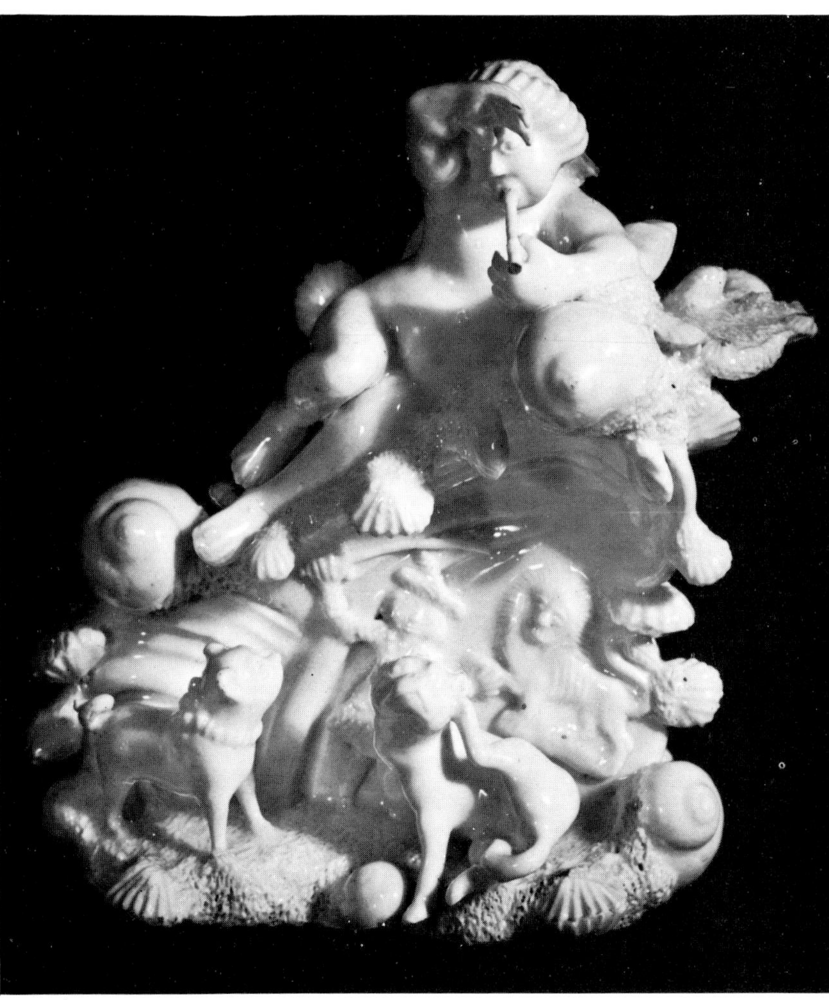

Plate 131. *'Fame on the crest of the wave' (O10) with Bonny Prince Charlie, flanked by two pugs, shaking the paw of the British Lion. Longton Hall c.1750 (Snowman model).* George Savage and Sigmund Katz collection

example a round patch upon the back is visible which corresponds to the oval medallion bearing the raised anchor mark. The other shows the goddess holding a child on her lap. Shou-lao may be recognised by his bulging bald pate, symbolising his intellectural prowess, and by the fan he carries. The Taoist Immortal, Chung-li Ch'uan is bearded and stands in long robes holding a whisk. He closely resembles the Lund's Bristol model traditionally called Lu-tung Pin who should carry a sword but who also has a whisk so that this may be a case of mistaken identity! A heron with one wing displayed (O23) is solid cast and this, together with an 'Indian Crane' (O22) and a parrot are surely reflections of the Oriental influence. A delightful pair of recumbent horses (O19) are reminiscent of Ming jade and soapstone carvings but *blanc-de-Chine* examples were once included in the Ionodes Collection.[21]

By far the greater proportion of models echo Meissen originals. Thus the set of characters from the Commedia dell' Arte made by Peter Reinicke prompted Longton versions of 'Pantalone' (O5), 'Scapino' and 'Arlecchino' (O3), whilst 'Columbina seated playing a hurdy-gurdy' and the 'Avvocato' attired in cap and gown, reading a book (Plate 132) (O4) follow originals by J.J. Kändler. A turbanned 'Turk', standing with both thumbs tucked into his belt, and a 'Polish nobleman' wearing long robes and carrying a sword (Plate 134), are both after Kändler prototypes. A bagpiper seated with legs crossed, wearing a brimmed hat (O1) echoes a Meissen model based on a bronze by Giovanni da Bologna, whilst the source of a standing Dutch Piper (O2), an example of which is in the Victoria and Albert Museum, is unknown. Two seated putti, one with a lyre, the other holding a parchment scroll, representing 'Music' and 'Literature' (O13), are copied from figures by E.F. Meyer. A 'Ceres with putto' (O7) may be adapted from ivories carved by Belthazzar Permoser, though they were probably copied from the intermediate source of a Meissen group. The figure of the goddess was also adapted to provide the model of an 'Actress' (O8). Four standing rustics serve to portray the Four Seasons (O6) which are similar to the later red anchor Chelsea set and presumably both were copied from lost Meissen originals.

21. Sotheby's, 2-7-63, lot 31.

Meissen animals inspired the Longton Hall recumbent cow and bull (O20), the standing ewe and ram (Plate 133) (O17) which have heads turned to the right and characteristically broad backs, two groups of 'Ewe and Lamb' (O15)

Plate 132 (left). The 'Avvocato' (lawyer) (O4) from the Commedia dell 'Arte. 6¾ins. (17.1cm). Longton Hall c.1751, Snowman type.
George Savage

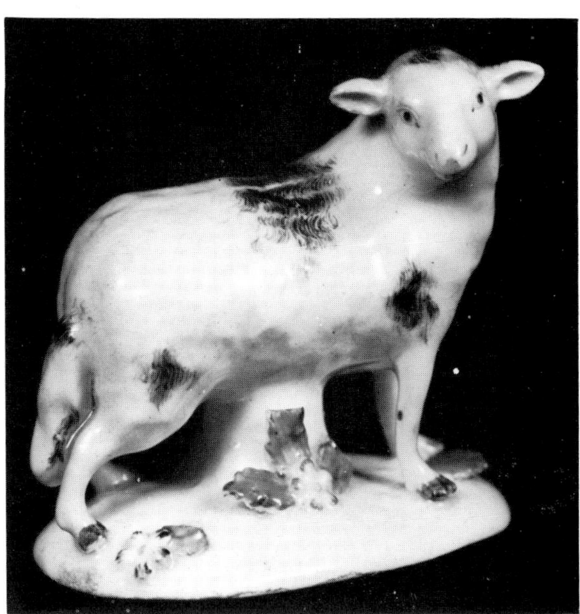

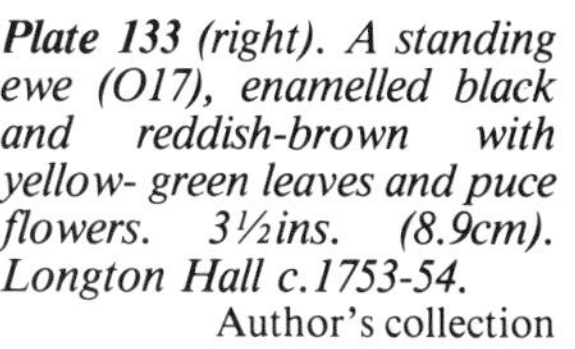

Plate 133 (right). A standing ewe (O17), enamelled black and reddish-brown with yellow- green leaves and puce flowers. 3½ins. (8.9cm). Longton Hall c.1753-54.
Author's collection

Colour Plate R. *'The Four Quarters of the Globe' (M200). 5¼ins. (13.3cm). Chelsea-Derby c.1780, incised 'No. 200'. Asia, Africa and Europe follow originals made at Meissen by F.E. Meyer of which there are also Chelsea versions. America was adapted from J.F. Eberlein's model of Diana.*
John and Diana Mould collection

Colour Plate S. *A gentleman, possibly a toper, reclining (O62). 5½ins. (14cm). Longton Hall c.1756. The deep yellow and yellow-green enamels, the light-red hair, and the heavy scrolled base typify the factory at this period.*
John and Diana Mould collection

and 'Goat suckling a Kid' (O16), and a pair of 'Pugs seated on cushions', which are decorated in underglaze manganese and are incised with the date 1750. Birds are represented by a 'Turkeycock' and 'Turkeyhen' wreathed in vine leaves and grapes (O23) of undetermined origin; 'Two Finches with cherries' and a 'Finch with a snail watched by a Pug' may be original. A pair of finely modelled Pheasants (O25) in Rous Lench Court[22] are apparently unique. Many of the first period snowman models are discussed and illustrated by Dr. Bernard Watney.[23]

There remain a handful of figures which traditionally have been ascribed to Longton Hall between the years 1752 and 1753. They include a seated pair of 'Gallant' and 'Lady' who are bare-headed and cross-legged, in front of candlesticks decorated with wreaths of leaves, and mounted on oddly shaped bases elevated upon six short legs (O26). These same two figures are known as an arbour group topped by a candle sconce. There is a Turk (O27), similar to the earlier snowman model, which may also be included. It seems most likely that all of these were made at West Pans, in Scotland, by William Littler after the closure of Longton Hall in 1760.

Plate 134. *Polish Nobleman after a Meissen original, 5¾ins. (14.6cm). Longton Hall 1753-54 (transitional period) ex McGregor Stewart collection.* Sotheby Parke Bernet

Longton Hall Figures made between 1754 and 1757

Paste and Glaze

According to most authorities the paste of the so called 'Middle Period' contains between 2 and 4 per cent of lead oxide, with little change in the proportions of other ingredients. The body has an opalescent waxy quality and contains numerous small air bubbles. The shortness of the material was reduced, but firecracks and surface tearing of the paste continued to be evident. Transillumination of flat wares discloses an opaque greenish colour and small zones of increased translucency known as tears. A few specimens have moons in thickly potted areas. The glaze is much thinner than on early wares but retains a glassy quality and presents a satin-like surface. The colour varies between a greyish hue and an opaque white. Dry patches and pinhole defects may be visible, together with sanding, though these defects become progressively less common. Ventilation holes are fairly large and cylindrical.

The Bases

Although a few models were, after the earlier fashion, mounted on simple mound or pad bases, the majority were moulded with rather clumsy scrolls arranged in asymmetrical patterns of the rococo style. This may be seen in the group of the 'Putti feeding a Goat' (Plate 136) (O33). Some others display an unusual appreciation of the rococo with tastefully arranged scrolls that commence at the inferior circumference of the base in front and ascend to incorporate the prop supporting the figure at the back. This comprehensive treatment of base and support is usually artistically successful and recalls the design of bases by that master of the Bavarian rococo, Franz Anton Bustelli of Nymphenburg. The upper surface of the bases are usually adorned with moulded leaves and flowers. The flowers are very large in scale to the model and take the form either of cabbages with ragged leaves, or of huge roses with strangely rectangular petals, whilst many of the leaves are cigar shaped. The under surfaces of bases are usually glazed and careful inspection may in some reveal faint radial lines or small dots caused by spurs. Many figures fail to stand securely owing to the unevenness of their bases.

Enamel Colouring and Decorative Style

Between 1754 and 1755, a distinctive palette was evolved which included a deep lemon yellow, a fine pink, which though slightly streaky is only marginally inferior to the rose-pink of Chelsea, a rather dry orange-red, an

22. See footnote 20.
23. 'Snowman Figures from Longton Hall, Staffordshire' by Bernard Watney, *Antiques,* August 1974, pp. 278-284. (See also Appendix O.)

opaque light blue with a mauvish cast, a purple, cold brown, mauve and black as well as a distinctive yellow-green. Often, these enamels would be used in combination with an inky and rather blotchy underglaze blue. The use of underglaze manganese seems to have been abandoned at a fairly early date. Flesh tints vary between a pale pink and faint daubs of orange-red applied to areas left in the white. Eyelids and eyelashes are suggested with pencilling in light red, a colour rarely seen about the eyes on models from other factories whilst the same distinctive colour may be used to represent hair. Irises may be painted grey, brown, or after the Meissen fashion in an orange-grey. Hair is usually indicated with a wash of grey, brown, buff, or light red over which very fine lines in purplish brown or a darker shade of the wash are laid. Scrolls upon bases invariably incorporate pink and yellow, though orange-red, Littler's underglaze blue, grey and red may be found in different combinations. The tips of the petals of flowers are often touched with red, yellow, and pink.

The painting of garments rarely includes floral sprigs though there are a few examples most beautifully enamelled in the style of the 'Trembly Rose' painter. More often patterns are created by combinations of circles, lines, dots, stars, crosses or more rarely stylised florettes superimposed upon a pale ground wash or on areas which are otherwise white. Gilding is present on a few models and is rather pale and usually rubbed. Although it is frequently stated that the honey gilding process was sometimes employed, judging by surviving examples this must have been rare for most exhibit the effects of mercury gilding.

The Marks

Models that are in part decorated with Littler's blue, may bear the device of crossed 'Ls' surmounting a vertical line of three or four dots in the same colour underglaze. Since most of these models were issued after the departure of Jenkinson from Longton Hall, it is hardly likely that the letters were intended to represent a 'J' crossed with an 'L' (Jenkinson and Littler).

The Modelling

The affinity between saltglaze stoneware figures and the Longton models has already been mentioned. There are several examples, including the model of the 'Indian Crane' (O22), various sportsmen and street traders, that are common to both disciplines. There is a stylistic resemblance too between the best Longton Hall figures and the lead glaze pottery models of Ralph Wood (1715-1772) and his immediate successors and associates. Both rejected the idealised representation of rustics, criers and artisans and favoured a commendable, if unflattering, realism. There are models of stocky peasants with broad shoulders and bellies bulging out above U-shaped folds of drapery and women with rounded cheeks, full figures and thick arms draped with shawls. These are amongst the most satisfactory porcelain models despite the limitations imposed by the shortness of the paste and the thickness of the glaze. The hand of at least one other far less accomplished modeller is evident. His preference for seated figures which lean slightly backwards and are both inclined and rotated to one side is exemplified by the seated 'Child Seasons' (O39). Paired models are in mirror positions, faces are round in outline and have flattened features, heads are flat topped and placed on squat necks, drapery is greatly simplified and unconvincing. Nevertheless, despite such naïve representation, many models have an unaccountable charm and the model, for instance, of 'Arlecchino' with bagpipes (O46) is in its way more pleasing than the Kändler original and the more competent copies made at Chelsea and Bow. The resemblance between the putti, emblematic of Music and Literature (O13) of the first period, and those of the middle period representing Music (O35), and Summer (O36), suggests that the artist responsible for some of the snowmen may have remained at the factory until at least 1757. Models of 'Liberty' and 'Matrimony' (O66) are portrayed in an altogether different style and are depicted with small heads, elongated torsos and limbs and are mounted on tall bases. Whether these stem from the hand of a third modeller at Longton, or simply reflect the style of lost prototypes such as might have been created by Friedrich Elias Meyer at Meissen, has not been determined.

The Models

Many Longton Hall models relate to mythology. The 'Twelve labours of Hercules' are represented by two groups, one of 'Hercules wrestling with the Nemean Lion' (Plate 135) (O28) which was probably based on a sixteenth century bronze,[24] the other of 'Hercules with the Keryneian Stag' (O29) which was inspired by an engraving.[25] Stylistically similar is a third group portraying 'Sampson wrestling with a Lion' (O37). The mirror image pair of groups depicting 'Cupid on a galloping Horse, and a baying Hound' (O30) were based on Francesco Fanelli's bronze of the Infant Hercules though the omission of the long-bow from the hand of the rider in the Longton versions impaired the meaning of the original. The group of 'Two Putti feeding a Goat' (Plate 136) (O33), possibly based on the bronze by Jacques Sarrazin, exists in two versions.[26] The least common one shows the two putti feeding flowers to the animal, whilst in the other grapes provide the provender. They may have been intended to represent respectively 'Summer' and 'Autumn'. Amongst the most pleasing are the 'Infant Artist' (Plate 137) (O32), who stands with palette and brush in hand before his easel, and the 'Infant Bacchus' (O31) in his chaplet of vine leaves holding a bunch of grapes up to his tiny mouth. Both probably follow Meissen originals and the first mentioned may have been modelled on one of a set of 'The Arts and Sciences'. Other copies of Meissen models include 'Music' (O35) and 'Summer' (O36).

24. *Europaische Bronzestatuetten* (West Germany, 1967) by H.R. Weihrauch, fig. 405.
25. 'Engravings as the Origin of Design and Decoration for English Eighteenth Century Ceramics' by Bernard Watney, *Burlington Magazine,* 1966, Vol. 108, No. 761, fig. 13.
26. *Sculpture, Renaissance to Rococo,* (London, 1969) by H. Keutner, no. 298.

Plate 135. *'Hercules and the Nemean Lion' (O28). 5¾ins. (14.6cm). Longton Hall c.1756.* Sotheby Parke Bernet

Plate 136. *'Two Putti feeding a Goat' with Flowers (O33). 5½ins. (14cm). Longton Hall c.1756.* Author's collection

Several different sets representing 'The Four Seasons' were issued. Reference has briefly been made to the seated 'Child Seasons' (O39) composed of Spring as a girl with a basket of flowers; Summer, a boy with corn (Plate 138); Autumn is a somewhat similar girl with a basket of grapes upon her knee; Winter is a bareheaded youth who warms his hands over a brazier. There are also standing 'Rustic Seasons' (O41) which are similar to the red anchor Chelsea 'Rustic Seasons' (C98) with alteration of the model of a man representing Winter so that he extends both hands out over a brazier. The standing 'Infant Seasons' (O38) are, oddly enough, better known in their Plymouth versions than in the Longton Hall originals. They are nude children scantily draped: Spring holds flowers; Summer stands beside a corn sheaf; Autumn holds grapes; Winter huddles in a cloak beside a brazier. There are also two groups representing seasons. Spring depicts a girl kneeling with flowers in her apron beside a youth who stands with posies in either hand, the two watched by a dog and a sheep; Autumn shows a girl kneeling and holding out her apron with both hands to receive grapes which are tipped from a tall pannier by a standing youth beside whom is a ewe and a lamb (O42). Candlestick versions of both are known though groups emblematic of Summer and Winter have not yet come to light. A delightful group of 'Two Children struggling with a Dolphin' (O34), like the Bow versions (G25) and Chelsea adaptations (C77), follow a Vincennes original.

The stage is represented by a model of an 'Actor reading his Script' (Plate 139) (O43) which he holds in both hands. Two models of 'Arlecchino' in mask

Plate 137. *'The Infant Artist' (O32). 5½ins. (14cm). Longton Hall c.1756.*
Author's collection

Plate 138. *A seated boy, emblematic of 'Summer' from the 'Child Seasons' (O39). 4½ins. (11.4cm). Longton Hall c.1756. The sickle is an example of faulty restoration.*
David Love

Plate 139. *'An Actor reading his script' (O43). Longton Hall c.1755-56.*
George Savage and Sigmund Katz collection

and motley show him wearing a conical hat and dancing (O44) and with slapsticks (O45). A seated 'Arleccchino with bagpipes', and 'Columbina with a hurdy-gurdy' (O46), like the more competently modelled Chelsea (C2) and Bow H10) versions, follow originals by Kändler. Musicians include a seated 'Gentleman' playing a lute and companion 'Lady with a Flute' (O47), a 'Gentleman' playing a violin and 'Lady' holding a musical score (O49) and these also reflect Meissen prototypes. A 'Dancing Girl' (O48) who wears a plumed hat and holds both arms in front of her in the position of the dance, is known in a contemporary Derby version (K4), and appears to be the prototype of the female partner to the so called 'New Dancers' (H34) which were to become such popular models at Bow. Foreign personages are represented by a model of a standing 'Turk' wearing a turban and cloak with arms akimbo, and a 'Levantine Lady' (O69). A pair of fine 'Prancing Chargers', one with a 'Blackamoor', the other with a 'Turk' in attendance (O68), followed Kändler's originals based on 'Les Chevaux de Marly' by N. Coustou.

Amongst the most outstanding Longton Hall products are models of peasants which in most cases seem to be original. A woman 'Cabbage Seller' (O53) personifies this group of figures. She stands in rustic dress, apron and shawl, holding a huge cabbage beneath her left arm and with a basket of vegetables at her feet. Her heavy facial features and thick waist suggest that she was modelled from life. A 'Fruit Seller' (Plate 140) (O55) sits wearing a wide-brimmed hat beside a basket of assorted wares with a bunch of grapes in one hand. There are fine models of 'Flower Sellers' (O54), who have panniers of blossoms and each hold posies, a 'Butter Seller' (O52), and a 'Boy' holding a bunch of grapes (O51). A pair of 'Cooks' (O60) hold saucepans and spoons, whilst a 'Gardener' stands leaning upon his spade holding a flower pot, and his companion 'Woman' holds a basket (O57). A short necked 'Farmer' (O56) stands holding a bird's nest. A rustic 'Piper' (O61), who wears a Tyrolean hat and stands cross-legged playing his instrument, is modelled after a Kändler original. The standing model of a 'Huntsman' wearing a peaked cap, holds a gun and a powder-flask, and his 'Lady' is portrayed with a game-bird in one hand (O59). A 'Goatherd' bearing a kid upon his neck (Pate 141) (O50) was adapted from Soldani's bronze of a 'Satyr with a Goat' after the antique.[27]

Less artistically successful are figures of a 'Gallant' who is depicted placing his hat upon the head of a dog, and a 'Lady' who also has a dog (Plate 142) (O67). These are too detailed and are rather similar to others issued at Champion's Bristol factory (P30) and at Derby (M362). A rare model of a gentleman reclining with one arm raised (Colour Plate S) (O62) is placed beside a hamper and may have been intended to represent a toper though no surviving example holds a glass. A 'Boy Toper' (O63) is portrayed astride a barrel after a Meissen original. Amongst the few examples of religious subjects translated into porcelain are a seated 'Monk' reading from a book, and companion 'Nun' likewise (O71) and 'Abbess reading a letter' (O70).

Two models, already mentioned, are in a completely different style. These are a gallant holding a nest of fledglings and companion girl with a lantern-like bird-cage (O66). They may possibly represent debased versions of 'Liberty and Matrimony' and stand nine and a half and ten inches tall on legged bases before wreaths of leaves and flowers. The size is unusually big for Longton Hall and their slender forms are also atypical. Bernard Watney has pointed out that they wear the fancy-dress of pilgrims, including capes adorned with shells which are the symbols of the Order of St. James of Compostella.

There remain a few animal and bird models of which the most delightful are leopards prowling on scrolled bases (O73), a pair of fierce tigers (O76), and some far less attractive pugs (O74). A rare pair of lions (O77) are in a private

27. *Europaische Bronzestatuetten,* op. cit., fig. 503.

collection. Two candlestick groups include a 'Ram with Ewe', and companion 'Nanny-Goat with Kid' (O75).

Longton Hall Figures made between 1758 and 1760

Paste and Glaze

Analysis of the paste of a model of 'Asia' (O79), cited by Bernard Watney[28] gave the following results: silica 62 per cent, lime 17.5 per cent, lead oxide 10 per cent, alumina coupled with iron 6 per cent, soda together with potash 3.7 per cent, and only traces of magnesia and phosphate. These results are somewhat unexpected showing a lead oxide content as high as that of the first period and in excess of that of the middle period of production. Indeed, it would suggest that a formula akin to that employed prior to 1754 was used. However, the number of analyses made of this late Longton Hall paste appear to have been very few. Chipped fragments show black specks indicative of careless preparation and transillumination, possibly only in flat ware, reveals a brownish colour. The glaze resembles that used during the middle period.

28. 'Porcelain Figures of the Snowman Technique', op. cit., p. 45.

Plate 140. *'A Fruit Seller' (O55). 5ins. (12.7cm). Longton Hall c.1756, ex collection of Sir William Young.* Sotheby Parke Bernet

Plate 141 *(right). Figure of a 'Goatherd' (O50), adapted from a bronze satyr. 9¾ins. (24.8cm). Longton Hall c.1756-57.* Sotheby Parke Bernet

The Bases

A minority of late Longton Hall models stand on simple bases such as 'Minerva' (O84) and a 'River God' (O87) both of whom stand upon plain rectangles. Others, such as the large standing 'Four Continents' (O79) have bases moulded with patterns of shells and scrolls arranged in a symmetrical fashion. At least one model (O78) of Britannia was provided with a detachable stand. A group, known as 'the Lovers' (O86), displays a legged base that recalls the style favoured at contemporary Bow. Indeed, some of these complex bases may have been created by artists migrating from the London porcelain factories at this time.

Enamel Colouring and Decorative Style

The colours of the earlier palette were retained and a reddish-brown was added. Delicate floral painting now appears upon the garments of some figures including a female musician (O85), and some examples of the 'Four Continents' (O79). The stand provided for the model of 'Britannia' (O78) was transfer printed with scenes from the Seven Years War by Sadler and Green. In addition, high quality gilding may be found on a few of the more important models such as the fine equestrian model of the 'Duke of Brunswick' (O81).

The Modelling

During the final phase of production some of the finest models were created in a larger scale and in more ambitious poses than had until this time been attempted. The late Longton Hall figures compare favourably with the best red anchor Chelsea and dry-edge Derby models.

The Models

The figure of 'Britannia' (O78) is depicted seated holding a medallion in the likeness of George II, and with a shield which bears the Union Jack minus the cross of St. Patrick. Mention has been made of the detachable base decorated with transfer prints. Some examples show that the prints have been touched up with a brush and enamel paint. The equestrian model of the 'Duke of Brunswick' (O81) is, perhaps, the finest of all Longton models. The duke is portrayed wearing the Order of the Garter, with which he was invested in August, 1759, after the victory at Minden, astride a dappled charger which prances upon French trophies of war. Unusually fine gilding may be seen upon the duke's hat, military decorations, saddle-cloth, stirrups, and upon the fleur-de-lys on the French flag. There are many similar Meissen models from which the Longton one may have been copied, but one made by Kändler, c.1745, of the Empress Elizabeth of Russia is the probable source.[29] She wears the uniform of an officer of her guards, with the star and ribbon of St. Alexander Nevski, and a tricorn hat and is shown astride a piebald horse. The poet Dryden (O80), is portrayed after the fashion of Scheemakers Shakespeare, and stands leaning on his right elbow upon a pile of books which rest upon a plinth, whilst holding a scroll in his dependent right hand. The model of David Garrick (Plate 142) (O82) is smaller, and mounted on a rectangular base; it shows him supporting a volume with his right hand upon a low pedestal, with a cloak thrown over his left shoulder. Inscribed upon the pages of the book are lines from the prologue of *The Tempest* "The cloud capped towers...". A head and shoulders of George III (O83) when he was Prince of Wales, stands upon a shaped plinth bearing the device of three feathers in high relief. This was once attributed to the Chelsea factory and makes an interesting comparison with the bust of George II (Q25) ascribed to Chaffer's Liverpool.

A group, known either as 'The Dancers', or 'The Lovers' (O86), depicts a gallant and a lady strolling arm in arm. The base has legs and is fenestrated with comma shaped windows, that recall the style favoured at Bow and,

29. Christie's, 28-3-77, lot 133.

indeed, the group was once ascribed erroneously to that manufactory. Perhaps they were based on an original by Friedrich Elias Meyer and copied by a former Bow employee. There is a fine pair of musicians (O85) which include a lady wearing a jaunty hat and carrying a tambourine who leans forward as though about to break into a dance, and a dancing man holding a lyre. They too display an unusual competence of modelling and have bases raised upon feet suggesting they may have been created by a former London artist. There is a most unusual 'River God' (O87), almost nude, who stands with a drape about his waist and upon his head a crown curiously formed from the prows of ships; he leans upon an up-turned urn from which water and fishes flow and there is a paddle at his left side. He may have represented 'Commerce' in some lost baroque bronze. The Longton Hall model of 'Minerva' (O84) is the most attractive of them all; she stands upon a rectangular base and was copied from a bronze finial on a clock made by Thomas Tompion for the bedchamber of William III at Hampton Court.[30] Arthur Lane has noted that a very similar Bow version is inscribed upon the helmet with the cypher of George III.[31]

The large standing Four Continents (Colour Plate T) (O79) stand about thirteen inches tall on highly sculptural bases with gilded rococo scrolls. America is a Red Indian girl depicted in the act of selecting an arrow from a quiver upon her back and holding a long-bow in her left hand; a tree-stump support to her left is covered with leaves, and at her feet there is a prairie dog. This figure was adapted from the Derby 'Diana', which echoes an original by Eberlein. Africa is a bare-headed negress who holds her elephant head-dress in her right hand whilst on her right there is a lion and a crocodile; Asia is a Levantine girl holding a perfume-burner standing beside a recumbent camel; Europe is a lady holding a book with artistic trophies and a small recumbent horse at her feet. These, together with many other Longton Hall models, later reappeared in the hard paste versions of Cookworthy's Plymouth factory.

30. *Thomas Tompion, His Life and Work* (London, 1951) by R.W. Symonds, fig. 33.

31. *Bow Porcelain* (London, 1926) by Frank Hurlbutt, pl. 56B, the Bow version of 'Minerva'.

***Plate 142.** David Garrick (O82), standing beside a plinth (left). 7½ins. (19.1cm). Longton Hall c.1759-60. A 'Lady' playing with a dog (O67). 8¾ins. (22.2cm). Longton Hall c.1757.* Sotheby Parke Bernet

Chapter X

The Plymouth and Bristol Factories of William Cookworthy and the Bristol Factory of Richard Champion

William Cookworthy (1707-1780) was born at Kingsbridge in south Devon, and was the eldest of seven children. When he was thirteen years of age his father, who was also called William, died leaving his mother, Edith, virtually penniless. The young boy secured an apprenticeship to the London firm of Bevans, Druggists and Chemists, the following year, and because the family were unable to raise the coach fare, he walked two hundred odd miles to the Metropolis to take up his appointment. He must have been a diligent worker and well liked, for upon the completion of his training his employers gave financial support enabling him to set up a business in Notte Street, Plymouth, under the name of Bevans and Cookworthy. Cookworthy was an active member of the Society of Friends, and having taught himself Latin and French, soon established a reputation for wisdom and learning. In 1735 he married Sarah Berry of Wellington, Somerset, who bore him five sons before her death in 1745. Cookworthy never remarried, but brought his mother into his home to live with him and the children for the remainder of her life. Amongst his many friends and acquaintances were numbered Dr. Samuel Johnson, Captain Cook and the explorer, Sir Joseph Banks, who became president of the Royal Society between 1778 and 1820, and John Narcarrow who was superintendent of Cornish Mines and also something of an engineer, whose knowledge of local rocks and clays must have been invaluable to Cookworthy in his quest for the raw materials with which to manufacture porcelain after the Chinese manner.

On 30th May, 1745, Cookworthy wrote to his friend, Richard Hingstone,[1] a surgeon from Penryn: "...I had lately with me the person who had discovered the china earth. He had several samples of china-ware of their making with him, which were, I think, equal to the Asiatic. It was found in the back of Virginia where he was in quest of mines: having read du Halde, discovered both petunse and kaulin. 'Tis the latter earth, he says, is the essential thing towards the success of the manufacture. He has gone for a cargo of it, having bought the whole country of the Indians where it rises. They can import it for £13 per ton, and by that means afford their china as cheap as stone ware..." It is clear, from this, that Cookworthy had himself read du Halde in which accounts had been given by Père D'Entrecolles relating to the manufacture of true or hard paste porcelain at Ching-tê Chên, in the province of Kangsi, in China. The person mentioned in his letter must surely have been André Duché, the potter from Savannah, Georgia, to whom reference has been made in Chapter VII. Cookworthy had been conducting experiments into the manufacture of porcelain after the Chinese manner, probably since 1745 or earlier. An undated memorandum, which seems to have been written c.1765, survives in Cookworthy's hand.[2] "It is now twenty years since I discovered that the ingredients used by the Chinese in the composition of their porcelain, were to

1. *The Ceramic Art of Great Britain* (London, 1878) by Llewellyn Jewitt, Vol. 1, pp. 320-321.
2. Ibid., pp. 323-326.

be got, in immense quantities, in the county of Cornwall; and as I have since that time, by abundance of experiments, clearly proved this to the entire satisfaction of many ingenious men, I was willing this discovery might be preserved to posterity, if I should not live to carry it into manufacture...I have lately discovered that in the neighbourhood of the parish of St. Stephen's, in Cornwall, there are immense quantities both of Petunse stone and the Caulin, and which, I believe, may be more commodiously and advantageously wrought than those of Tregonnin Hill, as, by the experiments I have made on them, they produce a much whiter body, and do not shrink so much, by far, in baking, nor take stains so readily from the fire. Tregonnin Hill is about a mile from Godolphin House, between Helston and Penzance. St. Stephen's lies between Truro, St. Austel, and St. Columb; and the parish of Dennis, the next to St. Stephen's, I believe, hath both the ingredients in plenty in it." This may have been on land leased from a 'Mr. R. Eadyvean, of Bodmin', which in contemporary documents is often referred to as the 'Mine at Addy Vein'. It may be deduced from this document that Cookworthy had originally discovered china clay on Tregonning Hill c.1745, and was accordingly not anxious to purchase the white earth from Duché. Further, that for some time the secret of china stone had eluded him until he found at some time about 1765 that the Growan or Moorstone was equivalent to the Chinese petuntse. At the same time, he seems to have found a more suitable china clay at St. Austel and was prepared to attempt manufacture on a commercial basis.

John Mallett[3] cites a number of letters and documents to support the contention that Cookworthy set up a small porcelain manufactory in Bristol in November 1765 which failed before Christmas of the same year. Joseph Banks, who was awaiting a passage to Newfoundland in 1766, noted in his diary for 18th April, 1766, "We went to Plymouth to Enquire about a Manufacture of China invented by a Mr. Cookworthy of that Place but did not see him...they told us that a manufactary had been set up at Bristol for the convenience of fewel [*sic*] but had sunk to the Partners (for several were Engag'd in it) about 600lb merely as they told us on account of their not being able to burn ware without Smoaking it they gave us specimens of three of the Principal ingredients used in the Composition (1) More Stone (a Kind of Granate) with white specks for that with black will by no means answer the Purpose (2) a Kind of Marl of a very saponaceous quality of Comeing near to the soapie rock in appearance but Much softer & (3) a stone that has much the appearance of chalk With some few metallick grains interspersed in its substance they were all raisd in a mine Calld Addy Vein near St. Austel in Cornwal..."[4]

On 7th November, 1765, Richard Champion of Bristol wrote to his brother-in-law, Caleb Lloyd telling him that he had sent samples of "Cherokee clay from America" to "a new work just established. Porcelain is composed of two materials, Clay and Stone. This new work is from a Clay and Stone discovered in Cornwall, which answers the description of the Chinese. But in burning there is a deficiency; though the Body is perfectly white within, but not without, which is always smoky. Their Clay is very much like, but not quite so fine as the Cherokee; however there can be no chance of introducing the latter as a Manufacture, when it can be so easily produced in Cornwall..."[5] On 28th February, 1766, Champion wrote to the Earl of Hyndford: "...The Proprietors of the work in Bristol having imagined they had discovered in Cornwall all the Materials similar to the Chinese; but though they burnt the body part tolerably well, yet there were impurities in the Glaze or Stone, which were insurmountable, even in the greatest fire they could give it and which was equal to a Glass House heat..." It has not been possible to identify products

3. 'Cookworthy's First Bristol Factory of 1765' by J.V.G. Mallet, *Transactions,* English Ceramic Circle, 1974, Vol. 9, Pt. 2, pp. 212-220.

4. *Joseph Banks in Newfoundland, his Diary, Manuscripts and Collections* (London, 1971), ed. A.M. Lysaght, p. 117.

5. *Two Centuries of Ceramic Art in Bristol* (London, 1873) by Hugh Owen, pp. 7-14, correspondence between Richard Champion, Caleb Lloyd and the Earl of Hyndford.

of the first Cookworthy porcelain factory at Bristol though it is likely that if any survive they will show severe smoke staining and, possibly, the 'Gardener holding a basket of fruit' and companion 'Lady holding a basket of flowers' (P11), which stand upon scrolled bases before bocages topped with candle sconces, now in the Victoria and Albert Museum, may be examples.[6]

Early in 1768, Cookworthy formed a consortium with a view to establishing a new porcelain factory at Plymouth. The main financial support came from Thomas Pitt, John and Joseph Hartford, Joseph Fry, Thomas Winwood, Edward Brice, Richard Champion, and Thomas Frank who had been associated with the manufacture of Bristol delftware. A company was floated with fourteen shares of which three were held by Cookworthy, one by his brother Philip, and one by his brother-in-law Thomas Were; other shareholders included Richard Champion, Philips, Bulteel and Wolcott. Premises were secured and a factory set up at Coxside, on the extreme angle that juts out into the water at Sutton Pool.[7] Cookworthy made application for a patent for "a kind of porcelain newly invented by me, composed of moorstone or growan, and growan clay...", which was granted on 17th March, 1768. Full details of the formulae for paste and glaze are provided by Llewellyn Jewitt.[8] "...The clay is prepared by diluting it with water, allowing the gravel and mica to subside, pouring the water, white with clay, into vessels, allowing the clay to settle. It is that the earth gives the ware its whiteness and infusability, and the stone its transparence and mellowness...The articles formed when biscuited, are dipped into a glaze made of levigated stone, with the addition of lime and fern ashes or magnesia alba, and then baked." Staining of the glaze remained troublesome, but was greatly reduced. However, the high temperature necessary to fire the body led to a number of defects such as spiral wreathing, firecracks, and sagging away from the perpendicular. The glaze also displayed blemishes such as pinhole defects and smoke staining whilst enamel colours applied overglaze tended to become muddy.

The former Bow repairer, Thibauld, or Tebo, probably came to work as modeller for Cookworthy in about the year 1769 but he had been employed at Worcester also as modeller at about the same time and the exact date of his arrival at Plymouth is not known. Most of the Plymouth models were cast from Longton Hall moulds so that his task would have been little more than that of a repairer. In 1774, Thibauld left Bristol to join Wedgwood at Etruria. Hugh Owen[9] gives the names of some of the other employees which included Anthony Amatt, a thrower and painter, Moses Hill, china maker, John Britain, foreman, and a German named B. Proeffel whose skills are not defined. Thomas Briand, possibly a descendent of Thomas Briand, who, in 1743, had been introduced to the Royal Society, was a 'flower modeller'. Philip James, of 30, Ellbroad Street, was a china painter and his wife is said to have been "employed modelling children's toys — lambs, &c."

Between March and November 1770, operations were transferred from the Coxside, Plymouth, to Castle Green, Bristol. The Plymouth Poor Rates of that year record a change of occupancy of 'Mr. Cookworthy's Mills'. The *Worcester Journal* of 22nd March, 1770, advertised for additional craftsmen at the new venue: "China Ware Painters wanted for the Plymouth New Invented Porcelain Manufactory. A number of sobre ingenious artists capable of painting in enamel or blue, may hear of constant employment by sending their proposals to Thomas Frank, Castle Green, Bristol". A number of items seem to have been made to commemorate the closure of the Plymouth works which are inscribed in light red enamel overglaze: "Mr Wm Cookworthys Factory Plym 1770".[10] Hugh Owen,[11] reproduces a drawing of an enamelling

6. 'Cookworthy's First Bristol Factory of 1765', op. cit., pl. 118.

7. *The Ceramic Art of Great Britain,* op. cit., p. 326.

8. Ibid., pp. 329-331.

9. *Two Centuries of Ceramic Art in Bristol,* op. cit., pp. 289-302.

10. Catalogue of the Bristol bicentenary exhibition, 1770-1970, figs. 11, 12 and 13.

11. *Two Centuries of Ceramic Art in Bristol,* op. cit., p. 19, pl. II.

kiln, dated 16th October, 1770, which might be a sketch made by Richard Champion intended to serve as a guide for similar kilns that were to be erected at Bristol. Written on the right hand side in calligraphy, said to be of Champion, are the words "Last burning of enamele Nov 27 1770". Many reasons have been advanced to explain the move including better communications, an available pool of labour accustomed to working in the glass industry, and the proximity of the coal fields of South Wales, but the likely cause was that Richard Champion resided in Bristol and had become the dominant influence in the manufactory. In 1770, the share owned by Thomas Were and Sons in the old Plymouth factory was sold to the "Proprietors of the New China Manufactory at Bristol".

Richard Champion (1743-1791) was the son of Joseph Champion and his wife Elizabeth, née Rogers, who died in 1745. They were a wealthy Bristol family with extensive business and shipping interests. Richard was educated in London between 1751 and 1762, when he was visited by his sister Sarah who was shocked at what she saw. In 1761, she wrote, "Many things made me heartily wish to return to my Friends in Bristol, nor did a sight of those things usually seen in London amuse me...The women's dresses hurt my natural modesty, their affectations disgusted me. The men were painted Fops, I could not help dispising..."[12] Champion returned to Bristol to work for his uncle whose businesses included a zinc works. He was something of a marine architect who twice submitted plans for the improvement of the Bristol docks. In 1764, he married Judith Lloyd and made his home in St. James's Square. The same year he met William Cookworthy in the house of Mr. Joseph Fry. His brother-in-law was Caleb Lloyd who resided in Charleston, South Carolina, with whom he endeavoured to build up an export trade to the American colonies. In 1765, Champion received a box of white china-clay from the territory of the Chirokee Indians from Lloyd and passed samples on to Richard Holdship at Worcester as well as to Cookworthy. Champion, like Cookworthy and many of their associates, was a Quaker. He must have corresponded with Cookworthy from shortly after the first attempt in 1765 to manufacture porcelain at Bristol. In 1768 he became one of the original shareholders in the Plymouth porcelain company and eventually came to invest some £15,000 of his fortune in the venture.

The first mention of the new Bristol manufactory was made in the journal of Sarah Champion, dated 3rd July, 1771: "After dinner visited the China work which was then carried on in Castle Green." The Bristol Poor Rate Assessments name as the occupants of Castle Green on 23rd September, 'William Cookworthy & Co.'. Cookworthy was by now an old man and in 1773 retired from the manufactory though the deed of transfer in ownership was not finalised until 16th May, 1774. The new proprietor was deeply interested in whig politics and an intimate friend of Edmund Burke the member of Parliament in whose election in 1774 he had taken such an active part. The occasion was celebrated by the presentation by Judith Champion of a Bristol tea service to Mrs. Burke.[13] A number of other sets of dinner and tea equipages from the Bristol factory, made for prominent local families, survive and are represented in the Bristol City Museum and Art Gallery. Champion retained the services of John Britain as foreman, and John Bolton as work's manager. Bolton had previously been at Kentish Town and Worcester and when in 1775 he appeared before the Parliamentary Commission, he was described as 'Gentleman'. Henry Bone of Truro was apprenticed painter in 1772 and later exhibited at the Royal Academy and became enameller and miniaturist to George IV. Another young Cornishman, William Stevens, who was also apprenticed painter on china, later created swags of rosebuds and

12. *Two Centuries of Ceramic Art in Bristol*, op.cit., p. 41.
13. Catalogue of the Bristol bicentenary exhibition, op. cit., fig. 78.

cameos in the neo-classical style on Bristol porcelain. A Monsieur Soqui (or Saqui) from Sèvres painted exotic birds on some of the finer cabinet pieces in the French taste. An advertisement in *Felix Farley's Bristol Journal* of 30th March, 1771, for a porcelain sale does not specify that it was of local manufacture. A second notice in the same journal on 15th August, 1772, was more specific and included "Very elegant Figures, beautiful Vases, Jars and Beakers, with all kinds of useful China, blue and white and enamelled. To be sold without reserve. J. Stephens, auctioneer..." On 28th November, 1772, there followed in the same organ, "at the Manufactory in Castle Green, Bristol, are sold various Kinds of True PORCELAIN, Both Useful and Ornamental Consisting of a New Assortment. The Figures, Vases, Jars, and Beakes, are very elegant, the Useful Ware exceedingly good. As this Manufactory is not at present sufficiently known, it may not be improper to remark, that this Porcelain is wholly free from the Imperfections in Wearing, which the English China usually has, and its composition is equal in fineness to the East Indian, and will wear as well. The enamell'd ware, which is rendered nearly as cheap as the English Blue and White, comes very near, and in Some Pieces equal the Dresden, which this Work most particularly imitates."

Champion was evidently dissatisfied with the relatively crude modelling efforts of Thibauld and sought his early replacement. On 27th February, 1772, Champion wrote to an unnamed modeller at Derby whom many have identified as Pierre Stephan.

> "I have seen the Four Elements which were made at Derby, they are very Beautiful, their dresses easy, the forms fine, two in particular Air and Water are charming figures. I apprehend that you made ye models and therefore hope for your execution the following Fancies will not look amiss.
>
> **The Seasons**
>
> **Spring,** a Nymph with a Coronet of flow'rs on her head in flowing Robes rather flying behind her, approaching with a smiling countenance as she advances the flow'rs appear to start up before her those at her feet higher those at a distance, which seems to be just Budding out on the side after a Plough or Harrow, which she points to with one hand, & with the other holds a small open Baskett fill'd with Seeds which she offers, from the Baskett falls a kind of Zone or Belt, on which are represented the sign of the Zodiac Aries Taurus Germines [*sic*].
>
> **Summer,** A Man in the Prime of Life loosly drap'd with a Belt round his Body, on which are represented the Signs of the Zodiac Cancer Leo Virgo A Pr. of Shears (Made use of in shearing Sheep) in one hand & with the other supports a Baskett of wool on his Shoulders, on the Ground a Scythe with Trusses of Hay scatter'd about.
>
> **Autumn,** A Matron with a kind of Coronet on her head from whence Spring Ears of Corn. Her robes not so flow [*sic*] as Spring being of a graver Cast, in one Hand a Sickle, she leans on a Thyrsis round which are twin'd Baskett of grapes & a Zone or Belt falling from it, on which are represented the signs of ye Zodiac Libra Scorpio Sagittarius, the grounds she treads on full of Corn & on a side of her a Baskett of fruit overturn'd.
>
> **Winter.** A Descriped [*sic*] old man his head bald & a long Beard leaning a Staff under one arm a Bundle of sticks, his robe schatted & clasp'd with a Belt, on which are represented the Three signs of the Zodiac, Capricorn, Aquarius, Pisces, the ground cover'd with bare branches of Trees, Frost and Snow & Icicles hanging down in different Places.
>
> **The Elements**
>
> **Fire.** A Vulcan forging a Thunderbolt in the attitude of striking with his anvil and Hammer, some pieces of Iron or coals or anything peculiar to a Blacksmith's Shop to be scatter'd about.
>
> **Water.** A Naiad crown'd with rushes, leaning with her arm on an urn from whence gushes out water. In the other had [*sic*] she holds a fishing Net, with fishes enclos'd in it, the ground ornamented with rushes, shells, Fishes or the Fancies peculiar to water.

Earth. A Husbandman digging with a spade a Baskett fill'd with Implements of Husbandry on ye Ground. The ground ornamented, with corn, acorns or Fruits.
Air. A winged Zephyr crown'd with Flow'rs treding on clouds which rise naturally about him, his robes flowing & flying behind him he holds in one Hand a Branch of a Tree, if any ornament behind are wanting, some Cherubim's heads blowing would not be amiss... All these figures to be about 10 inches high after having seen the Derby Figures, I did not recommend Ease & Elegance in the shaped dress, but the Latter I shall just mention as the antique Robes, are very easy and have a Propriety which is not to be met with in foreign Dresses, & as these figures are of a serious Cast I think such dresses will carry with them a greater Elegance. I shall be oblig'd to you to carry the designs into execution as soon as possible."

These original instructions written by a proprietor to a modeller display great attention to detail and few other examples have survived. Both sets of 'Classical Elements' (P35) and 'Classical Seasons' (P37) are illustrated in Plates 149 and 150, and can be seen to follow the specifications in the neo-classical style favoured by Champion.

The fourteen year patent assigned to Champion by Cookworthy in 1773, was due to expire in 1782 and in the autumn of 1774, he made application to have the normal term extended by another fourteen years, by Act of Parliament. At the preliminary hearing by a Special Committee, Josiah Wedgwood strongly opposed the renewal. However, Edmund Burke and others of Champion's friends ensured a bill was introduced into the House of Commons. Wedgwood elicited support from the Staffordshire potters and contended: "The discoverer and purchaser for want of skill and experience had not been able during the space of 7 years already elapsed to bring it to any useful degree of perfection, and that if Mr. Champion has at length perfected it, the unexpired term of seven years ought to be enough to enable him to reimburse himself."[14] Champion brought specimens of his ware, including decorative pierced baskets, for scrutiny and called John Bolton to give evidence on his behalf. He submitted to "a discerning and encouraging Legislature whether a 7 years' sale is likely to repay a 7 years' unproductive, experimental and chargeable labour, as well as the future improvement to grow from new endeavours. Until he was able to make porcelain in quantities to supply a market, it was rather an object of curiosity than a manufacture for national benefit."[15] Passage of the Bill through the Commons was obtained but difficulties arose in the House of Lords where the powerful advocacy of Earl Gower nearly defeated it. Eventually, the rights laid down in the original patent were extended for the extra fourteen years but were restricted to use of raw materials in translucent porcelain, thereby leaving Wedgwood and others free to incorporate china stone into creamware.

The cost of the hearing and extension of the patent by act of Parliament had cost a great deal of money and, for a while, Champion was unable to meet in full all his outstanding commitments. On 24th August, 1778, Wedgwood wrote to his partner, Thomas Bentley, "Poor Champion, you must have heard, is quite demolished; it was never likely to be otherwise, as he had neither professional knowledge, sufficient capital, nor scarcely any real acquaintance with the materials he was working upon. I suppose we might buy some growan stone and growan clay now upon easy terms, for they have prepared a large quantity of this last year."[16] Champion had too many rich and powerful friends to be 'demolished' and by the end of the year had been able to revoke his deed of assignment. However, times were not propitious for the Bristol manufactory with loss of trade and restriction of shipping due to the American War of Independence. During the years 1776-78, Champion had made numerous trips to London almost certainly with a view to finding a

14. *Marks & Monograms on European & Oriental Pottery & Porcelain,* (London, 1965) by W. Chaffers, Vol. II, p. 234.

15. Ibid.

16. *The Ceramic Art of Great Britain,* op. cit., p. 380.

partner, but his efforts seem to have been unsuccessful. It is likely that production of porcelain ceased in 1779, though a muffle-kiln was used possibly until 1780 to enable enamelling of factory stock to continue. Amongst the last figures to be decorated was one depicting Andromache weeping over the ashes of Hector (P45). This had been copied from the Chelsea-Derby original (M100) and was inscribed in gilt to commemorate the death of Champion's daughter, Eliza, in 1779.[17]

On 28th February, 1780, and for the two subsequent days, three hundred and two lots of Bristol porcelain were sold at auction by "Mess. Christie and Ansell, at their Great Room, next to Cumberland House, Pall Mall".[18] The contents of the sale did not include any figures and appears to have been composed of the accumulated stocks of the previous two years. In 1781, Champion sold the rights remaining under his renewed patent to a group of potters from Shelton. These included Samuel Hollins, red china potter, Anthony Keeling, the son-in-law of Enoch Booth, potter from Tunstall. John Turner of Lane End, Jacob Warburton son of William Warburton of Hot Lane, William Clowes potter of Pert Hill, and Charles Bagnall and potter from Shelton. Simeon Shaw[19] gives the date of the transaction erroneously as 1777. Between 5th November, 1781, and 8th April, 1782, Champion resided in Staffordshire, and it is believed was superintendent of a china company.[20] The Bristol factory was closed and the potters who had purchased the rights, set up the factory at New Hall. No models are known to have been manufactured from this works.

In April, 1782, Champion was appointed Deputy Paymaster General of the forces under the administration of the Marquis of Rockingham. This appointment had been engineered by Edmund Burke who held the ministerial post. The death of the Marquis brought about a change of ministers and Champion retained his office only until 31st July. In 1784, he emigrated to America and settled in Camden, South Carolina, some one hundred and fifty miles from Charleston where his relatives, the Lloyds, resided. There he became an honoured citizen and a Member of the State Legislature. He died on 7th October, 1791.

Cookworthy's Plymouth and Bristol Figures

The Paste and Glaze

Analyses of both the Plymouth and early Bristol pastes show them to be almost identical with silica 69.5 per cent, alumina 26 per cent, potash 2.5 per cent, soda 1.7 per cent and only a trace of magnesia. The fired body is very strong and has a greyish hue. However, within a very short time after having been moulded or thrown the unfired paste became quite hard and it proved difficult or impossible to smooth out surface irregularities by use of a wet brush. The rough, almost home spun, look of most models may depend upon this quality. Imperfect wedging failed to eliminate air bubbles from the mix which, in the heat of the kiln, expanded, ruptured and gave rise to pitting of the surface of the biscuit. The high temperatures necessary for firing of hard paste, probably about 1,400°C,[21] led to a number of defects such as distortion from unequal shrinkage, tearing and firecracks from lack of plasticity, drooping of models away from the perpendicular and sagging of projecting parts. Thus, the model of a 'Goatherd', in the City Museum and Art Gallery, Plymouth, looks as if his neck is broken for his head droops down upon his chest. The figure of an old man in the Bristol City Art Gallery and Museum, emblematic of Winter, from the 'Rustic Seasons', shows that a wedge of porcelain has been inserted between the foot and the upper surface of the base

17. *Two Centuries of Ceramic Art in Bristol,* op. cit., pp. 198 and 199, pl. VIII.
18. *Contributions towards the History of Early English Porcelain* (Salisbury, 1881) by J.E. Nightingale, pp. 101-112, sale catalogue.
19. *History of the Staffordshire Potteries* (Hanley, 1829) by Simeon Shaw.
20. *Two Centuries of Ceramic Art in Bristol,* op. cit., p. 259.
21. 'Cookworthy Plymouth and Bristol Porcelain' by Alex Cummings, *Connoisseur,* 1971, Vol. 176, No. 707, pp. 10-15.

owing to shrinkage of the leg in the biscuit kiln. The glaze is feldspathic, creamy, very hard and usually free of scratch marks and abrasions. Some early specimens, prior to 1770, display a rather thick glaze. Often it is stained an unpleasant yellow, grey or even brown colour. Iron impurities account for 'sanding', and the surface is often peppered with pinhole defects. Crazing and dry patches are rare. The glaze is fused intimately with the body in a manner never found when lead glaze is applied to soft paste.

The Bases

Many models taken from Longton Hall moulds appear on tall steep mounds bearing a symmetrical pattern composed of scrolls in slight relief picked out in vermilion. Some, such as the large 'Continents', may be mounted on exceptionally high bases decorated with deeply moulded 'C' and 'S' scrolls arranged in the taste of Louis XVI, which enhances their artistic impact. Small models of animals are on pad or shallow mounds whilst birds may be perched upon tall 'chimney-pot' stands with lower circumferences flared outwards and applied leaves and flowers in slip. The inferior surfaces are left open so that the smooth glazed interior can be seen thereby distinguishing them from their Longton Hall prototypes.

Enamel Colours

A high proportion of Plymouth figures were issued in the white. Those that are coloured display a characteristic enamel palette including a canary yellow, a blue-green, light red, both a dark and a light rather cold brown, and a spectrum that ranges from rose, through crimson to a deep vermilion. A streaky manganese pink resembles the gold purple of Bow. The most unsatisfactory colour is blue which has a greyish hue when it is light in shade and an inky black when it is dark. After about 1770 a dull turquoise was added. The decorative schemes are rather drab and this effect was aggravated by debasement of colours in the high temperatures necessitated in the muffle-kiln to fix the enamel to the feldspathic glaze. Flesh tints are generally pale with orange red touches to the lips and barely perceptible daubs on the cheeks. Irises of the eyes may be grey, brown, or orange-pink; eyelashes are suggested with lines drawn in a rather cold brown and hair is indicated with streaks of brown, yellow, and grey in varying combinations. Garments are covered mostly in plain washes and the irregular reserves found on Chelsea, Derby and Bow models of the mid- and late 1760s are not encountered. Perhaps Cookworthy, as a Quaker, disapproved of the fripperies of the high rococo. Dresses are often left white and adorned with widely spaced floral sprigs painted in the Oriental style. Gilding is rare on early Plymouth figures but there are a few examples, including the 'Infant Bacchus' (P5). It is usually pale and thin and rubbed, and often exhibits an almost greenish hue. Gold is restricted to scrolls upon bases and it is unusual to find it applied to buttons, shoe-buckles, etc. It may also be found on useful wares painted with exotic birds by the hand of Monsieur Soqui.

The Marks

Only a few models are marked. An impressed 'T' or 'To' is generally accepted as the mark of Monsieur Thibauld (or Tebo) who most probably repaired models cast in Longton Hall moulds. Similar marks are known on Bow and Worcester figures. The alchemists' sign for tin ♃ or ♃ may also be found, usually drawn in light red overglaze. Other marks include an X or crossed swords in a purplish underglaze blue which though evident on useful ware must be extremely rare on figures. Likewise, the letters B or K or Arabic numbers occasionally appear on models.

Modelling

Hard paste Plymouth models cast from Longton Hall moulds exhibit an unaccustomed sharpness of detail and in their drab colouring look very different from the originals. Sometimes one or two figures from a Longton group would be rearranged or issued individually to portray an entirely strange theme. Others were placed before bocages which are composed of large and rather flat leaves attached to a plate of paste. Upon this foliage, large numbers of flowers were placed with circumferences almost touching one another. Such blossoms usually have five or six oval or flame shaped petals radiating from a raised centre though sometimes they are no more than discs with saw-tooth edges. Most attractive are those with heads like bluebells which have the tips of their petals everted. Most human figures, such as 'Gardener' and companion 'Lady', various 'Musicians', and 'Topers' are portrayed in a robust style shared with Longton Hall and with the best of the Staffordshire earthenware potters. A very few, seem to be entirely original. There is a third group of figures which most closely resemble those made at Worcester by Monsieur Thibault and these are most probably by the same artist. They are stiffly posed, have long necks, and drapery is portrayed by simple folds or pleats that are unconvincing and ungainly. They date to the period 1769-1772 and so overlap the Plymouth and Bristol establishments. Small models of animals and birds, which mostly appear on mound or scrolled bases, are said to have been created by the wife of the Plymouth enameller, Philip James. They have a naïvety and simple charm rarely encountered except perhaps in some Bow animals. It is likely that some magnificent pheasants were copied from Oriental prototypes.

The Models

Moulds of the Longton Hall group, 'Two Putti feeding a Goat' (O33) were adapted to provide a number of variations. The original group was reissued

Plate 143. *'Two Putti feeding a Goat' with flowers (P2). 7ins. (17.8cm). Plymouth c.1768-70.* Plymouth City Museum and Art Gallery

virtually unaltered (Plate 143) (P2), or with added bocage (P1). A new group employed 'Two Putti holding between them a wreath' (P3), whilst the 'Goat' (P4) was produced as an individual model. The 'Infant Seasons' (P6) are better known in their Plymouth versions than in the Longton Hall prototypes, whilst the reverse is true of the 'Infant Bacchus' (Colour Plate V) (P5) crowned with vine leaves holding a bunch of grapes. Both Longton and Plymouth sets of 'The Four Continents' (P7 and O79) are displayed in the Plymouth City Museum and Art Gallery. The Cookworthy models are mounted on taller bases adorned with moulded and enamelled scrolls arranged in the symmetrical manner beloved of the Louis seize style. The figure emblematic of Africa has her elephant head-dress upon the ground instead of in her hand which is the case in the Longton version. An example of this negress in the Bristol City Museum and Art Gallery sports a feathered head-dress borrowed from America. The matt black flesh tint of the negress and inappropriate white of the Red Indian issued at Plymouth contrasts with the deep chocolate brown and light red exhibited by their Longton Hall sisters. A 'Boy astride a barrel', is unexpectedly paired with a seated 'Boy with pipe and tambourine' (Plate 144) (P10). A pair of seated musicians include a 'Boy with a flute' and a 'Girl with a mandoline' (P8). A 'Gardener holding a basket of fruit', and 'Lady holding a basket of flowers' (P11) are adapted from the Longton 'Flower Seller', and 'Cabbage Seller'.[22] They stand on scrolled bases before bocages topped with candle holders and exist in both white and enamelled versions.

A magnificent 'Putto seated upon a Dolphin' (Plate 145) (P12) which holds its tail erect, stands on a shell encrusted base and may be original. A boy and

22. *Longton Hall Porcelain* (London, 1957) by Bernard Watney, pl. 61c 'Flower Seller'; col. pl. C, 'Cabbage Seller'. 'Cookworthy's First Bristol Factory', op. cit., pl. 118, Plymouth 'Gardener and companion' (possibly from the Bristol factory of 1765).

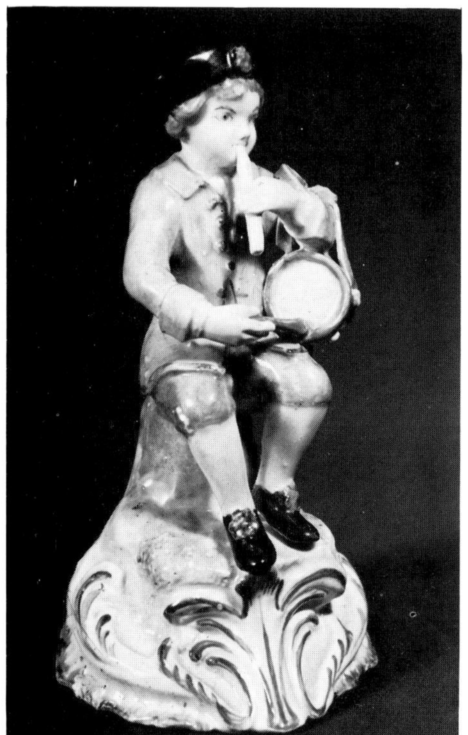

***Plate 144.** 'Boy with pipe and tambourine' (P10). 5¾ins. (14.6cm). Plymouth c.1768-70.*
Author's collection

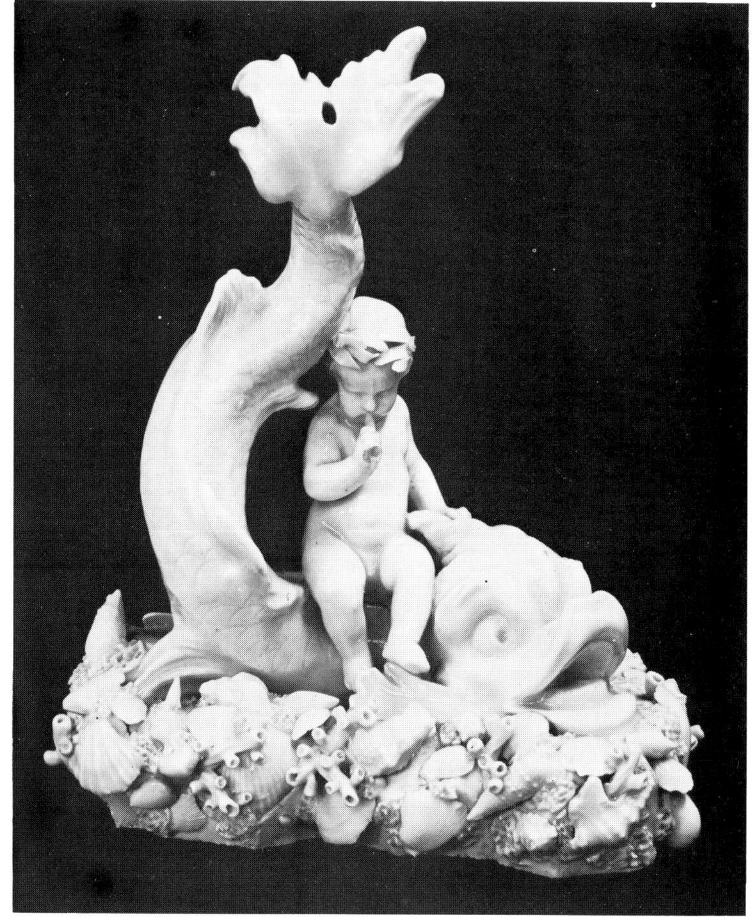

***Plate 145** (right). 'Putto seated upon a Dolphin' (P12). 8ins. (20.3cm). Plymouth c.1768-70.*
Plymouth City Museum and Art Gallery

companion girl in mirror poses, each seated beside a vase and extending a posy (P13), have heavy facial features suggesting they may be copies of German originals. Models of pheasants, both in the white (P20) and resplendent in bright red, blue, yellow, purple, and brown enamels (Colour Plate U) (P21) perch on tall flower-encrusted supports and most probably follow Oriental prototypes imported from Ching-tê Chên.[23] There are models of finches (Plate 146) (P17), pugs (P23) which have cropped ears, sheep (P24) on scrolled bases, a heifer (P15) and a pair of hares (P16) examples of which are in the County Museum, Truro, and the Plymouth City Museum and Art Gallery. A pair of dog-like seated lion and lioness (Plate 147) (P18) are overwhelmed by two superb standing lions (Plate 148) (P19) which may have been derived from terracottas made by John Bacon at Eleanor Coade's factory for Heaton Hall, Manchester.

23. Catalogue of the Exhibition of Porcelain in memory of Thomas Cookworthy, 1968, col. frontis., Plymouth pheasants.

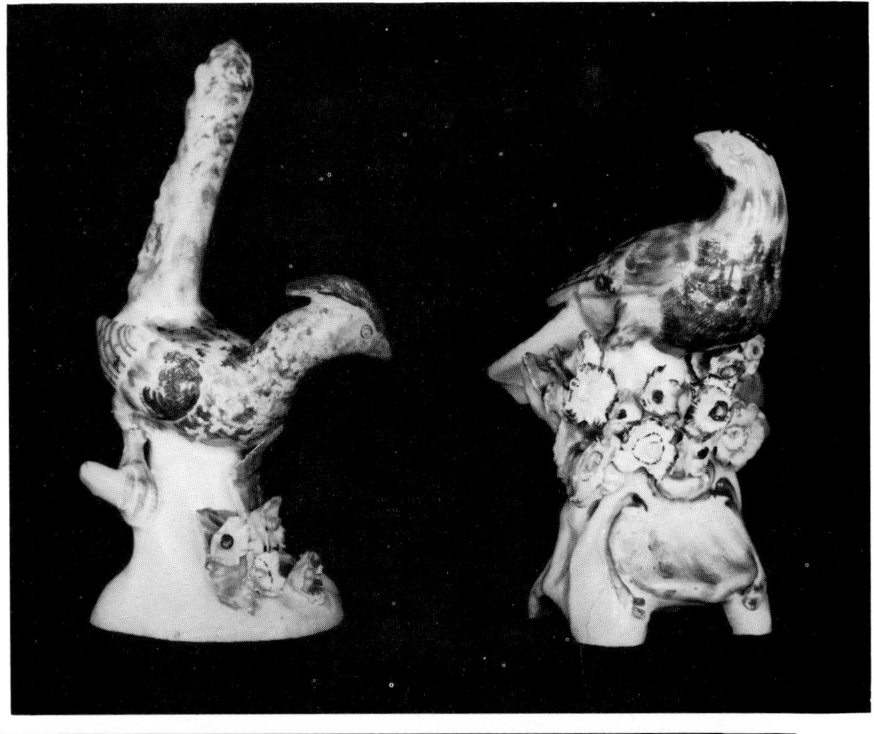

Plate 146. *A pair of finches on flower encrusted stands (P17). 5½ins. and 4¾ins. (14cm and 12.1cm). Plymouth c.1768-70.* Plymouth City Museum and Art Gallery

Plate 147. *A pair of recumbent lions (P18). 5⅛ins. and 4¾ins. (13cm and 12.1cm). Plymouth c.1768-70.* Plymouth City Museum and Art Gallery

Plate 148. *A pair of standing lions (P19). 11½ins. (29.2cm) long. Plymouth c.1770. Probably after terracottas by J. Bacon.* Plymouth City Museum and Art Gallery

Models ascribed to Tebo include a 'Shepherd' bagpiper in a tricorn hat, and 'Shepherdess' wearing a small hat and holding a crook (Colour Plate W) (P26). A smaller version of the same shepherd was issued with a different shepherdess holding flowers in her apron (P27). The long necked stiffly posed models, with naïve representation of drapery, bespeak poorly of their creator's skill in modelling. Many of the models described above are illustrated by F. Severne Mackenna.[24]

Champion's Bristol Figures

Paste and Glaze

There is very little difference on analysis in the ingredients of the Plymouth and Bristol pastes but to the naked eye the imperfections that are so evident upon the earlier figures become less common. The greyish hue of the initial venture was gradually eliminated to produce a whiter body and, though the surface tearing and firecracks were reduced they remain in evidence. Several models show quite severe sagging of projecting parts and lean away from the perpendicular. In the same way, there followed improvements in the appearance of the glaze which generally shows less pin-holing and smoke staining.

The Bases

Shortly after the move to Bristol the high bases, decorated with symmetrically arranged scrolls picked out in vermilion, were abandoned. In their place, are found rectangular bases with their circumference painted to simulate marble and upper surfaces covered in a dull turquoise. Others resemble the irregular rock-like pads after the fashion of contemporary Chelsea-Derby models though, unlike bases of that factory, these were mostly left uncoloured or exhibited a few touches of enamel and gilt. The inferior surface of almost all the bases was now covered with a flat plate of paste perforated by a small cylindrical ventilation hole and generally wiped free of glaze; some are slightly concave.

Enamel Colours and Decorative Style

There was an overall improvement in the quality of the enamel colours but little extension in the range of the palette. The blue enamel, which formerly had been most unattractive, now improved, and became cleaner and brighter though still retaining its purplish tint. Gilding was used especially to accent

24. *Cookworthy's Plymouth and Bristol Porcelain* (Leigh-on-Sea, 1946) by F. Severne Mackenna.

features upon the bases, but with great restraint and many figures are without any gilt. It was laid upon vermilion enamel so that it stands out from the surface in slight relief and has a rich sumptuous appearance very different from the rubbed greenish gold of the preceding era. Gilding was most frequently used on wares decorated with exotic birds, presumably by Monsieur Soqui.

The Modelling

There is a large group of Bristol figures which have many features in common and which may possibly stem from the hand of Pierre Stephan who at this time was supplying models as a freelance artist to Richard Champion. These take the form of overgrown children in adult dress. Foreheads are bulging, noses are small and button-like, cheeks are full and rounded whilst mouths have short thick lower lips with upper lips resembling Cupid's bows whilst their elevated corners impart the appearance of a smirk. The unattractive facial expression is aggravated by the dark red used on enamel specimens. The bodies of these figures are chubby and their heads are too large in scale. Other models including the 'Classical Seasons' (P37) and 'Classical Elements' (Plate 149) (P35) are depicted in a lumpish Louis seize style with correct anatomical proportions. It is difficult to accept that these have also been attributed to Pierre Stephan.

The Models

The detailed instructions written by Richard Champion to a former Derby modeller, possibly Pierre Stephan, have already been mentioned (p. 241) and the sets of figures known as the Classical Seasons and the Classical Elements

Plate 149. *The four 'Classical Elements' (P35). 10ins. to 11ins. (25.4cm to 27.9cm). Bristol c.1773, marked 'T°'.*
Sotheby Parke Bernet

follow the guide lines laid down by the proprietor. There are a few minor variations in some versions. For example, Autumn (Plate 150) may be portrayed standing with her reaping-hook beside an up-turned basket of grapes or of vegetables, whilst Summer (Plate 150) usually lacks the basket of wool on his shoulders together with the scythe and trusses of hay that had been proposed. However, it is interesting to see that the modeller accepted the suggestion that he might depict cherubims' heads blowing behind the figure emblematic of Air. These models look better in the white than in the rather drab colours of the Bristol palette.

The 'Rustic Seasons' (Plate 151) (P36) consist of four standing children which stylistically resemble the Chelsea-Derby 'French Seasons' (M123), also attributed to Stephan. The Bristol versions are the larger and less attractive. Spring is a girl with a pannier of flowers in her right hand who adjusts a diadem of flowers with her left hand; Summer is a youth who stands in his shirt sleeves barefoot beside a beehive and holds corn stalks; Autumn is a girl who holds basket of grapes in both hands; Winter is a boy wearing a tricorn hat who is skating with both arms folded. The pair representing 'Liberty and Matrimony' (P31) consists of a rustic swain holding a bird's nest in both hands and a companion girl with a lantern-like bird-cage; such emasculated adaptations of the satirical Meissen prototypes are meaningless, unlike the fine

Plate 150. *'Autumn', a lady with a reaping hook (missing) standing beside a vine, and 'Summer', a youth with shears (missing) standing beside a ram, from the 'Classical Seasons' (P37). 10ins. (25.4cm). Bristol c.1773.* Author's collection

Plate 151. *The 'Rustic Seasons' (P36), probably by Pierre Stephan. 11ins. (27.9cm). Champion's Bristol, c.1774.*
Plymouth City Museum and Art Gallery

Plate 152 (above left). A 'Shepherd' holding a bird standing beside a dog, companion 'Shepherdess' standing with flowers in her apron beside a lamb (P28). 7ins. (17.8cm). Bristol c.1774, probably modelled by P. Stephan. Sotheby Parke Bernet

Plate 153 (above right). A 'Girl with a puppy' in a plumed head-dress (P30). 7⅛ins. (18.1cm). Champion's Bristol c.1773-75. This model has china-blue eyes matching her sash. David Thorn collection

Plate 154 (left). 'Milton' standing beside a plinth (P42). 7¾ins. (19.7cm). Bristol c.1774-76. Plymouth City Museum and Art Gallery

Plate 155 (opposite page). 'Three Vestal Virgins' standing with their backs against a plinth upon which rests an urn (P43). 16ins. (40.6cm). Bristol c.1776-78. Plymouth City Museum and Art Gallery

Bow versions of 1752. A 'Shepherd' and 'Shepherdess' (P28) probably modelled by Stephan is shown in Plate 152. Other models in the same style include a 'Boy with a Puppy' upon the head of which he holds a tricorn hat, and a 'Girl with a puppy' in a plumed headdress (Plate 153) (P30) and in the example of the female figure in the collection of David Thorn, the eyes and plumes are both china-blue. A 'Girl holding up a musical triangle' and 'Boy with a Hurdy-gurdy' who leans forward with the instrument upon his knee (P29) are also in a similar style, as is the droll model of a 'Girl standing with a mouse-trap' with a cat (P34). Bernard Watney[25] has found the inspiration behind the model of a 'Boy frightened by a Dog' (P32) shown running with both arms elevated, to have been a painting of 'Tobias and the Fish' by Huygh Voskul (1592-1665), now in the Staatsgemäldesammlungen, Munich.

Some of the later Bristol models are in the style of the 'Classical Seasons' and 'Elements'. There is a rare model of a 'Peasant Woman' (P38) on her way to market, wearing bonnet, cloak, and an apron over her full skirt, in the Glaisher Bequest in the Fitzwilliam Museum. A group described in Lady Charlotte Schreiber's Journal[26] as "the fine double group purchased of Jacob some years ago" is 'Venus, Adonis and Cupid' (P40). This consists of Venus, who reclines upon a rock with a bouquet in her right hand, with her left hand resting on the shoulder of the seated Adonis who proffers a basket of flowers; Cupid with his quiver, lies naked before a rock holding his mantle with one hand. The example in the Shreiber Collection[27] is painted with very pale colours and, perhaps for this reason, is not entirely successful from the artistic viewpoint. Three models follow Chelsea-Derby prototypes and include 'Shakespeare', and 'Milton' (Plate 154) (P42) and the group 'Love subdued by Time' (P41). A pair of 'Sphinxes' (P44) are mounted on rectangular bases and modelled in the neo-classical style and hence create a very different appearance from those created earlier at Chelsea and at Bow. A group of 'Three Vestal Virgins' (Plate 155) (P43), stand back to back about a plinth upon which rests a vase. Traditionally, the last figure to have been made was a lady leaning against a plinth weeping and probably meant to represent Andromache weeping over the ashes of Hector (P45) which was copied from the Chelsea-Derby original (M100), adapted from Thomas Burke's engraving of a painting by Angelica Kauffmann 'Andromache and Hecuba weeping over the ashes of Hector'.[28] An example in the Fitzwilliam Museum, Cambridge is glazed but left white except for gilt sprigging. The Bristol model shows poor modelling on its reverse and is clearly intended to be viewed from the front. Llewellyn Jewitt[29] reproduces an engraving of another example, then in the collection of Mr. Desaussure of South Carolina, which had been inscribed in gilt to commemorate the tragic death of Champion's daughter, Eliza. The urn bears upon it "Eliza Chamion. O.B XIII OCTOB MDCCLXXIX aetat XIV". Below this her date of birth is recorded, 'Nat XXI Mart MDCCLXV', and upon the base is written "This Tribute to the Memory of an Amiable Girl was inscribed on her coffin the 16th October, 1779, by a Father who loved Her". This must have been appended to a model that had first been issued at least one year before the event. It will be recalled that Richard Champion emigrated to America where, in 1784, he settled in South Carolina. He must have taken the model with him. J.M. Desaussure of Camden, South Carolina, married a grand-daughter of Champion, and in his keeping the heirloom has been preserved. The reader will find many illustrations of Bristol wares and figures in Dr. F. Severne Mackenna's book.[30]

25. 'The Origins of Some Ceramic Designs' by Bernard Watney, *Transactions,* English Ceramic Circle, 1975, Vol. 9, pt. 3, pl. 181a, Bristol model; plate 181b, painting of Tobias and the Fish.

26. *Lady Charlotte Schreiber's Journals, Confidences of a Collector of Ceramics and Antiques throughout Britain, France, Holland, Belgium, Spain, Portugal, Turkey, Austria and Germany from 1869 to 1885* (London and New York, 1911) ed. M.J. Guest.

27. Schreiber Collection, pl,. 77, no. 768 (no. 731).

28. 'Some Parallels and Prototypes in Ceramics' by Bernard Watney, *Transactions,* English Ceramic Circle, Vol. 10, pt. 5, pp. 350-356, pl. 157b, Bristol model; pl. 157c. engraving by Thomas Burke, c.1772.

29. *Ceramic Art of Great Britain* (1883 second ed.), op. cit., p. 227, fig. 759.

30. *Champion's Bristol Porcelain* (Leigh-on-Sea, 1946) by F. Severne Kackenna.

Chapter XI

Miscellaneous English Factories that issued Porcelain Figures during the 18th Century

Figures made between 1768 and 1770 at Dr. Wall's Worcester Factory

The new soapstone formula purchased from Benjamin Lund enabled the new Worcester factory, established in 1752, to make crisply potted useful wares that would withstand the temperature of boiling water. These qualities gave Worcester an advantage over all other contemporary English factories, and it is hardly surprising that the proprietors decided to focus production on dinner and tea services and useful wares of all kinds to meet an insatiable public demand. Indeed, there was only one brief experiment made in the field of porcelain figures. The modeller seems to have been the former Bow repairer, Monsieur Thibauld. The mark To is found on Bow figures, such as the Muses, issued shortly after 1750. It is likely that he arrived in Worcester c.1768 where he created seven or eight figures before leaving to work for Cookworthy at Plymouth.

Plate 156. *A 'Lady' and companion 'Gardener' (Q14). 6¾ins. and 7ins. (17.1cm and 17.8cm). Worcester c.1768-70, probably modelled by Thibauld.* Sotheby Parke Bernet

Plate 157. *Standing young Turk holding a perfume vase (Q15). 5¼ins. (14.6cm). Worcester c.1768-70, probably modelled by Thibauld.* Sotheby Parke Bernet

Plate 158. *'Two Canaries' in a bocage candlestick (Q17). 9¾ins. (24.8cm). Worcester c.1768-70.*
Sotheby Parke Bernet

The body of a model of a sportsman, from the collection of the late H.R. Marshall, was analysed by Dr. A.D. Moss in 1949.[1] It revealed silica 67 per cent, magnesium oxide 13 per cent, alumina and iron oxide together 7 per cent, lead oxide 2 per cent, calcium oxide 3 per cent, and soda together with potash 8 per cent. The high magnesia content indicates inclusion of about 40 per cent soapstone in the mix. The paste is extremely hard and close grained and the thin, transparent, and brilliant glaze blends intimately with the body. Models are known both in white and enamel colour. The enamel palette includes deep yellow, a blue-green, rose-pink, iron-red, and both a dark and a light blue. Decoration of garments of figures was most often effected in the old Japanese style, with florettes, stars, crosses, and circles arranged in patterns dominated by dark blue, red and yellow. The models were press-moulded and hence are rather heavy in the hand. Modelling is undistinguished, and many examples have long necks, vacant expressions, and stand woodenly with artless representation of drapery and of other garments. Accessories, such as leaves, flowers, and the design of bases, are as might be expected from an ex-repairer, competently finished and reminiscent of earlier work at Bow.

Models include a 'Gardener' (Plate 156) wearing a tricorn hat, jacket, apron and breeches, holding a pot plant in his right hand and with the other leaning upon a spade; his companion is a 'Lady' who wears a small hat, laced bodice and skirt arranged in ungainly pleats, and has a basket over her left arm (Q14). They usually appear on mound bases adorned with leaves and flowers but some versions have bases with 'S' shaped legs with dependent 'U' scrolls and are mounted before bocages topped by candle holders after the style of Bow

1. *Worcester Porcelain and Lund's Bristol* (London, 1966) by F.A. Barrett, p.44.

models issued between 1765 and 1776.[2] A 'Sportsman' and companion 'Lady' (Q16) portray a man in a tricorn hat standing with his left hand upon his hip and holding in his right a dangerous fowling piece; his lady wears a brimmed hat, and a cloak over her riding habit, whilst she holds a powder flask in one hand and dead game in the other. There is a pair of Turks (Q15), one clean shaven carrying a perfume pot (Plate 157), the other, who is bearded, carrying a scimitar; both have turbans and loose robes decorated with floral painting in the style of *Indianische Blumen*. Most examples of the Sportsmen are on bases adorned with symmetrically arranged scrolls whilst the Turks are most often on mound bases adorned with leaves and flowers. There is also a bocage group of 'Two Canaries' (Plate 158) (Q17) which face one another in an arbour of leaves beneath a candle sconce.

A small model representing 'Cupid at Vulcan's Forge' (Q18), once erroneously attributed to Longton Hall, has now been ascribed to Dr. Wall's Worcester factory owing to the discovery of a matching shard on the factory site.[3]

Chamberlain's Worcester Figures

Only two models have been attributed to Chamberlain's Worcester factory. The first consists of a pair of kingfishers (Q20), perched on conical bases decorated with lobed saucer-shaped flowers, and moss in applied slip, and each with a fish on the upper surface. The under surface is concave. A pair may be seen in the Rissik Marshall Collection in the Ashmolean Museum, Oxford.[4] The second model, recognised by Dr. Bernard Watney,[5] is of a ram (Q19), which is also decorated with saucer-shaped flowers and moss and stands on a base that is concave underneath. Both are press-moulded, and display firecracks and iron staining upon a glistening glaze. No coloured examples have so far been recognised. Dr. Watney dates the models to the late 1780s or early 1790s.

A Group of Early Models, probably Experimental Derby, c.1750

Dr. Bernard Watney[6] has described a small group of soft paste models that share some unusual characteristics. They are slip-cast, and fashioned from a non-phosphatic, non-steatitic paste that has a lead oxide content of between 4 and 6 per cent. The group includes five models of putti seated with their knees widely separated and their legs obliquely placed, in a manner that is reminiscent of some Girl-in-a-Swing figures though they are not so expertly modelled as those of the London factory. Indeed, they are stiffly posed and have noses that are sharply outlined in profile, lips that appear to be slightly pursed, and eyes that are represented by elevated discs that are indented and placed below carefully delineated upper lids. Fingers are long, and the failure of the modeller to represent separation between individual digits makes them appear to be webbed. The models include 'Spring', a putto crowned with a wreath of flowers (Q1), and 'Winter', another putto with a brazier between his knees (Q2); both are mounted on rectangular bases which have chamfered upper edges, and display applied slip decoration. 'Summer', is a putto with wings, or perhaps a cupid, and sits with corn on a curiously octagonal base with scalloped concave edges (Q3). There are two further putti as musicians, one seated upon an octagonal plinth with a lyre, the other likewise, but holding a musical score (Q4). There is a crudely modelled standing 'Turk', and companion 'Lady' (Q5) which are mounted on flat octagonal bases, and the figure of a headless 'Actor' (Q7) in the Victoria and Albert Museum[7] which

2. *Porcelain Figurines* (London, 1975) by Nathaniel Harris, p. 62, Worcester 'Gardener' and 'Companion' on legged bases with bocage. *English Porcelain of the 18th Century* (London, 1952) by J.L. Dixon, pl. 82, 'Gardeners' on mound bases.

3. *The Illustrated Guide to Worcester Porcelain,* 1751-1793 (London, 1969) by Henry Sandon, pl. 129, 'Cupid at Vulcan's Forge'.

4. *Coloured Worcester Porcelain of the 18th Century* (London, 1954) by H.R. Marshall, pl. 40.

5. 'A Hare, a Ram, Two Putti and Associated Figures' by Bernard Watney, *Transactions,* English Ceramic Circle, 1972, Vol. 8, pt. 2, pp. 224-227, pl. 179a, Worcester 'Kingfisher'; pl. 179b, 'Worcester Ram'.

6. ibid.

7. Victoria and Albert Museum Catalogue, No. C.1410-1924.

Plate 159. *A 'Pug scratching' (Q6). 4¾ins. (12.1cm). 'Experimental Derby' c.1750.* George Savage

also shows webbed fingers and lastly, a version of a seated 'Pug scratching' (Plate 159) (Q6).

Two putti musicians (Q4) both have dry-edge glazing similar to that seen on Planché Derby models of the period 1750-55. The upper surfaces of the bases of the Turk, companion Lady, and of one putto, show fine semi-lunar incisions which were recognised as a feature on some Girl-in-a-Swing models by the late Arthur Lane, who called them 'fingernail parings'. Slip adornment of the bases of 'Spring', the 'Actor', and the 'Pug', takes the form of strawberry flowers with concave petals seen also on the non-phosphatic model of Kitty Clive (Plate 87), and on three early Derby creamers described in Chapter VIII. Thus, there are strong links between this small group and dry-edge Derby models, and possible connections with the Girl-in-a-Swing factory. It seems possible that they represent the first attempts by an early modeller at Derby, possibly André Planché, to create figures from a primitive glassy paste.

The So-called Transitional Derby Models

Another small group of figures have been labelled 'Transitional Derby' because they appear to date to the period 1755-56 during the transition between the management of André Planché and William Duesbury. It is possible that they are trial models made in parallel with the last dry-edge figures by an artist who did not have the skill of Planché and who later served under William Duesbury at Derby. The paste is glassy and one unconfirmed analysis gave a lead oxide content of about 4 per cent. The body has a greyish hue and assumes a dark brown colour in areas of exposed biscuit. Tearing of the surface of the paste and full thickness firecracks are common and most models lean away from the perpendicular and show sagging of projecting limbs. The glaze is thick and lacks lustre; it has an unattractive yellowish tinge and is both smoke stained and heavily sanded. Modelling is doll-like lacking the robust treatment of the Planché figures and bases are often elaborately sculptural with shell patterns and scrolls arranged in rather clumsy asymmetrical patterns. The under surfaces are usually ground and ventilation holes are intermediate in size and cylindrical in section. The figures are all decorated in a limited palette of debased colours which include a dirty puce-pink, a pale green, a dull orange, brown, purple, pale yellow, light blue which has a milky look about it, and black. Two models bear the mark of two triangles within a circle, one other has a 'Y' in a circle. All marks are incised.

A model of a 'Crested Pheasant' (Q8) serves as a taper-stick. An example in the Eckstein and Fodden Collection[8] has a small vignette painted upon the upper surface of the base containing figures in place of the more usual moulded flowers that resemble rosettes. Other examples are in the Untermyer Collection and there are at least two others in private collections. A 'Dancing Youth' (Q9) who wears a tricorn hat, stands with his right hand elevated upon a base adorned with scrolls, and is bedecked with large flowers and ribbons fashioned from slip. An example is in the Victoria and Albert Museum.[9] Two seated figures of a 'Youth wearing a tricorn hat' with a huge bird under his right arm, who pats a dog that leaps up on his left side (Q10) and of a bare-headed 'Girl seated with a dog', seem to have been issued as a pair and may be seen in the British Museum.[10] An adaptation of the youth seated without a hat and devoid of any bird is represented in the Fitzwilliam Museum, Cambridge. All appear on elaborately scrolled bases. There is also a model of a 'Chinese Boy climbing a creeper-like tree' (Q12) in the Fitzwilliam Museum.[11] Some authorities have included the rococo style watch stand (Plate 92) (J21) incorporating a Chinaman and a Chinese boy, as well as the model of the goddess Cybele (Colour Plate O) (J25) in this group. However, these are much heavier in the hand, and show a far higher degree of modelling competence whilst the glaze and enamel decoration of examples known to the author are totally dissimilar to the so called 'Transitional Derby Group'.

A Lund's Bristol Figure

In 1749 Benjamin Lund and William Miller established a small porcelain factory in Lowdin's Glass House at Bristol. The paste contained soapstone and was thus dissimilar from that of all other English factories of the day. A license to mine soapstone from a place known as Gew Graze, close to the Lizard peninsula, was obtained in 1748, though it is improbable that any porcelain was manufactured commercially until the following year. The venture was short-lived for, by 1751, negotiations were already in progress for the sale of the business to a group of gentlemen headed by Dr. Wall of Worcester. These were successfully concluded by 1752 when operations were transferred to Worcester, and the Bristol factory closed.

Only one model appears to have been made at Lund's Bristol factory, namely one of the Taoist Immortal known as 'Lu-tung Pin' (Q13). This was cast from a simple two-piece mould made by application to an Oriental *blanc-de-Chine* prototype, probably from Tê Hua. The Bristol version was press-moulded, and hence it is heavy in the hand for its size. It is left open at the base but inspection of the interior in most specimens shows it has been sponged smooth before glazing was effected. The modelling detail is blurred and shallow, and the thick glaze varies between models from a greenish hue to a pale cream colour. The mark BRISTOLL, sometimes with the date 1750 appended, is impressed upon the lower portion of the base at the back. Some are decorated upon the base with underglaze manganese. Examples may be seen in the Sigmund Katz Collection, in the Victoria and Albert Museum, and in the City Museum and Art Gallery at Bristol.

Lowestoft Figures

The porcelain factory at Lowestoft was established as an off-shoot from Bow, close to Grunton, where there were plentiful supplies of a good white clay. The paste, like that of Bow, was phosphatic, and commercial production commenced c.1757 under the proprietorship of Robert Brown. Most of the

8. *Derby Porcelain* (London, 1971) by F.A. Barrett and A.L. Thorpe, pl. 23.

9. *English Porcelain Figures of the 18th Century* (London, 1961) by Arthur Lane, pl. 62b.

10. ibid., pl. 62a.

11. *Derby Porcelain* (Barrett & Thorpe), op. cit., pl. 25.

early wares are tea services decorated in underglaze blackish blue. By the year 1760, the former greyish coloured paste became white, the glaze more brilliant, and production was diversified to include a number of small and rather artless models of birds and small animals. These include swans, a sheep, a ram, a seated cat and a tabby cat, and a seated pug (Q24). They have been recognised by matching wasters found upon the factory site. Some are decorated with underglaze manganese, all have bases glazed over their inferior surfaces and exhibit ventilation holes that are funnel-shaped like those seen on dry-edge Derby models.[12]

Excavations on the factory site have more recently revealed wasters and moulds of a few models of human subjects. These were press-moulded and are hence heavy in the hand, whilst bases are either mounds decorated with rather clumsy scrolls picked out in enamel colour or are elevated upon short S-shaped legs. The models include a 'Youth playing a Triangle' (Plate 160) who wears a tricorn hat, and companion 'Lady with a Mandoline' (Plate 161) (Q22) which may be seen in the Victoria and Albert Musem. At least one pair of a 'Dancing Man' and companion 'Dancing Girl' (Q23) have waist high bocages attached

12. *English Porcelain* (London, 1974) by John Cushion, p. 34, pl. 27, two swans, a pug and a tabby cat. *Connoisseur Year Book* (London, 1957) by Geoffrey Godden, p. 73, a sheep. Sotheby's sale catalogue, 13-11-73, lot 101, a ram; lot 28, a seated pug.

***Plate 160** (left). 'Youth playing triangle (missing) (Q22). 8ins. (20.3cm). Lowestoft c.1770-80.*
Sotheby Parke Bernet

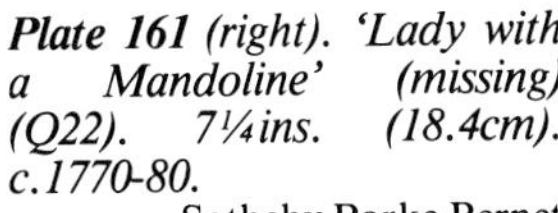

***Plate 161** (right). 'Lady with a Mandoline' (missing) (Q22). 7¼ins. (18.4cm). c.1770-80.*
Sotheby Parke Bernet

to radial spokes arising from the top of the base like a fan.[13] There is also a group of 'Two dancing Putti' (Q21) mounted on a single mound base.[14]

The problem posed by this small and undistinguished group of models is to distinguish them from their more sophisticated brothers and sisters from Bow. The Lowestoft paste is greyer in hue and both pinhole defects and sanding of the glaze are much more common. Modelling is less competent, heads are rounded and faces rather flat, whilst poses are stiff and lack any sense of movement. Moulded flowers applied to bases usually have five or six petals, and leaves which are thick, narrow and spiky may have incised branching dorsal veins which contrast with the moulded veins sometimes found at Bow. Reference has already been made to the shape of the ventilation holes. The Lowestoft palette includes lemon yellow, mauvish-pink, a poor turquoise with a brownish cast and a dull green and is far more restricted than the range of colours employed on most Bow models. Painting of garments may also make use of stylised florettes and scroll-like leaves which may either be attached to thin wandering curved stems or appear as widely spaced sprigs and sprays.

Richard Chaffer's Liverpool Figures

In 1968, Dr. Bernard Watney[15] brought together a miscellany of small models, a bust, and two plaques which he presented as the products of Chaffer's Liverpool factory. They were all fashioned from a soapstone paste which presents a rough texture when areas of biscuit are palpated. The body looks grey and most displayed numerous firecracks, due to the shortness of the paste, many of which had been filled in with frit. The glaze lacks the brilliance of Worcester and looks cold owing to its greenish cast. In some instances bluing of the glaze was present in the form of blue specks due either to imperfect mixing or to contamination of the glaze with blue used in the underglaze decoration of useful wares. Under surfaces of bases are unglazed, flat, and perforated by rather small ventilation holes. Dr. Watney dated the models to c.1755.

A model of a reclining Ariadne (Q30) in the Victoria and Albert Museum,[16] is derived from a copy of an ancient Roman figure now in the Archaeological Museum, Florence,[17] itself a copy of an antique Greek statue. Other versions are sometimes adapted by the addition of an asp entwined about the lady's left arm to serve as models of Cleopatra, and are known in black basaltes, marked G. Bentley 22nd. May, 1791, in late eighteenth century Ralph Wood pottery, and in yellow-glazed Swansea pottery when it may be paired with another model of Marc Antony.[18] Clearly replicas of the Roman model were widely available in England which served the potters at various establishments. The soapstone bust of George II (Plate 162) on a shaped plinth (Q25) stands eleven and three quarter inches tall. This was formerly attributed to Chelsea on account of the fine modelling but the result could easily have been achieved by applying plaster of Paris direct to a marble or bronze to form a mould. This, like the other figures, is press-moulded and very heavy. It seems likely that problems in firing a piece so large caused special treatment of the bust leading to almost a vitrification of the paste causing many in the past to believe it had been constructed of hard paste.

The remainder of the models are all copies of porcelain figures made at other factories and, by reason of their slightly smaller size, appear to have been cast from moulds applied directly to the surface of their prototypes. They include a 'Nurse breast-feeding a baby' (Q26) which is four and a half inches tall and was copied from the Chelsea model known as 'La Nourrice' (B50) which is about six and three quarter inches tall. Also, the figure of a 'Seated Nun reading from a book' (Plate 163) (Q27) which is four to five inches tall

13. 'Some Trifles from Lowestoft' by Geoffrey Godden, *Antique Dealer and Collector's Guide,* March 1970, pp. 64-68, fig. 5, Lowestoft 'Dancers'.

14. *Connoisseur Year Book,* op. cit., p. 73, no. 3, two putti.

15. 'The King, the Nun and Other Figures' by Bernard Watney, *Transactions,* English Ceramic Circle, 1968, Vol. 7, pt. 1, pp. 48-58.

16. Victoria and Albert Museum Catalogue, No. C.1-1932.

17. *Il Museo Archologico di Firenze* (1912) by L.A. Milani, p. 313, no. 40-41.

18. 'The King, the Nun and Other Figures', op. cit., pl. 82c.

Colour Plate T. 'The Four Continents' (O79). 12½ins. to 13¼ins. (31.8cm to 33.7cm). Longton Hall c.1759/60.
Plymouth Museum and Art Gallery

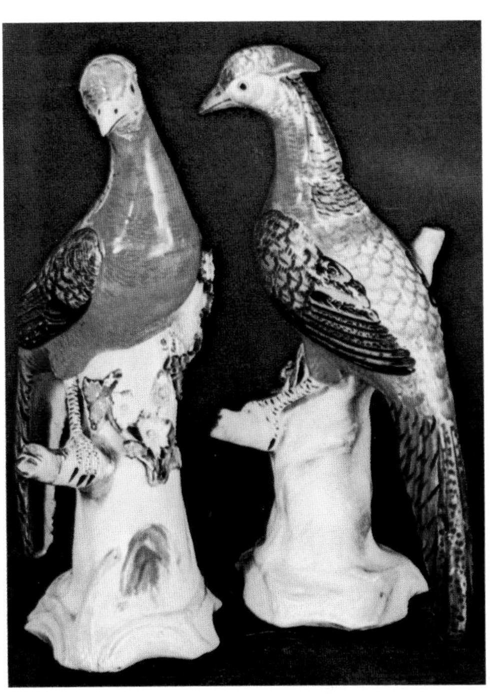

Colour Plate U. 'The Chinese Pheasants' (P21). 9ins. (22.9cm). Plymouth c.1768/70. Probably inspired by Chinese originals.
Plymouth Museum and Art Gallery

Colour Plate V. 'The Infant Bacchus' (P5). 5ins. (12.7cm). Plymouth c.1768/70. After a Meissen original.
John and Diana Mould collection

Colour Plate W. Shepherd and companion shepherdess (P26). 6⅞ins. (17.1cm). Bristol c.1772. Plymouth Museum and Art Gallery

Colour Plate X. 'Milton' (P42). 8¾ins. (22.2cm). Bristol c.1774. A copy of a Derby model probably based on a terracotta by Scheemakers.
B. and T. Thorn Antiques

Colour Plate Y. Four standing putti, emblematic of the 'Four Seasons' (Q37). 6½ins. (16.5cm). Gilbody's Liverpool. Plymouth Museum and Art Gallery

and follows a Bow prototype (H116) (Plate 78, Chapter VII) of five and three quarter inches based on a Meissen original. A 'Male Dancer' (Q28), four and a half inches in height, follows one of several models of the male figure in the pair known as the 'New Dancers' (H34) which were issued in several sizes. The enamelled Liverpool figure illustrated by Dr. Watney,[19] sports a moustache and a goatee beard which gives him a French appearance. Finally, there is a standing 'Turk' (Q29) in turban and cloak with arms akimbo which stands six and a half inches tall and may follow either the Longton Hall (O69) or a Bow original. The group also contains two wall plaques,[20] two wall brackets, and a 'Hare' tureen.

The method used in the construction of these models suggests that there was no skilled modeller on the staff of the factory of their origin. Further, it is possible to recognise the hand of certainly two, and possibly three, different independent artists in the matter of enamel decoration in coloured specimens. Dr. Watney considered that they were possibly decorated by John Bolton between 1752 and 1754 of Kentish Town, London, and by James Giles, who also worked in London, between 1755 and 1756. The different styles associated with these artists have been described in connection with outside decorated dry-edge Derby models (pages 180-181).

19. 'The King, the Nun and Other Figures', op. cit., pl. 55b.

20. ibid., pl. 54b, wall bracket depicting 'Fame crowning a Roman victor with Cupid in chains'; pl. 54c, wall bracket depicting 'Susanna and the Elders'.

Plate 162 (left). A bust of George II (Q25). 11¾ins. (29.8cm). Chaffers' Liverpool. George Savage and Dudley Delevingne collection

Plate 163 (below). 'A seated Nun' (Q27). 5ins. (12.7cm). Chaffers' Liverpool. Sotheby Parke Bernet

Plate 164. 'Winter' portrayed by a man in fur-lined hat and coat with a charcoal burner (Q34). 4¾ins. (12.1cm). Samuel Gilbody's Liverpool. Sotheby Parke Bernet

Philip Christian's Liverpool

There is a tureen made at Philip Christian's Liverpool factory, now in the Victoria and Albert Museum, with a lid on which the finial takes the form of a hare (Q33). This, most probably, dates to the late 1760s. The model seems to have been copied from a Chelsea version based on a Meissen original. There is also a model of a man standing wearing a fur-lined hat and overcoat carrying a basket of charcoal, emblematic of 'Winter' (Plate 164) (Q34). This seems to have been based on a figure in the Chelsea 'Rustic Seasons' (C98), which is also known in Longton Hall versions (O6 and O41).

Samuel Gilbody's Liverpool

Alan Smith[21] has published the outcome of limited excavations made upon the site of Samuel Gilbody's factory in Liverpool. Amongst the shards that were recovered were biscuit fragments of the model of a 'Shepherd standing beside a Dog' holding a basket of fruit (Q35). Later, a perfect specimen of the same model was found which had once been in the Dudley Delevingne Collection[22] and seems to be an exact copy of a slightly earlier Derby Shepherd[23] now in the collection of Bernard Watney. A second Gilbody figure exists in the collection of John Mallet of 'Minerva' (Q36) who stands in crested helmet wearing a cuirass and leaning upon a shield; in her right hand there appears to have been either a spear or a sword that is now missing.[24] The painted floral decoration upon the dress of the goddess corresponds with that on a spoon tray[25] in Bernard Watney's possession.[26]

A set of four putti in the Plymouth Museum and Art Gallery representing the 'Four Seasons' (Colour Plate Y) (Q37), together with other porcelain figures, are attributed to Gilbody's Liverpool factory by Bernard Watney. The figure representing Summer from this set is known also in a larger size. The same author illustrates a group depicting 'Ceres attended by Cupid' and a 'Turkish Lady', which appear to be copies of Longton Hall models (O7 and O69). He also illustrates a 'Peasant holding a basket of charcoal' emblematic of Winter, which echoes the red anchor Chelsea model (C98).

Seth Pennington's Liverpool

A press-moulded white glazed figure of a 'Negro Slave' (Q38) in the Plymouth City Museum and Art Gallery, has been attributed to Seth Pennington's Liverpool factory by Bernard Watney.[27] This has a blued glaze, stands about nine inches tall on a flat rectangular base and is incised 'India Slave 1772' (not '1779' as elsewhere stated).

William Reid's Liverpool

A small model of a 'Hound' (Q39), decorated in underglaze blue has been attributed by Bernard Watney to William Reid's Liverpool factory.[28]

Staffordshire Porcelain

After the failure of the Longton Hall factory in 1760, no porcelain was manufactured in Staffordshire for many years. The large number of models made both of animal and human subjects were made either of cream coloured earthenware covered with transparent polychrome lead glazes, after the manner of Ralph Wood, father and son, and Enoch Wood, or were fashioned in salt glazed stoneware. These lie beyond the province of the present work. However, from time to time, models that are familiar in pottery are found in porcelain versions and the majority of those made during the eighteenth century seem to date to the period 1780 to 1800. A few examples illustrated elsewhere are listed in the Appendices, Q40-43.

21. 'Samuel Gilbody, some recent finds at Liverpool' by Alan Smith, *Transactions,* English Ceramic Circle, 1969, Vol. 7, pt. 2, pp. 100-107, pls. 117 and 118.
22. 'Potting on Merseyside, 1700-1900' by Alan Smith, *Antique Collecting,* March 1976, pl. 16.
23. 'Samuel Gilbody, some recent finds at Liverpool', op. cit., pls. 119a, 119b and 119c.
24. 'A Hare, a Ram, two Putti and Associated Figures', op. cit., pl. 188a.
25. ibid., pl. 188b.
26. 'Gilbody Figures, 1754-1761, a Short Review' by Bernard Watney, *Transactions,* English Ceramic Circle, 1980, Vol. 10, pt. 5, pp. 346-347; pl. 144a, 'Turkish Woman', 3⅜ins.; pl. 144b, 'Putto representing Summer', 4½ins.; pl. 144c, set of the 'Four Seasons'; pl. 145a, 'Winter', 3¾ins.; pl. 145b, 'Ceres with Cupid', 5¼ins.
27. 'A Hare, a Ram, two Putti and Associated Figures', op. cit., pl. 178a.
28. *English Blue and White Porcelain of the 18th Century* (London, 1963) by Bernard Watney, p. 80, pl. 45a.

Chapter XII

The Decline of the English Porcelain Figure

In August 1786, Joseph Lygo wrote to William Duesbury regarding "the Great Stock of enamelled figures in the Warehouse, these must be sold first owing to the body being altered and the new figures of different size."[1] He most probably implied that it would be wise to clear the stock decorated in the old style before selling those which were presumably issued in the biscuit and were larger in scale. He mentioned in the same letter that the demand for porcelain figures in London had shown a sharp fall that year. The decline evidently continued steadily for, during the last fifteen years of the existence of the Derby factory in the Nottingham Road, very few new models were introduced. Although there were many causes of this, the most important was the emergence of the neo-classical style which, as will be shown, was essentially hostile to the small scale enamelled and gilded porcelain figure.

The ruins of Herculaneum had been discovered accidentally in 1719, although formal explorations of the site were delayed until 1738. In 1748, similar archaeological excavations began upon the site of the ancient Roman city of Pompeii which, like Herculaneum, had been overwhelmed by an eruption from the volcano, Vesuvius in A.D. 79. The ruins of Pompeii were unique because items of household furniture and pottery had been preserved in the volcanic dust. A number of vases and urns, thought at the time to be Etruscan, were of late Greek origin. In 1749 Abel François Poisson, Marquis de Vandières, and the brother of Madame de Pompadour, later to be created Marquis de Marigny, arrived in Rome at the head of a delegation intent on the study of the works of antiquity that had been recovered. The party included the painter and engraver Charles Cochin, the architect Jacques Germain Soufflot, and the Abbé Leblanc. The purpose of the visit was to provide the Marquis with the necessary knowledge and experience to enable him to qualify for the post of *Directeur des Bâtiment, Jardins, Arts et Manufactures Royaux,* to which he was to be appointed in 1755. After his return to France in 1751, he was later to retain the services of Cochin for supervision of "tout le détail de l'administration des arts". Soufflot became director of the Gobelins tapestry atelier and also designed a number of public buildings including the church of St. Genevieve in Paris which he modelled on the Pantheon in Rome. In 1754, Cochin published two articles in the *Mercure de France* in which he satirised the prevailing rococo taste and extolled the merits of the relics of antiquity. The same year, he published his *Observations sur les fouilles d'Herculaneum,* in which he made known to a wide public the artistic style of the archaeological discoveries. Meanwhile, Ann-Claude-Phillipe, Comte de Caylus, art connoisseur and collector, had been advocating a return to classical sources of inspiration in the arts since his election in 1731 to the position of *Conseilleur honoraire de l'Academie de Peinture.* In 1752, he published his magnum opus, *Recueil d'antiquités égyptiennes, étrusques, greques et romaines.* These folio volumes included detailed descriptions and engravings of works of Roman and Greek art both in his own collection and in the great museums of the day.

1. *Derby Porcelain* (London, 1971) by F.A. Barrett and A.L. Thorpe, p. 139.

Perhaps the loudest voice to be raised in praise of the works of art unearthed at Pompeii, Herculaneum, and also in Greece, was that of the scholar, Johann Joachim Winckelmann (1718-1768). Born the son of an impoverished cobbler of Stendal, he had somehow managed to acquire a fine education, but only after enduring great deprivation and suffering many humiliations heaped on him by a class-ridden society. He rose to become librarian to Count Bunau, the cultivated chancellor of Saxony, author and scholar, who was the proud possessor of more than 40,000 books in his château located in the outskirts of Dresden. Wickelmann was, by reason of his lowly birth, debarred from sitting at his master's dining-table which was almost certainly decorated, in the current fashion of the day, with enamelled and gilded porcelain figures. These must have become for Winckelmann the symbol of everything he loathed and detested and of the social forces that kept him for ever in an inferior position. Here, it may be recalled, Goethe was permitted to dine at court only after receiving letters patent of nobility in 1782, and that the master tailor of Heinrich von Brühl was lampooned in porcelain astride a bespectacled goat bearing the implements of his trade to the undoubted delight of the aristocratic throng.

Winckelmann become deeply interested in the new archaeological discoveries that were being made in Italy and Greece. In 1755 he left Saxony and became the secretary to Cardinal Albani in Rome, where he was afforded the opportunity of visiting Pompeii and Herculaneum. Many of the antiquities had, by this time, been removed by Charles IV, king of the Two Sicilies, to his private museum at Portici castle. Winckelmann's foreign nationality would have made it difficult for him to gain access to the royal domain but he made things worse for himself by criticising the manner in which the research had been supervised and ordered by the king and was, accordingly, banished from the castle. In 1763, Winckelmann was appointed Superintendent of Antiquities in Rome and, the following year, published his magnum opus *Geschichte der Kunst des Altertums* (The History of the Art of Antiquity). The undoubted success of this work was, in part, due to the wholehearted support given to the project by the Comte de Caylus. Thinking, perhaps, of Count Bunau's banquets, Winckelmann expressed all the pent up emotion and burning resentment of many years. Under the heading 'Notes on the plebeian taste of porcelain design', he wrote, "Connoisseurs of the beautiful must find such wares infinitely more splendid than all the popular pieces of porcelain, an exquisite material that has not yet been perfected by true art, and which expresses no worthy, uplifting image. Porcelain is generally modelled into ridiculous little puppets, and the childish taste it engenders has spread everywhere instead of reproducing eternal works of antiquity such as the Dioscorides and Solon and trying to teach through art. Copies of such perfection in porcelain would have contributed in no small measure to the sense of beauty, and would thus have stimulated good taste." Centuries of burial had removed almost all traces of pigment from the excavated marbles which, though Winckelmann and others did not know it, had once been painted in brilliant colours. Accordingly, he denigrated colour and extolled line and form. "Colour, light and shade make painting less estimable than noble contour alone..." He added "The noble simplicity and serene grandeur of Greek sculpture has never been surpassed by the hand of man...The arts of painting and sculpture are only justified by imitation of the Antique." Such advocacy proved catastrophic to the natural development of original art for nearly a quarter of a century. Winckelmann's second major work *Monumenti Antichi Ineditii,* published in 1766, expanded this thesis and sounded the death knell of the rococo style. In 1768, the man who had murdered the porcelain figure was himself slain in the waiting-room of a Trieste hotel by a person everybody vowed must have been a lunatic.

Many of the established arbiters of taste were, at this same time, fast leaving the stage. Madame de Pompadour, who had been such a strong *patronne* of the fine arts, died in 1764. Étienne Maurice Falconet, unwilling or unable to face mounting criticism of his work which failed to adapt to the new taste, left Sèvres to take up an appointment in Russia in 1766. In 1770 François Boucher, who for so long had been the centre of artistic endeavour at the French Court, died. During the closing years of the reign of Louis XV, the first signs of the so called *Louis seize* style became apparent. Decorative motifs and scrolls were arranged in tightly disciplined designs and the former studied asymmetry was considered to be ugly. The more exuberant curves and *bombé* shapes, together with the cabriole leg were abandoned in favour of rectangular shapes, flat surfaces and legs that were straight and fluted rather like a Grecian column that had been slimmed down. During the French revolution, the pace towards a new asceticism was hastened and in this every assistance was given by Jacques-Louis David. A nephew of Boucher, he was a Member of the Committee of Public Safety and narrowly escaped the guillotine to become Court Painter to Napoleon I. After the initial period of looting and unbridled destruction that accompanied the revolution, when tapestries were burned for the gold they contained and when fine bronzes and silver were melted down by a government that had no further use for them, an ascetic neo-classical style was evolved. Painted ceilings and murals were whitewashed, cartouches and gilded mirrors removed together with all reminders of the hated *ancien régime*. Many motifs derived from the antiquities of Rome and Greece were employed for the embellishment of simple furniture to which others from ancient Egypt were added following the Middle East campaigns of Napoleon Bonapart.

In England the baroque had very little effect upon the decorative and architectural styles. An Italian architect, Andrea Palladio (1518-1580) had introduced a style based on the *Ten Books of Architecture,* compiled c.15 B.C. by Vetruvius during the reign of the Roman emperor Augustus. This was published in his *Quattro Libri dell'architectura* in 1550 and greatly influenced Inigo Jones and, after the death of Sir Christopher Wren, successive architects such as Lord Burlington and Colin Campbell. The style was monumental, ponderous, and based upon strict Orders from which no deviation was allowed which resulted in fine basic proportions but very little variation and limited decoration. Since no Greek or Roman furniture was known to have survived prior to the excavations at Herculaneum, it was left to men like William Kent and Thomas Ripley to create tables, chairs and case furniture that would blend into the Palladian setting. The results were predictable. A massive scale was chosen and much use was made of designs incorporating the Vetruvian scroll, rams' masks, swags, and creatures like the eagle and the dolphin. Most of the work was heavily carved and gilded by Italian craftsmen. The advent of the altogether lighter designs of the new French rococo must have come as a welcome relief though, strangely, very few English country-houses followed the fashion. Perhaps one of the best examples was Chesterfield House built in 1749 though sadly demolished in 1937. Indeed, it can be said with some truth that in England the Palladian merged imperceptibly into the neo-classical style with only a trace, here and there, of the rococo.

Robert Adam (1728-1792) was the son of William Adam, a Scottish architect steeped in the Palladian tradition. In November 1754, Robert and his brother James went upon the 'Grand Tour' in the company of Lord John Hope. The party stayed for a few weeks in Paris in November of that year when the brothers visited museums, churches and royal palaces. They also met Cochin, recently returned from Italy, who must surely have shown them engravings of antiquities, some of which were to appear in *Observations sur les fouilles d'Herculanum*. Afterwards Robert went to Herculaneum whilst James visited Pompeii. They elicited the help of Charles Louis Clérisseau, a draughtsman, who made many sketches for them and Robert travelled to Spalatro in Dalmatia to view the ruins of the emperor Diocletian's palace. In Florence Robert Adam wrote: "We danced with all the greater Quality and with some of the greatest whores." After their return in 1758, the brothers commenced architectural and decorative work that was to transform the prevailing scene beyond recognition. Robert Adam wrote a folio volume with engravings *The ruins of the palace of the Emperor Diocletian at Spalatro,* published in 1764. He secured the collaboration of painters such as Antonio Zucchi and his wife, Angelica Kauffmann, stuccoists like Joseph Rose, the great specialist in English ormolu, Matthew Boulton, and many cabinet-makers including especially Thomas Chippendale, John Linnell, James Wyatt and Samuel Norman. Decorative schemes were effected within a tightly disciplined framework of geometrical shapes incorporating circles, ovals, rectangles, and octagons, together with motifs derived from antiquity. These included leaf scrolls, bell husks, swags, paterae, medallions, and urns, either painted upon flat surfaces or moulded in low relief. Favourite symbols were the amphora, vase, tripod, acanthus, anthemion, sphinx, and griffin. The delicacy of line and lightness of scale, owed much to the rococo, but unlike the former style, a strict symmetry was preserved. The fluted columns and the friezes on temples were scaled down to provide respectively the legs of chairs and case furniture and moulded ornament upon crest rails and overmantels. Between 1766 and 1770, the Adam brothers were engaged in building or remodelling many of the great country-houses. Their attention was turned towards the provision of comprehensive schemes that included designs for ceilings, internal architectural features, movable furniture, and in some cases even carpets and curtains. Examples of their work may be seen at Harewood House, Nostell Priory, Osterley, Syon House, and at Saltram House. In 1773, they published *The Works in Architecture of Robert and James Adam*. In this they state: "The massive entablature, the ponderous compartment ceiling, the tabernacle frame, almost the only species of ornament formerly known in this country are now universally exploded, and in their place, we have adopted a beautiful variety of light mouldings, gracefully formed, delicately enriched and arranged with propriety and skill. We have introduced a great diversity of ceilings, friezes and decorated pilasters, and have added grace and beauty to the whole, by a mixture of grotesque, stucco, and painted ornaments...we flatter ourselves, we have been able to seize with some degree of success, the beautiful spirit of antiquity, and to transfuse it with novelty and variety, through all our numerous works."

Within the setting of the new style, there was no place for the small enamelled and gilded porcelain figure. The plaster cast became the ideal of plastic beauty. At Meissen, Schonheit and Juchtzer were the chief modellers during the closing years of the eighteenth century. They created a number of small reproductions of the antique and for this purpose studied the vast collection of plaster casts in the collection of the Saxon Court Painter, Raphael Anton Mengs. The figures were little more than reduced imitations of large scale statues but presented a very hard cold appearance due to the high fired body. At Sèvres, the use of pâte tendre, which was an exquisitely beautiful substance, was abandoned c.1770 for the pâte dure which like the Meissen body was unsuitable for issue in the biscuit. In England, the leading exponent of the neo-classical style in ceramics was Josiah Wedgwood who created portrait busts in jasper of ancient personages including Aristotle, Cicero, Homer, Plato, Seneca and Virgil after the Roman style as well as others of characters ranging from Shakespeare to Handel.[2] His full length Queen's Ware models of dancing nymphs[3] were based on a Pompeian fresco. Wedgwood also introduced black basaltes which had a matt surface akin to that of 'Etruscan' vases and which in colour resembled bronze. This material was employed for free-standing models taken from many different sources. His 'Venus', was based on the Hellenistic, Venus de Medici; two dissimilar models of 'Bacchus' followed respectively work by Sansovino and Michelangelo, whilst five 'Sleeping Children' were derived from five terracottas by François Duquesnoy.[4] Many figures, including Grecian and Egyptian sphinxes, griffins, gods and goddesses, were mentioned in the Sale Catalogues of 1773, 1774, and later, imitated classical sculpture. Vases and urns in basaltes and in jasper, decorated with miniature friezes in white slip after the antique, provide the evidence that Wedgwood was eager to fulfil the role allocated to the pottery by Winckelmann, namely to copy the works of antiquity. Eventually, in 1790, Wedgwood reproduced in jasper a deep blue Roman glass vase, known as the Barberini or Portland vase, which was surely the ultimate prostitution of the potter's art even if it was a magnificent technical achievement. Meanwhile, at Derby, between 1771 and 1795 an ever increasing proportion of models and groups were issued in biscuit and related to the neo-classical style and subject matter. In such company the small rococo porcelain figure, resplendent in enamel and gilt, was unable to survive and became an unwelcome intruder.

Economic and social factors were also contributory to the change in porcelain taste. During the Napoleonic wars, the ports of Europe were closed to British shipping and the cost of living rose by three hundred per cent. The price of flour was so high that it was cheaper to buy an imitation creamware piecrust made by Wedgwood than the real thing. Soaring inflation and steeply rising wages made it unprofitable to construct porcelain models laboriously by hand in unstable soft paste requiring not less than three passages through the kiln in which a high proportion became wasters. By 1810, Derby had adopted a bone china body and within a few years a tough stoneware was employed by Copeland, Mintons, and Coalport simulating Parian marble. This material allowed knife edges to be modelled and greatly reduced kiln wastage. The number of moulds required for each model were reduced to the minimum to ensure maximum cost effectiveness and this eventually led to the Staffordshire flat-back figure, cast from a two-piece mould.

The social structure was profoundly altered by the industrial revolution that followed the discovery of steam power backed up by plentiful supplies of cheap coal. A merchant class grew up with artistic tastes very different from those of the aristocracy and landed gentry who alone had comprised the market before. In addition, perhaps for the first time in European history, the craftsman and artisan, though not yet the unskilled labourer, were able to earn more than was necessary simply to keep body and soul together. They demanded plentiful inexpensive goods and the means of mass-production were there to meet their demands. Towards the end of the eighteenth and beginning of the nineteenth century, a number of small artless porcelain models were made clad in dark enamel colours and brash gilding to satisfy the taste of the new social order. Improved methods of manufacture and better raw materials created many articles formerly regarded as luxuries for the enjoyment of a wide public. Deeply cut crystal and, for the less affluent, press-moulded glass from Nailsea, Stourbridge and Newcastle flowed into the market. Beautiful

2. *Decorative Wedgwood in Architecture and Furniture* (London, 1965) by Alison Kelly, pp. 29-33, portrait busts and figures.

3. *The Story of Wedgwood* (London, 1975) by Alison Kelly, pl. 15, the 'Dancing Nymphs'.

4. *Decorative Wedgwood in Architecture and Furniture,* op. cit., cites sales catalogue of 1773.

translucent bone china, created by Spode, Copelands and their successors in brilliant glazes and decorated with an almost unlimited range of enamels, became available. Transfer printing reduced the cost of both blue and white and polychromes, whilst inexpensive creamware attractively painted was issued by Josiah Wedgwood, and the potters of Leeds, Staffordshire and Liverpool. These embellishments of the dining-table made other adornment superfluous and the porcelain figure became redundant.

Although aesthetic, social, and economic factors all combined to the demise of the rococo porcelain model, there were also more subtle psychological reasons. The introduction first of the colza lamp and subsequently of electric light, destroyed for ever in the hearts of men the illusion of fairyland that once, in the flickering glow of wax candles, had been their delight. The delectable fancy dress in miniature in which porcelain lords and ladies acted out their roles of shepherd and shepherdess in the myth of the erotic pastoral, the gaiety and mirth provoked by singerie and 'Love in disguise for desart', and the wish fulfilment of the chinoiserie, found no place in the harshly lit world of reality. They became like the long treasured toys of a child who after returning from his first term at a boarding school discovers they have lost their magic. Instead, for the next fifty or more years these child-like delights were to be ousted by the colourless asceticism of the neo-classical style in which a pretentious and nervous self-consciousness usurped the robust hedonism of a former age.

Chapter XIII

Reproductions, Fakes, Restoration and Collecting

Reproductions

Sooner or later the collector will encounter reproductions of eighteenth century English porcelain figures made during the nineteenth or twentieth century. Amongst the earliest were those issued from the small manufactory set up in King Street, Derby, in 1848, following the closure of the main factory in the Nottingham Road. Many of the craftsmen and artists who had been employed by Robert Bloor and Thomas Clarke, joined the new establishment, including William Locker, who served as manager between 1848 and his death in 1859. Between 1859 and 1866, the proprietors were a former draper named Stevenson and the painter and gilder, Sampson Hancock. The old Derby mark of the crown, crossed batons, and the script letter 'D' was retained and flanked by the initials 'S' and 'H'. Following the death of Stevenson, the same letters continued to be used and they referred to Sampson Hancock. Many models were cast from old Derby moulds purchased at the sale of the Nottingham Road works in 1848. A bone china body and a feldspathic glaze were employed. Enamel colours are generally brighter and more glossy and include an opaque chrome yellow-green, whilst there seems to have been a preference

Plate 165. *'Shepherd' feeding two dogs from a scrip slung over one shoulder (right); companion 'Shepherdess' holding a lamb and flowers (left) (D75). 11¾ins. (29.8cm). Chelsea c.1765.*
Victoria and Albert Museum

for deep tan flesh tints and china-blue eyes. Models are often smaller than their originals and a high proportion are mounted on octagonal bases decorated with a Greek key fret pattern in slight relief which may be picked out in brassy gilding. Modelling is generally debased and there is a general blunting of moulded detail.

Some of the works catalogues survive and portions of these have been reproduced by Geoffrey Godden,[1] and by John Twitchet and Betty Bailey.[2] Models include 'The Four Elements' (M3), after Stephan, a 'Toper', a 'Tinker', a 'Beggarwoman', a 'Girl cleaning her shoes', and a 'Girl kneeling on a cushion'. Many of the models created by Edward Keys representing 'Dr. Syntax' were reissued, and also the group depicting a 'Cobbler whistling to a caged starling', after Cyfflé, which was also copied by George Cocker at Friar Gate in biscuit. The 'French Seasons' (M123), were copied, both free-standing and mounted, beside candlesticks when they are most often white and stand on the pierced and scrolled bases which were so popular during the period of the late rococo revival. In 1935 the manufactory was absorbed into the Royal Crown Derby Porcelain Manufactory in the Osmaston Road, where further reproductions, bearing the factory device in red, are still being made.

During the 1850s and '60s, the Coalport factory made reproductions of both Sèvres and gold anchor Chelsea vases, as well as the triangle marked Chelsea 'Goat and Bee' creamers (A1). Dr. Severne Mackenna[3] has listed the characteristics of the originals and their copies. The replicas are more thickly potted with less elegant handles and display a uniformly brilliant white which has a rather cold tone. Their glaze is tight-fitting, transparent, and tough and may extend to include the under surface which is often concave. This contrasts with the flat unglazed areas of the prototypes. Further, if any mark is found, it

1. *An Illustrated Encyclopaèdia of British Pottery and Porcelain* (London, 1966) by G.A. Godden, p. 309.

2. *Royal Crown Derby* (London, 1976) by John Twitchet and Betty Bailey, pp. 20-34.

3. *Chelsea Porcelain, the Triangle and Raised Anchor Wares* (Leigh-on-Sea, 1948) by F. Severne Mackenna, pp. 69-71, pl. 54, figs. 105 and 106.

Plate 166. *Samson copies of Chelsea Shepherd and Shepherdess (D75). See Plate 165 for originals.* Christie's

will take the form of an impressed triangle and lacks the heaped up edges of the incised device. Transillumination of the reproduction produces a faintly pink colour and the pin-point areas of increased translucency are not encountered. The tails of the Coalport goats droop, instead of being up-turned, their manes are thicker, and their horns are both longer and slimmer. Moulded flowers and leaves are much thicker and the petals of flowers are concave instead of convex. Coloured examples are decorated in a much brighter palette, whilst the bees may be painted with alternating horizontal bands of black and yellow, like a wasp, on the copies.

The vast majority of reproductions, however, stem from the factory founded in 1848, by Edmé Samson, in the Rue Vendôme (subsequently renamed Rue Béranger) in Paris. Originally the works were concerned only with enamelling porcelain which had been purchased in the white from other factories. Under the influence of the proprietor's son, Émile, additional land was acquired in the Montreuil-sous-Bois, upon which seven kilns were erected. A resumé of the history of the factory and some of the models that were issued are given by John Cushion.[4] Between 1870 and 1913, when Émile Samson died, reproductions were made of faience, European and Oriental useful wares, and of eighteenth century porcelain figures, including many created in England. Moulds were taken directly from original models so that the Samson versions are slightly smaller than their originals. Differences in both paste and glaze serve to distinguish original from copy, whilst the more even and glossy enamels found on the Samson models stand out upon the glaze in slight relief, creating an entirely different effect to the streaky pale colour that seems to have sunk deeply into the glaze of the eighteenth century figures. Although it is piously stated that Samson models always bear a factory mark, such as 'SAMSON', the two letter 'Ls' back to back, or a gilt swastika, this is evidently untrue. On May 24th, 1971, there was a sale at Christie's of "an interesting series of wares and figures after English originals from the Samson factory, Rue Béranger, Paris, used as working models in the factory". A few bore spurious gold anchors, though the majority were unmarked. Quite apart from the qualities of paste and glaze there are other, more subtle, differences between Samson copies and their prototypes. Firstly, the dynamic appearance of the originals, especially those from the Bow manufactory, is almost entirely lost. For example, Bow models of a 'Seated Male 'cellist', and companion 'Lady with a hurdy-gurdy' (H53) display a magnificent sense of movement, whilst their Samson copies[5] appear to be posing for a still photograph before a long exposure camera. Likewise, the elegance and grace of the Derby 'Ranelagh Dancers' (K52) was lost in the stiffly posed imitations.[6] The illustrations of a pair of gold anchor Shepherd and Shepherdess (Plate 165) (D75) and their Samson versions (Plate 166), here serve as examples. Although the copyists were often only children, the factory did not hesitate to issue copies of the most complex groups, such as the gold anchor Chelsea 'Dancing Lesson' (D63). Frequently, however, accessory decoration was simplified to spare expense and this is evident in some of the copies made of the Chelsea 'Fable' groups. The original Chelsea 'Cock with a jewel on a dung-hill' (D94), for example, is placed on a highly sculptural base before a huge bocage that is topped by a pierced candle holder; the copy has a simpler and flatter base, a solid candle sconce and the bocage is replaced by a wreath of leaves. More rarely, as in the 'Two Foxes beneath a fruiting vine' (D98), the original conception is faithfully reproduced (Plate 167). Familarity with eighteenth century English figures will reveal many errors in the copies. The flowers that were moulded at Bow were usually large, saucer-shaped, and had pointed petals, whereas those applied to Samson's 'Stag' and 'Doe' (Plate 168) more closely

4. 'Fake or Collector's Piece' by J.P. Cushion, *Antique Collecting*, 1975, Vol. 10, No. 3, pp. 22-25.

5. ibid., figs. 5 and 5a.

6. ibid., fig. 8.

Plate 167. *Samson versions of three gold anchor Chelsea fable groups: left, 'Cock with a jewel upon a dung hill'; centre, 'Fox and vixen with sour grapes'; right, group of 'Cat and a Peacock'.* Christie's

Plate 168. *Samson versions of Bow models: left and right, 'A Stag and a Doe'; centre, 'A seated Cat'. The original Bow deer usually appear on mound bases.* Christie's

resemble those of a stawberry plant. The very beautiful dry-edge Derby group of a huntsman flautist with a lady (Plate 169) (J17) normally appears on a simple pad base devoid of any embellishment. The Samson version (Plate 170), heedless of period or style, is mounted on a wide flat base edged with scrolls in front of a bocage. Also, the enamel decoration employed does not accord with that found on originals, whilst the rather brassy gilding is totally dissimilar from the honey gilding of Chelsea. Until 1924, when Bernard Rackham first drew attention to the association between patch marks and the Derby factory,[7] many Derby models were wrongly ascribed to Chelsea. Further, it was not until 1926 that the dry-edge became accepted as a trait peculiar to models made before 1756 at Derby.[8] Since nearly all Samson's reproductions were issued prior to 1913, it is not surprising that many copies of figures and groups made at Derby carry a spurious Chelsea mark which in most instances is a gold anchor. Undoubtedly hard paste copies of English models were made at other Continental factories, particularly those located in Germany and Austria. There are some artless models that are stiffly posed and which make no pretence to follow any eighteenth century prototypes but carry large gold anchor marks. These stem from the Fitzendorft manufactory in Thuringia and are unlikely to deceive anyone familiar with the products of the eighteenth century.

All the reproductions cited so far are constructed of either bone china or Continental hard paste and so their confusion with English soft paste figures is unlikely. Occasionally, however, a highly skilled craftsman may turn his attention towards making more convincing copies intended to deceive. The skill that is demanded, together with the time and expense, limits the exercise to forgeries of a handful of rare and costly models. During the second decade of the present century, Mr. and Mrs. Sigmund Katz purchased a rare and possibly unique model of 'Dottore Baloardo' (B34) based upon an engraving

7. *Catalogue of the Burlington Fine Arts Club of Counterfeits, Imitations, and Copies of Works of Art* (London, 1924) by Bernard Rackham, p. 31.

8. 'Early Derby Porcelain' by W.B. Honey, B. Rackham and H. Read, *Burlington Magazine*, 1926, Vol. 49, No. 285, pp. 294-297.

***Plate 169.** 'Huntsman in peaked cap playing a flute beside a Lady' who has one hand upon his sleeve (J17). 6¼ins. (15.9cm). Dry-edge Derby c.1755.* N.C. Ashton collection

after Watteau. Prior to the completion of this transaction, the model had passed through the hands of a well-known porcelain restorer in London. Afterwards, shortly before the First World War, several reproductions appeared in the salerooms.[9] The Chelsea original[10] stands eleven and a half inches tall and is fashioned in the characteristic glassy, non-phosphatic paste of the raised anchor period. The copies stand nine and a half inches and are made of a highly phosphatic material. One of the copies now resides beside the original in the Sigmund Katz Collection, in the Boston Museum of Fine Arts; another found its way into the Lady Ludlow Collection, once in Luton Hoo, near Bedford.[11]

During the early 1950s several reproductions appeared on the market which seemed to have emanated from the Torquay area. George Savage[12] relates how, when he first examined some primitive models of birds, he tentatively dated them to c.1752-1754 and, by a process of reasoned elimination, thought they might have been created at Derby. However, when this attribution was shown to be untenable owing to the phosphatic nature of the paste revealed by analysis, a more thorough scrutiny showed them to be modern. Subsequently other examples, mostly canaries and finches, which are mounted on tall chimney-pot bases adorned with leaves and flowers in enamelled slip, have come to light. Some of them have funnel-shaped ventilation holes, others incised numbers that do not accord with the description of the models in Haslem's Derby factory list. Most are betrayed by their colouring which is too brilliant, and by weak modelling. George Savage[13] also mentions a reproduction in the same phosphatic semi-porcelain of the Girl-in-a-Swing 'Dancing Girl' (E3). This was painted in a palette and style found upon a genuine model which had been issued in the white and decorated in modern

9. Personal communication from George Savage.
10. *Eighteenth Century English Porcelain* (London, 1952) by George Savage, pl. 10.
11. *Catalogue of the Lady Ludlow Collection* (London, 1932) by A. Hayden, pl. 66, no. 158.
12. *Forgeries, Fakes, and Reproductions* (London, 1963) by George Savage, pp. 175-176.
13. ibid., p. 176.

Plate 170. *Samson copy of a dry-edge Derby group (J17), showing inappropriate flat and scrolled base and a bocage.* Christie's

times! Arthur Lane[14] has listed some of the features by which the Torquay reproductions may be recognised. They are made of a light-weight and rather chalky earthenware which, on palpation, feels much the same as soft paste. Unglazed portions of the body, such as the interior, are stained a blackish or a deep brown colour, whilst the glaze presents a greasy appearance and lacks lustre. Unfortunately, only a small proportion of examples display these peculiarities. Moreover, there are not only wide variations between models of paste and glaze, but also in modelling competence and style. Though it remains possible that these variations might represent a spectrum of individual experience, the natural suspicion is raised that more than one artist may have been responsible. The most common reproductions are of the dry-edge Derby 'Florentine Boars' (Plate 171) (J1). Originals may be seen in the Franks Collection,[15] in the Derby City Museum and Art Gallery[16] and examples are illustrated. The Torquay versions (Plate 172), which are slightly smaller, sag out of alignment in an exaggerated manner and display weak modelling which completely fails to recapture the magnificent animation of the originals. The inferior surface of one example is not discoloured but shows both a large irregular shaped ventilation hole and a pseudo screwhole which ends blindly in the substance of the base (Plate 173). Copies of the dry-edge 'Stag' and 'Doe'

14. *English Porcelain Figures of the 18th Century* (London, 1961) by Arthur Lane, p. 98, footnote 2.

15. 'English Porcelain in the British Museum — Part I, Early Derby' by William King, *Country Life,* 19th January, 1929, pp. 99, fig. 3.

16. *Derby Porcelain* (London, 1971) by F.A. Barrett and A.L. Thorpe, pls. 18 and 19.

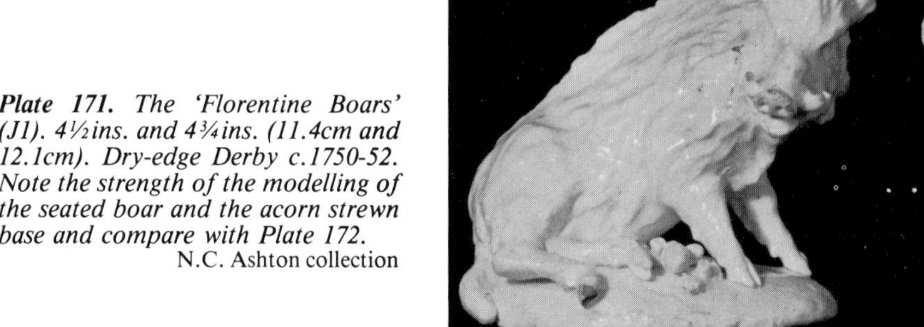

***Plate 171.** The 'Florentine Boars' (J1). 4½ins. and 4¾ins. (11.4cm and 12.1cm). Dry-edge Derby c.1750-52. Note the strength of the modelling of the seated boar and the acorn strewn base and compare with Plate 172.*
N.C. Ashton collection

***Plate 172.** Torquay reproduction of the dry-edge Derby seated wild boar (J1). Note weak modelling, sagging out of alignment, oddly shaped ears compared to the original in Plate 171.*

***Plate 173.** The inferior surface of the base of the Torquay reproduction of the dry-edge Derby wild boar, showing irregular ventilation hole in the centre and a second pseudo screw-hole which ends blindly near the lower edge. Note the absence of discoloration of the exposed paste.*

at lodge (J2) are shown in Plate 174, and are amongst the most competent, as judged from their prototypes in the Derby City Museum and Art Gallery.[17] Here, the glaze is brilliant though faintly crazed, the sideways drooping is less evident, whilst the ventilation hole, like that of its original, is large and cylindrical. It is betrayed, however, by the blackish discoloration of the body and by the enamel decoration, of which more will be said later. The Derby factory under Planché also created a number of models of goats,[18] of which the 'Billy-Goat' (Plate 176) and 'Nanny-Goat suckling a Kid' (Plate 175) (J4) are perhaps the best known. The Torquay artist preferred to copy a lesser known model, also following a Meissen original, of a 'Recumbent Billy-Goat' (Plate 177). Here, the more usual irregular pad base is replaced by one edged with scrolls, picked out in rubbed gilt and adorned with applied flowers of saucer shapes enamelled puce and opaque medium blue. Such embellishments, though often found on Meissen models of the period, rarely appear on dry-edge Derby.

Enamel decoration is effected in a palette and style employed by at least one independent decorator who painted Derby figures. Representation of fur or hide is accomplished with short lines of black or brown laid upon a peach coloured ground. These lines are thicker and fewer in number upon Torquay reproductions, whilst the wash of yellow-green applied to the superior surface of bases is also thicker, more glossy, and lacking in the blotchy appearance of prototypes. The delicately painted representations of grass, leaves and flowers, which may often be placed upon the props supporting the bellies of animals, are not encountered in copies. Further, although Torquay versions may display continuous rings in light brown enamel about the eyes of the beasts, these lack the reddish tinge found on original models. Although Torquay reproductions pose a threat to the collector, the danger is more apparent than real for few have been deceived.

17. *Derby Porcelain,* op. cit., pl. 21.
18. 'Early Derby Porcelain', op. cit., pl. 11F.

Plate 174. *Torquay reproduction of dry-edge Derby model of a doe, from the pair of a 'Stag and Doe at lodge' (J2). Note firecracks, sagging, a brilliant glaze with slight crazing, and the short comma shaped lines used to denote hide which are placed upon a peach coloured ground. The interior of this model is a greyish-white.*

***Plate 175.** 'Nanny-Goat suckling her Kid' (J4), companion to 'Billy-Goat' shown in Plate 176. 6½ins. (16.5cm). Dry-edge Derby c.1753.* N.C. Ashton collection

***Plate 176.** 'Billy-Goat' (J4), companion to 'Nanny-Goat' shown in Plate 175. 6½ins. (16.5cm). Dry-edge Derby c.1753.* N.C. Ashton collection

***Plate 177.** Torquay reproduction of the dry-edge Derby model of a seated billy-goat. Note the dull greasy looking glaze, rather clumsy scrolls and poor quality gilding upon the base. The interior is discoloured a deep blackish-brown. Both eyes are ringed with a continuous brown line.*

Fakes

The term 'Fake' is traditionally reserved to describe a genuine piece that has been altered at some time after manufacture in a manner calculated to enhance its market value. This regrettable practice, which is less commonly seen on figures than useful wares, may entail application of enamel to a model issued in the white, embellishment of existing decoration, the addition of a spurious factory mark, or the removal of an unwanted one such as that of the Samson Factory. The whole subject has been reviewed both by Wallace Elliot[19] and by George Savage.[20]

When a lead glaze is reheated in a muffle kiln, many years after its glost firing, so that enamels may be affixed to the surface, many tell-tale blemishes are produced. These may include the appearance of myriads of tiny air bubbles within its substance, loss of lustre, staining and heavy sanding. Such defects may not be especially severe if refiring is effected within a few months of issue. However, similar but slight blemishes were mentioned by Josiah Wedgwood in his correspondence with Sadler and Green to whom he had sent creamware for transfer printing. The defects are also found on enamelled examples of figures issued by the Derby factory prior to 1756 and on those from the Girl-in-a-Swing manufactory. Here, it should be recalled, probably all models were issued in the white so that coloured specimens that survive might most properly be deemed fakes! When the process of enamelling is delayed for over two hundred years, the results may be catastrophic, for both paste and glaze absorb foreign particles which profoundly alter their physical properties. Soft paste becomes discoloured a dark brown or black, and both any existing colour and freshly applied enamels become debased. Dr. Severne Mackenna[21] describes these results seen on a raised anchor Chelsea bust of the Duke of Cumberland (B49) that an unknown modern faker had attempted to enamel. These hazards are usually sufficient, mercifully, to deter such artists from turning their unwelcome attentions towards eighteenth century English porcelain figures.

The more common examples of faking consist of useful wares to which a rare ground colour, such as claret for Chelsea or apple green for Worcester, has been appended. The high prices paid during the earlier part of this century for Chinese vases with black ground, called *famille noire,* diverted the attentions of fakers to this form of decoration which had the additional advantage of serving to conceal any other unwanted adornment. Familiarity with the true colours, and debasement of any surviving eighteenth century decoration may assist identification, whilst weakness in drawing, over-crowding of design and unevenness of the surface will also facilitate exposure of fakes. Clobbering, especially with 'foul red' on top of underglaze blue, may also be encountered, whilst gilding may be added to an otherwise banal piece. The latter is frequently rather brash and never displays the sumptuous appearance of the gold on Chelsea wares and figures. The number of English porcelain figures treated in this fashion must be exceedingly small.

It is, of course, a very simple matter to add a spurious factory mark in enamel overglaze. The collector is advised to ignore all marks and devices that do not accord with an opinion based on other data. Reproductions of Chelsea plates may often bear gold anchors that do not accord with style and period but occasionally a faked mark may be found upon a genuine piece. Sometimes there may be an irony about spurious marks, as when I saw a most beautifully decorated red anchor Chelsea dish which sported a large gold anchor upon the inferior surface of its base. The perpetrator of this double crime was not only ignorant of the nature of his possession but also ran the risk that it might be rejected as no more than a reproduction on account of the obviously phoney

19. 'Reproductions and Fakes' by W. Elliot, *Transactions,* English Ceramic Circle, 1939, Vol. 2, No. 7, pp. 67-82.

20. *Forgeries, Fakes and Reproductions,* op. cit., p. 71.

21. *Chelsea Porcelain, the Triangle and Raised Anchor Wares,* op. cit., p. 71.

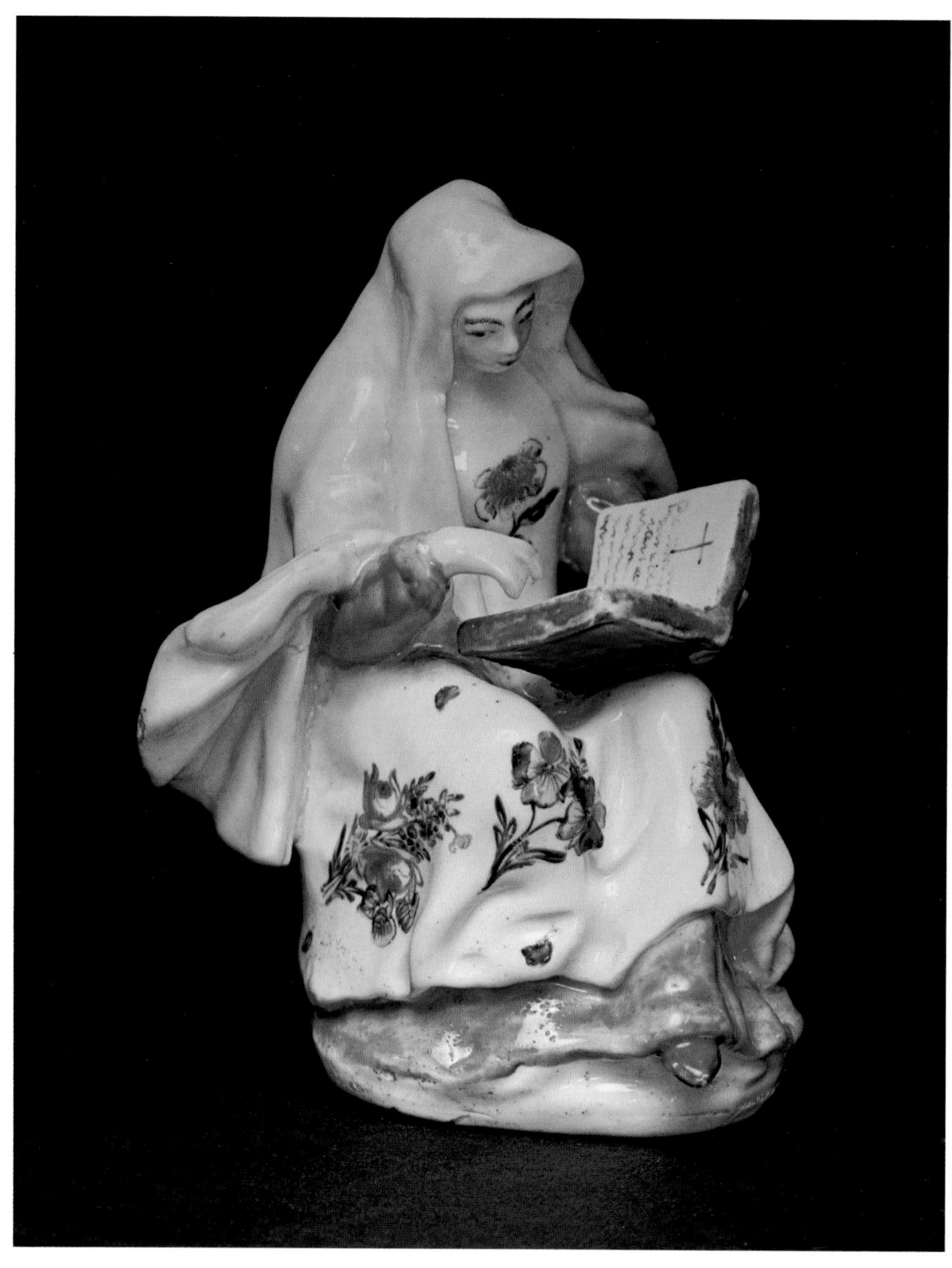

Colour Plate Z. *'A nun seated reading from a book' (Q27). 4¾ins. (12.1cm). Chaffers' Liverpool c.1758. The palette and style of enamel painting has been associated with John Bolton of Kentish Town.* David Thorn collection

mark! Unwanted marks, such as those relating to the Samson factory, may be scraped away and the surface gloss restored by a touch of varnish. More sophisticated fakers remove the mark with hydrofluoric acid. When the results of such handiwork are viewed obliquely beneath a bright light, the altered surface texture and sometimes also the ghost outline of the mark may be seen.

Marks may also be cut into the inferior surface of a model with a fine drill such as that used by a dental surgeon. The dry-edge Derby model of the a snuff taker (J33) from the author's collection, received this attention when some former owner cut the letters 'D.V.' (duc de Vilroi) doubtless in the hope that the figure might be mistaken for one created at Mennecy. Nearly always, there is a cleanness and freshness about these modern incisions which contrast with the discoloration of other zones of unglazed body. Fakers may sometimes add the mark of a triangle to Chelsea models and wares in order to suggest that they were made prior to 1749 and, hence, to increase their desirability. It is, of course, impossible to reproduce the heaped up edges of an incised mark upon porcelain once it has emerged from the biscuit kiln. I have actually seen a first period Chelsea beaker, which had been unmarked, bearing a phoney incised triangle. Strangely enough, faked raised anchor marks are exceptionally rare despite the fact that they should not be too difficult to make and lute on to a figure.

Damage and Restoration

It is salutary to recall how, in 1976, a raised anchor Chelsea model of 'Scapino' (B37), in near mint condition, fetched over £5,000 at auction, whilst an exactly similar but heavily restored figure realised only £500 in that same year. Clearly the identification of damage, together with assessment of restoration, are skills essential to anybody who wishes to collect antique porcelain especially such objects as fragile figures. Nearly always restoration is effected in a composition which, in modern times, usually includes a hypoxy resin that sets extremely hard. Before it has set completely, it is smoothed over with a very fine glass paper and painted with oil pigments. Owing to the difficulty in matching exactly surviving colours, it is necessary to overpaint to a greater or lesser extent areas that are undamaged. The work of the most highly skilled restorer is identifiable by the smallest amount of overpainting. Several coats of a very thin, transparent, clear varnish are then sprayed over the area, each application being carried slightly wider than the preceding one, thereby concealing as far as possible the junction between varnish and normal glaze. Sometimes, portions of a badly damaged model may be pirated as spare parts and the author has seen a segment from the brim of a lady's hat used to replace the peak of a jockey cap worn by a huntsman, and the gun taken from a Derby huntsman transferred to a similar model from Bow. Prior to the advent of very strong modern glues, metal pillars were often used to attach a decapitated head to the torso and, unless these were made of stainless steel, corrosion or rust often caused problems. Damage to a very rare piece may, exceptionally, be made good with a porcelain prosthesis. The missing part is modelled in wax or clay and a plaster of paris mould constructed. The casting, which is usually constructed from a hard paste formula, is glazed and given a single firing before enamels are fixed to the surface in a muffle kiln. When the figure is otherwise in perfect condition, the last process may be carried out after luting the appendage to the model, but, if there is any danger of disintegration in the muffle kiln, the coloured section is later cemented into position.

Varnish feels slightly tacky to the exploring finger and warmer than lead glaze to the tip of the tongue. There may be a distinct smell of turpentine about a newly repaired figure, whilst old varnish becomes discoloured yellow. When porcelain is struck with metal lightly, it will emit a resonant ping, whereas if areas replaced by composition are tapped, they give a dull note. If any doubt remains, provided permission has been granted, a pin-point may be dragged over the surface which will scarcely mark even a soft glaze but will cut deeply into varnish. One dealer, I know, prefers to bite suspect zones of a model though not everybody is equipped to give this demonstration of dental prowess. The marriage of parts from different models may be betrayed by minor differences of scale and colour and more rarely by the absurdity of the graft when a fishing net may replace a spade! Hard paste prostheses are evident from the colder tone of the glaze, poorly matching colours and sometimes by brilliant brassy gilding which are most often seen in replacement of sconces and candle holders.

The ultra-violet lamp is a most valuable adjunct to the assessment of restoration and several portable mains models are advertised in relevant journals. The apparatus is easy to handle and, even in the hands of a novice, completely reliable and safe. The light is propagated within a quartz tube filled with mercury vapour and is screened with tinted glass. There are two different models. The first passes maximum radiation at 2,537 Angstrom units because it is fitted with a short-wave filter, and is more suited for research into the nature of pastes and glazes than for revealing restoration. The second, which is the standard model and which has no short-wave filter, and is best suited for detection of restoration, operates at 3,660 Angstrom units. All surface dust and dirt must be removed from the object to be examined which is then viewed in a darkened room within one to two feet of the lamp. Hard paste clad in a feldspathic glaze will fluoresce a deep purple; soft paste covered with a lead glaze will appear as a purplish blue; whilst composition and varnish will show up a whitish-yellow. The finest hair line at the site of a clean break to a limb that has been stuck together will be immediately apparent. Under the mercury-lamp the widest extent covered by varnish will be revealed but this may be very much greater than the underlying restoration. An examination with an ultra violet lamp of a Chelsea-Derby shepherdess which had been restored, showed that the only remaining area of purplish-blue fluorescence was the brim of the maiden's hat! Recently a pair of Bow 'Elements' which appeared to have been extensively repaired and overpainted, were sold at auction for £160. The new owner removed the varnish and paint and found very little damage. His purchase was probably worth £350. This is a situation in which an ultra-violet lamp would not have helped a would-be purchaser and anyway it is not always possible to use them in auction room premises.

X-rays may, very occasionally, prove helpful, for they will usually show reduced density of composition compared to the porcelain body and will also uncover metal pillars inserted into a detached head to secure it to the neck. However, the grave dangers associated with gamma irradiation must be appreciated and none but a qualified radiologist or radiographer should ever use this method. The high radio-density of porcelain, especially that which contains bone ash, is such that by plain radiography it may be difficult even to determine whether a model has a central cavity or is solid cast and the irregular contours of the figure add to the difficulties. However, Dr. Ronald Grainger and the author adapted the procedure of tomography to show that an early Bow Turk was cast solid.[22] In essence, by moving the plate and X-ray tube in a circle, whilst maintaining their relative positions, it is possible to blur out of focus all radiological details other than those pertaining to the zone lying equidistant between the two. In this manner, it is possible to obtain radiographs which are, in effect, horizontal penny slices of the model at any level desired.

An appreciation of the extent of damage and restoration must be followed

22. 'Evidence that some Bow Figures were cast Solid' by Peter Bradshaw and Ronald Grainger, *Journal of the Northern Ceramic Society*, 1972-73, Vol. 1, pp. 41-44.

by a decision whether to accept or reject the model. Few such fragile objects are likely to have survived in pristine condition after the passage of two hundred years and to insist on rare perfection may tempt others to supply the need by artificial means. Owing to the obvious vulnerability of figures and because they were issued in relatively small numbers, more damage is tolerated by collectors than would be acceptable in useful wares. It would, today, be impossible to form an interesting collection of figures in mint condition even with unlimited funds. Obviously, rather more damage is acceptable on a rare or exceptionally beautiful model than upon a commonplace item such as the Chelsea-Derby 'Milton' or 'Shakespeare'. However, it is wise to strive to obtain models only in the best possible state that the collector can afford. It is far better to own a small collection of interesting figures in fine condition than to be the sad possessor of several cabinets full of heavily restored porcelains.

Clean fractures across the neck, or involving limbs, are not especially serious for, it will be recalled, the head and limbs were separately cast and then luted to the main section before the biscuit firing. Fragmentation of adjacent areas of face and head, portions of the trunk, or of whole segments of limbs necessitating their replacement with composition, seems generally unacceptable. Missing finger tips, chips to edges of garments, flaking of leaves off the superior surface of the base, broken flower petals and even quite extensive breakage involving bocage and sconces, do not impair the artistic impact of the model itself and may be tolerated. It should be remembered that it is extremely difficult to restore damage involving figures in the white, whether glazed or biscuit, convincingly, and when damage is evident which would be obtrusive without repair, such figures are best left to less discerning collectors.

Almost invisible restoration can be effected on enamelled models though, for aesthetic reasons, repair should be restricted to the minimum and involve the least possible overpainting. Missing fingers are easily replaced and it is no great task to treat chipped edges in a way that makes these blemishes less noticeable. Accessories necessary for proper identification of subject, or which are characteristic of a particular model, must be either replaced if missing or restored if damaged. It would seem to the author patently ridiculous leaving a model of a musician lacking his musical instrument or a huntsman devoid of his gun. Sometimes, however, a missing accessory may seem almost irrelevant, for example, the loss of the reaping hook from the hand of the lady representing Autumn (Plate 150, Chapter X) from the set of Champion's Bristol 'Classical Seasons'. Here, the identity of the lady is assured by the fruiting vine at her side and up-turned basket of grapes at her feet and any restoration would be superfluous. Conversely, the model of a Blackamoor stepping over a lion, emblematic of Africa (Plate 113, Chapter VIII), which was issued both by the Chelsea and Derby factories, is immediately recognised by his elephant head-dress. The protruding trunk is especially vulnerable and when missing should be replaced, for to leave it will prove to be a continuing source of irritation. Few would contemplate purchase of a model missing a head, arm or leg for it would be like possessing a table with three legs; artistically unacceptable and serving no useful purpose. However, the model of an 'Actor' lacking a head, attributed to the Derby factory, now in the Victoria and Albert Museum, is unique and most collectors would, given the opportunity, purchase such a model. Clearly restoration would be impossible without knowledge of a specimen with head complete. Restoration is a highly skilled art and it is better to leave damage as it is rather than to accept the services of a second class repairer. Most reputable dealers will be able to recommend a porcelain restorer who will restrict his work to the minimum necessary to make the figure appear at its best, and this will command an appropriate fee.

Firecracks are almost a mark of authenticity and unless they are prominently located across the front of a figure, they are best left alone. Figures with unsightly firecracks should most often be rejected. Smoke staining and sanding may be characteristic of certain phases of a particular factory and, for this reason, some may wish to include examples in their collection. However, such blemishes will be reflected in lower costs. There is nothing commendable about dirt. Models should be placed upon a soft cloth in a plastic bowl and washed with soap solution in tepid water. An old fashioned shaving-brush is an invaluable aid. Staining of soft paste usually cannot be removed but dirt and grease may be bubbled out of crevices or firecracks with a solution of hydrogen peroxide available from most chemist shops without prescription.

Collecting

Before embarking upon a hobby that will entail the outlay of several hundreds of pounds per annum, it is wise to review eighteenth century English porcelain figures in depth. This may be achieved by visits to national and private collections. The widest range available in London is displayed in the Victoria and Albert Museum which contains the Schreiber, Statham, Allen and Broderip collections. Important early models are in the London Museum, whilst in the British Museum is housed the Franks collection. Some interesting figures may also be found in the Lady Binning collection in Fenton House, Hampstead. There is a fine display of Derby models in the City Museum and Art Gallery of that city, and many later examples can be seen in the Museum of the Royal Crown Derby Porcelain Company. Cookworthy's Plymouth and Bristol, and Champion's Bristol figures are amply represented both in the Plymouth and Bristol City Museum and Art Galleries and a seasoning of like models are contained in the County Museum, Truro. The rare Worcester figures in the Rissik Marshall Collection are in the Ashmolean Museum, Oxford, and also in the Dyson Perrins Museum in Worcester. Lord Fisher's magnificent collection of English figures includes many Meissen prototypes and may be viewed in the Fitzwilliam Museum, Cambridge. The Cecil Higgins Collection, in Bedford, displays a feast of rare Chelsea and other English groups and models, as well as a spectrum of Meissen and other Continental figures. Lord Bearsted's Collection, in Upton House, near Bambury, Warwickshire, contains an imposing array of gold anchor Chelsea groups including Fable groups and a set of Apollo and the Nine Muses, not to mention other models from Derby and Bow. Sadly, much of the Lady Ludlow Collection at Luton Hoo House, near Luton, Bedfordshire, has been dispersed. There is an assortment of Meissen, Chelsea, Bow and Plymouth figures in Saltram House, Plympton, Devon, and another distributed about the rooms of Temple Newsam House, Leeds. Continental porcelains and figures are seasoned with a few made in this country in the magnificent collections in Waddeston Manor, Buckinghamshire.

In the United States of America, English porcelain figures are concentrated in the Museum of Fine Arts, Boston, Massachusetts, where the Sigmund Katz and Alfred Hutton Collections are to be found. The great collection of Judge Irwin Untermyer is in the Metropolitan Museum, New York. Exquisite porcelains, including many early Chelsea models, are in the Colonial Williamsburg Foundation, Williamsburg, Virginia, whilst a selection of English models is displayed in the Rhode Island School of Design, Providence.

Scholarship is an essential ingredient in the development of a collection. Initially books that give general coverage of the subject will meet the need but, before very long, more detailed and specialised works will be required. Public libraries and others attached to technical colleges and universities will often be able to obtain obscure references in short supply via the inter-libraries loan service or to supply photocopies from elsewhere on payment of a small fee. Sooner or later most collectors will want to gather together their own reference shelf containing standard textbooks and sundry items of interest, and a Bibliography for further reading is given at the end of this book.

Book learning and the viewing of porcelain through glass are both worthless unless the collector can gain familiarity with figures and wares by handling them. This facility can be obtained by visits to private collections, dealers' premises, antique fairs and auction previews. The collector is advised to make a friend of a reputable dealer and to build up mutual confidence by making regular purchases and consultations. Once this has been established, most dealers will allow stock to be handled and will answer serious inquiries by practical instruction based on long personal experience. They will, almost certainly, visit the London salerooms and bid on commission for a client. This is a most valuable service for those who reside outside London and who would otherwise have to entail considerable expense to make a personal inspection of the condition of a potential purchase before the auction. The more important auctions are advertised in the national press and in periodicals covering the field of the fine arts. Catalogues may be purchased by application to the auction rooms, either to cover a particular sale or by subscription for coverage of all sales pertaining to a special subject.

It is necessary to be able to add to a collection at least once a year if interest is to be sustained. Availability is, therefore, of paramount importance for it would be futile to attempt to collect Chippendale furniture in outer Mongolia or Sung pottery in Iceland. English eighteenth century porcelain figures are still plentiful in the United Kingdom, though annually they become more difficult to obtain. There are not many who live outside the British Isles who collect them and this contrasts with the world market for the porcelains of France, Germany and from the Orient. Thus, in times when our national currency has been debased, there are unlikely to be many foreign buyers, whose countries enjoy more robust economies, pricing the home based collector out of the bidding except, perhaps, for the most exceptional or rare pieces. Indeed, it is probably true to say that many eighteenth century English porcelain figures are less expensive than some of the more sophisticated modern figurines. Rising prices need not necessarily be a disincentive to the collector, for nobody but a fool or a millionaire would deliberately purchase items that were declining in value. Nevertheless, inflation may stimulate interest in the fine arts by those who have lost faith in their national currency. One dealer in the South West once told me how a stranger had come to him with a cheque made out for £3,000 and asked him to buy items of porcelain up to that figure less commission which he thought would be a good hedge against inflation. In due course when the goods had been obtained, the dealer telephoned his client to inform him that the porcelain was now available for his inspection. He received the staggering reply: "Oh no. I have absolutely no interest in china. Just have it packed up in a good stout box and send it to the strong room of my bank!" So it is that beautiful things are debased to the level of share certificates and salted away from the eyes of those who would greatly appreciate them. It is small comfort to learn that of the 1,500 pictures painted by Vincent van Gogh there are 3,000 in the New World or that more antique English furniture crosses the Atlantic ocean in one year than could possibly have been made during the entire eighteenth century!

A large proportion of the pleasure in collecting is the sharing of knowledge with friends and interested acquaintances. There are numerous clubs and societies which provide suitable facilities including journals, news letters, general meetings and lectures. Also many arrange annual seminars, often in association with technical colleges and universities, where collectors may meet experts in their field of interest. A collection differs from a mere accumulation of objects only by the presence of a theme that connects the items. Many relating to subject matter have already been described in earlier chapters. Alternatively, themes may concern materials such as models in the white but glazed, in the biscuit, or in enamel and gilt. Collectors may prefer to specialise in the work of a particular modeller or decorative artist, or, perhaps in baroque, rococo or neo-classical style. It would be difficult today to emulate Lady Charlotte Schreiber and form a collection representative of all English porcelain factories of the eighteenth century. In fact, in the light of modern scholarship, her collection was not particularly illustrative of her avowed aim. Nowadays it is famed for the beauty of the porcelain it contains. It should always be possible for an informed viewer to suggest what might next be purchased for inclusion in a collection and, equally, what would be inappropriate. Omission of the work of Nicolas François Gauron, or a group inspired by a painting by Angelica Kauffmann, in a collection of Derby biscuit would be obvious gaps to be filled, whilst an enamelled Meissen figure would be a stranger in such company.

Prices

Less than fifty years ago, W.B. Honey wrote: "Bow figures in fair condition cost £10 or more, but may be less . . . early Derby figures rarely exceed £10 and the commoner Chelsea-Derby £5 or £6 . . ."[23] In 1980 a Bow model of a 'Levantine Lady' (H14) was sold for £580, a Derby chinoiserie group emblematic of 'Feeling' (J34) for £6,800, and a Chelsea-Derby biscuit group portraying 'Two Virgins awakening Cupid' (M195) realised £450. Inflation has for a very long time been a feature of free economies and it is likely to remain with us whatever politicians may say or do, so that any review of fine art prices will assuredly be obsolete before it is printed. However, a few remarks of a general nature about prices may prove helpful to the collector.

Auction prices of eighteenth century English porcelain figures will depend on the competitiveness of bidding, scarcity, condition and quality, all of which are closely linked to the factory of origin, subject and the style of presentation. Though it is obvious that two rich men bidding against one another will create a high price, it is less well appreciated that dealers' prices may vary from one area to another where the item may hold special interest for local collectors. Rockingham porcelain is, for example, likely to be far more expensive in the North Midlands, and Plymouth or Bristol wares to be more expensive in the South West of England. The all important matter of condition has already been mentioned in an earlier section of this chapter and here values for figures in fine condition are discussed. Scarcity may enhance value despite the lack of artistic merit. In 1977 an ugly long-necked pair of white Worcester 'Gardeners' (Q14) was auction for £5,000, whilst in 1981 the rare Girl-in-a-Swing 'Britannia lamenting the death of Frederick Prince of Wales' (E16) sold for £10,000. Longton Hall 'Snowmen' models rarely come up for sale but would probably fetch more than £600. A crudely fashioned white nun reading a book (Q27), attributed to the Chaffers' manufactory, was sold in 1976 for £200; following a resurgence of interest in Liverpool porcelains, an identical figure was sold six months later for £480. However, exceptional bargains may still be had by those with special knowledge; in 1980 a pair of putti, representing Spring and Summer, most probably from Gilbody's Liverpool factory but

23. *English Pottery and Porcelain* (London, 1933) by W.B. Honey, pp. 243-253, 'Collecting'.

wrongly catalogued as Derby, was sold for £200.

Quality is linked especially with red anchor Chelsea figures and wares and this is reflected by auction prices which in the period 1979-80 included: 'Mezzotino' (C8) £2,300; a pair of seated 'Monk' and 'Nun' (C105) £1,250; a peasant woman representing 'Summer' (C98) £950; and a 'Girl playing a piccolo' (C51) £550. The increasing shortage of red anchor figures for sale has prompted wealthy collectors to seek dry-edge Derby and in 1980 prices included: a chinoiserie group portraying 'Smell' (J34) £6,750; a lady eating fruit symbolising 'Taste' (J33) £760; an old man representing 'Winter' (J32) £540. A few Bow figures of quality, like the seated nun reading a book (see Plate 78, Chapter VII) which cost £680, may be dear but the vast majority are undervalued, probably because no book on the manufactory has been published since 1926.[24] A Bow sportsman and companion (H68) was sold for £750 in 1978 and in the same year a 'Boy Toper' (H26) realised £450, whilst in 1981 a complete set of white 'Rustic Seasons' (H92) of c.1755 was auctioned for £1,100. Figures of the Derby Pale Family may cost £300 to £450 and even pairs may be obtained for £650 to £750, with pairs of sheep or cattle at £200 to £350. Derby figures of 1760-70 may be obtained for about £200 to £300 and pairs for around £450. However, once again the few examples that display quality may cost a great deal more, like the pair of 'Italian Farmer' holding a cockerel and 'Wife' with a hen (K56) which was auctioned for £860. Chelsea-Derby figures are amongst the cheapest ranging from £90 to £250, though some groups may be priced at £450. Complete sets, often assembled from singles or pairs, are never cheap and the Chelsea-Derby 'Four Elements' (M3) were sold for £650, the 'French Seasons' (M123) for £600, and the 'Four Quarters of the Globe' (M200) for £850, all in 1978-80. Longton Hall figures of peasants of the period 1753-57, and other figures of 1758-60, display quality and are scarce and therefore are likely to command prices in excess of £600.

The earliest models are, not surprisingly, the most expensive. A stiffly fashioned Chelsea 'Ceres' (A13) of 1749, was sold recently for £3,000, the ungainly Bow Muse 'Erato' (G14) for £750 and the Derby 'Lady seated with a mandolin' (K14) for £680. Subject also affects price; at the cheapest end of the scale are models of putto, cupids and children, notables and mythological themes. A transitional Derby 'Cybele' (J25) sold in 1978 for £160, 'Britannia' (K78) for £120, 'Milton' (M297) for £95, a Bow pair of Neptune and Ceres (representing Earth and Water) (H100) for £275, and even a red anchor Chelsea 'Cupid in Disguise' (C115) was sold in 1980 for £250. Intermediate in price are pastoral subjects, dancers, musicians, notables, monks and nuns. A pair of gold anchor shepherd and shepherdess would cost about £550 to £650, a Bow version £450 to £550 and Derby examples a little less. Turks and Levantines are more expensive and a Bow pair (H14) sold in 1980 for £980. At the dearest end of the price range are raised anchor Chelsea birds, which rarely obtain less than £5,000 a pair and may fetch up to £10,000. Beggars, peasants from the Cries of Paris and characters from the Italian Comedy are also expensive, and in 1979-80 the red anchor models of the 'Jewish Pedlar' (C30) and 'Dottore Baloardo' (C7) were sold respectively for £10,000 and £3,300. Somewhat oddly Bow figures of the Commedia dell' Arte are far cheaper, and in 1978 a white 'Pantalone' was purchased for £200, and an enamelled 'Pedrolino' (H8) was offered for £500. The best representations of chinoiserie are very dear, whilst the dry-edge Derby animals also attract wealthy collectors; in 1981 a pair of 'Florentine Boars' (J1), one with a missing leg, fetched £1,300.

The style of presentation will also affect price. Only the best biscuit figures make more than £150 though fine groups are around £450, whilst white glazed

24. *Bow Porcelain* (London, 1926) by Frank Hurlbutt.

figures are cheaper than those which are enamelled. Finely modelled figures on simple bases in the baroque style are the most expensive, and some of the earlier examples of the rococo which retain something of baroque simplicity, are greatly admired. Later rococo figures and groups on highly sculptured based with huge bocages, some with attached candle sconces, have lost the appeal of earlier years when rich collectors bid huge sums to secure examples, and the neo-classical style is no longer eagerly sought after.

The collector is advised to rely more on his own taste than to accept blindly the opinions expressed by self-acclaimed experts or academics whose opinions are just as fickle as those of the general public. Had an aspiring collector heeded their promptings in the late nineteenth or early twentieth centuries, and purchased gold anchor Chelsea groups, he would, in terms of real money, have made a very poor investment. Good taste has no firm anchorage and varies from one generation to another, between individuals and cultures. It may be born of love, nurtured by experience and salted with scholarship. George Savage[25] has reminded us that good taste may be defined as an intuitive feeling for what is artistically and socially right and that it depends upon the appreciation of quality of design, in craftsmanship and in materials. This order of precedence is of paramount importance, for otherwise an object made of gold would always be esteemed above one fashioned from bronze, regardless of workmanship. It is, of course, true that good workmanship is rarely lavished upon inferior materials or used to execute a poor design, for a fine craftsman is incapable of bad taste. The collector should first seek quality and then, should his taste alter and assuredly it will, there can be little difficulty in the exchange of old loves for new.

There is a tale of a connoisseur who in a long life had assembled a series of ceramic collections, each one of which expressed a stage in the maturation of his taste. Eventually he sold everything he had ever possessed and purchased a single white vase of exquisite form, clad in an immaculate glaze, which had been made in the eleventh century for the Imperial Sung Court. This was ultimate perfection!

25. *Forgeries, Fakes and Reproductions*, op. cit., p. 247.

The Appendices

Appendices A-P list the figures of the various manufactories. The figures are numbered, titled and described and, where possible, a source from which further information may be sought, and in many cases in which an illustration may be found, is quoted. The size given for the figure is that which appears in the work referred to. The reader should bear in mind that the size of a figure may vary considerably due to the vagaries of the firing process. Where the entry ends *See Plate 00,* this refers to an illustration in the present volume.

Appendix R illustrates and describes the marks used by the Manufactories. Appendix S gives additional information on the Commedia dell 'Arte, and Appendix T lists the mythological figures used extensively as the subjects of 18th century porcelain figures.

The following abbreviations are used:

Books and other Publications

Barrett: *Worcester Porcelain* (London, 1953) by F.A. Barrett.

Barrett & Thorpe: *Derby Porcelain* (London, 1971) by F.A. Barrett and A.L. Thorpe.

Bradley: *Ceramics of Derbyshire 1770-1975* (Tiverton, 1977) edited by H.G. Bradley.

Bristol City Mus. Cat: Catalogue of the exhibition of 'Bristol Porcelain to celebrate the bicentenary 1770-1970' held at the City Museum and Art Gallery, Bristol.

Bryant: *Chelsea Porcelain Toys* (London, 1925) by G.E. Bryant.

Cheyne Book: *The Cheyne Book of Chelsea China and Pottery* (London, 1973) edited by Reginald Blunt.

Cushion (A): *Porcelain* (London, 1973) by J.P. Cushion.

Cushion (B): *English Porcelain* (London, 1974) by J.P. Cushion.

E.C.C., 1948 ex. cat: Commemorative catalogue of an 'Exhibition of English Pottery and Porcelain' of members of the English Ceramic Circle, held at the V & A.

English Ceramics: *English Ceramics 1580-1830* (London, 1977) edited by R.J. Charleston and D. Towner, published as a 'Commemorative Catalogue of Ceramics and Enamels to celebrate the 50th Anniversary of the English Ceramic Circle, 1927-1977'.

Foster: 'Chelsea Scent Bottles — Girl in a Swing and Another Type' by Kate Foster, *Transactions,* E.C.C., 1967, Vol. 6, pt. 3, pp. 284-291.

Gilhespy (A): *Crown Derby Porcelain* (Leigh-on-Sea, 1951) by F. Brayshaw Gilhespy.

Gilhespy (B): *Derby Porcelain* (London, 1961) by F. Brayshaw Gilhespy.

Godden (A): *Connoisseur Year Book* (London, 1957) by Geoffrey Godden.

Godden (B): *An Illustrated Encyclopaedia of British Pottery and Porcelain* (London, 1966) by Geoffrey Godden.

Harris: *Porcelain Figurines* (Maidenhead, 1975) by N. Harris.

Herbert Allen: *Catalogue of the Herbert Allen Collection of English Porcelain* (London, 1917) by B. Rackham.

Hobson: *Catalogue of English Porcelain in the British Museum* (1905) by R.L. Hobson.

Honey (A): *Old English Porcelain* (London, 1928) by W.B. Honey.

Honey (B): *English Pottery and Porcelain* (London, 1933) by W.B. Honey.

Hughes (B): *English Pottery and Porcelain Figures* (London, 1964) by G.B. Hughes.

Hughes (B & T): *English Porcelain and Bone China* (London, 1955) by G.B. and Therle Hughes.

Hurlbutt (A): *Old Derby Porcelain, its artists and workmen* (London, 1925) by Frank Hurlbutt.

Hurlbutt (B): *Bow Porcelain* (London, 1926) by Frank Hurlbutt.

King (A): *Chelsea Porcelain* (London, 1922) by William King.

King (B): *English Porcelain Figures of the 18th Century* (London, 1924) by William King.

Lane: *English Porcelain Figures of the 18th Century* (London, 1961) by Arthur Lane.

Lane & Charleston: 'Girl in a Swing Porcelain and Chelsea' by A. Lane and R.J. Charleston, *Transactions,* English Ceramic Circle, 1962, Vol. 5, pt. 3, pp. 111-144.

Ludlow: *Catalogue of the Lady Ludlow Collection* (London, 1932) by Arthur Hayden.

Mackenna (A): *Chelsea Porcelain, the triangle and raised anchor wares* (Leigh-on-Sea, 1943) by F. Severne Mackenna.

Mackenna (B): *Chelsea Porcelain, the red anchor Wares* (Leigh-on-Sea, 1951) by F. Severne Mackenna.

Mackenna (C): *Chelsea Porcelain, the gold anchor Wares* (Leigh-on-Sea, 1952) by F. Severne Mackenna.

Mackenna (D): *Cookworthy's Plymouth and Bristol Porcelain* (Leigh-on-Sea, 1946) by F. Severne Mackenna.

Mackenna (E): *Champion's Bristol Porcelain* (Leigh-on-Sea, 1946) by F. Severne Mackenna.

Marshall: *Coloured Worcester Porcelain of the 18th Century* (London, 1954) by H.R. Marshall.

Morley-Fletcher: *Investing in Pottery and Porcelain* (London, 1968) by Hugo Morley-Fletcher.

Plymouth City Mus. Cat: Catalogue of the Exhibition of Porcelain in Memory of Thomas Cookworthy, held at the Plymouth City Art Gallery and Museum in 1968.

Ramsey: *Complete Encyclopaedia of Antiques* (London, 1962) ed. L.G.G. Ramsey.

Rice: *Rockingham Ornamental Porcelain* (London, 1965) by D.G. Rice.

Rosenfeld: *Porcelain Figures of the 18th Century* (New York, 1949) by David Rosenfeld.

Sandon: *The Illustrated Guide to Worcester Porcelain* (London, 1969) by Henry Sandon.

Savage (A): *Eighteenth Century English Porcelain* (Bungay, 1952) by George Savage.

Savage (B): *A Dictionary of Antiques* (London, 1970) by George Savage.

Savage, Newman & Cushion: *Dictionary of Ceramic Terms* (London, 1974) by George Savage, Harold Newman and John Cushion.

Schreiber: *Catalogue of English Porcelain, Earthenware, Enamels, etc., collected by Charles Schreiber, Esq., M.P., and the Lady Charlotte Elizabeth Schreiber and presented to the Victoria and Albert Museum in 1884* (London, 1915) by Bernard Rackham, Vol. 1, Porcelain.

Scott: *Antique Porcelain Digest* (Bath, 1961) by Cleo M. and G. Ryland Scott.

Sotheby's: Sotheby's Auction Sales Catalogues.

Stoner: *Chelsea, Bow and Derby Porcelain Figures* (Newport, 1955) by Frank Stoner.

Tait (A): Catalogue of the Exhibition of Bow Porcelain 1744-66, by H.G. Tait, held at the British Museum, October 1959-April 1960.

Tait (B): *Porcelain* (London, 1962) by H.G. Tait.

Trans. E.C.C.: Transactions of the English Ceramic Circle.

Trans. E.P.C.: Transactions of the English Porcelain Circle.

Treasures of the National Trust: *Treasures of the National Trust* (London, 1976) edited by R. Fedden.

Twitchett: *Derby Porcelain* (London, 1980) by John Twitchett.

Untermyer: *Chelsea and Other English Porcelain, Pottery and Enamels in the Irwin Untermyer Collection* (Cambridge, Mass., 1957) by Yvonne Hackenbroch.

Watney (A): *Longton Hall Porcelain* (London, 1957) by Bernard Watney.
Watney (B): 'The King, the Nun and Other Figures' by Bernard Watney, *Transactions,* English Ceramic Circle, 1968, Vol. 7, pt. 2, pp. 48-58.
Williamsburg: *Chelsea Porcelain at Williamsburg* (Williamsburg, Virginia, 1977) edited by John C. Austin.
Williams (A): Catalogue of an Exhibition of Early Derby Porcelain 1750-1770 by Winifred Williams, held at 3 Bury St., St. James's, London, 9th-18th January, 1973.
Williams (B): Catalogue of an Exhibition of White 18th Century European Porcelain, by Winifred Williams, held at 3 Bury St., St. James's, London, 10th-27th June, 1975.

Museums and Collections

Ashmolean – Ashmolean Museum, Oxford.
Ashton Col. — Norman C. Ashton Collection (private).
BM — British Museum, London.
Castle Mus. — Castle Museum, Nottingham.
Cecil Higgins Mus. — Cecil Higgins Art Gallery, Bedford.
Bristol City Mus. — City Museum and Art Gallery, Bristol.
Derby Mus. — City Museum and Art Gallery, Derby.
Derby Porc. Co. Mus. — Royal Crown Derby Porcelain Company Museum, Derby.
Fitzwilliam — Fitzwilliam Museum, Cambridge.
Lord Bearsted col. — Lord Bearsted's Collection, Upton House, Warwickshire.
Nat. Mus. Ireland — National Museum of Ireland, Dublin.
Saltram House — Saltram House, Plympton, Devon.
Sigmund Katz col. — Sigmund Katz Collection, Boston Museum of Fine Art, U.S.A.
Temple Newsam — Temple Newsam House, Leeds.
Truro Mus. — County Museum, Truro.
V & A — Victoria and Albert Museum, London.

Other Private Collections mentioned in the Appendices and and the Text

Dudley Delevingne Collection (now dispersed).
Dr. H.G.M. Edwards.
Mr. Leslie Godden.
Mr. and Mrs. John Mould.
Mrs. Margaret Newton.
Mr. Simon Spero.
Mr. David Thorn.
Mr. Robert Williams.

APPENDIX A
Chelsea Figures made prior to 1750

A1 Goat and Bee Creamer. Mackenna (A) pl. 1, fig. 1.
A2 'Seated Chinaman holding a Guinea Fowl' (teapot). Ibid., pl. 5, fig. 11. 'Seated Chinaman holding a Snake' (teapot). Ibid., pl. 5, fig. 12. 'Seated Chinaman holding a Parrot' (teapot). Williamsburg, pl. 2.
A3 'Seated Chinaman as Tea Caddy'. Untermyer, pl. 2, fig. 7.
A4 'Grotesque Chinaman', after the sage, Pu-tai Ho-shang (pastil burner). Lane, pl. 2A. *See Plate 13.*
A5 'Boy asleep upon a mattress', 6½ins. long. Ibid., pl. 2C.
A6 'Boy seated with a reed-pipe', 6ins. Ibid., pl. 2B.
A7 A pair of models of a boy seated upon rocks, 6ins. Sotheby's, 18-5-54, lot 138. One example in Fitzwilliam Museum.
A8 'Chinaman' standing before a table upon which rests a teapot, about 6ins. Trans. E.C.C., 1939, Vol. 2, No. 6, pl. XIA, porcelain figure; pl. XIB, engraving after Boucher. Note, this is probably a fragment of the Bow group (G44), emblematic of 'Fire', wrongly ascribed to Chelsea.
A9 'Chinese Fisherman', 8¾ins. Lane, pl. 3.
A10 'Rustic Lovers' (group); youth in tricorn hat faces a girl who sits upon his right knee restraining his left hand which lies upon her knee, 9ins. Ibid., pl. 4. See also E12.
A11 'Print Seller', after Cries of Paris by Bouchardon, 4½ins. Harris, p. 47, Chelsea model and Meissen prototype.
A12 'Milton', standing beside a plinth, after Scheemakers, 10ins. *Apollo,* 1943, Vol. 37, and Sotheby's, 18-5-54, lot 126.
A13 'Ceres' crowned with corn ears holding a sheaf and pruning hook, 12¼ins. Lane, pl. 1. *For later version see Plate 36.*
A14 Bust of the Duke of Cumberland (triangle mark), 5½ins. Trans. E.C.C., No. 3, 1933, pl. XVIIIA. *For later version see Plate 19.* Ibid; pl. XVIIIB, Staffordshire pottery version.
A15 Sphinxes (pair), with female busts and heads. *Apollo,* June 1960, p. 184, fig. V.
A16 'Reclining Greyhounds' (pair). Trans. E.C.C., 1960, Vol. 6, fig. 23.
A17 'Finches' (pair), after Vincennes prototypes, 6ins. Sotheby's, 19-5-70, lot 154. Saltram House No. 266T, a canary in similar paste and style, possibly Chelsea.
A18 'Squirrel eating a nut', 3⅜ins. Williamsburg, pl. 104.
A19 'Tawny Owls' (pair) 6ins. Sotheby's 27-4-76, lot 112.

APPENDIX B
Chelsea Figures made between 1750 and 1753

Birds modelled after illustrations in *A History of Uncommon Birds* **by George Edwards.** The plate numbers used in the first two volumes of the four issued, are those given in brackets after the title of the birds.

B1 'Arabian Bustards' (Pl. 12) 7ins. Christie's, 12-5-69, lot 173.
B2 'Black and White Chinese Pheasants' (Pl. 66) 8¼ins. Mackenna (A), pl. 32, fig. 67; pl. 33, fig. 68.
B3 'Blue Creeper and Golden-Headed Titmouse', perched on a single branch (Pl. 13) 5ins. Cheyne Book, pl. 13, no. 286.
B4 'Blue and Green Daws' (Pl. 236) 7¼ins. Untermyer, pl. 10, fig. 17.
B5 'Chinese Teals' (Pl. 102) 5⅝ins. Ibid., pl. 11, fig. 24.
B6 'Crested Red Butcher Bird' and 'Common Fork-Tailed Butcher Bird' (Pl. 54) 6¾ins. Cheyne Book, pl. 13, no. 285. *See Plate 15.*
B7 'Dusky Spotted Ducks' (Pl. 99) 5¼ins. Mackenna (A), pl. 34, fig. 70.
B8 'Greater Bullfinches' (Pl. 82) 4¾ins. Cheyne Book, pl. 13, no. 300.
B9 'Greater Indian Cranes' (Pl. 45) 9¼ins. Untermyer, pl. 13, fig. 15.
B10 'Greated Spotted Cuckoos' (Pl. 57) 7¾ins. Ibid., pl. 8, fig. 16.
B11 'Great Indian Flycatchers' (Pl. 79) 4⅛ins. Ibid., pl. 10, fig. 21.
B12 'Grey-Headed Woodpeckers' (Pl. 65) 5¼ins. Cheyne Book, pl. 13, no. 299.
B13 'Green Winged Doves' (Pl. 14) 5½ins. Untermyer, pl. 11, fig. 18.
B14 'Guan; or Quan' (Pl. 13) 8½ins. Cheyne Book, pl. 13, no. 298.
B15 'Little Brown and White Ducks' (Pl. 157) 3¼ins. Untermyer, pl. 10, fig. 20.
B16 'Little Black and White Ducks' (Pl. 100) 4¼ins. Ibid., pl. 11, fig. 19.
B17 'Little Hawk Owls' (Pl. 63) 7ins. Cheyne Book, pl. 13, No. 297.
B18 'Little White Partridges' (Pl. 72) 6ins. Untermyer, pl. 7, fig. 23.
B19 'Parakeets' (Pl. 6) 5ins. Ibid., pl. 11, fig. 22. *See Plate 14.*
B20 'Red Bellied Blue Birds' (Pl. 22) 7ins. Cheyne Book, pl. 13, No. 272.
B21 'Touracos' (Pl. 7) 8¼ins. Trans. E.P.C., 1931, No. III, plate IX.
B22 'Whip-Poor-Wills or Lesser Goat-Suckers' (Pl. 63) 6½ins. Ibid., pl. XI with copy of illustrative plate. *See Plate 16.*

Bird Models from Other Sources

B23 'Blue Tits', 4½ins. Cheyne Book, pl. 14, no. 271.
B24 'Buntings' (pair) 6¾ins. Ludlow, pl. 61, no. 143.
B25 'Canaries' (pair) 4¾ins. Trans. E.C.C., 1962, Vol. 5, pl. 132C; also Saltram House 368.T.
B26 'Crossbill', 3ins. Cheyne Book, pl. 14, No. 281.
B27 'Finches' (pair) 6ins. Trans. E.C.C., 1962, Vol. 5, pl. 133A, 133B, 133C.
B28 'Hen Harriers' (pair) 8ins. Scott, pl. 139, figs. 465, 466.
B29 'Parrots' (pair) 2⅞ins. Williamsburg, fig. 110.
B30 'Peacock'; and companion model of 'Peahen', 8ins. Cheyne Book, pl. 13, nos. 284 and 298; Mackenna (A), pl. 34, fig. 69.
B31 'Pheasant' (after oriental model) 6½ins. Mackenna (A), pl. 35, fig. 73.
B32 'Swans: Cob and Pen with cygnet', 8ins. Cheyne Book, pl. 13, no. 280.

Italian Comedy Characters
B33 'Dottore Baloardo' (after Reinicke) 7¼ins. Untermyer, pl. 39, fig. 14.
B34 'Dottore Baloardo' (after Watteau) 11½ins. Savage (A), pl. 10. Note, Ludlow, pl. 66, no. 158, illustrates a modern copy.
B35 'Isabella' (after Vecellio) 9½ins. Mackenna (A), pl. 38, fig. 78. *See Plate 17.*
B36 'Pantalone', bearded in skull-cap and gown holding a purse, 4½ins. Untermyer, pl. 21, fig. 13.
B37 'Scapino' (after Reinicke) 4½ins. Morley-Fletcher (A), p. 83. *See Colour Plate A.*
B38 'Scaramuzzi' (after Reinicke), in cap and tabaro dancing, 4½ins. Mackenna (A), pl. 39, fig. 79.

Chinese and Levantine Characters
B39 Chinoiserie group, 'Lady with Child and a Cat playing with a string toy' (after Boucher) 9¼ins. Lane, pl. 7.
B40 Chinoiserie group, 'Lady pouring chocolate from jug into a cup held by a Boy; A separate crouching Boy with fruit' *(en suite)* (after Boucher) 9ins. Mackenna (A), pl. 36, fig. 76.
B41 'Boy in leaf-shaped hat, cloak and cheeks puffed out' (after Watteau) 5ins. Ibid., pl. 36, fig. 74.
B42 'Chinese Boy holding a gourd over his shoulder' (after Oriental model) 4½ins. Ibid., pl. 36, fig. 75.
B43 Kuan Yin (after Oriental model) 4½ins. Godden (B), p. 73, fig. 126; *Connoisseur,* Dec. 1926, p.237.
B44 'Dame of Constantinople', a lady in a turban and sumptuous robes; 'Lady of the Levant', likewise, 10½ins. *Connoisseur,* Vol. 145, pp. 145-151, figs. 1-4, models and engravings after Boucher.

Allegorical and Commemorative
B45 'Europa and the Bull' (group). Honey (A), pl. 2G.
B46 'Britannia mourning for Frederick Prince of Wales', 10ins. Lane, pl. 8.
B47 'Sphinxes' (pair) with female busts and bewigged heads, draped, 6⅛ins. Savage (A), pl. 38.
B48 'Head of a Smiling Girl'. Mackenna (A), pl. 40, fig. 83.
B49 'Bust of the Duke of Cumberland', 4½ins. Ibid., pl. 14, fig. 35. *See Plate 19.*

Peasant and Pastoral
B50 'La Nourrice' (nurse seated breast feeding an infant) 7¼ins. Mackenna (A), pl. 40, figs. 81, 82. *See Plate 21.*
B51 'Rose Seller' in lace cap and dress with ruffle at the neck, 8ins. Stoner, pl. 2.
B52 'Gardener's Companion' in brimmed hat, 9ins. Mackenna (A), pl. 42, fig. 85. *See Plate 20.*
B53 'Peasant seated upon the ground with a hurdy-gurdy', 5¾ins. Ibid., pl. 37, fig. 77.
B54 'Peasant standing with a hurdy-gurdy' (included amongst the Meissen 'Cries of Paris'), 5ins. Harris, p. 44.
B55 'A standing Peasant Toper', 8½ins. *See Plate 23.*
B56 'Dwarf in tall hat', 6ins. Mackenna (A), pl. 39, fig. 80.

Animals
B57 'Pug dog seated upon a square tasselled cushion', 3½ins. Mackenna (A), pl. 30, fig. 64; Williamsburg, pl. 111.
B58 'Seated Hound' (one of a pair). Honey (A), pl. 2F.
B59 'Trump', the pet pug of William Hogarth (after Roubiliac). Harris, p. 46; Victoria and Albert Museum Bul., Vol. III, No. 2, pp. 45-53. *See Plate 22.*
B60 'Two Goats' (group), 6½ins. Sotheby's, 17-10-72, lot 17.
B61 'Two recumbent Kids' (group) 2¼ins. Schreiber, no. 206 (no. 132); Williamsburg, pl. 112.
B62 'Lion', recumbent, 3½ins. Ibid., no. 145 (no. 8).
B63 Sheep: 'Ewe and companion Ram standing heads turned'; 'Ewe and Lamb' (group) and 'Ram and Lamb' (group); 'Recumbent Ewe' and companion 'Recumbent Ram'. Private collections, illustrations unknown to author.

Addendum
B64 'Toper', 8½ins. *See Plate 23.*

APPENDIX C
Chelsea Figures 1753-1757 (Red Anchor Period)

Italian Comedy Characters
C1 'Arlecchino', in round hat, mask, and motley carrying slap-sticks, 6½ins. Savage (B), p. 78.
C2 'Arlecchino, seated with bagpipes wearing conical hat; Columbina seated with hurdy-gurdy', 5¼ins. Cheyne Book, pl. 11, no. 157.
C3 'Avvocato' (lawyer), in doctor's cap and gown, 6ins. Mackenna (B), pl. 67, fig. 134.
C4 'Columbina', in round hat dancing, 5½ins. Ibid., pl. 67, fig. 133.
C5 'Columbina seated playing a lute whilst Pantalone stands with musical score and waves a baton' (group), 6¼ins. King (B), fig. 30.
C6 'Crinolined Lady', possibly Isabella, holding mask and fan, 6ins. Cheyne Book, pl. 11, No. 161; King (B), fig. 24. 'Companion Gallant', in tricorn hat and large waistcoat, hand in pocket, 6ins. Savage (B), p. 9. *See Colour Plate B.*
C7 'Dottore Baloardo' in broad brimmed hat and long cloak striking a histrionic pose, 5½ins. Mackenna (B), pl. 65, fig. 130. *See Plate 24.*
C8 'Mezzetino walking', 5½ins. Sotheby's, 19-5-70, lot 147.
C9 'Narcissino' in brimmed hat, linen tabs at neck, baggy breeches, and cloak thrown over his left shoulder. Known at Chelsea as 'The Captain', 5½ins. Mackenna (B), pl. 65, fig. 130. *See Plate 25.*
C10 'Pantalone' in skull-cap, long cloak leaning forwards holding a purse, 5¾ins. Sotheby's, 22-2-72, lot 36. *See Plate 26.*
C11 'Pedrolino' (Pierrot) in brimmed hat, ruff, loose jacket and trousers with hands raised in surprise, 6½ins. Sotheby's, 26-11-63, lot 65; Cheyne Book, pl. 11, no. 161.
C12 'Pedrolino standing with end-flute and tambourine', 6½ins. E.C.C. 1948 ex. cat., pl. 59, no. 270.
C13 'Pedrolino seated with drum on his left and fife held to his lips', 6ins. Cheyne Book, pl. 8, no. 195.
C14 'Scaramuzzi' (Scaramouche) in soft cap, jacket with ruffle and a tabaro, walking with mincing gait, 5¾ins. Mackenna (B), pl. 65, fig. 130.
C15 'Scaramuzzi standing with his tabaro slipping from off his shoulders', 5¾ins. Scott, pl. 143, fig. 478.

The Cries of Paris and Other Vendors
C16 'Ballad Singer', a woman seated with song sheet in hand and a child on her lap, 6½ins. King (B), fig. 25.
C17 Beggar, known as 'the Blind Beggar', in head scarf, ragged breeches and cloak, holding out tricorn hat for alms, 7½ins. Lane, pl. 16; Cheyne Book, pl. 6, no. 176. *See Plate 29.*
C18 'Beggar', known as 'Italian', in brimmed hat, ragged breeches and shirt-sleeves standing arms folded, 7½ins. Stoner, pl. 6.
C19 'Beggar', also called 'Italian', standing in tricorn hat, blanket gathered about him and extending a pouch for alms, 7½ins. Untermyer, pl. 20, fig. 44; Stoner, pl. 6. *See Plate 29.*
C20 'Beggarwoman', in linen cap holding a basket of vegetables in both hands, 7½ins. Cheyne Book, pl. 6, no. 176B.
C21 'Birdcatcher'; companion 'Wife', each with basket cages upon their backs, 9½ins. Stoner, pl. 25 (wife only).
C22 'Carpenter' standing in brimmed hat with toolbag slung over one shoulder, 8ins. Mackenna (B), pl. 72, fig. 143.
C23 'Cooks', a woman in cap; companion man in turban, each carrying a platter of food, 10½ins. King (B), fig. 9.
C24 'Fisherman standing in peaked cap removing catch from a net between his knees', 6½ins. *Treasures of the National Trust* (1976), pl. 122; Saltram House, 267.T.
C25 'Fisherman astride an eel-trap', drunk with shirt stuffed full of his catch, 7ins. Ibid., pl. 122; Saltram House 267.T.
C26 'Fisherman holding a live carp' in his left hand, 7¾ins. Untermyer, pl. 27, fig. 41.
C27 'Fisherman with fish in right hand and a huge net' over his left shoulder (after the Borghese Warrior), 7ins. King (B), fig. 28.
C28 'Fishwife', in cap, apron and holding platter of fish before her, 6ins. Lane, pl. 17. *See Plate 28.*
C29 'Flower Seller', with basket of flowers and 'kerchief about her head, 8½ins. Mackenna (B), pl. 74, fig. 148.
C30 'Jewish Pedlar' in fur hat with tray slung from neck with ribbons and trinkets; companion 'Trinket seller', a lady with box attached to waist belt, 7¼ins. Untermyer, pl. 27, fig. 43.
C31 'Musician in hat turned up at one side with a hurdy-gurdy', 8½ins. Mackenna (B), pl. 73, fig. 145; Harris, p. 49.
C32 Musician, called 'Itinerant Musician', with bagpipes, child and a dog (group), 8ins. Stoner, pl. 18.
C33 'Print Seller' with pack on back and samples in either hand, 8ins. Mackenna (B), pl. 72, fig. 144.
C34 'Rat Catcher' seated with trap and a rat, 5¾ins. Cheyne Book, pl. 8, no. 191. *See Plate 27.*
C35 'Savoyard Drummer', in tricorn hat with fife to lips and drum at his right side slung from his waist, 6ins. Sotheby's 10-12-73, lot 213.

Peasant and Pastoral
C36 'Boy Fisherman' standing beside up-ended rectangular basket of fish; companion 'Girl with two fish in a fold of her apron' and a basket of fish at her side, 5⅛ins. and 5¼ins. Schreiber, pl. 1, no. 1 (no. 51).
C37 'Boy in conical hat seated holding a bird', 7¼ins. Cheyne Book, pl. 11, no. 173.
C38 'Carter' in brimmed hat and trousers gathered at knees, holding a mug of ale, 4½ins. Christie's, 16-5-75, lot 52. *See Plate 30.*
C39 'Cooper' in brimmed hat seated upon a cask with barrel hoops over his left shoulder, 5¼ins. Cushion (A), col. pl. 5.

C40 'Dutch Dancers' (group); farmer dancing, arms linked with his wife, rather stiffly portrayed, 7½ins. Untermyer, pl. 32, fig. 37.

C41 'Fisherman' and companion model of 'Fishwife', each seated, he with a basket between his knees, she with the top of her lap perforated to serve as flower holders, 8ins. Cheyne Book, pl. 11, no. 159; Harris, p. 45, col. pl.

C42 'Fruit Sellers': Male and companion female peasants seated in mirror positions beside baskets with one hand extended proffering fruit (after S. le Clerk). One version has basket filled with porcelain fruit, another is intended as a sweetmeat receptacle, 9ins. and 9½ins. Stoner, pl. 20; Untermyer, pls. 22 and 23, fig. 35 in col. *See Plates 31 and 32.*

C43 'The Maypole Dancers'. Standing fiddler and a drunk upon a central mound surrounded by a horseshoe of dancers facing outwards; lord in wig, lady, baliff and his wife and a peasant and his woman, 14ins. Lane, pl. 20; Stoner, pl. 19. Fitzwilliam Museum.

C44 'Ostler' with his pipe in his hat band and a whip in his hand, 4½ins. Christie's, 16-6-75, lot 51. *See Plate 30.*

C45 'Peasant', drunk wearing brimmed hat turned back to front, left hand in pocket, right holding an empty tankard, 6½ins. Sotheby's, 13-11-73, lot 119.

C46 Peasant, known as 'Irish Peasant', dancing, 7¾ins. Mackenna (B), pl. 73, fig. 146.

C47 'Peasant Woman in headscarf standing with a mandoline', 8ins. Ibid., pl. 74, fig. 147.

C48 'Tyrolean Dancers' (group); a peasant girl and rustic in a mask whirl one another about in a gavotte (after Eberlein), 7ins. Untermyer, pl. 32, fig. 38.

Musicians, Dancers and Sportsmen

C49 'Actor, seated with hand on breast singing', 7ins. Cheyne Book, pl. 11, no. 183.

C50 'Boy, in Pierrot costume, seated blowing fife' and beating a drum; 'Girl in linen cap with a flute', 6ins. Ibid., pl. 10, no. 138.

C51 'Boy, in soft cap seated playing a reed-pipe'; 'Girl playing a piccolo', 6½ins. Mackenna (B), pl. 66, figs. 131, 132.

C52 'Man, in tricorn hat, seated with salt-box' slung by a strap diagonally from his left shoulder, playing a reed-pipe, 6ins. Cheyne Book, pl. 9, no. 143.

C53 'Dancing Girl', holding out her skirts in a fan with both hands, 6ins. Untermyer, pl. 25, fig. 12.

C54 'Huntsman in peaked cap kneeling before a Lady who has a bird's nest in her lap' (group), 7¼ins. Ibid., pl. 34, fig. 40.

C55 'Huntsman with tricorn hat in hand'; companion 'Lady in riding habit with a whip', 6¾ins. Mackenna (B), pl. 71, fig. 142; E.C.C. 1948 ex. cat., pl. 60, nos. 268, 269.

C56 'Shepherd Boy seated with end-flute', with its case and a pouch hanging behind him, 6ins. Cheyne Book, pl. 6, no. 172.

C57 'Shepherd in tricorn hat playing a recorder standing cross-legged beside his dog'; 'Shepherdess with flowers in her apron holding a posy', 6¾ins. Stoner, pl. 17. *See Plate 48.*

C58 'Shepherd in tricorn hat standing playing bagpipes beside a dog'; companion 'Shepherdess with a lamb', 9¼ins. Ibid. pl. 17.

C59 'A Troubador with head-scarf playing a guitar', with a sword and hat at his feet; companion 'Lady playing a piccolo', 6½ins. Cheyne Book, pl. 9, no. 150.

Foreign Personages

C60 'Chinaman' in conical hat and long robes standing with arms folded, 6ins. Honey (A), pl. 11B.

C61 'Chinaman' seated with hands concealed in long sleeves, 5ins. Mackenna (B), pl. 51, fig. 102.

C62 'Chinaman' standing bare-headed with huge moustache and arms folded, 7ins. Sotheby's, 25-10-66, lot 374. *See Plate 34.*

C63 'Chinese Boy with fife'; 'Girl with drum', each seated on a rocky base, 6½ins. Stoner, pl. 12.

C64 'Chinese Boy in cloak and leaf-shaped hat dancing'. Savage (A), pl. 11B.

C65 'Chinese Musicians' (group); small boy with a bell, youth with two bells, small girl with a drum and teenage girl with a flute, all in a circle facing outwards, 14ins. Lane, pl. 21; Untermyer, pl. 29, 30, fig. 39 (col.).

C66 'Negro in a turban', with left arm raised and a quiver of arrows on his back; companion 'Negress in crown and cloak', with right hand elevated to her face. Also known as 'the Indian Prince and Queen', 7½ins. Mackenna (B), pl. 51, fig. 101.

C67 'Man in a Chinese mask', 7¼ins. National Museum of Wales, Cadiff. *See Plate 35.*

C68 'Polish Lady in head scarf and crinoline lifting her skirt to reveal her petticoat', 6¾ins. King (B), fig. 24; Mackenna (B), pl. 68, fig. 135.

C69 'Turk in tall hat' and loose robes standing; 'Levantine Lady' in high head-dress with left hand raised and right holding the edge of her coat, 6½ins. Untermyer, pl. 21, fig. 36. *See Plate 33.*

C70 'Turk in plumed turban seated'; companion 'levantine Lady likewise', each holding a shell container, 6ins. Mackenna (B), pl. 50, fig. 99.

C71 'Spanish Sportsman' and companion 'Lady' dressed in sumptuous attire each holding a gun, 8½ins. Cheyne Book, pls. 7, 9A, no. 186; King (B), figs. 22, 23.

Allegorical and Mythological

C72 'Apollo' standing in laurel wreath with a lyre, 11ins. Lane, pl. 10.

C73 'Bacchus' standing, vine leaves on brow holding grapes and a goblet, 14ins. Ibid., pl. 112; Mackenna (B), pl. 54, fig. 107.

C74 'Bustos of four Pagan Gods' on plinths, 5ins. Ibid., pl. 54, fig. 108.

C75 'Boy astride a Seal', 8¼ins. Mackenna (B), pl. 54, fig. 107.

C76 'Ceres' in wreath of corn husks standing holding a reaping hook, beside a cornsheaf, 12¾ins. Ibid., pl. 56, fig. 112; Lane, pl. 11. *See Plate 36.*

C77 'Two children, struggling with a fish', 9½ins. Mackenna (B), pl. 48, fig. 95.

C78 'Boy riding a Hippocampus', 10ins. Ibid., pl. 53, fig. 105.

C79 'Diana' with long-bow and hound, 9¼ins. Savage (A), pl. 23C.

C80 'Flora with two Cupids', 17ins. Stoner, col. frontis.

C81 'Galatea with a child Triton' (group), 6ins. Untermyer, pl. 28, fig. 52.

C82 'Jupiter' with an Eagle. Eckstein Bequest, Brit. Mus.

C83 'Leda kneeling beside a dolphin', 9½ins. Mackenna (B), pl. 53, fig. 106.

C84 'Leda with Cupid and Swan' (group), 11⅝ins. Scheiber, pl. 20, no. 171 (no. 134). *See Plate 47* (gold anchor version).

C85 'Mars', as a Roman centurion bare-headed with cloak and shield, 10½ins. Mackenna (B), pl. 55, fig. 109.

C86 'Mercury' standing in winged sandals and helmet holding a caduceus, 11ins. Savage (A), pl. 11B.

C87 'Perseus and Andromeda' (group), 11ins. Cheyne Book, pl. 7, no. 200. Sotheby's, 6-5-69, lot 122.

C88 'Rape of the Sabines' (group), 9½ins. Stoner, pl. 15.

C89 'River God' and companion 'Godess', reclining, 5¼ins. Mackenna (B), pl. 52, figs. 103, 104.

C90 'Saturn' (or 'Cronus'), devowering one of his children (group), 9⅜ins. Ibid., pl. 57, fig. 114; King (B), fig. 20.

C91 'Una' standing beside a lion, 26ins. Stoner, pl. 23.

C92 Vases (rococo), one with 'Meleager' holding the boar's head, the other with 'Atalanta' and her hound. Trans. E.C.C., Vol. 4, 1957, figs. 9, 10.

C93 'Venus holding a flaming heart', 10¼ins. Savage (A), pl. 22A.

The Five Senses

C94 Five seated adult figures in classical robes:
'Taste', a lady with a basket of fruit upon her knee.
'Sight', a man with an eagle holding a spyglass.
'Hearing', a lady with a lute beside a recumbent deer.
'Feeling' a lady with a falcon in her lap and a tortoise at her feet.
'Smell', a man beside a perfume vase with a hound.
Models 11¾-12¼ins. Trans. E.P.C., 1929, No. II, pl. I, II (whole set); Morley-Fletcher (A), p. 87; Mackenna (B), pl. 58, fig. 115; Savage (A), pl. 18A for individual illustrations.

The Arts and Sciences

C95 'Astronomy', depicted as a draped nude putto seated upon a plinth with a celestial globe, 4¾ins. Harris, p. 45. *See Plate 37.*
'Geography', ditto in mirror image with a terrestial globe, 4¾ins. Cheyne Book, pl. 8, no. 196.

C96 'Painting', a putto standing holding a picture, 5½ins. Schreiber, pl. 18, no. 173 (no. 135).
'Astrology', a putto holding a canvas upon which are depicted planetary symbols, 5½ins. Godden (A), pl. 133.

The Four Quarters of the Globe

C97 Two groups, each of two seated Children:
'America', a Red Indian girl seated on an alligator, or a seal, facing 'Europe', a girl seated upon a plinth.
'Africa', a Blackamoor wearing an elephant headdress seated upon a lion, paired with 'Asia', a Levantine girl wearing a stocking cap. Groups 11ins. Stoner, pl. 21; Mackenna (B), pl. 69, figs. 136, 137.

The Four Seasons

C98 Individual standing figures of rustics *(See Plate 38).*
'Spring', a lady in brimmed hat with a posy in her right hand and a basket of flowers over her right arm.
'Summer', a woman wearing a linen cap, holding a sheaf of corn in both hands.
'Autumn', a youth with stockings rolled down with a fruiting vine.
'Winter', a man in fur-lined hat with a basket of charcoal, 5-5½ins. Lane, pl. 18.

C99 Standing adult figures, each on rococo scroll base, before a plinth which is a candlestick. Mackenna (B) pl. 63, figs. 124, 125.

C100 Four groups, each of two children, beside a rococo candlestick:
'Spring', a girl with a basket of flowers and child with a posy.
'Summer', a girl with corn and child attendant, (not illustrated).
'Autumn', a youth with grapes and girl with grapes in her lap.
'Winter', a youth fixing skates to his boots and a child huddled in a blanket. Mackenna (B), pl. 64, figs. 126, 127, 128.

C101 Putti representing the Seasons:
Group of four putti with appropriate accessories upon a mound beneath a leafing tree, 8ins. Ibid., pl. 62, figs. 122, 123.
Two groups, each of two putti:
'Spring' seated with basket of flowers beside 'Summer' standing with cornsheaf.
'Autumn' standing with grapes beside 'Winter' seated in cloak before a brazier, 8½ins. Savage (A), pl. 30A, 30B.

Religious Subjects

C102 'Pietà', Virgin seated holding dead body of Christ with an attendant Angel, 10ins. Mackenna (B), pl. 60, fig. 119; *Burlington Magazine,* 1972, Vol. 114, No. 837, fig. 4.

C103 'Madonna seated with Holy Child' standing upon a terrestial globe, 8¾ins. Mackenna (B), pl. 59, fig. 118; Ludlow, pl. 67. No. 159; Cecil Higgins Mus., Bedford.

C104 Standing figures of religious:
'Abbess of Cologne' in habit and ruff, 7½ins. Dixon, pl. 22; Sotheby's, 8-11-60, lot 147.
'Nun, standing with breviary and rosary', 7½ins. Savage (A), pl. 28B. *See Plate 39.*
'Monk, standing with breviary', 6ins. Ibid., plate 62C.

C105 Seated religious:
'Nun seated upon a coffer with book' in left hand, 5½ins. Cheyne Book, pl. 9, no. 120.
'Nun seated with book in both hands', 5¼ins. Honey (A), pl. 11A.
'Nun seated with book'; companion 'Monk' likewise, 5¼ins. Lane, pl. 19B.

Grotesques

C106 'Female dwarf' in high hat (after Calotto), 6ins. Mackenna (A), pl. 58. fig. 116.

C107 'Aesop as a hunchback negro wearing a gold freed man's chain', 10½ins. Scott, pl. 138, fig. 462.

C108 'A Fox dressed as a Poacher' holding a chicken by the neck, 5¾ins. Untermyer, pl. 21, fig. 45.

C109 'Monkey Musicians' (after Kändler's 'Affenkapelle'):
'Conductor', in periwig and coat holding a scroll in right hand with left arm raised, 8ins.
'Musician' in tricorn hat and jacket with French horn, 6ins.
'Musician' in tricorn hat and jacket with drum and pipe, 6¼ins.
'Musician', as above, holding drum sticks in either hand and companion likewise with drum upon his back, 5⅞ins. *See Colour Plate D.*
'Musician' in wig and jacket standing behind an unclad monkey bearing an organ upon its back, 5⅞ins.
'Lady musician' in cap and dress holding a hurdy-gurdy, 5¾ins.
'Musician' in wig and jacket playing a shawm, 5⅝ins.
'Lady vocalist' seated with score upon her lap, 5⅛ins. *See Colour Plate D.*
'Lady vocalist' seated with musical book in her left hand, 5⅛ins.
Williamsburg, pl. 121-129 for complete set of ten figs.; other illustrations. Lane, pl. 22; Untermyer, pl. 28, fig. 26; Scott, pl. 142, fig. 475.

Family Groups

C110 'Musical Entertainment'; a seated lady with lyre beside a boy and youth with a fife, 6¼ins. Untermyer, pl. 37, fig. 50.

C111 'Musical Entertainment'; lady seated with score beside a child and a youth with a hurdy-gurdy, 6½ins. Ibid., pl. 37, fig. 50.

C112 'Alfresco Meal'; woman with babe opposite father seated upon tubs before an inverted tub as a table, and a child with a bowl who squats, 5ins. Ibid., pl. 37, fig. 51.

C113 'Fisherman seated before a trestle table' with a platter and a basket of fish, 4½ins. Lane, pl. 24B.

C114 'Fruit Gatherers', four figures, two seated, one standing and another kneeling, gathering fruit, 6¼ins. Lane, pl. 24A.

Cupids in Disguise

C115 'Cupid as a wounded soldier', 4¾ins. Lane, pl. 23A.
'Cupid with a musical-box'. *Apollo,* 1955, Vol. 61, No. 364, p.183.
'Cupid with flat drum and drum-sticks'. Ibid., p. 183.
'Cupid with a hurdy-gurdy'. Ibid., p. 184.
'Cupid as a cook' tasting contents of a saucepan over a brick oven. Mackenna (B), pl. 76, fig. 152.
'Cupid as a cook' bearing a platter of food. Ibid., pl. 76, fig. 152.
See also Appendix D1.

Animals

C116 'Cow', walking, 4¾ins. Sotheby's, 6-6-72, lot 69.

C117 'Cow', recumbent, 5¾ins. Ibid., 14-5-74, lot 113.

C118 'Nanny-Goat and Kid' (group), 2¼ins. Schreiber, no. 206 (no. 132).

C119 'Lions' (pair), each with one paw upon a ball, 10ins. long. Trans. E.C.C., 1969, Vol. 7, pl. 130D. *See Plate 40.*

C120 'Ewe', standing and companion 'Ram' likewise, 5ins. Cheyne Book, pl. 2, No. 219.

C121 'Lamb' lying down, 1ins. Schreiber, pl. 18, no. 208 (no. 133).

C122 'Squirrel eating a nut', 4½ins. *See Plate 41.*

C123 'Pugs', seated with roses in their collars (pair), 4ins. Schreiber pl. 33, no. 209 (no. 308).

Birds

C124 'Barn Owls', 8¾ins. Schreiber, no. 221 (no. 149).

C125 'Bullfinches' (pair), 4¾ins. Ludlow, pl. 62, no. 147.

C126 'Bullfinches' (pair), 6ins. Cheyne Book, pl. 14, no. 274.

C127 'Buntings' (pair), 6¾ins. Ibid., pl. 61, no. 143.

C128 'Canary', 6½ins. Ibid., pl. 62, no. 148.

C129 'Cockerel' and companion 'Hen', 5⅝ins. and 5⅞ins. Schreiber, pl. 18, no. 219 (no. 147).

C130 'Goldfinches' (pair), 6½ins. Ludlow, pl. 60, no. 142.

C131 'Greenfinches' (pair), 6½ins. Schreiber, pl. 18, no. 218 (no. 146).

C132 'Parroquets' (pair), 5½ins. Ludlow, pl. 59, no. 138.

C133 'Partridges' (group of two), 4⅛ins. Schreiber, no. 220 (no. 228)

C134 'Peacock' and companion 'Peanhen', 7ins. Untermyer, pl. 12, fig. 47.

C135 'Pheasants' (pair), 5½ins. and 4¾ins. Cheyne Book, pl. 14, no. 289. *See Plate 42.*

C136 'Pheasants' (pair), 5ins. and 6ins. Sotheby's, 21-7-64, lot 131.

C137 'Yellowfinch', 4ins. E.C.C., 1948 ex. cat., pl. 57, no. 259.

Miscellaneous

C138 'Seated Chinaman beside a vase'; companion 'Chinese Lady' likewise, 8ins. Cheyne Book, pl. 19, no. 233.

C139 'A Boy wearing a silver crown standing stiffly upright'; possibly a devotional piece representing a saint, 9½ins. Ibid., pl. 6, no. 184. Cecil Higgins Mus., Bedford.

APPENDIX D
Chelsea Figures 1759-1769 (Gold Anchor Mark)

Cupids in Disguise

D1 'Cupid as Pastry Cook' with a platter, 4¾ins. *Apollo,* June 1955, p. 187.
'Cupid with bandage on head with a hurdy-gurdy', 4½ins. Ibid.
'Cupid in brimmed hat with money-bag' (money changer), 4¾ins. Ibid., p. 183.
'Cupid as a Nurse Maid with baby in a crib', 4½ins. Ibid., p. 188.
'Cupid as a Farmer', 4¾ins. Ibid., p. 188.
'Cupid as a Camp Follower', 4¼ins. Ibid., p. 188.
'Cupid as a Gallant', 4½ins. Ibid., p. 184.
'Cupid as a drummer', 4½ins. Ibid., p. 184.
'Cupid as a Water Carrier' with bottle and glass in hands and tank on back, 5ins. Cheyne Book, pl. 5, no. 3.
'Cupid in tricorn hat with flail over his shoulder', 5ins. Ibid., pl. 16, no. 111.
'Cupid with a Basket', 4¾ins. Mackenna. (C), pl. 58, fig. 111.
'Cupid as a Cook with saucepan'. Ibid., pl. 50, fig. 117.
'Cupid with a Musical-Box'. Ibid.
'Cupid as a Chimney Sweep'. Ibid.
'Cupid as a Scholar in wig and gown'. Fitzwilliam Mus.
'Cupid as a Fishwife'. Fitzwilliam Mus.
'Cupid with a Fiddle'. Fitzwilliam Mus.

Non-winged Cupids or Putti

D2 'Cupid with garland of grapes with a tambourine', possibly representing 'Bacchus'. Mackenna (C), pl. 58, fig. 114.
'Cupid with flaming heart in either hand'. Cheyne Book, pl. 16, no. 112.
'Cupid with wreath of flowers'. Ibid.
'Cupid with hands clasped'. Ibid.

Miscellaneous Putti and Cupids

D3 'Three Putti', one with a bird, each on a legged base. Mackenna (C), pl. 58, fig. 112.

D4 'Group of four Putti playing musical instruments'. Ibid., pl. 58, fig. 113.

D5 Porcelain clock case in rococo style, four putti, one at each corner playing a musical instrument, with lady attended by a putto as the finial, 20½ins. Ludlow, pl. 106, no. 213.

D6 Vases decorated with applied models of putti, one emblematic of 'Summer', the other of 'Autumn', 12ins. Mackenna (C), pl. 24, figs. 47 and 48.

Family Groups

D7 'Lovers, as Pilgrims beneath a tree' in which Cupid lurks, 12½ins. Untermyer, pl. 40, fig. 58; Ludlow, pl. 84, no. 187.

D8 'Alfresco Meal', with father, mother and an infant seated on chairs at a table, with a child upon the ground, 8ins. King (B), fig. 32.

D9 Similar group to above but with inverted tubs serving as table and chairs, 8½ins. Ibid., fig. 33.

D10 'Group of Fruit Gatherers', (see C114) in gold anchor version.

D11 Group of 'Fisherman seated beneath a tree' with table on which are fish before him, and 'Fishwife' with fish in her left hand whilst supporting a net with her right, 6¾ins. Sotheby's, 17-10-67.

D12 'Family group seated beneath a tree' before a table upon which lie plucked hens, 9ins. Ludlow, pl. 83, no. 185.

D13 'Milk Maid with two Children selling milk', 6¾ins. Cheyne Book, pl. 11, no. 240.

D14 'Youth with two Children selling grapes', 6¾ins. Ibid., pl. 11, no. 240.

D15 'Boy seated on upturned basket eating cherries with a Girl standing stooping over him', 7½ins. Ibid., pl. 16, no. 147.

D16 'Lady in hat, jacket and skirt seated beside a man in a tall fur hat within an arbour', 8½ins. Sotheby's, 2-4-68, lot 46.

Italian Comedy Characters

D17 'Arlecchino' in round hat and motley holding slapsticks, standing beside Columbina in bodice and full skirt which she holds out to reveal her petticoat, 9ins. N. Harris, p. 24-25.

Cries of Paris

D18 'Night Watchman' with basket of provisions and lantern; companion 'Lady' likewise, 5¾ins. Untermyer, pl. 21, fig. 55. *See Plate 43.*

Grotesques and Freaks

D19 'David Gaborisco in a Cossack's uniform' as the 'Prussian Dwarf', 11ins. Morley-Fletcher (A), p. 92; Ludlow, pl. 95, no. 199.

D20 'John Coan in a Beefeater's uniform' with a dog as the 'English Dwarf', 11ins. Mackenna (C), pl. 49, fig. 96; Ludlow, pl. 92, no. 198.

D21 'The Dog Orchestra', conductor, female singer and musicians who respectively play pipes of Pan, French horn and violins, 7½ins. Savage, Newman and Cushion, p. 98.

Ranelagh Masqueraders

D22 'Man in balaclava' and stocking cap, jacket, breeches and boots, with powder cask beneath left arm and rifle across his back; companion 'lady' in head scarf and tricorn hat, masked and wearing a cloak, drum at right side and rifle across back as a vivandiere, 7⅞ins. and 8¼ins. English Ceramics, pl. IX.

D23 'Jack O'Green' in leaf covered jerkin and bearded facemask, holding a faggot in left hand with right arm akimbo; companion 'lady' in leafed bodice and skirt adorned with garlands, left hand holding mask to her face, right behind her back, 7⅞ins. and 7¾ins. Williamsburg, pl. 130.

D24 'Man in Pierrot costume', sword at his side, leaning upon a cane and gesticulating with his right hand, 8¼ins. Ibid, pl. 139; Mackenna (C), pl. 55, fig. 106.

D25 'Lady in tall head-dress, masked with crinoline', holding out her skirt with her left hand and with a fan in her right, described as a 'French Princess', 8⅜ins. Ibid., pl. 55, fig. 106; Williamsburg, pl. 134.

D26 'Man in brimmed hat dancing wearing a Chinese mask', 7⅞ins. Ibid., pl. 138.

D27 'Lady adjusting her veil' with her left hand dancing having a hurdy gurdy at her waist; companion 'Fiddler in mask' and soft hat, cloak, breeches and sash about his waist dancing, 8¼ins. Ibid., pl. 132; Mackenna (C), pl. 54, fig. 105.

D28 'Lady standing bare-headed in bodice, elbow sleeves, panier skirt and apron wears a white mask and holds out her apron', 8ins. Williamsburg, pl. 135.

D29 'Man in tricorn hat and mask, playing a flageolet', 7⅞ins. Ibid., pl. 137.

D30 'Lady in tricorn hat and mask, standing holding out her coat in both hands to reveal three-quarter skirt over a full skirt', 8⅛ins. Ibid., pl. 133.

D31 'Man in brimmed hat, ruff and cloak, dancing with flask in one hand and goblet in the other', 8ins. Lane, pl. 25.

D32 'Lady in mask, plumed head-dress', bodice and skirt with left arm extended horizontally holding out her skirt with her right, 8¼ins. Lane, pl. 25.

Vauxhall Revellers

D33 'Man in Turkish costume', turban, jacket, breeches and boots, left arm akimbo, right upraised; 'Lady in Levantine dress', masked holding a flower in her left hand and her dress in her right, 12¾ins. Mackenna (C), pl. 56, fig. 108.

D34 'Vauxhall Singers'; man in soft plumed hat, cloak and breeches, holding a mask in his left hand; companion Lady in Turkish dress with stocking cap, fur-lined cloak and a crescent suspended by a cord about her neck, 12½ins. Ludlow, pl. 104, no. 211.

Allegorical and Mythological

D35 'Apollo' wearing a laurel chaplet and robes holding a lyre. Mackenna (C), pl. 53, fig. 103.

D36 The Nine Muses:
Calliope', standing in laurel crown holding a scroll.
'Clio', standing with trumpet in hand and left hand on her hip.
'Erato', standing in laurel crown holding a quill and a scroll.
'Euterpe', dancing and playing a flute.
'Melpomene', wearing a stocking cap holding a goblet in her hand.
'Polyhymnia', standing and making a dramatic gesture.
'Terpsichore', standing with a tambourine.
'Thalia' standing with both hands outstretched as if asking a question.
'Urania', holding a celestial globe in both hands.
The set, 11½ins-15ins. Mackenna (C), pl. 53, fig. 103.

D37 'Venus seated with Cupid' in a bocage, 13ins. Untermyer, pl. 45, fig. 71.

D38 'Leda and the Swan' with an attendant Cupid, in a bocage, 10¼-13 ins. Ibid., pl. 45, fig. 71. *See Plate 44.*

D39 'Una and the Lion', 27ins. Cheyne Book, pl. 11A,no. 3; Stoner, pl. 23 (reissue of C91).

D40 'Hercules spinning beside Omphale' who holds his club, attended by Cupid (group), 12¼ins. Upton House Porcelain Cat., no. 26, pl. 28.

D41 'Hercules slaying the Hydra' with an axe, 'Iolaus' holding a brand (group), 12¾ins. Ibid., no. 26, pl. 28.

D42 'Jupiter' with an eagle in a chariot, 9½ins. Cheyne Book, pl. 22, no. 261.

D43 'June' with a peacock in a chariot, 9¾ins. Cecil Higgins Mus.

D44 'Winged Mercury' wearing a cloak beside a reclining 'Venus' (two different groups). Mackenna (C), pl. 50, fig. 97.

D45 'Mars' standing in Roman uniform wearing a helmet; companion 'Venus' holding aloft a mirror to which a Cupid reaches up, 7½ins. *See Plate 45.*

D46 'Mars seated facing Venus' (group). Morley-Fletcher (A), col. pl., facing p. 88.

D47 'Flora' represented as a lady standing holding a posy to her nose beside a plinth upon which rests a perfume burner, 10½ins. Cecil Higgins Mus.

D48 'Roman Charity' (group); Pero breast-feeding Cimon in chains, on detachable base, 21ins. Lane, pl. 28.

D49 'Charity' (group); a woman seated and breast-feeding an infant with two children at her side, 7¼ins. *See Colour Plate C.*

D50 'Modesty and Liberality' (group); two draped standing nude women, 16½ins. Mackenna (C), pl. 47, fig. 91.

D51 'Mercury and Argus' (group), 11ins. V & A.

D52 'Neptune' holding a paddle, 13ins. Mackenna (C), pl. 56, fig. 109.

D53 'Perseus and Andromeda' chained to a rock before a monster, a cupid in attendance, 11½ins. Cheyne Book, pl. 7, no. 200.

The Four Seasons

D54 Two groups each of two figures:
'Spring', a lady with a basket of flowers, standing beside 'Winter', a man wearing a hat and coat and holding a muff.
'Summer', a lady with a corn-sheaf, standing with one hand upon the shoulder of 'Autumn', a youth with a basket of grapes, 9½ins. Mackenna (C), pl. 50. fig. 96.

D55 A set of four seated figures:
'Spring', a lady wearing a hat, bodice, skirt and apron, holding a posy in one hand and with blossoms upon her lap.
'Summer', a lady in very similar attire with corn stalks in her lap beside a cornsheaf.
'Autumn', a youth with a basket of grapes and a bunch of grapes in his hand.
'Winter', a man in an overcoat beside a brazier.
Models all about 6ins. Mackenna (C), pl. 52, fig. 100, for Autumn and Spring; Ludlow, pl. 80, no. 181, for Summer.

D56 Seated youths and girls:
'Spring', a lady in a picture hat tied with a scarf beneath her chin with flowers in her lap and at her side.
'Summer', a lady in very similar attire holding corn stalks beside a cornsheaf.
'Autumn', a youth wearing a cocked hat with a fruiting vine and grapes.
'Winter', a youth wearing gaiters and a cloak blowing upon the fingers of his right hand and holding his left over a brazier.
Models about 5¼ins-5½ins. Stoner, pl. 57.

D57 'The Allegorical Seasons' (two groups, each of two figures).
'Winter', a man wearing a stocking cap, fur-edged coat and boots, who is skating beside 'Spring', a girl standing with flowers in her apron.
'Autumn', a gardener holding fruit and vegetables in his apron and with his hat in his right hand, beside 'Summer', a lady who has her left hand upon his shoulder and a cornsheaf under her right arm.
Models 12¾ins. Schreiber, pl. 25, no. 193 (no. 198).

D58 Group of four putti with appropriate accessories upon a mound base beneath a tree, 9ins. Stoner, pl. 28.

D59 Two groups, each of two putti:
'Autumn', a putto holding a bunch of grapes, standing beside 'Winter' depicted as a reclining putto warming his hands over a brazier.
'Spring', and 'Summer', unknown to author. Mackenna (C), pl. 48, fig. 91.

The Four Quarters of the Globe

D60 Four individual standing children:
'Africa', a blackamoor wearing an elephant head-dress and cloak, holding a crab and cornucopia and stepping over a lion.
'Asia', a Levantine girl holding a perfume vase beside a crouching camel.
'America', a Red Indian girl wearing feathered head-dress and skirt, holding a longbow, beside a prairie dog.
'Europe', a white girl wearing a crown, and holding an orb and sceptre in either hand.
Models about 9½ins. Lane, pl. 22B, 23B.

The Four Elements

D61 Standing adult figures in classical robes:
'Fire', a youth, possibly Vulcan, standing beside a flaming urn upon a flower-encrusted plinth.
'Air', a woman, possibly Juno, her veil and garments blown out by the wind, standing beside an eagle.
'Water', Neptune beside a dolphin pouring water from a vase beneath his left arm.
'Earth' Ceres beside a lion, holding a cornucopia.
Models about 9ins. Mackenna (C), pl. 57, fig. 110. *See Plate 46.*

The Five Senses

D62 Reissue of seated adult figures(C94) with added bocages:
'Hearing', a lady, with a lute, beside a recumbent deer.
'Taste', a lady with a basket of fruit in her lap, 14ins. Mackenna (C), pl. 46, figs. 88, 89.
'Sight', a man with a spyglass and an eagle.
'Feeling', a lady, holding a parrot, with a tortoise at her feet.
'Smell', a man with a dog and a perfume vase.
Illustrations of the last three in gold anchor versions unknown to the author.

Pastoral, Huntsmen and Gallants

D63 'Dancing Lesson' (group); a girl teaching a dog to dance upon a plinth, before a huge bocage with her Swain beside her, 16ins. Lane, pl. 29. London Mus.

D64 'Gallant seated with large bow in his hat' holding a cup; companion 'Lady in round hat', bodice and skirt, each before bocage flanked by candle holders, 10ins. Mackenna (C), pl. 51, fig. 99.

D65 'Gallant seated leaning back upon a plinth holding a net'; companion 'Lady, holding a basket of flowers', each before a bocage. Scott, pl. 152, figs. 517, 518.

D66 'Gallant seated with birdcage on his knee and left hand outstretched'; companion 'Lady with her left arm about a dog and right outstretched', each before wreath-like bocage, 10ins. *Apollo,* 1934, Vol. 20, No. 118, p. 119, fig. X.

D67 'Gardener' in headscarf and tricorn hat seated with vegetables in his apron; companion 'Lady' likewise with flowers, 7ins. Cheyne Book, pl. 19, no. 243.

D68 'Gardener' standing bare-headed, holding a stave in both hands; companion 'Lady' in linen cap, bodice and skirt, holding a pot plant to her breast, 6ins. Stoner, pl. 31.

D69 'Huntsman' in coat and breeches, standing booted holding a gun in left hand and game in right; companion 'Lady' wearing crossed belts, with her left hand behind her back and a basket of flowers in her right, 10½ins. Ludlow, pl. 100, no. 206.

D70 'Huntsman standing gun in hand with two dogs beside a seated lady' (group), before bocage flanked by sconces, 10⅞ins. Untermyer, pl. 51, fig. 70.

D71 'Huntsman seated cross-legged hat in left hand beside a Lady also seated who pats dogs' (group), before a bocage flanked by candle sconces, 10⅞ins. Ibid., pl. 50, fig. 70.

D72 'The Music Lesson' (group); a seated swain teaches a peasant girl to play an end-flute, with dogs and sheep about them in a bocage, 15ins. Untermyer, frontis., fig. 75 (col.). *See Plate 50a.*

D73 'Reaper standing with trousers rolled up holding a scythe'; companion 'Lady in bodice and apron', each with small bocage, 9ins. Mackenna (C), pl. 48, fig. 92.

D74 'Reaper in tricorn hat' standing in shirtsleeves, with sheaf of corn in both hands. Hughes (B), pl. 14.

D75 'Shepherd in cockaded hat', cloak and knickerbockers, feeding a dog from a scrip; companion 'Shepherdess' beside a sheep, holding a lamb under her left arm and a posy in her right hand, 11¾ins. Lane, pl. 26, 27; Morley Fletcher (A), p. 92. *See Plate 165.*

D76 'Shepherd' in round hat, open coat, breeches and boots, with one hand outstretched; companion 'Shepherdess' in threequarter coat over which are crossed belts, holding a basket of flowers beneath her right arm, 11ins. Morley-Fletcher (A), p. 93.

D77 'Shepherd in tricorn hat playing the bagpipes' standing beside a dog; companion 'Shepherdess in brimmed hat holding a crook' and proffering an apple with her right hand, 10¼ins. Stoner, pl. 35 and pl. 22, red anchor version.

D78 'Shepherd in tricorn hat holding a sheep' beneath his right arm, and extending a flower in his left hand; 'Shepherdess in hat bodice, skirt and apron' in which she secures blossoms with her right hand whilst holding a posy in her left. known as 'The French Shepherds', 9ins. Herbert Allen, pl. 11, No. 36 (in this example the basket contains eggs). Also issued as 'Chamber Candlesticks'. Scott, pl. 152, fig. 514.

D79 'The Imperial Shepherds'; shepherd in tricorn hat standing with scrip attached to a diagonal belt holding crook in left hand and a posy in his right; Shepherdess in small hat holding blossoms both in her apron and in a basket under her right arm, 10¼ins. Cheyne Book, pl. 17, no. 247.

D80 'Shepherd playing a recorder' standing cross-legged beside his dog; companion 'Shepherdess with flowers' in her apron held with her right hand and a posy in her left, 7½ins. Also in a bocage, 11ins. F. Stoner, pl. 29, and pl. 17 red anchor version. *See Plate 47.*

Foreign Personages

D81 'Chinaman seated beside a vase'; companion 'Lady' likewise, 8ins. Cheyne Book, pl. 19, no. 233.

D82 'Chinese Coolie' standing with basket in his left hand. Mackenna (C), pl. 52, fig. 102.

D83 'Chinese Lady seated with flute held to her lips'; companion 'Chinaman with lute', each in trellissed arbour topped by a cupola and flanked with sconces, 13¾ins. Stoner, pl. 40.

D84 'Blackamoors' (pair), each kneeling with arms elevated to support a candle sconce. Harris, p. 43.

Musicians

D85 'Negro seated playing a French horn'; companion 'white man' likewise, 5½ins. Sotheby's, 2-4-68, lot 45.

D86 'Gentleman with a cello'. Mackenna (C), pl. 52, fig. 101.

D87 'Male rustic in soft cap seated playing the flute'; companion 'Lady playing a lute', the two in a trellissed arbour flanked with candle sconces, 12ins. Mackenna (C), pl. 47, fig. 90.

D88 'Musician' standing in tricorn hat holding fife to lips with left hand and banging drum suspended from left sleeve, 6ins. Cheyne Book, pl. 19, no. 244.

Fable group Candlesticks

D89 'Goat in the well looking to Fox for assistance', 10¾ins. Also . . .

D90 'Fox in the well looking up to the Wolf for help', 10¾ins. Upton House Porcelain Cat., no. 31; also Sotheby's, 6-5-69, lot 126.

D91 'Dog in a manger barking at a brown and white Ox', 12½ins. Also . . .

D92 'Ass laden with provender eating thistles beside a dog', 12½ins. Upton House Porcelain Cat., no. 30; Sotheby's, 10-5-66, lot 167.

D93 'Vain Jackdaw' (actually a magpie) amongst Peacocks, 10½ins. Also . . .

D94 'Cock with a jewel on a dung-hill', 10½ins. Untermyer, pl. 46, fig. 76. (N.B. these have been attributed to Chelsea-Derby).

D95 'Maid killing the Cock', 10¾ins. Cheyne Book, pl. 17, no. 231.

D96 'Dog with a Clog', 10¾ins. Trans. E.C.C., 1942, No. 8, p. 142, pl. XLVIII.

D97 'Fox attacked by a hound whilst the Cat takes refuge in a tree'. Also . . .

D98 'Two Foxes beneath a fruiting vine', 9½ins. Upton House Porcelain Cat., no. 29.

D99 'Dog attacking a Fox watched by a Hen', 8ins. Also . . .

D100 'Crow with cheese in its mouth and a Fox', 8ins. Ibid., no. 32.

D101 'Leopard boasting to the Fox', 12ins. Also . . .

D102 'Tiger attempting to remove an arrow head from its flank and a Fox', 12ins. Ibid., no. 28; Stoner, pls. 39, 102; Mackenna (C), pl. 44, fig. 85.

Other Animal and Bird Candlestick groups

D103 'Leopard, assailed by two Dogs'; companion 'group of Wild Boar attacked by hounds', 12½ins. Mackenna (C), pl. 44, fig. 84.

D104 'Fox with Game'; companion group 'Dog with Game', 9ins. Ibid., pl. 45, fig. 86.

D105 'Cat with a Dog', 7½ins. Sotheby's 3-11-62, lot 62.

D106 'Two Rabbits within a bocage' (paired groups), 9¼ins. Mackenna (C), pl. 43, fig. 83. *See Plate 51.*

D107 'Leopard assailed by three Hounds', 15¾ins. Ludlow, pl. 97, no. 203.

D108 'Stag assailed by three Hounds, 15¾ins. Ibid., pl. 98, no. 204.

D109 'Partridge in wreath of flowers' (pair of candlesticks). Mackenna (C), pl. 43, fig. 82.

D110 'Pair of Finches in a bocage', 7¾ins. Ludlow, pl. 64, no. 153.

D111 'Finches' (pair of candlestick birds), 6¼ins. Ibid., pl. 65, no. 156 (marked with a red anchor but in style of gold anchor).

D112 'Pair of Thrushes with Fledglings in cherry bush', 14ins. Untermyer, pl. 44, fig. 69.

Miscellaneous

D113 'George III and Queen Charlotte attended by a Page, 14ins. Untermyer, pl. 43, fig. 57.

D114 'Young Lady consulting a Gipsy woman who has a babe upon her back and a child at her side', 12ins. *Apollo,* August 1969, p. 109, pl. 11; Upton House, Porcelain Cat., no. 43.

D115 'Pair of standing figures' in rustic dress holding open the lids of hampers, with small bocages. Mackenna (C), pl. 51, fig. 98. (Sweetmeat containers).

D116 'Gallant standing beside a dog'; companion 'Lady beside a lamb', each beside oval baskets. Harris, p. 48 (Sweetmeat containers).

D117 Lady dressed in classical robes beside a Perfume Vase', 10½ins. Cheyne Book, pl. 6, no. 180.

D118 'Farmyard Group of clock tower, farm, dog, game and a fox, 8½ins. Sotheby's, 2-4-68, lot 97.

D119 'Arbour group with Hussar'; companion group with 'Lady', 8½ins. Sotheby's, 5-10-76, lot 97.

APPENDIX E
Girl-in-a-Swing Figures Circa 1749-1750

E1 'Girl seated on a swing slung between two tree-stumps,', 6½ins. Lane & Charleston, pl. 126; Lane, pl. 30B; Mackenna (A), pl. 50, fig. 99. *See Plate 52.*

E2 'Male Musician standing in round plumed hat' with a hurdy-gurdy, square base, 5¾ins. Lane, pl. 31B (white); Tait (B), pl. 28 (col.). *See Plate 53.*

E3 'Dancing Girl' standing upon rectangular base holding out her skirt in a fan, 5⅝ins. Lane, pl. 31B (white); Tait (B), pl. 28 (col.). *See Plate 53.*

E4 'Girl standing with basket' in both hands before a flowering tree-stump, 7½ins. Lane & Charleston, pl. 131A (col.).

E5 'Boy in tricorn hat holding a fish' in both hands whilst leaning against a treestump, 7½ins. Ibid., pl. 131B (col.), pl. 131C engraving of 'Water'.

E6 'Girl (as in E4) standing beside a Youth who reclines with legs crossed' holding a bird upon his right thigh and stroking with his left hand another smaller bird, emblematic of 'Air', 8⅝ins. Lane & Charleston, pl. 130A.

E7 'A Youth standing bare-headed with a basket upon his back, before a Girl seated with a basket of fish at her side', emblematic of 'Water', 7⅝ins. Ibid., pl. 130B.

E8 'Gallant kneeling and presenting a bird's nest to a seated Lady who has one hand upon his shoulder', 6⅝ins. Ibid., pl. 129A; Lane, pl. 33.

E9 The 'Mater Dolorosa', portrayed by the Virgin Mary in a veil arms crossed over her breast, 7¾ins. Lane & Charleston, pl. 129; Lane, pl. 31A.

E10 'Boy seated on ground before a Girl seated upon a rock fondling a lamb', 4ins. V & A Cat. no. C.75-1925; Trans. E.C.C., Vol. 4, No. 5, 1959, pl. 23B.

E11 'Boy and Girl as above in mirror positions fondling a dove', 4ins. Ibid., pl. 23A.

E12 'Rustic Lovers depicting a Swain with a Girl facing him upon his knee', 6⅝ins. Lane and Charleston, pl. 135C, pl. 135B Chelsea version of group.

E13 'Hercules and Omphale' (after Vincennes group), 8¾ins. Lane, pl. 34.

E14 'Ganymede and the Eagle', 5⅝ins. Lane, pl. 30.

E15 'Europa and the Bull' (companion to E14), 7⅛ins. Savage (A), pl. 37C.

E16 'Britannia lamenting the death of Frederick Prince of Wales', handkerchief to eyes in right hand, seated beside a shield, lion, and cameo of the prince, 9ins. Untermyer, pl. 1, fig. 9 (with well modelled lion); Lane and Charleston, pl. 126B (with crudely modelled lion).

E17 'Girl leaning against a tree-stump with a bunch of grapes', 4½ins. Untermyer, pl. 9, fig. 2 (col. pl.).

E18 'Boy in round hat leaning against a panier of grapes' (companion to E17), 5¼ins. Ibid., pl. 9, fig. 2.

E19 'Girl reclining against a tree-stump asleep', 4½ins. Untermyer, pl. 9, fig. 1.

E20 'Boy leaning against a tree-stump with finger to his lips' (companion to E19), 4½ins. Ibid., pl. 9, fig. 1.

E21 'Boy holding aloft a bunch of grapes' as a taper-stick, emblematic of 'Autumn', 4½ins. Sotheby's 15-2-45, lot 55.

E22 'Boy seated upon tree-stump blowing upon his fingers to warm them (companion to E21), emblematic of 'Winter', 4½ins. Trans. E.C.C., Vol. 5, pt. 3, 1962. pl. 135A.

E23 'Gallant seated wearing a very large tricorn hat', 4½ins. Sotheby's, 19-3-63, lot 160 (attributed to Longton Hall); Williams (B), fig. 32 (tentatively ascribed to Girl-in-a-Swing).

E24 'The Holy Family' (after Raphael), seated Virgin Mary with Holy Child standing on her left leaning across to greet the infant St. John held by a kneeling St. Elizabeth, 8¼ins. *Connoisseur,* 1968, Vol. 168, No. 676, p. 97, fig. 1.

E25 'Figure of Lady in classical robes standing before a plinth upon which a lamp burns', possibly after a Vincennes model of 'Amitiée'. *See Plate 54.*

E26 'Fox and Stork at the well', 5½ins. Mackenna (A), pl. 50, fig. 100.

E27 'Bird' mounted upon a hexagonal base, looking towards the left, 5¼ins. Ibid., pl. 53, 103.

E28 'Bird', as above, looking to the right, 6¼ins. Ludlow, pl. 60C, no. 142.

E29 'Bird' looking to the right with one wing displayed, 6¼ins. Trans. E.C.C., 1962, Vol. 5, pt. 3, pl. 133B.

E30 'Bird' looking to the right, 4ins. Savage (A), pl. 3A.

E31 'Hunting Dog', 4½ins. Trans. E.C.C., 1962, Vol. 5, pt. 3, pl. 134A.

APPENDIX F
Miniature Figures and Scent Bottles

Chelsea Miniature Figures (2¼ins-3ins)

'Gallant with tricorn hat' under left arm and right in his breeches pocket. Untermyer, pl. 71, fig. 191.
'Gallant with left hand upon heart' in the act of making a deep salutation, hat in right hand. Mackenna (C), pl. 62, fig. 123.
'Gardener in stocking cap with a hoe'. Ibid., pl. 62, fig. 123.
'Gardener with watering-can'. Ibid., pl. 62, fig. 123.
'Gardener pushing a wheel-barrow filled with grass'. Untermyer, pl. 71, fig. 192.
'Gardener' pushing a garden roller. Ibid., pl. 71, fig. 193.
'Girl with a dove and a dalmatian'. Ibid., pl. 71, fig. 169.
'Highlander in jacket and kilt', walking. Ibid., pl. 71, fig. 194.
'Huntsman, leaning upon his gun'. Mackenna (C), pl. 62, fig. 123.
'Huntsman walking with gun at the ready'. Ibid., pl. 62, fig. 123.
'Lady in a hat bending over a crib'. Ibid., pl. 62, fig. 123.
'Lady riding a galloping horse'. Untermyer, pl. 71, fig. 196.
'Lady in hat, bodice', and skirt dancing (possibly Columbina). Mackenna (C), pl. 62, fig. 123.
'Lady in fur trimmed muff'. Untermyer, pl. 71, fig. 197.
'Man who appears to be bending a metal pipe over one knee'. Mackenna (C), pl. 62, fig. 123.
'Poet seated upon a treestump writing in a book'. Untermyer, pl. 71, fig. 198.
'Putti, two beside a small vase'. Mackenna (C), pl. 62, fig. 123.
'Cockerel' (small). Mackenna (C), pl. 62, fig. 123.
'Monkey seated upon a green mound'. Untermyer, pl. 71, fig. 202.

Chelsea Scent Bottles

'Boy, masked playing a flute'. Untermyer, pl. 72, fig. 102.
'Boy Huntsman with a dog'. Ibid., pl. 65, fig. 106.
'Boy with a Goat'. Ibid., pl. 65, fig. 105.
'Boy with a mandoline'. Ibid., pl. 73, fig. 107.
'Chinese Lovers with wine'. Ibid., pl. 73, fig. 116.
'Chinese Musicians'. Ibid., pl. 73, fig. 119.
'Chinese family group'. Ibid., pl. 73, fig. 117.
'Chinese Lady with a parasol'. Ibid., pl. 67, fig. 118.
'Cupid at the altar of Love'. Ibid., pl. 66, fig. 122.
'Cupid with a Dog'. Ibid., pl. 66, fig. 128.
'Cupid upon a Cloud'. Ibid., pl. 66, fig. 125.
'Cupid impaling a Heart'. Ibid., pl. 62, fig. 133.
'Cupid with a Globe'. Ibid., pl. 62, fig. 131.
'Cupid with a Devil'. Ibid., pl. 66, fig. 127.
'Cupid as a Sculptor'. Ibid., pl. 66, fig. 142.
'Cupid with Rose-buds'. Untermyer, pl. 66, fig. 140.
'Cupid as an Artist'. Ibid., pl. 66, fig. 138.
'Cupid with a Key'. Ibid., pl. 66, fig. 135.
'Cupid with a Lion'. Ibid., pl. 66, fig. 136.
'Cupid with a Donkey'. Ibid., pl. 66, fig. 129.
'Cupid on Crutches'. Ibid., pl. 66, fig. 126.
'Cupid with Doves'. Ibid., pl. 66, fig. 130.
'Cupid and a Nymph beside a Clock'. Ibid., pl. 66, fig. 137.
'Cupids at a Furnace'. Ibid., pl. 66, fig. 110.
'Cupid at a Grindstone'. Ibid., pl. 66, fig. 132.
'Cupid with a Cross-Bow'. Ibid., pl. 66, fig. 123.
'Cupid with billing Doves'. Bryant, pl. 26, No. 1.
'Cupid with Drums'. Ibid., pl. 10, no. 2.
'Cupid as a River God'. Ibid., pl. 22, no. 4.
'Cupid with an Urn'. Ibid., pl. 24, no. 1.
'Cupid with Venus and a Clock'. Foster,pl. 231A.
'Cupids, two in masks with an Urn'. Sotheby's, 4-7-60.
'Cupids, three back to back, with a basket'. Untermyer, pl. 61, fig. 237.
'Cupid with a Panther'. Ibid., pl. 61, fig. 139.
'Cupids, two at a Fountain'. Ibid., pl. 65, fig. 109.
'Cupids, three with a flower vase'. Ibid., pl. 61, fig. 237.
'Friar, carrying a woman'. Ibid., pl. 67, fig. 142.
'Friar, carrying a sack'. Ibid., pl. 67, fig. 145.
'Friar, standing'. Ibid., pl. 67, fig. 144.
'Girl, playing a tambourine'. Ibid., pl. 71, fig. 114.
'Girl dancing'. Sotheby's, 4-5-65, lot 15.
'Girl as a Gardener'. Untermyer, pl. 65, fig. 170.
'Girl and Boy writing a letter'. Ibid., pl. 65, fig. 108.
'Girl, gathering Grapes'. Ibid., pl. 73, fig. 171.
'Girl with a basket of Roses'. Ibid., pl. 71, fig. 166.
'Graces, three'. Ibid., pl. 61, fig. 238.
'Harlequin attacked from behind by a rooster'. Ibid., pl. 62, fig. 159.
'Harlequin chasing a Cock'. Ibid., pl. 62, fig. 160.
'Harlequin dancing in Motley'. Ibid., pl. 62, fig. 158.
'Harlequin and Columbine'. Ibid., pl. 62, fig. 162.
'Lovers, a pair'. Ibid., pl. 61, fig. 179.
'Lovers with a Bird-cage'. Bryant, pl. 25, no. 3.
'Monk with a basket and a Sack'. Sotheby's, 4-5-65, lot 35.
'Orpheus'. Untermyer, pl. 61, fig. 189.
'Polish Hussar'. Foster, pl. 214I.
'Polish Soldier dancing'. Ibid., pl. 214B.
'Portia'. Sotheby's, 1-5-65, lot. 59.
'Priest with a Missal'. Untermyer, pl. 67, fig. 146.
'Shakespeare'. Untermyer, pl. 67, fig. 186.
'Shepherdess', seated. Ibid., pl. 73, fig. 172.
'Turk'. Ibid., pl. 67, fig. 121.
'Turk, seated with a pipe'. Ibid., pl. 67, fig. 120.
'Woman feeding a Child'. Sotheby's, 4-5-65, lot 523.
'Youth playing a Mandoline'. Untermyer, pl. 73, fig. 107.
'Cat'. Untermyer', pl. 64, fig. 79.
'Dog'. Ibid., pl. 64, fig. 80.
'Dolphins'. Ibid., pl. 64, fig. 81.
'Doves'. Ibid., pl. 61, fig. 84; pl. 63, fig. 83.
'Fish in a Net'. Ibid., pl. 64, fig. 153.
'Hen with Chickens'. Ibid., pl. 63, fig. 89.
'Monkey with a Basket'. Ibid., pl. 63, fig. 90.
'Monkey with Vase'. ibid., pl. 63, fig. 91.
'Parrot'. Ibid., pl. 63, fig. 94.
'Squirrel'. Ibid., pl. 64, fig. 98.
'Urn, with Caryatid Handles'. Bryant, pl. 24, no. 3.

Girl-in-a-Swing Scent Bottles

'Chinaman standing with a Dove'. Untermyer, pl. 67, fig. 115.
'Chinese Lady with a Basket'. Foster,pl. 208A; Sotheby's, 26-11-74, lot 129.
'Cupid with a Dalmatian upon his knee'. Foster, pl. 208D.
'Girl with a Hurdy-Gurdy'. Ibid., pl. 208B.
'Girl with a Basket of Flowers'. Ibid., pl. 69B.
'Girl with a covered Basket'. Untermyer, pl. 67, fig. 174.
'Harlequin beside a Barrel'. Ibid., pl. 62, fig. 161.
'Lady Dancing'. Foster, pl. 139.
'Pierrot'. Untermyer, pl. 71, fig. 163.
'Sleeping Girl, with a mastiff'. Bryant, pl. 8, no. 3.
'Troubadour'. Untermyer, pl. 73, fig. 187.
'Cat seated with a Mouse'. Foster, pl. 208E.
'Cochin China Parrot and Cock'. Bryant, pl. 4, no. 1.
'Goldfinch'. Trans. E.C.C., Vol. 6, pt. 3, pl. 208G.
'Hawk'. Ibid., pl. 208F.
'Monkey with a Bottle'. Sotheby's, 4-7-60, lot 30.
'Parrot'. Untermyer, pl. 63, fig. 94.
'Pug Dog'. Sotheby's, 4-7-60, lot 30.
'Raven and Fox' (Fable group). Untermyer, pl. 63, fig. 86.
'Rooster'. Ibid., pl. 63, fig. 97.
'Swan'. Ibid., pl. 63, figs. 99, 100.

Note: a further 25 scent bottles relate to porcelain flowers and are not included.

APPENDIX G
Bow Figures made between 1750 and 1754

Theatrical Subjects.

G1 Kitty Clive as 'Mrs Riot', 9ins. Lane, pl. 37 (white); Untermyer, pl. 76, fig. 241; Savage (A), pl. 53 (enamelled).
G2 Henry Woodward as the 'Fine Gentleman', 10¾ins. Lane, pl. 36; Untermyer, pl. 77, fig. 241; Savage (A), pl. 52.
G3 David Garrick as 'Falstaff', 7ins. Hughes, pl. 8.
G4 'An Actor', possibly Garrick, 7ins. Sotheby's, 25-8-39, lot 203.
G5 'Actor in Turkish Dress' with sword; companion 'Actress in Levantine Costume', 8¼ins. Stoner, pl. 68; Savage (A), pl. 43A, 43B. *See Plate 55.*
G6 'Arlecchino', in plumed hat, mask and motley with right arm raised to his shoulder, 6¼ins. Stoner, pl. 71.
G7 'Columbina' in picture hat with basket of grapes, 6¼ins. *Country Life,* June 1970, p. 1138, fig. 9.
G8 'Columbina' in plumed hat, bodice and skirt, dancing, 6¼ins. Savage (A), pl. 54; Hurlbutt, pl. 43A.
G9 'Pulcinella' in conical cap leaning against a tree stump. *Apollo,* 1963, Vol. 78, p. 271, fig. 12.
G10 'Scapino' cap in hand, 4⅞ins. — *Apollo,* 1963, Vol. 78, p. 267, fig. 12; with mask in hand. Sotheby's, 5-6-68, lot 32.
G11 'Indiscretions of Arlecchino'. Arlecchino lying on ground regarding ankle of Columbina as she sits upon the knee of Mezzetino. 7⅝ins. E.C.C., ex. cat., pl. 36, no. 166.
G12 'Arlecchino in mask and motley with left arm about the waist of Columbina and right hand raised', 7⅝ins. Trans. E.C.C., Vol. 2, pl. CIIId.
G13 'The Italian Musicians', 7ins. King (B), fig. 6.

Allegorical and Mythological

G14 Apollo and the nine Muses, 6⅛ to 7¼ins. 'Apollo' wearing a laurel wreath and loose robes stands holding a lyre in his left hand. Sigmund Katz Col., Mus. of Fine Arts, Boston, U.S.A., later version Hurlbutt, pl. 63a.
'Thalia' wearing a laurel wreath and robes holding a mask in her left hand. Ibid.
'Calliope', example unknown to author.
'Clio' seated before an open book holding a quill in her right hand.
'Erato' seated with flowers in her lap attended by Eros.
'Euterpe' seated with musical instruments at her feet holding a recorder in her left hand.
'Melpomene' standing, a goblet in one hand and a dagger in the other.
'Polyhymnia' who has wings, seated holding a chaplet in her left hand over an obelisk to which she points with her right. *See plate 56.*
'Terpsichore' dancing with her left arm raised.
'Urania' stooped over a globe holding a pair of dividers.
The above seven models are illustrated in *Burlington Magazine,* 1929, Vol. 54, pl. I, figs. A, B, C; pl. II, figs. A, B, C, D.
G15 'Charity' (group); a woman standing with babe upon her left arm, handing an apple to a child that stands at her right side, 9¾ins. Lane, pl. 42; King (B), fig. 5. *See Plate 57.*
G16 'Hope' a lady in classical robes leaning upon the shaft of an anchor, 8¾ins. Sotheby's, 7-5-68, lot 121. *See Plate 58.*
G17 'Juno' and her peacock, 5¾ins. Stoner, pl. 65; G. Savage (A), pl. 55B.
G18 'Justice' leaning upon a pile of books bearing a short sword in right hand and scales in left, 8½ins. *Connoisseur* 1960, Vol. 145, p. 68; Sotheby's, 7-5-68, lot 121.
G19 'Mercury' (Hermes), standing in winged helmet and sandals with the caduceus, 7ins. Savage (A), pl. 55B.
G20 'Minerva' depicted as goddess of Wisdom, in cap and long sleeved dress, 8¼ins. Savage (A), pl. 51.
G21 'Minerva' depicted in crested helm, and cuirass, as a warrior goddess holding a shield upon which is the head of Medusa, 6¾ins. Lane, pl. 41B.
G22 'Neptune' astride a dolphin, 7ins. Savage (A), pl. 49B.
G23 'Sphinxes' (pair), with heads and beasts in the likeness of 'Peg Woffington' mounted on Rococo bases, 4¾ins. Schreiber, pl. 9, no. 143 (no. 6) in the white; Savage (A), pl. 39, in enamel.
G24 'Sphinxes' (pair), with head and breasts of an unidentified woman, with a drape over their backs on rectangular bases, 4¾ins. E.C.C. 1949 ex. cat., pl. 36, no. 37 white; Sotheby's, 5-10-75, lot 109 enamelled.
G25 'Two Putti struggling with a dolphin'. Harris, p. 51.

Peasant and Pastoral

G26 'Absinth Seller' in tricorn hat with tray of bottles, 7½ins. Sotheby's, 3-12-68, lot 147.
G27 'Beggar standing with hurdy-gurdy', 5ins. Ibid., 26-11-74, lot 133; companion 'Beggar Woman', V & A.
G28 'Beggar' standing in wide-brimmed hat, short trousers and stockings rolled down; companion 'Beggar Woman' in bonnet secured beneath chin, bearing a basket in both hands, 6¾ ins. Savage (A), pls. 49A, 49C. *See Plate 59.*
G29 'Beggar Woman' standing holding a child in a crib, 6½ins. Sotheby's, 27-4-76, lot 68.
G30 'Fruit Vendors', man in brimmed hat, with basket over left arm proffering an apple with his right hand; companion woman in a lace cap, holding fruit in her apron with both hands, 8¾ins. Stoner, pl. 69.
G31 'Gipsy Fortune Teller with a young lady' known as 'La Bonne Aventure', 6¾ins. Hurlbutt, pl. 42; King (B), fig. 2.
G32 'Gallant seated upon a bench beside a Fishergirl' 7½ins. Tait (A), fig. 18.
G33 'Huntsman seated upon a bench beside a Lady' in riding habit, about 7ins. Nat. Mus. Ireland.
G34 'Lady in cap and apron, seated sewing', 5¼ins. Temple Newsam.
G35 'Lady in crinoline with plumes in hair, seated with a lyre', 6½ins. *Apollo* 1960, Vol. 71, No. 705, p. 97, fig. IX; see also Sigmund Katz Col.
G36 'Lady in lace cap and crinoline accepting refreshments proffered by a Page' (group), 7ins. Honey (B), 1933, pl. 14A.
G37 'Liberty and Matrimony', sportsman standing holding a bird aloft in right hand, beside a ram and a dog; companion Lady holding open door of an empty bird-cage, 9¾ins. Tait (A), figs. 95, 96; variant of sportsman with gun, Lane, pls. 44, 45.
G38 'Print Seller' with pack on back and samples in either hand, 5¾ins. Sotheby's, 30-5-67, lot 147.
G39 'Sailor in tricorn hat' and trousers, left hand on hip; companion 'Lass' in head scarf holding out apron with left hand, 5½ins. Lane, pl. 40; Savage (A), pl 61B (in the white).
G40 'Thames Waterman' with badge of 'fouled anchor' on shoulder, 7ins. Lane, pl. 41A.
G41 'Vintner' standing in brimmbed hat, legs crossed beside panier of grapes holding a bunch, 6¼ins. Lane, pl. 40B.
G42 'Lovers seated with a birdcage' (group), 7½ins. Ibid., pl. 38.
G43 'Sportsman seated with gun', companion 'Lady with dog', 5ins. Trans. E.C.C., 1969, Vol. 7, pls. 129B, C.

Foreign Personalities

G44 Chinoiserie groups: 'Air'; Chinese lady holding aloft a bird, leaning on a bird-cage, beside a Chinaman seated with another bird and a flying-fish. 'Fire'; a Chinaman pouring tea from a pot standing beside a stove, and a seated Chinaman with a cup, both 7¾ins. Untermyer, pl. 74, fig. 239.
G45 'Goddess Ki Mao Sao' flanked by two kneeling Chinamen (group), 6¾ins. Untermyer, pl. 80, fig. 243.
G46 'Mongolian Prince'; companion 'Princess' (busts), 10½ins. King (B), fig. 4; Untermyer, pl. 79, fig. 242.
G47 'Negress standing beside a basket' with a lid, 8¾ins. Tait (A), fig. 6.
G48 'Turk in plumed turban', kneeling beside a container (sucrier), 4¾ins. Sotheby's, 27-2-68, lot 169.

Animals

G49 'Ewe reclining with a lamb' (group), 2½ins. Savage (A), pl. 46C; Hurlbutt, pl. 1A.
G50 'Nanny-Goat reclining with a Kid', 3ins. Savage (A), pl. 46B.
G51 'Fox with game', 5¾ins long. Trans. E.C.C., Vol. 7, pt. 1, pl. 2B.
G52 'Lions' (pair), each seated with one paw upon a tree stump, 4⅛ins. Savage (A), pl. 47A. *See Plate 60.*
G53 'Lions' (pair), each lying with heads turned to one side. Ibid, pl. 47B.
G54 'Lions' (pair), each with one paw upon a terrestial glove, 3¼ins. Sotheby's, 26-11-74, lot 140.
G55 'Lion' modelled after a Florentine marble, 11ins. long. Trans. E.C.C., 1968, Vol. 7, pt. 3, pl. 130A.
G56 'Pugs' (pair), recumbent upon tasselled cushions, one looking upwards, the other facing his rump, 5⅛ins. and 5⅝ins. long. Schreiber, pl. 9, no. 147 (no. 4).

G57 'Pug standing' 2¾ins. Schreiber, no. 148 (no. 3).
G58 'Pug seated on square base', 1¼ins. Hughes (B&T), pl. 9.
G59 'Retriever, standing with dead game', 4⅜ins. long. Schreiber, pl. 9. no. 701 (no. 21).

Birds
G60 'Crane', 1¾ins. Hughes (B&T), pl. 9.
G61 'Grotesque Birds' (pair), possible intended as cormorants, 7ins. Savage (A), pl. 40B.
G62 'Heron', 6ins. Hurlbutt, pl. 2.
G63 'Ostrich', 6ins, pl. 9, no. 151 (no. 9).
G64 'Owls' (pair). 8¼ins. Trans. E.C.C., 1968, Vol. 6, pt. 2, pl. 56.
G65 'Pheasant' standing upon a rocky mound, 2¾ins. Hughes (B&T), pl. 9.

Miscellaneous
G66 Candlesticks in the form of boys standing with flower pots upon their heads, 14⅞ins. Lane, pl. 43.

APPENDIX H
Bow Figures made between 1755 and 1765

Theatrical
H1 'Arlecchino' masked, in round hat and motley, with slapsticks and left hand upon his left shoulder, 6½ins. E.C.C. 1949 ex. cat., pl. 40, no. 174.
H2 'Columbina' in round hat, laced bodice and skirt, dancing, 6½ins. Ibid., pl. 40, no. 175; Hughes (B&T), pl. 10.
H3 'Pantalone' in long cloak leaning forward with right hand raised before him, 4ins. *See Plate 61.*
H4 'Dottore Baloardo' in wide brimmed hat and long cloak, right arm akimbo and left hand elevated, 6½ins. Sotheby's, 5-10-76, lot 120 (mound base); Hughes (B), pl. 4 (legged base).
H5 'Isabella' standing bare-headed in long skirt, 7½ins. Hughes (B), pl. 4.
H6 'Mezzetino', in soft cap, ruffle, and striped costume, walking, 6⅛ins. E.C.C. 1948 ex. cat., pl. 37, no. 181 (A.R. mark).
H7 'Narcissino', (labelled 'The Captain'), in brimmed hat, linen tabs at neck, cummerbund and baggy breeches, with cloak over his left shoulder, 8ins. E.C.C. 1948 ex. cat., pl. 41, no. 184.
H8 'Pedrolino' in hat with brim turned back, ruffle and loose jacket and trousers, holding up both hands in astonishment, 6½ins. Hughes (B&T), pl. 10; Saltram House, no. 260.T.
H9 'Scaramuzzi', 6½ins. Sotheby's, 3-12-68, lot 146.
H10 'Arlecchino in conical hat seated with bagpipes'; companion 'Columbina seated with hurdy-gurdy' 4¾ins. Hurlbutt, pl. 61.
H11 'David Garrick as Falstaff', 9½ins. Hurlbutt, pl. 33.
H12 'Boy, in fancy-dress of Arlecchino'; companion 'Girl dressed as Columbina', 5ins. *Antique Dealer & Collector's Guide,* February 1973, p. 102.

Foreign Personalities
H13 'Chinese Magician with a bear and a Child standing upon a chair' (group), 7¾ins. Hurlbutt, pl. 43B.
H14 'Turk' standing in plumed turban and fur-edged cloak over trousers, left hand on hip, right outstretched; companion 'Levantine Lady adjusting her head-dress' with her right hand, 7½ins. Morley-Fletcher (A), p. 100. *See Plate 62 and Colour Plate F.*
H15 'Turk seated in plumed turban'; companion 'Levantine Lady in tall head-dress', each beside a shell sweetmeat container, 7ins. Untermyer, pl. 80, fig. 245.
H16 'Turkish Boy' wearing a turban, waistcoat and trousers; companion 'Lady' in tall head-dress, coat and jewelled sash, 8¼ins. Sotheby's, 10-12-73, lot 161.
H17 'Youth in Turkish costume', with his right hand upon his breast, 7¾ins. Ramsey. Ludlow, pl. 49, no. 112.
H18 'Turkish Dancing Girl', 7½ins., Ramsey, pl. 354. Companion 'Turk' in turban and cloak, 7¾ins. V & A.
H19 'Boy in Turkish costume'; 'Girl in Levantine dress', 5ins. Sotheby's, 10-12-73, lot 160.
H20 'Turkish Lady being proferred refreshments by a Negro Page', (group), 10ins. Grosvenor Antique Fair Cat., 1976, fig. 283.
H21 'Negro' standing with bow slung across back, and thumbs in his belt; companion 'Negress in a crown' and drapes, her right arm elevated, 7ins. Private coll.
H22 'Blackamoor' in a turban, holding a cup and saucer upon a tray; companion 'Negress' with a basket over her left arm and right hand elevated to her face, 7¼ins. Hurlbutt, pl. 34.

Peasant and Artisan
H23 'Alchemist' with a bottle in his left hand and a tray of bottles under his right arm, 8ins. Sotheby's, 18-4-67, lot 178.
H24 'Boy Fish-Seller', standing beside an upturned square basket of fish; 'Girl', standing beside a pail of fish, 6ins. E.C.C., 1948 ex. cat., pl. 40, no. 186, male model; Fitzwilliam, female model.
H25 'Boy Toper astride a barrel', 5½ins. Herbert Allen, pl. 2, no. 3; Sotheby's, 5-10-76, lot 121.
H26 'Boy Toper' seated, on a tree-stump, 5½ins. *See Plate 65.*
H27 'Male Cook', wearing turban and apron, carrying a brace of ducks on a platter; 'Female Cook', wearing linen cap and apron with a platter of lamb, 7ins. Stoner, pl. 73. *See Plate 63.*
H28 'Male Cook wearing a stocking cap' and apron, standing beside a brick oven with a saucepan, tasting his forefinger, 6ins. Sotheby's, 5-10-76, lot 123.
H29 'Dutch Peasant' dancing; companion 'Dutch Woman' dancing, each beside a candlestick, 9¾ins. Stoner, pl. 83.
H30 'Knife-Grinder'. Trans. E.C.C., 1968, Vol. 7, pt. 1, 'Miscellany of Pieces' (not illustrated).
H31 'Fisherman standing with a net' held in both hands, 7ins. Savage (A), pl. 60C.
H32 'Itinerant Male Musician', with magic lantern upon his bank, turning the handle of a barrel-organ, 5½ins. Sotheby's, 7-5-68, lot 22.
H33 'Gentleman seated' wearing a tricorn hat, coat and breeches, drinking from a bottle; companion 'Lady' drinking from a glass, each beside a sweetmeat container, 6½ins. Stoner, pl. 81.
H34 'New Dancers'; boy in brimmed hat with arms elevated; girl in picture hat likewise, 6¾ins. Hurlbutt, pl. 45; Saltram House 261T. *See Plate 66.*
H35 'Pedlar with a begging bowl'; companion 'Woman with box of trinkets' suspended from a strap around her neck, 6¾ins. Stoner, pl. 79.
H36 'Peasant dancing arms akimbo'; companion 'Girl likewise' 6ins. Hughes (B&T), pl. 10.
H37 'Piedmontese Bagpiper' in wide brimmed plumed hat, cloak and bearing bagpipes, 9½ins. Savage (A), pl. 57.
H38 'Pilgrim with scrip and pack on his back', 6⅝ins. Lane, pl. 49.
H49 'Rat-Catcher seated ferret in hand and monkey' on his shoulder, 8ins. Sotheby's, 18-4-67, lot 49.
H40 'Sailor' in small hat, scarf, jacket and trousers, dancing, 8½ins. King (B), fig. 11.
H41 'Sailor's Lass' (lady with a Handkerchief), 7½ins. Stoner, pl. 76. Companion 'Sailor'. Bemrose Col. *See Plate 67.*
H42 'Tinker', with pots and pans. Trans. E.C.C., 1968, Vol. 7, pt. 2, pl. 2A.
H43 'Tyrolean Dancers' (group); male and female peasants in a gavotte, 8¼ins. Stoner, pl. 85; King (B), fig. 8.
H44 'Woodman sawing' a log on trestle; companion chopping wood with an axe, 5¾ins. Sotheby's, 5-10-76, lot 122. *See Plate 64.*

Musicians
H45 'Idyllic Musicians', man in plumed hat with pipe and tambour; woman in plumed head-dress with a triangle, 7¾ins. Hurlbutt pl. 62. *See Plate 69.*
H46 Same figures as H45 on single base before a bocage, 9¼ins. Untermyer, pl. 83, fig. 246.
H47 Same figures adapted beside baskets as sweetmeal containers, 8ins. Stoner, pl. 99.
H48 'Boy in plumed had beating a drum'; companion playing a flute, both on plinths, 10ins. Untermyer, pl. 82, fig. 247.
H49 'Lady seated with dulcimer', 7¼ins. Sotheby's, 28-10-69, lot 104.
H50 'Lady seated with zither'; companion 'Boy with drum and fife', 6ins. Stoner, pl. 78.
H51 'Lady seated with mandoline'; 'Gentleman with flute', 7ins. *Antique Dealer & Collector's Guide,* March 1973, p. 74. *See Plate 68.*
H52 'Standing male trumpeter'; companion 'Lady with triangle'. Hughes (B&T), pl. 7.
H53 'Seated Male cellist'; companion 'Lady with a hurdy-gurdy', 6¾ins. Stoner, pl. 86.
H54 'Gentleman standing with violin'; 'Lady with guitar', 9ins. Stoner, pl. 90.
H55 'Lady seated with flute'; 'Gentleman with salt-box', 5ins. Savage (A), pl. 50.
H56 'Lady standing with flute', 8¾ins. Sotheby's, 27-4-76, lot 65.
H57 'Lady seated with tambourine'; 'Boy with reed-pipe', 9ins. Untermyer, pl. 89, fig. 248 (col. pl.).
H58 'Lady seated with mandoline'; 'Boy in stocking cap with drum and fife', 8¼ins. Stoner, pl. 82.

Sporting and Pastoral
H59 'Lady in brimmed hat', bodice and skirt, with posy in right hand and a basket of flowers over her right arm. (Similar to 'Spring' in Chelsea 'Rustic Seasons' (C98), 6½ins. Saltram House no. 260.T, where model is identified as 'Columbina'.
H60 'Boy Sheperd piper' in brimmed hat with a dog; companion 'Dancing Shepherdess with a lamb', 6¼ins. *See Plate 70.*
H61 'Gardener' standing with one hand upon the shoulder of a 'Lady' who gathers flowers in her apron and holds a posy (group), 10ins. Sotheby's, 5-10-76, lot 107. *See Plate 72.*
H62 'Gardener' leaning upon his spade. *Antique Dealer & Collector's Guide,* November 1971, p. 36.
H63 'Liberty and Matrimony'; a Sportsman holding a nest of fledglings; companion Lady holding an empty bird-cage, 7½ins. Savage (A), pl. 63; Sotheby's, 10-12-73, lot 162.

H64 'Pugalists' (pair), 6½ins. Stoner, pl. 98.
H65 'Shepherd in tricorn hat standing with bagpipes'; 'Shepherdess with blossoms in her apron beside a lamb', 10½ins. Lane, pls. 46, 47.
H66 Shepherd in tricorn hat standing cross-legged beside his dog and playing a recorder; Shepherdess with flowers and a lamb, 9ins. Stoner, pl. 97.
H67 'Sportsman in a peaked cap' standing with a gun; Lady in riding habit with a falcon, 7½ins. *See Plate 71.*
H68 'Sportsman in tricorn hat standing with gun' and 'Lady with a falcon' (group), within a bocage, 6¼ins. Hurlbutt, pl. 46B.
H69 'Sportsman in tricorn hat with gun held at the trail'; 'Lady holding a pistol', 5½ins. Sotheby's, 22-10-68, lot 64. *See Colour Plate G.*

Allegorical and Mythological

H70 'Apollo' wearing a laurel wreath and loose robes, holding a lyre, 7ins. Sotheby's, 26-11-74, lot 137.
H71 'Bellona' standing in armour beside an owl, 7½ins. Hurlbutt, pl. 56B.
H72 'Charity' (group); a woman seated breast-feeding an infant with a seated and a standing child beside her, 5½ins. Sotheby's, 1-7-75, lot 88.
H73 'Charity' (reissue of G15), 11ins. Sotheby's, 13-11-73, lot 44.
H74 'Clio' standing with music in her hand, 15ins. Stoner, pl. 102. (Illustrations of other Muses are unknown to author.)
H75 'Cybele' (or Ceres) standing with a cornucopia beside a lion, 11ins. King (B), fig. 13.
H76 'Diana' holding a long-bow in her left hand with right hand raised beside her hound, 7¾ins. Hurlbutt, pl. 63.
H77 'Fame', as a winged angel with a trumpet, 7½ins. *See Plate 73.*
H78 'Flora', a lady standing holding a posy to her nose, beside a plinth on which rests a perfume vase, 10ins. Hurlbutt, pl. 36; Hughes (B), pl. 4B.
H79 'Flora Farnese', 18ins. King (B), fig. 10.
H80 'Juno' standing with her left breast bared, holding a sceptre, with a peacock, 5⅞ins. Sotheby's 13-11-73, lot 49.
H81 'Jupiter' standing holding a thunderbolt, beside an eagle, 6ins. Ibid., lot 49.
H82 'Jupiter' astride an eagle, 6ins. Savage (A), pl. 80C.
H83 'Mars' standing in Roman armour which has lion epaulettes, holding an oval shield, 10ins. Ibid., lot 137.
H84 'Minerva' standing in helmet and cuirass, 14ins. Hurlbutt, pl. 56A.
H85 'Mercury', in winged helmet bearing the caduceus, 7½ins. Sotheby's, 26-11-74, lot 137.
H86 'Neptune' standing beside a dolphin, 9ins. Scott, pl. 155, fig. 530.
H87 'Pluto' stepping over Cerberus, 7¾ins. Private col.
H88 'Venus' standing with doves at her feet, 10ins. Schreiber, pl 2, no. 9 (no. 88); Hughes (B&T). pl. 10.
H89 'Venus' standing with left breast bared, holding a torch, 10ins. Sotheby's, 13-11-73, lot 44.
H90 'Venus' reclining with a mirror, 7½ins. Ibid., 28-10-69, lot 96.

The Four Seasons

H91 'Antique Seasons' represented by standing adults beside vases.
'Spring', Flora beside a vase of flowers.
'Summer', Ceres holding corn beside a vase of fruits and leaves.
'Autumn', Bacchus beside a vase of grapes and vine leaves.
'Winter', Vulcan in a cloak beside a flaming urn.
Models 9½ins. Hurlbutt, pl. 51A (Bow); pl. 51B (Meissen).
H92 'Rustic Seasons' represented by seated adults:
'Spring', a lady wearing a picture hat with a posy and basket of flowers.
'Summer', a lady in similar dress and hat with corn in her lap.
'Autumn', a youth seated on a pannier with grapes and a goblet.
'Winter', a man in hooded coat warming his hands over a brazier. *See Colour Plate G.* Models about 5ins. Savage (A), pl. 64: Stoner, pl. 88.
H93 Standing youths and girls in contemporary dress:
'Spring', a girl in brimmed hat, laced bodice and skirt holding a posy beside a basket of flowers.
'Summer', a girl in a round hat and dress holding corn.
'Autumn', a youth in tricorn hat holding a basket of fruit, and with a bunch of grapes in his right hand.
'Winter', a youth wearing a tricorn hat to which ear-flaps are attached, holding a fur muff. About 7ins. Hurlbutt, pl. 49 (Winter); Untermyer, pl. 84, fig. 252 (paired groups).
H94 Standing 'Rustic Seasons':
'Spring', a lady in a hat with a posy in her hand and blossoms gathered in her apron.
'Summer', a girl in cap and apron holding a corn-sheaf.
'Autumn', a man in a brimmed hat, holding grapes and a goblet, beside a fruiting vine and a barrel.
'Winter', a man in a round hat and coat warming his hands over a charcoal burner attached to his belt.
Models about 9ins. Stoner, pl. 87.
H95 'Classical Seasons' represented by an adult and child in robes:
'Spring', Flora standing beside a seated putto with flowers.
'Summer', Ceres holding corn stooped over a seated putto.
'Autumn', Bacchus garlanded with vine leaves and grapes standing beside a seated putto with a basket of grapes.
'Winter', Vulcan, standing in a cloak and soft cap warming his hands over a brazier with a putto seated likewise.
Models beside Rococo candlesticks, 11ins. Morley-Fletcher (A), p.101; Hurlbutt, pl. 50A (Autumn), pl. 50B (set of Meissen prototypes).
H96 Paired examples of 'Seated Rustic Seasons', (two groups): Spring paired with Winter; Autumn paired with Summer. *Antique Dealer & Collector's Guide,* October 1968, p.17.
H97 Four individual standing Putti with appropriate accessories, 6ins. Ludlow, pl. 51, no. 116. *See Plate 74.*
H98 Four small busts on plinths: Flora, Ceres, Bacchus and Saturn, 5⅝ins. Hurlbutt, pl. 47A. *See Plate 75.*

The Five Senses

H99 A set of five seated adults in contemporary dress:
'Taste', a man seated with a bunch of grapes. *See Colour Plate G.*
'Smell', a girl with flowers. Morley-Fletcher (A), p.100.
'Sight', a lady looking into a mirror.
'Hearing', a man with a lute.
'Feeling', a lady stroking a dog. *See Plate 76.*
Models about 6 to 6½ins. Illustrations of 'Taste' and 'Hearing' not known to the author.

The Four Elements

H100 Individual models reissued as a set:
'Earth', Ceres (H75).
'Water', Neptune with a dolphin (H86).
'Air', Jupiter astride an eagle (H82), or Juno with her veil and garments blown out by the wind standing by an eagle.
'Fire', Vulcan standing beside a flaming urn.
Models about 7½ins Savage (A), pls. 65A, 66B; E.C.C. 1948 ex. cat., pl. 43, nos. 198, 199, 200. *See Colour Plate E, 'Water' and 'Earth'.*

Gallants, Ladies and Notables

H101 Frederick the Great. 9⅝ins. Stoner, pl. 80.
H102 'Gallant' wearing a dressing-gown, leaning forwards to blow a kiss; 'Lady' wearing a frilled skirt holding a fan, 8¼ins. Untermyer, pl. 99, fig. 250; Stoner, pl. 89.
H103 'Gallant' wearing a bow tie, large waistcoat, jacket and breeches, holding his hat beneath one arm; 'Lady' wearing jacket with elbow length sleeves and skirt divided to reveal a petticoat, holding a fan, 6¼ins. Stoner, pl. 75.
H104 'Gallant', wearing a tricorn hat standing with one hand in his pocket, 7¾ins. Herbert Allen, pl. 37, no. 185; Savage (A), pl. 88A. Companion 'Lady in a crinoline and holding a fan', 7½ins. *See Plate 77.*
H105 'Gallant' with right arm raised and left extended before him; 'Lady' in plumed hat, holding out her skirts in a fan, 7½ins. King (B), fig. 9.
H106 'Gallant', and companion 'Lady', holding open the lids of square hampers. *Country Life,* June, 1970, p.1138.
H107 The Marquis of Granby, in the uniform of the 'Blues', hatless with bald pate. Hughes (B), pl. 6A.
H108 'Hussar' standing in shako, tunic and fur-lined dolman, 4⅛ins. Schreiber, pl. 33, no. 199 (no. 92).
H109 General Wolfe, 13⅞ins. Lane, pl. 53; Hughes (B), pl. 6D.

Religious subjects

H110 'Bishop', standing in mitre and cope, with right hand raised in blessing. Schreiber, pl. 2, no. 24 (no. 91).
H111 'A Nun' standing holding an open book in her left hand with her right hand outstretched; 'Priest' wearing biretta and vestment, 5½ins. Lane, pl. 51A.
H112 Nun standing reading from a book'. Fitzwilliam, no. 3050.
H113 'Nun standing with right hand upon her chest, left arm at her side, wearing habit with rosary attached; companion 'Monk', 7ins. Savage (A), pl. 62B (nun). *See Plates 79a and 79b.*
H114 'Nun seated with cross' in her lap held by left hand and with a rosary in her right; companion 'Monk', seated holding an open book in his left hand and showing the text by pointing with his right, 4⅜ and 4¼ins. Lane, pl. 51B.
H115 'Nun' seated; companion 'Monk' likewise, each holding a book in both hands. Morley-Fletcher (A), p. 100.
H116 'A seated nun'; companion 'Monk', (in 'mirror' poses) each holding a book at arms length with one hand, the other hand poised in the air about to turn a page, 5¾ins. Herbert Allen, pl. 3, no. 6. *See Plate 78.*
H117 'Nun' seated; companion 'Monk' (in mirror poses) each holding a book in one hand, with the other hand resting upon the lap. Savage (A), pl. 73B.

Putti

H118 'Putto riding a nanny goat which suckles a kid whilst a second putto garlands the animal with flowers'; companion group of 'Three Putti garlanding a billy-goat with flowers', about 7ins. Mr. & Mrs. John Mould col. *See Colour Plate H.*
H119 Similar pair of groups but mounted on legged bases, with candle holders and brass stems terminating in porcelain flowers, 13ins. Stoner, pl. 94.
H120 'Putto, seated upon recumbent Leopard' feeding it with grapes, 4¾ins. Fitzwilliam, no. 93.
H121 Single standing putti:
'Holding a Puppy' 4¾ins. Savage (A), pl. 65C. *See Plate 81.*
Holding a basket of flowers' in his left hand, 4¾ins. Scott, pl. 171, figs. 627 & 628.
'Holding a basket of flowers in both hands'. Savage (A), pl. 65A.
H122 Seated putto, male; companion female, each draped beside flower encrusted candlesticks, 7½ins. Sotheby's 26-11-74, lot 7. *See Plate 80.*

Birds

H123 'Bullfinches', 5ins. Ludlow, pl. 47, no. 109.
H124 'Buntings' (yellow), 2½ins. Untermyer, pl. 87, fig. 258.
H125 'Buntings', 3⅝ins. Ibid., pl. 87, fig. 257. *See Plate 77.*
H126 'Buntings', a pair, upon a 'Y' shaped tree stump adorned with leaves and flowers, below which is a small dog, 7ins. Ludlow, pl. 46, no. 105.
H127 'Two Buntings in a cherry tree' with a nest of fledglings topped by a candle holder, 9½ins. Sotheby's, 18-6-71, lot 115.
H128 'Cockerel', and companion 'Hen', 6½ and 5½ins. Untermyer, pl. 92, fig. 256.
H129 'Finches' (pair) on tall bases, 6ins. Hurlbutt, pl. 29.
H130 'Finches' (pair), 3½ins. Stoner, pl. 107.
H131 'Finches' (pair) on mound bases, 4ins. Hurlbutt, pl. 29.
H132 'Goldfinch', 3½ins. Sotheby's, 4-2-75, lot 137.
H133 'Goldfinch' with one wing displayed, 6ins. Ibid. 14-5-75, lot 61.
H134 'Goldfinches' (pair), on tall bases, 5¼ins. Ibid., 2-4-68, lot 14.
H135 'Goldfinches' (pair), 3¾ins. E.C.C., 1949 ex. cat., pl. 38, nos. 191, 192.
H136 'Kestrel', 6ins. Sotheby's, 14-5-74, lot 60.
H137 'Owl', tawny, 7¼ins. Untermyer, pl. 78, fig. 259.
H138 'Owls' (pair), 9½ins. Stoner, pl. 105.
H139 'Parrots eating fruit' (pair), 7ins. *Treasures of the National Trust* (1976), pl. 115; Ludlow, pl. 50, no. 115.
H140 'Parrots' (pair), 7½ins. Untermyer, pl. 92, fig. 260.
H141 'Peacock', and companion 'Peahen', 7¼ins. Stoner, pl. 108.
H142 'Peacock', 4ins. Hurlbutt, pl. 29,
H143 'Pheasants' (pair), 6⅞ins. Untermyer, pl. 87, fig. 262.
H144 'Pheasants' (pair), 10¼ and 10¾ins. Sotheby's, 23-2-64, lot 120.
H145 'Pheasant' in a bocage (candlestick), 10ins. Sotheby's, 23-2-71, lot 76.
H146 'Pigeon', 1¼ins. Ludlow, pl. 49, no. 114.
H147 'Rooster', and companion 'Hen with three chicks', 4ins. Schreiber, no. 226 (no. 60).
H148 'Song Birds' (two) in a nest in a bocage (candlestick), 8½ins. Untermyer, pl. 86, fig. 253.
H149 'Warblers' (pair), 5ins. Ludlow, pl. 47, no. 107.

Animals

H150 'Cats', seated (pair) one with a mouse, 3 and 3½ins. Schreiber, no. 33 (no. 99).
H151 'Cats' (pair) seated, 2⅝ins. *Connoisseur,* Vol. 137, p.90, fig. 1.
H152 'Cow', standing, and companion 'Bull', 4ins. Stoner, pl. 104.
H153 'Dog begging beside a Rooster and recumbent mongrel' (group), 4⅝ins. Untermyer, pl. 75, fig. 254.
H154 'Dog with a recumbent Goat and a Squirrel' (group), in a bocage, 7½ins. Sotheby's, 26-11-74, lot 138.
H155 'Ewe' standing, companion 'Ram', 4¾ins. Private col.
H156 Fable group of 'Fox dining with the Stork', 9½ins. Grosvenor House Antiques Fair Cat. p.25 (illustration).
H157 Fable group of 'Stork dining with the Fox', 10½ins. Ibid.
H158 'Hounds' (pair) seated on mound bases, 3¼ins. Grosvenor House Antiques Fair, 1964, cat. p. 84, pls. 4, 5.
H159 'Hounds', dismal puppies, (pair), 5¾ins. *Antique Dealer & Collector's Guide,* April 1967, p. 8.
H160 'Lions' (pair), 5ins. Tait (A), fig. 58.
H161 'Monkey' eating nuts, companion 'Female' with a baby upon her back, 3½ins. Schreiber, no. 31 (no. 58).
H162 'Monkeys' (two) with a 'Squirrel' in a bocage (group). Sotheby's, 26-11-74, lot 138.
H163 'Pug' seated, 4½ins. Private col.
H164 'Squirrels eating nuts' (pair), 8ins. Stoner, pl. 110.
H165 'Stag' recumbent beneath a bocage (candlestick), companion 'Doe', 9ins. Ibid., pl. 109 (Stag).

Miscellaneous

H166 'The Tea Party' (group); a lady seated with a teacup in her hand beside a plinth upon which rests a vase of flowers, and a gentleman standing beside a blackamoor who holds a tray, 9½ins. Godden (B), p. 37, fig. 69.
H167 'Monkey dressed as a Gallant'; companion dressed as a 'Lady', each seated beside a sweetmeat container, 6¼ins. Stoner, pl. 106.
H168 Decorative vase with moulded figures, commemorating the death of the composer Handel. Three putti mounted around the base emblematic of 'Music', 'Drama', and the 'Dance'. Tait (A), Fig. 36.

APPENDIX I
Bow Figures Made Between 1766 and 1776

Theatrical

I 1 'Arlecchino' wearing motley standing beside 'Columbina' upon a legged base before a bocage (reissues of models H1 and H2). Morley-Fletcher (A), p. 91. col. pl.
I 2 'Arlecchino' wearing a pointed cap and motley, dancing; companion 'Columbina', also dancing, mounted upon tall bases with vertical slot-like fenestrations, 6⅞ins. Untermyer, pl. 90, fig. 249. The same models married upon a single flat, wide base edged with scrolls, 6ins. Stoner, pl. 101.

Foreign Personages

I 3 'Chinese Magician with a child' who stands upon a chair, the two mounted on a scrolled base within a gazebo, topped by a cupola (reissue of H13 omitting bear), 11ins. Stoner, pl. 93.

Allegorical and Mythological

I 4 'Two Putti decking a Billy Goat with garlands'; companion group of 'two Putti decking a Nanny Goat' which suckles a kid with flowers (reissue of groups H118 adapted as candlesticks), 13ins. Stoner, pl. 94.
I 5 'The Muse Clio', standing with a scroll in her left hand, mounted on a circular base fitted with a detachable stand, a copy of the Chelsea model D36, 15ins. with stand. Ibid., pl. 102.
I 6 'Mars' standing in Roman armour wearing a helmet from which four plumes arise; 'Minerva' in crested helmet and armour, 7¾ins. Private col.

The Four Seasons

I 7 'Standing adult Rustics' (reissue of H94), 7ins. Hurlbutt, pl. 54. *See Plate 82.*
I 8 'Standing Youths and Girls in contemporary dress', reissue of H93, with Autumn paired with Summer, and Spring with Winter. Pairs mounted upon legged bases, before bocages, flanked by candle sconces, 9⅝ins. Untermyer, pls. 84, 85, fig. 252.
I 9 Large standing single figures:
'Spring', a lady, wearing a hat, holding a posy with flowers gathered in her apron and 'Autumn' a gardener holding fruit with vegetables gathered in his apron. Models derived from those on the Chelsea 'Allegorical Seasons' (D57) and issued separately, 13ins. Stoner, pl. 103. (Illustrations or models of Summer and Autumn unknown to the author.) *See Plate 83.*

Pastoral subjects

I 10 'Huntsman wearing a peaked cap holding a gun'; 'Lady wearing riding habit holding game and a falcon' (reissues of H65 with addition of a large standing hound to each figure), 7½ins. Untermyer, pl. 90, fig. 251.
I 11 'Shepherd playing a recorder', standing cross-legged beside a dog; 'Shepherdess holding a posy' with flowers gathered in her apron (reissue of H66), 9ins. Untermyer, pl. 83, fig. 246.
I 12 'Huntsman and Lady seated before a fountain' (group), mounted on a scrolled base before a bocage, 11ins. Plymouth City Mus.
I 13 'Fortune telling group'; a lady having her palm read by a gipsy woman who has a babe upon her back and a child at her side (similar to Chelsea group D114), 10¾ins. Stoner, pl. 92.

Musicians

I 14 'Gentleman standing with a violin beside a seated Lady who plays the hurdy-gurdy', mounted on a scrolled base before a bocage flanked by candle sconces; derived from 'Male Violinist' (H54) and 'Columbina' (H10), formerly unrelated to one another. 8½ins. Stoner, pl. 91.
I 15 'The Idyllic Musicians', mounted as a group before a bocage, (reissue of separate models, H47), 9¼ins. Untermyer, pl. 83, fig. 246.
I 16 'The New Dancers', adapted from models (H34) to stand holding open the lids of sweetmeat containers, 8ins. Stoner, pl. 99.

The Four Quarters of the Globe:

I 17 Four small individual figures, each mounted upon a pierced plinth before a small bocage, 5⅜ins.-5¼ins. Saltram House. *See Plate 84:*
'Africa', a Negress with a lion.
'Asia', a Levantine girl with a casket.
'Europe', represented by Britannia.
'America', a Red Indian standing with one foot on an alligator.
The same figures are paired on either side of two chamber candlesticks. Lord Bearsted's col. cat., no. 4.'
I 18 'A Hussar', standing, 4ins. Schreiber, pl. 33, no. 199 (no. 92).

APPENDIX J
Derby Figures Made Prior to 1756

Animals

J1 'Florentine Boars' (pair), one seated, the other running, 4¼ins. Barrett & Thorpe, pls. 18, 19. *See Plate 171.*

J2 'Stag', and companion 'Doe', at lodge, 5ins. Ibid., pl. 21.

J3 'Charging Bulls' (pair), 5½ins. Ibid., pl. 20.

J4 'Billy Goat', and companion 'Nanny Goat suckling a Kid', 6½ins. Gilhespy (A), fig. 137. Stoner, pl. 44. *See Plates 175 and 176.*

J5 'Nanny Goat being milked by a naked Boy', 8½ins. Herbert Allen, pl. 1, no. 2. Note: now attributed to Longton Hall.

J6 Sheep, a standing 'Ewe' and companion 'Ram', 4½ins. (other sizes known). Ashton col. *See Plate 85.*

J7 'Ewe and Lamb' (group). *Connoisseur,* 1960, Vol. 146, p. 261, fig. 4; also in Derby Mus.

J8 'Dog', and companion 'Cat', both seated. V & A.

J9 'Lions' (pair), 3½ins. Ashton col. *See Plate 86.*

Human Subjects

J10 'Kitty Clive as Mrs Riot', 9¾ins. Barrett & Thorpe, pl. 3. *See Plate 87.*

J11 'Arlecchino' leaning against a tree-stump, left arm raised and right behind his back; companion 'Columbina' dancing. *Antique Dealer & Collector's Guide,* January 1973, p. 23.

J12 'An Actor' in wide brimmed hat and cloak, with right hand raised and left arm akimbo, 6¾ins. Ashton col. *See Plate 88.*

J13 'Boy Shepherd Piper' in brimmed hat with a dog; companion 'Dancing Shepherdess' beside a lamb, 6½ins. Gilhespy (B), col. pl. VIII. *See Plate 89 and Colour Plate I.*

J14 'Dancing Girl' holding a mask aloft in her right hand and her full skirt in her left; companion 'Male in pierrot costume' and cocaded hat, with left arm raised and right extended, 6½ins. Untermyer, pl. 96, fig. 271.

J15 'Gentleman standing bare-headed playing a recorder', 6½ins. Gilhespy (B), pl. 15.

J16 'Bagpipers' (pair), seated bare-headed. *Connoisseur,* September 1927, formerly in Wallace Elliott col.

J17 'Huntsman in peaked cap playing a flute beside a lady' seated on the ground who has one hand upon his sleeve (group), 6¼ins. Lane, pl. 56B. *See Plate 169 and Colour Plate P.*

J18 'Lady Vegetable Seller' with basket over her left arm, 7⅛ins. Lane, pl. 61B.

J19 'Male Absinth Seller' in tricorn hat with tray of bottles, 6¾ins. Lane, pl. 61C.

J20 'Print Seller', standing in a tricorn hat, a pack on his back, and samples in either hand, 6¼ins. Gilhespy (B), fig. 1. *See Plate 90.*

J21 'Chinaman in a conical hat with a Boy', adapted as a watchstand, 9ins. Gilhespy (A), fig. 140. *See Plate 92.*

J22 'St Philip', as a bearded man, wearing a soft cap and tattered cloak, standing barefoot regarding a cruxifix, 9½ins. Lane, pl. 59.

J23 'St Thomas', in Roman uniform, bareheaded and wrapped in a mantle, with an orb and broken sword at his feet, 9½ins. Schreiber, pl. 10, no. 137 (no. 287). *See Plate 91.*

Allegorical and Mythological

J24 'The Arts', represented by a standing figure of a man wearing a laurel chaplet and robes, with palette, brushes, tomes, and musical instruments at his feet, 6½ins. Barrett & Thorpe, pl. 10. *See Plate 94.*

J25 'Cybele', wearing a crown standing beside a lion holding a cornucopia, 6ins. Trans. E.C.C., !968, Vol. 7, pt. 1, pl. 57D. *See Plate 105 for version mounted on tall base and Colour Plate O.*

J26 'Mars', standing in Roman armour leaning upon his shield, 5⅝ins. Gilhespy (B), fig. 2. *See Plate 93.*

J27 'Minerva', in crested helmet and armour holding a shield upon which is the head of Medusa, 7ins. Bradley, no. 10.

J28 'Neptune' with a dolphin, 6¾ins. Gilhespy (B), fig. 2.

J29 'Pluto stepping over Cerberus', 6⅝ins. Lane, pl. 60A.

J30 'Venus', holding aloft a mirror towards which 'Cupid' reaches up, 7½ins. Gilhespy (A), fig. 141. *See Colour Plate K.*
Note: 'Jupiter' and his eagle, and 'Juno' and her peacock, both described in William Duesbury's London Account Book, have not been identified.

The Four Seasons:

J31 Four individual seated and draped putti:
'Spring', holding a basket of flowers upon a rock on his left side.
Summer', holding ears of corn beside a corn-sheaf.
'Autumn', with a bunch of grapes, seated upon an upturned basket.
'Winter', in a cloak, warming his hands over a charcoal burner.
Models average 5ins. Lane, pls. 56A, B. *See Plate 95.*

J32 Four pairs of standing Rustics:
'Spring'; a girl adjusting her brimmed hat, who secures flowers in her apron with her right hand and a gardener wearing a cocked hat, holding a basket of flowers and a posy, 7½ins. Stoner, pl. 47. *See Colour Plate J.*
'Summer'; a woman with a bird's nest in her left hand and a man holding a corn-sheaf in both hands, 6ins. Barrett & Thorpe, pls. 5, 6. *See Plates 96, 97 and 98 and Colour Plate J.*
'Winter'; an old woman wearing a headscarf extending her hands over a basket of charcoal, and an elderly man, likewise, holding a muff, 6 and 7¼ins. Lane, pl. 60B. *See Plate 99 and Colour Plate J.*

The Five Senses

J33 A set of five seated figures in contemporary dress:
'Feeling', a lady stroking a parrot upon her knee, 6½ins. Barrett & Thorpe, pl. 8.
'Taste', a lady with a basket of fruit in her lap eating grapes, 6½ins. Ibid., pl. 8. *See Colour Plate N.*
'Sight', a gentleman in cap and dressing-gown looking into a hand mirror, 6¼ins. Ibid., pl. 14. *See Colour Plate M.*
'Smell', a gentleman taking a pinch of snuff, 6¼ins. Ibid., pl. 14. *See Colour Plate L.*
'Hearing', a lady seated with a musical score (possibly also once held a musical instrument), 6ins. Royal Crown Derby Porcelain Co. Mus., Frontis. of museum guidebook.

J34 A set of chinoiserie groups, each of two figures:
'Feeling', a Chinaman in a conical hat cuffing a boy upon the cheek, 9¼ins. Schreiber, pl. 17, no. 140 (no. 284). *See Plate 100.*
'Taste', a Chinaman standing examining a phial, and a boy leaning over a basket containing bottles that lies upon its side, 8¼ins. Lane, col. pl. D; Ludlow, pl. 113, no. 241.
'Sight', a Chinese lady holding aloft a bird, whilst gesticulating with her right hand to a seated Chinaman, 7¼ins. Stoner, col. pl. 2.
'Smell', a Chinese youth holding a flower to his nose and a child who reaches up to grasp it, 8½ins. Barrett & Thorpe, pl. 17. *See Plate 101.*
'Hearing', a Chinese lady holding a lyre standing beside a seated child, 8¾ins. Sotheby's, 25-5-38, lot 317, late Wallace Elliot col.

The Four Elements

J35 'Water', a seated Chinese boy beside a basket of fish, both hands are extended before him and in one he probably once held a cup.
'Air', a seated Chinese boy with one hand raised, which may once have held a bird, both 8ins. Barrett & Thorpe, pl. 13 (the pair complete with brass fitments); Bradley, no. 4, illustrates an enamelled pair in the Leslie Godden col.

APPENDIX K
Derby Figures made between 1756 and 1769

The Pale Family 1756-1759

K1 'Arlecchino in round hat and motley standing beside Columbina' on a wide flat base, 6½ins. Williams (A), fig. 45 (col.).

K2 'Arlecchino in modley standing making playful gestures to a child also in motley held by Columbina', 6½ins. Barrett & Thorpe, col. frontis.

K3 'Boy in tricorn hat holding a posy kicking his legs'; companion 'Girl seated with her hat on her lap', the two seated, 4¾ins. Williams (A), fig. 24. *See Plate 106.*

K4 'Boy in hat', jacket and trousers standing with both arms raised before him; companion 'Girl' likewise (prototypes of Bow 'New Dancers', H34), 4½ and 4¾ins. Ibid., fig. 20.

K5 'Boy in tricorn hat standing with fife and tambourine', 5½ins. Barrett & Thorpe, pl. 49.

K6 'Boy in tricorn hat playing an end-flute', 4ins. Morley-Fletcher (A), p. 107.

K7 Candlestick group: bird perched in 'V' of branched candlestick with boy, girl and a dog, mounted upon the base, the whole encrusted with flowers, 10ins. Barrett & Thorpe, pl. 30.

K8 Candlestick group: two dogs begging regarding a squirrel in a leafing tree, 9ins. Ibid., pl. 58.

K9 Candlesticks (pair): 'Arlecchino' dancing and companion 'Pulcinella' carrying a lantern, 9½ins. Gilhespy (B), fig. 25.

K10 'Candlestick of seated putto eating grapes' (dry-edge prototype J31, 'Autumn'), 9ins. Gilhespy (B), fig. 22. *See Plate 107.*

K11 'Diana' with long-bow and hound, taking an arrow from a quiver, 10ins. Dixon, pl. 38.

K12 'Gentleman in hat playing a flute' (dry-edge prototype J15), 7ins. Gilhespy (B), fig. 15. *See Plate 104.*

K13 'Gardener' in tricorn hat with basket of fruit, extending an apple in his right hand; companion 'Girl' holding corn in her apron with both hands, 4¾ins. Barrett & Thorpe, pl. 52.

K14 'Lady seated with a mandoline' (dry-edge prototype of 'Taste' J34), 5½ins. Gilhespy (B), fig. 23. *See Plate 103.*

K15 'Male dancer in Pierrot costume' (dry-edge prototype J14); companion 'Lady standing holding out her apron' with her right hand with left elevated (new model), 6½ and 6ins. Barrett & Thorne, pl. 51.

K16 'Seated Gentleman holding a shell container'; companion 'Lady', likewise (salts), 7ins. Williams (A), fig. 13.

K17 Standing 'Rustic Seasons'; a peasant in wide-brimmed hat with basket of grapes holding a bunch in his right hand; companion woman with basket of flowers proffering a posy, about 5ins. Derby Mus.

K18 'Seated Seasons': 'Spring' a girl wearing a floral crown holding a garland; 'Summer' a boy with a crown of corn stalks with corn in his hand, 4½ins. Barrett & Thorpe, pl. 48. *See Plate 105.*

K19 'Shepherdess stooping to caress a lamb' the front legs of which are on her knee; 'Shepherd with right hand on hip and a posy in his left', 5½ins. *Antique Dealer & Collectors's Guide,* July 1969, p. 30.

K20 'Naked Child seated beside a vase', 3ins. Williams (A), fig. 23.

K21 'Two Lovers and a Clown', 5ins. Gilhespy (B), fig. 23; Williams (A), col. pl.

The Main Stream of Production 1760-1769

Theatrical

K22 'Arlecchino' in round hat and motley, with his right hand on his breast and stapsticks in his left, 7ins. Sotheby's 12-3-74, lot 157.

K23 'Arlecchino, Columbina and Pulcinella' addorsed, each with a shell container, 9¾ins. Stoner, pl. 59.

K24 'Boy dressed as Arlecchino'; 'Girl attired as Columbina', 4½ins. Gilhespy (A), fig. 149. Bocaged version, 5½ins. Ibid.

K25 'An actress dressed as a Street Seller', wrongly identified as 'Colly Cibber', 8¾ins. Cushion (B), col. pl. 12; Hughes (B), pl. 11.

K26 'Duet Singers', male with right hand on hip and left elevated, female in mirror position, 8¾ins. Barrett & Thorpe, pl. 68.

K27 'Falstaff' in plumed hat, holding an oval shield and a sword, 5¼ins. Barrett & Thorpe, pl. 62.

K28 'Milton', standing beside a plinth, 11ins. King (B), fig. 40.

K29 'Shakespeare', standing beside a plinth, 11½ins. Ibid., fig. 41.

K30 'Tancred' wearing a fur hat and dolman, 9ins. Cushion (B), col. pl. 12; Barrett & Thorpe, pl. 63.

K31 'Two Lovers with a Clown' (group) in a bocage, 12ins. Barrett & Thorpe, pl. 57.

Foreign Personages

K32 'Abyssinian Archer', 11¾ins. Gilhespy (A), fig. 186; Cushion (A), pl. 67, Meissen prototype.

K33 'Blackamoor' in a long cloak and turban; 'Negress' in tall hat and cloak, 8¼ins. Barrett & Thorpe, pl. 65.

K34 'Blackamoor', and companion 'Negress', each bearing a shell. Cushion (A), pl. 91.

K35 'Four Blackamoors' addorsed, each with a shell, 9ins. *Antique Dealer & Collector's Guide,* June 1971, p. 87, pl. 3.

K36 'Boy in Turkish costume'; 'Girl' likewise, the two standing, 8ins. Stoner, pl. 51. Miniature versions 3½ins. tall later issued by Robert Bloor.

K37 'Turk', wearing turban and long cloak, walking with right arm upraised; 'Levantine Lady' in long coat with elbow length sleeves, dancing. Honey (A), pls. 44A, 44C.

K38 'Negress' with right hand elevated to adjust tall head-dress and proffering an apple with her left (probably pair to K32), 12ins. Herbert Allen, pl. 10, no. 33.

K39 'Chinese Boys playing about rococo candlestick' (pair), 10¼ins. Untermyer, pl. 107, fig. 289.

Musicians and Dancers

K40 'Gentleman, seated with cello', 6½ins. Stoner, pl. 56.

K41 'Gentleman, seated with violin', 5¼ins. Untermyer, pl. 96, fig. 273.

K42 'Idyllic Musicians'. Male in tricorn hat playing three holed pipe and beating a tambourine suspended from his sleeve; companion Lady in plumed head-dress playing a triangle, 7¼ins. Fitzwilliam, nos. C64, C65, 'Flambé Musicians'.

K43 'Lady in plumed head-dress playing a mandoline'; companion 'Man seated with bagpipes', each in a gazebo topped by a chinoiserie cupola, 12ins. Morley-Fletcher (A), p. 138.

K44 'Lady seated playing hurdy-gurdy', 6¼ins. Stoner, pl. 56.

K45 'Male piper', standing cross legged beside a dog; companion 'Dancing Girl', each as a candlestick, 9¼ins. Hurlbutt (A), pl. 10.

K46 'Youth in soft cap, standing cross legged with pipe to his lips and a tambourine' suspended from his sleeve. Honey (A), 45B.

K47 'Youth seated in soft cap', breeches gathered with ribbons at the knees, playing bagpipes. Stoner, pl. 63.

K48 'Dancing Lesson' (after van Loo); a girl with plumes in her hair, stands holding a dog upon its hind legs which is dressed in motley whilst boy plays hurdy-gurdy, 11ins. Schreiber, pl. 22, no. 178 (no. 299).

K49 'Singing Lesson' (after van Loo); a girl holds unclad dog upon a plinth with its mouth open and boy holds song sheet, 11ins. Lane, pl. 67.

K50 'Male Dancer', in plumed cap, jacket, breeches and hose, short cloak over right arm; companion 'Girl holding out skirts with right hand' and with left elevated, 9½ins. Stoner, pl. 55.

K51 'Minuet Dancers' (after Watteau); boy and companion girl leaning backwards in cloaks, dancing, 11⅛ins. King (B), col. pl. II.

K52 'Ranelagh Dancers'; male, sumptuously attired, left arm akimbo, proffering a letter inscribed 'Domini Lucretiae'; companion lady in plumes and cloak with a miniature cameo suspended from her shoulder (after Duchess of Ancaster), 11½ins. Stoner, pl. 57.

K53 'Tyrolean Dancers' (group) after Eberlein, 7ins. Stoner, pl. 54.

Peasant and Pastoral

K53A 'Boy Shepherd Bagpiper'; companion 'Dancing Shepherdess', (see J13 for dry-edge prototype), updated to wear Scottish dress, 7ins. Morley-Fletcher (A), p. 136.

K54 'Farmer holding a pig'; 'Wife holding a baby'; 'Parson'. Three separate models representing the 'Tithe Pig', 9½ins. Gilhespy (A), fig. 152; Stoner, pl. 50. *See Plate 120 for later group.*

K55 'Grape Vendors': Man in cocked hat seated with basket of grapes; companion Woman in round hat, likewise, 4¾ins. *See Plate 115.*

K56 'Italian Farmer', holding a cockerel; companion 'Wife' with a hen, 7½ins. V & A cat. nos. C673-1925 (early versions), C1002-1917 (later versions). *See Colour Plate Q.*

K57 'Peasant Woman standing with grapes gathered in her apron beside a Man in a hat who has his right arm about her waist', 6¼ins. Barrett & Thorpe, pl. 71. *See Plate 116.*

K58 'Shepherd', and companion 'Shepherdess' singing, each holding musical score in one hand and wearing wide brimmed hats respectively with a dog and a lamb, 6¾ins. Royal Crown Derby Porc. Co. Mus.

K59 'Shepherdess', in small hat, leaning forwards with flowers and garlands about her, 7½ins. Barrett & Thorpe, pl. 27.

K60 The 'Dresden Shepherds'; shepherd standing in cocked hat with posy in his left hand and sheep under his arm; shepherdess in brimmed hat with flowers secured in her apron with her left hand and a basket of blossoms over her right arm, 8ins. Honey (A), pls. 45A, 45C. *See Plate 108.* Similar models adapted as candlesticks, 9½ins. Scott, pl. 152, fig. 514.

K61 'Shepherd standing beside a seated dog'; companion 'Shepherdess placing a garland about the neck of a lamb', each before waist tall bocages, 5¼ and 5⅜ins. Herbert Allen, pl. 13, no. 39.

K62 'Shepherd in cocked hat' proffering posy with right hand and holding a basket in his left; companion 'Shepherdess' with flowers gather in her apron, 8½ins. Hughes (B), pl. 9. *See Plate 109.*

K63 'Shepherd proffering an apple' with his right hand, wearing a tricorn hat, standing with basket of fruit held to his chest with his left hand; companion 'Shepherdess with a crook' in small hat, with apron hooked up to her waist, both on bases cut away with two inverted 'Us', 10ins. Barrett & Thorpe, pl. 53.

K64 'Shepherd playing a recorder', standing cross-legged beside a dog; 'Shepherdess holding flowers' in her apron and a posy beside a lamb, 6½ins. *Antique Dealer & Collector's Guide,* March 1971, p. 5. *See Plate 109.*

K65 'Shepherd seated with his dog'; 'Shepherdess seated with a bird-cage', each flanked by candle sconces, emblematic of 'Liberty and Matrimony' 9½ins. Stoner, pl. 62.

K66 'Shepherdess' holding out her skirt with both hands to contain flowers, 9¼ins. Barrett & Thorpe, pl. 70.

K67 'The Welsh Tailors'; a tailor holding a pair of scissors astride a goat with a pannier of kids upon his back; wife holding a baby riding a nanny-goat suckling a kid, 7½ins. Ibid., pls. 123, 124.

Street Vendors and Others

K68 'A Gallant' standing beside a hound; 'Lady' standing beside a sheep, each holding open the lid of a hamper, 9ins. Gilhespy (A), fig. 144.

K69 'Gallant' seated beside a dog; companion 'Lady', likewise, beside a sheep, each holding oval containers shaped like shells. Hughes (B & T), pl. 13.

K70 'Jewish Pedlar', standing in fur-lined hat, bottle in hand, and a tray of small bottles slung by a strap about his neck; 'Woman with a box of trinkets' attached to her belt, 10½ins. — Untermyer, pl. 98, fig. 276.

K71 'Print seller with map on his back' and companion 'Lady holding a map', 6½ins. Barrett & Thorpe, pl. 68. *See Plates 111 and 112.*

The Five Senses

K72 A set of five seated youths and girls with creatures:
'Taste', a boy eating grapes beside a leopard.
'Sight', a boy with a spyglass beside an eagle.
'Feeling', a girl attended by Cupid whose quiver hangs from a tree stump.
'Smell', a boy holding a posy to his nose beside a hound.
'Hearing', a girl playing a lute beside a swan.
Models about 9½ins. Cheyne Book, pl. 23, no. 252 (erroneously ascribed to Chelsea).

The Four Quarters of the Globe (Continents)

K73 Four individual standing children:
'Africa', a Blackamoor wearing an elephant head-dress and cloak, holding a cornucopia and a crab, stepping over a lion. *See Plate 113.*
'Asia', a Levantine girl holding a perfume vase in her left hand beside a crouching camel. *See Plate 113.*
'America', a Red Indian girl wearing a feathered head-dress and skirt, holding a long-bow in her left hand, beside a prairie dog.
'Europe', a white girl wearing a crown and robes, holding an orb and a sceptre in either hand.
Models about 7¼ins. Morley-Fletcher (A), p. 137; Derby City Mus.

The Four Seasons

K74 A set of four single seated putti:
'Spring', wearing floral wreath with a basket of blossoms.
'Summer', wearing a wreath of corn ears, beside a corn-sheaf.
'Autumn', crowned with vine leaves with a bunch and a basket of grapes.
'Winter', wearing a cloak, with a brazier balanced on his knee.
Models about 6½ins. Cushion (B), fig. 56.

K75 'The Classical Seasons' represented by standing adults each with a child: 'Spring', Flora with a putto carrying a basket of flowers.
'Summer', Ceres with a putto carrying in both hands a corn-sheaf.
'Autumn', Bacchus and a putto with grapes.
'Winter', Vulcan standing in cloak with arms folded and a putto carrying faggots for a lighted brazier.
Models about 9ins. Gilhespy (B), figs. 19, 20 (Meissen prototypes). *See Plate 114.*

K76 'The Antique Seasons' represented by standing figures in classical robes, each beside a vase:
'Spring', Flora beside a vase of flowers. Barrett & Thorpe, pl. 56.
'Autumn', Bacchus beside a vase of grapes. Temple Newsam.
'Summer', Ceres beside a vase of grapes, and 'Winter', Vulcan beside a flaming vase. Illus. unknown to author.

Allegorical and Mythological

K77 'Aphrodite' standing beside a dolphin, 10½ins. Stoner, pl. 53.
K78 'Britannia', in helmet, armour and holding a shield, 7½ins. Cushion (B), pl. 88; large model 13½ins. *See Plate 118.*
K79 'Diana' (reissue of K11), 13¼ins.
K80 'Europa and the Bull' (group), 11⅜ins. Lane, pl. 66.
K81 'Juno and the peacock', 13¾ins. King (B), fig. 45.
K82 'Jupiter and the eagle', 15ins. Derby City Mus.
K83 'Jupiter in a chariot' with an eagle, 11ins. Sotheby's 14-5-70, lot 132; Ashmolean.
K84 'Juno in a chariot' with a peacock, 10½ins. Sotheby's 14-5-70, lot 132; Ashmolean.
K85 'Justice' with sword and scales, 10ins. Hughes (B), pl. 9.
K86 'Leda and the Swan', 11½ins. Barrett & Thorpe, pl. 59.
K87 'Mars' and companion 'Minerva', 13½ and 15ins. Scott, pl. 168, figs. 615, 616.
K88 'Mars' and companion 'Venus with a Cupid', each as a candlestick, 10¾ins. Ludlow, pl. 190, no. 100. *See Plate 118.*
K89 'Muse Clio', reclining with a quill attended by Cupid who holds a parchment scroll, 8¼ins. Tait (B), pl. 45.
K90 'Muse Erato', reclining with a tambourine attended by a Cupid with flowers, 7½ins. Tait (B), fig. 30.
K91 'Neptune standing beside a dolphin', 16ins. Derby Mus.
K92 'Pluto, stepping over the three headed dog, Cerberus', 7ins. Barrett & Thorpe, pl. 47. *See Plate 117.*
K93 'St. Philip' (reissue of J22), 13ins. V & A.
K94 'St. Thomas' (reissue of J23), 13ins. Ibid., both C299-1940.
K95 'Venus seated with a dolphin upon which a Cupid sits', 8¾ins. Barrett & Thorpe, pl. 60.
K96 'Vulcan' with a thunderbolt and a brazier, 15ins. King (B), fig. 44.
K97 'War', a youth standing beside a canon with trophies of war at his feet, 8½ins. Barrett & Thorpe, pl. 61.

Birds

K98 'Blue Tit', 2¾ins. Sotheby's, 18-4-67, lot 30.
K99 'Blue Tits' (pair), 5ins. Ibid., 3-4-73, lot 72.
K100 'Bullfinches', 4½ins. Stoner, pl. 61.
K101 'Buntings' (pair), 3¾ins. Untermyer, pl. 110, fig. 28 (col.).
K102 'Buntings', two in a bocage with flowers topped by a candle holder (pair), 10½ins. Sotheby's, 21-7-64, lot 70.
K103 'Canaries' (pair), 5¾ins. Stoner, pl. 60.
K104 'Canaries', 5⅜ins. Untermyer, pl. 110, fig. 283 (col.).
K105 'Canary', 2⅞ins. Sotheby's, 6-5-69, lot 110.
K106 'Chaffinches' (pair), 6ins. Williams (A), pl. 56.
K107 'Dove', 2¾ins. Barrett & Thorpe, pl. 54.
K108 'Finches' (pair), 3⅞ins. Untermyer, pl. 105, fig. 284.
K109 'Goldfinches', 2½ins. E.C.C. 1948 ex. cat., pl. 67, nos. 312, 313.
K110 'Goldfinches' (pair), 4ins. Sotheby's, 14-5-67, lot 7.
K111 'Goldfinches, 2½ins. Ibid., 25-3-74, lot 175.
K112 'Great Tits', 4¾ins. Stoner, pl. 60.
K113 'Owl', 2½ins. Sotheby's, 22-3-74, lot 186.
K114 'Parrot', 3¼ins. Ibid., 18-4-74, lot 29.
K115 'Peacock', 3¾ins. Ibid., 25-3-74, lot 46.
K116 'Peacock'; companion 'Peahen', each with a bocage. *Antique Dealer & Collector's Guide,* September 1969, p. 80.
K117 'Song Bird', 5ins. Untermyer, pl. 110, fig. 286 (col.).
K118 'Tit', 3⅛ins. Sotheby's, 18-4-67, lot 22.
K119 'Titmice' (pair), 4⅝ins. Untermyer, pl. 110, fig. 285 (col.).
K120 'Tomtits' (pair), 4¾ins. Barrett & Thorpe, pl. 54.
K121 'Warblers' (pair), 4½ and 4ins. Untermyer, pl. 105, fig. 287.
K122 'Woodpecker', 6¼ins. Sotheby's, 6-5-69, lot 111.
K123 'Woodpecker', 5¼ins. Untermyer, pl. 110, fig. 288 (col.).
K124 'Two Finches with a nest of fledglings' in a cherry tree, 9¾ins. Sotheby's, 10-12-73, lot 206.
K125 Two 'Fabulous Birds' in a bocage topped by candle holder, 9⅜ins. Ibid., 30-5-67, lot 67.

Animals

K126 'Bull', charging, 2¾ins. Gilhespy (B), fig. 151.
K127 'Bull', charging (after dry-edge model J3), 2¾ins. Derby Porc. Co. Mus.
K128 'Cow suckling a calf'; companion 'Bull', 5½ins. Sotheby's, 25-3-74, lot 193.
K129 'Cow, recumbent' before a small bocage, 3½ins. Gilhespy (B), fig. 151.
K130 'Dog', standing within a wreath like bocage, beneath a candle holder, 9ins. Gilhespy (A), fig. 145.
K131 'Goats' (group), seated. Savage (A), pl. 68.
K132 'Goats', 3¾ and 4¼ins. Sotheby's, 25-3-74, lot 192.
K133 'Horse', standing, 3¾ins. Ibid., lot 194A.
K134 'Leopards' (pair), on mound bases, 5½ins. Gilhespy (B), fig. 54.
K135 'Monkey, playing a French Horn'; 'companion playing a Violin', 7ins. Sotheby's, 22-10-68, lots 81 and 82.
K136 'Pointer', 4⅛ins. (6½ins. long). Schreiber, pl. 41, no. 433 (no. 363).
K137 'Pug seated upon a cushion', 2¾ins. Sotheby's, 25-3-74, lot 170.
K138 'Pug, recumbent', 3¾ins. Ibid, lot 171.
K139 'Pug seated' upon a tasselled cushion, 4¾ins. Savage (A), 89B.
K140 'Ram with Lambs' (group), 5½ins. Sotheby's, 25-3-74, lot 190.
K141 'Sheep lying upon a mound base', 2¾ins. Gilhespy (B), fig. 151.
K142 'Sheep', lying before a small bocage, 4½ins. Sotheby's, 3-4-73, lot 79.
K143 'Sheep', recumbent upon an oval base, 2⅜ins. Ibid., 25-3-74, lot 188.
K144 'Ewe, suckling a Lamb' (group); companion 'Ram with a Lamb' (group), 5ins. Williams (A), fig. 58.
K145 'Squirrels, red, holding nuts' (pair), 3½ins. Sotheby's, 10-12-73, lot 208; Schreiber, no. 434, (no. 364).
K146 'Stag', before a small bocage upon a mound base, 3½ins. Gilhespy (B), fig. 151.
K147 'Stag'; and companion 'Doe', at lodge, 4½ins. Williams (A), fig. 58.

Putti

K148 'Putto' standing with diadem of flowers, proffering a posy in either hand, 4¼ins. *See Plate 102.*
K149 'Seated Putto', holding posy in outstretched hand, on a rococo base, beneath a candlestick (pair), 6¾ins. *See Plate 110.*

APPENDIX L
Derby Figures 1770-1795, not listed by Haslem: also models by Gauron, Bacon and Stephan

Notables

L1 'Admiral Lord Rodney'; companion figure of 'Admiral Hood', about 10½ins. *Ceramic Americana of the 18th Century,* Part IV, pp. 55-56, figs. 10, 11.*
L2 An 'Admiral', possibly Adam Duncan, standing left arm akimbo with baton in left hand before two Cupids and naval trophies, 11¾ins. Upton House, Porc. Cat. no. 59.
L3 'General Drinkwater'. Cited by Lane, illus. unknown to author.
L4 'Charles Pratt, the Baron Camden', in bell-bottomed wig and robes of Lord Chancellor, leaning on a tome inscribed 'Coke Vol. I' upon a plinth decorated with the mask of 'Justice' (after Ravenet), 12⅝ins. Lane, pl. 72.
L5 'Field Marshal Conway' holding a baton, leaning against a cannon beside a Cupid holding a shield with the device of a Saracen's head, 12ins. Barrett & Thorpe, col. pl. D.

* Footnote
Ceramic Americana of the 18th Century, Art in America, by R.T.H. Hasley (1916), Vol. V, p. 53. A black basaltes version of 'Admiral Lord Rodney' stands wearing a cocked-hat and full dress naval uniform, his right hand resting upon a cannon, pointing with his left in the direction of the enemy; companion figure of 'Admiral Hood' stands likewise before a cannon and naval trophies, a baton in his left hand and a sword in his right. Also illustrated at two Chelsea-Derby porcelain versions of 'Admiral Lord Howe', which are wrongly identified as representing Admiral Rodney. See figures 11b, 10, 11a and 12 respectively.

L6 'William Pitt, the Lord Chatham', standing beside a plinth and a kneeling Red Indian Girl, 13ins. King (B), fig. 36.
L7 Three groups, en suite, of the Royal Family after Zoffany: 'George III' standing beside a plinth upon which rest crown and sceptre on a cushion, 14ins. Lane, pl. 73.
'Queen Charlotte with two Royal Children'. Trans. E.C.C., no. 4, pp. 23-27, pl. IX; pl. X, painting by Johann Zoffany.
'Four Royal Children'. Ibid.
L8 'Bust of Jean Jacques Rousseau' after J.H. Tarval's painting, 6¼ins. Schreiber, pl. 41, no. 432 (no. 361).
L9 'Bust of Alexander Pope' after G. Kneller's portrait, 6¾ins. Ibid., pl. 41, no. 431 (no. 360).

Allegorical Subjects

L10 'Astronomy', a lady in classical robes leaning upon a barometer and a cupid holding a sextant. Barrett & Thorpe, pl. 102.
L11 'Minerva, portrayed by a cupid, crowning Constancy' who is another cupid, part of a composite group. Schreiber, pl. 44, no. 413 (no. 422). Reverse depicts Cupid as 'Hercules slaying a Hydra', overall 11ins. Trans. E.C.C., 1969, Vol. 7, pl. 122C.
L12 'Neptune' in crown and cloak beside a dolphin, the base decorated with shells, 9¾ins. Upton House, Porc. cat. no. 64.

L13 'The Three Arts'; draped nude ladies standing back to back about a plinth upon which rests an urn, 12ins. Trans. E.C.C., Vol. 7, pl. 128A, Derby group; pl. 128B, engraving after Raphael.

L14 'A Lesson in Love' (group), Cupid lecturing to a group of three young ladies, after Boucher's 'L'Education Sentimentale', 9ins. King (B), fig. 52.

L15 'Putto', bedecked in garlands, standing stiffly, holding a flower basket before him in both hands. 4¾ and 5½ins. Barrett & Thorpe, pl. 88.

L16 Small Bustos: 'Spring', a lady wreathed in flowers; 'Winter', a bearded man cowled and in a cloak, 3¾ and 3⅜ins. Schreiber, pl. 41, nos. 430, 431 (nos. 359, 360).

Pastoral and Peasant

L17 'Shepherdess seated with a lamb in her lap, resisting the attempts of a standing Gallant to stroke her cheek', after Boucher's 'Le Mouton Favorite', 6ins. Lane, pl. 70A.

L18 'Shepherd and Shepherdess reclining' beneath a leafing tree on a mound base about which stand eight putti, two emblematic of each of the Four Seasons, 13½ins. King (B), fig. 55. (This may possibly be a French biscuit group.)

L19 'Sportsman with gun' standing before a holly bush, 7⅛ins. Herbert Allen, pl. 26, no. 96.

L20 'The Russian Shepherds' (group); a bearded peasant in tunic, trousers and boots, sits playing a guitar beside a standing lady. A third figure of a seated youth playing a pipe may be seen at the back. 13ins. Lane, pl. 75.

L21 'Boy dancing with a Girl' (group) in the position adopted in a reel, after 'La Danse Allemande' created at Sèvres, 6¼ins. Schreiber, pl. 41, no. 415, (no. 348).

L22 'Boy Gardener standing with his back to a lady companion', amidst fruit, flowers, vegetables and garden implements, 8ins. Barrett & Thorpe, pl. 100.

L23 'Gardener standing leaning upon his spade', in tricorn hat with a posy in his right hand. This model appears to have been adapted from M3, a gardener by Stephan in a set of Elements, by omission of the plinth and flower pot, 7½ins. Mackenna (C), pl. 63, fig. 124.

L24 'Boy dressed in turban and cloak with a leaping dog' which has a hat upon its head, 6ins. Barrett & Thorpe, pl. 89.

Miscellaneous

L25 'The Three Marys' (group). The Virgin Mary stands with hands clasped before two other figures, one standing with right arm outstretched as if to support the cross, the other seated in contemplation. At the back is a socket, presumably to take a crucifix, 9½ins. Schreiber, pl. 19, no. 170 (no. 295).

L26 'Gallant' standing and holding open the lid of a rectangular hamper; companion 'Lady', likewise (in mirror poses), 9ins. Gilhespy (A), fig. 144.

Animals and Birds

L27 'Reclining Buck' with tall antlers; companion 'Doe', 6ins. Bradley, no. 20.

L28 'Pugs' (pair) seated, 3½ins. V & A, No. I-308.

L29 'Bull' standing beneath a tree; companion 'Cow with a calf', 5ins. Private Col.

L30 'A Spanish Pointer', 4½ins. Schreiber, pl. 41, no. 433 (no. 363).

L31 'A Recumbent Setter' (incised W. Coffee) 4⅛ins. long. Bradley, no. 42. *Note:* a list of Small Animal Models provided by John Haslem includes the following: 'Pug Dogs', large and small; 'Begging Pugs'; 'Begging French Dogs'; a variety of 'Sheep', including 'Ewes', 'Rams' and 'Lambs', standing and lying; 'Canary Birds'; 'Tomtits'; 'Linnets'; 'Birds on branches'. Some of these may relate to the period 1770-95.

Models attributed to Nicolas Gauron

'Minerva crowning Constancy and Hercules killing the Hydra' (L11), known in a Tournai version ascribed to Gauron.

'The Four Elements', represented by four groups, each of two Cupids (M48), known in Tournai versions ascribed to Gauron.

Attributed to Gauron only on grounds of modelling style: 'The Four Seasons', represented by four putti on a mound beneath a tree (M388); 'The Knot in the Cravat', after Falconet (M177 and M255); 'The Alpine Shepherdess' after Falconet (M178 and M256); 'The Grape Gatherers' after Falconet (M176).

Models attributed to John Bacon

'The Royal Ramily', consisting of three groups issued en suite after Zoffany (L7). Note the details of the upper portion of the king's dress correspond with those upon a bust of the monarch by John Bacon, now in Christ Church, Oxford.

'David Garrick as Richard III' (M21) and 'James Quinn as Falstaff' (M231) are also attributed to Bacon by John Haslem.

Models attributed to Pierre Stephan

'Admiral Lord Rodney' (L1), known in a Wedgwood black basaltes version by Stephan.

'Admiral Lord Howe' (M384), signed 'P. Stephan'.

'The Four Elements' (M3), according to John Haslem.

'Pastoral Group' (M12).

'The Five Senses' (M59).

'The French Seasons' (M123), inferior copies of four models from a set of eight made at Tournai by Gauron.

The following have been ascribed to Stephan for stylistic reasons: Admiral Sir Adam Duncan (L2); 'Prudence and Discretion' (M15 and M38); 'Renaldo and Armida' (group) (M76); 'Procris and Cephalus' (group) (M75); 'Two Virgins awakening Cupid' after Angelica Kauffmann (group) (M195); 'Bacchantes adorning a bust of Pan' after Angelica Kauffmann (group) (M196); 'Three Graces distressing Cupid' after Angelica Kauffmann (group) (M235); 'A Gardener with a Girl' (group) (L22).

Models related to the Wilkes scandal were first issued prior to the arrival of Stephan in England but have sometimes been linked with his name. The later Chelsea-Derby versions include: 'Charles Pratt, the Baron Camden' (L4); 'Catherine Macaulay' (M88); 'John Wilkes' (M88 and M126); 'Field Marshal Conway' (L5); 'William Pitt, the Lord Chatham' (L6).

APPENDIX M
Haslem's List of Derby Figures (modified), c.1772-1795

M1 'The Three Virtues' (group), 11½ins.

M3 'The Four Elements': 10½, 9¼ and 7⅛ins. 'Water', a fishergirl standing with a net; 'Earth', a gardener holding a spade, standing beside a pot plant upon a plinth; 'Fire', a youth igniting a faggot by means of a burning-glass; 'Air', a girl holding aloft a bird. Gilhespy (B), fig. 143. *See Plates 123 and 124.*

M4 'A Pastoral Group'.

M5 'The Antique Seasons', 8, 6½ and 4⅛ins., standing figures on plinths of 'Flora', 'Ceres', 'Bacchus' and 'Vulcan'. Private col.

M6 'The Four Seasons'.

M7 Girl wearing a brimmed hat, standing with flowers in her apron, her right elbow against a plinth upon which rests a watering can; companion Gardener holding a spade (listed as 'Gardening'), 6¾ and 5ins. Derby Mus., cat. no. 645.

M8 Boy seated, holding fruit in his up-turned hat on his lap; girl seated, posy in hand, with a basket of flowers on her lap (listed as 'Fruit and Flowers'), 5¾ins. Trans. E.C.C., Vol. 7, pls. 124a, 124b.

M9 Girl standing holding a mandoline; boy standing with a French horn (listed as 'Music'), 6¼, 6 and 4⅝ins. Derby Mus., cat. nos. 1519, 395.

M10 Boy standing with a flute; girl standing with a hurdy-gurdy (listed as 'Flute and Cymbal'), 6¼, 5⅞ and 4⅝ins. Herbert Allen, pl. 26, no. 97.

M11 Boy seated, playing a flute, 6¾ions. Derby Mus., cat. no. 358; companion girl seated, playing a guitar. Barrett & Thorpe, pl. 130.

M12 'Pastoral Group' depicting a sleeping shepherdess beneath an urn on a plinth, and a shepherd standing playing a reed-pipe, 12¼ins. Barrett and Thorpe, pl. 97.

M13 'Cupid' riding a goat; 'Bacchus' riding a stag, 7ins. V & A cat. no. C.1291-1919.

M14 A girl holding a knife standing before a plinth upon which lies a sacrificial lamb, 6ins. Barrett & Thorpe, pl. 90; companion Youth likewise with a sacrificial goat (listed as 'Sacrifice Figures'), private col.

M15 'Prudence', a draped girl looking into a hand mirror with a snake entwined about her arm; 'Discretion', a cupid holding one finger to his lips, both beside urns on plinths, 8⅛ins. Schreiber, pl. 41, no. 410 (no. 344).

M16 Boy in a tricorn hat dancing with a girl in a lace cap (listed as 'Dancing Group'), 6⅝ins. Derby Mus.

M17 Boy, bare-headed, dancing with a Girl likewise, 7ins. Hughes (B and T), pl. 14c.

M19 Child with a basket of fruit. Cited by Barrett & Thorpe.

M20 A boy standing with a basket of flowers holding a posy; a girl standing with a basket of fruit holding an apple, 6¼, 5¾ and 4⅝ins. Derby Mus., no. 654.

M21 'David Garrick as Richard III', 9¾ins. Cushion (B), pl. 13; Schreiber, pl. 40, no. 205 (no. 342).

M23 'Swiss Boy' in a wide brimmed hat and short trousers, walking; 'Swiss Girl', holding a basket in her left hand and faggots beneath her right arm. Rice, pl. 102 (Rockingham versions).

M25-M34 Ten figures, each on pierced stands, of 'Apollo and the Muses', 6ins. Barrett & Thorpe, pl. 93, 'Calliope'.

M35 'The Rustic Seasons', represented by single standing adolescents: 'Spring', a girl with a basket of flowers; 'Summer', a girl with a cornsheaf, 6ins. Herbert Allen, pl. 26, no. 101. 'Autumn', a youth with grapes; 'Winter', a youth skating. David Love Antiques.

M36 A Boy seated on an upturned basket, posy in hand, and flowers in his inverted hat upon his lap; Girl seated with blossoms in her lap and a posy in her hand, 5⅝ins. Herbert Allen, pl. 33, no. 126.

M37 'Jason' in armour, and his wife 'Medea', standing before 'Diana' who is posed upon a plinth, 12¾ins. Sotheby's, 31-7-79, lot 102; Derby Mus.

M38 'Prudence and Discretion', 5½ins., probably a reissue of M15.

M39-M45 Seven Groups representing 'Arts and Sciences', each composed of two cupids upon a pierced rectangular stand, 7ins.
'Commerce', a cupid taking money from a scrip as his companion writes upon a slate supported by parcels. Barrett & Thorpe, pl. 101.
'Astronomy and Geometry', Cupid with a spyglass and companion holding dividers over a globe. Ibid.
'Arithmetic', a cupid writing in a ledger supported by a companion who also holds an ink-well. Ibid.
'Music' (M40), a cupid playing a lute and companion holding a musical score. Trans. E.C.C., 1967, Vol. 6, pt. 3, pl. 223b.
'Painting and Sculpture' (M42), a cupid sculpting a bust and companion seated with a sketchbook. Private col.
'Architecture', two cupids, one standing, the other sitting, amidst classical ruins. Private col.
'Geography'. Group unknown to author.

M46 Boy in a tricorn hat dancing a reel with a girl (group), 6¼ins. Schreiber, pl. 41, no. 415 (no. 348).

M47 'The Grotesque Seasons', represented by truncated figures of rustics: 'Spring', a girl with a basket of flowers and a posy; 'Summer', a boy securing a corn-sheaf'; 'Autumn', a girl with a bunch of grapes; 'Winter', a boy in a hat, shovelling coal. Gilhespy (A), fig. 161.

M48 'The Four Elements' represented by four groups, each of two putti beneath a tree: 'Air', two cupids, one with a cage, robbing a nest; 'Earth', two cupids, one with a spade, the other holding a garland; 'Fire', two cupids at a grindstone; 'Water', a cupid with a fishing-net and companion with baskets of fish, 8¾ins., figs. 617-620.

M49 A kneeling boy embracing a dog; girl likewise, with a cat, 5¾ and 5⅜ins. Schreiber, pl. 41, no. 416 (no. 349).

M50 Sportsman in a brimmed-hat, standing with a gun; lady holding a basket of flowers, 5¾ins. Trans. E.C.C., 1959, Vol. 7, pt. 2, pls. 124c, 124d.

M51 Boy standing barefoot and bareheaded, holding a puppy in his right hand and with his left upraised; Girl likewise with a lamb (listed as the 'French Shepherds'), 5ins. Derby Museum.

M52 Dragon Candlesticks, 5ins.

M53 Griffin Candlesticks, 5ins.

M54 'Justice', standing with scales and a short sword, 9½ins. Hughes (B), pl. 9.

M55 'The Dresden Shepherds'; shepherd standing with a basket held to his breast with his left hand, proffering an apple with his right; shepherdess with flowers gathered in her apron, proffering a posy in her left hand, 9ins. *Antique Dealer & Collector's Guide,* June 1966, p. 58.

M56 'Shepherds with Garlands', 6¾, 7⅝, 9 and 9¾ins.

M57 'The French Shepherds'. A boy standing bareheaded and barefoot, supporting with his right hand a puppy that has both paws upon his chest, and attracting its attention with a ball held in his left; girl, likewise, holding in both arms a lamb which has a rosette attached to its neck, in six sizes. Derby Mus.; author's col. *See Plate 121.*

M58 Shepherd in a brimmed-hat standing, playing an end-flute, a dog at his feet, 6½ins. Herbert Allen, pl. 26, no. 100.

M59 'The Five Senses'. Seated figures of: 'Smell', a youth holding a posy beside a hound; 'Taste', a youth holding grapes beside a leopard; 'Feeling', a girl attended by Cupid whose quiver hangs from a tree stump; 'Sight', a youth with a spyglass beside an eagle; 'Heating', a girl with a lute beside a swan, 9½ins. (reissue of K72). Cheyne Book, pl. 23, no. 252 (wrongly attributed to Chelsea).

M60 'The Singing Shepherds', shepherd standing, left hand upraised, right upon his hip; shepherdess in mirror position, the two singing, 5⅝, 7 and 8ins. Herbert Allen, pl. 12, no. 95.

M61 'The Four Seasons', possibly a reissue of M35.

M62 'The Welsh Tailors', tailor holding scissors, astride a billy-goat, wife holding a baby, riding a nanny-goat which suckles a kid, 5½ and 9ins. Barrett & Thorpe, pls. 123, 124.

M63 Boy Turk in turban and cloak; girl in stocking-cap and cloak, 3½ins. Gilhespy (A), fig. 181.

M64 'The Four Seasons', individual standing figures.

M65 'Diana', 6½ and 8ins. *Antique Dealer & Collector's Guide,* Sept. 1972, p. 38; Ford House Antiques.

M66 'Venus and Cupid' (group), 6½ins. Barrett & Thorpe, pl. 60.

M67 'Venus', Chelsea model.

M68 'The Four Seasons'; two groups, each of two figures: 'Spring', a girl with a basket of flowers over her right arm, holding a posy, and 'Winter', a youth with his left hand upon his breast holding a gun in his right; companion group 'Summer', a girl in a round hat, laced bodice and apron, holding a corn-sheaf under her arm, and 'Autumn', a bare-headed boy with a basket of grapes over his right arm and a bunch of grapes in his left hand, 8½ins. Schreiber, pl. 41, no. 417 (no. 350).

M69 Gentleman seated with a flute; companion lady with a lute (listed as 'Sitting Flute Figures'), 6½ins. Ibid., pl. 41, no. 424 (no. 356).

M70 Figure of 'Christie', 12⅛ins.

M71 Boy in a tricorn hat seated on a stool, with a dog in his lap; girl seated, feeding a cat with a spoon that she holds by the forepaws, 5½ins. *Connoisseur,* December 1949, p. xxxiii.

M72 Pastoral group with goat, 5⅝ins.

M73 Pastoral group with dog, 5⅝ins.

M74 Dancing group of two figures, 6½ins.

M75 'Procris and Cephalus' (group); the shepherd Cephalus bends over the dying Procris whose breast he has pierced with his javelin (after Monet's engraving), 8½ins. Gilhespy (A), fig. 153.

M76 'Renaldo and Armida' (group); the sourceress Armida covers the sleeping Renaldo with flowers, 8½ins. *Connoisseur,* 1924, Vol. 69, p. 212, no. III.

M77 A Girl seated in a gilded chair mending a stocking, 5½ins. *Antique Dealer & Collector's Guide,* May 1963, p. 25.

M78 'The Shoe Maker' (group after Falconet); a cobbler kneels to fit a shoe to a lady, 7ins. Barrett & Thorpe, pl. 131.

M79 'The Stocking Mender' (group after Falconet); a maid darns the stocking of a standing gallant, 6¾ins. Derby Mus.

M80 'Spinning', a group of two figures.

M81 'The Shoe Black' (group after Falconet); a maid kneels to clean the shoes of a standing gallant, 6½ins. Gilhespy (B), fig. 63.

M82 'Fury', a group of two figures with a broken fiddle.

M83 'Fury', a group composed of a man and a woman fighting with a broken chair, 5⅝ins. V & A, cat. no. 3016-1901.

M84 'The Hair Dresser' (group after Falconet); a man servant dresses the hair of a seated lady, 6½ins. Gilhespy (B), fig. 63.

M85 'A Macaroni' (a dude).

M86 'The Four Elements', represented by two groups, each of two figures, similar to M3. Private col.

M87 A pair of saluation figures, 4¾ins.

M88 'John Wilkes', standing beside a plinth from which hang scrolls inscribed 'Bill of Rights', and 'Magna Charta'; companion model of 'Catherine Macaulay' standing leaning upon volumes of her historical work, pen in hand, 12ins. Gilhespy (A), fig. 158.

M89 'Fury Group Family', possibly reissue of either M82 or M83.

M90 'A Cook and Companion'.

M91 'A Female Macaroni' (i.e. a fine lady), presumably a pair to M85.

M92 'Three Figures Learning Music'; a music teacher in a tricorn hat sits beside a lady who wears a hat and plays a recorder, his arm about her shoulders, whilst a seated boy plays a pipe (group). *Antique Dealer & Collector's Guide,* April 1974, p. 10.

M93 'A Game of Hazard' (group after Falconet); a boy operates a foretune telling device whilst the pointer is observed by a boy, a girl, and a dog, 6¾ins. Derby Mus.

M94 'A Raree Shaw' (after Falconet); a boy acts as showman with a peepshow watched by a girl holding a basket of bread, and a small boy, 6¾ins. Ibid.

M95 'Sphinx Candlestick'.

M96 'Sphinx Vase'.

M97 'Griffin Vase'.

M98 'Group of Prudence and Discretion', 11½ins.

M99 'Aesculapius', a bearded man in long robes leaning on a club and holding a scroll, 6¾ins. Schreiber, pl. 41, no. 418 (no. 351).
'Hygieia', a lady standing and holding in both hands a drap across her back, 6¾ins. Trans. E.C.C., 1969, Vol. 7, pl. 126c.

M100 'Andromache', a veiled weeping woman leaning upon an urn containing the ashes of 'Hector', 9¼ins. *Apollo,* 1955, June, p. 78.

M101 'Grotesque Boy and Girl'; a boy, with a basket of fruit over his arm eats an apple; a girl eats curds-and-whey with a spoon from a bowl, 4½ins. B. & T. Thorn Antiques.

M102-M113 Twelve figures of monks and nuns, including:
A standing 'Monk holding a skull'; companion 'Nun holding a book'. Cushion (B), pl. 16.
A seated monk holding a book, 4½ins. *Antique Dealer & Collector's Guide,* April 1971, p. 12. Companion nun, 5ins. Gilhespy (A), fig. 155. (Both are incised No. 105.)
Two 'Confessional Groups', one with a nun kneeling before an abbot, K. Chappell Antiques; the other a nun kneeling before an abbess, both 5ins. Lane, pl. 70a.

M114 'Mars', 6½ins. Bradley, fig. 36.

M115 'Venus and Cupid', 6¼ins. Private collection.

M116 'Apollo' standing with a lyre, 6¾ins. Derby Mus.

M117 'Jupiter' holding a thunderbolt beside an eagle, 7½ins. Barrett & Thorpe, pl. 91.

M118 'Neptune' beside a dolphin, 6¾ins. Derby Mus.

M119 'Juno' beside a peacock, 6½ins. Barrett & Thorpe, pl. 91.

M120 'The New Diana', 6½ins. Hurlbutt (A), pl. 13.

M121 'Minerva', wearing a crested helmet, cuirass and sandals, holding a shield, 6ins. Schreiber, pl. 19, no. 187, (no. 302).

M122 'Aesculapius' standing leaning upon a club and holding a scroll (listed as 'Hercules'), 6¼ins. See M99.

M123 'The French Seasons', four standing children: 'Spring', a boy in a tricorn hat holding a posy between both hands; 'Summer', a bare-headed girl in a dress standing beside a corn-sheaf; 'Autumn', a girl in a headscarf, laced bodice, skirt and apron, with a basket of grapes and a bunch of grapes in either hand; 'Winter', a boy bearing faggots upon his left shoulder, 7½ and 4ins. Gilhespy (A), fig. 160. *See Plate 125.*

M124 'Time', portrayed by an old man, 'clipping the wings of Love', in the guise of Cupid (group), 7½ins. Barrett & Thorpe, pl. 92.

M125 'The Chelsea Seasons': 'Spring', a lady holding a basket of flowers, and 'Winter', a sportsman holding a gun (M50); 'Summer', a girl with a corn-sheaf beneath her arm. Derby Mus.; 'Autumn', a youth with a pannier of grapes, average 5ins. Private col.

M126 'John Wilkes', 12ins. Barrett & Thorpe, col. pl. D.

M127 Small figures (unspecified).
M137 'The Prudent Mother'; a woman seated reading a book with a child at her side (listed wrongly as 'Madonna, a Group'), 8¼ins. B. & T. Thorn Antiques.
M138 'Madonna and Child', a seated lady in classical robes, a baby and flowers upon her lap (listed wrongly as 'Prudent Mother'), 8¼ins. B. & T. Thorn Antiques.
M139 'Music', a group of two figures, 6½ins.
M140 'The Prudent Mother', 8¼ins. Either M137 or M138.
M141 Pair of 'Fighting Boys', 3½ins.
M142 'Boy riding a Dolphin', 5ins. Barrett & Thorpe, pl. 87.
M143 Companion 'Girl riding a Swan'.
M146 Bust of Virgil wearing a laurel wreath, 8¾ins. *Connoisseur,* 1928, Vol. 82, p. 30, no. II.
M147 Bust of Addison, 8¾ins. Ibid.
M159 Bust of a philosopher wearing a beret, smiling, 6ins. Sotheby's, 20-11-79, lot 121.
M160 Companion bust of a philosopher in a headscarf, frowning, 6ins. Ibid.
M161 'The Antique Figure of Wisdom'; a tall lady standing,dressed in a helmet, classical robes, and sandals, proffering an orb in her right outstretched hand, 8½ins. Plymouth Mus., reserve collection.
M162 'The Antique Figure of Justice'; a slender lady, bare-headed, standing blindfold in classical dress and sandals, holding a sword with lowered point, 8½ins. Ibid.
M163 'The Antique Figure of Plenty'; a lady wearing a coronet and loose robes, standing holding fruit and leaves in her right hand, and a cornucopia in her left, 9⅞ and 8½ins. Schreiber, pl. 41, no. 419 (no. 424).
M164 'The Antique Figure of Peace'; a lady in classical robes holding a dove and an olive branch, 9⅞ and 8½ins.
M175 A pair of boy and girl figures, 4ins.
M176 'The Grape Gatherers' (group after Falconet); a seated shepherd beside a shepherdess eating grapes, with a sheep that eats the posy in the youth's hand, 8½ins. Schreiber, pl. 43, no. 423 (no. 355).
M177 'The Knot in the Cravat' (group after Falconet); a seated lady adjusts the cravat of a gallant who squats before her, 8¼ins. Trans. E.C.C., 1969, Vol. 7, pl. 125.
M178 'The Alpine Shepherdess' (group after Falconet). A gallant seated on the green sward holds the hand of a seated shepherdess, 12ins. Ibid., pl. 123.
M179 'Music Group', composed of four children holding respectively a French horn, reed-pipe, tambourine and a fiddle, standing around a tree, 13¼ins. Derby Mus.
M180 A pair of boys, representing 'Spring and Autumn', 6ins. Private col.
M182 A pair of 'cupids' riding bucks, holding bows and arrows, about 5ins. Derby Mus., cat. no. 378.
M183 'Prudence' and 'Discretion', possibly a reissue of M15.
M184 Boy seated, bare-headed, with legs crossed, reading a book; girl seated with her hat upon her lap. *Connoisseur,* December 1949, p. xxxiii.
M185 'Cupid riding a Dolphin'; companion 'Cupid riding a Swan', probably re-issues of M142 and M143.
M189 'Boy riding a Sea-Horse', 4½ins.
M190 'A Triton', 2¾ins. Schreiber, pl. 40, no. 414, (no. 347) (illus. of a large triton).
M193 'Bacchus' (after Sansovino) standing wreathed in vine leaves holding a bunch of grapes and a goblet, 7½, 8¼ and 9ins. Trans. E.C.C., 1969, Vol. 7, pl. 127a.
M194 'Ariadne' wearing a cloak. Derby Mus.
M195 'Two Virgins awakening Cupid' (group after Angelica Kauffmann), 11½ins. Lane, pl. 71. *See Plate 126.*
M196 'Two Bacchantes adorning a bust of Pan' with a garland (group after Angelica Kauffmann), 11½ins. Barrett & Thorpe, pl. 98.
M197 'Cupid riding a Sea-Lion', 2¾ins.
M198 A pair of 'Haymakers'; standing figures of a rustic wearing a tricorn hat, jacket and breeches, carrying a keg attached to a stave over his left shoulder; a woman wearing a lace cap, dress and apron, holding a wine flask in her right hand, 6½ins. Burnley Antiques (both); female figure, V & A.
M199 'Harlequin' standing in plumed hat, mask and motley; 'Columbine' dancing, 5½ins. Bryan Bowden Antiques.
M200 'The Four Quarters of the Globe', four standing children (after Elias Meyer):
Africa, a Blackamoor wearing an elephant head-dress and cloak, holding a crab and a cornucopia, stepping over a lion;
Asia, a Levantine girl wearing a stocking-cap, dress and cloak, holding a perfume vase, beside a kneeling camel;
America, a Red Indian girl in feathered skirt and head-dress, holding a long-bow, beside a prairie dog;
Europe, a crowned girl with orb and sceptre, 5½-6ins. Gilhespy (B), fig. 149. *See Colour Plate R.*
M201-M202 A pair of 'Cupids', 4ins.
M203 A pair of 'Cupids with Dog and Falcon'.
M204 'A Pair of Gardeners', 5ins. Possibly Derby Mus., cat. no. 359, 456.
M205-M206 A pair of 'Cupids', 4½ins.
M207 'A Sea Nymph riding a Dolphin', 4⅛ins.
M208 'A Sea Nymph' playing a tambourine, 3ins.
M209 'A Syren' with a shell, 2½ins.
M210 'A Triton', 3ins.
M213-M214 'Cupid with a Dog'; 'Cupid with a Falcon', 4⅜ins. Barrett & Thorpe, pl. 89 (example illus. 6¼ins.).
M216 'Musical Group'; a lady in classical robes standing bare-headed playing a flute; two cupids, one seated with a musical score, the other standing with a fiddle, all before a ruined column upon which lies a tambourine, 9¾ins. Schreiber, pl. 40, no. 424 (no. 356).
M217 'Poetry Group'; a lady standing before a ruined column on which lie books; beside her are two cupids, one carrying a quill, the other a scroll, 9¾ins. Derby Mus., cat. no. 317.
M220-M221 A pair of basket figures, 5½ and 6½ins.
M222 'Winged Time'; a bearded man standing with a scythe beside an hour-glass, 6½ins. Trans. E.C.C., Vol. 7, 1969, pl. 127c.
M227 A pair of 'Grotesque Dwarfs' wearing tall-brimmed hats upon which are advertisements (after engravings by Calotto), 7ins. Barrett & Thorpe, pl. 133.
M229 'Neptune' standing holding a trident beside a dolphin, 8ins. Ibid., pl. 96.
M231 'James Quinn as Falstaff', wearing a plumed hat, cuirass and baggy trousers, and bearing an oval shield, 15ins. Harris, p. 61; Derby Mus.
M233 'Cupid disguised as a Sportsman' holding a leashed hound, 3⅜ins. Schreiber, pl. 41, no. 429 (no. 423).
M234 'Four Cupids Bird's-Nesting' (group), grouped about a tree on a mound base, 9ins. Barrett & Thorpe, pl. 94.
M235 'Three Graces distressing Cupid' who is tied to a tree (group after Angelica Kauffmann, 13ins. Ibid., pl. 99.
M236-M237 A pair of cupids, 4ins.
M239 'The Virgin Mary', 10½ins., possibly a reissue of M138.
M240 'A Pastoral Group' of two figures, 7¾ins.
M243 'Apollo', standing holding a lyre, 9½ins. Derby Mus. (a 19th century version).
M244 'Plenty', 9⅞ins., possibly reissue of M163.
M245 'Peace', 9¼ins., possibly reissue of M164.
M247 'A Pastoral Group' of two figures, 12¼ins.
M248 'The Four Antique Seasons' (group), composed of standing figures of Flora, Ceres, Bacchus and Vulcan around a tree (same models as M5), 11⅛ins. V & A.
M249-M250 'The Four Elements', represented by two groups each of two figures beneath a leafing tree upon a rock-like base. These are 'Air and Earth' and 'Fire and Water' including the same figures as M3, 9½ins. *Connoisseur,* 1928, Vol. 82, p. 33, nos. III, IV.
M251 'Four Cupids Hunting' (group); each wears a tricorn hat and is scantily draped, one with two leashed hounds, one holding a gun and a wallet, one holding a hunting horn, and one with a flute resting upon a cage, 7⅞ins. Herbert Allen, pl. 32, no. 117. *See Plate 127.*
M252 'A Group of three Cupids', 9ins.
M253 Cupid with a leashed dog; Cupid with a bird's cage (same models as M251), 3¾ins. Private col.
M254 'A Pastoral Group' of two figures, 13¼ins.
M255 'The Knot in the Cravat' (group), after Falconet (reissue of M177 with added tree), 12ins. Schreiber, pl. 42, no. 420 (no. 352).
M256 'The Alpine Shepherdess' (group), after Falconet (reissue of M178 with added tree), 12ins. Ibid., pl. 42, no. 420 (no. 352).
M257 'A Group of Four Cupids': one holding two hounds, one bearing a torch, one carrying a quiver full of arrows, one sharpening an arrow, 8¼ins. Herbert Allen, pl. 32, no. 118.
M258 'A Pair of Sitting Boy Candlesticks', 6½ins.
M259 'Britannia', standing in crested helmet and armour holding a trident in her right hand and leaning upon a shield with her left, beside a lion, in three sizes. Trans. E.C.C., 1969, Vol. 7, pl. 126a; Derby Mus.
M260 'A Boy Crying'; companion girl, likewise, 8½ins. Sotheby's, 22-10-68, lot 106.
M262-M278 Seventeen 'Cupids in Disguise'.
Examples at the Fitzwilliam: 'Cupid with a Dog', 'Cupid with a Trumpet', 'Cupid with a Hawk', 'Cupid with a Hurdy-Gurdy', 'Cupid as a Lady's Maid' and 'Cupid as a piping Shepherdess'.
Illus. in Gilhespy (B), fig. 146: 'Cupid wearing a wig, playing a pipe', 'Cupid carrying a Box', 'Cupid as a Cook, with stocking cap and saucepan' and 'Cupid as a Nurse-Maid holding a crib'.
M279 A pair of candlesticks with shepherd and shepherdess. Sotheby's, 19-4-66.
M280 A pair of candlesticks with piper and lady guitarist, 8½ins. Models probably M301.
M281 A pair of 'Spring' candlesticks, 6⅛ins. Twitchett, fig. 73.
M282 A pair of small 'Fame' and 'mercury' candlesticks, 8½ins.
M283 A pair of gardener candlesticks, 6⅞ins.
M284 A pair of piper and guitar candlesticks, 9½ins. See models M301.
M285 Ditto, 8ins.
M287 Pair of 'Garland Shepherd' candlesticks, 9½ins. Models possibly the same as M56.
M288 Pair of 'Mars' and 'Venus' candlesticks, 8ins. Ludlow, pl. 190, no. 200 (earlier examples).
M291 'James Quinn as Falstaff', in five sizes. See M231.
M292 Gardener standing in a stocking cap, shirt, breeches and apron, carrying a basket in both hands; companion woman in linen cap likewise, 5½ins. and 4⅜ins. Gilhespy (A), fig. 180. *See Plate 119.*
M293 'The Tithe Pig Group'; a farmer holds the tithe pig as his wife proffers their tenth child to the parson; mounted on a pad base beneath a tree, 7ins. Barrett & Thorpe, pl. 67. *See Plate 120.*

M294 'The Four Seasons' (group); two youths and two girls in rustic dress, bearing appropriate accessories, stand about an obelisk, 8ins. Morley-Fletcher (A), p. 138.
M295 'The Four Quarters of the Globe' (group); four children (see M200) stand about an obelisk upon a mound base, 10ins. Sotheby's 22-10-68, lot 107.
M296 'A Pair of Haymakers', 9¼ins. (probably reissue M198).
M297 'Milton', leaning against a plinth upon which rest a pile of books (after Scheemakers), 10¼ins. Trans. E.C.C., 1969, Vol. 7, pl. 126b. *See Plate 122.*
M298 'Minerva' standing wearing a crested helmet, cuirass and sandals, holding a spear and a shield upon which is the device of Medusa's head, 10ins. Upton House, Porc. cat., no. 66.
M299 'Neptune' standing on a rocky pedestal, 9¼ins. Reissue of M229.
M300 Ditto, 5⅜ins. Sotheby's, 31-7-79, lot 89.
M301 Gentleman seated in a chair playing an end-flute; lady seated likewise with a guitar, 8½, 6¼ and 5⅜ins. Reissue M69.
M302 'Fame', represented by a standing winged angel with a trumpet; companion 'Mercury' wearing winged sandals and helmet, and a cloak, bearing a money bag, 13¼ins. Schreiber, pl. 40, no. 179 (no. 340).
M303 Gentleman seated with a reed-pipe; companion lady likewise with a tambourine, 7¼ and 6⅜ins. Reissue of M284 without candlesticks.
M305 'Shakespeare' standing beside a plinth upon which rest a book and scroll, 10½ins. King (B), fig. 41.
M307 'The Four Seasons', represented by two seated shepherds and two shepherdesses, 5ins. Private col.
M309 'Music', represented by four standing adult musicians about an obelisk, 10ins. Derby Mus.
M311 Gentleman seated with an end-flute; companion Lady seated with a tambourine, 8¼ins. Reissue of M303 (listed as 'Pipe and Tambour').
M314 Boy wearing a wig, seated in a chair with his legs crossed, his cocked-hat under one arm, reading a book; companion girl tatting with a shuttle, a basket on her lap, 5½ins. Herbert Allen, pl. 33, no. 127.
M315 'The Four Seasons', 7ins. Possibly a larger version of M307.
M316 Sailor standing in jacket and trousers; companion lass dancing, in three sizes. *See Plate 130.*
M317 Pair of Dancing Figures.
M318 Ditto.
M322 Pair of men and chicken candlesticks, 6¼ins.
M323 Pair of Cupid and Flora candlesticks, 8¾ins.
M325 'The Four Elements', 8¾ins., not identified.
M326 Shepherd with one arm raised, hand on hip, singing; companion shepherdess in mirror pose likewise, in four sizes. Herbert Allen, pl. 12, no. 95.
M331 Pair of bird and dog candlesticks, 11¾ins.
M332 'The Four Quarters of the Globe', in three sizes. Reissue of M200. *See Colour Plate R.*
M333 'Music', represented by four boys wearing hats, jackets and breeches, two standing with an end-flute and a French horn, two seated with a tambourine and a fife (group), 9ins. Derby Mus.
M334 Three boys, one descending from a tree, one holding a nest of fledglings, one with a cage, 9ins. Barrett & Thorpe, pl. 94.
M335-M359 Twenty-five of Spangler's and Coffee's figures and groups: Of these only the following have been identified:
M358 'Cupid disarmed by Euphrosyne' (group), by Spengler after Angelica Kauffmann. *Connoisseur,* 1978, Vol. 198, figs. 8a, 8b.
M359 A 'Gardener' standing with flowers in a pot upon a plinth, by Spengler, 9¾ins. Ibid., fig. 6. Also a 'Gardener' with a spade in one hand and his hand to his face, by Coffee, 5⅝ins. Ibid., fig. 7.
M360 'Johnny Wapstraw and Companion'.
M361 Gardener, and companion lady. Possibly reissue of M204.
M362 A bare-headed girl seated upon a stool, feeding a cat, which she holds by the forepaws, with a spoon; boy in a tricorn hat seated, holding another hat upon the head of a dog dressed in a jacket (listed as 'Pair, sitting Cat and Dog, William and Mary'), 8ins. Derby Mus., cat. no. 537.
M363 A girl in bonnet and dress, leaning against an empty cage, holding a dead bird; youth digging a grave, 8ins. Lane, pl. 74b.
M364 'A Group of Figures Waltzing'; a youth in tie-wig, jacket and breeches dances with a lady wearing a hat and dress, his left hand in her right, 6½ins. Derby Mus., cat. no. 455.
M365 'A Pair of Dancing Figures'. In fact three figures; a girl with cymbals, a girl with a tambourine, and a boy with a French horn, 6¼ins. Two illustrated in the 'Exhibition of People and Pots' cat., no. 69, held at Manchester University, 1976.
M366 'Palemon' and Lavinia'; Palemon stands holding the hand of his beloved Lavinia, as she turns away in shame (group after Angelica Kauffman) (listed as 'A Spanish Group'), 12ins. *Connoisseur,* 1978, Vol. 198, p. 148, fig. 3.
M368 Pair of dancing figures.
M369 Shepherd standing before a plinth, playing a flute, 10ins. Bradley, fig. 38. Companion shepherdess, likewise, 10ins. V & A, cat. no. 3014-1901. *See Plate 128.*
M370 'Belisarius and his Daughter'; a bearded blind old man, with staff in his right hand, holding on to the shoulder of his youthful daughter with his left hand (group), 13ins. *Burlington Magazine,* 1927, Vol. 51, pl. 11b.
M372 'The Proposal'; a gallant leans forward with one hand upon his heart and the other outstretched; companion model of a lady has one hand elevated in protestation, 7 and 7½ins. Bradley, figs. 39, 40 (listed wrongly as 'Sailor and Lass').
M376 'Bacchus standing beside three Nymphs', one seated with a babe upon her lap, the other two standing (listed as 'Bacchus with Nymphs on mount Ida'), 9½ins. *Connoisseur,* 1928, Vol. 82, p. 36, no. IX
M378 A Scotsman standing in a kilt; companion lass. Gilhespy (A), pl. 5, fig. 67 (poor illus.).
M379 A group including 'Apollo', by Coffee according to Jospeh Lygo.
M380 'Poetry, Science and Art' (group); three ladies in classical dress, standing with their backs to a ruined column upon which rests an urn surrounded by trophies, 13ins. Derby Mus., cat. no. 629.
M382 A 'Dancing Girl' standing wearing a headband, left hand upon her hip, and holding out her skirt with her right hand, 6½ins. *Connoisseur,* 1978, Vol. 198, fig. 13.
M384 'Admiral Lord Howe', standing wearing a cocked-hat and full naval uniform, his left hand resting on a cannon, a sextant and a compass at his feet, 11¼ins. V & A, cat. no. C134-1937 (incised 'P. Stephan'). Bradley, fig. 41.
M385 'Hygieia' standing wearing a cloak, 10ins., possibly a reissue of M99.
M388 'The Four Seasons', represented by four putti: 'Spring', a putto with flowers; 'Summer', a putto with corn; 'Autumn', a putto with grapes; 'Winter', a putto beside a brazier, all grouped about a tree (group), 10½ins. Barrett & Thorpe, pl. 120.
M389 A shepherd wearing a hat, standing playing an end-flute; companion shepherdess dancing (after the 'Alpine Shepherds', by Angelica Kauffmann). *Connoisseur,* 1978, Vol. 198, fig. 12b.
M390 A lady standing bare-headed before a ruined Grecian column, holding in either hand the ends of a U-shaped garland, probably representing 'Flora' (listed as 'Gaultherus and Griselda'), 11¼ins. *See Plate 129.*
M391 'The Duke of York', wearing a cockaded hat, tunic and breeches, 11¼ins. Upton House Porc. cat., no. 57.
M395 A lady in a bonnet leaning upon a rustic gate to feed a sheep with hay (after 'Adelaide'), 12ins. Lane, pl. 77; Gilhespy (B), fig. 141.
M396 A shepherd leaning against a tree trunk with his hat in his right hand, a dog and a sheep at his feet, 13½ins. Lane, pl. 76.
M397 Cupid running with hands outstretched towards a lady attired in classical robes who welcomes him (listed as 'Cupid embracing a Virgin'), 12½ins. Derby Mus., cat. no. 1250.

Note: *Derby Porcelain* (London, 1980) by John Twitchett contains some important information and illustrations relating to Derby figures, but appeared since the manuscript of this book was completed.

APPENDIX N
Derby Figures Made Between 1790 and 1848

Models attributed to Jean-Jacques Spengler, 1790-1795.
L10 'Astronomy' (group).
Not yet identified: 'Morning', a lady beside a vase; 'Noon', a lady beside a vase; 'The Three Graces' (group).
L20 'The Russian Shepherds' (group).
M358 Cupid disarmed by 'Euphrosyne' (group), after Angelica Kauffman.
M359 A gardener (one of a pair)
M363 A girl holding a dead bird leaning against an empty bird-cage; companion model of a youth digging a grave.
M366 'Palemon and Lavinia' (group), after Angelica Kauffmann.
M369 Shepherd flautist and companion shepherdess with a flute, adapted from the 'Capitoline Faun'.
M370 'Belisarius and his Daughter' (group), after a Luneville group by Louis-Paul Cyffle.
M376 'Bacchus and Nymphs on mount Ida' (group).
M382 A 'Dancing Girl'.
M389 A shepherd playing an end-flute and companion shepherdess dancing, after Angelica Kauffman.
M395 A lady leaning upon a rustic gate feeding a sheep with hay.
M396 A shepherd leaning against a tree trunk, hat in hand, after a terracotta of 'Antinous'.

Models attributed to William Coffee, 1791-1795.
L30 'A Spanish Pointer', after Stubbs.
L31 'A Recumbent Setter' (signed W. Coffee).
M359 A gardener (one of a pair), according to Joseph Lygo "the most stupid thing I ever saw".
M379 A group including the figure of 'Apollo' (not identified), according to Joseph Lygo "very vulgar about the bosom . . .".
M378 A 'Scotsman' and companion model of his 'Lass'.
Probably numerous sundry models of animals.

Models attributed to Samuel Keys (fils), 1815-1830.
Liston, in the role of 'Mawworm'.
Liston, in the role of 'Domini Sampson'.
Liston, in the role of 'Paul Pry'. Gilhespy (B), fig. 144.
Madam Vestris singing 'Buy a broom'. For Rockingham example see *Rockingham Pottery and Porcelain* (1971), by D. G. Rice, pl. 15.
Billy Waters, the one-legged Negro fiddler. Gilhespy (A), fig. 170.
Grimaldi the clown. Cat. of an 'Exhibition of Clowning', no. 145, held on 11th June to 4th September, 1977, in the Nottingham Castle Mus.
'The Industrious Boy', seated writing in a book; and 'Industrious Girl' sewing, 5ins. Rice, pl. 106.
Boy standing cross-legged before a rocky plinth on which is an pitcher; girl holding a basket and a lamb in her apron, 5¼ins. Ibid., pl. 105 (female figure is Rockingham).
'Hebe' holding a ewer and basin standing beside a plinth; 'Innocence', holding a sheep upon a plinth, 28ins. Gilhespy (B), figs. 167, 168.
Sundry models of Animals.

Models attributed to Edward Keys, 1815-c.1826.
'Dr. Syntax walking', Derby Mus.; 'Dr. Syntax riding a horse', Derby Mus.; 'Dr. Syntax landing at Calais', Barrett & Thorpe, pl. 175; 'Dr. Syntax seated sketching', Bradley, pl. 329 (Stevenson & Hancock version); 'Dr. Syntax in the Green Room'; 'Dr. Syntax at York'; 'Dr. Syntax at the Book-Sellers'; 'Dr. Syntax retiring to bed'; 'Dr. Syntax tied to a tree'; 'Dr. Syntax scolding his Landlady'; 'Dr. Syntax chased by a Bull'; 'Dr. Syntax crossing a Lake'; 'Dr. Syntax's Landlady'.
'A Pair of Archers'.
'Six Paris Cries'.
Grotesques representing 'Comedy' and 'Tragedy'.
A set of vicars, wardens and curates.
'Dusty Bob' and 'African Sal'.
The Emperor Napoleon I.
Busts of Napoleon I and Lord Nelson.
A set of grotesque monkey musicians, 4½ins. Barret & Thorpe, pl. 152 (three examples); Twitchett, fig. 391 (14 examples).
A set of grotesque bear musicians, 5½ins. B. & T. Thorn Antiques.
Sundry models of Animals including: 'Elephant', 'Elephant and Driver', 'Sitting Foxes', 'New Sitting Pugs', and 'Lean Cows'.

Models attributed to John Whitaker, c.1818-c.1848.
An Angel.
Boy, and companion girl, each with a dog; Twitchett, fig. 336.
Boy with a Greyhound, and girl with a falcon. Possibly M203.
The Duke of Wellington, seated. Castle Mus., Nottingham, no. 1893-51.
Queen Victoria wearing a bonnet (c.1837). ibid., no. 1903-31.
An Eastern lady. Hughes (B), pl. 42d.
The Virgin Mary. Possibly M239.
A Child seated in a chair. Derby Mus; Twitchett, fig. 286.
A Boy seated with a Guitar. Derby Mus.
A Sleeping Nymph. — Godden (B), p. 143, fig. 233.
'Mazeppa' upon a wild horse chased by wolves (group), 5½ins. Barrett & Thope, pl. 175.
A Peacock amidst flowers, 6½ins. Ibid., pl. 128.
Sundry models of Animals including: a 'Leaping Stag', groups of 'Stags and Dogs', and a 'Parrot'.

Models made by George Cocker, at Friar Gate, 1826-1840.
A boy playing a hurdy-gurdy, standing beside a Monkey which holds a switch (after Meissen original), 6ins. Gilhespy (A), fig. 172.
A bearded Man (after Cyffle's 'Belisarius', standing beside a lady wearing a bonnet and Regency dress, 8ins. Gilhespy (B), fig. 67.
A cobbler whistling to a caged Starling (group), 5ins. Ibid., fig. 66.
'The Rape of the Sabines' (group).
Busts of Daniel O'Connel; Sir Robert Peel; Douglas Fox; the Duke of Wellington; Admiral Lord Nelson.
William Wilberforce, seated holding a book, 7½ins. Gilhespy (A), fig. 171.
Hannah More, seated wearing a crimped cap and long dress, 7½ins. Ibid., fig. 171.
A boy standing beside a plinth upon which a dog sits; companion girl standing beside a fountain, holding a lamb under her arm, 5ins. Herbert Allen, pl. 32, no. 120.
A girl seated, cleaning her shoes; companion girl kneeling upon a tasselled cushion, 3¾ins. Ibid., pl. 33, no. 129.
A relief plaque of a sleeping girl, 6ins. long. Gilhespy (B), fig. 145.

Models made by George Cocker in London, 1840-1842.
A Roman matron.
'Three Topers' including: two obese bare-headed standing men, one with both hands upon his stomach, the other with one hand inside his waistcoat and his other hanging at his side, about 5ins. Derby Mus. Gallery; 'A Dying Drunk'. Brighton Mus.

APPENDIX O
Longton Hall Figures

The 'First Period' 1749-August 1753

01 'Bagpiper', seated in brimmed hat, after Giovanni da Bologna, 4ins. *Connoisseur,* April 1957, fig. 8D.
02 'Dutch Piper', standing. V & A.
03 'Arlecchino' in conical hat dancing, 5½ins. *Connoisseur,* April 1957, fig. 7A.
04 'Avvocato', in cap and gown reading from a book 6¾ins. Watney (A), pl. 5A. *See Plate 132.*
05 'Pantalone', in cap, long gown, with right hand raised and left behind his back, 4½ins. *Connoisseur,* April 1957, fig. 7.
06 'Rustic Seasons': 'Summer', a peasant girl with a sheaf of corn; 'Winter', man in fur hat with charcoal basket, 5½ins. Watney (A), pls. 4B, C. 'Autumn', a youth with vine, and 'Spring', a girl with a basket of flowers. *Antiques,* Aug. 1974, figs. 21, 23.
07 'Ceres with Putto and cornsheaf', 6⅝ins. Watney (A), pl. 5A; 'Ceres incorporated into a candlestick', 10ins. Ibid., pl. 18C; 'Ceres in centre of triple salt', 7¼ins. Ibid., pl. 10A.
08 'Actress', standing, adapted from Ceres, 5½ins. *Connoisseur,* April 1957, fig. 10.
09 'Gallant' and companion 'Lady', each seated cross-legged beside a candlestick (enamelled), 8ins. Watney (A), pls. 18A, 18B.
010 'Fame on the crest of a wave' (group), below which is Bonny Prince Charlie shaking by the paw the British Lion and flanked by two Pugs. Ibid., pl. 1. *See Plate 131.*
011 'Cupid at Vulcan's Forge', 7¼ins. ibid., two versions, one standing, the other seated, pls. 2A, B.
012 'Columbine, seated with a hurdy-gurdy', 7¾ins. *Connoisseur,* April 1957, fig. 8A.
013 'Music', represented by seated putto with a lyre; companion 'Literature', portrayed by putto seated with a scroll, 4ins. Sotheby's, 21-11-67, lot 118.
014 'Kuan Yin', a seated Chinese goddess, 5¼ins. Williams (B), fig. 40; *Connoisseur,* April 1957, fig. 3B. Sigmund Katz Col., version holding a child on her lap.
015 'Ewe and Lamb', (group) recumbent facing opposite ways, 4¾ins. *Connoisseur,* April 1957, fig. 4A.
016 'Goat, recumbent, suckling a Kid' (group), 4ins. Sotheby's, 18-6-74, lot 197.
017 'Ewe and companion Ram', standing with heads turned to the right, 3½ins. *Connoisseur,* April 1957, fig. 12. *See Plate 133.*
018 'Two Sheep recumbent', side by side (group), 4½ins. *Connoisseur,* April 1957, fig. 6.
019 'Horses', recumbent, (pair); Honey (A), pl. 55B.
020 'Cow', and companion 'Bull', recumbent (pair), 4ins. Private col.
021 'Pug', seated upon a cushion, 2ins. long. Watney (A), pl. 3C.
022 'Indian Crane', as taper stick holder, 5ins. Honey (A), pl. 55A.
023 'Heron preening'. 4¼ins. Watney (A), pl. 3B.
024 'Turkeycock', with wreath about its neck, 7¾ins. Ibid., pl. 3A; 'Turkeyhen'. *Connoisseur,* April 1957, fig. 1.
025 'Pheasants' (pair), 7¼ins. *Connoisseur,* April 1957, fig. 2.

The following additional models are discussed and most are illustrated by Bernard Watney, in 'Snowman Figures from Longton Hall, Staffordshire'. *Antiques,* August 1974, pp. 278-284.
'Columbina', seated playing a hurdy-gurdy, 4½ins. Fig. 19.
'Scapino', standing cap in hand laughing, 4¾ins. Sotheby's, 14-2-67.
Polish Nobleman in a long robe bearing a sword, 5ins. Sigmund Katz col. *See Plate 134.*
Turk, standing in long robes wearing a turban, both thumbs tucked into his belt, 5¼ins. Ibid.
'Shou-lao', standing in long robes, holding a fan, 7¾ins. Sigmund Katz col.
'Chung-li Ch'uan', as a bearded sage, standing holding a fly-wisk, 7¾ins. Fig. 20.
Pug, seated (pair), 2¾ins. Fig. 18.
Parrot, 2¼ins. Fig. 14.
Two Finches with cherries, 7ins. Fig. 12.
Finch upon a branch with a snail, beside a pug (group), 4ins. Fig. 13.
Cormorant, 5¾ins. Fig. 10.

The Transitional Period 1753-1754

026 'Lady' seated bare-headed with legs crossed; companion 'Gallant' likewise (same as 09), each on legged base before candlestick adorned with circlets of leaves, 10ins. Watney (A), pls. 26A, B. Also, the same figures as a group in arbour of leaves topped by a candleholder, 8¾ins. Ibid., pl. 26C.
027 'Turk' standing arms akimbo in turban and cloak, 5¾ins.

The Middle Period 1754-1757

028 'Hercules wrestling with the Nemean Lion', 5¾ins. Savage (A), pl. 18B. *See Plate 135.*
029 'Hercules with the Keryneian Stag', 5¾ins. *Burlington Magazine,* 1966, Vol. 108, p. 404, fig. 10.
030 'Cupid on galloping horse, and a baying hound' (pair), 5⅞ins. Lane, pl. 81B.
031 'Infant Bacchus' crowned, with grapes in hand, 5ins. Watney (A), pl. 52. For Plymouth version *see Colour Plate U.*
032 'Infant Artist', 5ins. Ibid., pl. 51. *See Plate 137.*
033 'Two Putti feeding a Goat with Flowers' (group), 5½ins. *See Plate 136.* 'Two Putti feeding a Goat with Grapes' (group), 5½ins. Lane, pl. 81A.
034 'Two Children struggling with a Dolphin' (group) with drip-pan for taper stick in fish's mouth, 8½ins. Sotheby's, 13-11-73, lot 23.
035 'Putto seated with lyre', emblematic of 'Music', 5ins. Watney (A), pl. 56A.
036 'Putto standing with cornsheaf as Summer', 4½ins. Ibid., pl. 56C.
037 'Sampson wrestling with a Lion' (group), with detachable stand, 7½ins. Ibid., pl. 59A.
038 'The Four Infant Seasons', on high scroll bases, 5¾ins. Ibid., pl. 75. For Plymouth versions see (P6).
039 'The Four Child Seasons', represented by seated figures in contemporary dress: 'Spring', a girl with basket of flowers; 'Summer' a boy with corn; 'Autumn', a girl with grapes; 'Winter', a boy warming his hands over a brazier, 4½ins. Ibid., pls. 30A, B, C, D. *See Plate 138.*
040 Seasons represented by seated Youth and Girl: 'Summer' a youth with cork stalks in lap and around head as a chaplet, 4¾ins. *See Plate 138;* 'Spring', a girl with flowers and crown of the same both stiffly modelled. Hughes (B), pl. 14.
041 'Rustic Seasons'. Standing peasant figures: 'Summer', a woman in headscarf and apron holding a sheaf of corn; 'Winter', a man in overcoat and fur hat warming his hands over a brazier, 5ins. Private col. 'Autumn', a youth standing bare-headed carrying fruiting vines. Morley-Fletcher (A), p. 139.
042 'Groups emblematic of Spring', depicting a girl kneeling with flowers in her apron beside a standing youth with dog and a sheep; also 'Autumn', a girl kneeling with apron outstretched to accept grapes tipped from a panier by a standing youth, watched by a goat, 5¾ins. Untermyer, pl. 91, fig. 304. Similar to above but incorporating rococo candlesticks. Watney (A), pls. 61A, 61B.

Theatrical, Musical and Notable.

043 'Actor reading his script' held in both hands. Watney (A), pl. 45. *See Plate 139.*
044 'Arlecchino', in conical hat and mask, wearing a suit adorned with playing cards, right hand elevated to his face, 5ins. Ibid., pl. 40C.
045 'Arlecchino', masked and in motley, holding slapsticks, 5¾ins. Sotheby's, 27-4-76, lot 69.
046 'Arlecchino', in conical hat, seated with bagpipes; 'Columbina, seated with hurdy-gurdy', 5¼ins. Watney (A), pl. 40A.
047 'Gentleman', seated bare-headed playing a lute; companion 'Lady, with a flute', 6¾ins. Ibid., pls. 29A, 29B; Savage (A), pls. 80E, 82B.
048 'Girl Dancer', in plumed hat, laced bodice, skirt and apron with hands held before her (See Bow female 'New Dancer'). Watney (A), pl. 56A.
049 'Lady', holding a musical score; companion 'Gentleman' with a violin, 5¾ins. E.C.C., 1948 ex. cat., pl. 78, nos. 353, 354.

Peasant and Pastoral.

050 'Goatherd', with kid carried upon his neck, 10½ins. King (B), fig. 59. *See Plate 141.*
051 'Boy', seated and holding a bunch of grapes aloft in his left hand, 4⅞ins. Lane, pl. 80A.
052 'Butter Seller', a woman with a basket of wares, holding out a sample in her left hand, on high rococo styled base. Watney (A), pl. 55A.
053 'Cabbage Seller', a woman standing bare-headed in her apron with a cabbage beneath her arm and a basket at her feet, 7¾ins. Watney (A), col. pl. C.
054 'Flower Sellers'; a Boy seated with posy in his left hand and a basket of flowers in his right; Girl in mirror pose, on scrolled bases. Ibid., pls. 37A, 37B.
055 'Fruit Seller', a Woman wearing a hat seated beside a pannier of fruit with grapes in her right hand, the base adorned with roses. Ibid., pl. 31A. *See Plate 140.*
056 'Farmer' standing holding a bird's nest, 5¾ins. Ibid., pl. 53.
057 'Gardener' standing with a spade and a flower-pot; companion 'Woman' with a basket of flowers, 4¾ins. and 4¼ins. Ibid., pls. 55B, 55C.
058 'Girl standing to gather flowers', 5ins. Ibid., pl. 34A.
059 'Huntsman' wearing a peaked cap standing with a gun; 'Lady' with her right hand on her hip and holding game in her left, 8ins. Sotheby's, 7-5-68, lot 179.
060 'Cooks' a Woman wearing a hat holding a bowl; companion Man seated with a bowl and stirring the contents with two spoons, 6ins. Savage (A), pl. 83; Watney (A), pls. 57B, C.
061 'Piper' standing cross-legged in a Tyrolean hat beside a dog, 5¾ins. Watney (A), pl. 50.
062 'Toper', a Man reclining beside a hamper with his right hand elevated, 5½ins. Honey (B), pl. XVb. *See Colour Plate S.*
063 'Boy Toper' seated beside a barrel in a feathered hat, 5¼ins. Savage (A), pl. 48; E.C.C. ex., cat. 1948, pl. 79, no. 348.
064 'Rustic Musician' in a hat seated with a violin, 5¼ins. Sotheby's, 27-4-76, lot 70.
065 'Man seated reading a book'; companion 'Lady' likewise, 3¾ins. and 3ins. Watney (A), pls. 45B, 45C.
066 'Liberty and Matrimony'; a Gallant holding a nest of fledglings and companion Girl with a cage, each standing before a candlestick wreathed with leaves, 9½ins. and 10ins. Ibid., pls. 66B, 66C.
067 'Gallant' holding his hat upon the head of a dog; companion 'Lady' with her right arm encircling a puppy on a plinth, 9ins. and 8¾ins. Ibid., pls. 67A, 67B. *See Plate 142.*

Foreign Personages.

068 'Prancing Chargers' (pair), each with a standing groom, the one a 'Blackamoor', the other a 'Turk', 8¼ins. Watney (A), pls. 63B, 63C; Schreiber, pl. 1, no. 29 (no. 441).
069 'Turk' standing in a turban with both thumbs in his belt; 'Lady in Levantine dress' with a fur-edged coat and tall head-dress, 7¼ins. Watney (A), pls. 42, 43; Sotheby's, 13-11-73, lot 29.

Religious.

070 'Abbess', reading a letter, 5ins. Watney (A), pl. 57A.
071 'Nun', seated holding a book in one hand; companion 'Monk', in mirror image, 5¾ins. Sotheby's, 7-5-68, lot 180.

Animals and Birds.

072 'Bird candlesticks' (pair), 5½ins. Watney (A), pl. 44A.
073 'Leopards' on scrolled bases (pair), 4ins. Savage (A), pl. 76.
074 'Seated Pugs' (pair), 3½ins. and 4ins. Watney (A), pl. 35; E.C.C., 1948 ex. cat., pl. 79, no. 346.
075 'Ram with Ewe'; companion 'Nanny-Goat with Kid', each as a candlestick, 5½ins. Watney (A), pls. 65B, 65C.
076 'Tigers' prowling (pair), 4ins. Sotheby's, 10-5-66, lot 83.
077 'Lions'.

The Final Period, October 1757 to September 1760

078 'Britannia', seated with medallion in likeness of George II, on detachable base bearing scenes of the Seven Years War, 16ins. (overall). Lane, pl. 84.
079 'The Four Continents'; 'Europe', a lady holding a book beside a recumbent horse; 'Asia', a lady holding a casket with recumbent camel; 'America', a Red Indian girl with feathered head-dress and bow and arrows, beside a prairie dog; 'Africa', a negress holding an elephant head-dress and a spear, beside a crocodile, 12¼-13¼ins. Watney (A), pls. 80A-D. *Colour Plate T.*
080 'Dryden' standing with elbow resting on a plinth, 11ins. Lane, pl. 79.
081 'Duke of Brunswick' astride a prancing white charger with military trophies at his feet, 8¾ins. Lane, pl. 80A; Watney (A), col. frontis.
082 'David Garrick', standing beside a plinth on which hangs a scroll inscribed with lines from the Prologue of the Tempest. 8¼ins. Hughes (B), pl. 15. *Plate 142.*
083 Bust of George III when Prince of Wales on shaped stand, 11ins. Lane, pl. 9.
084 'Minerva' standing on square base, 7½ins. Watney (A), pl. 78.
085 'Musicians'; 'Girl playing tambourine'; 'Boy with a lyre', on legged bases, 11¾ins. Lane, pls. 74A, B.
086 'The Lovers' (group); a gallant and lady walking hands joined, on tall base, 10¾ins. Lane, pl. 82.
087 'River God', standing with one foot upon a parcel beside an overturned ewer from which water flows, crowned holding a paddle, 16½ins. Lane, pl. 85.
088 'Zephyr', a slender figure draped in a cloak, his head turned to the left, holding a flaming torch in his left hand, and a cherub's mask with windswept hair in his right, 15¼ins. Sotheby's, 12-5-81, lot 40.

APPENDIX P

Cookworthy's Plymouth and Bristol: Champion's Bristol Figures

Plymouth 1768-1770.

Figures taken from Longton Hall moulds.

P1 'Two Putti feeding a Goat with grapes' before a bocage, 9ins. Hughes (B&T), pl. 32.
P2 'Two Putti feeding a Goat with flowers', 7⅞ins. King (B), fig. 69. *See Plate 143.*
P3 'Two Putti holding between them a floral wreath', 8ins. Rosenfeld, p. 114; King (B), fig. 65.

P4 'Goat' (taken from P1 and 2 groups), 4ins. Tait, pl. 50.
P5 'Infant Bacchus' in wreath of vine leaves eating grapes, 5ins. *See Colour Plate V.*
P6 'The Infant Seasons', represented by four nude draped children with appropriate accessories on tall bases, 6½ins. Plymouth City Mus., cat. no. 27.
P7 'Large standing Continents'. Note 'Africa' is altered so that she no longer holds the elephant head-dress which is, instead, upon the base, 10½-11¼ins. Mackenna (D), figs. 91-94; an example in Plymouth City Mus., cat. no. 27, shows 'Africa' in feathered head-dress.
P8 'Boy seated playing a flute'; companion 'Girl with a mandoline', on tall bases, 5½ins. King (B), fig. 64.
P9 'Boy toper', astride a barrel, drinking; companion 'Girl, leaning against a wine cask goblet in hand', 6⅛ins. and 6ins. King (B), fig. 70.
P10 'Boy in tricorn hat seated with pipe and tambourine'; companion also a 'Boy astride a barrel' with glass raised and a bottle at his feet, 5¾ins. Schreiber, no. 686 (no. 698). *See Plate 144.*
P11 'Gardener holding a basket of fruit'; companion 'lady holding a basket of flowers', each on a scrolled base before a large bocage topped by a candleholder, 10⅝ins. Hughes (B), pls. 17C, 17D; Trans. E.C.C., 1974, Vol. 9, pl. 118.

Figures of uncertain origin.
P12 'Putto seated upon a Dolphin' with tail erect on a shell encrusted base, 8ins. *Connoisseur,* 1971, Vol. 176, no. 707, p. 12, pl. 1. *See Plate 145.*
P13 'Boy, seated beside a vase of flowers'; companion 'Girl' in mirror pose, each on scrolled base, 7¼ins. Hughes (B&T), pl. 32.

Animal and Bird Models.
P14 'Cows' (pair), 5ins. Plymouth City Mus.
P15 'Heifer', recumbent, 5½ins. Schreiber, pl. 74, no. 698 (no. 686).
P16 'Hares' (pair), 4¾ins. Truro Mus.
P17 'Finches' (pair), 5½ins. and 4¾ins. Plymouth City Mus. *See Plate 146.*
P18 'Lions' (pair), seated upon oval bases, 3ins. Schreiber, pl. 74, no. 698 (no. 686). *See Plate 147.*
P19 'Lion', and companion 'Lioness', 11½ins. long. Sotheby's, 7-11-67, lot 144. *See Plate 148.*
P20 'Pheasants' upon flower encrusted stands, 9½ins. Hughes (B&T), pl. 31; E.C.C., 1948 ex. cat., pl. 117, nos. 527, 528.
P21 'Pheasants' (enamelled), on tall bases, 9ins. Plymouth City Mus. *See Colour Plate U.*
P22 'Phoenixes' (pair) with outstretched wings; 8¼ins. Ludlow, pl. 119, no. 263.
P23 'Pug with cropped ears' and one paw raised, seated, 3¼ins. Plymouth City Mus. cat. no. 28.
P24 'Recumbent Ewe', and companion 'Ram', each on a scrolled base, 2½ins. Schreiber, no. 700 (no. 706); Plymouth City Mus.
P25 'Ram standing beside a recumbent lamb'; companion group of Ewe suckling a lamb'. 4½ins. Plymouth City Mus.

Bristol 1770-1780.

Models ascribed to Monsieur Thibauld.
P26 'Shepherd' in tricorn hat standing with bagpipes; companion 'Shepherdess' in hat holding a crook in her right hand and a posy in her left, 12ins. King (B), fig. 68; Schreiber, no. 733 (no. 732). *Colour Plate W.*
P27 'Shepherd' (as above but smaller); companion 'Shepherdess' with flowers gathered in her apron, 6¾ins. Mackenna (D), fig. 95.

Models ascribed to Pierre Stephan.
P28 'Shepherd' in tricorn hat standing barefoot with a bird in his hand beside a dog; 'Shepherdess', also barefoot, holding up her skirts with her left hand and with her right raised in wonder, 6⅞ins. Schreiber, pl. 73, no. 735 (no. 733). *See Plate 152.*
P29 'Boy standing holding a hurdy-gurdy'; 'Girl with a triangle', 7¼ins. Schreiber, pl. 81, no. 738 (no. 749); Hughes (B&T), pl. 33.
P30 'Boy standing holding his hat upon the head of a puppy'; 'Girl with a puppy' on a plinth, 7⅛ins. Schreiber, pl. 81, no. 737 (no. 748); Morley-Fletcher (A), p. 141. *See Plate 153.*
P31 'Boy holding a bird's nest'; 'Girl with a bird-cage', possibly intended as a debased version of 'Liberty and Matrimony', 8ins. Rosenfeld, p. 115; Bristol City Mus., cat. no. 43.

P32 'Boy standing with arms raised, frightened by a dog', 8⅞ins. King (B), fig. 71.
P33 'Goatherd', with kid upon his shoulder; companion 'Milkmaid' with a milk-churn, 12ins. Lane, pls. 94, 95.
P34 'Girl standing with a mousetrap', 7½ins. Cushion, pl. 50.
P35 Classical Elements: 'Water', girl standing with rustic net in left hand beside an upturned vase from which water flows; 'Fire', Vulcan forging thunderbolts upon an anvil; 'Air', a lady in floral wreath her garments blown out by the wind with cherubs blowing; 'Earth', a man one foot upon a spade beside an upturned basket of fruit and flowers, 10ins. Schreiber, pl. 77, no. 731 (no. 743); Mackenna (E), figs. 100-103. *See Plate 149.*
P36 'Rustic Seasons': standing children including 'Spring', a girl with a basket of blossoms in her right hand placing a flower in her hair with her left; 'Summer', a boy with corn in his right hand standing beside a bee-hive; 'Autumn', a girl dancing with a basket of grapes and bunch in hand; 'Winter', a boy in tricorn hat with arms folded, skating, 11ins. Schreiber, pl. 78, no. 729 (no. 745). *See Plate 151.*
P37 'Classical Seasons', standing figures in classical robes: 'Spring', a lady with flowers; 'Summer', a youth with a ram and shears; 'Autumn', a girl with fruiting vine, reaping-hook and upturned basket of fruit; 'Winter', an old man bearded in cloak with a stick, 10ins. Schreiber, pl. 79, 80, no. 730 (no. 742). *See Plate 150.*

Figures of Uncertain Origin.
P38 'Peasant Woman' in a bonnet, wearing a cloak, and apron over a full skirt which she holds with her left hand, carrying a basket. Glaisher Bequest, Fitzwilliam, no. 3095-1928.
P39 'Huntsman with gun' standing beside a dog; 'Lady also with gun', 7¼ins. Fitzwilliam, cat. no. 3131A & B.
P40 'Venus, Adonis and Cupid' (group), 10¼ins. mackenna (E), fig. 90; Schreiber, pl. 79, no. 729 (no. 745).
P41 'Love subdued by Time' (group), 10¼ins. Plymouth City Mus.
P42 'Shakespeare' standing beside a plinth; companion 'Milton' likewise (after Derby originals), 7¼ins. Ibid. *See Plate 154 and Colour Plate X.*
P43 'Three Vestal Virgins' with backs to a plinth upon which is an urn, 11¼ins. Bristol City Mus., cat. no. 40. *See Plate 155.*
P44 'Sphinxes' (pair), with female breasts and heads, 6¼ins. Mackenna (E), fig. 73; Trans. E.C.C., 1972, Vol. 8, pt. 2, pls. 184A, 184B, 185.
P45 'Lady' standing weeping leaning against a plinth on which is an urn (after Derby model of 'Andromache', M100), 12⅜ins. *Connoisseur,* 1956, Vol. 134, p. 185, fig. 1. Bristol City Mus., cat. no. 49.

The following models and groups are known to the author only from photographs in *A Catalogue of Bristol and Plymouth Porcelain, with Examples of Bristol Glass and Pottery, forming the Collection made by Mr Alfred Trapnell* (London, 1912), preface by A. W. Oxford.
P46 'A Vestal Virgin', 13ins. Pl. XXXI, no. 148. This is different from the group of three figures (P43) and is said to be in the likeness of one of Richard Champion's daughters.
P47 'Edmund Burke', depicted as a young man standing holding a cane; he is bewigged but hatless and wears a jacket, waistcoat, breches and shoes. Pl. XLIII, no. 465.
P48 'Minerva' standing wearing a crested helmet, armour and sandals, leaning upon a curiously scrolled shield upon which is painted the head of Medusa, 7½ins. Pl. XLVIII, no. 149.
P49 A Chinaman standing barefoot and bare-headed, his hands concealed in wide sleeves, carrying a boy upon his back. Pl. XLVIII, no. 528.
P50 A Lady standing, holding a posy in her right hand to her breast, with her left hand upon her hip; she has plumes in her hair, and wears a cloak, jacket and skirt. The model resembles the Derby 'Ranelagh Dancer' (K51) with important differences. Pl. XLIV, no. 459.
P51 'A Rustic Group'; a bare-headed youth holds a bird's nest at arms' length in his right hand and a girl, also bare-headed, in a laced bodice, dress, and apron, attempts to recover it, 5ins. Pl. XLVIII, no. 458.
P52 A Peasant Girl standing wearing a headscarf, dress and apron, holding a box containing a rabbit, 5ins. Pl. XLVIII, no. 152.
P53 'A Peacock'. Pl. LII, no. 604.
P54 'Seated Goats' (pair). Pl. X, no. 525.

APPENDIX Q
Miscellaneous Models made at Other Factories

Experimental Derby (possibly).
Q1 Putto seated with legs apart on rectangular base, crowned with flowers, emblematic of 'Spring', 4¼ins. Trans. E.C.C., 1972, Vol. 8, pt. 2, pl. 181A.
Q2 Putto with head shawl seated with a brazier between his knees, emblematic of 'Winter', 4¾ins. Ibid., pl. 181B.
Q3 Winged putto seated with corn upon an octagonal base, emblematic of 'Summer', 5⅝ins. Ibid., pl. 181C.
Q4 'Putto playing a lyre', in cloak seated upon a shaped plinth which has an octagonal base; companion figure of 'Putto holding a song-sheet', 4ins. Ibid., pl. 182B.
Q5 'Turk', standing upon an octagonal base, in turban, loose robes, with left arm akimbo and right hand outstretched; companion 'Lady in robes' and head-dress likewise on octagonal base, 6ins. Ibid., pl. 182A.
Q6 'Pug Dog seated, scratching' with left hind leg. Ibid., pl. 181. *See Plate 159.*
Q7 'An Actor' (headless figure), 6½ins. Ibid., pl. 183D.

Transitional Derby (so-called)

Q8 'Crested Pheasant' adapted as a taper-stick holder, 8½ins. Barrett & Thorpe, pl. 23.

Q9 'Dancing Youth', adorned with ribbons and flowers modelled in slip, 7¼ins. Lane, pl. 62B; V & A cat. no. C.540-1921.

Q10 'Youth, wearing a tricorn hat', seated with swan-like bird beneath his right arm; companion 'Girl, seated with a dog', the two mounted on scroll bases, 7¼ins. Lane, pl. 62B.

Q11 'Youth, bare-headed, seated with a dog', mounted upon a scroll base, 6ins. Barrett & Thorpe, pl. 26.

Q12 'Chinese Boy, climbing a creeper-like tree', 8¾ins. Ibid., pl. 24.

Lund's Bristol.

Q13 'Lu-tung Pin', a Taoist Immortal, modelled after a *blanc-de-Chine* Oriental prototype, 6¾ins. King (B), fig. 60; Barrett, pl. 2A.

Dr. Wall's Worcester.

Q14 'Gardener' standing in tricorn hat holding a pot plant and leaning upon his spade; companion lady in hat, carrying a basket of blossoms and a posy, 6¼ins. Barrett, pl. 87B; for example mounted upon legged base, Harris, pl. 62. *See Plate 156.*

Q15 'Turk' in turban, loose robes leaning upon a scimitar; companion 'Turkish youth carrying a perfume pot', 4¾ins. King (B), fig. 62; Barrett, pl. 86B. *See Plate 157.*

Q16 'Sportsman' in tricorn hat, standing left arm akimbo with a gun in his right hand; companion 'Lady' with powder flask in one hand and game in the other, 7ins. Barrett, pl. 85.

Q17 'Two Canaries facing one another within a bocage' topped by a candleholder. Morley-Fletcher (A), col. pl. facing p. 106. *See Plate 158.*

Q18 'Cupid at Vulcan's Forge', 4ins. Sandon, pl. 129.

Chamberlain's Worcester.

Q19 'Ram', recumbent beneath a flowering tree, on an oval base, 4ins. Trans. E.C.C., 1972, Vol. 8, pt. 2, pl. 179B.

Q20 'Kingfisher' (pair), with a fish, mounted upon a conical base decorated with saucer-shaped flowers and moss, 4½ins. Ibid., pl. 179A.

Lowestoft Figures.

Q21 'Two Dancing Putti upon a single pad base', 6ins. Godden (A), p. 73, fig. 3.

Q22 'Youth in tricorn hat with triangle' in hand dancing; companion 'Girl with a mandoline', both upon legged bases, 7¼ins. and 8ins. V & A cat. no. C245-1940; Harris, p. 72 (male figure only). *See Plates 160 and 161.*

Q23 'Male Dancer in tricorn hat'; companion 'Dancing Girl' in jacket and coat, 7¼ins. *Antique Dealer & Collector's Guide,* March 1970, p. 68.

Q24 Small animal and bird models:
'Cats', seated, 1⅜ins. Ludlow, pl. 108, no. 490.
'Cat, Tabby', 2¼ins. Cushion (A), pl. 27.
'Lamb', recumbent, 1⅜ins. Ludlow, pl. 108, no. 491.
'Pugs', seated (pair) on square bases, 3½ins. Sotheby's, 13-11-73, lot 28.
'Ram', 1⅝ins. Ibid., 14-5-74, lot 101.
'Sheep', 2¼ins. Godden (A), p. 73.
'Swans' (pair), 2¼ins. Ludlow, pl. 489, no. 488; Cushion (A), pl. 27.

Richard Chaffers' Liverpool.

Q25 'Bust of George II' upon a shaped plinth, 13ins. Trans. E.C.C., 1968, Vol. 7, pt. 1, pl. 51. *See Plate 162.*

Q26 'Nurse breast-feeding a baby' (La Nourrice), 4½ins. Ibid., pl. 52.

Q27 Seated Nun, reading from a book', 4½ins. Ibid., pl. 56. *See Plate 163 and Colour Plate Z.*

Q28 'Standing figure of a Male Dancer (after the Bow 'New Dancer'), 4½ins. Ibid., pl. 55B

Q29 'Turk', in loose robes and turban (after Bow model), 6½ins. Ibid., pl. 55A.

Q30 'Ariadne', reclining (after the antique), 6ins. Ibid., pl. 52C.

Q31 Wall bracket, portraying the infant Britannia beside a cupid with a trumpet emblematic of 'Fame', 11¼ins. Trans. E.C.C., 1972, Vol. 8, pt. 2, pl. 177.

Q32 Wall bracket, portraying a 'Panther with fruit', 5¼ins. Ibid., pl. 178B.

Philip Christian's Liverpool.

Q33 'A Hare', as the knob on a tureen lid. Trans. E.C.C., 1968, Vol. 7, pt. 1, pl. 53A.

Q34 Man in fur-lined hat and overcoat holding a basket of charcoal, emblematic of 'Winter' (after Chelsea original), 4¾ins. Sotheby's, 16-12-75, lot 96. *See Plate 164.*

Samuel Gilbody's Liverpool.

Q35 'Shepherd standing beside a lamb and a dog', with a basket of fruit (after a Derby prototype). Trans. E.C.C., 1971, Vol. 8, pt. 1, pls. 62-64; *Antique Collecting,* March 1976, pl. 16.

Q36 'Minerva', standing in crested helm and cuirass, leaning upon a shield with her right arm elevated (after Derby prototype), 5¾ins. Trans. E.C.C., 1972, Vol. 8, pt. 2, pl. 188A, an enamelled version from J. V. G. Mallet col.

Q37 Set of four standing putti, emblematic of the 'Four Seasons': 'Spring', holding a posy with basket of flowers wearing diadem and cross belt of flowers; 'Summer', likewise with corn; 'Autumn', likewise with goblet and grapes in hands; 'Winter', with fur-edged cloak over head and about nude body, about 4½ins. Plymouth City Mus. (reserve collection) identified by Dr. Bernard Watney. *Colour Plate Y.*

'Gilbody Figures, 1754-1761, A Short Review' by Bernard Watney, Trans. E.C.C., 1980, Vol. 10, pts. 4 & 5, pp. 346-347, gives information and illustrations of further Gilbody figures:
'A Turkish Lady', standing wearing a head-dress, robe and cloak, 3⅛ins. plate 144a.
'Winter', represented by a standing man wearing a hat and overcoat, holding a basket of charcoal (C98 Chelsea version; 06 Longton Hall version), 3¾ins. pl. 145a.
'Ceres', standing crowned with cornhusks, holding a corn-sheaf in her right hand accompanied by 'Cupid' (group), 5¾ins. pl. 145b.

Seth Pennington's Liverpool.

Q38 'Negro Slave', standing upon a square base, incised 'India Slave 1772' (not 1779 as elsewhere stated), 9ins. Trans. E.C.C., 1972 Vol. 8, pt. 2, pl. 178A; Plymouth City Mus.

William Reid's Liverpool.

Q39 Small 'Hound', decorated in underglaze blue. Watney, *English Blue and White Porcelain of the 18th Century,* p. 80, pl. 45A.

Staffordshire Porcelain of the 18th Century.

Q40 'Charity', a lady in classical robes standing with babe in arms and a child standing at her right side, 8½ins. Lane, pl. 96.

Q41 'Neptune', standing crowned beside a dolphin, 9ins. Scott, pl. 171, fig. 631.

Q42 'Venus', a lady standing in classical robes with a child and a dolphin, 8½ins. King (B), fig. 72.

Q43 'Apollo', standing with lyre, 8⅛ins. Ibid., fig. 72.

APPENDIX R
Marks on English Porcelain Figures

Chelsea

1. Chelsea 1745 — Chelsea, sometimes with the date '1745', incised in script on 'Goat and Bee' creamers.

2. An incised triangle (emblematic of 'Fire') appears on several models made before 1749.

3. A crown and trident, in underglaze blue, appears on the group known as 'The Rustic Lovers'.

4. An embossed anchor within an oval upon an applied medallion appears on some models made between 1749 and 1752. *See Plate 9.* The same device is enamelled red on some models made between 1752 and 1753. A violet enamel is used on one model of Isabella (B35).

5. June ye 26 1746. — 'June ye 26, 1746' incised on the model of a 'Boy asleep on a mattress'.

6. A red enamelled anchor. Drawn with a ring, cross-piece, rounded crown* through which the shaft fails to penetrate, and carefully drawn barbs. Many figures issued between 1753 and 1757. Similar anchors may appear in brown enamel or underglaze blue though rarely if ever on figures.

7. A red enamelled anchor. Drawn often without either ring or crosspiece or both, a pointed crown* through which the shaft usually penetrates, and often without barbs. Appears on many figures issued between 1759 and 1769
Note that miniature figures and scent-bottles may have two red anchors, or a red and a gold anchor, and very occasionally one in underglaze blue.

*the word crown as used here refers to the bottom of the anchor.

8. A gold anchor, similar to the red anchor described.

9. R — 'R' in gilt, appears upon groups known as the 'Allegorical Seasons'.

Bow

1. Symbol for Mercury, incised.
2. Symbol for Mars, incised.
3. Symbol for Copper, incised.

(1–3) appear on models made between 1750 and 1754.

4. The incised mark of the repairer Tebo, or Thibauld.

5. Another mark of the repairer Tebo or Thibauld.

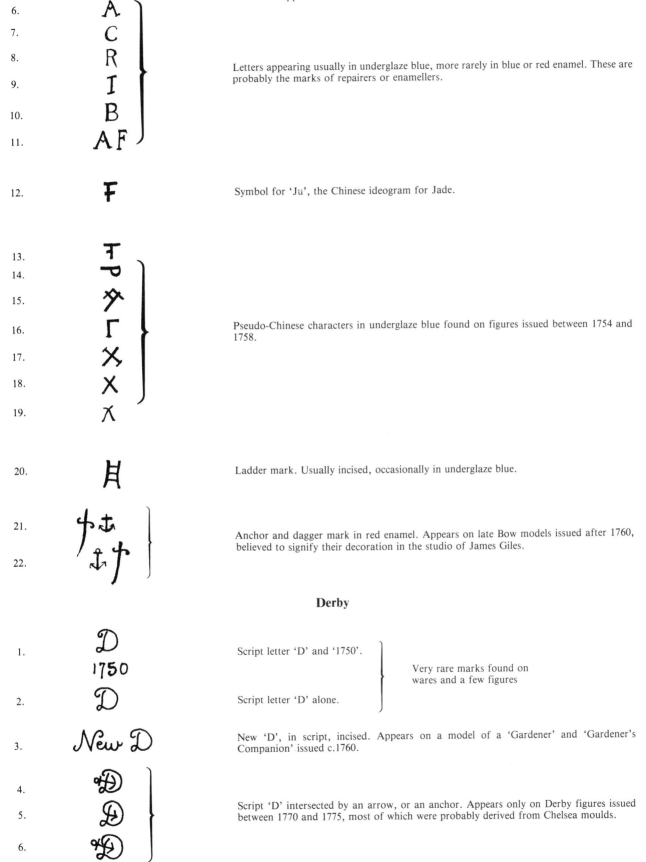

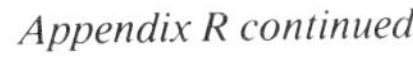

No.	Mark	Description
6.	A	Letters appearing usually in underglaze blue, more rarely in blue or red enamel. These are probably the marks of repairers or enamellers.
7.	C	
8.	R	
9.	I	
10.	B	
11.	AF	
12.		Symbol for 'Ju', the Chinese ideogram for Jade.
13.		
14.		Pseudo-Chinese characters in underglaze blue found on figures issued between 1754 and 1758.
15.		
16.	Γ	
17.		
18.	X	
19.		
20.		Ladder mark. Usually incised, occasionally in underglaze blue.
21.		Anchor and dagger mark in red enamel. Appears on late Bow models issued after 1760, believed to signify their decoration in the studio of James Giles.
22.		

Derby

1.	D 1750	Script letter 'D' and '1750'.	Very rare marks found on wares and a few figures
2.	D	Script letter 'D' alone.	
3.	New D	New 'D', in script, incised. Appears on a model of a 'Gardener' and 'Gardener's Companion' issued c.1760.	
4.		Script 'D' intersected by an arrow, or an anchor. Appears only on Derby figures issued between 1770 and 1775, most of which were probably derived from Chelsea moulds.	
5.			
6.			

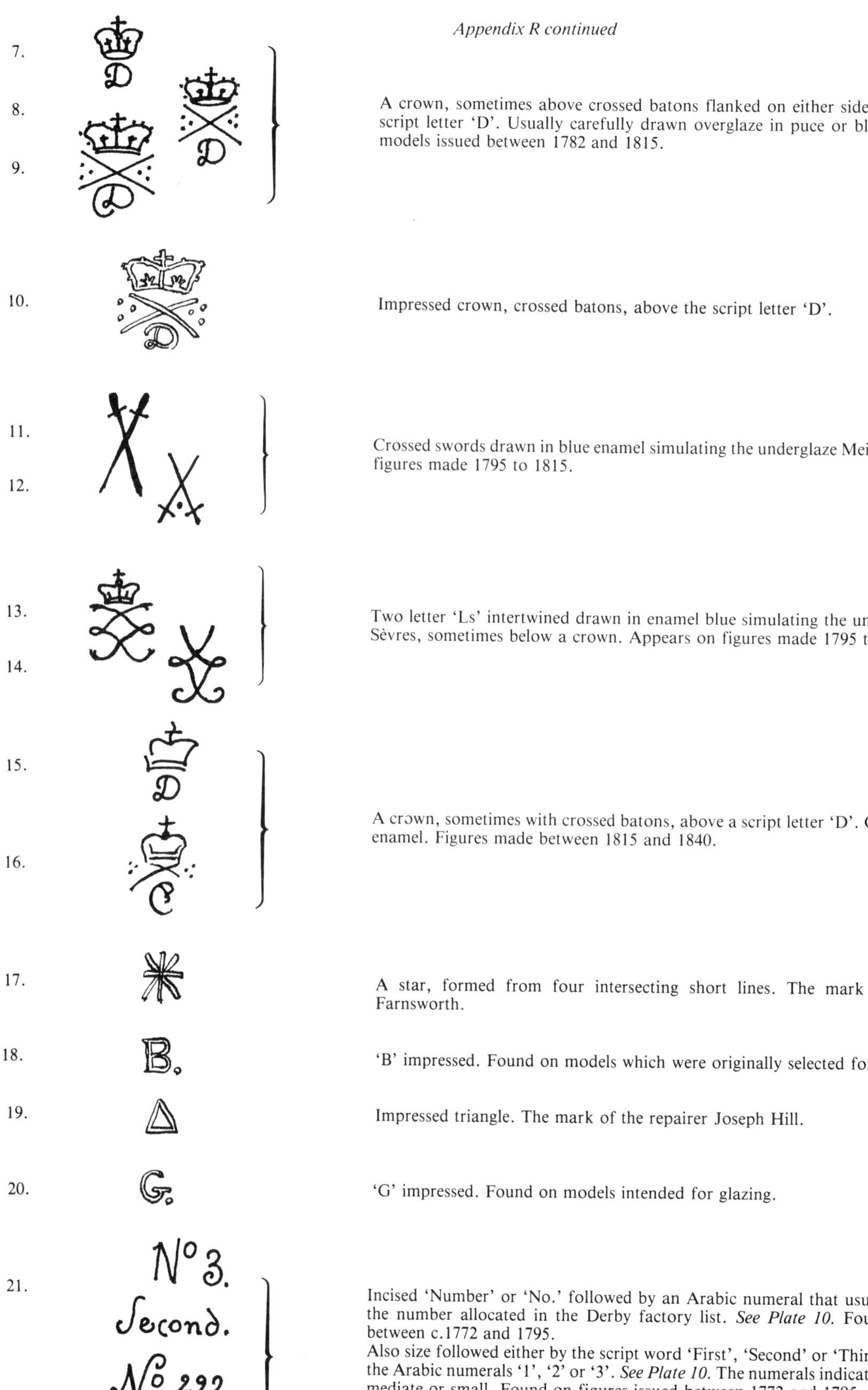

7.–9. A crown, sometimes above crossed batons flanked on either side by three dots, above a script letter 'D'. Usually carefully drawn overglaze in puce or blue enamel. Appears on models issued between 1782 and 1815.

10. Impressed crown, crossed batons, above the script letter 'D'.

11.–12. Crossed swords drawn in blue enamel simulating the underglaze Meissen mark. Appears on figures made 1795 to 1815.

13.–14. Two letter 'Ls' intertwined drawn in enamel blue simulating the underglaze blue mark of Sèvres, sometimes below a crown. Appears on figures made 1795 to 1815.

15.–16. A crown, sometimes with crossed batons, above a script letter 'D'. Carelessly drawn in red enamel. Figures made between 1815 and 1840.

17. A star, formed from four intersecting short lines. The mark of the repairer Isaac Farnsworth.

18. 'B' impressed. Found on models which were originally selected for issue in biscuit.

19. Impressed triangle. The mark of the repairer Joseph Hill.

20. 'G' impressed. Found on models intended for glazing.

21.–22. Incised 'Number' or 'No.' followed by an Arabic numeral that usually corresponds with the number allocated in the Derby factory list. *See Plate 10.* Found on models issued between c.1772 and 1795.
Also size followed either by the script word 'First', 'Second' or 'Third', or alternatively by the Arabic numerals '1', '2' or '3'. *See Plate 10.* The numerals indicate the sizes large, intermediate or small. Found on figures issued between 1772 and 1795.

Longton Hall

1. [mark]

2. [mark]

Two 'Ls' intersecting one another in mirror image, below which is a vertical line formed by two, three or four dots, drawn in underglaze blue. Found on figures which include decoration in underglaze blue issued between 1754 and 1760.

3. + A cross, in underglaze blue.

4. Crossed swords in underglaze blue found on a few animal models of the period 1752 to 1754.

Plymouth

Alchemists' sign for tin.

Lund's Bristol

BRISTOLL.

Impressed BRISTOLL sometimes with the date 1750.

Transitional Derby

An incised circle containing two triangles one inside the other, or the letter 'Y'.

APPENDIX S
The Commedia Dell'Arte (Italian Comedy)

Some have traced the origins of the Italian Comedy back to the band of comedians formed in the 8th century B.C. in Icaria by Susarion; others to the chariot-load of besmeared vagabonds used by Thespis to recite comic poems to music. Certainly, the *Ethlogi* (parodists), *cinaedologi* (obscene), and *simodi* who, together with the *hilarodi* wore white robes and sang to their own musical accompaniment, have parallels in the Commedia dell'Arte. Most will agree that the Italian Comedy developed from the farces enacted at Atella, or *Fabulae Atellanae,* which provided welcome entertainment for a populace in ancient Rome that had grown weary of the classical dramas of Greece. The slave characters, known as *sannio,* and the clowns or *funambulae,* appeared with faces blackened with soot bearing the phallus and have a striking resemblance to the Italian *zanni* figures, such as 'Arlecchino', who wore black masks and carried slapsticks. The lecherous merchant 'Papus', may be the forebear of 'Pantalone', the hunchback 'Marcus mimus albus' of 'Pulcinella', whilst 'Manducus', the *miles gloriosus* seems to be the ancestor of 'Il Capitano'. During the 3rd and 4th centuries A.D., the impromptu dialogues of the players laced with bawdy humour incurred the censorship of the Catholic church, and subsequently during the Dark Ages, the drama like other arts suffered a decline.

During the Renaissance, renewed interest was shown in the theatre and men like Beolio (1502-1542) and Cecchi (1518-1587) wrote scenarios which were performed by groups of strolling players. Many of the *dramatis personae* were drawn from folk-lore, or were based on living characters who frequented the great cities. Thus, we find 'Beltrame', 'Brighella' and 'Scapino' from Milan, 'Pulcinella' and 'Scaramuzzi' from Naples, 'Pantalone' from Venezia and 'Corviello' from Calabria. During the 16th and 17th centuries, troupes of actors were formed under the patronage of a nobleman, such as the Duke of Mantua and the Duke of Modena, which were based upon a large city. These toured the surrounding countryside and, when there was no suitable building, gave their performances upon portable stages before a back drop in the marketplace. In the late 16th century, a few troupes visited other European countries where they received acclaim.

Actors were drawn from the educated middle class though they would rarely include a person of noble birth. A specific role, with costume and face-mask, was allocated to each player which he retained until retirement or death. A scenario was usually posted in the wings a few hours before the curtain rose and, with no predetermined script, a dialogue was improvised as the plot unfolded. When this flagged, recourse was had to *lazzi* (stage tricks), which consisted of slapstick, mime, juggling, song and dance. Almost every member of the cast was an acrobat and able to play at least one musical instrument. Coverage of the face with a mask necessitated recourse to gesture and the skills demanded of a comedy actor were vastly different from those required on the conventional stage. Humour was often very coarse and though this frequently gave offence to the middle class, it was generally appreciated by the aristocracy and peasantry alike. In 1695, the troupe of the Duke of Modena played before the court of Louis XIV and when the jokes were translated into French, they seemed extravagant and licentious, and outraged the queen. The following year the king's minister wrote ". . . and if they chance to present indecent postures or speak lewd words or do anything which may be against propriety, his Majesty will dismiss them and send them back to Italy". In May 1697, M. de Pontchartrain wrote again to the chief of police, "The King has discharged his italian Comedians, and His Majesty has commanded me to write to you to have their theatre permanently closed . . ." However, the same year the king gave permission to both Tortoriti and Cadet each to form a troupe of their own but forbade either to come within thirty leagues of Paris. There can be little doubt that such drastic action had been prompted by the queen who, perhaps, thereby betrayed her own bourgeois origins. She had been first the wife of a cripple, M. Scarron, then governess to the royal children, and finally as madame de Maintenon appeared in the eyes of the court to "enjoy the honour of the King's adultery" though, in fact, she had satisfied the dictates of her conscience by a secret marriage to her lover.

Until the 17th century women were forbidden by Canon Law from appearing upon the boards and their roles were played by boys or clean shaven youths. Later, when the ban was lifted, actresses playing the role of 'Inamorata' wore small black velvet masks called *loups* which, at the time, were normal street wear and designed to preserve that milk-white complexion which was then the hallmark of beauty. *Servetta,* or servants, were without masks and might be referred to as *cantarinas* or *ballerinas* according to their chief function.

'Arlecchino da Bergamo' (Harlequin) was the most famous of all Comedy characters. Initially he wore loose garments decorated with braid arranged in diamond patterns, later, a costume to which were applied coloured triangular patches, and finally, a tight fitting dress of coloured lozenges known as the 'motley'. He sported a round plumed hat and a leather face mask of tan or black. Most of his time on stage was spent plotting mischief, in amorous intrigue or performing *lazzi*. His companion was the hunchback 'Pulcinella' (Punch) who wore a grey cap, white trousers and jacket gathered with a belt into which was thrust a wooden sword. His mask had a hook nose, bristling moustache and beard. He too was mischievous but his pranks usually had cruel or sinister undertones and, when he was in a black mood, Arlecchino was swift to elude him. 'Pantalone' (Pantaloon), was originally a lecherous and niggardly merchant of Venice who was mocked by his inamorata both for his meanness and impotence. Later, he developed into a respected head of family, the husband of 'Dame Ragonda', and the father of 'Isabella'. He usually wore a skull-cap, seedy red doublet, breches and hose and sported a black cloak. Sometimes he carried a money-bag to underline his miserly qualities. His mask had a hooked nose, thin drooping moustache and protuberant beard. His friend and companion was often a doctor of medicine, known as 'Il Dottore' or more specifically 'Baloardo', 'Hippocraso' or 'Balanzone', who haled from Bologna. Dressed all in black, relieved only by a white ruffle at the neck, he too wore a long cloak and was represented carrying learned books. He might wear either a skull-cap or doctor's hat and his black mask traditionally covered only his forehead and nose. A pompous, inept character, he was much given to misquoting Latin to conceal his ignorance. Sometimes his place was taken by a doctor of law, the 'Avvocato', an even more tedious fellow who wore a long gown decorated with rosettes and occasionally trimmed with sable. He had a tricorn hat and a white or black mask covered his face. The 'Capitano', passed by such names as 'Rodomondo', 'Cocodrillo', 'Rinoceronte' or 'Spavento'. He was a bully, a braggart and a coward. he was said to have come from Spain or France and his early dress included helmet, cuirass and boots. He evolved via a ruffian in Spanish styled plumed hat and starched ruff, to become a courtier in tricorn hat, jacket, tight fitting breeches and boots with a gigantic sword. His mask was flesh coloured with prominent menacing nose, up-turned moustache and a short beard. The character 'Scaramuzzi da Napoli' (Scaramouche or the Skirmisher), was a minor variant of the captain whilst another was 'Giangurgolo' (big-mouth).

'Brighella da Milano' was the archetype cut-throat who did not scruple to use his dagger in his adversary's back and yet could play a guitar and sing in a mellifluous tone. His entrance sent a chill down the spine. He wore a jacket gathered with a belt with purse and dagger, loose trousers and a tabaro or short cloak. His garments were decorated with green braid and his mask was an olive shade of the same colour, half mawkish, half cynical, with thick sensuous lips, sloe eyes, hook nose, and a chin bristling with a sparse beard and moustache. This epitome of evil was the forefather of lesser rogues, who wore similar costumes and played the roles of servants. Thus, there was 'Beltrame da Milano', a wilfully blind husband; 'Bagulin'; 'Scapino' and his double 'Mezzetino'. They both wore black costumes adorned with vertical stripes, respectively green and white or red and white thereby facilitating instant recognition by the audience. Another varlet was the dreamy, enigmatic 'Narcissino', who first appeared during the 17th century. He wore a brimmed hat, linen tabs at the neck, rather baggy breeches, sash, and tabaro. Perhaps the most loveable of all was the Scillian 'Pedrolino' (Pierrot). A faithful simpleton, he was always the unfortunate one to be caught when the schemes of Arlecchino and Pulcinella misfired. Dressed in loose jacket with ruffle, trousers and a soft hat turned back in front, his face was heavily powdered, but maskless. The costume of the coarse buffoon 'Pagliacco' was somewhat similar, though his garments were looser, the sleeves longer, and he sported a tall hat. 'Corviello' was a character akin to Arlecchino. The role of inamorato (lover) went by such names as 'Cinthio del Sole', 'Mario', 'Lelio', 'Flavio' or 'Octavo' and the part was played without a mask in the dress of a contemporary young man of fashion. The role of inamorata (loved one), included both fine lady and courtesan dressed in feminine fripperies and wearing the *loup*. They might be called 'Isabella', often the daughter of Pantalone, 'Flaminia', or 'Lavinia'. *Servetta*, or maids, included 'Columbina', the wife or mistress of Arlecchino, 'Violetta', 'Olivetta' and others. Prior to 1700, *servetta* wore an apron but subsequently this was replaced by a large bow worn in the hair. Occasional roles were 'Dame Ragonda', the wife of Pantalone, and 'La Ruffinia' the gossip or 'go-between'. A few characters were peculiar to only one troupe but the majority were common to all companies.

Giacomo Calotto (1592-1635) spent much of his short but adventurous life in Italy where he created etchings of theatrical characters, including those of Commedia dell'Arte, published in *Belli di Sfessania*. These were dramatically posed in the Mannerist style. Later, they were adapted and engraved by Joullain to illustrate *Histoire du Théâtre italien . . .*, by Luigi Riccoboni, published between 1827 and 1733 in Paris. During the visit of the troupe of the Duke of Modena to the court of Louis XIV in 1694, their colourful costumes prompted paintings of the subject by Claude Gillot (1673-1722) who published scenes from plays in a folio volume *Le Théâtre italien*. Gillot's pupil, Antoine Watteau, also turned his attention towards the Italian Comedy and his representations together with other work were published by his friend in a folio of engravings by various artists entitled *Recueil Julienne* in 1735. These were the main sources of inspiration upon which the porcelain modellers of the 18th century drew. There was, however, one notable exception, namely Nymphenburg. Here, c. 1760, a series of eight pairs of Comedy figures were created by Franz Anton Bustelli and the source upon which these were based has not been identified. Although the more usual characters normally associated with Commedia dell'Arte are represented such as Arlecchino, Pantalone, Capitano Spavento and Pedrolino, there are others such as 'Lalage', 'Julia', 'Lucinda', 'Donna Martina', and 'The Curé' that are unique. It has been suggested that the names of the ladies may be those of actresses who enacted the roles. A full set of the Bustelli Comedy Models is still available from the Nymphenburg factory which sells high quality reproductions.[1]

1. Christie's Sale Catalogue, 28th March 1977, Lots 157-171. Complete set of original Bustelli models c. 1760.

APPENDIX T

Greek and Roman Mythology Portrayed in Porcelain.

During the 18th century almost every educated gentleman spoke Latin and Greek and was familiar with classical literature. Many had completed a Grand Tour of Europe, during which they had surveyed the ruins of antiquity. It was, therefore, only natural that porcelain factories of those days should find a ready market for models relating to mythology. Many of us born between two world wars have but 'small Latin and less Greek', whilst those of the succeeding generation are frequently unfamiliar with even diminutive Latin and find the mythology of Greece and Rome a closed book. Perhaps, for this reason, porcelain figures illustrating mythological subjects command lower prices than others. However, since there are a great number of them it would seem appropriate to include a few short notes.

Greek Mythology

Aesculapius was the son of Apollo and was reared by a centaur (half man, half horse) called Chiron from whom he learned the art of healing. One remedy given to him by Athene was composed of the blood of the monster, Medusa. When Aesculapius began to restore life to the dead, Hades complained to Zeus that he was being robbed of his kingdom, and Zeus accordingly struck him dead with a thunderbolt.

Aphrodite probably originated as a Mother Goddess but evolved to become the guardian of love. She was the daughter of Zeus and Dione, and is usually portrayed with a hand-mirror or an apple, and may be attended by either Eros, or the Three Graces, Aglaea, Euphrosyne, and Thalia.

Apollo was the sun of Zeus and Leto and originated as a sun god; he later became concerned with pastoral care, prophecy, and the musical arts. He is depicted as a clean-shaven youth with either a lyre, or a shepherd's crook, or a long-bow and quiver.

Athene. The birth of this goddess was very odd! When Zeus had eaten his first wife, Metis, together with her unborn child, he developed a headache. This was cured by Prometheus who, cleaved open his head with a bronze axe and, from the gaping wound sprang Athene who became Zeus's favourite child. She fought with him against the Giants, slew Pallas who had attempted to ravish her, and became a warrior goddess. She was protector of the Argonauts on their quest for the Golden Fleece and was involved in the Trojan war. She is

depicted wearing a crested helmet, and a breastplate fringed with serpents given to her by Zeus, and with a shield upon the centre of which was the head of Medusa presented to her by Perseus. *See also* Hygieia.
Cephalus *see* Procris and Cephalus.
Cerberus was the three-headed dog that guarded the entrance to the underworld.
Charon was a ferryman who took those entering the underworld across the river Styx in his boat. Upon the far shore was the kingdom of Hades through which ran a number of rivers. Those who drank from the river Lethe enjoyed a state of forgetfulness or oblivion.
Cronus was the supreme deity who dwelt on mount Olympus before he was ousted by Zeus. His spouse was the primitive Earth Goddess, Rhea. Having heard a prophecy that one day he would be deposed by his own son, Cronus devoured each one of his new born male children. Rhea sought the advice of her parents, Uraneus and Gaea and, when she became pregnant again, they devised a plan by which the child was to be concealed and a stone wrapped in swaddling bands presented to Cronus. In this way the child Zeus was saved, and Cronus, presented with the stone, swallowed it.
Cybele was originally a Phrygian Earth Goddess of caverns and of land as distinct from cultivated soil; she became part of Greek mythology and was equated with Rhea. She is usually depicted wearing the turret crown of a mother goddess in a chariot drawn by lions or attended by two lions which suggest she may have originated in Africa. Some held that she was the spouse of Gordius, king of Phrygia.
Demeter represented cultivated soil, the fields, and the crops. Her daughter, Persephone, sometimes called Kore, was carried off to the underworld by Hades. Demeter is depicted crowned with corn stalks, holding a reaping-hook or a sceptre or perhaps a torch, standing beside a corn sheaf. The distinction between Cybele, Demeter and Persephone is not always evident in porcelain models.
Europa was the daughter of Agenor, king of Phoenicia. One day, whilst playing in the water-meadows, she saw a beautiful black bull and, as she approached it, the beast knelt down before her. After caresssing it, she placed garlands about its neck when it suddenly reared up and carried her off to Crete, where she was ravished. The bull turned out to be Zeus in disguise. The fruits of the union were Minos, Rhadamanthys, and Sarpedon.
Galatea was a water-spirit, or Nereid, who was courted by Polyphemus, one of the Cyclops, but preferred the youthful herdsman called Acis. Polyphemus surprised the two lovers in a rocky bower and crushed Acis with a huge boulder. However, Acis was transformed into a river in which Galatea and her tritons frolicked.
Ganymede was the son of Tros, the king of Phrygia, and Callirrhoe. Distinguished by his great beauty he attracted the attention of Zeus who, disguised as an eagle, carried him off to Olympus where he replaced Hebe to become bearer of the cup of nectar for the gods.
Graces. The three Graces, Aglaea, Euphrosyne, and Thalia, were nymphs in the train of Aphrodite. They are usually portrayed nude, with their arms about one another's shoulders.
Hera, the daughter of Cronus and Rhea, became the symbol of conjugal love and fertility. She wore a tall cylindrical crown and might be attended by a peacock emblematic of the stars in the firmament and carried a pomegranate representing fruitfulness. Her daughter was Hebe, cup bearer of the gods.
Hercules, the son of Zeus and Alcmene, was the twin brother of Iphicles. Hera, the third wife of Zeus, was jealous of Hercules and sent Lyssa, the spirit of madness, to him. He beame deranged and slew both his wife Megra, and all of his children. Eurytheus sentenced him to perform Twelve Labours for the expiation of this crime and three of these are illustrated in English porcelain.

1. Hercules was commanded to slay the **Nemean Lion** and to bring its skin back to Eurytheus. Hercules fired arrows at the beast which failed to penetrate its hide. He then attacked it with his club which proved useless for this task and finally strangled it with his bare hands. He retained the skin for himself and this rendered him invulnerable.

2. Hercules was ordered to kill the **Hydra** which dwelt in the marshes of Lerna in the Peloponese, where it ravaged the cattle. The monster had nine heads and if any one was severed, two more grew from the stump of the neck, whilst its breath was poisonous. Accompanied by Iolaus, the son of Iphicles, Hercules forced the brute into the open with flaming arrows. He severed each of the nine heads with a bronze axe and, as he did, so, Iolaus sealed the neck with a red hot iron.

3. Hercules was commanded to capture the **Keryneian Stag,** which had hooves of bronze and antlers made of gold. He did so after a chase that lasted a year.

Hercules is depicted as a muscular strong man wearing a lion's skin and bearing a club. However, when he was employed by Omphale, the queen of Lydia, he became besotted by her and allowed her to wear his lion's skin and to carry his club. He became effeminate, wore women's clothes and performed women's work. This scene is portrayed in porcelain when he is depicted holding the distaff whilst Omphale bears his club.
Hermes was the son of Zeus and Maia and, when he was still an infant, he escaped from his cradle to steal fifty oxen from a herd belonging to Apollo to the huge delight of Zeus. He became the messenger of the gods and went about his business in winged sandals and winged helmet bearing the caduceus, a wand entwined by a serpent, with which he would quieten Cerberus.
Hygieia a title sometimes assumed by Athene after her miraculous healing of Mnesicles, who had fallen off a building in the Propylaea. She may then be depicted with a scroll emblematic of medical learning and leaning upon a tree.
Jason And The Golden Fleece. Phrixus and Helle, children of Athamas the king of Boeotia, fearing they would be murdered by their step-mother, fled upon a ram provided by Hermes which was endowed with intelligence and able to speak. Helle fell off the back of the ram and was drowned in the sea now known as the Hellespont. Phrixus reached Colchis on the Black Sea where he sacrificed the ram to Zeus and gave its Golden Fleece to king Aeetes, who hung it upon a tree guarded by a dragon.

In Thessaly, Pelias had seized the throne from his brother Aeson. Pelias had been warned by the oracle that he should beware of a man who came to him wearing only one sandal. Therefore, when Jason, who was the son of Aeson, came before him clad in this manner to claim part of the kingdom, he promised to cede him his due provided he could bring back the Golden Fleece and hoped that thereby he would be rid of him. Jason built the fifty-oared ship, **Argo,** and gathered about him the Heroes who included Amphion, the Dioscuri, Hercules, Orpheus, Peleus, Theseus, and Meleager, and obtained the protection of Athene. After surviving many perils they arrived at Colchis where king Aeetes agreed to hand over the Golden Fleece in exchange for the successful performance of certain tasks. These including the sowing of the dragon's teeth. Medea, who was Aeetes's daughter, fell in love with Jason and showed him how the dangerous tasks might be accomplished. They obtained the Golden Fleece and returned to Thessaly, only to find that Pelias had killed Aeson during their absence. Medea suggested to the aging Pelias that she could rejuvenate him if he first submitted to being cut into small pieces and being roasted. He readily agreed and in this way the murder of her lover's father was revenged. The couple withdrew to Corinth but, after a decade, Jason deserted Medea to marry Creusa. Medea wrought vengeance by murdering all their children and sending the bride a wedding robe which caused her to be consumed by flames. She fled to Athens where she married Aegeus.
Meleager was the son of Oeneus and Althaea. The Fate, Atropos, told Meleager that he would live only as long as it took a brand burning on the hearth to be consumed in the flames. Althaea immediately extinguished the faggot and concealed it. Later, when Oeneus forgot to offer the first fruits of his harvest to Artemis, the god became enraged and sent a ferocious wild boar to ravage the land of Aetolia, where he resided. Meleager invited some of the most celebrated heroes to help him eradicate the nuisance. Many who joined him were slain by the beast. Eventually Atalanta wounded it with an arrow, and Meleager finished it off with his spear. A disagreement arose among the victors about the distribution of the boar's remains, which Meleager had already given to Atalanta. When Meleager's uncles endeavoured to remove parts of the beast, he slew them. Whereupon Althaea, disgusted at her son's impulsive behaviour, found and burned the faggot she had concealed for so long and thereby caused his death. Meleager is generally depicted with the boar's head and Atalanta with a long-bow and a hunting hound.
Muses. After the victory of the Olympians over the rebellious Titans, the gods petitioned Zeus asking him to create divinities who would enliven their celebrations. Zeus then slept with a Titaness named Mnemosyne who, in due course, gave birth to nine daughters known as the Muses. They provided music, poetry, song, and dance at the celestial feasts on mount Olympus, though they preferred to live on mount Helicon. At first, they were most chaste and, when Pyreneos who was king of Daulis, attempted to ravish them, they grew wings and flew away to safety. The wretched monarch attempted to follow them and fell to his death. Later, they enjoyed both lovers, who included Apollo, and husbands. They were formidable creatures not to be trifled with for, when the nine daughters of the Emanthian king, the Pierides, were foolish enough to compete with them for a prize in poetry, they were transformed into magpies for their presumption.

Thamyris, the Thracian bard, boasted that he could surpass them and was struck blind and deaf for his temerity. They were named: Calliope (Epic Poetry), Clio (History), Erato (Love Poetry), Euterpe (Lyric Poetry), Melpomene (Tragedy), Polyhymnia (Sacred Music), Terpsichore (Dance), Thalia (Comedy), and Urania (Astronomy). They may be depicted with, or without, wings with accessories appropriate to their functions.

Persephone was the daughter of Zeus and Demeter. Whilst she was in the fields gathering spring flowers, the ground opened up and Hades appeared who bore her off to the underworld. Forbidden to bring anything from the world into the shades, she had managed to conceal some pomegranate seeds about her person and because of this was permitted to visit her mother for seven months each year.

Perseus was the son of Danae who was seduced by Zeus disguised as a shower of gold. The outraged husband, Acrisius, placed mother and child in a chest, which he cast into the sea. The castaways were washed ashore at Seriphos where they came under the protection of Polydectes. Perseus grew up to become a robust warrior and, anxious to achieve fame, announced he would slay a Gorgon and bring back its head. He first visited the three old sisters, called the Graeae, who shared one eye and one tooth between them. Perseus stole both, and in exchange for their return, obtained the knowledge he sought, as well as a magic wallet and the dark helmet which made him invisible. Two of the Gorgons, Stheno and Euryale, were immortal, so Perseus attacked the third, who was Medusa. All three had large tusks, serpents for hair, bronze hands, and wings of gold; anybody who looked at one of them was immediately turned to stone. Wearing the dark helmet, Perseus observed Medusa's reflection in his shield and was able with one blow from his sickle to sever her head. He placed it in his wallet and later presented the head to Athene, who attached it to her shield, and gave the dark helmet to Hermes.

When Perseus reached Ethiopia he found that queen Cassiopeia had offended the Ocean Nymphs by proclaiming that she was the more beautiful. Poseidon took the side of the Nymphs and punished the queen by sending a sea-monster to pillage the land. When Cepheus, the king, consulted the oracle, he was told that the only way he could appease Poseidon was by sacrificing his daughter, Andromeda, to the monster. Perseus arrived to find Andromeda chained to a rock being threatened by the monster which he turned into stone by showing it the head of Medusa.

Poseidon was the son of Cronus and Rhea. Immediately after his birth he had been swallowed by his father but, when his mother Metis who had been councilled by Zeus gave him a draught, he regurgitated many of his children including Poseidon. After the war in which Zeus with the help of Poseidon and Hades defeated the Titans, sovereignty was divided between the victors. Zeus took the heavens, Hades the underworld, and Poseidon became lord of all the waters. he is generally depicted with a beard, crowned with laurel leaves, holding a trident with emblems of his kingdom, such as a dolphin, fish and shells, about him.

Procris and Cephalus. When the goddess Eos became besotted by Totonus who was a mortal, she begged Zeus to grant him eternal life but forgot to ask also for perpetual youth for her lover. Totonus became aged and impotent and Eos's covetous eye lighted on Procris, the son of Hermes who had only recently married Cephalus. Eos abducted Procris but he remained true to his wife so that she was forced to release him. However, before she did so, she placed in his heart the seeds of distrust. Wishing, one day, to test the fidelity of Procris, Cephalus disguised himself and proffered jewels to his unsuspecting wife if she would accept his favours. After refusing him, she eventually gave in to his advances. Disgusted at her weakness, Procris threw off his disguise and Cephalus fled to seek refuge with Artemis. Artemis gave her a hound that never lost the scent of a quarry, and a javelin that never missed its mark. Armed with these, she returned to her husband in disguise and offed them to him if he would be her lover. Following the realisation that both had been unfaithful, the two were reunited. However, some years later, Cephalus's suspicions about her husband's fidelity were roused once more and she followed him, concealing herself behind a shrub. Procris, seeing the bush move, threw his javelin which pierced the heart of Cephalus.

Tritons were men with scaly bodies, sharp fangs, forked fish tails and claws in place of nails.

Zeus. The birth of this god has already been described. he was reared in secret upon the slopes of mount Ida, with a goat acting as wet-nurse. Later, in gratitude, Zeus placed the goat in the constellations, but retained one of its horns from which any food or drink that might be desired could be obtained. This was the Cornucopia. Following the death of Cronus, and the defeat of both the Titans and Giants, Zeus became the supreme being upon mount Olympus. His first wife was Metis, goddess of Wisdom. Warned by Uranus that his child by Metis would be wiser than he, Zeus killed Metis and the unborn child and ate them both. His second wife was Themis, goddess of Law, by whom he had children called Horae (The Seasons), Eunomia (Wise Legislation), Dike (Justice), Eirene (Peace) and the Moreae (Fates). Themis seems to have remained adviser to Zeus, even though she was put aside for Hera, who became his third wife. Zeus was not slow to have torrid love affairs with both goddesses and mortal women. Very often he incurred the wrath of Hera, who usually punished the objects of her husband's affection or, when this proved to be impracticable, their offspring. One of the best known of the romances of Zeus involved Leda, the wife of Tyndareus. Zeus seduced the lady disguised as a swan and, since Leda had intercourse with Tyndraeus that same night, she subsequently produced two eggs; from one of these were hatched Pollux and Helen, who were divine, from the other Castor and Clytemnestra, who were mortal.

Roman Mythology

Many of the gods and goddesses of ancient Rome were based on those of Greece and differ from their prototypes only in minor detail and by their names.

Bacchus was the Roman equivalent of the Greek god of wine, Dionysus. It seems unnecessary here to relate the complex origin and evolution of this divinity. He was associated with Bacchanalian revels which caused the cult to be banned at one time in Rome. Bacchus is generally depicted crowned and decked with vine leaves, holding a bunch of grapes and a goblet, and may be accompanied by a leopard.

Ceres was the equivalent of the Greek Demeter, the goddess of crops and vines, and is usually represented crowned with corn husks holding a sickle and standing beside a corn-sheaf.

Diana was the virgin huntress of woodland glades and forests, and is usually depicted with a long-bow, quiver, and a hunting-dog. She corresponds to the Greek Artemis.

Ferona *see* Venus.

Flora *see* Venus.

Juno was both sister and consort to Jupiter. She was the female personification of light, patron of women in child-birth, and became the epitome of the Roman matron. She may be shown with a child in her arms, or with a peacock emblematic of the stars in the firmament, which was sacred to herself. She was the Roman equivalent of Hera.

Jupiter may be equated with Zeus and was the supreme being. He was originally controller of the weather, rain, flood, thunder, sun, wind etc, and later became a warrior-god who symbolised tutelary power. He was liable to hurl thunderbolts at miscreants first to warn them, then if they failed to take notice, to strike them dead. He is often depicted with an eagle, one of the symbols of Rome, carrying thunderbolts, or riding a chariot.

Mars held a very special place in Rome, for he was the father of the founding fathers, Romulus and Remus. He was, firstly, protector of agriculture but became the symbol of military prowess. He was usually depicted in the armour of a centurion, with a shield and sword and was sometimes accompanied by Bellona, goddess of war, who preceeded him into battle and who might be either his sister, or daughter, or spouse.

Mercury was the Roman equivalent of Hermes and, like him, wore winged helmet and sandals and carried the caduceus.

Minerva arose as a goddess who was the protector of trade and commerce, but she evolved to become a warrior-goddess and was worshipped together with Mars. Like Athene, she often carried a screech owl, and might bear the device of Medusa's head upon her shield.

Neptune was most probably a deity who guarded against drought but later assumed sway over the oceans, and was the Roman equivalent of Poseidon. He too, is represented with trident, dolphin and other emblems of the sea.

Saturn was protector of vines, crops and vegetation. He was driven from the heavens by Jupiter, much as Cronus was expelled by Zeus, with whom he may be confused. He may be portrayed with corn, vines or holding a sickle.

Venus, Flora and Ferona were three deities symbolic of Spring and were represented surrounded by budding flowers and fruits. Venus became the symbol of love and was often attended by Cupid who was her son. She carried a mirror signifying feminine beauty and an apple.

Vulcan was a god who controlled thunder and extinguished fires and who represented the sun before the arrival of Jupiter who expelled him. After his fall, he became the deity of metalworkers and his workshops were located on various volcanic islands. He is usually depicted with thunderbolts beside an anvil, holding tongs and a blacksmith's hammer.

Bibliography

General

Chaffers, William, *Marks and Monograms on English and Oriental Pottery and Porcelain* (London, 1965), vols. I & II.

Cushion, John, *English Porcelain* (London, 1975).

Cushion, John, *Animals in Pottery and Porcelain* (London, 1966).

Dixon, J., *English Porcelain of the 18th Century* (London, 1952).

Harris, Nathaniel, *Porcelain Figurines* (London, 1975).

Hayden, R.L., *Old English Porcelain in the Lady Ludlow Collection* (London, 1932).

Hobson, R.L., *Catalogue of English Porcelain in the British Museum* (London, 1905).

Honey, W.B., *English Pottery and Porcelain* (London, 1933).

Hughes, Bernard G., *English Pottery and Porcelain* (London, 1964).

Hughes, Bernard G., and Hughes, Therle, *English Porcelain and Bone Chine, 1743-1850* (London, 1952).

Jewitt, Llewellyn, *The Ceramic Art of Great Britain* (London, 1877), vols. I & II.

King, William, *English Porcelain Figures of the 18th Century* (London, 1924).

Lane, Arthur, *English Porcelain Figures of the Eighteenth Century* (London, 1961).

Nightingale, J.E., *Contributions towards the History of Early English Porcelain* (Salisbury, 1881).

Rackham, Bernard, *Catalogue of English Porcelain .... collected by Charles Schreiber .... and Lady Charlotte Elizabeth Schreiber,* Vol. I Porcelain, Victoria and Albert Museum (London, 1915).

Savage, George, *Eighteenth Century English Porcelain* (London, 1952).

Savage, George, *A Dictionary of Antiques* (London, 1968).

Scott, C.M. and Scott, G.R., *Antique Porcelain Digest* (Newport, 1967).

Stoner, Frank, *Chelsea, Bow and Derby Porcelain Figures* (Newport, 1955).

Chelsea and Girl-in-a-Swing

Austin, John C., *Chelsea Porcelain at Williamsburg* (Charlottesville, U.S.A., 1977).

Blunt, Reginald (ed.), *The Cheyne Book of Chelsea China and Pottery* (London, 1924).

Briant, G.E., *Chelsea Toys* (London, 1925).

Hackenbroch, Yvonne, *Chelsea and Other English Porcelain, Pottery and Enamel in the Irwin Untermyer Collection* (Cambridge, Mass., U.S.A., 1957).

King, William, *Chelsea Porcelain* (London, 1922).

Mackenna, F. Severne, *Chelsea Porcelain, the Triangle and Raised Anchor Wares* (Leigh-on-Sea, 1948).

Mackenna, F. Severne, *Chelsea Porcelain, the Red Anchor Wares* (Leigh-on-Sea, 1951).

Mackenna, F. Severne, *Chelsea Porcelain, the Gold Anchor Wares* (Leigh-on-Sea).

Bow

Hurlbutt, Frank, *Bow Porcelain* (London, 1926).

Mew, Egan, *Old Bow China* (London, 1910).

Tait, Hugh G., *Catalogue of the Exhibition of Bow Porcelain, 1744-1776,* held at the British Museum, October 1959 to April 1960 (London, 1959).

Derby

Barrett, F.A., and Thorpe, A.L., *Derby Porcelain* (London, 1971).

Bradley, H.G. (ed.), *Ceramics of Derbyshire, 1750-1975* (Tiverton, 1975).

Gilhespy, F. Brayshaw, *Crown Derby Porcelain* (Leigh-on-Sea, 1951).

Gilhespy, F. Brayshaw, *Derby Porcelain* (London, 1961).

Haslem, John, *The Old Derby China Factory* (London, 1876, reprinted Wakefield, 1973).

Hobson, R.L., *Derby Porcelain* (London, 1922).

Hurlbutt, Frank, *Old Derby Porcelain and its Artist Workmen* (London, 1925).

Twitchett, John, and Bailey, Betty, *Royal Crown Derby* (London, 1976).

Twitchett, John, *The Story of Royal Crown Derby* (London, 1976).

Twitchett, John, *Derby Porcelain* (London, 1980).

Plymouth and Bristol

Catalogue of The Exhibition of Porcelain in memory of Thomas Cookworthy, held in the City Museum and Art Gallery, Plymouth, 1968.

Catalogue of The Exhibition of Bristol Porcelain to celebrate the Bicentenary 1770-1970, held in the City Museum and Art Gallery, Bristol, 1970.

Mackenna, F. Severne, *Cookworthy's Plymouth and Bristol Porcelain* (Leigh-on-Sea, 1946).

Mackenna, F. Severne, *Champion's Bristol Porcelain* (Leigh-on-Sea, 1946).

Owen, Hugh, *Two Centuries of Ceramics in Bristol* (London, 1878).

Longton Hall

Bemrose, William, *Longton Hall Porcelain* (London, 1906).

Watney, Bernard, *Longton Hall Porcelain* (London, 1957).

Worcester

Barrett, Franklin A., *Worcester Porcelain and Lund's Bristol* (London, 1966).

Marshall, H. Rissik, *Coloured Worcester Porcelain of the Eighteenth Century* (London, 1954).

Sandon, Henry, *The Illustrated Guide to Worcester Porcelain* (London, 1969).

Lowestoft

Godden, Geoffrey, *The Illustrated Guide to Lowestoft Porcelain* (London, 1969).

William Reid's Liverpool

Watney, Bernard, *English Blue and White Porcelain of the Eighteenth Century* (London, 1963).

Index

Modelling subjects continued